D0044016

# Fodor's

# EUROPEAN PORTS OF CALL

2nd Edition

Where to Stay and Eat
for All Budgets

Must-See Sights
and Local Secrets

Ratings You Can Trust

Excerpted from *Fodor's Complete Guide to European Cruises*
Fodor's Travel Publications   New York, Toronto, London, Sydney, Auckland
**www.fodors.com**

## FODOR'S EUROPEAN PORTS OF CALL

**Editors:** Douglas Stallings

**Editorial Contributors:** Lindsay and Pete Bennett, Linda Coffman, Jane Foster, Ralph Grizzle, Marlise Elizabeth Kast, Paul Rubio, Dorota Wąsik

**Production Editor:** Carrie Parker

**Maps & Illustrations:** David Lindroth, *cartographer;* Bob Blake, Rebecca Baer, *map editors;* William Wu, *information graphics*

**Design:** Fabrizio La Rocca, *creative director;* Guido Caroti, Siobhan O'Hare, *art directors;* Tina Malaney, Chie Ushio, Ann McBride, Jessica Walsh, Nora Rosansky, *designers;* Melanie Marin, *senior picture editor*

**Cover Photo:** (Old City, Ibiza, Balearic Islands, Spain): Walter Bibikow/age fotostock

**Production Manager:** Angela L. McLean

2nd Edition

ISBN 978–0–307–48051–4

ISSN 1941–0204

## SPECIAL SALES

This book is available at special discounts for bulk purchases for sales promotions or premiums. Special editions, including personalized covers, excerpts of existing books, and corporate imprints, can be created in large quantities for special needs. For more information, write to Special Markets/Premium Sales, 1745 Broadway, MD 6-2, New York, NY 10019, or e-mail specialmarkets@randomhouse.com.

## AN IMPORTANT TIP & AN INVITATION

Although all prices, opening times, and other details in this book are based on information supplied to us at press time, changes occur all the time in the travel world, and Fodor's cannot accept responsibility for facts that become outdated or for inadvertent errors or omissions. So **always confirm information when it matters,** especially if you're making a detour to visit a specific place. Your experiences—positive and negative—matter to us. If we have missed or misstated something, **please write to us.** Share your opinion instantly through our online feedback center at fodors.com/contact-us.

PRINTED IN THE UNITED STATES OF AMERICA

10 9 8 7 6 5 4 3 2 1

# Be a Fodor's Correspondent

Your opinion matters. It matters to us. It matters to your fellow Fodor's travelers, too. And we'd like to hear it. In fact, we need to hear it.

When you share your experiences and opinions, you become an active member of the Fodor's community. That means we'll not only use your feedback to make our books better, but we'll publish your names and comments whenever possible. Throughout our guides, look for "Word of Mouth," excerpts of your unvarnished feedback.

Here's how you can help improve Fodor's for all of us.

Tell us when we're right. We rely on local writers to give you an insider's perspective. But our writers and staff editors—who are the best in the business—depend on you. Your positive feedback is a vote to renew our recommendations for the next edition.

Tell us when we're wrong. We're proud that we update most of our guides every year. But we're not perfect. Things change. Hotels cut services. Museums change hours. Charming cafés lose charm. If our writer didn't quite capture the essence of a place, tell us how you'd do it differently. If any of our descriptions are inaccurate or inadequate, we'll incorporate your changes in the next edition and will correct factual errors at fodors.com immediately.

Tell us what to include. You probably have had fantastic travel experiences that aren't yet in Fodor's. Why not share them with a community of like-minded travelers? Maybe you chanced upon a beach or bistro or B&B that you don't want to keep to yourself. Tell us why we should include it. And share your discoveries and experiences with everyone directly at fodors.com. Your input may lead us to add a new listing or highlight a place we cover with a "Highly Recommended" star or with our highest rating, "Fodor's Choice."

How to reach us. Share your opinion instantly through our online feedback center at fodors.com/contact-us.

You and travelers like you are the heart of the Fodor's community. Make our community richer by sharing your experiences. Be a Fodor's correspondent.

Happy Traveling!

Tim Jarrell, Publisher

**4** ‹

# CONTENTS

# ABOUT THIS BOOK

## Our Ratings

Sometimes you find terrific travel experiences and sometimes they just find you. But usually the burden is on you to select the right combination of experiences. That's where our ratings come in.

As travelers we've all discovered a place so wonderful that its worthiness is obvious. And sometimes that place is so experiential that superlatives don't do it justice: you just have to be there to know. These sights, properties, and experiences get our highest rating, **Fodor's Choice.**

By default, there's another category: any ship, experience, or establishment we include in this book is by definition worth your time, unless we say otherwise. And we will.

Disagree with any of our choices? Care to nominate a ship or suggest that we rate one more highly? Visit our feedback center at www.fodors.com/feedback.

## Budget Well

Hotel and restaurant price categories from ¢ to $$$$ are defined in the opening pages of each chapter. For attractions, we always give standard adult admission fees; reductions are usually available for children, students, and senior citizens. Want to pay with plastic? **AE, D, DC, MC, V** following restaurant and hotel listings indicate if American Express, Discover, Diners Club, MasterCard, and Visa are accepted.

## Restaurants

Unless we state otherwise, restaurants are open for lunch and dinner daily. We mention dress only when there's a specific requirement and reservations only when they're essential or not accepted—it's always best to book ahead.

## Hotels

Hotels have private bath, phone, TV, and air-conditioning and operate on the European Plan (aka EP, meaning without meals), unless we specify that they use the Continental Plan (CP, with a continental breakfast), Breakfast Plan (BP, with a full breakfast), or Modified American Plan (MAP, with breakfast and dinner), or are all-inclusive (including all meals and most activities). We always list facilities but not whether you'll be charged an extra fee to use them, so when pricing accommodations, find out what's included.

## Many Listings
- ★ Fodor's Choice
- ★ Highly recommended
- ✉ Physical address
- ✛ Directions or Map coordinates
- 🏠 Mailing address
- ☎ Telephone
- 📠 Fax
- 🌐 On the Web
- ✉ E-mail
- 💰 Admission fee
- 🕐 Open/closed times
- Ⓜ Metro stations
- 💳 Credit cards

## Hotels & Restaurants
- 🏨 Hotel
- 🛏 Number of rooms
- 🛁 Facilities
- 🍴 Meal plans
- ✕ Restaurant
- 📅 Reservations
- 👔 Dress code
- ⚲ Smoking
- BYOB

## Outdoors
- ⛳ Golf
- ⛺ Camping

## Other
- 🕐 Family-friendly
- ⇨ See also
- ✉ Branch address
- ☞ Take note

# Cruising in Europe

## WORD OF MOUTH

"We based our decision [about which European cruise to take] on where the cruise went. We wanted to see Athens, so we chose [a] cruise that included Athens. . . . You can explore most ports on your own. That way you can do what you want and spend as much time on shore as you want. Research is the key."

—BarbAnn

Updated by
Linda Coffman

Second only to the Caribbean in popularity with cruise passengers, Europe has it all—beautifully preserved castles, romantic gardens, fabulous art treasures, antiquities, and some of the world's most breathtaking scenery. Great cities flourished along all the coasts of the continent, which makes it possible to explore many of Europe's treasures by ship.

Every year major North American cruise lines satisfy the seasonal demand for what amounts to an old-fashioned Grand Tour afloat by repositioning a large portion of their Caribbean fleets to Europe. They join European-based ships that are ported in the Baltic for the summer and the Mediterranean year-round. The largest vessels generally stick to predictable routes that include major cities along the coasts such as Amsterdam, Venice, Barcelona, and Athens, or those, like Rome, close enough to visit during a port call. Small to midsize ships offer the advantage of visiting ports off the beaten path of the large ships and can call at intriguing destinations like the less-visited Greek Isles and jet-set favorite Ibiza without the necessity of tendering passengers ashore.

# CHOOSING YOUR CRUISE

Are you intrigued by the glory that is Rome or the antiquities of Greece? Do you want to venture behind the former Iron Curtain and unlock the mysteries of Russia? Unlike the "if it's Tuesday, this must be St. Thomas" nature of predictable Caribbean sailings, European itineraries come in shapes and sizes to suit a variety of interests. One voyage might emphasize the highlights of Baltic capital cities, while another focuses on classic Mediterranean cultures and cuisine. Equally rewarding, they nonetheless offer different experiences. Where to go is a highly personal decision and one of the first you must make.

After giving some thought to your itinerary and where in Europe you might wish to go, the ship you select is the most vital factor in your cruise vacation. Big ships offer stability and a huge variety of activities and facilities. Small ships feel more intimate—more like a private club. For every big-ship fan there is someone who would never set foot aboard a "floating resort." Examine your lifestyle to see which kind of ship best meets your needs. But realize also that the size of your ship will also influence which ports you visit as well as how you see them. Big ships visit major ports of call such as Barcelona, Civitavecchia (for Rome), Amsterdam, and Venice; when they call at smaller, shallower ports, passengers must disembark aboard shore tenders (small boats that ferry dozens of passengers to shore at a time). Or they may skip these smaller ports entirely. Small and midsize ships can visit smaller ports, such as Monte Carlo, Monaco, more easily; passengers are often able to disembark directly onto the pier without having to wait for tenders to bring them ashore.

# ITINERARIES

Ship size and cruise length have the greatest impact on the number of ports you can visit, but the itinerary type and embarkation port will also determine the number and variety of ports. **One-way cruises** are much more prevalent in European sailings than in the Caribbean. and will allow you to visit a wider variety of ports and travel farther from your port of embarkation. **Loop cruises** begin and end at the same point and often visit ports in relatively close proximity to one another. After deciding where to go, take a hard look at the number of hours your preferred itinerary spends in individual ports. You don't want to be frustrated by a lack of time ashore to do what you've come so far to accomplish. A late departure or overnight stay may be attractive if you wish to enjoy the local nightlife in a particular port.

## NORTHERN EUROPE AND BALTIC ITINERARIES

Typical one-week to 12-night cruises include a day or two at sea, but ships on these itineraries spend as much time as possible docked in Baltic capitals and major cities. Departing from such ports as Dover (U.K.), Amsterdam, Copenhagen, or Stockholm, highlights of Baltic itineraries may include Amsterdam, Oslo, Helsinki, Tallinn (Estonia), and St. Petersburg (Russia); ships calling on St. Petersburg often dock for two or three nights there. Some itineraries may focus on a theme or specific region, such as cruises around the British Isles or Norwegian fjords and North Cape.

## WESTERN MEDITERRANEAN ITINERARIES

Some of the most popular Mediterranean itineraries, especially for first-time cruisers to Europe, are one-week sailings that embark in Barcelona and stop in southern European ports that range from Nice to Civitavecchia (Rome) and may include more exotic off-the-beaten-path destinations like Malta and Corsica. A sea day might include a cruise through the narrow Strait of Messina or sailing past the volcanic island of Stromboli. Longer one-way itineraries can even start in Lisbon and end as far away as Venice, while possibly calling at not only Gibraltar, the French Riviera, and Sicily, but Dubrovnik (Croatia) as well.

## EASTERN MEDITERRANEAN AND GREEK ISLES ITINERARIES

The most exotic and port-intensive cruises are those embarking in Venice, Athens, and Istanbul. Often one-way voyages, these cruises visit coastal centers of antiquity such as Kuşadası (Ephesus) in Turkey and Katakolon (Olympia) in Greece, but also the Roman outposts of Dubrovnik and Korčula, Croatia. For a transit through Greece's historic Corinth Canal, you'll have to select an itinerary on one of the high-end, small cruise ships, such as Seabourn or SeaDream cruise lines' yacht-size vessels. A sea day might be spent cruising past the grandeur of Mount Athos after leaving Istanbul or along the coastline in the Adriatic Sea. Best explored by small ship—preferably one with sails that add to the allure—Greek Island itineraries that include Santorini, Corfu, Rhodes, and Mykonos are popular with honeymooners and couples for the romantic ambience of sun-splashed beaches and leisurely alfresco meals accompanied by local wines and breathtaking sea views, but these ports

Major European
Cruise Ports

**1**

are also visited by the larger ships, which must usually tender their passengers ashore.

## WHEN TO GO

Baltic cruises are scheduled from May through September, midsummer being high season, when the weather is predictably more pleasant. Temperatures throughout the Baltic are somewhat unpredictable, but can range from balmy mid- to high-70s F on sunny days to chilly 50s F in the evening, even if the sun doesn't set until well into the night. Mediterranean cruises are available year-round, with high season from late April through October when temperatures range from the upper 70s to mid-90s F, depending on your ports of call. Early spring and late fall aren't the best times to cruise in the Mediterranean if your plans include spending time on the beaches, yet the cooler temperatures are ideal for touring. Weather can be unpredictable and damp in fall and winter, but days often warm up when the sun is shining.

## CRUISE COSTS

Average cruise fares vary considerably by itinerary and season, as well as by the category of accommodations you select. Published rates are highest for the most unusual and desirable itineraries, as well as for cruises during peak summer months, when most North Americans plan for vacations in Europe. Europeans are known to prefer late-summer holidays, August being the busiest month. Typical daily per diems on a luxury line such as Silversea or Seabourn can be as much as three times or more the cost of a cruise on a mainstream line such as Royal Caribbean or even a premium Celebrity Cruises ship. It goes without saying that longer cruises are more expensive.

Solo travelers should be aware that single cabins have virtually disappeared from cruise ships, although they are available on P&O's *Azura*, the brand new *Norwegian Epic* (in a particularly successful format), and a few older vessels. Taking a double cabin can cost up to twice the advertised per-person rates (which are based on double occupancy). Some cruise lines will find same-sex roommates for singles; each then pays the per-person, double-occupancy rate.

Although the overall price you pay for your cruise is always a consideration, don't think of the bottom line in terms of the fare alone. You also have to figure in the cost of other shipboard charges beyond the basic fare. However, the ultimate cost isn't computed only in dollars spent; it is in what you get for your money. The real bottom line is value. Many cruise passengers don't mind spending a bit more to get the vacation they really want.

## TIPS

One of the most delicate—yet frequently debated—topics of conversation among cruise passengers involves the matter of tipping. Who do you tip? How much? What's "customary" and "recommended?"

Should parents tip the full amount for children or is just half adequate? Why do you have to tip at all?

When transfers to and from your ship are a part of your air-and-sea program, gratuities are generally included for luggage handling. In that case, do not worry about the interim tipping. However, if you take a taxi to the pier and hand over your bags to a stevedore, be sure to tip him. Treat him with respect and pass along the equivalent of at least $5.

During your cruise, room-service waiters generally receive a cash tip of $1 to $3 per delivery. A 15% to 18% gratuity will automatically be added to each bar bill during the cruise. If you use salon and spa services, a similar percentage might be added to the bills there as well. If you dine in a specialty restaurant, you may be asked to provide a one-time gratuity for the service staff.

There will be a "disembarkation talk" on the last day of the cruise that explains tipping procedures. If you are expected to tip in cash, small white "tip" envelopes will appear in your stateroom that day. If you tip in cash, you usually give the tip envelope directly to each person on the last night of the cruise. Tips generally add up to about $10 to $12 per person per day. You tip the same amount for each person who shares the cabin, including children, unless otherwise indicated.

Most cruise lines now either automatically add gratuities to passengers' onboard charge accounts or offer the option. If that suits you, then do nothing further. However, you are certainly free to adjust the amounts up or down to more appropriate levels or ask that the charge be removed altogether if you prefer distributing cash gratuities.

## EXTRAS

In addition to the cost of your cruise there are further expenses to consider, such as airfare to the port city. These days virtually all cruise lines offer air add-ons, which are sometimes—but not always—less expensive than the lowest available airline fare. Airfares to Europe can be considerably more expensive from May through September than during the rest of year.

Shore excursions can also be a substantial expense; the best shore excursions are not cheap. But if you skimp too much on your excursion budget you'll deprive yourself of an important part of the European cruising experience. European shore excursions can be as simple as a stroll through Copenhagen's fanciful Tivoli Gardens or as splendid as tours through the imperial residences of the czars in St. Petersburg. You can inspect the architecture of Gaudí in Barcelona, take an all-day guided tour of Rome with a stop at Vatican City, and climb to the top of the Acropolis in Athens. One of the most popular excursions is from the port of Kuşadası (Turkey) to the ancient excavated city of Ephesus. You will walk along the marble road that Mark Antony's and Cleopatra's chariots once passed over to reach the Great Theater, where gladiatorial contests entertained up to 24,000 spectators and where St. Paul addressed the Ephesians. If you want to take a ship-sponsored shore excursion, prebooking is highly recommended, as they can sell out weeks before you reach the ship.

But you don't necessarily have to take the tour offered by your ship. Although there's a distinct advantage these days to having your shore excursions priced in dollars rather than euros, you can still have a high-quality (though perhaps not cheaper) experience by banding together with a group of like-minded travelers to arrange a private tour rather than relying on the ship's big-bus experience. Or if you are more intrepid, you can simply hop in a taxi or onto public transportation and do some independent exploring. Whether you choose to take ship-sponsored tours or go it alone, you do need to budget for off-ship touring, because that's the reason you came to Europe in the first place.

Finally, there will be many extras added to your shipboard account during the cruise, including drinks (both alcoholic and nonalcoholic), activity fees (you pay to use that golf simulator), dining in specialty restaurants, spa services, gratuities, and even cappuccino and espresso on most ships.

# BEFORE YOU GO

To expedite your preboarding paperwork, some cruise lines have convenient forms on their Web sites. As long as you have your reservation number, you can provide the required immigration information (usually your citizenship information and passport number), prereserve shore excursions, and even indicate any special requests from the comfort of your home. Less-wired cruise lines might mail preboarding paperwork to you or your travel agent for completion after you make your final payment and request that you return the forms by mail or fax. No matter how you submit them, be sure to make hard copies of any forms you fill out and bring them with you to the pier to smooth the embarkation process.

## DOCUMENTS

It is every passenger's responsibility to have proper identification. If you arrive at the airport without it, you will not be allowed to board your plane. Should that happen, the cruise line will not issue a fare refund. Most travel agents know the requirements and can guide you to the proper agency to obtain what you need if you don't have it.

Everyone must have a valid passport to travel to Europe. Additionally, some countries to which cruise ships call require visas, though it's also true that tourist visas are sometimes not required for cruise passengers, even if they are generally required to visit a particular country. For instance, a visa is not necessary in Russia if you book all your shore excursions through your cruise line, but a visa is required if you tour independently. If your itinerary requires a visa of *all* passengers prior to boarding, you should receive an information letter from your cruise line with instructions and, possibly, application forms. It is your responsibility to obtain all necessary visas. Visa information and applications may also be obtained through the local embassy or consulate of the country you will be visiting. Visas can be obtained through embassies and consulates, but although you can do it yourself, a more hassle-free route is to use a visa service, such as Zierer Visa Service or Travisa, that specializes in the process. ■ **TIP➜ If you arrive at the pier without a required visa, you will not be allowed to board your ship, and the cruise line will not issue a fare refund.**

**Contacts Travisa** (⊕ *www.travisa.com*). **Zierer Visa Service** (⊕ *www.zvs.com*).

Children under the age of 18—when they are not traveling with *both* parents—almost always require a letter of permission from the absent parent(s). Airlines, cruise lines, and immigration agents can deny children initial boarding or entry to foreign countries without proper proof of identification and citizenship *and* a notarized permission letter from absent or noncustodial parents. Your travel agent or cruise line can help with the wording of such a letter.

## MONEY

On board your ship you won't have any worries about money, but you will need cash while ashore. If you have not arranged for transfers from the airport to the ship, you will need taxi fare in the local currency, which is the euro for most embarkation cities and the British pound in Great Britain. The Scandinavian countries Denmark, Norway, and Sweden also have their own currencies.

Currency exchange can be more costly in your home country than at your foreign destination, but many banks, as well as the American Automobile Association (AAA), American Express, and Travelex bureaus offer the service. In addition, you may find a currency exchange booth in the international terminal at your departure airport. However, the simplest, and usually least expensive, method of obtaining local currency is from an ATM. VISA and MasterCard debit and credit cards are widely accepted at ATMs throughout the world; however, some banks impose a fee for international withdrawals. Before leaving home, make sure you have a PIN (personal identification number) for your card and understand any fees associated with its use. You might also be wise to notify the credit-card company that you will be using your card overseas, so they don't refuse your charges when they notice its repeated use in foreign locales.

For days in port you will also want some cash on hand for beverages, snacks, and small souvenir purchases. Your cruise ship may offer a foreign currency exchange service onboard, but, like hotels, the exchange rate is not always the most favorable. We suggest, instead of carrying large amounts of cash when ashore, using a credit card for major purchases.

## INSURANCE

It's a good idea to purchase travel insurance, which covers a variety of possible hazards and mishaps, when you book a cruise. One important concern for cruise passengers is being delayed en route to the port of embarkation and missing the ship. Another major consideration is lost luggage—or even the delay of luggage. Both of these possibilities should be covered by your policy. You may miss the first day or two of your cruise, but all will not be lost financially. A travel policy will ensure that you can replace delayed necessities secure in the knowledge that you will be reimbursed for those unexpected expenditures. Save your receipts for all out-of-pocket expenses to file your claim, and be sure to get an incident report from the airline at fault.

No one wants his or her cruise vacation spoiled by a broken arm, heart attack, or worse, but if one of life's tragedies occurs, you want to be covered. The medical insurance program you depend on at home might not extend coverage beyond the borders of the United States. Medicare assuredly will not cover you if you are hurt or sick while abroad. It is worth noting that all ships of foreign registry are considered to be "outside the United States" by Medicare. If there is any question in your mind, check your cruise-ship's registry—with very few exceptions, it will *not* be the United States. Without basic coverage, travelers should be prepared to pay for any care they require, either by credit card or wire transfer of funds to the provider.

Some independent insurers such as Travel Guard, Access America, or CSA offer comprehensive policies at attractive rates. Nearly all cruise lines offer their own line of insurance. Compare the coverage and rates to determine which is best for you. Keep in mind that insurance purchased from an independent carrier is more likely to include coverage if the cruise line goes out of business before or during your cruise. Although it is a rare and unlikely occurrence, you do want to be insured in the event that it happens.

**U.S. Travel Insurers Access America** (☎ *800/284–8300* ⊕ *www. accessamerica.com*). **CSA Travel Protection** (☎ *800/711–1197* ⊕ *www. csatravelprotection.com*). **HTH Worldwide** (☎ *610/254–8700 or 888/243–2358* ⊕ *www.hthworldwide.com*). **Travelex Insurance** (☎ *800/228–9792* ⊕ *www. travelex-insurance.com*). **Travel Guard International** (☎ *715/345–0505 or 800/826–4919* ⊕ *www.travelguard.com*). **Travel Insured International** (☎ *800/243–3174* ⊕ *www.travelinsured.com*).

## CUSTOMS AND DUTIES

### TAXES

If you make any purchases while in Europe, you should ask for a V.A.T. refund form and find out whether the merchant gives refunds—not all stores do, nor are they required to. Have the form stamped like any customs form by customs officials when you leave the country or, if you're visiting several European Union countries, when you leave the EU. This has to be done at the airport on the day you are flying home. After you're through passport control, take the form to a refund-service counter for an on-the-spot refund (which is usually the quickest and easiest option), or mail it to the address on the form (or the envelope with it) after you arrive home. You receive the total refund stated on the form, but the processing time can be long, especially if you request a credit-card adjustment.

Global Refund is a Europe-wide service with 225,000 affiliated stores and more than 700 refund counters at major airports and border crossings. Its refund form, called a Tax Free Check, is the most common across the European continent. The service issues refunds in the form of cash, check, or credit-card adjustment.

**V.A.T. Refunds Global Refund** (☎ *800/566–9828* ⊕ *www.globalrefund.com*).

## U.S. CUSTOMS

Each individual or family returning to the United States must fill out a customs declaration form, which will be provided before your plane lands. If you owe any duties, you will have to pay them directly to the customs inspector, with cash or check. Be sure to keep receipts for all purchases; and you may be asked to show officials what you've bought. If your cruise is a transatlantic crossing, U.S. Customs clears ships sailing into arrival ports. After showing your passport to immigration officials, you must collect your luggage from the dock, then stand in line to pass through the inspection point. This can take up to an hour.

ALLOWANCES  You're always allowed to bring goods of a certain value back home without having to pay any duty or import tax. But there's a limit on the amount of tobacco and liquor you can bring back duty-free. The values of so-called "duty-free" goods are included in these amounts. When you shop abroad, save all your receipts, as customs inspectors may ask to see them as well as the items you purchased. If the total value of your goods is more than the duty-free limit, you'll have to pay a tax (most often a flat percentage) on the value of everything beyond that limit. For U.S. citizens who have been in Europe for at least 48 hours, the duty-free exemption is $800. But the duty-free exemption includes only 200 cigarettes, 100 cigars, and 1 liter of alcohol (this includes wine); above these limits, you have to pay duties, even if you didn't spend more than the $800 limit.

**U.S. Information U.S. Customs and Border Protection** (⊕ *www.cbp.gov*).

SENDING
PACKAGES
HOME
Although you probably won't want to spend your time looking for a post office, you can send packages home duty-free, with a limit of one parcel per addressee per day (except alcohol or tobacco products or perfume worth more than $5). You can mail up to $200 worth of goods to yourself, or $100 worth of goods to a friend or relative; label the package "personal use" or "unsolicited gift" (depending on which is the case) and attach a list of the contents and their retail value. If the package contains your used personal belongings, mark it "personal goods returned" to avoid paying duty on your laundry. You do not need to declare items that were sent home on your declaration forms for U.S. Customs.

# CRUISE LINES

Just as trends and fashion evolve over time, cruise lines embrace the ebb and flow of change. To keep pace with today's lifestyles, some cruise lines strive to include something that will appeal to everyone on their ships. Others focus on narrower elements and are more traditional. Today's passengers have higher expectations, and they sail on ships that are far superior to their predecessors. And they often do so at a much lower comparable fare than in the past.

So which cruise line is best? Only you can determine which is best for you. You won't find ratings by Fodor's—either quality stars or value scores. Why? Ratings are personal and heavily weighted to the reviewer's opinion. Your responsibility is to select the right cruise for you—no one knows your expectations better than you do yourself. It's your time, money, and vacation that are at stake. No matter how knowledgeable your travel agent is, how sincere your friends are, or what any expert can tell you, you are the only one who really knows what you like. The short wait for a table might not bother you because you would prefer a casual atmosphere with open seating; however, some people want the security of a set time at an assigned table served by a waiter who gets to know their preferences. You know what you are willing to trade off in order to get what you want.

## MAINSTREAM CRUISE LINES

The mainstream lines are the ones most often associated with modern cruising. They offer the advantage of something for everyone and nearly every available sports facility imaginable. Some ships even have ice-skating rinks, 18-hole miniature golf courses, bowling alleys, and rock-climbing walls.

Generally speaking, the mainstream lines have two basic ship sizes—large cruise ships and megaships—in their fleets. These vessels have plentiful outdoor deck space, and many have a wraparound outdoor promenade deck that allows you to stroll or jog the ship's perimeter. In the newest vessels, traditional meets trendy. You'll find atrium lobbies and expansive sun and sports decks, picture windows instead of portholes, and cabins that open onto private verandas. For all their resort-style innovations, they still feature cruise-ship classics—afternoon tea, complimentary room service, and lavish pampering. The smallest ships carry 1,000 passengers or fewer, while the largest accommodate more than 5,000 passengers and are filled with diversions.

These ships tend to be big and boxy. Picture windows are standard equipment, and cabins in the top categories have private verandas. From their casinos and discos to their fitness centers, everything is bigger and more extravagant than on other ships. You'll pay for many extras on the mainstream ships, from drinks at the bar to that cup of cappuccino, to spa treatments, to a game of bowling, to dinner in a specialty restaurant. You may want to rethink a cruise aboard one of these ships if you want a little downtime, since you'll be joined by 1,500 to 5,000 fellow passengers.

## PREMIUM CRUISE LINES

Premium cruise lines have a lot in common with the mainstream cruise lines, but with a little more of everything. The atmosphere is more refined, surroundings more gracious, and service more polished and attentive. There are still activities like pool games, although they aren't quite the high jinks typical of mainstream ships. In addition to traditional cruise activities, onboard lectures are common. Production shows are somewhat more sophisticated than on mainstream lines.

Ships tend to be newer midsize to large vessels that carry fewer passengers than mainstream ships and have a more spacious feel. Decor is usually more glamorous and subtle, with toned-down colors and extensive original art. Staterooms range from inside cabins for three or four to outside cabins with or without balconies to suites with numerous amenities, including butlers on some lines.

Most premium ships offer traditional assigned seatings for dinner. High marks are afforded the quality cuisine and presentation. Many ships have upscale bistros or specialty restaurants, which usually require reservations and command an additional charge. Although premium lines usually have as many extra charges as mainstream lines, the overall quality of what you receive is higher.

## LUXURY CRUISE LINES

Comprising only 5% of the market, the exclusive luxury cruise lines, such as Crystal, Cunard, Oceania, Regent Seven Seas, Seabourn, SeaDream, and Silversea offer high staff-to-guest ratios for personal service, superior cuisine in a single seating (except Crystal, with two assigned seatings, and Cunard, with dual-class dining assignments), and a highly inclusive product with few onboard charges. These small and midsize ships offer much more space per passenger than you will find on the mainstream lines' vessels. Lines differ in what they emphasize, with some touting luxurious accommodations and entertainment and others focusing on exotic destinations and onboard enrichment.

If you consider travel a necessity rather than a luxury and frequent posh resorts, then you will appreciate the extra attention and the higher level of comfort that luxury cruise lines offer. Itineraries on these ships often include the marquee ports, but luxury ships also visit some of the more uncommon destinations. With an intimate size, the smaller luxury ships can visit such ports as Marbella, Spain, and Korčula, Croatia.

## EUROPEAN CRUISE LINES

With more similarities to American-owned cruise lines than differences, these European-owned-and-operated cruise lines compare favorably to the mainstream cruise lines of a decade ago. Many lines have embarked on shipbuilding programs that rival the most ambitious in the cruise industry, but some European fleets still consist of older, smaller, yet well-maintained vessels. These cruises cater to Europeans—announcements may be broadcast in as many as five languages—and Americans are generally in the minority. English is widely spoken by the crew, however.

## RIVER CRUISES

Riverboats and barges present an entirely different perspective on European cruising. Smaller than even the smallest ocean cruise ships, they offer a convenient alternative to bus tours—you only unpack once—while navigating the rivers and canals to reach legendary inland cities. Just as on cruise ships, accommodations and meals are included. Some shore excursions might be part of the package as well.

## OTHER CRUISE LINES

A few small cruise lines sail through Europe and offer boutique to nearly bed-and-breakfast experiences. Notably, Star Clippers, Lindblad Expeditions, and Hurtigruten appeal to passengers who eschew mainstream cruises. Most of these niche vessels accommodate 200 or fewer passengers, and their focus is on soft adventure; Hurtigruten's ships and itineraries are perfectly suited for scenic coastal cruising and have few other onboard amenities. Other lines cruise between nearby ports and drop anchor so passengers can swim and snorkel directly from the ship (as on Star Clippers), and they have itineraries that usually leave plenty of time for exploring and other activities on- or offshore. Many of these cruises schedule casual enrichment talks that often continue on decks, at meals, and during trips ashore.

## AZAMARA CLUB CRUISES

✉ *1050 Caribbean Way, Miami, FL* ☎ *877/999–9553* ⊕ *www.azamara-clubcruises.com* ☞ *Cruise Style: Premium.*

In something of a surprise move, parent company Royal Caribbean International announced the formation of an all-new, deluxe cruise line in 2007. Two vessels originally slated for service in the Celebrity Cruises fleet, which were built for now-defunct Renaissance Cruises and acquired with the purchase of the Spanish cruise line Pullmantur, were the basis for the new line, Azamara Cruises. Designed to offer exotic destination-driven itineraries, Azamara Cruises presents a more intimate onboard experience while allowing access to the less-traveled ports of call experienced travelers want to visit.

When a cruise line sets a course to break the mold in an industry where the product falls into traditional categories—mainstream, premium, luxury—it's an exciting opportunity for experienced travelers who may want more than what a traditional cruise can deliver. More interested in traveling than cruising, they may still prefer the comfort and convenience that only a cruise ship can deliver in some exotic locales. Azamara Cruises gives this underserved group of travelers what they want—a cruise experience that's a bit different. Not quite luxury but more than premium, Azamara offers a deluxe cruise with concierge-style amenities for which you'd have to upgrade to a suite on other cruise lines.

In addition, since its launch, Azamara Club Cruises has added a number of more inclusive amenities to passengers' fares, with no charge for a specific brand of bottled water, specialty coffees and teas; shuttle bus service to/from port communities, where available; house wine served at lunches and dinners; and complimentary self-service laundry.

Extensive overhauls of two ships that formerly sailed for the now-defunct Renaissance Cruises have resulted in interiors that are brighter with the addition of light, neutral carpeting throughout, and splashes of bold color in the upholstery and drapes. Areas that once appeared stuffy are now welcoming, with contemporary artwork further enhancing the decor. Each vessel weighs in at 30,277 tons and carries only 694 passengers. Although the size affords a high level of intimacy and makes the ships easy to navigate, there is no skimping on features normally abundant on larger ships, such as private balconies and alternative dining. Cruisers may feel that they've checked into an upscale boutique hotel that just happens to float.

One distinguishing feature of Azamara is a wide range of enrichment programs to accompany the destination-rich itineraries. Popular programs include guest speakers and experts on a wide variety of topics, including destinations, technology, cultural explorations, art, music, and design. Lectures might include how to get the best photos from your digital camera or the proper way to pair wine and food, as taught by resident sommeliers. An onboard "excursion expert" can not only help you select shore excursions based on your personal interests but also will serve as a destination guide, offering information about the culture and history of each port of call. Entertainment, on the other hand, leans toward cabaret-size production shows and variety entertainers in the main lounge. Diverse musical offerings throughout the ships range from upbeat dance bands to intimate piano bar entertainers.

**Food:** Expect dinner favorites to have an upscale twist, such as gulf shrimp with cognac and garlic, or a filet mignon with black truffle sauce. Azamara chefs bring a fresh approach in contemporary and lighter cuisine—a reflection of what's happening all over the United States. Even though the menus list some trendier items, there will always be classic dishes available. Prime rib and other favorites will continue to be featured on the menu.

**Your Shipmates:** Azamara is designed to appeal to discerning travelers, primarily American couples of any age who appreciate a high level of service in an unstructured atmosphere.

**Dress Code:** Passengers who choose to wear formal attire are certainly welcome to do so, but there are no scheduled formal nights. The nightly dress code is simply "sophisticated" casual—a jacket and tie are never required, but you may see many men who are accustomed to wearing them do so anyway.

**Tipping:** Housekeeping and dining gratuities are included in the fare. A standard 18% is added to beverage charges. It is recommended that a $5 per person gratuity be extended when dining in the specialty restaurants.

## CARNIVAL CRUISE LINES

✉ *3655 N.W. 87 Ave., Miami, FL* ☎ *305/599–2600 or 800/227–6482* ⊕ *www.carnival.com* ☞ *Cruise Style: Mainstream.*

The world's largest cruise line originated the Fun Ship concept in 1972 with the relaunch of an aging ocean liner, which got stuck on a sandbar during its maiden voyage. In true entrepreneurial spirit, founder Ted Arison shrugged off an inauspicious beginning to introduce superliners a decade later. Sporting red-white-and-blue flared funnels, which are easily recognized from afar, new ships are continuously added to the fleet and rarely deviate from a successful pattern. If you find something you like on one vessel, you're likely to find something similar on another.

Each vessel features theme public rooms, ranging from ancient Egypt to futuristic motifs. More high-energy than cerebral, the entertainment consists of lavish Las Vegas–style revues presented in main show lounges by a company of singers and dancers. Other performers might include magicians, jugglers, acrobats, and even passengers taking part in the talent show or stepping up to the karaoke microphone. Live bands play a wide range of musical styles for dancing and listening in smaller lounges. Each ship has a disco, piano bar, and a comedy club.

Arrive early to get a seat for bingo and karaoke. Adult activities, particularly the competitive ones, tend to be silly and hilarious and play to full houses. Relaxing poolside can be difficult when bands crank up the volume or the cruise director selects volunteers for pool games; fortunately, it's always in fun and mostly entertaining. There's generally a quieter second pool to retreat to.

Carnival is so sure passengers will be satisfied with their cruise experience that it is the only cruise line to offer a Vacation Guarantee. Just notify them before arriving at the first port of call if you're unhappy for any reason. Should you choose to disembark at the ship's first non-U.S. port, Carnival will refund the unused portion of your cruise fare and pay for your flight back to your embarkation port. It's a generous offer for which they get few takers.

**Food:** Carnival ships have both flexible dining options and casual alternative restaurants. Although the tradition of two set mealtimes for dinner prevails on Carnival ships, the line's experiments with an open seating concept—Your Time Dining—have proved so successful that it has been implemented fleet-wide.

**Your Shipmates:** Carnival's passengers are predominantly active Americans, mostly couples in their mid-thirties to mid-fifties. Many families enjoy Carnival cruises in the Caribbean year-round. Holidays and school vacation periods are popular with families, and you'll see a lot of kids in summer. More than 600,000 children sailed on Carnival ships in 2010—a sixfold increase in 12 years.

**Dress Code:** Two "cruise elegant" nights are standard on seven-night cruises; one is the norm on shorter sailings. Although men should feel free to wear tuxedos, dark suits (or sport coats) and ties are more prevalent. All other evenings are "cruise casual," with jeans and dress shorts permitted in the dining rooms. All ships request that no short-shorts or cutoffs after 6 PM, but that policy is often ignored.

**Tipping:** A gratuity of $10 per passenger per day is automatically added to passenger accounts, and gratuities are distributed to stewards and waitstaff. Passengers may adjust the amount based on the level of service experienced. All beverage tabs at bars get an automatic 15% addition.

## CELEBRITY CRUISES

✉ *1050 Caribbean Way, Miami, FL* ☎ *800/647–2251* ⊕ *www. celebritycruises.com* ☞ *Cruise Style: Premium.*

The Chandris Group, owners of budget Fantasy Cruises, founded Celebrity in 1989. Initially utilizing an unlovely, refurbished former ocean liner from the Fantasy fleet, Celebrity gained a reputation for professional service and fine food despite the shabby-chic vessel where it was elegantly served. The cruise line eventually built premium sophisticated cruise ships. Signature amenities followed, including large standard staterooms with generous storage, fully equipped spas, and butler service. Valuable art collections grace the fleet.

Entertainment has never been a primary focus of Celebrity Cruises, although a lineup of lavish revues is presented in the main show lounges. In addition to shows featuring comedians, magicians, and jugglers, bands play a wide range of musical styles for dancing and listening in smaller lounges. You'll find guest lecturers on every Celebrity cruise. Presentations may range from financial strategies, astronomy, wine appreciation, photography tips, and politics to the food, history, and culture of ports of call. Culinary demonstrations, bingo, and art auctions are additional diversions throughout the fleet. There are plenty of activities, all outlined in the daily program of events. There are no public address announcements for bingo or hawking of gold-by-the-inch sales. You can still play and buy, but you won't be reminded repeatedly.

Although spacious accommodations in every category are a Celebrity standard, ConciergeClass, an upscale element on all ships, makes certain premium ocean-view and balcony staterooms almost the equivalent of suites in terms of service. A ConciergeClass stateroom includes numerous extras such as chilled champagne, fresh fruit, and flowers on arrival, exclusive room-service menus, evening canapés, luxury bedding, pillows, and linens, upgraded balcony furnishings, priority boarding and luggage service, and other VIP perks. At the touch of a single telephone button, a ConciergeClass desk representative is at hand to offer assistance. Suites are still the ultimate, though, and include the services of a butler to assist with unpacking, booking spa services and dining reservations, shining shoes, and even replacing a popped button.

**Food:** Aside from the sophisticated ambience of its restaurants, the cuisine has always been a highlight of a Celebrity cruise. However, in early 2007, Celebrity and longtime chef Michael Roux ended their affiliation. His hands-on involvement—personally creating menus and overseeing all aspects of dining operations—was integral in helping the line achieve the reputation it enjoys today. Happily, every ship in the fleet has a highly experienced team headed by executive chefs and food and beverage managers who have developed their skills in some of the world's finest restaurants and hotels.

**Your Shipmates:** Celebrity caters to American cruise passengers, primarily couples from their mid-thirties to mid-fifties. Many families enjoy cruising on Celebrity's fleet during summer months and holiday periods, particularly in the Caribbean. Lengthier cruises and exotic itineraries attract passengers in the over-sixty age group.

**Dress Code:** Two formal nights are standard on seven-night cruises. Men are encouraged to wear tuxedos, but dark suits or sport coats and ties are more prevalent. Other evenings are designated "smart casual and above." Although jeans are discouraged in formal restaurants, they are appropriate for casual dining venues after 6 PM. The line requests that no shorts be worn in public areas after 6 PM, and most people observe the dress code of the evening, unlike on some other cruise lines.

**Tipping:** Gratuities are automatically added daily to onboard accounts in the following amounts (which may be adjusted at your discretion):

$11.50 per person per day for passengers in stateroom categories; $12 per person per day for ConciergeClass and AquaClass staterooms; and $15 per person per day for Suites. An automatic gratuity of 15% is added to all beverage tabs.

## COSTA CRUISES

✉ *200 S. Park Rd., Suite 200, Hollywood, FL ☎ 954/266–5600 or 800/462–6782 ⊕ www.costacruise.com ☞ Cruise Style: Mainstream.*

Europe's number-one cruise line combines a continental experience, enticing itineraries, and Italy's classical design and style with relaxing days and romantic nights at sea. Genoa-based Costa Crociere, parent company of Costa Cruise Lines, had been in the shipping business for more than 100 years and in the passenger business for almost 50 years when it was bought by Airtours and Carnival Corporation in 1997. In 2000 Carnival completed a buyout of the Costa line and began expanding the fleet with larger and more dynamic ships.

Italian-style cruising is a mixture of Mediterranean flair and American comfort, beginning with a *buon viaggio* celebration and topped off by a signature Roman Bacchanal Parade and zany toga party. The supercharged social staff works overtime to get everyone in the mood and encourages everyone to be a part of the action.

Festive shipboard activities include some of Italy's favorite pastimes, such as playing games of bocce, dancing the tarantella, and tossing pizza dough during the Festa Italiana, an Italian street festival at sea. Other nights are themed as well—a welcome-aboard celebration (*Benvenuto A Bordo*), hosted by the captain on the first formal night, and *Notte Tropical*, a tropical deck party with a Mediterranean twist that culminates with the presentation of an alfresco midnight buffet. When it is time to say good-bye, Costa throws a Roman Bacchanal.

There's also a nod to the traditional cruise ship entertainment expected by North American passengers. Pool games, trivia, bingo, and sophisticated production shows blend nicely with classical concerts in lounges where a wide range of musical styles invite dancing or listening. Italian language, arts and crafts, and cooking classes are extremely popular. Every ship has a small chapel suitable for intimate weddings, and Catholic Mass is celebrated most days.

Acknowledging changing habits (even among Europeans), Costa Cruises has eliminated smoking entirely in dining rooms and show lounges. However, smokers are permitted to light up in designated areas in other public rooms, as well as on the pool deck.

An ongoing shipbuilding program has brought Costa ships into the 21st century with innovative large-ship designs that reflect their Italian heritage and style without overlooking the amenities expected by modern cruisers.

**Food:** Costa is noted for theme dinner menus that convey the evening's mood. Dining features regional Italian cuisines: a variety of pastas, chicken, beef, and seafood dishes, as well as authentic pizza. European chefs and culinary school graduates, who are members of Chaîne des

Rôtisseurs, provide a dining experience that's notable for a delicious, properly prepared pasta course, if not exactly living up to gourmet standards. Vegetarian and healthy diet choices are also offered, as are selections for children. Alternative dining is by reservation only in the upscale supper clubs, which serve traditional Italian cuisine.

**Your Shipmates:** Couples in the 35- to 55-year-old range are attracted to Costa Cruises; on most itineraries up to 80% of passengers are European, and many of them are of Italian descent. An international air prevails on board and announcements are often made in a variety of languages. The vibe on Costa's newest megaships is most likely to appeal to American tastes and expectations.

**Dress Code:** Two formal nights are standard on seven-night cruises. Men are encouraged to wear tuxedos, but dark suits or sport coats and ties are appropriate and more common than black tie. All other evenings are resort casual, although jeans are discouraged in restaurants. It's requested that no shorts be worn in public areas after 6 PM.

**Tipping:** A standard gratuity of €6.50 per adult per day for cruises up to eight nights or €5 per adult per day on longer cruises is automatically added to shipboard accounts and distributed to cabin stewards and dining room staff. The applicable charge for teens between the ages of 14 and 17 is 50% of those amounts; there is no charge for children under the age of 14. Passengers can adjust the amount based on the level of service experienced. An automatic 15% gratuity is added to all beverage tabs, as well as to checks for spa treatments and salon services.

## CRYSTAL CRUISES

✉ *2049 Century Park E, Suite 1400, Los Angeles, CA* ☎ *888/799–4625 or 310/785–9300* ⊕ *www.crystalcruises.com* ☞ *Cruise Style: Luxury.*

Winner of accolades and too many hospitality industry awards to count, Crystal Cruises offers a taste of the grandeur of the past along with all the modern touches discerning passengers demand today. Founded in 1990 and owned by Nippon Yusen Kaisha (NYK) in Japan, Crystal ships, unlike other luxury vessels, are large, carrying upward of 900 passengers. What makes them distinctive are superior service, a variety of dining options, spacious accommodations, and some of the highest ratios of space per passenger of any cruise ship.

Beginning with ship designs based on the principles of feng shui, the Eastern art of arranging your surroundings to attract positive energy, no detail is overlooked to provide passengers with the best imaginable experience. Just mention a preference for a certain food or beverage and your waiter will have it available whenever you request it.

The complete roster of entertainment and activities includes Broadway-style production shows and bingo, but where Crystal really shines is in the variety of enrichment and educational programs. Passengers can participate in the hands-on Computer University@Sea, interactive Creative Learning Institute classes, or attend lectures featuring top experts in their fields: keyboard lessons with Yamaha, language classes by Berlitz, wellness lectures with the Cleveland Clinic, and an introduction to tai chi with the Tai Chi Cultural Center. Professional ACBL Bridge instructors are on every cruise, and dance instructors offer lessons in contemporary and social dance styles.

**Food:** The food alone is reason enough to book a Crystal cruise. Dining in the main restaurants is an event starring a continental-inspired menu of dishes served by European-trained waiters. Off-menu item requests are honored when possible, and special dietary considerations are handled with ease. Full-course vegetarian menus are among the best at sea. Casual poolside dining beneath the stars is offered on some evenings in a relaxed, no-reservations option. A variety of hot and cold hors d'oeuvres are served in bars and lounges every evening before dinner and again during the wee hours.

But the specialty restaurants really shine. Contemporary Asian cuisine is served in Silk Road and the Sushi Bar, featuring the signature dishes of Nobu Matsuhisa. Both ships also have Prego, which serves regional Italian cuisine by Piero Selvaggio, owner of Valentino in Los Angeles and Las Vegas.

**Your Shipmates:** Affluent, well-traveled couples, from their late-thirties and up, are attracted to Crystal's destination-rich itineraries, shipboard enrichment programs, and elegant ambience. The average age of passengers is noticeably higher on longer itineraries.

**Dress Code:** Formal attire is required on at least two designated evenings, depending on the length of the cruise. Men are encouraged to wear tuxedos, and many do, although dark suits are also acceptable. Other evenings are informal or resort casual; the number of each is based on the number of sea days. The line requests that dress codes be observed in public areas after 6 PM, and few, if any, passengers disregard the suggestion. Most, in fact, dress up just a notch from guidelines.

**Tipping:** Tips may be distributed personally by passengers on the last night of the cruise or charged to shipboard accounts. Suggested gratuity guidelines per person per day are: senior waiter $5; waiter $3; cabin stewardess $5 (single travelers, $6); and (for suite occupants only) butler $5. Tips for the maître d', headwaiter, assistant stewardess, and room service personnel are discretionary. Passengers may adjust the amount based on the level of service experienced. All beverage tabs include an automatic 15% gratuity. A minimum of $7 per person per dinner is suggested for the servers in specialty restaurants; a 15% gratuity is suggested for spa and salon services.

## CUNARD LINE

✉ *24303 Town Center Dr., Valencia, CA* ☎ *661/753–1000 or 800/728–6273* ⊕ *www.cunard.com* ☞ *Cruise Style: Luxury.*

One of the world's most distinguished names in ocean travel since 1840, the Cunard Line has a long history of deluxe transatlantic crossings and worldwide cruising. The line's ships are legendary for their comfortable accommodations, excellent cuisine, and personal service. After a series of owners tried with little success to revive the company's flagging passenger shipping business, Carnival Corporation offered an infusion of

**1**

ready cash and the know-how to turn the line around in 1998. Exciting new ships have followed.

Entertainment has a decidedly English flavor, with nightly production shows or cabaret-style performances and even plays. An authentic pub gives the liners an even more British air, while music for dancing and listening is played in other bars and lounges. In *Queen Mary 2's* first-ever shipboard planetarium, high-tech presentations and virtual-reality shows offer a virtual ride through space.

Cunard's fine enrichment programs include lectures by experts in their fields, including top designers, master chefs, and artists. Even seaman-ship and navigation courses are offered to novice mariners. Passengers can plan their activities prior to departure by consulting the syllabus of courses available online at Cunard Line's Web site.

Delightful daily events include afternoon tea and the maritime tradition of sounding the ship's bell at noon. The line offers North Atlantic cross-ings and seasonal shorter cruises, including some Caribbean itineraries.

**Food:** Dining aboard a Cunard ship is by class, so dining room assign-ments are made according to the accommodation category booked. You can get as much luxury as you are willing to pay for on Cunard liners, where passengers in Junior Suites are assigned to the single-seating Princess Grill; the posh Queen's Grill serves passengers booked in duplex apartments and the most lavish suites. All other passengers are assigned to one of two seatings in the dramatic, multideck-high Britannia Restaurant.

**Your Shipmates:** Discerning, well-traveled American and British couples from their late-thirties to retirees are drawn to Cunard's traditional style and the notion of a cruise aboard an ocean liner. The availability of spacious accommodations and complimentary self-service laundry facilities makes Cunard liners a good option for families, although there may be fewer children on board than on similarly sized ships.

**Dress Code:** Glamorous evenings are typical of Cunard cruises, and speci-fied attire includes formal, informal, and casual. Although resort casual clothing prevails throughout the day, Cunard vessels are ocean liners at heart and, as expected, are dressier than most cruise ships at night. To maintain their high standards, the cruise line requests passengers to dress as they would for dining in fine restaurants.

**Tipping:** Suggested gratuities of $13 per person per day (for Grill Restau-rant accommodations) or $11 per person per day (all other accommoda-tions) are automatically charged to shipboard accounts for distribution to stewards and waitstaff. An automatic 15% gratuity is added to bever-age tabs for bar service. Passengers can still tip individual crew members directly in cash for any special services.

## DISNEY CRUISE LINE

*✉ 210 Celebration Pl., Suite 400, Celebration, FL ☎ 407/566–3500 or 888/325–2500 ⊕ www.disneycruise.com ☞ Cruise Style: Mainstream.*

With the launch of Disney Cruise Line in 1998, families were offered yet another reason to take a cruise. The magic of a Walt Disney resort vacation plus the romance of a sea voyage are a tempting combination, especially for adults who discovered Disney movies and the Mickey Mouse Club as children. Mixed with traditional shipboard activities, who can resist scheduled opportunities for the young and young-at-heart to interact with their favorite Disney characters?

A Disney cruise begins even before embarkation if you opt to use bus transfers from the Orlando airport or Walt Disney World. A slick orientation video passes the time and gets everyone revved up for their first view of the ship. Passengers who added a precruise stay at Walt Disney World seamlessly complete their cruise check-in before leaving the resort; check-in for the balance of passengers is handled in the efficient Port Canaveral terminal designed especially for Disney. While waiting to board, capture your children's attention by pointing out the cutaway model of a Disney ship and a map of the Bahamas and Caribbean inlaid in the floor. Shipboard entertainment leans heavily on popular Disney themes and characters. Parents are actively involved in the audience with their children at production shows, movies, live character meetings, deck parties, and dancing in the family nightclub. Teens have a supervised, no-adults-allowed club space in the forward fake funnel, where they gather for activities and parties. For adults, there are traditional no-kids-allowed bars and lounges with live music, dancing, theme parties, and late-night comedy, as well as daytime wine-tasting sessions, game shows, culinary arts and home entertaining demonstrations, and behind-the-scenes lectures on animation and filmmaking.

A giant LED screen has been affixed to the forward funnels of both original ships. Passengers can watch movies and special broadcasts while lounging in the family pool area. For many passengers, the short itineraries are a three- or four-night extension of a Walt Disney World vacation, while week-long sailings more resemble a traditional seven-night cruise with a Disney twist. All Bahamas and Caribbean cruises call at Castaway Cay, Disney's private Bahamian island with its own pier for convenient dockside debarkation.

**Food:** Don't expect top chefs and gourmet food. This is Disney, and the fare in the two casual restaurants is all-American for the most part, with a third restaurant being a bit fancier, with French-inspired dishes on the menus. Naturally, all have children's menus with an array of favorite sandwiches and entrées. Vegetarian and healthy selections are also available in all restaurants. A bonus is complimentary soft drinks, lemonade, and iced tea throughout the sailing. A beverage station in the buffet area is always open; however, there is a charge for soft drinks ordered from the bars and room service.

**Your Shipmates:** Disney Cruises appeal to kids of all ages—the young and not so young, singles, couples, and families. Multigeneration family groups are the core audience for these ships, and the facilities are ideal for family gatherings. What you might not have expected are the numerous newlywed couples celebrating their honeymoons on board.

**Dress Code:** Three- and four-night cruises are casual; no formal wear is required, and resort casual is the evening dress code for dinner in the more laid-back dining rooms. A sport coat is appropriate for the restaurants designated as fancier, as well as the adults-only specialty restaurants; however, you won't be turned away and could probably get by without the sport coat. In addition to the guideline for shorter cruises, one-week cruises schedule a semiformal evening and a formal night, during which men are encouraged to wear tuxedos, but dark suits or sport coats and ties are acceptable for both.

**Tipping:** Suggested gratuity amounts are calculated on a per person–per cruise rather than per night basis, and can be added to onboard accounts or offered in cash on the last night of the cruise. Guidelines include gratuities for your dining room server, assistant server, head server, and stateroom host/hostess for the following amounts: $36 for three-night cruises, $48 for four-night cruises, and $84 for seven-night cruises. Tips for room-service delivery, spa services, and the dining manager are at passenger's discretion. An automatic 15% gratuity is added to all bar tabs.

## FRED. OLSEN CRUISE LINES

✉ *Fred. Olsen House, Whitehouse Rd., Ipswich, UK* ☎ *01/473/742–424* ⊕ *www.fredolsencruises.com* ☞ *Cruise Style: Mainstream.*

Family-owned Fred. Olsen Cruise Lines proudly boasts a Norwegian heritage of seamanship and a fleet of small ships that offer an intimate cruising experience. Although the fleet doesn't consist of new vessels, all were well constructed originally and have been refitted since 2001. Two sister ships from the defunct luxury Royal Viking Line, *Royal Viking Star* and *Royal Viking Sky,* have reunited under the Fred. Olsen house flag and now sail as *Black Watch* and *Boudicca.* And while the line is destination-focused—itineraries are seldom repeated within any cruise season—itinerary planning is versatile.

Shipboard ambience is friendly, relaxed, and unabashedly British. As Fred. Olsen Cruise Lines expands, the line takes pride in maintaining the consistency their passengers prefer and expect, both on board and ashore. Activities and entertainment are traditional cruise-ship fare with a laid-back tempo, though on a much smaller scale than you find on the typical American megaship. Ballroom dancers outnumber the late-night disco set, and shows are more cabaret than Vegas. Particular favorites with most passengers are theme nights and the crew show. Cruises range from four-night "mini-breaks" to lengthier 7- to 78-night sailings. British pounds are used for all transactions on board.

**Food:** Attractively presented and above-average in quality, a wide variety of menu options is available in the dining rooms and buffets. Vegetarian selections are always available, and other special dietary considerations can be fulfilled with three to four weeks' advance notice. The line's Norwegian ownership is clearly evident in the high quality of seafood and fish dishes offered. A fairly extensive and quite affordable wine list enhances the cuisine.

**Your Shipmates:** Well-traveled, mature British passengers who enjoy the time-honored shipboard environment with a formal style make up the majority on board Fred. Olsen sailings. However, it's not unusual to find several generations of families all cruising together during summer months and school holiday breaks, when children's activity programs are offered to please grandparents who wish to spend quality time with their extended families.

**Dress Code:** Requested attire is appropriately casual during the day and consists of three types of traditional shipboard evening dress—formal, informal, and casual.

**Tipping:** Recommended gratuities, which may be added to your onboard account, are £2 passenger per day for your cabin steward and the same amount for your dining room waiter.

## HOLLAND AMERICA

> ✉ *300 Elliott Ave. W, Seattle, WA* ☎ *206/281–3535 or 800/577–1728* ⊕ *www.hollandamerica.com* ☞ *Cruise Style: Premium Deluxe.*

Holland America Line has enjoyed a distinguished record of traditional cruises, world exploration, and transatlantic crossings since 1873—all facets of its history that are reflected in the fleet's multimillion dollar shipboard art and antiques collections. Even the ships' names follow a pattern set long ago: all end in the suffix *dam* and are either derived from the names of various dams that cross Holland's rivers, important Dutch landmarks, or points of the compass. The names are even recycled when vessels are retired, and some are in their fifth and sixth generation of use.

Noted for focusing on passenger comfort, Holland America Line cruises are classic in design and style, and with an infusion of younger adults and families on board, they remain refined without being stuffy or stodgy. Following a basic design theme, returning passengers feel as at home on the newest Holland America vessels as they do on older ones.

Entertainment tends to be more Broadway-stylish than Las Vegas–brash. Colorful revues are presented in main show lounges by the ships' companies of singers and dancers. Other performances might include a range of cabaret acts: comedians, magicians, jugglers, and acrobats. Live bands play a wide range of musical styles for dancing and listening in smaller lounges and piano bars. Movies are shown daily in cinemas that double as the Culinary Arts Centers.

Holland America Line may never be considered cutting-edge, but the Signature of Excellence concept introduced in 2003 sets it apart from other premium cruise lines. An interactive Culinary Arts Center offers cooking demonstrations and wine-tasting sessions; Explorations Café (powered by the *New York Times*) is a coffeehouse-style library and Internet center; and the Explorations Guest Speakers Series is supported by in-cabin televised programming on flat-screen TVs in all cabins; the traditional Crow's Nest observation lounge has a new nightclub-disco layout, video wall, and sound-and-light systems; and facilities for children and teens have been greatly expanded. Although the initial Signature of Excellence upgrades were completed on the entire Holland America fleet in 2006, additional enhancements are ongoing.

**1**

**Food:** Holland America Line chefs, led by Master Chef Rudi Sodamin, utilize more than 500 different food items on a typical weeklong cruise to create the modern continental cuisine and traditional favorites served to their passengers. Vegetarian options as well as health-conscious cuisine are available, and special dietary requests can be handled with advance notice. Holland America's passengers used to skew older than they do now, so the sometimes bland dishes were no surprise. But the food quality, taste, and selection have greatly improved in recent years. A case in point is the reservations-required Pinnacle Grill alternative restaurants, where fresh seafood and premium cuts of Sterling Silver beef are used to prepare creative specialty dishes. The $20 per person charge for dinner would be worth it for the Dungeness crab cakes starter and dessert alone. Other delicious traditions are afternoon tea, a Dutch Chocolate Extravaganza, and Holland America Line's signature bread pudding.

Flexible scheduling allows for early or late seatings in the two-deck, formal restaurants. An open seating option from 5:15 to 9 has been introduced fleet-wide.

**Your Shipmates:** No longer just your grandparents' cruise line, today's Holland America sailings attract families and discerning couples, mostly from their late-thirties on up. Holidays and summer months are peak periods when you'll find more children in the mix. Comfortable retirees are often still in the majority, particularly on longer cruises. Families cruising together who book five or more cabins receive perks such as a fountain-soda package for each family member, a family photo for each stateroom, and complimentary water toys at Half Moon Cay (for Caribbean itineraries that call at the private island). If the group is larger than 10 cabins or more, the Head-of-Family is recognized with an upgrade from outside stateroom to a veranda cabin. It's the best family deal at sea, and there's no extra charge.

**Dress Code:** Evenings on Holland America Line cruises fall into two categories: smart casual and formal. For the two formal nights standard on seven-night cruises, men are encouraged to wear tuxedos, but dark suits or sport coats and ties are acceptable, and you'll certainly see them. On smart–casual nights—expect the type of attire you'd see at a country club or upscale resort. It's requested that no T-shirts, jeans, swimsuits, tank tops, or shorts be worn in public areas after 6 PM.

**Tipping:** Eleven dollars per passenger per day is automatically added to shipboard accounts, and gratuities are distributed to stewards and waitstaff. Passengers may adjust the amount based on the level of service experienced. Room-service tips are usually given in cash (it's at the passenger's discretion here). An automatic 15% gratuity is added to bar-service tabs.

## HURTIGRUTEN

✉ *405 Park Ave., Suite 904, New York, NY* ☎ *800/323–7436* ⊕ *www.hurtigruten.us* ☞ *Cruise Style: Small-ship.*

Originally intended as a communications and travel link between the villages on Norway's western coast, Hurtigruten (formerly known in the U.S. as Norwegian Coastal Voyage) provides an up-close look at the fascinatingly intricate fjords, mountains, and villages that not too long ago were isolated and difficult to navigate. Sailing with comfortable cruise ships that still do double-duty transferring cargo and the occasional village-to-village passenger, the Hurtigruten itineraries are often described as "the world's most beautiful voyage," as they provide access to some of the most stunning scenery and the unique cultures of Norway, many of them above the Arctic Circle.

Nine modern Hurtigruten ships are committed year-round to Norwegian coastal itineraries, known in Norway as "Hurtigruten," the word from which the cruise line's name is derived. Options include 6-night northbound, 5-night southbound, or 11-night round-trip sailings, calling at 34 ports in each one-way segment. In summer the Millennium, Contemporary, and Mid-Generation ships follow this route; in winter, *Nordnorge* and *Nordkapp* reposition, joining the company's newest ship, MS *Fram,* in the southern hemisphere to sail Antarctic and Chilean Fjord itineraries, replaced in Norway by *Lofoten* and *Nordstjernen.* The *Polar Star* and *Nordstjernen* make summer voyages to Spitsbergen, an island midway between Norway and the North Pole. The MS *Fram* makes summer expeditions to Greenland as well as a 67-day longitudinal world cruise in the fall.

**Food:** The itinerary is the primary point of emphasis on these cruises, and dining takes a far less prominent role than on cruises for the American market. There are two dinner seatings, and the three-course dinners allow no individual selection—everyone on a given evening will have the same appetizer, entrée, and dessert. There is a 24-hour café, but it is not a free amenity; passengers must pay for their meals there. Liquor, wine, and beer, priced in Norwegian *kroner,* are expensive, but the line allows guests to bring their own alcohol on board.

**Your Shipmates:** Americans are usually in the minority on these sailings. Travelers who find this kind of cruising attractive are usually sophisticated yet unpretentious individuals who can be comfortable in an internationally diverse group. They tend to be independent folks who are comfortable controlling their vacation experiences and are perfectly content enjoying spectacular scenery and visiting picturesque communities, mostly on their own.

**Dress Code:** Hurtigruten ships are truly casual, with no dress-up nights.

**Tipping:** There is a "no tipping required" policy, and the mostly Norwegian crew does not expect gratuities. If you want to tip a crew member for exceptional service, however, it is at your discretion.

## LINDBLAD EXPEDITIONS

*Lindblad Expeditions, 96 Morton St., New York, NY 10014* 212/765–7740 or 800/397–3348 *www.expeditions.com.*

Founded in 1979 as Special Expeditions by Sven-Olof Lindblad, the son of Lars-Eric Lindblad, the company changed its name in 1984 to Lindblad Expeditions. Every cruise is educational, focusing on soft adventure and environmentally conscientious travel through ecologically sensitive regions of Alaska. Since 2004 the line has partnered with *National Geographic* to enhance the experience by including *National Geographic* experts and photographers on board; forums to discuss current events and world issues; and participation by fellowship-funded teachers of geography and other subjects.

The ships of Lindblad Expeditions spend time looking for wildlife, exploring out-of-the-way inlets, and making Zodiac landings at isolated beaches. Each ship has a fleet of kayaks as well as a video-microphone: a hydrophone (underwater microphone) is combined with an underwater camera so passengers can listen to whale songs and watch live video of what's going on beneath the waves. In the evening the ships' naturalists recap the day's sights and adventures over cocktails in the lounge. A video chronicler makes a DVD of the entire cruise that you may purchase.

Every Lindblad itinerary has flexibility built into the schedule. In fact, entire days are left open for exploring on some itineraries. So, for example, if a blue whale or a school of dolphins are encountered, there will be time to stop and watch rather than having to rush to get to the next port of call.

**Food:** Breakfast is buffet-style, although you can order eggs and omelets from the kitchen, and lunch is served family-style. Afternoon tea features sandwiches and sweets, and hors d'oeurves are served during the cocktail hour. The open seating dinner typically consists of two entrées—meat or fish—as well as several always-available items such as steak and chicken. The "Seafood for Thought" program ensures that sustainable seafood is being served.

**Your Shipmates:** Lindblad attracts active, adventurous, well-traveled over-forties, and quite a few singles, as the line charges one of the industry's lowest single supplements. They are making a push, however, to be more family-friendly by adding cruises aimed specifically at families and children. To that end, staff members have undergone extensive training to tailor activities toward children.

**Dress Code:** Casual and comfortable attire is always appropriate.

**Tipping:** Although gratuities are at your discretion, tips of $12–$15 per person per day are suggested; these are pooled among the crew at journey's end. Tip the massage therapist individually following a treatment.

## MSC CRUISES

✉ *6750 N. Andrews Ave., Fort Lauderdale, FL* ☎ *800/666–9333* ⊕ *www.msccruisesusa.com* ☞ *Cruise Style: Premium.*

More widely known as one of the world's largest cargo shipping companies, MSC has operated cruises with an eclectic fleet since the late 1980s. When the line introduced two graceful, medium-size ships in 2003 and 2004, it ushered in an era of new shipbuilding that has seen the fleet grow faster than any other European cruise line.

MSC blankets the Mediterranean nearly year-round with a dizzying selection of cruise itineraries that allow a lot of time in ports of call and include few, if any sea days. In summer months several ships sail off to northern Europe to ply the Baltic. Itineraries planned for reposition-ing sailings visit some intriguing, off-the-beaten-track ports of call that other cruise lines bypass.

No glitz, no clutter—just elegant simplicity—is the standard of MSC's seaworthy interior decor. Extensive use of marble, brass, and wood reflects the best of Italian styling and design; clean lines and bold colors set their modern sophisticated tone.

MSC adopts some activities that appeal to American passengers without abandoning those preferred by Europeans (you should be prepared for announcements in Italian as well as English while on board). In addition to the guest lecturers, computer classes, and cooking lessons featured in the enrichment programs, Italian-language classes are a popular option. Nightly shows accentuate the cruise line's Mediterranean heritage; there might be a flamenco show in the main showroom and live music for listening and dancing in the smaller lounges, while the disco is a hap-pening late-night spot.

MSC entertainment staff members shine off stage as well as in front of the spotlight. They seek out passengers traveling solo, who might be looking for activity or dance partners, so that they feel fully included in the cruise.

Regardless of the itinerary, be prepared for a very Italian-influenced experience. Also expect to hear announcements in several languages.

**Food:** Dinner on MSC ships is a traditional multiple-course event cen-tered on authentic Italian fare. Menus list Mediterranean regional specialties and classic favorites prepared from scratch. Some favorites include lamb-and-mushroom quiche (a Tuscan dish) and veal scaloppini with tomatoes and mozzarella (a recipe from Sorrento in Campania). Although food is still prepared the Italian way, in a nod to American tastes, broiled chicken breast, grilled salmon, and Caesar salad are addi-tions to the dinner menu that are always available. Healthy Choice and vegetarian items are offered as well as tempting sugar-free desserts. A highlight is the bread, freshly baked on board daily. Pizza served in the buffet is some of the best at sea. The nightly midnight buffet is a retro food feast missing from most of today's cruises. Room service is always available, though the options are somewhat limited.

**Your Shipmates:** Most passengers are couples in the 35- to 55-year-old range, as well as some family groups who prefer the international atmo-sphere prevalent on board. More than half the passengers on Caribbean itineraries are North Americans, but expect a more international mix on European cruises, with North Americans in the minority.

**Dress Code:** Two formal nights are standard on seven-night cruises, and three may be scheduled on longer sailings. Men are encouraged to wear dark suits, but sport coats and ties are appropriate. All other evenings are casual, although jeans are discouraged in restaurants. It's requested that no shorts be worn in public areas after 6 PM.

**Tipping:** Customary gratuities are added to your shipboard account in the amount of $12 per person per day for adults and half that amount for children. You can always adjust these amounts at the reception desk or even pay in cash, if you prefer. Automatic 15% gratuities are incorporated into all bar purchases. You may also reward staff in the spa and casino for exceptional service.

# NORWEGIAN CRUISE LINE

✉ *7665 Corporate Center Dr., Miami, FL* ☎ *305/436–4000 or 800/327–7030* ⊕ *www.ncl.com* ⌕ *Cruise Style: Mainstream.*

Norwegian Cruise Line (NCL) set sail in 1966 with an entirely new concept: regularly scheduled Caribbean cruises from the then obscure port of Miami. Good food and friendly service combined with value fares established NCL as a winner for active adults and families. With the introduction of the now-retired SS *Norway* in 1979, NCL ushered in the era of cruises on megasize ships. Innovative and forward-looking, NCL has been a cruise-industry leader for four decades, and is as much at home in Europe as it is in the Caribbean.

Noted for top-quality, high-energy entertainment and emphasis on fitness facilities and programs, NCL combines action, activities, and a variety of dining options in a casual, free-flowing atmosphere. Freestyle cruising has meant an end to rigid dining schedules and dress codes. NCL ships now offer a host of flexible dining options that allow passengers to eat in the main dining rooms or any of a number of à la carte and specialty restaurants at any time and with whom they please. Now co-owned by Genting Hong Kong Limited and Apollo Management, a private equity company, NCL continues to be an industry innovator.

More high jinks than high-brow, entertainment after dark features extravagant Las Vegas–style revues presented in main show lounges by lavishly costumed singers and dancers. Other performers might include comedians, magicians, jugglers, and acrobats. Passengers can get into the act by taking part in talent shows or step up to the karaoke microphone. Live bands play for dancing and listening passengers in smaller lounges, and each ship has a lively disco. Some ships include shows by Chicago's world-famous Second City improvisational comedy company. With the launch of *Norwegian Epic* in 2010, the Blue Man Group and Cirque Productions (a U.S.-based company somewhat similar in style to Cirque du Soleil) join NCL's talent line-up.

Casinos, bingo sessions, and art auctions are well attended. Adult games, particularly the competitive ones, are fun to participate in and provide laughs for audience members. Goofy pool games are an NCL staple, and the ships' bands crank up the volume during afternoon and evening deck parties.

From a distance, most cruise ships look so similar that it's often difficult to tell them apart, but NCL's largest, modern ships stand out with their distinctive use of hull art. Each new ship is distinguished by murals extending from bow to midship.

When others scoffed at winter cruises to the Caribbean, Bahamas, and Florida from New York City, NCL recognized the demand and has sailed with such success that others have followed in its wake. A Winter Weather Guarantee is offered should foul weather threaten to spoil your vacation plans. If departure from New York is delayed for more than 12 hours due to weather, you will receive an onboard credit of $100 per person on your current departure, or, if you decide to cancel your cruise, you will receive a cruise credit equal to the amount you paid to use on a future NCL cruise within one year and any reasonable incidental expenses you incur in rearranging your travel plans.

**Food:** Main dining rooms serve what is traditionally deemed continental fare, although it's about what you would expect at a really good hotel banquet. Health-conscious menu selections are nicely prepared, and vegetarian choices are always available. Where NCL really shines is the specialty restaurants, especially the French-Mediterranean Le Bistro (on all ships), the pan-Asian restaurants, and steak houses (on the newer ships). As a rule of thumb, the newer the ship, the wider the variety, because new ships were purpose-built with as many as 10 or more places to eat. You may find Spanish tapas, an Italian trattoria, a steak house, and a pan-Asian restaurant complete with a sushi and sashimi bar and teppanyaki room. Almost all carry a cover charge or are priced à la carte and require reservations. An NCL staple, the late-night Chocoholic Buffet continues to be a favorite event.

**Your Shipmates:** NCL's mostly American cruise passengers are active couples ranging from their mid-thirties to mid-fifties. Many families enjoy cruising on NCL ships during holidays and summer months. Longer cruises and more exotic itineraries attract passengers in the over-55 age group.

**Dress Code:** Resort casual attire is appropriate at all times; the option of one formal evening is available on all cruises of seven nights and longer. Most passengers actually raise the casual dress code a notch to what could be called casual chic attire.

**Tipping:** A fixed service charge of $12 per person per day is added to shipboard accounts. An automatic 15% gratuity is added to bar tabs. Staff members may also accept cash gratuities. Passengers in suites who have access to concierge and butler services are asked to offer a cash gratuity at their own discretion.

## OCEANIA CRUISES

✉ *8300 N.W. 33rd St., Suite 308, Miami, FL* ☎ *305/514–2300 or 800/531–5658* ⊕ *www.oceaniacruises.com* ☞ *Cruise Style: Premium.*

This distinctive cruise line was founded by Frank Del Rio and Joe Watters, cruise-industry veterans with the know-how to satisfy the wants of inquisitive passengers. By offering itineraries to interesting ports of call and upscale touches—all for fares much lower than you would expect—they are succeeding quite nicely. Oceania Cruises set sail in 2003 to carve a unique, almost boutique niche in the cruise industry by obtaining mid-size R-class ships that formerly made up the popular Renaissance Cruises fleet. The line is now owned by Prestige Cruise Holdings.

Intimate and cozy public spaces reflect the importance of socializing on Oceania ships. Indoor lounges feature numerous conversation areas, and even the pool deck is a social center. The Patio is a shaded slice of deck adjacent to the pool and hot tubs. Defined by billowing drapes and carpeting underfoot, it is furnished with plush sofas and chairs ideal for relaxation. Evening entertainment leans toward light cabaret, solo artists, music for dancing, and conversation with fellow passengers; however, you'll find lively karaoke sessions on the schedule as well. The sophisticated, adult atmosphere on days at sea is enhanced by a combo performing jazz or easy-listening melodies poolside.

Although thickly padded single and double loungers are arranged around the pool, if more privacy appeals to you, eight private cabanas are available for rent. Each one has a double chaise longue with a view of the sea; overhead drapery can be drawn back for sunbathing, and the side panels can be left open or closed. Waiters are on standby to offer chilled towels or serve occupants with beverages or snacks. In addition, you can request a spa service in your cabana.

Varied, destination-rich itineraries are an important characteristic of Oceania Cruises, and most sailings are in the 10- to 12-night range. Before arrival in ports of call, lectures are presented on the historical background, culture, and traditions of the islands.

Culinary demonstrations by guest presenters and Oceania's own executive chefs are extremely popular. Lectures on varied topics, computer courses, hands-on arts and crafts classes, and wine or champagne seminars round out the popular enrichment series on board.

**Food:** Several top cruise-industry chefs were lured away from other cruise lines to ensure that the artistry of world-renowned master chef Jacques Pépin, who crafted five-star menus for Oceania, is properly carried out. The results are sure to please the most discriminating palate. Oceania simply serves some of the best food at sea, particularly impressive for a cruise line that charges far less than luxury rates. The main restaurant offers trendy, French-continental cuisine with an always-on-the-menu steak, seafood, or poultry choice and a vegetarian option.

Intimate specialty restaurants require reservations, but there's no additional charge for Toscana, the Italian restaurant, or Polo Grill, the steak house. On Marina, passengers have those and more restaurants from which to choose—Jacques, the first restaurant to bear Jacques Pépin's name, serves French cuisine; Red Ginger features contemporary interpretations of Asian classics; Privée hosts private, seven-course menu degustation dinners for a single party of up to 10; and La Reserve serves exclusive wine and food pairings.

**Your Shipmates:** Oceania Cruises appeal to singles and couples from their late-thirties to well-traveled retirees who have the time for and prefer longer cruises. Most are American couples attracted to the casually sophisticated atmosphere, creative cuisine, and high level of service. Many are past passengers of the now-defunct Renaissance Cruises who are loyal to their favorite ships, which now offer a variety of destination-rich itineraries.

**Dress Code:** Leave the formal wear at home—attire on Oceania ships is country-club casual every evening, although some guests can't help dressing up to dine in the beautifully appointed restaurants. A jacket and tie are never required for dinner, but many men wear sport jackets, as they would to dine in an upscale restaurant ashore. Jeans, shorts, T-shirts, and tennis shoes are discouraged after 6 PM in public rooms.

**Tipping:** Gratuities of $12.50 per person per day are added to shipboard accounts for distribution to stewards and waitstaff; an additional $4 per person per day is added for occupants of suites with butler service. Passengers may adjust the amount based on the level of service experienced. An automatic 18% gratuity is added to all bar tabs for bartenders and drink servers and to all bills for salon and spa services.

## P&O CRUISES

*⊠ Richmond House, Terminus Terrace, SouthamptonUK ☎ 0845/678–0014 ⊕ www.pocruises.com ☞ Cruise Style: Mainstream.*

P&O Cruises (originally the Peninsular & Oriental Steam Navigation Company) boasts an illustrious history in passenger shipping since 1837. While the company's suggestion that they invented cruising may not be entirely accurate, P&O is assuredly a pioneer of modern cruising. Having set aside such throwbacks as passenger classes, the company acquired Princess Cruises in 1974. P&O then purchased Sitmar Cruises and merged it with Princess in 1988, and the passenger-cruise business—known as P&O Princess—was spun off in 2000.

P&O Cruises remains Britain's leading cruise line, sailing the U.K.'s largest and most modern fleet. The ships are equipped with every modern facility you could think of, from swimming pools to stylish restaurants, spas, bars, casinos, theaters, and showrooms. An abundance of balcony and outside cabins ensures that a view to the sea is never far away. P&O ships, with accommodation from inside cabins to lavish suites, cater to a wide cross-section of budgets and tastes. In view of U.K. laws banning smoking in public places, smoking is only allowed on private balconies and designated areas of open decks; all staterooms and ship interiors are no-smoking.

To offer passengers a variety of choices, P&O has adapted their fleet to match their preferences. Although most of the fleet caters to families as well as couples and singles of all ages, *Arcadia* and *Artemis* are adults-only ships. It has been announced that Artemis will leave the fleet in April 2011 and Adonis (formerly Royal Princess) will be added. No specifics about Adonis were available at this writing.

**Food:** P&O has jumped on the choice bandwagon in dining and offers a somewhat dizzying number of options, although actual menu offerings vary quite a bit across the fleet. Club Dining, with assigned seating, is available on all ships; Select Dining in specialty restaurants requires reservations and carries a small charge; Freedom Dining is an open seating dinner offered in certain restaurants on *Arcadia, Oceana, Azura,* and *Ventura.*

**Your Shipmates:** Count on fellow passengers to be predominantly British singles, couples, and families, although you may find Scandinavians, Americans, and Australians aboard for some sailings. Passengers must be 18 or older to sail aboard the all-adult ships,.

**1**

**Tipping:** The recommended gratuity is £3.10 per passenger (age 12 and older) per day for dining-room service, which is charged to the onboard accounts of *Arcadia, Oceana,* and *Ventura* passengers who opt for Freedom Dining and paid in cash by all others.

## PRINCESS CRUISES

✉ *24305 Town Center Dr., Santa Clarita, CA* ☎ *661/753–0000 or 800/ 774–6237* ⊕ *www.princess.com* ☞ *Cruise Style: Premium.*

Princess Cruises may be best known for introducing cruise travel to millions of viewers, when its flagship became the setting for *The Love Boat* television series in 1977. Since that heady time of small-screen stardom, the Princess fleet has grown both in the number and size of ships. Although most are large in scale, Princess vessels manage to create the illusion of intimacy through the use of color and decor in understated yet lovely public rooms graced by multimillion-dollar art collections.

Princess has also become more flexible; Personal Choice Cruising offers alternatives for open seating dining (when you wish and with whom you please) and entertainment options as diverse as those found in resorts ashore.

The roster of adult activities still includes standbys like bingo and art auctions, but also enrichment programs featuring guest lecturers, cooking classes, wine-tasting seminars, pottery workshops, and computer and digital photography classes. Nighttime production shows tend toward Broadway-style revues presented in the main show lounge, and performers might include comedians, magicians, jugglers, and acrobats. Live bands play a wide range of musical styles for dancing and listening, and each ship has a disco.

On Pub Night the cruise director's staff leads a rollicking evening of fun with passenger participation. At the conclusion of the second formal night, champagne trickles down over a champagne waterfall, painstakingly created by the arrangement of champagne glasses in a pyramid shape. Ladies are invited to join the maître d' to assist in the pouring for a great photo op.

Lovely chapels or the wide-open decks are equally romantic settings for weddings at sea with the captain officiating.

**Food:** Personal choices regarding where and what to eat abound, but because of the number of passengers, unless you opt for traditional assigned seating, you might have to wait for a table in one of the open seating dining rooms. Menus are varied and extensive in the main dining rooms, and the results are good to excellent considering how much work is going on in the galleys. Vegetarian and healthy lifestyle options are always on the menu, as well as steak, fish, or chicken. A special menu is designed especially for children.

Alternative restaurants are a staple throughout the fleet but vary by ship class. Grand-class ships have upscale steak houses and Sabatini's, an Italian restaurant; both require reservations and carry an extra cover charge. Sun-class ships offer complimentary sit-down dining in the pizzeria and a similar steak-house option, although it's in a sectioned-off area of the buffet restaurant. On *Caribbean, Crown, Emerald,* and *Ruby Princess,* a casual evening alternative to the dining rooms and usual buffet is Café Caribe—adjacent to the Lido buffet restaurant, it serves cuisine with a Caribbean flair. With a few breaks in service, Lido buffets on all ships are almost always open, and a pizzeria and grill offer casual daytime snack choices. The fleet's patisseries and ice-cream bars charge for specialty coffee, some pastries, and premium ice cream. A daily British-style pub lunch served in the ships' Wheelhouse Bar has been introduced fleet-wide with the exception of the Sun-class and smaller ships.

**Your Shipmates:** Princess Cruises attract mostly American passengers, ranging from their mid-thirties to mid-fifties. Families enjoy cruising together on the Princess fleet, particularly during holiday seasons and summer months, when many children are on board. Longer cruises appeal to well-traveled retirees and couples who have the time.

**Dress Code:** Two formal nights are standard on seven-night cruises; an additional formal night may be scheduled on longer sailings. Men are encouraged to wear tuxedos, but dark suits are appropriate. All other evenings are casual, although jeans are discouraged, and it's requested that no shorts be worn in public areas after 6 PM.

**Tipping:** A gratuity of $10.50 per person per day ($11 for passengers in suites and minisuites) is added to shipboard accounts for distribution to stewards and waitstaff. Passengers may adjust the amount based on the level of service experienced. An automatic 15% is added to all bar tabs for bartenders and drink servers; gratuities to other staff members may be extended at passengers' discretion.

# REGENT SEVEN SEAS CRUISES

✉ *1000 Corporate Dr., Suite 500, Fort Lauderdale, FL* ☎ *954/776–6123 or 877/505–5370* ⊕ *www.rssc.com* ☞ *Cruise Style: Luxury.*

The 1994 merger of Radisson Diamond Cruises and Seven Seas Cruise Line launched Radisson Seven Seas Cruises with an eclectic fleet of vessels that offered a nearly all-inclusive cruise experience in sumptuous, contemporary surroundings. The line was rebranded as Regent Seven Seas Cruises in 2006, and ownership passed to Prestige Cruise Holdings (which also owns Oceania Cruises) in 2008.

Even more inclusive than in the past, the line has maintained its traditional tried-and-true formula—delightful ships offering exquisite service, generous staterooms with abundant amenities, a variety of dining options, and superior lecture and enrichment programs. Guests are greeted with champagne upon boarding and find an all-inclusive beverage policy that offers not only soft drinks and bottled water, but also cocktails and select wines at all bars and restaurants throughout the ships.

The cruises are destination-focused, and most sailings host guest lecturers—historians, anthropologists, naturalists, and diplomats. Spotlight cruises center around popular pastimes and themes, such as food and wine, photography, history, archaeology, literature, performing arts, design and cultures, active exploration and wellness, antiques, jewelry and shopping, the environment, and marine life. Passengers need no urging to participate in discussions and workshops led by celebrated experts. All passengers have access to these unique experiences on board and on shore.

Activities and entertainment are tailored for each of the line's distinctive ships with the tastes of sophisticated passengers in mind. Don't expect napkin-folding demonstrations or nonstop action. Production revues, cabaret acts, concert-style piano performances, solo performers, and comedians may be featured in show lounges, with combos playing for listening and dancing in lounges and bars throughout the ships. Casinos are more akin to Monaco than Las Vegas. All ships display tasteful and varied art collections, including pieces that are for sale.

**Food:** Menus may appear to include the usual beef Wellington and Maine lobster, but in the hands of Regent Seven Seas chefs the results are some of the most outstanding meals at sea. Specialty dining varies within the fleet, but the newest ships, *Seven Seas Voyager* and *Seven Seas Mariner,* have the edge with the sophisticated Signatures, featuring the cuisine of Le Cordon Bleu of Paris. Prime 7, on all three ships, is a contemporary adaptation of the classic American steak house offering a fresh, distinctive decor and an innovative menu of the finest prime-aged steak and chops, along with fresh seafood and poultry specialties. In addition, Mediterranean-influenced bistro dinners that need no reservations are served in La Veranda, the venue that is the daytime casual Lido buffet restaurant.

**Your Shipmates:** Regent Seven Seas Cruises are inviting to active, affluent, well-traveled couples ranging from their late-thirties to retirees who enjoy the ships' chic ambience and destination-rich itineraries. Longer cruises attract veteran passengers in the over-sixty age group.

**Dress Code:** Formal attire is required on designated evenings. Men are encouraged to wear tuxedos, and many do so; dark suits are acceptable. Cruises of 7 to 10 nights usually have one or two formal nights; longer cruises may have three. Other evenings are informal or resort casual; the number of each is based on the number of sea days. It's requested that dress codes be observed in public areas after 6 PM.

**Tipping:** Gratuities are included in the fare, and none are expected. To show their appreciation, passengers may elect to make a contribution to a crew welfare fund that benefits the ship's staff.

## ROYAL CARIBBEAN

✉ *1050 Royal Caribbean Way, Miami, FL* ☎ *305/539–6000 or 800/327– 6700* ⊕ *www.royalcaribbean.com* ☞ *Cruise Style: Mainstream.*

Big, bigger, biggest! More than two decades ago, Royal Caribbean launched Sovereign-class ships, the first of the modern megacruise liners, which continue to be an all-around favorite of passengers who enjoy traditional cruising ambience with a touch of daring and whimsy tossed in. Plunging into the 21st century, each ship in the current fleet carries more passengers than the entire Royal Caribbean fleet of the 1970s and has features—such as new surfing pools—that were unheard of in the past.

All Royal Caribbean ships are topped by the company's distinctive signature Viking Crown Lounge, a place to watch the seascape by day and dance away at night. Expansive multideck atriums and the generous use of brass and floor-to-ceiling glass windows give each vessel a sense of spaciousness and style. The action is nonstop in casinos and dance clubs after dark, while daytime hours are filled with poolside games and traditional cruise activities. Port talks tend to lean heavily on shopping recommendations and the sale of shore excursions.

A variety of lounges and high-energy stage shows draws passengers of all ages out to mingle and dance the night away. Production extravaganzas showcase singers and dancers in lavish costumes. Comedians, acrobats, magicians, jugglers, and solo entertainers fill show lounges on nights when the ships' companies aren't performing. Professional ice shows are a highlight of cruises on Voyager-, Freedom-, and Oasis-class ships—the only ships at sea with ice-skating rinks.

**Food:** Dining is an international experience with nightly changing themes and cuisines from around the world. Passenger preference for casual attire and a resortlike atmosphere has prompted the cruise line to add laid-back alternatives to the formal dining rooms in the Windjammer Café and, on certain ships, Johnny Rockets Diner; Seaview Café evokes the ambience of an island beachside stand. Royal Caribbean offers you the choice of early or late dinner seating and has introduced an open seating program fleet-wide.

**Your Shipmates:** Royal Caribbean cruises have a broad appeal for active couples and singles, mostly in their thirties to fifties. Families are partial to the newer vessels that have larger staterooms, huge facilities for children and teens, and seemingly endless choices of activities and dining options.

**Dress Code:** Two formal nights are standard on seven-night cruises; one formal night is the norm on shorter sailings. Men are encouraged to wear tuxedos, but dark suits or sport coats and ties are more prevalent. All other evenings are casual, although jeans are discouraged in restaurants. It's requested that no shorts be worn in public areas after 6 PM, although there are passengers who can't wait to change into them after dinner.

**Tipping:** Tips can be prepaid when the cruise is booked, added on to shipboard accounts, or given in cash on the last night of the cruise. Suggested gratuities per passenger per day are $3.50 for the cabin steward ($5.75 for suites), $3.50 for the waiter, $2 for the assistant waiter, and $0.75 for the headwaiter. An 15% gratuity is automatically added to all bar tabs.

## SEABOURN CRUISE LINE

✉ *6100 Blue Lagoon Dr., Suite 400, Miami, FL* ☎ *305/463–3000 or 800/929–9391* ⊕ *www.seabourn.com* ☞ *Cruise Style: Luxury.*

Seabourn was founded on the principle that dedication to personal service in elegant surroundings would appeal to sophisticated, independent-minded passengers whose lifestyles demand the best. Lovingly maintained since their introduction in 1987—and routinely updated with new features—the original megayachts of Seabourn and their new fleet mates have proved to be a smashing success over the years. They remain favorites with people who can take care of themselves but would rather do so aboard a ship that caters to their individual preferences.

Recognized as a leader in small-ship, luxury cruising, Seabourn delivers all the expected extras—complimentary wines and spirits, a stocked minibar in all suites, and elegant amenities. Expect the unexpected as well—from exclusive travel-document portfolios and luggage tags to the pleasure of a complimentary mini-massage while lounging at the pool. If you don't want to lift a finger, Seabourn will even arrange to have your luggage picked up at home and delivered directly to your suite—for a price.

Dining and evening socializing are generally more stimulating to Seabourn passengers than splashy song-and-dance revues. Still, proportionately scaled production shows and cabarets are presented in the main showroom and smaller lounge. Movies Under the Stars are shown on the wind-protected Sun Deck at least one evening on virtually all cruises as long as the weather permits. The library stocks not only books but also movies for those who prefer to watch them in the privacy of their suites—popcorn will be delivered with a call to room service.

The Dress Circle Series enrichment program features guest appearances by luminaries in the arts, literature, politics, and world affairs; during Chef's Circle sailings you can learn the secrets of the world's most innovative chefs. Due to the size of Seabourn ships, passengers have the opportunity to mingle with presenters and interact one-on-one.

Peace and tranquillity reign on these ships, so the daily roster of events is somewhat thin. Wine-tastings, lectures, and other quiet pursuits might be scheduled, but most passengers are satisfied to simply do what pleases them.

One don't-miss activity is the daily team trivia contest. Prizes are unimportant: it's the bragging rights that most guests seek.

Although the trio of original Seabourn ships has been upgraded with new features over the years, the line has begun a program to build a new set of larger, even more luxurious triplets to be introduced in 2009 (*Seabourn Odyssey*), 2010 (*Seabourn Sojourn*), and an as-yet-unnamed vessel in 2011. There is no word about whether the original megayachts will be retired when *Seabourn Odyssey* launches as the line's flagship.

**Food:** Exceptional cuisine created by celebrity chef Charlie Palmer is prepared *à la minute* and served in open seating dining rooms. Upscale menu offerings include foie gras, quail, fresh seafood, and jasmine crème brûlée. Dishes low in cholesterol, salt, and fat, as well as vegetarian selections, are prepared with the same artful presentation and attention to detail. Wines are chosen to complement each day's luncheon and dinner menus, and caviar is always available. A background of classical music sets the tone for afternoon tea. The weekly Gala Tea features crêpes Suzette.

**Your Shipmates:** Seabourn's yachtlike vessels appeal to well-traveled, affluent couples of all ages who enjoy destination-intense itineraries, a subdued atmosphere, and exclusive service. Passengers tend to be fifty-plus and retired couples who are accustomed to evening formality.

**Dress Code:** At least one formal night is standard on seven-night cruises and three to four nights, depending on the itinerary, on two-week cruises. Men are required to wear tuxedos or dark suits after 6 PM, and the majority prefer black tie. All other evenings are elegant casual, and slacks with a jacket over a sweater or shirt for men and a sundress or skirt or pants with a sweater or blouse for women are suggested.

**Tipping:** Tipping is neither required nor expected.

## SILVERSEA CRUISES

✉ *110 E. Broward Blvd., Fort Lauderdale, FL* ☎ *954/522–4477 or 800/722–9955* ⊕ *www.silversea.com* ✆ *Cruise Style: Luxury.*

Silversea Cruises was launched in 1994 by the former owners of Sitmar Cruises, the Lefebvre family of Rome, whose concept for the new cruise line was to build and sail the highest-quality luxury ships at sea. Intimate ships, paired with exclusive amenities and unparalleled hospitality are the hallmarks of Silversea cruises. All-inclusive air-and-sea fares can be customized to include not just round-trip airfare but all transfers, porterage, and deluxe precruise accommodations as well.

Personalization is a Silversea maxim. Their ships offer more activities than other comparably sized luxury vessels. Take part in those that interest you, or opt instead for a good book and any number of quiet spots to read or snooze in the shade. Silversea's third generation of ships will introduce even more luxurious features when the 36,000-ton *Silver Spirit* launches late in 2009.

Guest lecturers are featured on nearly every cruise; language, dance, and culinary lessons and excellent wine appreciation sessions are always on the schedule of events. Silversea also schedules culinary arts cruises and a series of wine-focused voyages that feature award-winning authors, international wine experts, winemakers, and acclaimed chefs from the world's top restaurants. During afternoon tea, ladies gather for conversation over needlepoint, and the ranks of highly competitive trivia teams increase every successive afternoon.

After dark, the Bar is a predinner gathering spot and the late-night place for dancing to a live band. A multitiered show lounge is the setting for talented singers and musicians, classical concerts, magic shows, big-screen movies, and folkloric entertainers from ashore. A small casino offers slot machines and gaming tables.

**Food:** Dishes from the galleys of Silversea's master chefs are complemented by those of La Collection du Monde, created by Silversea's culinary partner, the world-class chefs of Relais & Châteaux. Menus include hot and cold appetizers, at least four entrée selections, a vegetarian alternative, and Cruiselite cuisine (low in cholesterol, sodium, and fat). Special off-menu orders are prepared whenever possible, provided that the ingredients are available on board. In the event that they aren't, you may find after a day in port that a trip to the market was made in order to fulfill your request.

Chef Marco Betti, the owner of Antica Pasta restaurants in Florence, Italy, and Atlanta, Georgia, has designed a new menu for La Terrazza that focuses on one of the most luxurious food trends, the "slow food" movement. The goal of the movement is to preserve the gastronomic traditions of Italy through the use of fresh, traditional foods, and it has spread throughout the world. At La Terrazza (by day, a casual buffet) the menu showcases the finest in Italian cooking, from classic favorites to Tuscan fare. The restaurant carries no surcharge. Seating is limited, so reservations are a must to ensure a table—it's one reservation you'll be glad you took the time to book.

**Your Shipmates:** Silversea Cruises appeal to sophisticated, affluent couples who enjoy the country-club-like atmosphere, exquisite cuisine, and polished service on board, not to mention the exotic ports and unique experiences ashore.

**Dress Code:** Two formal nights are standard on seven-night cruises and three to four nights, depending on the itinerary, on longer sailings. Men are required to wear tuxedos or dark suits after 6 PM. All other evenings are either informal, when a jacket is called for (a tie is optional, but most men wear them), or casual, when slacks with a jacket over an open-collar shirt for men and sporty dresses or skirts or pants with a sweater or blouse for women are suggested.

**Tipping:** Tipping is neither required nor expected.

## STAR CLIPPERS

✉ *7200 N.W. 19th St., Suite 206, Miami, FL* ☎ *305/442–0550 or 800/ 442–0551* ⊕ *www.starclippers.com* ☞ *Cruise Style: Sailing Ship.*

In 1991 Star Clippers unveiled a new tall-ship alternative to sophisticated travelers, whose desires included having an adventure at sea but not on board a conventional cruise ship. Star Clippers vessels are four- and five-masted sailing beauties—the world's largest barkentine and full-rigged sailing ships. Filled with modern, high-tech equipment as well as the amenities of private yachts, the ships rely on sail power while at sea unless conditions require the assistance of the engines. Minimal heeling, usually less than 6%, is achieved through judicious control of the sails.

A boyhood dream became a cruise-line reality when Swedish entrepreneur Mikael Krafft launched his fleet of authentic re-creations of classic 19th-century clipper ships. The day officially begins when the captain holds an informative daily briefing on deck with a bit of storytelling tossed in. Star Clippers are not cruise ships in the ordinary sense with strict agendas and pages of activities. You're free to do what you please day and night, but many passengers join the crew members topside when the sails are raised or for some of the lighthearted events like crab-racing contests, scavenger hunts, and a talent night. The informality of singing around the piano bar typifies an evening on one of these ships, although in certain ports local performers come on board to spice up the action with an authentic taste of the local music and arts.

The lack of rigid scheduling is one of Star Clippers' most appealing attractions. The bridge is always open, and passengers are welcome to peer over the captain's shoulder as he plots the ship's course. Crew members are happy to demonstrate how to splice a line, reef a sail, or tie a proper knot.

As attractive as the ships' interiors are, the focal point of Star Clippers cruises is the outdoors. Plan to spend a lot of time on deck soaking in the sun, sea, and sky. It doesn't get any better than that. Consider also that each ship has at least two swimming pools. Granted, they are tiny, but they are a refreshing feature uncommon on true sailing ships and all but the most lavish yachts.

Although the Star Clippers ships are motorized, their engines are shut down whenever crews unfurl the sails (36,000 square feet on *Star Clipper* and *Star Flyer*, and 56,000 square feet on *Royal Clipper*) to capture the wind. On a typical cruise, the ships rely exclusively on sail power any time favorable conditions prevail.

As the haunting strains of Vangelis's symphony "1492: Conquest of Paradise" are piped over the PA system and the first of the sails is unfurled, the only thing you'll hear on deck is the sound of the music and the calls of the line handlers until every sail is in place. While the feeling of the wind powering large ships through the water is spine-tingling, you will miss the wondrous sight of your ship under sail unless the captain can schedule a photo opportunity utilizing one of the tenders. It's one of the most memorable sights you'll see if this opportunity avails itself. However, when necessary, the ships will cruise under motor power to meet the requirements of their itineraries.

**Food:** Not noted for gourmet fare, the international cuisine is what you would expect from a trendy shoreside bistro, albeit an elegant one. All meals are open seating in the formal dining room during scheduled hours; breakfast and lunch—an impressive spread of seafood, salads, and grilled items—are served buffet-style, while dinners are leisurely affairs served in the European manner. Hint: If you want your salad *before* your main course, just ask; the French style is to serve it after the main course. Menus, created in consultation with chef Jean Marie Meulien (who has been awarded Michelin stars throughout his career), include appetizers, soups, pasta, a sorbet course, at least three choices of entrées, salad, cheese, and, of course, dessert. Mediterranean-inspired entrées, vegetarian, and light dishes are featured. A maître d' is present at the more formal evening meals to seat passengers, but it isn't uncommon on these small ships for them to arrange their own groups of dinner company.

**Your Shipmates:** Star Clippers cruises draw active, upscale American and European couples from their thirties on up, who enjoy sailing but in a casually sophisticated atmosphere with modern conveniences. Many sailings are equally divided between North Americans and Europeans, so announcements are made in several languages accordingly.

This is not a cruise line for the physically challenged; there are no elevators or ramps, nor are staterooms or bathrooms wheelchair accessible. Gangways and shore launches can also be difficult to negotiate.

**Dress Code:** All evenings are elegant casual, so slacks and open-collar shirts are fine for men, and sundresses, skirts, or pants with a sweater or blouse are suggested for women. Coats and ties are never required. Shorts and T-shirts are not allowed in the dining room at dinner.

**Tipping:** Gratuities are not included in the cruise fare and are extended at the sole discretion of passengers. The recommended amount is €8 per person per day. Tips are pooled and shared; individual tipping is discouraged. You can either put cash in the tip envelope that will be provided to you and drop it at the Purser's Office or charge gratuities to your shipboard account. An automatic 15% gratuity is added to each passenger's bar bill.

## WINDSTAR CRUISES

✉ *2101 4th Ave., Suite 1150, Seattle, WA* ☎ *206/292–9606 or 800/258–7245* ⊕ *www.windstarcruises.com* ☞ *Cruise Style: Luxury.*

Are they cruise ships with sails or sailing ships designed for cruises? Since 1986, these masted sailing yachts have filled an upscale niche. They often visit ports of call inaccessible to huge, traditional cruise ships and offer a unique perspective of any cruising region. However, Windstar ships seldom depend on wind alone to sail. Nevertheless, if you're fortunate and conditions are perfect, as they sometimes are, the complete silence of pure sailing is heavenly. Stabilizers and computer-controlled ballast systems ensure no more than a mere few degrees of lean.

When you can tear yourself away from the sight of thousands of yards of Dacron sail overhead, it doesn't take long to read the daily schedule of activities on a typical Windstar cruise. Simply put, there are few scheduled activities. Diversions are for the most part social, laid-back, and impromptu. You can choose to take part in the short list of daily activities; borrow a book, game, or DVD from the library; or do nothing at all. There's never pressure to join in or participate if you simply prefer relaxing with a fully loaded iPod, which you can check out on board.

Evening entertainment is informal, with a small dance combo playing in the main lounges. Compact casinos offer games of chance and slot machines, but don't look for bingo or other organized contests. A weekly show by the crew is delightful; attired in the traditional costumes of their homelands, they present music and dance highlighting their cultures. You may find occasional movies in the main lounges, which are outfitted with state-of-the-art video and sound equipment. Most passengers prefer socializing, either in the main lounge or an outdoor bar where Cigars Under the Stars attracts not only cigar aficionados but stargazers as well.

Welcome-aboard and farewell parties are hosted by the captain, and most passengers attend those as well as the nightly informational sessions regarding ports of call and activities that are presented by the activities staff during predinner cocktails.

A multimillion-dollar Degrees of Difference initiative enhanced each ship from stern to stern in 2006–07. The Yacht Club, which replaced the library on *Wind Surf,* is designed to be the social hub of the ship, with computer stations, a coffee bar, and a more expansive feel than the room it replaced. You will be able to join other passengers in comfortable seating around a large flat-screen TV to cheer on your favorite team during sporting events. In addition, all accommodations and bathrooms have been remodeled with updated materials; new weights and televisions were added to the gym; a couples massage room enhances the *Wind Surf* spa; the casual Veranda was expanded; the decks now have Balinese sun beds; and cooling mist sprayers are near the pools. Subsequent updates to *Wind Spirit* and *Wind Star* are similar but on a smaller scale.

**Food:** Dining on Windstar ships is as casually elegant as the dress code. There's seldom a wait for a table in open seating dining rooms where tables for two are plentiful. Whether meals are taken in the open and airy top-deck buffet, with its floor-to-ceiling windows and adjacent tables outside, or in the formal dining room, dishes are as creative as the surroundings. Expect traditional entrées but also items that incorporate regional ingredients, such as plantains, for added interest. Save room for petits fours with coffee and a taste of the fine cheeses from the after-dinner cheese cart.

**Your Shipmates:** Windstar Cruises appeal to upscale professional couples in their late-thirties to sixties and on up to retirees, who enjoy the unpretentious, yet casually sophisticated atmosphere, creative cuisine, and refined service.

Windstar's ships were not designed for accessibility, and are not a good choice for the physically challenged. Although every attempt is made to accommodate passengers with disabilities, *Wind Surf* has only two elevators, and the smaller ships have none. There are no staterooms or bathrooms with wheelchair accessibility, and gangways can be difficult to navigate, depending on the tide and angle of ascent. Service animals are permitted to sail if arrangements were made at the time of booking.

**Dress Code:** All evenings are country-club casual, and slacks with a jacket over a sweater or shirt for men, and sundresses, skirts, or pants with a sweater or blouse for women are suggested. Coats and ties for men are not necessary, but some male passengers prefer to wear a jacket with open-collar shirt to dinner.

**Tipping:** For many years Windstar sailed under a "tipping not required" policy. Windstar has now changed that policy. A service charge of $12 per guest per day (including children) is now added to each shipboard account. A 15% service charge is added to all bar bills. All these proceeds are paid directly to the crew.

# Western Mediterranean

PORTS IN FRANCE, ITALY, MALTA, PORTUGAL, & SPAIN

## WORD OF MOUTH

"My wife and I are going on a trip of a lifetime next June—12-day Mediterranean/Greece cruise starting [in] Rome and ending in Venice. . . . Probably our biggest dilemma is in Naples. With only one day, do you go to Isle of Capri, try to see Pompeii and Mount Vesuvius, or see the Amalfi Coast?"

—MurrayMartin

Lindsay
Bennett

If you're a first-time cruiser in Europe and want to stop at some of the most popular European destinations, a Western Mediterranean itinerary might be ideal for you.

Western Mediterranean itineraries often begin in either Barcelona or Civitavecchia (for Rome) and may be one-way or round-trip cruises. One-week cruises in Europe tend to be one-way cruises, while those of 10 days or more are sometimes loop cruises. A few of these itineraries may take you as far as Venice, though that city is a more popular jumping-off point for cruises through the Adriatic and Aegean. Although some of the ports included in this chapter (such as Venice or Bari in Italy) are more likely to be on Eastern Mediterranean itineraries, others (such as Le Havre or Bordeaux in France) may be a part of some Northern European cruise routes. We've kept all the ports in Italy and France together in this chapter to make them easier to find. Larger ships will be limited in the ports at which they can call, but smaller ships may hit some of the lesser-visited spots on the French or Italian Riviera.

## ABOUT THE RESTAURANTS

All the restaurants we recommend serve lunch, and many also serve dinner. If your cruise ship stays late in port, you may choose to dine off the ship. Although the cuisine in Europe is varied, one thing is constant across the continent: Europeans tend to eat a leisurely meal at lunch. In most ports there are quicker and simpler alternatives for those who just want to grab a quick bite before returning to the ship.

| WHAT IT COSTS IN EUROS | | | | |
|---|---|---|---|---|
| | ¢ | $ | $$ | $$$ | $$$$ |
| Restaurants | under €11 | €12–€17 | €18–€23 | €24–€30 | over €30 |

Restaurant price categories are based on the average price of a main course at dinner.

# A CORUÑA, SPAIN (FOR SANTIAGO DE COMPOSTELA)

One of Spain's busiest ports, A Coruña (La Coruña in Castilian) prides itself on being the most progressive city in the region. The weather can be fierce, wet, and windy—hence the glass-enclosed, white-pane galleries lining the houses lining the harbor. This is one of two main ports at which cruise ships call so they can offer an overland trek to the pilgrimage city of Santiago de Compostela; the other is Vigo (⇨ *Vigo, below, for information on Santiago de Compostela, including a map*). Though at 57 km (35 mi) to the north, A Coruña is marginally closer. Occasionally, a cruise ship will offer an overland excursion beginning in one port and ending in the other.

## ESSENTIALS

CURRENCY    The euro (€1 to US$1.36 at this writing).

HOURS    Museums are generally open from 9 until 7 or 8, many are closed on Monday, and some close in the afternoon. Most stores are open Monday through Saturday 9 to 1:30 and 5 to 8, but tourist shops may open in the afternoon and also on Sunday between May and September.

INTERNET    **CMC Informatica** ⊠ *c/Pio XII no 10 bajo, A Coruña* ☎ *881/894685* ⊕ *www.comunicopy.com* ☯ *Weekdays 10–2 and 4–8, Sun. 10–2.* **Estrella Park Street** (⊠ *Estrella 12, A Coruña* ☎ *981/229070*).

TELEPHONES    Most tri- and quad-band GSM phones work in Spain, which has a 3G-compatible network. Public kiosks accept phone cards that support international calls (cards sold in press shops, bars, and telecom shops). Major companies include Vodafone.

### COMING ASHORE

Ships dock at Liners Quay in the interior of the port. There are few services at the port itself, but from the port entrance you can explore the town on foot.

Bus 1 runs from the port to the main bus station every 20 minutes for €1.10. There is at least one train per hour to Santiago de Compostela. Journey time is 50 minutes, and tickets cost approximately €9 return.

A tourist tram operates around the town of A Coruña throughout the year (weekends only October through June). Tickets cost €2. Taxis wait at the port entrance and can be hired by the day for tourist itineraries. Renting a car would allow you to explore Santiago de Compostela plus the rugged countryside of this wild corner of Spain, but prices are expensive. Expect to pay €75 per day for a manual economy vehicle.

## EXPLORING A CORUÑA

**Castillo de San Antón.** At the northeastern tip of the Old Town is St. Anthony's Castle, a 16th-century fort. Inside is A Coruña's **Museum of Archaeology,** with remnants of the prehistoric Celtic culture that once thrived in these parts. ☎ *981/189850* ▦ *€2* ☯ *July and Aug., Tues.–Sat. 10–9, Sun. 10–3; Sept.–June, Tues.–Sat. 10–7, Sun. 10–2:30.*

**Church of Santiago.** The 12th-century church is the oldest church in A Coruña, and was the first stop on the *camino inglés* (English route) toward Santiago de Compostela. Originally Romanesque, it's now a hodgepodge, with Gothic arches, a baroque altarpiece, and two 18th-century rose windows. ⊠ *Pl. de la Constitución s/n.*

**Colegiata de Santa María.** This Romanesque beauty from the mid-13th century is often called Santa María del Campo (St. Mary of the Field) because it was once outside the city walls. A quirk of this church is that, because of an architectural miscalculation, the roof is too heavy for its supports, so the columns inside lean outward, and the buttresses outside have been thickened. ⊠ *Pl. de Santa María.*

**Dársena de la Marina.** To see why sailors once nicknamed A Coruña *la ciudad de cristal* (the glass city), stroll what is said to be the longest seaside promenade in Europe. Although the congregation of boats is charming, the real sight is across the street: a long, gracefully curved row of houses. Built by fishermen in the 18th century, the houses actually face *away* from the sea. Nets were hung from the porches to dry, and fish was sold on the street below. The **glass galleries** ultimately spread across the harbor and eventually throughout Galicia.

↻ **Domus/Casa del Hombre.** The slate-covered Museum of Mankind was designed by Japanese architect Arata Isozaki. In the shape of a ship's sail, this museum is dedicated to the study of the human being, and particularly the human body. ✉ *C. Santa Teresa 1* ☎ *981/189840* ⊕ *www. casaciencias.org* ✎ *Museum €2, IMAX €1* ⊙ *Daily 10–7.*

**Museo de Bellas Artes.** The Museum of Fine Arts, housed in a converted convent on the edge of the old town, has French, Spanish, and Italian paintings and a curious collection of etchings by Goya. ✉ *C. Zalaeta s/n* ☎ *981/223723* ✎ *Free* ⊙ *Tues.–Fri. 10–8, Sat. 10–2 and 4:30–8, Sun. 10–2.*

**Plaza de María Pita.** The focal point of the *ciudad vieja* (Old Town) is this expansive plaza. Its north side is given over to the neoclassical **Palacio Municipal,** or city hall, built in 1908–12. The **monument** in the center, built in 1998, depicts the heroine herself, Maior (María) Pita, holding her lance. When England's notorious Sir Francis Drake arrived to sack A Coruña in 1589, the locals were only half finished building the defensive Castillo de San Antón, and a 13-day battle ensued. When María Pita's husband died, she took up his lance, slew the Briton who tried to plant the Union Jack here, and revived the exhausted Coruñesos.

**Torre de Hercules.** Much of A Coruña sits on a peninsula, on the tip of which is the oldest still-functioning lighthouse in the world. Originally built during the reign of Trajan, the Roman emperor born in Spain in AD 98, the lighthouse was rebuilt in the 18th century and looks strikingly modern; all that remains from Roman times are inscribed foundation stones. Scale the 245 steps for superb views of the city and coastline. ✉ *Ctra. de la Torre s/n* ☎ *981/223730* ⊕ *www.torrehdeerculesacoruna. com* ✎ *€2.50* ⊙ *July and Aug., Sun.–Thurs. 10–9, Fri. and Sat. 10–midnight; Apr.–June and Sept., daily 10–7; Oct.–Mar., daily 10–6.*

## SHOPPING

The main shopping streets in A Coruña are Calle Canzones, Calle San Andres, and Calle Real.

**Adolfo Dominguez.** Galicia has spawned some of Spain's top designers, notably Adolfo Dominguez. ✉ *Av. Finisterre 3* ☎ *981/252539.*

**José López Rama.** Authentic Galician *zuecos* (hand-painted wooden clogs) are still worn in some villages to navigate mud; the cobbler José López Rama has a workshop 15 minutes south of A Coruña in the village of Carballo. ✉ *Rúa do Muiño 7, Carballo* ☎ *981/701068.*

**Sastrería Iglesias.** For hats and Galician folk clothing, stop into this shop—founded 1864—where artisan José Luis Iglesias Rodrígues sells his textiles. ✉ *Rego do Auga 14, A Coruña* ☎ *981/221634.*

## WHERE TO EAT

**$** ╳ **Adega o Bebedeiro.** Steps from the ultramodern Domus, this tiny res-
SPANISH taurant is beloved by locals for its authentic food and low prices. It
★ feels like an old farmhouse, with stone walls and floors, a fireplace, pine
tables and stools, and dusty wine bottles (*adega* means "wine cellar").
Appetizers such as *setas rellenas de marisco y salsa holandesa* (wild
mushrooms with seafood and hollandaise sauce) are followed by fresh
fish at market prices and an ever-changing array of delicious desserts.
✉ *C. Ángel Rebollo 34* ☎ *981/210609* ▭ *AE, DC, MC, V* ☉ *Closed
Mon., last 2 wks in June, and last 2 wks in Dec. No dinner Sun.*

**¢–$** ╳ **La Penela.** The smart, contemporary, bottle-green dining room is the
SEAFOOD perfect place to feast on fresh fish while sipping Albariño—try at least a
★ few crabs or mussels with béchamel, for which this restaurant is locally
famous. If shellfish isn't your speed, the roast veal is also popular. The
restaurant occupies a modernist building on a corner of the lively Praza
María Pita. Some tables have views of the harbor, or you can eat in a
glassed-in terrace on the square. ✉ *Praza María Pita 12* ☎ *981/209200*
▭ *AE, DC, MC, V* ☉ *Closed Sun. and Jan. 10–25.*

# AJACCIO, CORSICA

Guy de Maupassant called Corsica "the mountain in the sea." A vertical
granite world plopped down in the Mediterranean between Provence
and Tuscany, Corsica's gifts of artistic and archaeological treasures,
crystalline waters, granite peaks, and pine forests add up to one of
France's most unspoiled sanctuaries. Mountain people born and bred,
true Corsicans are highland spirits, at home in the all-sustaining chest-
nut forest, the Laricio pines, or the dense undergrowth of the *maquis*,
a variety of wild and aromatic plants that gave Corsica one of its sobri-
quets, "the perfumed isle." Its strategic location 168 km (105 mi) south
of Monaco and 81 km (50 mi) west of Italy made Corsica a prize
hotly contested by a succession of Mediterranean powers. Their vestiges
remain in impressive citadels, churches, bridges, and medieval watch-
towers. The Italian influence is also apparent in the Corsican language,
which is a combination of Italian, Tuscan dialect, and Latin.

### ESSENTIALS

CURRENCY The euro (€1 to US$1.36 at this writing).

HOURS Stores are open Monday–Saturday 9–7, but many close at lunchtime
(usually noon–2 or 3), and some open later and on Sunday during July
and August. Museums are open 10–5, but most are closed on either
Monday or Tuesday.

TELEPHONES Tri-band GSM phones work in France. You can buy prepaid phone
cards at telecom shops, newsvendors, and tobacconists in all towns and
cities. Phone cards can be used for local or international calls. France
Telecom and Orange are leading telecom companies.

### COMING ASHORE

Ships dock in Ajaccio port, a short walk from the town of Ajaccio. Cafés
and shops can be found immediately outside the port gates.

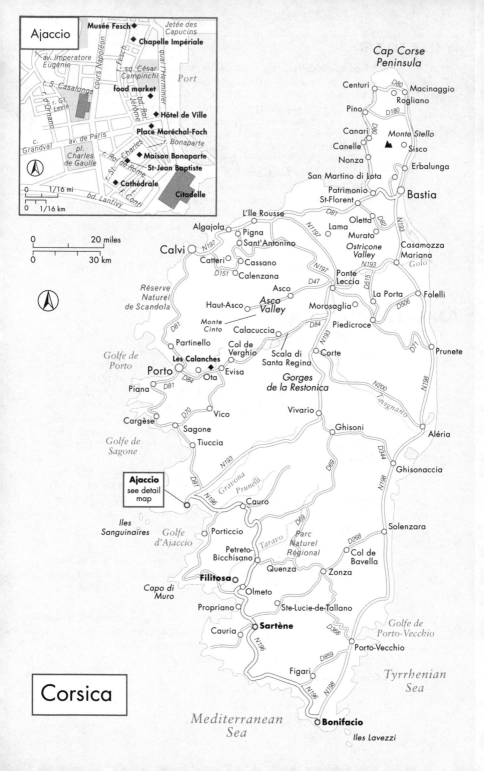

## Ajaccio

Musée Fesch ◆
Chapelle Impériale ◆
*Jetée des Capucins*
av. Impérator Eugénie
*sq. César Campinchi*
food market ■
*Port*
Hôtel de Ville ◆
Place Maréchal-Foch ◆
Maison Bonaparte ◆
St-Jean Baptiste
Cathédrale ◆
Citadelle

1/16 mi
1/16 km

20 miles
30 km

## Corsica

**Cap Corse Peninsula**

Centuri • D80 • Macinaggio
Pino • D180 • Rogliano
Canari • D80 • *Monte Stello* ▲
Canelle • Sisco
Nonza
San Martino di Lota
Patrimonio • **Bastia**
St-Florent
Oletta
Lama • Murato
*Ostricone Valley*
Casamozza
Mariana
*Golo*
L'Ile Rousse
Algajola
Pigna • Sant'Antonino
**Calvi**
Catteri • Cassano
Calenzana
Ponte Leccia
La Porta • Folelli
*Réserve Naturel de Scandola*
Asco • *Asco Valley*
Haut-Asco
*Monte Cinto*
Calacuccia
Morosaglia
Piedicroce
Prunete
Partinello
Col de Verghio
Scala di Santa Regina
**Corte**
**Les Calanches**
Evisa
**Porto**
Ota
*Golfe de Porto*
Piana
*Gorges de la Restonica*
Vico
Vivario
Ghisoni
Cargèse
Sagone
Tiuccia
Aléria
*Golfe de Sagone*
Ghisonaccia
**Ajaccio** see detail map
Cauro
Porticcio
Solenzara
*Iles Sanguinaires*
*Golfe d'Ajaccio*
Petreto-Bicchisano
*Parc Naturel Régional*
Col de Bavella
**Filitosa**
Quenza
Zonza
Olmeto
Propriano
Ste-Lucie-de-Tallano
Capo di Muro
Cauria
**Sartène**
*Golfe de Porto-Vecchio*
Porto-Vecchio
Figari
*Tyrrhenian Sea*
**Bonifacio**
*Iles Lavezzi*
*Mediterranean Sea*

The local bus network is geared to residents, who take it to school and work. At least two buses a day connect all the southern towns with Ajaccio, but timetables may not coincide with your ship's departure time, so check carefully. Renting a vehicle would allow you to explore several towns and surrounding attractions during your stay on the island; however, be aware that travel times may be longer than map distances suggest, because the mountain roads can be narrow and winding. Vehicle rental costs approximately €60 per day for an economy manual car. Delivery to the port will be an additional charge. Hertz serves the entire island; its 18 offices are at all airports and harbors and in the major towns. Be sure to reserve at least two weeks in advance in July and August.

## CORSICA BEST BETS

**Bonifacio.** Rising seemingly out of the living rock, this medieval stronghold is now a maze of tourist-friendly cafés and shops.

**The Calanques de Piana.** Russet red inlets of jagged rocks lapped by azure waters, this vista, which you can see if you drive between Ajaccio and Calvi, is truly breathtaking.

**Calvi.** A picture-perfect little town topped by a walled citadel, Calvi also offers some of the finest beaches on the island.

# EXPLORING CORSICA

## AJACCIO

Ajaccio, Napoléon's birthplace and Corsica's modern capital, is a busy, French-flavored town with a bustling port and ancient streets. The city has a long history dating back to its founding in 1492, and some of the original buildings can still be seen on rue Roie-de-Rome, near the Musée du Capitellu.

**Cathédrale.** The 16th-century baroque cathedral where Napoléon was baptized is at the end of rue St-Charles. The interior is covered with trompe-l'oeil frescoes, and the high altar, from a church in Lucca, Italy, was donated by Napoléon's sister Eliza after he made her princess of Tuscany. Eugène Delacroix's *Virgin of Sacré Coeur* hangs above the altar. ⊠ *Rue F.-Conti.* ☎ *04–95–21–41–14* ✉ *Free* ⊘ *Daily 9–11* AM.

**Chapelle Impérial.** The Renaissance-style Imperial Chapel was built in 1857 by Napoléon's nephew, Napoléon III, to accommodate the tombs of the Bonaparte family (Napoléon Bonaparte himself is buried in the Hôtel des Invalides in Paris). The Coptic crucifix over the altar was taken from Egypt during the general's 1798 campaign. The chapel is undergoing a renovation at this writing that is expected to be finished by 2012. ⊠ *50 rue Fesch* ✉ *€1.50* ⊘ *Tues.–Sat. 10–12:30 and 3–7.*

**Food market.** A good place to start any visit is at the spectacular food market held every morning except Monday across the quai from the ferry port. This is an excellent opportunity to admire an enticing parade of Corsican cheeses, pastries, sausages, and everything from traditional chestnut-flour beignets to prehistoric *rascasse* (red scorpion fish) at the fish market tucked in under the Hôtel de Ville. ⊠ *Pl. Campinchi* ⊙ *Tues.–Sun. 7 AM–12:30 PM.*

**Hôtel de Ville** *(Town Hall)*. Ajaccio's town hall has an Empire-style grand salon hung with portraits of a long line of Bonapartes. You'll find a fine bust of Letizia, Napoléon's formidable mother; a bronze death mask of the emperor himself; and a frescoed ceiling depicting Napoléon's meteoric rise. ⊠ *Pl. Maréchal-Foch* ☎ *04–95–51–52–67* ☜ *€2.30* ⊙ *Weekdays 9–noon and 2–6.*

**Fodor's Choice** **Maison Bonaparte** *(Bonaparte House)*. Two short blocks left of the statue
★ of Napoléon on place Maréchal-Foch is the house where Napoléon Bonaparte was born on August 15, 1769. Today this large (once middleclass) house contains a museum with portraits of the entire Bonaparte clan. Search out the two family trees woven out of actual human hair. Most of the salons are 20th-century redos and hommages to the emperor's favored Empire neoclassical style. Several are distressingly bare, others flaunt antiques created under King Louis-Phillipe (his sworn enemy), while only one—the Chambre à Alcôve—seems to evince the life of the little giant, since legend has it he spent his nights here when after his conquest of Egypt. Still, fans of the man—and connoisseurs of *le style empire à la ajaccienne*—will find this worthwhile. ⊠ *Rue St-Charles* ☎ *04–95–21–43–89* ⊕ *www.musee-maisonbonaparte.fr* ☜ *€6* ⊙ *Tues.–Sun. 10–noon and 2–5.*

★ **Musée Fesch.** Adjacent to the Chapelle Impérial, this museum houses a fine collection of Italian masters, ranging from Botticelli and Canaletto to De Tura—part of a massive collection of 30,000 paintings bought at bargain prices by Napoléon's uncle, Cardinal Fesch, archbishop of Lyon, following the French Revolution. Thanks to his nephew's military conquests, the cardinal was able to amass (steal, some would say) many celebrated Old Master paintings, the most famous of which are now in the Louvre. ⊠ *50 rue Fesch* ☎ *04–95–21–48–17* ⊕ *www.musee-fesch. com/* ☜ *€5.50* ⊙ *Apr., June, Sept., and Oct., Wed.–Mon. 9:30–noon and 3–6:30; July and Aug., Tues.–Sat. 9–midnight, Sun. and Mon. 9:30–noon and 3–6:30; Nov.–Mar., Wed.–Mon. 9:30–noon and 2:30–6.*

**Place Maréchal-Foch.** Rows of stately palm trees lead up to a marble statue of Napoléon on the city's main square. The neighboring Place de Gaulle (also known as Place de Diamant) is a large square surrounded by sandwich shops, cafés, and a small carousal. Marking the center is a bronze statue of Napoléon surrounded by his four brothers.

**St-Jean Baptiste.** At the corner of rue St-Charles and rue Roi-de-Rome, opposite this tiny church, are the city's oldest houses. They were built shortly after the town was founded in 1492.

## FILITOSA
★ *71 km (43 mi) southeast of Ajaccio off N196.*

Filitosa is the site of Corsica's largest grouping of megalithic menhir statues. Bizarre, life-size stone figures of ancient warriors rise up mysteriously from the undulating terrain, many with human faces whose features have been flattened over time by erosion. A small museum on the site houses archaeological finds, including the menhir known as

*Scalsa Murta,* whose delicately carved spine and rib cage are surprisingly contemporary for a work dating from some 5,000 years ago. The guidebook in English (€5) by experts Cesari and Acquaviva is supplemented by information in English at each site. ⊠ *Contact Centre Préhistorique Filitosa* ☎ *04–95–74–00–91 for information* ⊕ *www.filitosa.fr* 🎫 *Guided tours in English €5* ⊗ *June–Aug., daily 8–7.*

## SARTÈNE
*27 km (16 mi) southeast of Filitosa on N196.*

Described as the "most Corsican of all Corsican towns" by French novelist Prosper Mérimée, Sartène, founded in the 16th century, has survived pirate raids and bloody feuding among the town's families. The word "vendetta" is believed to have originated here as the result of a 19th-century family feud so serious that French troops were brought in to serve as a peacekeeping buffer force. Centuries of fighting have left the town with a somewhat eerie and menacing atmosphere. Perhaps adding to this is the annual Good Friday *catenacciu* (enchaining) procession, in which an anonymous penitent, dragging ankle chains, lugs a heavy cross through the village streets.

Surrounded by ancient ramparts, **Vieux Sartène** (Old Sartène) begins at place de la Libération, the main square. To one side is the **Hôtel de Ville** (town hall), in the former Genoese governor's palace. Slip into the Middle Ages through the tunnel under the Town Hall to place du Maggiu and the ancient **Santa Anna** quarter, a warren of narrow, cobbled streets lined with granite houses. Scarcely 100 yards from the Hôtel de Ville, down a steep and winding street, is a 12th-century *tour de guet* (watchtower). Sartène is a key link to Corsica's prehistory, thanks to its proximity to Pianu de Levie's dolmens and megalithic statues.

**Musée Départemental de Préhistoire Corse** *(Regional Museum of Corsican Prehistory).* Some of the island's best prehistoric relics are in this museum in what was once the town's prison. ⊠ *Rue Croce* ☎ *04–95–77–01–09* ⊕ *www.prehistoire-corse.org* 🎫 *€4* ⊗ *Mon.–Sat. 10–noon and 2–6.*

## BONIFACIO
**Fodor's**Choice *52 km (31 mi) southeast of Sartène via N196.*
★ The ancient fortress town of Bonifacio occupies a spectacular clifftop aerie above a harbor carved from limestone cliffs. It's 13 km (8 mi) from Sardinia, and the local speech is heavily influenced by the accent and idiom of that nearby Italian island. Established in the 12th century as Genoa's first Corsican stronghold, Bonifacio remained Genoese through centuries of battles and sieges. As you wander the narrow streets of the **Haute Ville** (Upper Village), inside the walls of the citadel, think of Homer's *Odyssey.* It's here, in the harbor, that scholars place the catastrophic encounter (Chapter X) between Ulysses's fleet and the Laestrygonians, who hurled lethal boulders down from the cliffs.

**Bastion de l'Étendard** *(Bastion of the Standard).* From place d'Armes at the city gate, enter the Bastion de l'Étendard, where you can still see the system of weights and levers used to pull up the drawbridge. The former garrison now houses life-size dioramas of Bonifacio's history. 🎫 *€2* ⊗ *Mid-June–mid-Sept., daily 9–7.*

★ **Dragon Grottoes.** From Bonifacio you can take a boat trip to the Dragon Grottoes and **Venus's Bath** (the trip takes one hour on boats that set out every 15 minutes during July and August) or the **Lavezzi Islands**. ✉ *Boats leave from outside Hôtel La Caravelle* ☎ *04–95–75–05–93 for information.*

**Ste-Marie-Majeure.** In the center of the maze of cobbled streets that makes up the citadel is the 12th-century church with buttresses attaching it to surrounding houses. Inside the church, note the Renaissance baptismal font, carved in bas-relief, and the 3rd-century white-marble Roman sarcophagus. Walk around the back to see the loggia, which is built above a huge cistern that stored water for use in times of siege, as did the circular stone silos seen throughout the town.

## PORTO–LES CALANCHES
*5 km (3 mi) west of Ota, 30 km (19 mi) south of Calvi.*

The flashy resort town of Porto doesn't have much character, but its setting on the crystalline **Golfe de Porto** (Gulf of Porto), surrounded by massive pink-granite mountains, is superb. Activity focuses on the small port, where there is a boardwalk with restaurants and hotels. A short hike from the boardwalk will bring you to a 16th-century Genoese tower that overlooks the bay. Boat excursions leave daily for the **Réserve Naturel de Scandola**.

## CALVI
*92 km (58 mi) north of Piana, 159 km (100 mi) north of Ajaccio.*

Calvi, Corsica's slice of the Riviera, has been described by author Dorothy Carrington as "an oasis of pleasure on an otherwise austere island." Calvi grew rich by supplying products to Genoa; its citizens remained loyal supporters of Genoa long after the rest of the island declared independence. Calvi also claims to be the birthplace of Christopher Columbus. During the 18th century the town endured assaults from Corsican nationalists, including celebrated patriot Pasquale Paoli. Today Calvi sees a summertime invasion of tourists, drawn to the 6-km (4-mi) stretch of sandy white beach, the citadel, and the buzzing nightlife.

**Citadelle.** The Genoese citadel perched on a rocky promontory at the tip of the bay competes with the beach as a major attraction. An inscription above the drawbridge—CIVITAS CALVI SEMPER FIDELIS (The citizens of Calvi always faithful)—reflects the town's unswerving allegiance to Genoa. At the welcome center, just inside the gates, you can see a video on the city's history and arrange to take a guided tour given in English (three times a day) or a self-guided walking tour. ✉ *Up hill off av. de l'Uruguay* ☎ *04–95–65–36–74* 🖥 *Guided tour and video show €9* ☉ *Tours Easter–early Oct., daily at 10, 4:30, and 6:30.*

**St-Jean-Baptiste.** Stop in at the 13th-century church of John the Baptist; it contains an interesting Renaissance baptismal font. Look up to see the rows of pews screened by grillwork: the chaste young women of Calvi's upper classes sat here. ✉ *Pl. d'Armes.*

### L'ILE ROUSSE

*10 km (6 mi) northeast of Algajola, 37 km (22 mi) southwest of St-Florent.*

L'Ile Rousse, famous for its market and named for the island of reddish rock now connected to the town by a causeway, is a favorite for vacationers who come to bask in its Riviera-like mise-en-scène. A small two-car train runs along the coast to Calvi, delivering sun-worshippers to beaches not accessible by road.

## SHOPPING

Traditional handicrafts are found in abundance in the shopping streets of the major towns. Until the mid-20th century most Corsicans had to be relatively self-sufficient, and this has led to all manner of crafts from knives and walking sticks to warm winter sweaters. Look for pottery, for which the island is known. Corsican knives are a specialty item, and the finest examples have exquisite blades and handles. Also look for items carved from wood and bone, some practical, some ornate. Because food had to be put back for the winter, preserved foods became very important parts of the Corsican diet, and are now well known; the charcuterie is excellent—in addition to a range of hams and salamis, you'll find aromatic dried herbs, numerous cheeses, plus fragrant jams and honey. Don't forget to sample a bottle of Corsican wine.

The citadel of Bonifacio has excellent boutiques set in historic stone cottages and cellars. Both Ajaccio and L'Isle Rousse have excellent markets, and in Calvi the major shopping streets are rue Clemenceau and boulevard Wilson.

**Librairie la Marge.** Much more than just a bookstore specializing in books about Corsica, this is a hub of Corsican culture, where you can also buy music and attend poetry readings. ⊠ *4 rue Emmanuelle-Arène, Ajaccio* ☎ *04–95–51–23–67.*

**Paese Nostru.** This store sells Corsican crafts of all kinds. ⊠ *Passage Guinguetta, Ajaccio* ☎ *04–95–51–05–07*

**U Stazzu.** This is a good source for Corsican meat, cheese, and wine. ⊠ *1 rue Bonaparte, Ajaccio* ☎ *04–95–51–10–80.*

**U Tilaghju.** One of several artisanal shops near the cathedral, U Tilaghju has an impressive collection of ceramics. ⊠ *Rue Forcioli Conti, Ajaccio*

## ACTIVITIES

The area around Bonifacio is ideal for water sports, including windsurfing and sea kayaking. The island also has several golf courses for those who can't bear to be away from the greens. In summer, sailing is a major pastime, with wealthy French and Italians plying a course to the chic harbors and the secluded rocky coves. Well-being is also taken very seriously, with several excellent spas.

**Club Atoll.** For water sports, contact this company. ⊠ *Rte. de Porto-Vecchio* ☎ *04–95–73–02–83.*

**Institut de Thalassothérapie** (Institute of Thalassotherapy). Across the Prunelli River south of Ajaccio, Porticcio is the capital's upscale suburb and luxurious beach resort town. It's primarily notable for its seawater cures at this spa in the Sofitel Porticcio. ✉ *Domaine de la Pointe Golfe d'Ajaccio, Porticcio* ☏ *04–95–29–40–00* ⊕ *www.accorthalassa.com.*

**Sperone.** The best golf course on Corsica (and one of the best in the Mediterranean), a 20,106-foot, par-72 gem designed by Robert Trent Jones, is at this club just east of Bonifacio. ✉ *Domaine de Sperone* ☏ *04–95–73–17–13* ⊕ *www.sperone.com.*

## BEACHES

There are fine Riviera-like strands north of Calvi reached by a little train service that runs around the bay to L'Isle Rousse. These do get busy between late July and the end of August, but can be delightfully peaceful early or late in the season. In summer there are numerous cafés and restaurants for refreshment. Note that topless sunbathing is acceptable here, and you will find bare breasts at every beach.

**Plage d'Ostriconi.** This beach is at the mouth of the Ostriconi River. ✉ *20 km [13 mi] north of L'Isle Rousse.*

**Plage Saleccia.** This wild, undeveloped beach that is frequented by nudists was used as a location for the 1960s film *The Longest Day.* ✉ *St-Florent.*

## WHERE TO EAT

**$–$$**

FRENCH

✗ **20123.** This well-loved Ajaccio favorite is known for its traditional cuisine, fresh fish from the nearby market, and, in season, game specials such as *civet de sanglier* (wild boar stew) with *trompettes de la mort* (wild mushrooms) served in a bubbling earthenware casserole. The setting, resembling a French village, is equally inviting, with a "starry sky," antique lanterns, live music, and a stone fountain where guests pour water into ceramic jugs. Placed onto checkered tablecloths are cutting boards with fresh-baked loaves of wheat bread. Three-course fixed menus are offered in two seatings at 7:30 and 9:30, and include an exquisite cheese platter with figs. ✉ *2 rue Roi-de-Rome, Ajaccio* ☏ *04–95–21–50–05* ⊕ *www.20123.fr* ▤ *MC, V* ☉ *Closed Mon. and Jan. 15–Feb. 15. No lunch June 15–Sept. 15.*

**$$–$$$**
★

✗ **Le Voilier.** This popular year-round restaurant in the port serves carefully selected and prepared fish and seafood, along with fine Corsican sausage and traditional cuisine from *soupe corse* to *fiadone* (cheesecake). ✉ *Quai Comparetti, Bonifacio* ☏ *04–95–73–07–06* ▤ *AE, DC, MC, V* ☉ *Closed Mon. No dinner Sun.*

# BARCELONA, SPAIN

Capital of Catalonia, 2,000-year-old Barcelona commanded a vast Mediterranean empire when Madrid was still a dusty Moorish outpost on the Spanish steppe. Relegated to second-city status only in 1561, Barcelona has long rivaled and often surpassed Madrid's supremacy.

Catalans jealously guard their language and their culture. Barcelona has long had a frenetically active cultural life. It was the home of architect Antoni Gaudí, and the painters Joan Miró and Salvador Dalí. Pablo Picasso also spent his formative years in Barcelona. Native musicians include cellist Pablo (Pau, in Catalan) Casals, opera singers Montserrat Caballé and José (Josep) Carreras, and early-music master Jordi Savall. One of Europe's most visually stunning cities, Barcelona balances its many elements, from the medieval intimacy of its Gothic Quarter to the grace of the wide boulevards in the Moderniste Eixample. In the 21st century innovative structures, such as the Ricardo Bofill *Vela* (sail) hotel, demonstrate Barcelona's insatiable appetite for novelty and progress.

### ESSENTIALS

CURRENCY  The euro (€1 to US$1.36 at this writing).

HOURS  Museums are generally open from 9 until 7 or 8; many are closed on Monday and some close in the afternoon. Most stores are open Monday through Saturday 9 to 1:30 and 5 to 8, but a few remain open all afternoon. Virtually all close on Sunday.

INTERNET  **Easy Internet Café** ⊠ *La Rambla 31* ☏ *93/301–7507.*

SAFETY  Barcelona has a reputation for active pickpocketing and scamming, especially around La Rambla. The risk is much greater at night than during daylight hours, but it always pays to be vigilant to avoid becoming a victim. Keep bags and purses closed, and carry them across the front of your body (this includes backpacks); thieves tend to cut bag straps to steal your belongings. Be aware of any approach by a stranger; it's better to walk away from all such encounters. And certainly don't carry any cash or valuables that you do not need.

The best way to avoid being targeted by scams and pickpockets is to act with confidence. Thieves often target travelers who seem confused or lost. And don't dress like a tourist. People in Barcelona dress smartly and rarely wear shorts and T-shirts.

TELEPHONES  Spain has good land and mobile services. Public kiosks accept phone cards that support international calls (cards sold in press shops, bars, and telecom shops). Mobile services are GSM and 3G compatible. Major companies include Vodafone.

### COMING ASHORE

Barcelona is one of Europe's busiest cruise ports. Vessels dock at the Port Vell facility, which has seven terminals catering to cruise-ship traffic. All terminals are equipped with duty-free shops, telephones, bar/restaurants, information desks, and currency-exchange booths. The ships docking closest to the terminal entrance are a 10-minute walk from the southern end of Las Ramblas (the Rambla), but those docked at the farthest end have a long walk or must catch a shuttle bus to the port entrance. The shuttle, which runs every 20 minutes, links all terminals with the public square at the bottom of the Rambla. If you walk up Las Ramblas, after about 10 minutes you'll reach Drassanes metro station for onward public transport around the city. A single metro or bus ticket is €1.40; a day ticket (T-Dia) is €6.

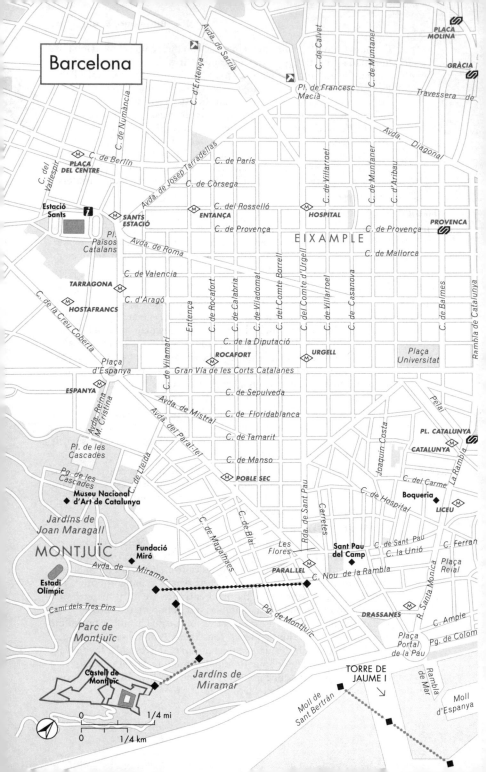

If you intend to explore Barcelona, don't rent a car. Public transportation and taxis are by far the most sensible options. City buses run daily from 5:30 AM to 11:30 PM. The FCG (Ferrocarril de la Generalitat) train is a comfortable commuter train that gets you to within walking distance of nearly everything in Barcelona; transfers to the regular city metro are free. The Barcelona Tourist Bus is another excellent way to tour the city. Three routes (Roman, Modernisme, and Gausi) cover just about every place you might want to visit, and you can hop on and off whenever you want. A one-day ticket is €22; you can buy online at ⊕ *www.tmb.net.*

If you plan to explore the Spanish coast or countryside, a vehicle would be beneficial, but even an economy car (manual transmission) is expensive at approximately €90 per day.

### GETTING TO THE AIRPORT
Barcelona's main airport is El Prat de Llobregat, 14 km (9 mi) south of Barcelona. If you choose not to purchase airport transfers from your cruise line, the simplest way to get from the airport to the cruise port is to take a taxi from the airport to the port (about €30).

There are public transport options, but transfers between bus, metro, or rail stations do involve up to 10 minutes of walking, and this may be impractical with many pieces of luggage. If you only have light baggage, this will certainly be a less expensive option.

The Aerobus leaves El Prat for Plaça de Catalunya in downtown Barcelona every 10 minutes (6 AM–11 PM) on weekdays and every 30 minutes (6:30 AM–10:30 PM) on weekends. From Plaça de Catalunya, it leaves for the airport every 15 minutes (5:30 AM–10 PM) on weekdays and every 30 minutes (6:30 AM–10:30 PM) on weekends. The fare is €5 (round-trip €9).

From the Plaça de Catalunya you'll need to transfer to the Metro and take the service to Drassanes station (2 stops) at the bottom La Rambla, a 10-minute walk from the port entrance.

The TMB bus number 46 runs between the airport and Plaça d'Espanya every 50 minutes between 5 AM and 12:15 AM. Ticket prices are €1.40. From the bus depot it's necessary to take the Metro from Plaça d'Espanya to Drassanes (three stops).

The RENFE airport train is inexpensive and efficient, but also runs only every 20 to 30 minutes. From the airport, the RENFE station is a 10- to 15-minute walk (with moving walkway) from the port gates. Trains run between 6 AM and midnight, stopping at the Estació de Sants. The one-way fare is €2.90. The 10-ride T-10 Metro ticket (⇨ *By Bus*) includes service to the airport station for the price of a single ride. From there it's necessary to transfer to the Metro for the journey to Drassanes station (five stops).

## EXPLORING BARCELONA

Barcelona's Old City includes **El Barri Gòtic** (the Gothic Quarter). Although this section of the city is being cleaned up, bag-snatching is common here, so keep your wits about you, and if at all possible, carry nothing in your hands. Nearby is Sant Pere, which was once Barcelona's old textile neighborhood.

Barcelona's best-known promenade, **La Rambla,** is a constant and colorful flood of humanity with flower stalls, bird vendors, mimes, musicians, and outdoor cafés. Federico García Lorca called this street the only one in the world that he wished would never end; traffic plays second fiddle to the endless *paseo* (stroll) of locals and travelers alike. The whole avenue is referred to as Las Ramblas (Les Rambles, in Catalan) or La Rambla, but each section has its own name: Rambla Santa Monica is at the southeastern, or port, end; Rambla de les Flors is in the middle; and Rambla dels Estudis is at the top, near Plaça de Catalunya.

**BARCELONA BEST BETS**

**La Sagrada Família.** Gaudí's stalagmites, stalactites, and cylindrical towers add up to the city's most surprising architectural marvel.

**Santa Maria del Mar.** Peerless Mediterranean Gothic style: a sweeping display of form and line. Hearing Renaissance polyphony in this architectural gem is the ultimate.

**Stroll along the Rambla.** This fine avenue is the place to feel Barcelona's heartbeat with milling throngs of cool urbanites, families, and elderly city dwellers all out to see and be seen.

North of Plaça de Catalunya is the checkerboard known as the **Eixample.** With the dismantling of the city walls in 1860, Barcelona embarked upon an expansion scheme. The street grid was the work of urban planner Ildefons Cerdà; much of the building here was done at the height of Modernisme. The Eixample's principal thoroughfares are Rambla de Catalunya and Passeig de Gràcia, where the city's most elegant shops vie for space among its best art nouveau buildings.

Once Barcelona's pungent fishing port, **Barceloneta** retains much of its maritime flavor. Nearby is **La Ciutadella,** once a fortress but now the city's main downtown park. **Montjuïc,** a hill to the south of town, may have been named for the Jewish cemetery that was once on its slopes.

## WHAT TO SEE

**Fodor's Choice ★** **Boqueria.** Barcelona's most spectacular food market, also known as the Mercat de Sant Josep, is an explosion of life and color sprinkled with delicious little bar-restaurants. ⊠ *La Rambla 91, Rambla* ⊕ *www. boqueria.info* ⊗ *Mon.–Sat. 8–8:30* Ⓜ *Liceu.*

**★** **Fundació Miró.** The Miró Foundation was a gift from the artist Joan Miró to his native city, and is one of Barcelona's most exciting showcases of contemporary art. The late-20th-century building makes a perfect setting for Miró's unmistakably playful and colorful style. ⊠ *Av. Miramar 71, Montjuïc* ☎ *93/443–9470* ⊕ *www.bcn.fjmiro.es* 🎟 *€8.50* ⊗ *Tues., Wed., Fri., and Sat. 10–7 (until 8 July–Sept.), Thurs. 10–9:30, Sun. 10–2:30.*

**Fodor's Choice ★** **Manzana de la Discòrdia.** On this city block you can find three main Moderniste masterpieces. **Casa Lleó Morera** (No. 35) has a facade covered with ornamentation and sculptures of female figures using the modern inventions of the age: the telephone, the telegraph, the photographic camera, and the Victrola. The pseudo-Flemish **Casa Amatller** (No. 41) was built by Josep Puig i Cadafalch in 1900 with decorative elements by Eusebi Arnau.

At No. 43 the colorful and bizarre **Casa Batlló** is Gaudí at his most spectacular, with its mottled facade resembling anything from an abstract pointillist painting to rainbow sprinkles on an ice-cream cone. Nationalist symbolism is at work here: the motifs are allusions to Catalonia's Middle Ages, with its codes of chivalry and religious fervor. ⊠ *Passeig de Gràcia 43, between Consell de Cent and Aragó, Eixample* ☎ *93/216– 0306* ⊕ *www.casabatllo.es* ⊠ *€17.80* ☉ *Daily 9–8* Ⓜ *Passeig de Gràcia.*

ↂ **Museu d'Història de Catalunya.** Built into what used to be a port warehouse, this state-of-the-art museum traces 3,000 years of Catalan history. The rooftop cafeteria, open to the general public, has excellent views over the harbor. ⊠ *Pl. Pau Vila 3, Barceloneta* ☎ *93/225–4700* ⊕ *www.mhcat.net* ⊠ *€4; free 1st Sun. of month* ☉ *Tues. and Thurs.– Sat. 10–7, Wed. 10–8, Sun. 10–2:30* Ⓜ *Barceloneta.*

**Fodor's Choice** **Museu Nacional d'Art de Catalunya** *(MNAC; Catalonian National Museum*
★ *of Art).* Housed in the imposing **Palau Nacional,** built in 1929 as the centerpiece of the World's Fair, this superb museum was renovated in 1995 by Gae Aulenti, architect of the Musée d'Orsay in Paris. The eclectic collection spans from the Romanesque period to the 20th century and includes works by Rubens, Tintoretto, and Velázquez. Pride of place, however, goes to the Romanesque exhibition, the world's finest collection of Romanesque frescoes, altarpieces, and wood carvings. ⊠ *Mirador del Palau 6, Montjuïc* ☎ *93/622–0376* ⊕ *www.mnac.es* ⊠ *€8:50* ☉ *Tues.–Sat. 10–7, Sun. 10–2:30* Ⓜ *Plana Espanya.*

**Fodor's Choice** **Museu Picasso.** Picasso spent key formative years (1895–1904) in Barce-
★ lona, and this 3,600-work permanent collection is strong on his early production. Displays include childhood and adolescent sketches, works from Picasso's Blue and Rose periods, and the famous 44 cubist studies based on Velázquez's *Las Meninas.* ⊠ *Carrer Montcada 15–23, Born-Ribera* ☎ *93/319–6310* ⊕ *www.museupicasso.bcn.es* ⊠ *Permanent collection €9, temporary exhibits €5.80, combined ticket €9.50; free 1st Sun. of month* ☉ *Tues.–Sun. 10–8* Ⓜ *Arc de Triomf, Liceu, Jaume I.*

**Fodor's Choice** **Palau de la Música Catalana.** A riot of color and form, Barcelona's Music
★ Palace is the flagship of the city's Moderniste architecture. Designed by Lluís Domènech i Montaner in 1908, the Palau's exterior is remarkable in itself, but the interior is an uproar. Wagnerian cavalry erupts from the right side of the stage over a heavy-browed bust of Beethoven, and Catalonia's popular music is represented by the flowing maidens of Lluís Millet's song *Flors de Maig (Flowers of May)* on the left. Overhead, an inverted stained-glass cupola seems to offer the divine manna of music; painted rosettes and giant peacock feathers explode from the tops of the walls. Even the stage is populated with Muse-like art nouveau musicians, each half bust, half mosaic. ⊠ *Ticket office, Calle Palau de la Musica 4–6, Sant Pere* ☎ *902/442–882* ⊕ *www.palaumusica.org* ⊠ *Tour €12* ☉ *1-hr tours daily* Ⓜ *Urquinaona*

**Fodor's Choice** **Santa Maria del Mar.** This pure and classical space enclosed by soaring
★ columns is something of an oddity in ornate and complex Moderniste

Barcelona. Santa Maria del Mar (Saint Mary of the Sea) was built from 1329 to 1383, in fulfillment of a vow made a century earlier by Jaume I to build a church to watch over all Catalan seafarers. The architect, Montagut de Berenguer, designed a bare-bones basilica that is now considered the finest existing example of Catalan (or Mediterranean) Gothic architecture. ⊠ *Pl. de Santa Maria, Born-Ribera* ☎ *93/310–2390* ⊙ *Daily 9–1:30 and 4:30–8:30* Ⓜ *Catalunya, Jaume I.*

**Fodor's Choice**    **Temple Expiatori de la Sagrada Família.** Barcelona's most unforgettable
★    landmark, Antoni Gaudí's Sagrada Família was conceived as nothing short of a Bible in stone. The cathedral is comprised of a series of magnificent monumental tableau, drawing inspiration from the long tradition of medieval allegory in church design and decoration yet standing firmly in the Modernist era in its delivery. This landmark is one of the most important architectural creations of the 19th to 21st centuries but remained unfinished at the time of Gaudí's death. Controversy surrounds subsequent work to complete the structure. ⊠ *Mallorca 401, Eixample* ☎ *93/207–3031* ⊕ *www.sagradafamilia.org* 🎫 *€12, bell tower elevator €2.50* ⊙ *Oct.–Mar., daily 9–6; Apr.–Sept., daily 9–8* Ⓜ *Sagrada Família.*

# SHOPPING

Between the surging fashion scene, a host of young clothing designers, clever home furnishings, delicious foodstuffs including wine and olive oil, and ceramics, art, and antiques, Barcelona is the best place in Spain to unload extra ballast from your wallet.

Barcelona's prime shopping districts are the Passeig de Gràcia, Rambla de Catalunya, Plaça de Catalunya, Porta de l'Àngel, and Avinguda Diagonal up to Carrer Ganduxer. For high fashion, browse along Passeig de Gràcia and the Diagonal between Plaça Joan Carles I and Plaça Francesc Macià. There are two-dozen antiques shops in the Gothic Quarter, another 70 shops off Passeig de Gràcia on Bulevard dels Antiquaris, and still more in Gràcia and Sarrià. For old-fashioned Spanish shops, prowl the Gothic Quarter, especially **Carrer Ferran.** The area around the church of Santa Maria del Mar, an artisans' quarter since medieval times, is full of cheerful design stores and art galleries. The area surrounding **Plaça del Pi,** from the Boqueria to Carrer Portaferrissa and Carrer de la Canuda, is thick with boutiques and jewelry and design shops. The **Barri de la Ribera,** around Santa Maria del Mar, especially the Born area, has a cluster of design, fashion, and and food shops. Design, jewelry, and knickknack shops cluster on Carrer Banys Vells and Carrer Flassaders, near Carrer Montcada.

**Art Escudellers.** This gallery has ceramics from all over Spain, with more than 200 different artisans represented and maps showing where the work is from. ⊠ *C. Escudellers 23–25, Barri Gòtic* ⊕ *www.escudellers-art.com.*

**Bulevard dels Antiquaris.** The Eixample's antiques shopping district contains 75 stores. ⊠ *Passeig de Gràcia 55, Eixample* ⊕ *www.bulevard-delsantiquaris.com.*

**Galeria Joan Prats.** This is a veteran gallery known for the quality of its artists' works. ⊠ *La Rambla de Catalunya 54, Eixample* ⊕ *www. galeriajoanprats.com.*

## BEACHES

**Sant Pol.** Five kilometers (3 mi) of beaches now run from the Platja (beach) de Sant Sebastià, a nudist enclave, northward through the Barceloneta, Port Olímpic, Nova Icària, Bogatell, Mar Bella, Nova Mar Bella, and Novíssima Mar Bella beaches to the Fòrum complex and the rocky Illa Pangea swimming area. Next to the mouth of the Besòs River is Platja Nova. Topless bathing is common. The beaches immediately north of Barcelona include Montgat, Ocata, Vilasar de Mar, Arenys de Mar, Canet, and Sant Pol de Mar, all accessible by train from the RENFE station in Plaça de Catalunya. Especially worthy is Sant Pol, with clean sand and a handsome old part of town and Carme Ruscalleda's famous **Sant Pau,** one of the top three restaurants in Catalonia. ⊠ *Passeig Maritim 59* ☎ *93/665–1347.*

## WHERE TO EAT

$ ✕ **Cal Pep.** A two-minute walk east from Santa Maria del Mar toward

TAPAS  the Estació de França, Pep's has Barcelona's best and freshest selection

**Fodor's**Choice  of tapas, cooked and served piping hot in this boisterous space. ⊠ *Pl.*

★  *de les Olles 8, Born-Ribera* ☎ *93/319–6183* ⊕ *www.calpep.com* ☉ *No dinner. Closed Mon. and Aug.* Ⓜ *Jaume I.*

$$–$$$ ✕ **Cuines Santa Caterina.** A lovingly restored market designed by the

ECLECTIC  late Enric Miralles and completed by his widow Benedetta Tagliabue provides a spectacular setting for one of the city's most original dining operations. Under the undulating wooden superstructure of the market, the breakfast and tapas bar, open from dawn to midnight, offers a variety of culinary specialties cross-referenced by culture (Mediterranean, Asian) and product (pasta, rice, fish, meat), all served on sleek counters and long wooden tables. ⊠ *Av. Francesc Cambó, Barri Gòtic* ☎ *93/268–9918* ▭ *AE, DC, MC, V* Ⓜ *Catalunya, Liceu, Jaume I.*

## WHERE TO STAY

$$$–$$$$ 🏨 **Duquesa de Cardona.** This refurbished 16th-century town house over-

**Fodor's**Choice  looking the port has ultracontemporary facilities with designer touches,

★  all housed in an early-Renaissance structure. The exterior rooms have views of the harbor, the World Trade Center, and the passenger-boat terminals. The hotel is a 10-minute walk from everything in the Gothic Quarter or Barceloneta and no more than a 30-minute walk from the main Eixample attractions. The miniature rooftop pool, more for a dip than a swim, is cooling in summer. **Pros:** contemporary technology in a traditional palace at a key spot over the port; roof terrace with live music in summer. **Cons:** rooms on the small side; roof terrace tiny; sea views restricted by Maremagnum complex. ⊠ *Passeig de Colom 12, Rambla* ☎ *93/268–9090* 📠 *93/268–2931* ⊕ *www.hduquesadecardona.*

*com* ⏚ *44 rooms* ⏚ *In-room: Wi-Fi. In-hotel: restaurant, pool* ▤ *AE, DC, MC, V* 🍴 *EP* Ⓜ *Drassanes.*

**$$$$**
**Fodor's Choice**
**★**

🔳 **Hotel Neri.** Built into a 17th-century palace over one of the Gothic Quarter's smallest and most charming squares, Plaça Sant Felip Neri, the Neri is a singular counterpoint of ancient and avant-garde design. The facade and location are early Barcelona, but the cavernous interior spaces are unfailingly contemporary and edgy. Rooms stress straight lines, sheer and angular precision, and expanses of wood and stone with Mark Rothko–like artwork. **Pros:** central location; design; roof terrace for cocktails and breakfast. **Cons:** noise from the echo-chamber square can be a problem on summer nights (and winter morning school days); impractical design details such as the hanging bed lights. ⊠ *St. Sever 5, Barri Gòtic* ☎ *93/304–0655* 🖷 *93/304–0337* ⊕ *www.hotelneri.com* ⏚ *22 rooms* ⏚ *In-room:refrigerator, Wi-Fi. In-hotel: restaurant, bar, Internet terminal, Wi-Fi hotspot* ▤ *AE, DC, MC, V* 🍴 *EP* Ⓜ *Liceu, Catalunya.*

**$$**
**Fodor's Choice**
**★**

🔳 **Sant Agustí.** In a leafy square just off the Rambla, the Sant Agust has long been popular with musicians performing at the Liceu opera house. Rooms are small but graceful and attractively designed, with plenty of bright wood trim and clean lines. **Pros:** central location near the Boqueria market, the Rambla, and the opera house; cozy, wood-beamed, traditional design. **Cons:** noisy square usually requiring closed windows; short on amenities and room service. ⊠ *Pl. Sant Agustí 3, Raval* ☎ *93/318–165893/317–2928* ⊕ *www.hotelsa.com* ⏚ *77 rooms* ⏚ *In-room: a/c, safe, Wi-Fi. In-hotel: bar, Wi-Fi hotspot* ▤ *AE, DC, MC, V* 🍴 *EP* Ⓜ *Liceu.*

# BARI, ITALY

Puglia is one of three regions making up the heel and toe of Italy's boot, and informally known collectively as the *mezzogiorno,* a name that translates literally as "midday." It's a curiously telling nickname because midday is when it's quietest here. This is Italy's deep south, where whitewashed buildings stand silently over the turquoise Mediterranean, castles guard medieval alleyways, and grandmothers dry their handmade orecchiette pasta in the mid-afternoon heat. At every turn, Puglia boasts unspoiled scenery, a wonderful country food tradition, and an openness to outsiders. Beyond the cities, seaside resorts, and the few major sights, there's a sparsely populated countryside with expanses of silvery olive trees, vineyards of *primitivo* and *aglianico* grapes, and giant prickly-pear cacti. Puglia still doesn't make it onto the itineraries of most visitors to Italy. This translates into an unusual opportunity to engage with a rich culture and landscape virtually untouched by mass tourism. Bari is at the top of the boot; it's the biggest city in the Mezzogiorno, a lively, quirky, and sometimes seamy port city on the Adriatic coast.

## ESSENTIALS

**CURRENCY** The euro (€1 to US$1.36 at this writing).

**HOURS** Shops are generally open from 8 AM until noon or 1 PM, then again from 3 or 4 until 8, perhaps opening later in summer. Most shops are closed

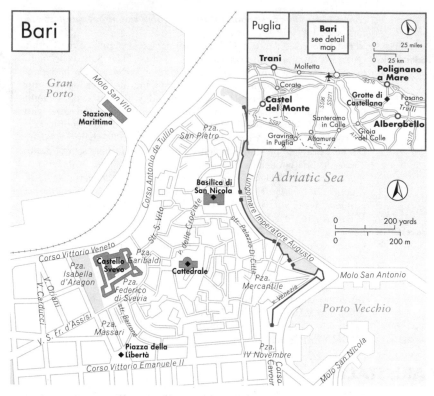

on Sunday. Most museums and attractions open throughout the day, though some, particularly churches, close in the afternoon.

**INTERNET** **Bit Stop di Signorile Andrea** (✉ *Via Pasubio 222* ☎ *080/556–4269* ⊕ *www. bitstop-bari.it*) is closed on Sunday.

**TELEPHONES** Tri-band GSM phones work in Italy. You can buy prepaid phone cards at telecom shops, news vendors, and tobacconists in all towns and cities. Phone cards can be used for local or international calls.

## COMING ASHORE

Bari is a large port, and has a dedicated cruise terminal; ships dock, giving passengers only a short walk to the port entrance. From here, it is a further short walk into the city, where you can explore on foot.

Bari is linked by rail to all the major towns in the region. Trani can be reached in 34 to 50 minutes; there are two trains per hour and the single fare is €2.60. Polignano a Mare is less than 30 minutes from Bari by train; there is one service per hour and a single fare costs €2.10. Alberobello is a journey time of 80 to 100 minutes, and tickets cost €4. All train tickets—except those to Alberobello—can be bought online at www.trenilatia.com and retrieved from machines in Bari station. Buy tickets for Alberobello from the Ferrovie Sud-Est office at Bari railway station. Renting a vehicle would allow you to explore the Puglia countryside at your own pace. An economy manual vehicle costs approximately €54 per day, but delivery to the port may cost more.

## EXPLORING BARI AND PUGLIA

### BARI

The biggest city in the Mezzogiorno, Bari is a major port and a transit point for travelers catching ferries across the Adriatic to Greece, but it's also a cosmopolitan city with one of the most interesting historic centers in the region. Most of Bari is set out in a logical, 19th-century grid, following the designs of Joachim Murat (1767–1815), Napoléon's brother-in-law and King of the Two Sicilies. By day, explore the old town's winding alleyways, where Bari's open-door policy offers a glimpse into the daily routine of southern Italy—matrons hand-rolling pasta with their grandchildren home from school for the midday meal, and handymen perched on rickety ladders, patching up centuries-old arches and doorways.

**Basilica di San Nicola.** In the città vecchia, overlooking the sea and just off Via Venezia, is the church that was built in the 11th century to house the bones of St. Nicholas, also known as St. Nick, or Santa Claus. His remains, buried in the crypt, are said to have been stolen by Bari sailors from Myra, where St. Nicholas was bishop, in what is now Turkey. The basilica, of solid and powerful construction, was the only building to survive the otherwise wholesale destruction of Bari by the Normans in 1152. ⊠ *Piazza San Nicola* ☎ *080/5737111* ⊕ *www.basilicasannicola. it* ⊗ *Daily 7:30–1 and 4–7:30.*

**Castello Svevo.** Looming over Bari's cathedral is this huge fortress. The current building dates from the time of Holy Roman Emperor Frederick II (1194–1250), who rebuilt an existing Norman-Byzantine castle to his own exacting specifications. Designed more for power than beauty, it looks out beyond the cathedral to the small Porto Vecchio (Old Port). Inside, a haphazard collection of medieval Puglian art is frequently enlivened by changing exhibitions featuring local, national, and international artists. Hours and admission are subject to change depending on the current exhibiton. ⊠ *Piazza Federico II di Svevia* ☎ *080/5286262* ⊡ *€2* ⊗ *Thurs.–Tues. 8:30–7:30. Last entrance at 6:30.*

**Cattedrale.** Bari's 12th-century cathedral is the seat of the local bishop, and was the scene of many significant political marriages between important families in the Middle Ages. The cathedral's solid architecture reflects the Romanesque style favored by the Normans of that period. ⊠ *Piazza dell'Odegitria* ☎ *080/5210605* ⊗ *Mon.–Sat. 8:30–12:30 and 4–7:30, Sun. 8–12:30 and 5–8:30.*

**Piazza della Libertà.** The heart of the modern town is this central piazza, but just beyond it, across Corso Vittorio Emanuele, is the *città vecchia* (Old Town), a maze of narrow streets on the promontory that juts out between Bari's old and new ports, circumscribed by Via Venezia, offering elevated views of the Adriatic in every direction. Stop for an outdoor drink at **Greta** (⊠ *Via Venezia 24*) for a commanding view of the port and sea.

## TRANI

*43 km (27 mi) northwest of Bari.*

Smaller than the other ports along this coast, Trani has a quaint Old Town with polished stone streets and buildings, medieval churches, and a harbor filled with fishing boats. Trani is also justly famous for its sweet dessert wine, Moscato di Trani.

**Castle.** The boxy, well-preserved Castle was built by Frederick II in 1233. ⊠ *Piazza Manfredi 16* ☎ *0883/506603* ⛶ *€2* ☉ *Daily 8:30–7.*

**Duomo.** The stunning, pinkish-white-hue 11th-century Duomo is considered one of the finest in Puglia, is built on a spit of land jutting into the sea. ⊠ *Piazza Duomo* ☎ *No phone* ☉ *Daily 8–12:30 and 3–7:30.*

**Via Sinagoga.** A Jewish community flourished here in medieval times, and on Synagogue Street two of the four synagogues still exist: **Santa Maria Scolanova** and **Santa Anna,** both built in the 13th century; the latter still bears a Hebrew inscription.

## POLIGNANO A MARE

*40 km (24 mi) southeast of Bari.*

With a well-preserved whitewashed Old Town perched on limestone cliffs overlooking the Adriatic, Polignano a Mare is only a half-hour train ride down the coast from Bari. The town is virtually lifeless all winter, but becomes something of a weekend hot spot for city dwellers in summer.

## CASTEL DEL MONTE

★ *56 km (35 mi) southwest of Bari.*

Built by Frederick II in the first half of the 13th century on an isolated hill, Castel del Monte is an imposing octagonal castle with eight austere towers. Little is known about the structure, since virtually no records exist. The gift shop has many books that explore its mysterious past and posit fascinating theories based on its dimensions and Federico II's love of mathematics. It has none of the usual defense features associated with medieval castles, so it probably had little military significance. Some theories suggest it might have been built as a hunting lodge, or may have served as an astronomical observatory, or even as a stop for pilgrims on their quest for the Holy Grail. ⊠ *On signposted minor road 18 km (11 mi) south of Andria* ☎ *0883/569997, 0883/592283 tour reservations* ⊕ *www.casteldelmonte.beniculturali.it* ⛶ *€3* ☉ *Mar.–Sept., daily 10:15–7:45; Oct.–Feb., daily 9:15–6:45. Last entrance 30 mins before closing.*

---

**BARI BEST BETS**

**Soaking in the atmosphere in Bari's Old Town.** The dramas of life in Italy's deep south are not a show put on for tourists but a fascinating daily performance for lovers of people-watching.

**Exploring Polignano a Mare.** This whitewashed village's roots are well in sync with the Mediterranean heartbeat.

**Touring Trulli country.** These unique humble stone buildings surrounded by vines are one of Italy's most unusual architectural treasures.

### ALBEROBELLO

*59 km (37 mi) southeast of Bari.*

Although Alberobello is something of a tourist trap, the amalgamation of more than 1,000 *trulli* (beehive-shape homes) huddled together along steep, narrow streets is nonetheless an unusual sight (as well as a national monument and a UNESCO World Heritage Site). The origins of the beehive-shape trulli go back to the 13th century and maybe further. The trulli, found nowhere else in the world, are built of local limestone, without mortar, and with a hole in the top for escaping smoke. As one of the most popular tourist destinations in Puglia, Alberobello has spawned some excellent restaurants (and some not-so-excellent trinket shops).

**Trullo Sovrano.** Alberobello's largest trullo is up the hill through the trulli zone (head up Corso Vittorio Emanuele past the obelisk and the basilica). Though you can go inside, where you can find a fairly conventional domestic dwelling, the real interest is the structure itself.

**Via Alberobello–Martina Franca.** The trulli in Alberobello itself are impressive, but the most beautiful concentration of trulli is along Via Alberobello–Martina Franca. Numerous conical homes and buildings stand along a stretch of about 15 km (9 mi) between those two towns. Amid expanses of vineyards, you'll see delightfully amusing examples of trulli put to use in every which way—as wineries, for instance.

## SHOPPING

Puglia is Italy's second most-productive wine region, so taste a few, including the famed dessert wine Moscato di Trani, and buy some bottles of your favorite. Olives are grown in great abundance, too. The virgin olive oil pressed here is of excellent quality. Other souvenirs include ceramics in a range of styles, from practical terracotta to beautiful glazed ornaments. Miniature trulli take on many forms, from faithfully finished stone copies to kitsch plastic fridge magnets. Italian styling is very much in evidence in the streets of Bari.

The main shopping streets in Bari are Via Argiro and Via Sparano. Souvenir shops are numerous in the narrow streets of the Old Town. Alberobello has many trulli that have been converted into souvenir shops.

**Louis Vuitton.** The French luxury-goods company has a full range of original fashion items and accessories at this store, and it's probably much less visited than the ones in larger Italian cities. ⊠ *Via Sparano 127, Bari* ☎ *080/5245499.*

## WHERE TO EAT

$$$ ✕ **La Regia.** This small hotel-restaurant occupies a 17th-century palazzo superbly positioned in front of the Duomo, on a swath of land jutting out into the sea. The restaurant has attractive stonework and vaulted ceilings incorporated into its contemporary decor. Regional specialties are presented imaginatively: try the baked crepes (similar to cannelloni) or grilled fish. Reservations are essential for Sunday lunch

ITALIAN

★

and for dinner on summer weekends. ⊠ *Piazza Mons. Addazi 2, Trani* ☎ *0883/584444* ⊕ *www.hotelregia.it* ☰ *MC, V* ⊘ *Closed Mon.* |◯| *BP.*

**$$$$** ✕ **Ristorante al Pescatore.** This is one of Bari's best fish restaurants, in
SEAFOOD the Old Town opposite the castle and just around the corner from the cathedral. Summer cooking is done outside, where you can sit amid a cheerful clamor of quaffing and dining. Try a whole grilled local fish, accompanied by crisp salad and a carafe of invigorating local wine. Reservations are essential in July and August. ⊠ *Piazza Federico II di Svevia 6, Bari* ☎ *080/5237039* ⊕ *www.ristorantealpescatorebari.com* ☰ *AE, DC, MC, V* ⊘ *Closed Mon.*

# BORDEAUX, FRANCE

Bordeaux as a whole, rather than any particular points within it, is what you'll want to visit in order to understand why Victor Hugo described it as Versailles plus Antwerp, and why, when he was exiled from his native Spain, the painter Francisco de Goya chose it as his last home (he died here in 1828). The capital of southwest France and the region's largest city, Bordeaux remains synonymous with the wine trade, and wine shippers have long maintained their headquarters along the banks of the River Garonne at the heart of town. As a whole, Bordeaux is a less exuberant city than many others in France. The profits generated by centuries of fine vintages have been carefully invested in fine yet understated architecture, and an aura of 18th-century elegance permeates the downtown core. Conservative and refined, the city rewards visitors with its museums, shopping, and restaurants.

## ESSENTIALS

CURRENCY The euro (€1 to US$1.36 at this writing).

HOURS Museums are open 10–5, but most close on Monday or Tuesday. Stores are open Monday–Saturday 9–7, but some close for lunch (usually noon–2).

INTERNET **Art Obas** (⊠ *7 rue Maucoudinat* ☎ *05–56–44–26–30*). **Cyber Evasion** (⊠ *62 cours Pasteur* ☎ *06–98–49–64–18*). **La Cyb** (⊠ *23 cours Pasteur south of cathedral* ☎ *05–56–01–15–15*).

TELEPHONES Tri-band GSM phones work in France. You can buy prepaid phone cards at telecom shops, news vendors, and tobacconists in all towns and cities. Phone cards can be used for local or international calls. France Telecom and Orange are leading telecom companies.

## COMING ASHORE

Cruise ships sail up the Gironde River and dock directly on the city waterfront within walking distance of all the major city attractions. Because of its proximity to the downtown core, there are no facilities specifically for cruise-ship passengers at the dock site.

Bordeaux is a compact city, and there will be no need to rent a vehicle unless you want to tour the many vineyards in the surrounding countryside independently. Cost of rental is approximately €70 per day for an economy manual vehicle. Taxis are plentiful and can provide tourist itineraries. For single-journey tariffs, rates are €2.30 for pick-up

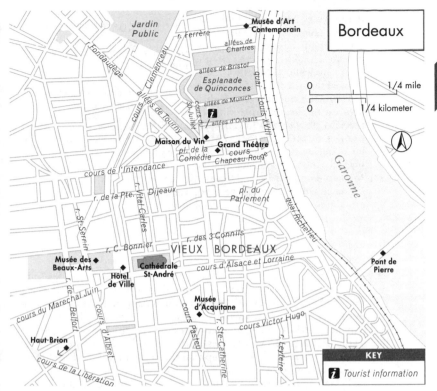

followed by €0.73 per km. There's an hourly rental fee of €26.90 if you should choose to take a taxi for a number of hours.

## EXPLORING BORDEAUX

**Cathédrale St-André.** This hefty edifice isn't one of France's finer Gothic cathedrals, but the intricate 14th-century chancel makes an interesting contrast with the earlier nave. Excellent stone carvings adorn the facade. You can climb the 15th-century, 160-foot **Tour Pey-Berland** for a stunning view of the city. ⊠ *Pl. Pey-Berland* 🏛 *Tower €5* ⊘ *Tower, June–Sept., daily 10–1:15 and 2–6; Oct.–May, Tues.–Sun. 10–12:30 and 2–5:30.*

**Grand Théâtre.** The city's leading 18th-century monument was designed by Victor Louis and built between 1773 and 1780. It's the pride of the city, with an elegant exterior ringed by graceful Corinthian columns and a dazzling foyer with a two-winged staircase and a cupola. The theater hall has a frescoed ceiling with a shimmering chandelier composed of 14,000 Bohemian crystals. ⊠ *Pl. de la Comédie* 🕾 *05–56–00–85–95* ⊕ *www.opera-bordeaux.com* 🎟 *€3* ⊘ *Wed. and Sat. 3, 4, and 5.*

**Haut-Brion.** One of the region's most famous wine-producing châteaux is actually within the city limits: Follow N250 southwest from central

Bordeaux for 3 km (2 mi) to the district of Pessac, home to Haut-Brion, producer of the only non-Médoc wine to be ranked a *premier cru* (the most elite wine classification). It is claimed that the very buildings surrounding the vineyards create their own microclimate, protecting the precious grapes and allowing them to ripen earlier. The white château looks out over the celebrated pebbly soil. The wines produced at **La Mission–Haut Brion (Domaine Clarence Dillon)**, across the road, are almost as sought-after. ✉ *133 av. Jean-Jaurès, Pessac* ☎ *05–56–00–29–30* ⊕ *www.haut-brion.com* ✉ *Free 1-hr visits by appointment, weekdays only, with tasting* ⊗ *Closed mid-July–mid-Aug.*

> ### BORDEAUX BEST BETS
>
> **Opening a bottle of a fine wine.** Bordeaux is famed more for its wines than anything else, so indulge your olfactory sense and your taste buds with a vintage from an excellent château.
>
> **Touring the vineyards.** Not only is it wonderful to watch the grapes maturing on the vines, but to tour the historic châteaus and their extensive cellars is to understand the understated essence of this small region of France.

★ **Maison du Vin.** Run by the CIVB (Conseil Interprofessionnel des Vins de Bordeaux), the headquarters of the Bordeaux wine trade (the city tourist office is just across the street from here) is right in the heart of Bordeaux. Before you set out to explore the regional wine country, stop at the Maison to gain clues from the (English-speaking) person at the Tourisme de Viticole desk, who has helpful guides on all the various wine regions. More important, tasting a red (like Pauillac or St-Émilion), a dry white (like an Entre-Deux-Mers, Graves, or Côtes de Blaye), and a sweet white (like Sauternes or Loupiac) will help you decide which of the 57 wine appellations (areas) to explore. You can also make purchases at the **Vinothèque** opposite. ✉ *8 cours du XXX-Juillet* ☎ *05–56–00–43–47* ⊕ *www.la-vinotheque.com* ✉ *Free* ⊗ *Mon.–Sat. 10–7:30, wine bar Mon.–Sat. 11–10.*

**Musée d'Aquitaine.** This excellent museum takes you on a trip through Bordeaux's history, with emphases on Roman, medieval, Renaissance, port-harbor, colonial, and 20th-century daily life. Aquitaine is the region in which Bordeaux sits, so there are many artifacts from the surrounding countryside. The detailed prehistoric section almost saves you a trip to the Lascaux II, as the magnificent ancient cave paintings found there are reproduced here in part. The collection of religious objects from Africa and the Middle East forms an interesting contrast to the more parochial galleries. ✉ *20 cours Pasteur* ☎ *05–56–01–51–00* ✉ *Free* ⊗ *Tues.–Sun. 11–6.*

**Musée d'Art Contemporain** *(Contemporary Art Center)*. Imaginatively housed in a converted 19th-century spice warehouse, the Entrepôt Lainé, this museum is just north of the sprawling Esplanade des Quinconce. Many shows here showcase cutting-edge artists who invariably festoon the huge expanse of the place with hanging ropes, ladders, and large video screens. ✉ *7 rue Ferrère* ☎ *05–56–00–81–50* ✉ *Free* ⊗ *Tues. and Thurs.–Sun. 11–6, Wed. 11–8.*

**Musée des Beaux-Arts.** Across tidy gardens behind the ornate Hôtel de Ville (town hall), Bordeaux's biggest art museum has a collection of works spanning the 15th to 21st centuries, with important paintings by Paolo Veronese (*St. Dorothy*), Camille Corot (*Bath of Diana*), and Odilon Redon (*Apollo's Chariot*), and sculptures by Auguste Rodin. The museum has one of the largest collections of Dutch and Flemish paintings outside their native region, including works by Rubens, Van Dyck, and Ruysdael. ⊠ *20 cours d'Albret* ☎ *05–56–10–20–56* ⊒ *Free* ⊘ *Wed.–Mon. 11–6.*

**Pont de Pierre.** For a view of the picturesque quayside, stroll across the Garonne on this bridge that was built on the orders of Napoléon between 1810 and 1821 and until 1965 the only bridge across the river.

## SHOPPING

Between the cathedral and the Grand Théâtre are numerous pedestrian streets where stylish shops and clothing boutiques abound—Bordeaux may favor understatement but there's no lack of elegance. Couture is well in evidence here for both women and men. Wines are of course a must if you haven't bought direct from the château, or indulge in France's other culinary obsession—cheese (perhaps for a picnic lunch).

**Jean d'Alos Fromager-Affineur.** For an exceptional selection of cheeses, go to this shop. ⊠ *4 rue Montesquieu* ☎ *05–56–44–29–66.*

**La Maison des Millésimes.** This wine store has a wide range of great wines and will deliver to anywhere in the world. ⊠ *37 rue Esprit-des-Lois* ☎ *05–56–44–03–92.*

**Vinothèque.** This store sells top-ranked Bordeaux wines. ⊠ *8 cours du XXX-Juillet* ☎ *05–57–10–41–41.*

## WHERE TO EAT

If you are looking for just a small bite to eat or a refreshment stop, the trendy **Museum Café** (⊠ *7 rue Ferrère*) next to the art library on the top floor of the Musée d'Art Contemporain, offers a good choice of beverages and snacks, and fine views over the Bordeaux skyline. It's open Tuesday through Sunday, noon until 6.

**$–$$**
FRENCH
✕ **Café Français.** For more than 30 years, Madame Jouhanneau has presided over this venerable bistro in the heart of the Vieille Ville hard by the Cathédrale St-André. The interior, with large mirrors and plush curtains, is sober, the mood busy. But it's the food, solidly based on fresh regional specialties, that counts, and, for solid sustenance at reasonable prices, it's hard to beat. Try for a table on the terrace: the view over Place Pey-Berland is never less than diverting. ⊠ *5–6 pl. Pey-Berland* ☎ *05–56–52–96–69* ⊟ *AE, DC, MC, V.*

# CÁDIZ, SPAIN (FOR SEVILLE AND JEREZ)

Gypsies, bulls, flamenco, horses—Andalusia is the Spain of story and song, the one Washington Irving romanticized in the 19th century. Andalusia is, moreover, at once the least and most surprising part of Spain: Least surprising because it lives up to the hype and stereotype that long confused all of Spain with the Andalusian version, and most surprising because it is, at the same time, so much more. All the romantic images of Andalusia, and Spain in general, spring vividly to life in Seville. Spain's fourth-largest city is an olé cliché of matadors, flamenco, tapas bars, gypsies, geraniums, and strolling guitarists. The smaller cities of Cádiz—the Western world's oldest metropolis, founded by Phoenicians more than 3,000 years ago—and Jerez, with its sherry cellars and purebred horses, have much to explore as well.

## ESSENTIALS

CURRENCY   The euro (€1 to US$1.36 at this writing).

HOURS   Museums generally open 9 until 7 or 8, many are closed on Monday and some close in the afternoon. Most stores are open Monday through Saturday 9 to 1:30 and 5 to 8, but a few stay open in the afternoon. Virtually all close on Sunday.

INTERNET   **Enrada2** ⊠ *Calle Sacramento 36* ☎ *95/680–8181.*

TELEPHONES   Spain has good land and mobile services. Public kiosks accept phone cards that support international calls (cards sold in press shops, bars, and telecom shops). Mobile services support most tri-band GSM phones and are 3G compatible. Major companies include Vodafone.

## COMING ASHORE

Vessels dock at the Alfonso XIII quay in the Cádiz Port, which is in the heart of the city. The passenger terminal has a restaurant, press outlet, phones, and taxi kiosk. From the port, the sights of downtown Cádiz are all within walking distance.

If you wish to travel independently, there is one train per hour from Cádiz to Seville. The journey takes between 1½ and 2 hours. Tickets cost €12.90 single. Taxi fare from Cádiz to Seville is currently €95 each way—a vehicle takes four people. There is also one train per hour to Jerez. The journey takes 45 minutes, and the ticket price is €4.90 one-way. A car rental would open up much of the region to you, but parking and navigation in the cities is difficult. The price for an economy manual vehicle is approximately €60 per day.

## EXPLORING CÁDIZ, SEVILLE, AND JEREZ DE LA FRONTERA

### CÁDIZ

Founded as Gadir by Phoenician traders in 1100 BC, Cádiz claims to be the oldest continuously inhabited city in the Western world. Hannibal lived in Cádiz for a time, Julius Caesar first held public office here, and Columbus set out from here on his second voyage, after which the city became the home base of the Spanish fleet. During the 18th century Cádiz monopolized New World trade and became the wealthiest port in Western Europe. Most of its buildings—including the cathedral, built

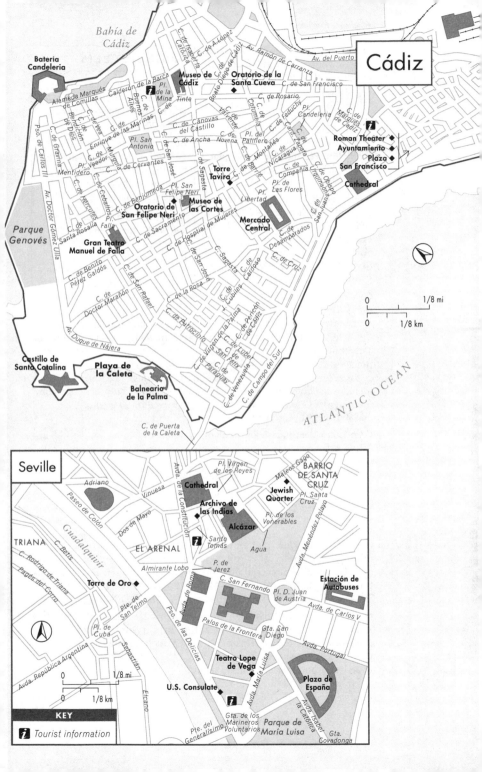

# Cádiz

Bahía de
Cádiz

Av. del Puerto

Bateria
Candeleria

Alameda Marqués
de Comillas

Museo de
Cádiz

Oratorio de la
Santa Cueva

C. de San Francisco

Pl.
de la
Mina

Roman Theater
Ayuntamiento
Plaza
San Francisco

Cathedral

Torre
Tavira

Parque
Genovés

Oratorio de
San Felipe Neri

Museo
de las Cortes

Pl.
Libertad

Mercado
Central

Gran Teatro
Manuel de Falla

0                1/8 mi
0           1/8 km

Castillo de
Santa Catalina

Playa de
la Caleta

Balneario
de la Palma

ATLANTIC OCEAN

C. de Puerta
de la Caleta

# Seville

Adriano

Pl. Virgen
de los Reyes

BARRIO
DE SANTA
CRUZ

Cathedral

Jewish
Quarter

Pl. Santa
Cruz

Archivo de
las Indias

Pl. de los
Venerables

Alcázar

TRIANA

Santo
Tomás

EL ARENAL

Agua

Guadalquivir

Almirante Lobo

Torre de Oro

P. de
Jerez

Estación de
Autobuses

C. San Fernando

Pl. D. Juan
de Austria

Gta. San
Diego

Teatro Lope
de Vega

Plaza de
España

U.S. Consulate

Parque de
María Luisa

0           1/8 mi
0           1/8 km

## KEY

**i** *Tourist information*

in part with gold and silver from the New World—date from this period. Today the old city is African in appearance and immensely intriguing—a cluster of narrow streets opening onto charming small squares. The golden cupola of the cathedral looms above low white houses, and the whole place has a charming if slightly dilapidated air.

**Ayuntamiento.** Cádiz's impressive city hall overlooks the Plaza San Juan de Diós, one of Cádiz's liveliest hubs. Built in two parts, in 1799 and 1861, the building is attractively illuminated at night. ⊠ *Pl. de San Juan de Dios s/n.*

**Cathedral.** Five blocks southeast of the Torre Tavira is Cádiz's cathedral, with its gold dome and baroque facade. Construction of the cathedral began in 1722, when the city was at the height of its power. The cathedral **museum**, on Calle Acero, displays gold, silver, and jewels from the New World, as well as Enrique de Arfe's processional cross, which is carried in the annual Corpus Christi parades. The entrance price includes the crypt, museum, and church of Santa Cruz. ⊠ *Pl. Catedral* ☎ *956/259812* ⊠ *€5* ⊙ *Mass Sun. at noon; museum Tues.–Fri. 10–2 and 4:30–7:30, Sat. 10–1.*

**Gran Teatro Manuel de Falla.** Four blocks west of Santa Inés is the Plaza Manuel de Falla, overlooked by an amazing neo-Mudejar redbrick theater. The classic interior is impressive as well; try to attend a performance. ⊠ *Pl. Manuel de Falla* ☎ *956/220828.*

**Museo de Cádiz.** A good place to begin your explorations of Cádiz is the Plaza de Mina, a large, leafy square with palm trees and plenty of benches. On the east side of the Plaza de Mina is the *provincial museum.* Notable pieces include works by Murillo and Alonso Cano as well as the *Four Evangelists* and set of saints by Zurbarán, which have much in common with his masterpieces at Guadalupe, in Extremadura. The archaeological section contains Phoenician sarcophagi from the time of this ancient city's birth. ⊠ *Pl. de Mina* ☎ *956/212281* ⊠ *€2, free for EU citizens* ⊙ *Tues. 2:30–8:30, Wed.–Sat. 9–8, Sun. 9:30–2:30.*

**Museo de las Cortes.** Next door to the Oratorio de San Felipe Neri, this small but pleasant museum has a 19th-century mural depicting the establishment of the Constitution of 1812. Its real showpiece, however, is a 1779 ivory-and-mahogany model of Cádiz, with all of the city's streets and buildings in minute detail, looking much as they do now. ⊠ *Santa Inés 9* ☎ *956/221788* ⊠ *Free* ⊙ *Oct.–May, Tues.–Fri. 9–1 and 4–7, weekends 9–1; June–Sept., Tues.–Fri. 9–1 and 5–8, weekends 9–1.*

---

**CÁDIZ BEST BETS**

**Explore Seville's Alcázar.** One of Spain's finest historic palaces was built to symbolize victory over the Moors.

**Be awe-inspired by Seville's Cathedral.** The largest Gothic building in the world and the third-largest church, this is a building of superlatives.

**Sip a glass of fine sherry in a sidewalk café accompanied by tasty tapas.** Your tastebuds will tingle, and you can watch the languorous life of southern Spain happen around your table.

**Oratorio de la Santa Cueva.** A few blocks east of the Plaza de Mina, next door to the Iglesia del Rosario, is this oval 18th-century chapel with three frescoes by Goya. ⊠ *C. Rosario 10* ☎ *956/222262* ☒ *€3* ⊙ *Tues.– Fri. 10–1 and 4:30–7:30, weekends 10–1.*

**Oratorio de San Felipe Neri.** Heading up Calle San José from the Plaza de la Mina, you see the church in which Spain's first liberal constitution was declared in 1812. ⊠ *Santa Inés 38* ☎ *956/211612* ☒ *€3* ⊙ *Mon.– Sat. 10–1:30.*

**Plaza San Francisco.** This plaza near the ayuntamiento is a pretty square surrounded by white-and-yellow houses and filled with orange trees and elegant street lamps. It's especially lively during the evening *paseo* (promenade).

**Roman Theater.** Next door to the church of Santa Cruz are the remains of a 1st-century BC Roman amphitheater that were discovered by chance in 1982; the theater is still under excavation. ⊠ *C. Rosario* ☒ *Free* ⊙ *Daily 10–2.*

**Torre Tavira.** At 150 feet, this tower, attached to an 18th-century palace that's now a conservatory of music, is the highest point in the old city. ⊠ *Marqués del Real Tesoro 10* ☎ *956/212910* ☒ *€4* ⊙ *Mid-June–mid-Sept., daily 10–8; mid-Sept.–mid-June, daily 10–6.*

## SEVILLE
*149 km (93 mi) northeast of Cádiz.*

Seville's whitewashed houses bright with bougainvillea, its ocher-color palaces, and its baroque facades have long enchanted both Sevillanos and travelers. Lord Byron's well-known line, "Seville is a pleasant city famous for oranges and women," may be true, but is far too tame. Seville's color and vivacity are legendary but best seen during one of the traditional *fiestas*, when modern dress is swapped for vivid ruffled costume, and the streets come alive with song and dance.

★ **Alcázar.** This palace was built by Pedro I (1350–69) on the site of Seville's former Moorish *alcázar* (fortress). Don't mistake the Alcázar for a genuine Moorish palace, like Granada's Alhambra—it may look like one, but it was commissioned and paid for by a Christian king more than 100 years after the reconquest of Seville. In its construction, Pedro the Cruel incorporated stones and capitals he pillaged from Valencia, from Córdoba's Medina Azahara, and from Seville itself. The palace serves as the official Seville residence of the king and queen. If the king and queen are not in residence, it is possible to visit their apartments by a guided tour (separate ticket from the Alcázar, mornings only). ⊠ *Pl. del Triunfo, Santa Cruz* ☎ *95/450–2324* ⊕ *www.patronato-alcazarsevilla. es* ☒ *€7.50* ⊙ *Tues.–Sat. 9:30–7, Sun. 9:30–5.*

**Archivo de las Indias** *(Archives of the Indies).* This dignified Renaissance building holds archives of more than 40,000 documents, including drawings, trade documents, plans of South American towns, even the autographs of Columbus, Magellan, and Cortés. ⊠ *Av. de la Constitución, Santa Cruz* ☎ *95/421–1234* ☒ *Free* ⊙ *Mon.–Sat. 10–4, Sun. 10–2.*

**Cathedral.** After Ferdinand III captured Seville from the Moors in 1248, the great mosque begun by Yusuf II in 1171 was reconsecrated and used as a Christian cathedral. But in 1401 the people of Seville decided to erect a new cathedral, one that would equal the glory of their great city. Today it is still the world's third-largest church, after St. Peter's in Rome and St. Paul's in London. The magnificent *retablo* (altarpiece) in the main chapel is the largest in Christendom (65 feet by 43 feet). It depicts some 36 scenes from the life of Christ, with pillars carved with more than 200 figures. Scientific studies have proved that the **monument to Christopher Columbus** houses some earthly remains of the great explorer, though not enough to be a complete skeleton. You can climb to the top of the **Giralda**, which dominates Seville's skyline. Once the minaret of Seville's great mosque, it was built between 1184 and 1196, and the Christians incorporated it into their new cathedral. ⊠ *Pl. Virgen de los Reyes, Santa Cruz* ☎ *95/421–4971* ⊕ *www.catedraldesevilla.es* ⊠ *Cathedral and Giralda €8* ⊙ *Cathedral July and Aug., Mon.–Sat. 9.30–4, Sun. 2.30–6; Sept.–June, Mon.–Sat. 11:15–5, Sun. 2.30–6.*

☼ **Plaza de España.** This grandiose half-moon of buildings was copied as Spain's centerpiece pavilion at the 1929 Barcelona Exposition. The brightly colored azulejo pictures represent the 50 provinces of Spain, while the four bridges symbolize the medieval kingdoms of the Iberian Peninsula. You can rent small boats for rowing along the arc-shape canal.

**Torre de Oro.** A 12-sided tower built by the Moors in 1220 to complete the city's ramparts, it served to close off the harbor when a chain was stretched across the river from its base to another tower on the opposite bank. In 1248 Admiral Ramón de Bonifaz broke through this barrier, and thus did Ferdinand III capture Seville. The tower now houses a small naval museum. ⊠ *Paseo Alcalde Marqués de Contadero s/n, El Arenal* ☎ *95/422–2419* ⊠ *€2* ⊙ *Tues.–Fri. 10–2, weekends 11–2.*

## JEREZ DE LA FRONTERA
*52 km (34 mi) northeast of Cádiz.*

Jerez, world headquarters for sherry, is surrounded by vineyards of chalky soil, whose Palomino grapes have funded a host of churches and noble mansions. Names such as González Byass, Domecq, Harvey, and Sandeman are inextricably linked with Jerez. At any given time more than half a million barrels of sherry are maturing in Jerez's vast aboveground wine cellars.

**González Byass.** If you have time for only one bodega, tour the González Byass, home of the famous Tío Pepe. This tour is well organized and includes La Concha, an open-air aging cellar designed by Gustave Eiffel. Your guide will explain the *solera* method of blending old wine with new, and the importance of the *flor* (a sort of yeast that forms on the surface of the wine as it ages) in determining the kind of sherry. You'll be invited to sample generous amounts of pale, dry fino; nutty *amontillado*; or rich, deep *oloroso,* and, of course, to purchase a few bottles. ⊠ *Calle Manuel Mar a Gonz lez* ☎ *956/357000, 902/440077 for visitor information* ⊕ *www.gonzalezbyass.com.*

**2**

Ⓒ **Real Escuela Andaluza del Arte Ecuestre** *(Royal Andalusian School of*
Fodor'sChoice *Equestrian Art)*. The school operates on the grounds of the Recreo de
★ las Cadenas, a 19th-century palace, which was designed by Charles
Garnier (also the architect of the Opera in Paris and the Monte Carlo
Casino). You can visit the stables and tack room of this prestigious
school and watch the horses being put through their paces with multilingual guided tours between 10:30 and 12:30 daily in summer. The
attached Carriage Museum displays a variety of international carriages
and tack. Every Tuesday and Thursday (as well as Friday in August
and some Saturdays in summer) the horses and skilled riders demonstrate intricate dressage techniques and jumping in the spectacular show
**"Cómo Bailan los Caballos Andaluces."** Reservations are essential.
✉ *Av. Duque de Abrantes s/n* ☎ *956/319635* ⊕ *www.realescuela.org*
🎫 *Stables and museum €10, museum only €4, dressage show €18–€25*
⊙ *Stables Mar.–Dec., Wed. and Fri. 9:30–1, Jan. and Feb., Mon, Tues.*
*9:30–1. Carriage Museum Mon.–Sat., 10–3. Dressage shows Tues. and*
*Thurs. noon (Aug. also Fri. and sometimes Sat. at noon).*

## SHOPPING

The region abounds with colorful souvenirs, including fine flamenco
costumes, classical guitars, ornate fans traditional to Andalusia. Look
out also for copious choices in ceramics, porcelain, and textiles, including beautiful hand-stitched embroidery (be aware that machine-embroi-
dered items have flooded the market). Don't forget a bottle or two of
excellent Jerez sherry, or Spanish olives and olive oil to augment your
larders back home.

Seville is the region's main shopping area and the place for arche-
typal Andalusian souvenirs, most of which are sold in the Barrio de
Santa Cruz and around the cathedral and Giralda, especially on Calle
Alemanes. The main shopping street for Sevillanos themselves is Calle
Sierpes, along with its neighboring streets Cuna, Tetuan, Velázquez,
Plaza Magdalena, and Plaza Duque—boutiques abound here. The
streets of old Cádiz are the place to browse and buy.

**Artesanía Textil.** You can find all kinds of blankets, shawls, and embroi-
dered tablecloths woven by local artisans at the two shops of Artesania
Textil, but the Centro branch is the most central option. ✉ *Sierpes 70,*
*Centro, Seville* ☎ *95/422–0125.*

**Casa Rubio.** This is Seville's premier fan store, no mean distinction,
with both traditional and contemporary designs. ✉ *Sierpes 56, Cen-*
*tro, Seville* ☎ *95/422–6872.*

**La Alacena.** La Cartuja china, originally crafted at La Cartuja Monastery
but now made outside Seville, is sold at this shop. ✉ *Alfonso XII 25,*
*San Vicente, Seville* ☎ *95/422–8021.*

## WHERE TO EAT

$ ✕**Casa Manteca.** Cádiz's most quintessentially Andalusian tavern is
SPANISH just down the street from El Faro restaurant and a little deeper into
the La Viña barrio (named for the vineyard that once stood here).

*Chacina* (Iberian ham or sausage), served on waxed paper, and Manzanilla (sherry from Sanlúcar de Barrameda) are standard fare at this low wooden counter that has served bullfighters and flamenco singers, as well as dignitaries from around the world since 1953. ⊠ *Corralón de los Carros 66, Cádiz* ☎ *956/213603* ▤ *AE, DC, MC, V* ⊘ *Closed Mon. No lunch Sun.*

$–$$
SPANISH
Fodor'sChoice
★

✕ **Enrique Becerra.** Excellent tapas and a lively bar await at this restaurant run by the fifth generation of a family of celebrated restaurateurs (Enrique's brother Jesús owns Becerrita). The menu focuses on traditional, home-cooked Andalusian dishes, such as *pez espada al amontillado* (swordfish cooked in dark sherry) and *cordero a la miel con espinacas* (honey-glazed lamb stuffed with spinach and pine nuts). Don't miss the cumin seed–laced *espinacas con garbanzos* (spinach with chickpeas) or the extensive wine list. ⊠ *Calle Gamazo 2, El Arenal* ☎ *95/421–3049* ▤ *AE, DC, MC, V* ⊘ *Closed Sun. and last 2 wks of July.*

# CANNES, FRANCE (WITH THE ILES DE LÉRINS AND ANTIBES)

A tasteful and expensive stomping ground for the upscale, Cannes is a sybaritic heaven for those who believe that life is short and sin has something to do with the absence of a tan. Backed by gentle hills and flanked to the southwest by the Estérel, warmed by dependable sun but kept bearable in summer by the cool Mediterranean breeze, Cannes is pampered with the luxurious climate that has made it one of the most popular and glamorous resorts in Europe. The cynosure of sun worshippers since the 1860s, it has been further glamorized by the modern success of its film festival. If you're a culture lover into art of the noncelluloid type you should look elsewhere. Come to Cannes for incomparable continental panache and as a stepping stone to attractions a little farther afield.

## ESSENTIALS

CURRENCY  The euro (€1 to US$1.36 at this writing).

HOURS  Most stores are open Monday–Saturday 9–7, but many close at lunchtime (usually noon–2 or 3) and some will open later and on Sunday during July and August. Museums are open 10–5, but most are closed on either Monday or Tuesday.

INTERNET  **Web Center** (⊠ *26 rue Hoche, Cannes* ☎ *04–93–68–72–37*).

TELEPHONES  Tri-band GSM phones work in France. You can buy prepaid phone cards at telecom shops, news vendors, and tobacconists in all towns and cities. Phone cards can be used for local or international calls. France Telecom and Orange are leading telecom companies.

## COMING ASHORE

Cruise vessels anchor offshore in Cannes, and passengers are tendered ashore to the Old Port. Ffrom there it is walking distance to all the city attractions. Taxis are on hand, and it's a five-minute ride to the train or bus station.

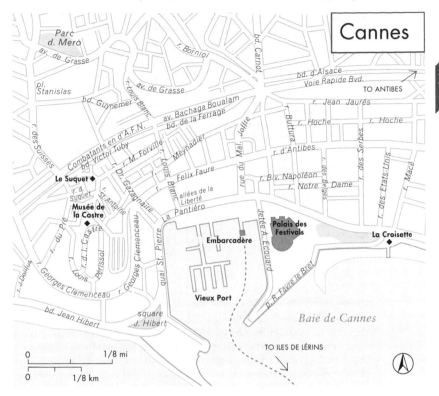

There will be no need to rent a vehicle unless you want to tour the surrounding Provençal countryside. The rental cost is approximately €70 per day for an economy manual vehicle. Taxis are plentiful and can provide tourist itineraries. For single journeys, tariffs are €2.80 at flag fall, then €0.84 per km. If you want to rent by the hour, the daytime tariff is €28.

Local trains are frequent; you can reach Nice in 20 minutes (€6.10 or €8.60 by faster TGV), Antibes in 10 minutes (€2.60 or €3.60 by faster TGV), and almost all other coastal towns can also be reached on a local train in less than an hour. Both RCA and TAM bus lines have frequent service (RCA's 200 bus between Cannes and Antibes runs every 20 minutes).

## EXPLORING CANNES

### CANNES

**La Croisette.** The most delightful thing to do in Cannes is to head to the famous mile-long waterfront promenade that starts at the western end by the Palais des Festivals and the town port, and allow the *esprit de Cannes* to take over. This is precisely the sort of place for which the verb *flâner* (to dawdle, saunter) was invented, so stroll among the palm trees and flowers and crowds of poseurs (fur coats in tropical weather, cell phones and Rollerblades, sunglasses at night). Head east past the broad expanse of private beaches, glamorous shops, and luxurious hotels (such as the wedding-cake Carlton, famed for its see-and-be-seen terrace-level brasserie). The beaches along here are almost all private, though open for a fee—each beach is marked with from one to four little life buoys, rating their quality and expense.

**Le Suquet.** Climb up Rue St-Antoine into the picturesque Vieille Ville neighborhood known as Le Suquet on the site of the original Roman *castrum.* Shops proffer Provençal goods, and the atmospheric cafés give you a chance to catch your breath; the pretty pastel shutters, Gothic stonework, and narrow passageways are lovely distractions.

---

### CANNES BEST BETS

**Stroll along the Croisette.** This seafront promenade is where all the beautiful people go for their walks. Check out the handprints of the stars set in clay on the pavement around the Palais des Festivals.

**Musée Picasso.** The medieval castle in nearly Antibes displays a fascinating array covering the many eras of the artist's long and successful career.

**Wander the streets of Vieux Antibes.** The narrow streets of the Old Town are wonderful for capturing images of life in languorous southern France.

---

**Musée de la Castre.** The hill called "Le Suquet," for which the neighborhood is named, is crowned by an 11th-century château that houses this museum and the imposing four-sided **Tour du Suquet** (Suquet Tower), built in 1385 as a lookout against Saracen-led invasions. ⊠ *Pl. de la Castre, Le Suquet* ☎ *04–93–38–55–26* 🖃 *€3* ☉ *Apr.–June, Tues.–Sun. 10–1 and 2–6; July and Aug., daily 10–7; Sept., Tues.–Sun. 10–1 and 2–6; Oct.–Mar., Tues.–Sun. 10–1 and 2–5.*

**Palais des Festivals.** Pick up a map at the tourist office, the scene of the famous Festival International du Film, otherwise known as the Cannes Film Festival. As you leave the information center, follow the Palais to your right to see the red-carpeted stairs where the stars ascend every year. Set into the surrounding pavement, the **Allée des Etoiles** (Stars' Walk) enshrines some 300 autographed imprints of film stars' hands—of Dépardieu, Streep, and Stallone, among others.

## ÎLES LÉRINS

*15–20 minutes by ferry off the coast of Cannes.*

When you're glutted on glamour, you may want to make a day trip to the peaceful Iles de Lérins (Lérins Islands); boats depart from Cannes's Vieux Port. Allow at least a half day to enjoy either of the islands; you can fit both in only if you get an early start. Access to the ferry is across the large parking in front of the Sofitel hotel, southwest from the Palais des Festivals. You have two ferry options.

**Tour Contacts Compangie Planaria.** This company goes to Ile St-Honorat. ⊠ *Quai Lauboeuf, port of Cannes, La Croisette, Cannes* ☎ *04–92–98–71–38* ⊕ *www.cannes-ilesdelerins.com.* **Trans Cote D'Azur.** This company goes to Isle St. Margueritte. ⊠ *Quai Lauboeuf, port of Cannes, La Croisette, Cannes* ☎ *04–92–98–71–30* ⊕ *www.trans-cote-azur.com.*

### ÎLES LÉRINS

**Ile St-Honorat.** This island can be reached in 20 minutes (€12 round-trip) from the Vieux Port. Smaller and wilder than Ste-Marguerite, it is home to an active monastery and the ruins of its 11th-century predecessor. Oddly enough, the monks are more famous in the region for their nonreligious activity: manufacturing and selling a rather strong liqueur called Lerina.

**Ile Ste-Marguerite.** This island is a 15-minute trip from Cannes by boat that costs €11.50 round-trip. Its **Fort Royal,** built by Richelieu and improved by Vauban, offers views over the ramparts to the rocky island coast and the open sea.

Behind the prison buildings is the **Musée de la Mer** *(Marine Museum),* with a Roman boat dating from the 1st century BC and a collection of amphorae and pottery recovered from ancient shipwrecks. It is more famous, however, for reputedly being the prison of the Man in the Iron Mask. Inside, you can see his cell and hear his story, and although the truth of his captivity is not certain, it is true that many Huguenots were confined here during Louis XIV's religious scourges. ☎ *04–93–43–18–17* 🖾 *€3.40* ۞ *Oct.–Mar., Tues.–Sun. 10:30–1:15 and 2:15–4:45; Apr.–mid-June, Tues.–Sun. 10:30–1:15 and 2:15–5:45; mid-June–Sept., daily 10:30–5:45.*

### ANTIBES

*11 km (7 mi) northeast of Cannes, 15 km (9 mi) southeast of Nice.*

**Fodor's**Choice
★
No wonder Picasso once called this home—Antibes (pronounced Awn-teeb) is a stunner. With its broad stone ramparts scalloping in and out over the waves and backed by blunt medieval towers and a skew of tile roofs, it remains one of the most romantic old towns on the Mediterranean coast. As gateway to the Cap d'Antibes, Antibes's Port Vauban harbor has some of the largest yachts in the world tied up at its berths—their millionaire owners won't find a more dramatic spot to anchor, with the tableau of the snowy Alps looming in the distance and the formidable medieval block towers of the Fort Carré guarding entry to the port. Stroll Promenade Amiral-de-Grasse along the crest of Vauban's sea walls, and you'll understand why the views inspired Picasso to paint on a panoramic scale. Yet a few steps inland you'll enter a souklike maze of old streets that are relentlessly picturesque and joyously beautiful.

To visit Old Antibes, pass through the **Porte Marine,** an arched gateway in the rampart wall. Follow Rue Aubernon to **Cours Masséna,** where the little sheltered market sells lemons, olives, and hand-stuffed sausages, and the vendors take breaks in the shoebox cafés flanking one side.

★ **Château Grimaldi.** Next door to the cathedral, the medieval château rises high over the water on a Roman foundation. Famed as rulers of Monaco, the Grimaldi family lived here until the Revolution, but this fine old castle was little more than a monument until in 1946 its curator offered use of its vast chambers to Picasso, at a time when that extraordinary genius was enjoying a period of intense creative energy. The result is now housed in the **Musée Picasso,** a bounty of exhilarating paintings, ceramics, and lithographs inspired by the sea and by

Greek mythology—all very Mediterranean. Even those who are not great Picasso fans should enjoy his vast paintings on wood, canvas, paper, and walls, alive with nymphs, fauns, and centaurs. The museum houses more than 300 works by the artist, as well as pieces by Miró, Calder, and Léger. ⊠ *Pl. du Château* ☎ *04–92–90–54–20* ⊡ *€6* ⊘ *Mid-June–mid-Sept., Tues.–Sun. 10–6; July and Aug., Wed. and Fri. until 8; mid-Sept.–mid-June, Tues.–Sun. 10–noon and 2–6.*

**Fodor'sChoice**   **Commune Libre du Safranier** *(Free Commune of Safranier).* A few blocks
★   south of the Château Grimaldi is this neighborhood, a magical little place with a character all its own. Here, not far off the seaside promenade and focused around the Place du Safranier, tiny houses hang heavy with flowers and vines and neighbors carry on conversations from window to window across the stone-stepped Rue du Bas-Castelet. It is said that Place du Safranier was once a tiny fishing port; now it's the scene of this sub-village's festivals.

★   **Église de l'Immaculée-Conception.** From Cours Masséna head up to the Church of the Immaculate Conception. The church's 18th-century facade, a marvelously Latin mix of classical symmetry and fantasy, has been restored in shades of ocher and cream. Its stout medieval watchtower was built in the 11th century with stones "mined" from Roman structures. Inside is a baroque altarpiece painted by the Niçois artist Louis Bréa in 1515. ⊠ *Pl. de la Cathédrale.*

**Musée Archéologique** *(Archaeology Museum).* The Bastion St-André, a squat Vauban fortress, now contains this museum. Its collection focuses on Antibes's classical history, displaying amphorae and sculptures found in local digs as well as salvaged from shipwrecks from the harbor. ⊠ *Bastion Saint-André, Av. Général-Maizières* ☎ *04–92–90–54–35* ⊡ *€3* ⊘ *Mid-Sept.–mid-June, Tues.–Sun. 10–1 and 2–6; mid-June–mid-Sept., Tues.–Sun. 10–noon and 2–8; July and Aug., Wed. and Fri. until 8.*

# SHOPPING

Cannes caters to the upmarket crowd with a wealth of designer boutiques such as Chanel and Dior, and high-class jewelers. But if you don't want to max out your credit cards there's a wealth of choice of less expensive ready-to-wear fashion. Boutiques also sell colorful crafts from the Provence region, including basketware, bright fabrics, olive-wood items, plus delicious olives, olive oils, honey, dried herbs, and quaffable local wines. Film buffs may also want to stock up on official Cannes Film Festival merchandise.

**Rue d'Antibes,** running parallel with the Croisette but two blocks inland, is Cannes's main high-end shopping street. At its western end is **Rue Meynadier,** packed tight with trendy clothing boutiques and fine food shops. Not far away is the covered **Marché Forville,** the scene of the animated morning food market. The narrow alleyways of **Le Suquet,** are also a great place to browse. Film Festival merchandise can be bought at the **Palais du Festivals,** but the official Film Festival shop is found on La Croisette, close to the Majestic Hotel.

Vicil Antibes has an excellent shopping, though you'll find far fewer designer boutiques than in Cannes. Small shops sell an excellent range of local crafts and foodstuffs and there are several galleries selling work by local artists.

## BEACHES

The pebble beach that fronts the full length of La Croisette has a chic atmosphere in summer. Most sections have been privatized and are owned by hotels and/or restaurants that rent out chaise longues, mats, and umbrellas to the public and hotel guests (who also have to pay). Public beaches are between the color-coordinated private beach umbrellas, and offer simple open showers and basic toilets. The restaurants here are some of the best places for lunch or refreshment, though you do pay extra for the location.

## WHERE TO EAT

**$$**  ✕**La Pizza.** Sprawling up over two floors and right in front of the Old
PIZZA Port, this busy Italian restaurant serves steaks, fish, and salads, but go there for what they're famous for: gloriously good right-out-of-the-wood-fire-oven pizza in hungry-man-size portions. There is an outpost in Nice as well. ⊠ *3 quai St-Pierre, La Croisette* 🕾 *04–93–39–22–56* 🗏 *AE, MC, V.*

**$$**  ✕**Le Petit Lardon.** Popular and unpretentious, this tiny bistro is feisty
FRENCH and fun. Watch for a great mix of seasonal Provençal and Burgundian flavors: escargots served with butter and garlic, roast rabbit *au jus* stuffed with raisins, and melt-in-your-mouth lavender crème brûlée. Busy, bustling, and friendly, it is ideal for a casual meal, but it is tiny, so reserve well in advance. ⊠ *Rue de Batéguier 3, La Croisette* 🕾 *04–93–39–06–28* 🗏 *AE, MC, V* ⊗ *Closed Sun.*

# CIVITAVECCHIA, ITALY (FOR ROME)

Rome is a heady blend of artistic and architectural masterpieces, classical ruins, and extravagant baroque churches and piazzas. The city's 2,700-year-old history is on display wherever you look; the ancient rubs shoulders with the medieval, the modern runs into the Renaissance, and the result is a bustling open-air museum. Julius Caesar and Nero, the Vandals and the Popes, Raphael and Caravaggio, Napoléon and Mussolini—these and countless other luminaries have left their mark on the city. Today Rome's formidable legacy is kept alive by its people, their history knit into the fabric of their everyday lives. Raphaelesque teenage girls zip through traffic on their *motorini*; priests in flowing robes stride through medieval piazzas talking on cell phones. Modern Rome has one foot in the past, one in the present—a fascinating stance that allows you to tip back an espresso in a square designed by Bernini, then hop on the metro to your next attraction.

### ESSENTIALS

CURRENCY  The euro (€1 to US$1.36 at this writing).

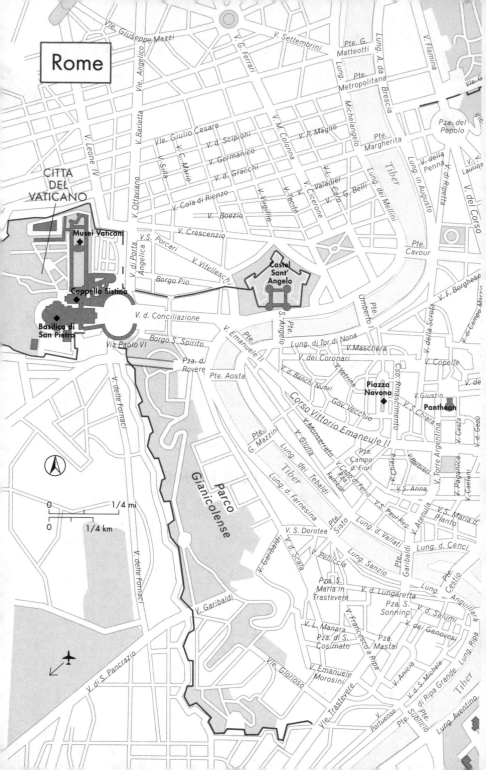

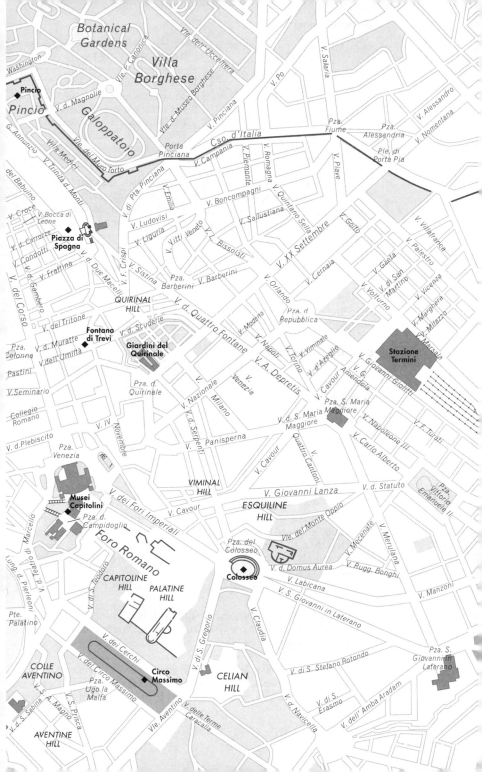

HOURS

Stores are generally open from 9 or 9:30 to 1 and from 3:30 or 4 to 7 or 7:30. There's a tendency for shops in central districts to stay open all day. Many places close Sunday, and some also close Monday morning from September to mid-June and Saturday afternoon from mid-June through August.

INTERNET

Internet cafés are relatively common in Rome. There are several centrally located spots near Piazza Navona and Campo dei Fiori. **Easy Internet Cafe** (⊠ *Via Barberini, Quirinale* ☎ *06/42903388*) is the biggest in the city.

TELEPHONES

Tri-band GSM phones work in Italy. You can buy prepaid phone cards at telecom shops, news vendors, and tobacconists in all towns and cities. Phone cards can be used for local or international calls.

---

### ROME BEST BETS

**The Colosseum.** Although jam-packed with tourists, this is still one of ancient Rome's most iconic relics and was the scene of some of its bloodiest contests.

**Basilica di San Pietro.** The mother church for all Catholics is redolent with spirit and filled with artistic masterpieces. Just remember that the Sistine Chapel can only be visited if you go to the Vatican Museums.

**Join the throng at Piazza Navona.** Visit this large square with its three fountains and immerse yourself in the energy that is modern Rome.

---

### COMING ASHORE

Civitavecchia is a large port, and you will be bused from the ship to the terminal area. There are passenger facilities such as cafés and information offices, but these are shared with commercial ferry traffic and can be crowded. A shuttle will take you to the railway station, where you can catch trains to Rome, or you can walk along the harborfront to the station in less than 10 minutes. Taxis charge around €20 for the journey to the train station. Train tickets to Rome cost approximately €9 round-trip. If you prebook on the Trenitalia Web site ⊕ *www.trenitalia.com*, you can print out your tickets at the station. There are three trains per hour, and the journey time is 1 hour 15 minutes. The cost for a private car with driver to Rome is approximately €150 one-way.

Taxis charge approximately €2.33 initially, then €0.78 per km (½-mi) with an increment of €0.11 per 140 meters (460 feet) when the taxi travels at less than 20 kph (12 mph). You shouldn't rent a car if you want to explore only Rome, because both traffic and parking are difficult; however, if you want to explore the countryside around Civitavecchia a car would be useful. Rental costs are approximately €50 per day for a compact manual vehicle.

Rome's metro (subway) is somewhat limited, but it's quick if you are headed somewhere that it goes. The public bus and tram system is slow. Taking the compact electric buses of Lines 117 and 119 through the center of Rome can save a lot of walking. A ticket valid for 75 minutes on any combination of buses and trams and one entrance to the metro costs €1. Tickets for the public transit system are sold at tobacconists, newsstands, some coffee bars; you can also buy them in the green machines positioned in metro stations and some bus stops. A BIG ticket, valid for one day on all public transport, costs €4.

**GETTING TO THE AIRPORT**

If you do not purchase airport transfers from your cruise line, the most practical option is to take a taxi or private transfer company to pick you up at the port and drop you at the airport. Costs for this are around €150 for either option, though the private transfer vehicle will be larger and can accommodate up to seven people.

**Dock Service.** This company can provide port to airport transfers (or vice versa) as well as guided land tours within Rome. ☎ *239/603–7469 in U.S., 338/9139644 in Italy* ⊕ *www.limoservicesrome.eu*

## EXPLORING ROME

★ **Basilica di San Pietro.** The largest church in the world, built over the tomb of St. Peter, is also the most imposing and breathtaking architectural achievement of the Renaissance (although much of the lavish interior dates to the baroque). The physical statistics are impressive: it covers 18,000 square yards, runs 212 yards in length, and carries a dome that rises 435 feet and measures 138 feet across its base. Its history is equally impressive: no less than five of Italy's greatest artists—Bramante, Raphael, Peruzzi, Antonio Sangallo the Younger, and Michelangelo—died while striving to erect this new St. Peter's.

The history of the original St. Peter's goes back to AD 349, when the emperor Constantine completed a basilica over the site of the tomb of St. Peter, the Church's first pope. In 1452 a reconstruction job was authorized, but it wasn't until 1626 that the basilica was completed and consecrated.

The basilica is filled with innumerable masterpieces, and the visit is free, but you must pay to enter the **Museo Storico** or to take in the view from the **roof.** The **Grotte Vaticane** (containing the tombs of the popes) has a separate line, but the exit is outside the church; it's best to leave this for last, after you've visited the basilica (though it's often possible to reenter the basilica by going directly up the steps). Be aware that you will have to pass through metal detectors and go through a bag-check before admission. This means that lines can form well into St. Peter's Square, but they tend to move fairly quickly. An audioguide is available in English to accompany your visit to the Basilica. St. Peter's is closed during ceremonies in the piazza (such as the Pope's weekly audience on Wednesday mornings). ⊠ *Piazza San Pietro* ☎ *06/69883712* ⊕ *www. vatican.va* ⊠ *Basilica free; Museo Storico €15; elevator to roof €7, stairs to roof €5* ⊙ *Apr.–Sept., daily 7–7; Oct.–Mar., daily 7–6:30.*

**Fodor's Choice** **Colosseo** *(Colosseum).* The most spectacular extant edifice of ancient
★ Rome, this sports arena was designed to hold more than 50,000 spectators for gory entertainments such as combats between wild beasts and gladiators. Designed by order of the Flavian emperor Vespasian in AD 72, the arena has a circumference of 573 yards. Among the stadium's many wonders was a *velarium,* an ingenious system of sail-like awnings

rigged on ropes and maneuvered by sailors from the imperial fleet, who would unfurl them to protect the arena's occupants from sun or rain.

Some experts maintain that it was in Rome's circuses, and not here, that thousands of early Christians were martyred. Still, tradition has reserved a special place for the Colosseum in the story of Christianity, and it was Pope Benedict XIV who stopped the use of the building as a quarry when, in 1749, he declared it sanctified by the blood of the martyrs. ⊠ *Piazza del Colosseo* ☎ *06/39967700* ⊕ *www.pierreci.it* ⌸ *€12* ⊗ *Daily 9–1 hr before sunset.*

**Fodor's Choice**
★
**Musei Vaticani** *(The Vatican Museums)*. Other than the pope and his papal court, the occupants of the Vatican are some of the most famous art works in the world, a collection so rich that you will only be able to skim the surface.

The gems of the Vatican's sculpture collection are in the **Pio-Clementino Museum,** with pieces rescued from ancient piazzas and palaces from around the city. In the **Octagonal Courtyard** is the *Laocoön* group, held to be possibly the single most important antique sculpture group in terms of its influence on Renaissance artists.

Rivaling the Sistine Chapel for artistic interest are the **Stanze di Raffaello** (Raphael Rooms). When people talk about the Italian High Renaissance, it's Raphael's frescoes they're probably thinking about. The **Segnatura Room** was painted almost entirely by Raphael himself. All the revolutionary characteristics of High Renaissance art are here: naturalism; humanism; and a profound interest in the ancient world, the result of the 15th-century rediscovery of archaeology and classical antiquity.

It's generally believed that Cesare Borgia murdered his sister Lucrezia's husband, Alphonse of Aragon, in the Room of the Sibyl in the **Borgia Apartments.** Other highly ornate rooms have religious scenes featuring many Borgia family members.

The paintings in the **Pinacoteca** (Picture Gallery) are almost exclusively of religious subjects, and are arranged in chronological order, beginning with works of the 11th and 12th centuries. Highlights include a Giotto triptych and Madonnas by the Florentine 15th-century painters Fra Angelico and Filippo Lippi along with further Raphael masterpieces.

**Fodor's Choice**
★
In 1508 the redoubtable Pope Julius II commissioned Michelangelo to fresco more than 10,000 square feet of the ceiling of the **Cappella Sistina** *(Sistine Chapel)*. The task took four years. The result was a masterpiece. Before the chapel was consecrated in 1483, its lower walls had been decorated by a group of artists including Botticelli, Ghirlandaio, Perugino, Signorelli, and Pinturicchio. More than 20 years later, Michelangelo was called on again, this time by the Farnese Pope Paul III, to add to the chapel's decoration by painting the *Last Judgment* on the wall over the altar. *Vatican Museums* ⊠ *Viale Vaticano* ☎ *06/69884947* ⊕ *www. vatican.va* ⌸ *€15* ⊗ *Mon. Sat. 9–6 (ticket office closes at 4), also open last Sun. of month 9–2 (ticket office closes at 12:20)* ☞ *Note: Ushers at entrance of St. Peter's and Vatican Museums will bar entry to people with bare knees or bare shoulders.*

**Fodor's Choice**
★ **Fontana di Trevi** *(Trevi Fountain).* Alive with rushing waters and marble sea creatures commanded by an imperious Oceanus, this aquatic marvel is one of the city's most exciting sights. The work of Nicola Salvi—though it's thought that Bernini may have been responsible for parts of the design—was completed in 1762, and is a perfect example of the rococo taste for dramatic theatrical effects. Usually thickly fringed with tourists tossing coins into the basin to ensure their return to Rome (the fountain grosses about €120,000 a year, most of it donated to charity). ⊠ *Piazza di Trevi.*

★ **Musei Capitolini.** If you have time for just one museum in Rome other than the Vatican Museums, make it this one. This immense collection, housed in the twin Palazzi del Museo Capitolino and Palazzo dei Conservatori buildings, which flank Michelangelo's piazza, is a greatest hits collection of Roman art through the ages, from the ancients to the baroque. After your tour of the museum, you can stroll through the Foro Romana (free) all the way up to the Colosseo. ⊠ *Piazza del Campidoglio* ☎ *060608* ⊕ *www.museicapitolini.org* ⊠ *€11* ⊙ *Tues.–Sun. 9–8.*

**Fodor's Choice**
★ **Pantheon.** This onetime pagan temple, a marvel of architectural harmony and proportion, is the best-preserved monument of imperial Rome. Dating from around AD 120, the most striking thing about the Pantheon is the remarkable unity of the building. You don't have to look far to find the reason for this harmony: the diameter described by the dome is exactly equal to its height. It's the use of such simple mathematical balance that gives classical architecture its characteristic sense of proportion and its nobility and timeless appeal. The great opening at the apex of the dome, the oculus, is nearly 30 feet in diameter, and was the temple's only source of light. It was intended to symbolize the "all-seeing eye of heaven." ⊠ *Piazza della Rotonda* ☎ *06/68300230* ⊠ *Free* ⊙ *Mon.–Sat. 8.30–7:30, Sun. 9–6.*

**Fodor's Choice**
★ **Piazza Navona.** Here everything that makes Rome unique is compressed into one beautiful baroque piazza. It has antiquity, Bernini sculptures, three gorgeous fountains, a magnificently baroque church (Sant'Agnese in Agone), and, above all, the excitement of people out to enjoy themselves—strolling, café-loafing, seeing, and being seen. The piazza's most famous work of art is the **Fontana dei Quattro Fiumi,** created for Innocent X by Bernini in 1651. ⊠ *Junction of Via della Cuccagna, Corsia Agonale, Via di Sant'Agnese, and Via Agonale.*

ⓒ **Piazza di Spagna** *(Spanish Steps).* Those icons of postcard Rome, the
**Fodor's Choice**
★ Spanish Steps, and the piazza from which they ascend both get their names from the Spanish Embassy to the Vatican on the piazza, in spite of the fact that the staircase was built with French funds in 1723. For centuries, the steps welcomed tourists: among them Stendhal, Honoré de Balzac, William Makepeace Thackeray, and Byron. ⊠ *Piazza di Spagna, Spagna.*

ⓒ **Pincio.** The Pincio gardens have always been a favorite spot for strolling. Even a pope or two would head here to see and be seen among the beau monde of Rome. From the balustraded Pincio terrace you can look down at Piazza del Popolo and beyond, surveying much of Rome. ⊠ *Piazzale Napoleone I and Viale dell'Obelisco, Villa Borghese.*

### SHOPPING

Italian style is everywhere in Rome, from couture clothing to fashion accessories by all the best names. Specialties of the city include excellent silks, linens, lace, and other fabrics. Edibles include wines, olive oils, pasta, and sweet biscotti, small hard biscuits.

★ The city's most famous shopping district, **Piazza di Spagna,** is a galaxy of boutiques selling gorgeous wares with glamorous labels. **Via del Corso,** a main shopping avenue, has more than a mile of clothing, shoes, leather goods, and home furnishings from classic to cutting-edge. **Via Cola di Rienzo** is block after block of boutiques, shoe stores, department stores, and mid-level chain stores, as well as street stalls and upscale food shops. **Via dei Coronari** has quirky antiques and home furnishings. Via Giulia and other surrounding streets are good bets for decorative arts. Should your gift list include religious souvenirs, shop between Piazza San Pietro and **Borgo Pio.** Liturgical vestments and statues of saints make for good window-shopping on **Via dei Cestari.**

## WHERE TO EAT

$-$$$  ✗ **Alle Fratte.** Here staple Roman trattoria fare shares the menu with
ITALIAN  dishes that have a southern Italian slant. Boisterous owner Francesco,
Fodor's Choice  his American relatives, and their trusted waiter Peppe make you feel at
★  home. ⊠ *Via delle Fratte di Trastevere 49/50* ☎ *06/5835775* ⊕ *www. allefratteditrastevere.com* ⊟ *AE, DC, MC, V* ⊘ *Closed Wed. and 2 wks in Aug.*

$$-$$$$  ✗ **Dal Bolognese.** The classic Dal Bolognese is a convenient shopping-
ITALIAN  spree lunch spot, and the tables on the expansive pedestrian piazza are prime people-watching real estate. Choose from delicious fresh pastas in creamy sauces and steaming trays of boiled meats. ⊠ *Piazza del Popolo 1, near Piazza di Spagna* ☎ *06/3611426* ⊟ *AE, DC, MC, V* ⊘ *Closed Mon. and Aug.*

## WHERE TO STAY

$$$$  ⛱ **Hassler.** When it comes to million-dollar views, this exclusive hotel
☾  has the best seats in the house. Which is why movie stars, money shak-
Fodor's Choice  ers, and the *nouveau riche* are all willing to pay top dollar (or top euro,
★  shall we say) to stay at the best address in Rome, just atop the Spanish Steps. The hotel is owned by the Wirth family, a famous dynasty of Swiss hoteliers who also own Il Palazzetto—a small yet stylish boutique hotel—and the International Wine Academy (also nearby), which offers wine tastings and wine appreciation courses. The exterior of the Hassler is rather bland, but the guest rooms are certainly among the world's most extravagant and lavishly decorated. You can get more standard rooms at the back of the hotel, which will spare you and your wallet of the VIP prices. Of course, even the lowest prices at the Hassler can't compare with what you could find somewhere else. The recently renovated penthouse boasts the largest terrace in Rome. The Rooftop Restaurant, the Imagò (which guests use for the breakfast buffet), is world-famous for its view, if not for its food; and the Palm Court Garden, which becomes the hotel bar in summer, is overflowing with

**2**

flowers. **Pros:** charming old-world feel; prime location and panoramic views at the top of the Spanish Steps; just "steps" away from some of the best shopping in the world. **Cons:** VIP prices; many think the staff is too standoffish; some say the cuisine at the rooftop restaurant isn't worth the gourmet price tag. ⊠ *Piazza Trinità dei Monti 6, Spagna* ☎ *06/699340* ⊕ *www.lhw.com* ⇒ *85 rooms, 13 suites* ⬧ *In-room: safe, refrigerator, Internet. In-hotel: restaurant, room service, bar, gym, spa, laundry service, public Wi-Fi, parking (paid), no-smoking rooms* ⊟ *AE, DC, MC, V* ⦿❙ *EP.*

$$$–$$$$  ⊞ **Scalinata di Spagna.** A longtime favorite of hopeless romantics, it's
**Fodor'sChoice**  often hard to snag a room at this tiny hotel, as it's often booked up
★  for months, even years at a time. And it's not hard to guess why. For starters, its prime location at the top of the Spanish Steps, inconspicuous little entrance, and quiet, sunny charm all add to the character that guests fall in love with over and over again. Rooms were renovated in a stylish manner, focusing on accentuated floral fabrics and Empire-style sofas. Rooms that overlook the Spanish Steps are the first to go. But don't fret if you don't snatch up the room of your choice. You can always escape to the hotel's extravagant rooftop garden and gaze over ancient Rome as you nibble on your *cornetto* and sip on your *cappuccino.* Amenities, such as breakfast service until noon and in-room Internet access, are a nice touch. **Pros:** friendly and helpful concierge; fresh fruit in the rooms; free Wi-Fi throughout the Scalinata. **Cons:** it's a hike up the hill to the hotel; no porter and no elevator; service can be hit-or-miss. ⊠ *Piazza Trinità dei Monti 17, Spagna* ☎ *06/6793006* ⊕ *www.hotelscalinata.com* ⇒ *16 rooms* ⬧ *In-room: safe, refrigerator, Wi-Fi. In-hotel: room service, laundry service, Internet terminal, public Wi-Fi, parking (paid), no-smoking rooms* ⊟ *AE, D, MC, V* ⦿❙ *BP.*

$$  ⊞ **Yes Hotel.** Don't let the contemporary coolness of this hotel fool you.
**Fodor'sChoice**  It is a budget hotel. It's situated just near Stazione Termini, which is
★  key for moving around, and also has plenty of dining options in the area. Yes also offers the kind of amenities that are usually found in more expensive hotels, including mahogany furniture, decorative art, electronic safes, flat-screen TVs, and air-conditioning. Wireless Internet access is available in the rooms and throughout the hotel for an extra fee. **Pros:** flat-screen TVs with satellite TV; it doesn't feel like a budget hotel, but it is; discount if you pay cash; great value. **Cons:** rooms are small; no individual climate control or refrigerators in the rooms. ⊠ *Via Magenta 15, San Lorenzo* ☎ *06/44363836* ⊕ *www.yeshotelrome.com* ⇒ *29 rooms, 1 suite* ⬧ *In-room: safe, Wi-Fi (paid). In-hotel: parking (paid) Wi-Fi (paid), no-smoking rooms* ⊟ *MC, V* ⦿❙ *CP.*

# GENOA, ITALY

Genoa (Genova, in Italian) claims that it was the birthplace of Christopher Columbus (one of several places that claim the explorer), but the city's proud history predates that explorer by several hundred years. Genoa was already an important trading station by the 3rd century BC, when the Romans conquered Liguria. Known as *La Superba* (The Proud), Genoa was a great maritime power in the 13th century, rivaling

Venice and Pisa. But its luster eventually diminished, and the city was outshone by these and other formidable cities. By the 17th century it was no longer a great sea power. It has, however, continued to be a profitable port. Genoa is now a busy, sprawling, and cosmopolitan city. But with more than two millennia of history under its belt, magnificent palaces and museums, the largest medieval city center in Europe, and an elaborate network of ancient hilltop fortresses, Genoa may be just the dose of culture you are looking for. Portofino can be visited on a day-trip from Genoa if your ship doesn't call there directly (⇨ *Portofino*).

## ESSENTIALS

CURRENCY   The euro (€1 to US$1.36 at this writing).

HOURS   Stores are generally open from 9 or 9:30 to 1 and from 3:30 or 4 to 7 or 7:30. Many shops close Sunday, though this is changing, too, especially in the city center. Many national museums are closed on Monday and may have shorter hours on Sunday.

INTERNET   There is passenger Internet access in the port terminal.

TELEPHONES   Tri-band GSM phones work in Italy. You can buy prepaid phone cards at telecom shops, news vendors, and tobacconists in all towns and cities. Phone cards can be used for local or international calls.

## COMING ASHORE

Genoa is a massive port, and cruise ships usually dock at one of two terminals, the Ponte dei Mille Maritime Station and Ponte Andrea Doria Maritime Station. Ponte dei Mille is a magnificent 1930s building (renovated 2001) with good passenger facilities that include shops, restaurants, an information center, and a bank. Neighboring Ponte Andrea Doria was refurbished in 2007 with similar facilities but on a slightly smaller scale. From here it's a few minutes' walk to the port entrance, from which you can also walk into the city; however, the streets around the port are workaday and gritty, so you may want to take a taxi rather than walk into the city proper.

With the occasional assistance of public transportation, the only way to visit Genoa is on foot. Many of the more interesting districts are either entirely closed to traffic, have roads so narrow that no car could fit, or are, even at the best of times, blocked by gridlock. A vehicle might be useful if you want to explore the Ligurian countryside and coastline around Genoa. Rental costs are approximately €45 per day for a compact manual vehicle.

Within Liguria local trains make innumerable stops. Regular service operates from Genoa's two stations: departures from Stazione Principe travel to points west and Stazione Brignole to points east and south. All the coastal resorts are on this line. If you buy tickets though Trenitalia's (Italian Railway's) Web site (⊕ *www.trenitalia.com*), you can print them out at self-service machines in Genoa station.

## EXPLORING GENOA

### THE MEDIEVAL CORE

The medieval center of Genoa, threaded with tiny streets flanked by 11th-century portals, is roughly the area between the port and Piazza de Ferrari. This mazelike pedestrian zone is officially called the Caruggi District, but the Genovese, in their matter-of-fact way, simply refer to the area as the place of the *vicoli* (narrow alleys). In this warren of narrow, cobbled streets extending north from Piazza Caricamento the city's oldest churches sit among tiny shops selling antique furniture, coffee, cheese, rifles, wine, gilt picture frames, camping gear, and even live fish. The 500-year-old apartment buildings lean so precariously that penthouse balconies nearly touch those across the street, blocking what little sunlight would have shone down onto the cobblestones. Wealthy Genovese built their homes in this quarter in the 16th century, and prosperous guilds, such as the goldsmiths for whom Vico degli Indoratori and Via degli Orefici were named, set up shop here.

**Galleria Nazionale.** This gallery, housed in the richly adorned **Palazzo Spinola** north of Piazza Soziglia, contains masterpieces by Luca Giordano and Guido Reni. The *Ecce Homo* by Antonello da Messina is a hauntingly beautiful painting, of historical interest because it was the Sicilian da Messina who first brought Flemish oil paints and techniques to Italy from his sojourns in the Low Countries. ⊠ *Piazza Pellicceria 1, Maddalena* ☎ *010/2705300* ⊕ *www.palazzospinola.it* ⊡ *€4, €6.50 including Palazzo Reale* ⊙ *Tues.–Sat. 8:30–7:30, Sun. 1:30–7:30.*

**Palazzo Bianco.** It's difficult to miss the splendid white facade of this town palace as you walk down Via Garibaldi, once one of Genoa's most important streets. The building houses a fine collection of 17th-century art, with the Spanish and Flemish schools well represented. ⊠ *Via Garibaldi 11, Maddalena* ☎ *010/5572193* ⊕ *www.museidigenova.it* ⊡ *€8, includes Palazzo Rosso and Palazzo Doria Tursi* ⊙ *Tues.–Fri. 9–7, weekends 10–7.*

**Fodor'sChoice** **Palazzo Reale.** Lavish rococo rooms provide sumptuous display space for
★ paintings, sculptures, tapestries, and Asian ceramics. The 17th-century palace—also known as Palazzo Balbi Durazzo—was built by the Balbi family, enormously wealthy Genovese merchants. Its regal pretensions were not lost on the Savoy, who bought the palace and turned it into a royal residence in the early 19th century. The gallery of mirrors and the ballroom on the upper floor are particularly decadent. Look for works by Sir Anthony Van Dyck, who lived in Genoa for six years, beginning in 1621, and painted many portraits of the Genovese nobility. The formal gardens, which you can visit for €1, provide a welcome respite from the bustle of the city beyond the palace walls, as well as great views of the harbor. ⊠ *Via Balbi 10, Pré* ☎ *010/2710236* ⊕ *www.palazzorealegenova.it* ⊡ *€4, €6.50 including Galleria Nazionale* ⊙ *Tues. and Wed. 9–1:30, Thurs.–Sun. 9–7.*

**Palazzo Rosso.** This 17th-century baroque palace was named for the red stone used in its construction. It now contains, apart from a number of lavishly frescoed suites, works by Titian, Veronese, Reni, and Van Dyck. ⊠ *Via Garibaldi 18, Maddalena* ☎ *010/2759185* ⊕ *www.*

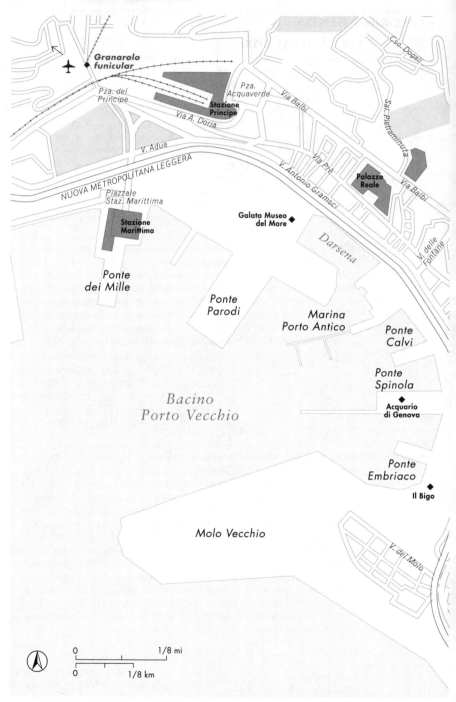

Granarolo funicular

Pza. del Principe

Pza. Acquaverde

Via Balbi

Cso. Dogali

Sal. Pietraminuta

Via A. Doria

Stazione Principe

V. Adua

NUOVA METROPOLITANA LEGGERA

Via Balbi

Via Prè

V. Antonio Gramsci

Palazzo Reale

Piazzale Staz. Marittima

Stazione Marittima

Galata Museo del Mare ◆

Darsena

V. delle Fontane

Ponte dei Mille

Ponte Parodi

Marina Porto Antico

Ponte Calvi

Ponte Spinola

Acquario di Genova ◆

*Bacino Porto Vecchio*

Ponte Embriaco

Il Bigo ◆

*Molo Vecchio*

V. del Molo

0        1/8 mi

0        1/8 km

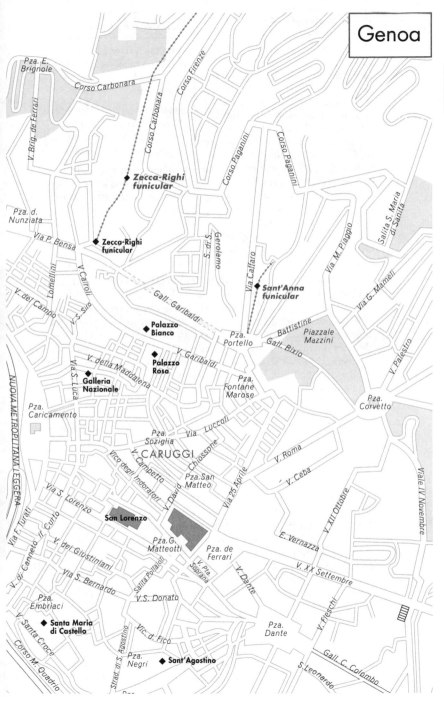

Genoa

2

Pza. E. Brignole
Corso Carbonara
Corso Carbonara
Corso Firenze
Corso Paganini
Corso Paganini
V. Brig. de Ferrari
Zecca-Righi funicular
Salita S. Maria di Sanità
Pza. d. Nunziata
Via P. Bensa
Zecca-Righi funicular
Gerolamo
S. D. S.
Via Caffaro
Sant'Anna funicular
Via M. Piaggio
Via G. Mameli
V. Carroli
Tomellini
V. del Campo
V. S. Siro
Gall. Garibaldi
Palazzo Bianco
V. Garibaldi
Pza. Portello
Battistine
Gall. Bixio
Piazzale Mazzini
V. Palestro
Palazzo Rosa
V. della Maddalena
Pza. Fontane Marose
Galleria Nazionale
V. S. Luca
Pza. Caricamento
Pza. Corvetto
NUOVA METROPOLITANA LEGGERA
Pza. Soziglia
CARUGGI
Via Luccoli
Chiossone
Pza. San Matteo
V. Roma
Vico degli Indoratori
V. Campetto
V. David
Via 25 Aprile
V. Ceba
Viale IV Novembre
Via S. Lorenzo
V. F. Turati
V. di Curto
San Lorenzo
Pza. G. Matteotti
Pza. de Ferrari
V. XII Ottobre
E. Vernazza
V. Fieschi
V. di Canneto il Curto
V. dei Giustiniani
Via S. Bernardo
Salita Pollaioli
V. Pta Soprana
V. Dante
V. XX Settembre
Pza. Embriaci
V.S. Donato
Pza. Dante
V. Santa Croce
Stra. di S. Agostino
Vic. d. Fico
Santa Maria di Castello
Pza. Negri
Sant'Agostino
Gall. C. Colombo
Corso Mr. Quadrio
S. Leonardo

*museidigenova.it* ✉ *€8, includes Palazzo Bianco and Palazzo Doria Tursi* ⊙ *Tues.–Fri. 9–7, weekends 10–7.*

**Zecca-Righi funicular.** This is a seven-stop commuter funicular beginning at Piazza della Nunziata and ending at a high lookout on the fortified gates in the 17th-century city walls. Ringed around the circumference of the city are a number of huge fortresses; this gate was part of the city's system of defenses. From Righi you can undertake scenic all-day hikes from one fortress to the next. At this writing, the funicular was closed for repair, but it reopened in

October 2010. ✉ *Piazza della Nunziata, Pré* ☎ *010/5582414* ⊕ *www. amt.genova.it* ✉ *€2, free with bus ticket* ⊙ *Daily 6 AM–11:45 PM.*

## SOUTHERN DISTRICTS AND THE AQUARIUM

Inhabited since the 6th century BC, the oldest section of Genoa lies on a hill to the southwest of the Caruggi District. Today, apart from a section of 9th-century wall near Porta Soprana, there is little to show that an imposing castle once stood here. Though the neighborhood is considerably run-down, some of Genoa's oldest churches make it a worthwhile excursion. No visit to Genoa is complete, however, without at least a stroll along the harborfront. The port was given a complete overhaul during Genoa's preparations for the Columbus quincentennial celebrations of 1992, and additional restorations in 2003 and 2004 have done much to revitalize the waterfront including a prehistoric Biosphere, Il Bigo panoramic lift (mentioned later in this section) with towering views over the town and port, and La Citta dei Bambino with over 90 interactive displays aimed especially at children. Combined tickets for these several attractions—marketed as Acquario Village and including entrance to the Aquarium and Galata Museo del Mare (listed below)—cost €39, but there are also several packages incorporating two or more of the individual attractions.

ⓒ ★ **Acquario di Genova.** Europe's biggest aquarium, second in the world only to Osaka's in Japan, is the third-most-visited museum in Italy, and a must for children. Fifty tanks of marine species, including sea turtles, dolphins, seals, eels, penguins, and sharks, share space with educational displays and re-creations of marine ecosystems, including a tank of coral from the Red Sea. Timed tickets permit entrance every half-hour. ✉ *Ponte Spinola, Porto Vecchio* ☎ *010/23451* ⊕ *www.acquario.ge.it* ✉ *€18* ⊙ *Mar.–June, weekdays 9–7:30, weekends 8:45–8:30; July and Aug., daily 8:30 AM–10 PM; Nov.–Feb., weekdays 9:30–7:30, weekends 9:30–8:30. Entry permitted every ½ hr; last entry 1½ hrs before closing.*

**Galata Museo del Mare.** Devoted entirely to the city's seafaring history, this museum is probably the best way, at least on dry land, to get an idea of the changing shape of Genoa's busy port. Highlighting the displays is a full-size replica of a 17th-century Genovese galleon. ✉ *Calata de Mari 1, Ponte dei Mille* ☎ *010/2345655* ⊕ *www.galatamuseodelmare.it* 🎫 *€11* ⊙ *Mar.–Oct., daily 10–7:30; Nov.–Feb., Tues.–Fri. 10–6, weekends 10–7:30; last entrance 1½ hrs before closing.*

🕛 **Il Bigo.** The bizarre white structure erected in 1992 to celebrate the Columbus quincentennial looks like either a radioactive spider or an overgrown potato spore, depending on your point of view. Its most redeeming feature is the **Ascensore Panoramico Bigo** (Bigo Panoramic Elevator), from which you can take in the harbor, city, and sea. Next to the elevator, in an area covered by sail-like awnings, there's an ice-skating rink in winter. ✉ *Ponte Spinola, Porto Vecchio* ☎ *010/23451, 347/4860524 ice-skating* 🎫 *Elevator €4, skating rink €8* ⊙ *Elevator Feb. and Nov., weekends 10–5; June–Aug., Tues., Wed., and Sun. 10–8, Thurs.–Sat. 10 AM–11 PM; Mar.–May and Sept., Tues.–Sun. 10–6; Oct., Tues.–Sun. 10–5; Dec. 26–Jan. 6, daily 10–5. Skating rink Nov. or Dec.–Mar., weekdays 8 AM–9:30 PM, Sat. 10 AM–2 AM, Sun. 10 AM–midnight.*

**San Lorenzo.** Contrasting black slate and white marble, so common in Liguria, embellished the cathedral at the heart of medieval Genoa—inside and out. Consecrated in 1118, the church honors St. Lawrence, who passed through the city on his way to Rome in the 3rd century. For hundreds of years the building was used for religious and state purposes such as civic elections. Note the 13th-century Gothic portal, fascinating twisted barbershop columns, and the 15th- to 17th-century frescoes inside. The last campanile dates from the early 16th century. The **Museo del Tesoro di San Lorenzo** (San Lorenzo Treasury Museum) housed inside has some stunning pieces from medieval goldsmiths and silversmiths, for which medieval Genoa was renowned. ✉ *Piazza San Lorenzo, Molo* ☎ *010/2471831* ⊕ *www.museidigenova.it* 🎫 *Cathedral free, museum €6* ⊙ *Cathedral daily 8–noon and 3–6:45. Museum Mon.–Sat. 9–noon and 3–6.*

**Sant'Agostino.** This 13th-century Gothic church was damaged during World War II, but it still has a fine campanile and two well-preserved cloisters that house an excellent museum displaying pieces of medieval architecture and fresco paintings. Highlighting the collection are the enigmatic fragments of a tomb sculpture by Giovanni Pisano (circa 1250–circa 1315). ✉ *Piazza Sarzano 35/r, Molo* ☎ *010/2511263* ⊕ *www.museidigenova.it* 🎫 *€4* ⊙ *Tues.–Fri. 9–7, weekends 10–7.*

**Santa Maria di Castello.** One of Genoa's most significant religious buildings, an early Christian church, was rebuilt in the 12th century and finally completed in 1513. You can visit the adjacent cloisters and see the fine artwork contained in the museum. Museum hours vary during religious services. ✉ *Salita di Santa Maria di Castello 15, Molo* ☎ *010/2549511* 🎫 *Free* ⊙ *Daily 9–noon and 3:30–6:30.*

# SHOPPING

In addition to the well-known Italian fine leather and haute couture, Liguria is famous for its fine lace, silver-and-gold filigree work, and ceramics. Look also for bargains in velvet, macramé, olive wood, and marble. Genoa is the best spot to find all these specialties. Don't forget the excellent wines, cheeses, dried meats, and olive oils.

In the heart of the medieval quarter, Via Soziglia is lined with shops selling handicrafts and tempting foods. Via XX Settembre is famous for its exclusive shops. High-end shops line Via Luccoli. The best shopping area for trendy but inexpensive Italian clothing is near San Siro, on Via San Luca.

**Pescetto.** This company sells designer clothes, perfumes, and gifts at its fancy shop. ⊠ *Via Scurreria 8, Molo* ☎ *010/2473433* ⊕ *www.pescetto.it.*

**Vinoteca Sola.** You can purchase the best Ligurian wines and have them shipped home. You can even buy futures for vintages to come. ⊠ *Piazza Colombo 13–15/r, near Stazione Brignole, Foce* ☎ *010/561329* ⊕ *www. vinotecasola.it.*

## WHERE TO EAT

$$$$   ✕**Da Domenico.** Don't be dismayed by the labyrinth of rooms and wood
ITALIAN   passages that lead to your table at this restaurant in a quiet square near Piazza Dante—you've found one of those hidden corners that only the Genovese know. Traditional seafood and meat dishes make up most of the menu. ⊠ *Piazza Leonardo 3, Molo* ☎ *010/540289* ⚠ *Reservations essential* ⊟ *AE, DC, MC, V* ⊙ *Closed Mon.*

$   ✕**Exultate.** When the weather permits, umbrella-shaded tables spread
ITALIAN   out from this tiny eatery into the nearby square. Its selection popular with locals, the restaurant's inexpensive daily menu is presented on a chalkboard for all to see, with elaborate salads and homemade desserts highlighting the list. The bar also serves five types of microbrews. ⊠ *Piazza Lavagna 15/r, Maddalena* ☎ *010/2512605* ⊟ *MC, V* ⊙ *Closed Sun.*

# GIBRALTAR

The tiny British colony of Gibraltar—nicknamed Gib, or simply the Rock—whose impressive silhouette dominates the strait between Spain and Morocco, was one of the two Pillars of Hercules in ancient times, marking the western limits of the known world and in an ace position commanding the narrow pathway between the Mediterranean Sea and the Atlantic Ocean. Today the Rock is like Britain with a suntan. There are double-decker buses, policemen in helmets, and bright red mailboxes. Gibraltar was ceded to Great Britain in 1713 by the Treaty of Utrecht, and Spain has been trying to get it back ever since. Recently, Britain and Spain have been talking about joint Anglo-Spanish sovereignty, much to the ire of the majority of Gibraltarians, who remain fiercely patriotic to the crown. Millions of dollars have been spent in developing the Rock's tourist potential, and Gibraltar's economy is further boosted by its important status as an offshore financial center.

### ESSENTIALS

CURRENCY Gibraltar uses the pound sterling (£1 to $1.51 at present exchange rate) but issues its own notes and coins, which are equivalent in value to British pounds. Euros can also be used in most of the shops, but the exchange rate may be unfavorable; U.S. currency is generally not accepted, but ATMs are common and credit cards are widely accepted.

HOURS Shops are open weekdays from 9:30 to 7:30 PM, Saturday from 10 to 1. Some shops open Sunday when a ship is in port. Attractions have varied hours, but these are generally weekdays from 10 to 5, and some may open weekends.

TELEPHONES 3G services are available on the island. GibTel is the main service provider. Public phones accept phonecards and credit cards.

### COMING ASHORE

There is a dedicated cruise terminal within Gibraltar's commercial port. The passenger terminal has a range of facilities, including a bar-café, souvenir shop, tourist information center, bank and currency exchange facilities, and an exhibition area. From here it is an easy walk into Gibraltar itself, where all the sites of town can be accessed on foot (or where you can take a bus to the attractions that are farther afield). You can also take a taxi; fares are £2.40 for pick-up and £0.15 per 200 meters or per minute of travel. On days when a number of cruise ships dock at the same time, taxis may be dfficult to find, and it would be wise to prebook a vehicle.

The town of Gibraltar is compact, and it's easy to walk around. Vehicles rented in Gibraltar can be taken over the border into Spain, so you could explore some of the southern Spanish coastline from here in a day. Vehicles are only rented to people between the ages of 23 and 70. The Official Rock Tour—conducted either by minibus or, at a greater cost, taxi—takes about 90 minutes and includes all the major sights, allowing you to choose which places to come back to and linger at later. Costs are around £18 to £25 per person (six-person max.).

The cable car to the top of the rock costs £8 round-trip.

## EXPLORING GIBRALTAR

The colorful, congested library is where the dignified Regency architecture of Great Britain blends well with the shutters, balconies, and patios of southern Spain. Shops, restaurants, and pubs beckon on busy Main Street; at the Governor's Residence, the ceremonial Changing of the Guard takes place six times a year and the Ceremony of the Keys takes place twice a year. Also, make sure you see the Law Courts,\ the Anglican Cathedral of the Holy Trinity, and the Catholic Cathedral of St. Mary the Crowned.

**Main Tourist Office.** Gibraltar's main tourist office is on Cathedral Square. ✉ *Duke of Kent House, Cathedral Sq.* ☎ *350/20074950* ⊕ *www. gibraltar.gi* ☉ *Weekdays 9–5:30, weekends 10–3.*

**Apes' Den.** The famous Barbary Apes are a breed of cinnamon-color, tailless monkeys native to Morocco's Atlas Mountains. Legend holds that as long as the apes remain in Gibraltar, the British will keep the Rock;

# Gibraltar

*Marina Bay*

Gibraltar
Town
see detail
map

*Gibraltar
Harbor*

*Devil's Tower Rd.*

Moorish
Castle

Great Siege
Tunnels

*Catalan Bay Rd.*

*Wiltis's Rd.*

*Old Queen's Rd.*

*Queen's Rd.*

Cable Car

Apes' Den

Wall of
Charles V

Botanical
Gardens

*Europa Rd.*

*Sir Herbert Miles Rd.*

*Sandy
Bay*

St. Michael's
Cave

*Engineer Rd.*

*Queen's Rd.*

*Dudley Ward Tunnel*

*Rosia
Bay*

Upper Rock
Nature Reserve

*Governor's
Beach*

*Camp
Bay*

*Europa Rd.*

*Europa Advance Rd.*

*Little
Bay*

Shrine of Our
Lady of Europe

Mezquita
Ibrahim-Al-Ibrahim

*Bay of
Gibraltar*

Europa
Point

*Mediterranean
Sea*

## Gibraltar Town

*Corral Rd.*

Casemates
Gate

*Smith Dorrien Av.*

*Corral Rd.*

*Fish Market Rd.*

Casemates
Sq.

*Crutchett's Ramp*

*Queensway*

*Cooperage Ln.*

*Castle Ramp*

American
War
Memorial

*Parliament Ln.*

*Tuckey's
Ln.*

*Irish Town*

*Engineer Ln.*

*Main St.*

*Bell
Ln.*

*Castle St.*

*Market Ln.*

*Line Wall Rd.*

John
Mackintosh
Sq.

*College Ln.*

*Cannon
Ln.*

*Governor's St.*

*Hospital
Ramp*

*Prince
Edward's Rd.*

St. Mary
the Crowned

*King St.*

*Gunner's
Ln.*

*Library St.*

*Governor's
Pde.*

*Library
Ramp*

Gibraltar
Museum

*Bomb House Ln.*

*King's St.*

*George's
Ln.*

Cathedral of
the Holy Trinity

*Cathedral
Sq.*

*Town Range*

*Prince Edward's Rd.*

Main Tourist
Office

*Governor's Ln.*

King's
Chapel

Governor's
Residence

*Queensway*

Nefusot
Yehudada
Synagogue

*Convent
Ramp*

0        1/16 mi

0        1/16 km

0                1/2 mi

0        1/2 km

2

Winston Churchill went so far as to issue an order for their preservation when the apes' numbers began to dwindle during World War II. They are publicly fed twice daily, at 8 and 4, at a rocky area down Old Queens Road and near the Wall of Charles V. Among the apes' mischievous talents are grabbing food, purses, and cameras. It's actually against the law for the public to feed them, since it encourages these bad behaviors. ⊠ *From Rosia Bay, drive along Queensway and Europa Rd. as far as Casino, above Alameda Gardens. Make a sharp right here, up Engineer Rd. to Jews' Gate, a lookout over docks and the Bay of Gibraltar toward Algeciras* 🎫 *£10 includes St. Michael's Cave, Great Siege Tunnels, Moorish Castle, and Military Heritage Center* ⊙ *Daily 9:30–7:15*

**GIBRALTAR BEST BETS**

**The town of Gibraltar.** Immerse yourself in a little piece of Britain far south of the white cliffs of Dover.

**Take in the panorama from the top of the Rock.** Look south to the northern coast of Africa and north to the southern coastal plains of Spain.

**Make friends with a Barbary ape.** These cheeky primates inhabit the slopes of the Rock. They have a penchant for stealing bags and sunglasses—so you have been warned!

★ **Cable Car.** You can reach St. Michael's Cave—or ride all the way to the top of Gibraltar—on this cable car. The car doesn't go high off the ground, but the views of Spain and Africa from the Rock's pinnacle are superb. It leaves from a station at the southern end of Main Street. 🎫 *Cable car £8 round-trip* ⊙ *Apr.–Oct. Daily 9:30–5:15; Nov.–Mar. Mon.–Sat. 9:30–5:15.*

**Casemates Square.** This square in the northern part of town is Gibraltar's social hub and has been pedestrianized. There are now plenty of places to sit out with a drink and watch the world go by. In the square is a branch of the **tourist office** (☎ *350/20045000* ⊙ *Weekdays 9–5:30, weekends 10–4*).

**Europa Point.** From here, have a look across the straits to Morocco, 23 km (14 mi) away. You're now standing on one of the two ancient Pillars of Hercules. In front of you, the lighthouse has dominated the meeting place of the Atlantic and the Mediterranean since 1841; sailors can see its light from a distance of 27 km (17 mi). ⊠ *Continue along coast road to Rock's southern tip.*

**Gibraltar Museum.** Housing a beautiful 14th-century Moorish bathhouse and an 1865 model of the Rock, Gibraltar's museum has displays that evoke the Great Siege and the Battle of Trafalgar. There's also a reproduction of the "Gibraltar Woman," the Neanderthal skull discovered here in 1848. ⊠ *Bomb House La.* ☎ *350/20074289* ⊕ *www. gibmuseum.gi* 🎫 *£2* ⊙ *Weekdays 10–6, Sat. 10–2.*

**Great Siege Tunnels.** The tunnels, formerly known as the Upper Galleries, were carved out during the Great Siege of 1779–82. You can plainly see the openings from whence the guns were pointed at the Spanish invaders. These tunnels form part of what is arguably the most impressive defense system anywhere in the world. ⊠ *From Rosia Bay, drive along Queensway and Europa Rd. as far as Casino, above Alameda Gardens. Make a sharp right here, up Engineer Rd. to Jews' Gate, a lookout over docks and Bay of Gibraltar toward Algeciras* ⚏ *£10 includes St. Michael's Cave, Ape's Den, Moorish Castle, and Military Heritage Center* ⊙ *Daily 9:30–7:15*

**Moorish Castle.** Built by the descendants of Tariq, who conquered the Rock in 711, the present Tower of Homage dates from 1333, and its besieged walls bear the scars of stones from medieval catapults (and, later, cannonballs). Admiral George Rooke hoisted the British flag from its summit when he captured the Rock in 1704, and it has flown here ever since. The castle is on Willis's Road. ⊠ *From Rosia Bay, drive along Queensway and Europa Rd. as far as Casino, above Alameda Gardens. Make a sharp right here, up Engineer Rd. to Jews' Gate, a lookout over docks and Bay of Gibraltar toward Algeciras* ⚏ *£10 includes St. Michael's Cave, Great Siege Tunnels, Ape's Den, and Military Heritage Center* ⊙ *Daily 9:30–7:15.*

**Nefusot Yehudada Synagogue.** The 18th-century synagogue on Line Wall Road is one of the oldest synagogues on the Iberian Peninsula, dating back to 1724. There are guided tours twice a day at 12:30 PM and 2:30 PM, accompanied by a short history of the Gibraltar Jewish community. ⊠ *Line Wall Rd.* ☎ *350/2007647* ⊙ *By appointment (call ahead).*

**Rosia Bay.** For a fine view, drive high above the bay to which Nelson's flagship, HMS *Victory,* was towed after the Battle of Trafalgar in 1805. On board were the dead, who were buried in Trafalgar Cemetery on the southern edge of town—except for Admiral Nelson, whose body was returned to England preserved in a barrel of rum. ⊠ *From Europa Flats, follow Europa Rd. back along Rock's western slopes.*

**Shrine of Our Lady of Europe.** This shrine has been venerated by seafarers since 1462. Once a mosque, the small Catholic chapel has a little museum with a 1462 statue of the Virgin and some documents. ⊠ *Just west of Europa Point and lighthouse, along Rock's southern tip* ⊕ *www.ourladyofeurope.net* ⚏ *Free* ⊙ *Mon.–Wed. and Fri. 10–1 and 2–6; Thurs. and Sat. 10–1 (subject to change).*

**St. Michael's Cave.** The largest of Gibraltar's 150 caves is a series of underground chambers hung with stalactites and stalagmites. It's an ideal performing-arts venue. Sound-and-light shows are held here most days at 11 AM and 4 PM. St. Michael's is on Queens Road. ⊠ *From Rosia Bay, drive along Queensway and Europa Rd. as far as Casino, above Alameda Gardens. Make a sharp right here, up Engineer Rd. to Jews' Gate, a lookout over docks and Bay of Gibraltar toward Algeciras.* ⚏ *£10 includes Great Siege Tunnels, Ape's Den, Moorish Castle and Military Heritage Center* ⊙ *Daily 9:30–7:15*

**Upper Rock Nature Preserve.** Accessible from Jews' Gate, the preserve includes St. Michael's Cave, the Apes' Den, the Great Siege Tunnels, the Moorish Castle, and the Military Heritage Center, which chronicles the British regiments who have served on the Rock. ⊠ *From Rosia Bay, drive along Europa Rd. as far as Casino, above Alameda Gardens. Make a sharp right here up Engineer Rd. to Jews' Gate, a lookout* *over docks and Bay of Gibraltar toward Algeciras ⛴£10, includes all attractions, plus £1.50 per vehicle ⊙ Daily 9:30–7:15.*

## SHOPPING

The quintessential Britishness of Gibraltar is reflected in its shopping. Many British main-street names can be found here, including Marks and Spencer, so you can stock up on marmalades, biscuits, and Cheddar cheese. Fine English china and glassware also make an appearance along with oodles of Royal memorabilia. Inexpensive items include Union Jack motifs and red double-decker buses printed on everything from T-shirts to coffee mugs. The island is tax-friendly so prices are cheaper than in Spain or the United Kingdom.

**Gibraltar Crystal.** The store sells a range of brightly colored glass pieces that have been produced in its factory on the island. ⊠ *Grand Casemates* ☎ *350/20050136* ⊕ *www.gibraltar-crystal.com.*

**Marks and Spencer.** This department store has all things British, from clothing to food. ⊠ *215 Main St.* ☎ *350/20075857.*

## WHERE TO EAT

$ 　 ✕ **14 On the Quay.** One of the Rock's more sophisticated new restaurants,
MEDITERRANEAN 　 14 On the Quay is appropriately located in Queensway Quay, which is less brash than nearby, newer Ocean Village. The menu changes with the seasons, but starters like lemon risotto with seared scallops and mains among the likes of roasted loin of wild boar with the classic British bubble and squeak are all served on locally produced exquisite crystal plates. Desserts such as the creamy malt-flavored mousse with a chocolate crust and shortbread are sublime. ⊠ *Queensway, Quay Marina* ☎ *200/43731* ⊕ *MC, V.*

¢ 　 ✕ **Sacarello's.** Right off Main Street, this place is as well known for its
BRITISH 　 excellent coffee and cakes as it is for its adjacent restaurant. There's a lavish daily salad buffet, as well as filled baked potatoes; panfried noodles with broccoli, mussels, and chicken; and rack of lamb with wine and fine herbs. Top your meal off with a specialty coffee with cream and vanilla. The restaurant has several rooms warmly decorated in English-pub style, with cozy corners, dark-wood furnishings, and low ceilings. ⊠ *57 Irish Town* ☎ *9567/20070625* ⊟ *MC, V* ⊙ *Closed Sun.*

# IBIZA, SPAIN

Sleepy from November to May, the capital of Ibiza is transformed in summer into Party Central for retro hippies and nonstop clubbers, but the town and the island have so much more to offer. Dalt Vila, the medieval quarter on the hill overlooking Ibiza Town, is a UNESCO World Heritage site with narrow alleyways brimming with atmosphere. Around the coastline the island has 50 sandy beaches. Ibiza was discovered by sun-seeking hippies in the late 1960s, eventually emerging as an icon of counter-culture chic. In the late 1980s and 1990s club culture took over. Young ravers flocked here from all over the world to dance all night and pack the sands of beach resorts all day. That Ibiza is still alive and well, but emblematic of the island's future are its growing numbers of luxury hotels, spas, and gourmet restaurants. Ibiza is toning down and scaling up.

## ESSENTIALS

CURRENCY  The euro (€1 to US$1.36 at this writing).

HOURS  Museums generally open 9 until 7 or 8, many are closed on Monday and some close in the afternoon. Most stores are open Monday through Saturday 9 to 1:30 and 5 to 8, but tourist shops may open in the afternoon and also on Sundays between May and September.

INTERNET  **Cibermatic** (⊠ *Cayetano Soler 3, Ibiza Town* ☎ *971303382*) is open from Monday to Saturday but closes from 1:30 to 5 in the afternoon.

TELEPHONES  Tri-band GSM phones should work in Spain, and mobile services are 3G compatible. Public kiosks accept phone cards that support international calls (cards sold in press shops, bars, and telecom shops). Major companies include Vodafone.

## COMING ASHORE

Boats dock on the town pier at the edge of town. From here you can walk into the capital without problem, and for this reason, facilities at the terminal are limited. You won't need transport to enjoy Ibiza Town, however if you rent a car, you can explore much of this small but fascinating island in a day. An economy rental car for one day is €80 (from July through September, you'll really need to book ahead). There are 25 buses a day between Ibiza Town, Sant Rafael, and San Antonio, several per day between Ibiza, Sant Jordi, Salinas, Cala Tarida, and Sant Eulalia. Fares start at €1.80, and all are under €5.

Taxis are also numerous and are metered. They can undertake tourist tours. Fares start at €0.98 per minute (min €3.25) and waiting time of €17.61 per hour. There is a small supplement (€1.65) for port pick-up.

# EXPLORING IBIZA

### IBIZA TOWN (EIVISSA)

Hedonistic and historical, Eivissa (Ibiza, in Catalan) is a city jam-packed with cafés and nightspots and trendy shops; looming over it are the massive stone walls of **Dalt Vila**—the medieval city was declared a UNESCO World Heritage site in 1999—and its Gothic cathedral. Squeezed between the north walls of the Old City and the harbor is **Sa Penya,** a long labyrinth of narrow stone-paved streets that offer the city's best exploring. What would the fishermen who used to live in this quarter have thought seeing so many of their little whitewashed houses transformed into bars and offbeat restaurants and boutiques with names like the Kabul Sutra Tantra Shop, and Good Times Jewelry, and Bitch?

One enters the Dalt Vila via a ramp through the **Portal de ses Taules,** the Old City's main gate. On each side stands a statue, Roman in origin and now headless: Juno on the right, an armless male on the left. Keep going up until you reach the sights.

# Ibiza Island

Cala Xarraca
Caló d'Es Porcs
Portinatx
Sant Vicent
Cala San Vicente
Puerto San Miguel
San Miguel
Sant Joan
Sant Mateo
Balafi
Sant Carles
Santa Agnes
Sant Llorenç
Bahía de Sant Antoni
Santa Gertrudis de Fruitera
Santa Eulària des Riu
Sant Antoni
Sant Rafael
Ibiza Town see detail map
Sant Josep
Sant Jordi
Playa d'En Bossa
Es Vedrà
Mitjorn
Es Cavallet
Ses Salines
Es Palmador
Trucadors
Estany Pudent
Puerto de La Sabina
Es Pujols
Estany d'es Peix
Sant Ferran
Sant Francesc Xavier
Cala Sahona
Formentera
Playa de Mitjorn
El Pilar
Cabo de Berbería

0    6 miles
0    9 km

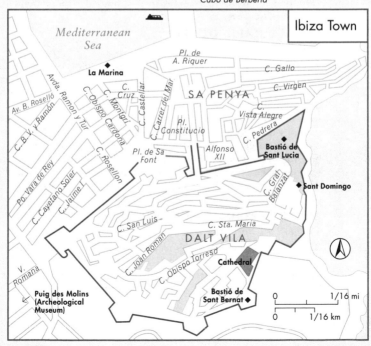

# Ibiza Town

Mediterranean Sea

La Marina
Pl. de A. Riquer
C. Gallo
C. Virgen
SA PENYA
C. Cruz
C. Montlan
C. Castellar
Carrer del Mar
Avda. Ramon y Ramón
Av. B. Roselló
C. Obispo Cardona
C. B.V. y Ramón
Pl. Constitucio
C. Vista Alegre
C. Pedrera
Pl. de Sa Font
Alfonso XII
Bastió de Sant Lucia
Po. Vara de Rey
C. Rosellon
Sant Domingo
C. Gral. Balanzat
C. Cayetano Soler
C. Jaime I
C. San Luis
C. Sta. Maria
C. Joan Roman
DALT VILA
V. Romana
C. Obispo Torresd
Cathedral
Puig des Molins (Archeological Museum)
Bastió de Sant Bernat

0    1/16 mi
0    1/16 km

**Bastió de Santa Llúcia.** Uphill from the contemporary art museum is a sculpture of a priest sitting on one of the stone seats in the gardens. On the left, the wide Bastion of St. Lucia has a panoramic view.

**Bastió de Sant Bernat.** Behind the cathedral, from the Bastion of St. Bernard, a promenade with sea views runs west to the bastions of Sant Jordi and Sant Jaume, past the Castell—a fortress formerly used as an army barracks, turned over to the city of Ibiza in 1973, and left to fall apart until 2006, when work

> ### IBIZA BEST BETS
>
> **Explore the narrow alleyways of Sa Penya.** Ibiza Town's most atmospheric quarter is great for browsing and shopping.
>
> **Bring your swim suit.** Spend an afternoon on one of Ibiza's trendy beaches.
>
> **Stroll uphill in Dalt Vila.** The quarter's architecture has been designated a World Heritage site.

began to transform it into a 70-room luxury parador, though that work still continues at this writing. The promenade ends at the steps to the **Portal Nou** (New Gate).

**Cathedral.** From the church of San Domingo, follow any of the streets or steps leading uphill to Carrer Obispo Torres (Carrer Major). The cathedral is on the site of religious structures from each of the cultures that have ruled Ibiza since the Phoenicians. Built in the 13th and 14th centuries and renovated in the 18th century, the cathedral has a Gothic tower and a baroque nave. ⊠ *Carrer Major* ☎ *971/312774* ۞ *Weekdays 10–1, Sun. 10:30–noon.*

**Sant Domingo.** If you wind your way up the promontory of Santa Llúcia, you'll come to this 16th-century church, its roof an irregular landscape of tile domes. Eivissa's city offices are now housed in the church's former monastery. ⊠ *Carrer de Balanzat.*

### SANTA EULÀRIA DES RIU
*15 km (9 mi) northeast of Eivissa.*

At the edge of this town on the island's eastern coast, to the right below the road, a Roman bridge crosses what is claimed to be the only permanent river in the Balearics (hence "des Riu," or "of the river"). Ahead, on the hilltop, are the cubes and domes of the church—to reach it, look for a narrow lane to the left, signed PUIG DE MISSA, itself so named for the hill where regular mass was once held. A stoutly arched, cryptlike covered area guards the entrance; inside are a fine gold reredos and blue-tile stations of the cross. Santa Eulària itself follows the curve of a long sandy beach, a few blocks deep with restaurants, shops, and holiday apartments. From here it's a 10-minute drive to **Sant Carles** and the open-air **hippie market** held there every Saturday morning.

### SANTA GERTRUDIS DE FRUITERA
*15 km (9 mi) north of Eivissa.*

Blink, and you miss it: that's true of most of the small towns in the island's interior—and especially so of Santa Gertrudis, not much more than a bend in the road from Eivissa to the north coast. But don't blink: Santa Gertrudis is strategic, and it's cute. From here you are only a few minutes' drive from some of the island's flat-out best resort hotels and spas. You are minutes from the most beautiful secluded north coves and beaches: **S'Illa des Bosc, Benirrás** (where they have drum circles to salute the setting sun), **S'Illot des Renclí, Portinatx, Caló d'En Serra.** Santa Gertrudis itself has offbeat shops, and laid-back sidewalk cafés, and good food. Artists and expats like it here: they've given it an appeal that now makes for listings of half a million dollars for a modest three-bedroom flat.

## SHOPPING

In the late 1960s and '70s Ibiza built a reputation for extremes of fashion. Little of this phenomenon survives, though the softer designs inspired by Smilja Mihailovich (under the Ad Lib label) still prosper. Clothing and beachwear plus fashion accessories of all kinds are the major buys here, including excellent leather goods, but there is also a community of artists working in glass, ceramics, and bronze. Along Carrer d'Enmig is an eclectic collection of shops and stalls selling fashion and crafts. Although the Sa Penya area of Eivissa still has a few designer boutiques, much of the area is now called the Mercat dels Hippies (hippie market), with more than 80 stalls of overpriced tourist ephemera.

**Heltor.** For leather wear, belts, bags, and shoes, go to Heltor. ⊠ *Madrid 12, Eivissa* ☏ *971/391225.*

**Ibiza Republic.** For trendy casual gear, sandals, belts, and bags, try this store. ⊠ *Carre Creu, Eivissa* ☏ *971/191305.*

## BEACHES

Immediately south of Ibiza Town is a long, sandy beach, the nearly 3-km (2-mi) **Playa d'en Bossa.** Farther on, a left turn at Sant Jordi on the way to the airport leads across the salt pans to **Es Cavallet** and **Ses Salines,** two of the best beaches on the island. Topless bathing is accepted all over Ibiza, but Es Cavallet is the official nudist beach. The remaining beaches on this part of the island are accessible from the Ibiza–Sant Josep–Sant Antoni highway, down side roads that often end in rough tracks. North of Sant Antoni there are no easily accessible beaches until you reach **Puerto San Miguel,** an almost rectangular cove with relatively restrained development. Next along the north coast, accessible via San Juan, is Portinatx, a series of small coves with sandy beaches, of which the first and last, **Cala Xarraca** and **Caló d'Es Porcs,** are the best. East of San Juan is the long, curved cove beach of **Cala San Vicente.** Popular with families, it has a more leisurely pace than Ibiza's other resorts. The beaches on the east coast have been developed, but **Santa Eulalia** remains attractive. The resort has a narrow, sloping beach in front of a pedestrian promenade that is much less frenetic than Sant Antoni.

## WHERE TO EAT

$ ✕ **Can Caus.** Ibiza might pride itself—justly—on its seafood, but there
SPANISH   comes a time for meat and potatoes. When that time comes, take the
20-minute drive from Eivissa to the outskirts of Santa Gertrudis, to
this informal, family-style roadside restaurant, and feast on skewers of
barbecued *sobrasada* (soft pork sausage), goat chops, lamb kebabs, or
grilled sweetbreads with red peppers, onions, and eggplant. For starters,
there's fried goat cheese with garden salad, and a great crusty bread with
garlic mayonnaise. Most people eat at the long wooden tables on the
terrace. ⊠ *Ctra. Sant Miquel, Km. 3.5, Santa Gertrudis* ☎ *971/197516*
⊟ *AE, MC, V* ⊘ *Closed Mon. Sept.–June.*

$ ✕ **Mezzanotte.** This charming little portside restaurant is a branch of the
SPANISH   popular Mezzanotte in Eivissa. There are 12 tables inside, softly lighted
with candles and track lights; in summer, seating expands to an interior
patio and tables on the sidewalk. The kitchen prides itself on hard-
to-find fresh ingredients flown in from Italy. The linguini with jumbo
shrimp, saffron, and zucchini—or with *bottarga* (dried and salted mullet roe from Sardinia)—is wonderful. ⊠ *Paseo de s'Alamera 22, Santa
Eulària* ☎ *971/319498* ⊟ *MC, V* ⊘ *Closed Jan., Feb., and Mon. No
lunch June–Aug.*

# LE HAVRE, FRANCE (FOR NORMANDY AND PARIS)

Le Havre, France's second-largest port (after Marseille), was destroyed
in World War II. You may find the rebuilt city bleak and uninviting; on
the other hand, you may admire Auguste Perret's audacious modern
architecture, which earned the city UNESCO World Heritage status in
2005. The city is the perfect starting point for some of the highlights
of Normandy, the French region of rolling verdant farmland and long,
sandy beaches. Tiny fishing villages dot the coves around the city, a
world away from the gritty urban feel of Le Havre itself. Normandy was
also the location of the D-Day invasion of Europe by Allied forces during WWII, the largest wartime seaborne invasion of all time. You can
visit the beach landing sites and evocative museums about the battle.
From Le Havre it's also possible to visit Paris, one of the world's most
famous cities.

### ESSENTIALS

CURRENCY   The euro (€1 to US$1.36 at this writing).

HOURS   Stores are generally open Monday through Saturday 9–7, but many
close at lunchtime (usually noon–2 or 3) and some will open later and
on Sunday during July and August. Museums open 10–5, but most are
closed on either Monday or Tuesday.

INTERNET   **Microminute** (⊠ *7 rue Casimir Perrier* ☎ *02-35-22-10-15* ⊕ *www.
microminute.com* ⊘ *Mon. 2–7, Tues.-Sat. 10–7*) has eight ports and
a games room.

TELEPHONES   Tri-band GSM phones work in France. You can buy prepaid phone
cards at telecom shops, news vendors, and tobacconists in all towns and

cities. Phone cards can be used for local or international calls. France Telecom and Orange are leading telecom companies.

## COMING ASHORE

Le Havre is a large port with vast amounts of freight traffic in addition to cruise ships. Disembarking passengers will find a small welcome center with practical information and multilingual staff, a small shop, plus taxi and tour services, including a shuttle service into the city, which stops at the railway station. If you intend to spend the day in Le Havre, it is only a few minutes' walk from the port entrance to the downtown area.

Le Havre is the main cruise port for visits to Paris; however, the city is a 2- to 2½-hour journey away depending on the service chosen. From the railway station there are hourly trains to Paris terminating at Gare St-Lazare. SNCF (⊕ *www.sncf.com*), the French railway company, is reliable and efficient. Prices are cheaper if you buy tickets in advance, but a second-class round-trip should be around €30 if purchased on the day of travel.

We would advise against renting a car just to make the trip into Paris (traffic and parking are both very difficult); however, a rental car is an ideal way to explore the rolling countryside of Normandy. An economy manual car costs around €75 per day. Taxis wait outside the port gates and can provide tourist itineraries. For single journeys, fares are €1.70 at pick-up, then €0.84 per km.

# EXPLORING NORMANDY AND PARIS

## LE HAVRE

**Cite Perret.** The postwar reconstruction of the city designed by architect Auguste Perret is a tour de force of moderism. Called the "poet of concrete," Perret's new town gained UNESCO World Heritage status for its unique and coherent whole. The style produces very different reactions in people; you either love or hate it. The tourist office in Le Havre organizes 90-minute walking tours of the area, and these can be booked from the cruise terminal welcome center.

The **Musée André-Malraux**, the city art museum, is an innovative 1960s glass-and-metal structure surrounded by a moat, and includes an attractive sea-view café. Two local artists who gorgeously immortalized the Normandy coast are showcased here—Raoul Dufy (1877–1953), through a remarkable collection of his brightly colored oils, watercolors, and sketches; and Eugène Boudin (1824–98), a forerunner of impressionism, whose compelling beach scenes and landscapes tellingly evoke the Normandy sea and skyline. ⊠ *2 bd. Clemenceau* ☎ *02–35–19–62–62* ⛭ *€5* ⊙ *Mon., Wed.–Fri. 11–6, weekends 11–7.*

## HONFLEUR

Fodor'sChoice
★ *24 km (15 mi) southeast of Le Havre via A131 and the Pont de Normandie.*

The town of Honfleur, full of half-timber houses and cobbled streets, was once an important departure point for maritime expeditions, including the first voyages to Canada in the 15th and 16th centuries.

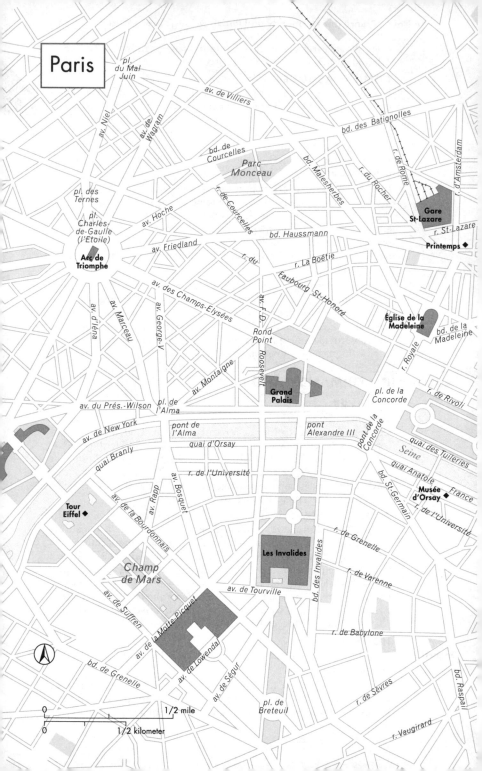

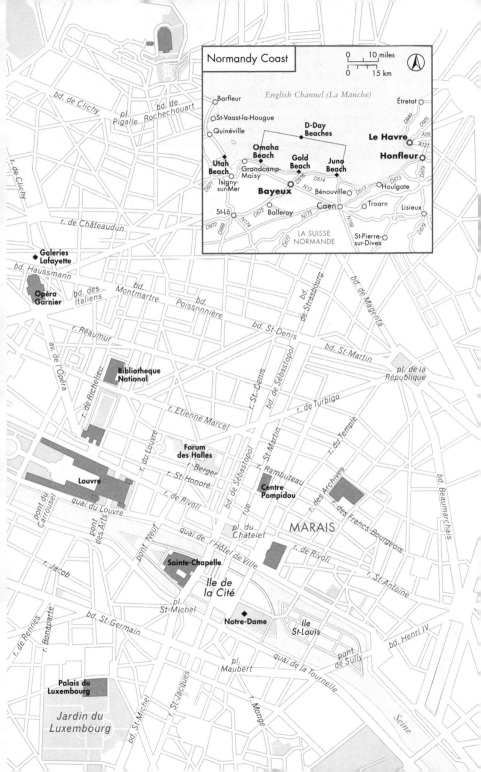

### Normandy Coast

| 0 | 10 miles |
| 0 | 15 km |

English Channel (La Manche)

Barfleur

St-Vaast-la-Hougue

Quinéville

**D-Day Beaches**

**Utah Beach**

**Omaha Beach**

Grandcamp-Maisy

**Gold Beach**

**Juno Beach**

Étretat

**Le Havre**

**Honfleur**

Isigny-sur-Mer

**Bayeux**

D516

D514

N13

Bénouville

Houlgate

D513

D513

St-Lô

D572

Balleroy

N175

Caen

Troarn

Lisieux

D972

N174

D577

N158

St-Pierre-sur-Dives

D579

LA SUISSE NORMANDE

D925

D940

A29

A131

D579

---

**Galeries Lafayette**

bd. Haussmann

**Opéra Garnier**

bd. de Clichy

pl. Pigalle

bd. de Rochechouart

r. de Clichy

r. de Châteaudun

bd. des Italiens

bd. Montmartre

bd. Poissonnière

r. Réaumur

av. de l'Opéra

**Bibliothèque National**

r. de Richelieu

r. Etienne Marcel

bd. St-Denis

r. St-Denis

bd. de Sébastopol

bd. St-Martin

bd. de Strasbourg

bd. de Magenta

pl. de la République

r. de Turbigo

**Forum des Halles**

r. Berger

r. St-Honoré

r. de Rivoli

r. du Louvre

**Louvre**

pont du Carrousel

pont des Arts

quai du Louvre

pont Neuf

quai de l'Hôtel de Ville

r. Rambuteau

r. St-Martin

rue

bd. de Sébastopol

**Centre Pompidou**

r. du Temple

r. des Archives

r. des Francs-Bourgeois

**MARAIS**

r. de Rivoli

r. St-Antoine

bd. Beaumarchais

pl. du Chatelet

**Sainte-Chapelle**

**Île de la Cité**

pl. St-Michel

bd. St-Germain

r. Bonaparte

r. de Rennes

r. Jacob

**Notre-Dame**

**Île St-Louis**

pont de Sully

bd. Henri IV

pl. Maubert

quai de la Tournelle

**Palais du Luxembourg**

bd. St-Michel

r. St-Jacques

r. Monge

Seine

*Jardin du Luxembourg*

The 17th-century harbor is fronted on one side by two-story stone houses with low, sloping roofs and on the other by tall, narrow houses whose wooden facades are topped by slate roofs. Note that parking can be a problem. Your best bet is the parking lot just beyond the Vieux-Bassin (Old Harbor) on the left as you approach from the land side.

★ **Ste-Catherine.** Soak up the seafaring atmosphere by strolling around the Old Harbor and paying a visit to the ravishing wooden church that dominates the tumbling square. The church and ramshackle belfry across the way were built by townspeople to show their gratitude for the departure of the English at the end of the Hundred Years' War, in 1453. ⊠ *Rue des Logettes* ☎ *02–31–89–11–83.*

> ### LE HAVRE BEST BETS
>
> **Honfleur.** Wander the tangled knot of cobbled alleyways of the old town and enjoy an alfresco lunch in the picturesque harbor.
>
> **D-Day Beaches.** The battles that took place on these beaches on June 6, 1944, were the turning point of WWII.
>
> **Paris.** The city of romance, Paris is a must-see; it will be a quick tour, but you can see some highlights in a day.

## BAYEUX

*10 km (6 mi) southwest of Arromanches via D516, 28 km (17 mi) northwest of Caen.*

Bayeux, the first town to be liberated during the Battle of Normandy, was already steeped in history—as home to a Norman Gothic cathedral and the world's most celebrated piece of needlework: the Bayeux Tapestry.

**Fodor's Choice**
★  **Bayeux Tapestry** *(Tapestry Museum).* Known in French as the *Tapisserie de la Reine Mathilde* (Queen Matilda's Tapestry), the Bayeux Tapestry depicts, in 58 comic strip–type scenes, the epic story of William of Normandy's conquest of England in 1066, culminating in the Battle of Hastings on October 14, 1066. It was probably commissioned from Saxon embroiderers by the count of Kent. It's showcased in the **Musée de la Tapisserie**; headphones are provided free for you to listen to an English commentary about the tapestry, scene by scene. ⊠ *Centre Guillaume-le-Conquérant, 13 bis rue de Nesmond* ☎ *02–31–51–25–50* ⊕ *www.tapisserie-bayeux.fr* ⊠ *€7.80, joint ticket with Musée Baron-Gérard* ⊙ *May–Aug., daily 9–7:15 Mar.–June and mid-Sept.–Nov., daily 9–6:30; mid-Nov.–mid-Mar., daily 9:30–12:30 and 2–6.*

**Cathédrale Notre-Dame.** Bayeux's mightiest edifice is a harmonious mixture of Norman and Gothic architecture. Note the portal on the south side of the transept that depicts the assassination of English archbishop Thomas à Becket in Canterbury Cathedral in 1170, following his courageous opposition to King Henry II's attempts to control the church. ⊠ *Rue du Bienvenu* ☎ *02–31–92–01–85* ⊙ *Daily 9–6.*

## THE D-DAY BEACHES

*Omaha Beach is 16 km (10 mi) northwest of Bayeux.*

History focused its sights along the coasts of Normandy at 6:30 AM on June 6, 1944, as the 135,000 men and 20,000 vehicles of the Allied troops made landfall in their first incursion in Europe in World War II. The entire operation on this "Longest Day" was called Operation Overlord—the code name for the invasion of Normandy.

**American Cemetery and Memorial.** The hilltop memorial, designed by the landscape architect Markley Stevenson, is a moving tribute to the fallen, with its Wall of the Missing (in the form of a semicircular colonnade), drumlike chapel, and avenues of holly oaks trimmed to resemble open parachutes. ⊠ *Colleville-sur-Mer.*

**Omaha Beach.** You won't be disappointed by the rugged terrain and windswept sand of Omaha Beach. Here you can find the **Monument du Débarquement** (Monument to the Normandy Landings) and nearby, in Vierville-sur-Mer, the **U.S. National Guard Monument.** ⊠ *16 km [10 mi] northwest of Bayeux.*

**Utah Beach Landing Museum.** Inspect the glitteringly modern Utah Beach Landing Museum, whose exhibits include a W5 Utah scale model detailing the German defenses. ⊠ *Ste-Marie-du-Mont* ☏ *02–33–71–53–35* ⊕ *www.utah-beach.com* 🖥 *€6* ⊙ *June–Sept. 9:30–7; Apr. May, and Oct. 10–6; Nov., Feb., and Mar. 10–5:30.*

## PARIS

A day trip to Paris of just a few hours can barely scratch the surface of what one of the world's greatest cities can offer, but that doesn't mean you won't find those few hours really worthwhile. Below are the highlights of the highlights.

★ **Arc de Triomphe.** Set on Place Charles-de-Gaulle—known to Parisians as L'Étoile, or the Star (a reference to the streets that fan out from it)—the colossal, 164-foot Arc de Triomphe was planned by Napoléon but not finished until 1836, 20 years after the end of his rule. A small museum halfway up the arch is devoted to its history. France's Unknown Soldier is buried beneath the archway. ⊠ *Pl. Charles-de-Gaulle, Champs-Élysées* ☏ *01–55–37–73–77* ⊕ *www.monuments-nationaux.fr* 🖥 *€9* ⊙ *Apr.–Sept., daily 10 AM–11 PM; Oct.–Mar., daily 10 AM–10:30 PM* Ⓜ *Métro or RER: Étoile.*

★ **Les Invalides.** Famed as the final resting place of Napoléon, the Hôtel des Invalides, to use its official name, is an outstanding monumental baroque ensemble, designed by Libéral Bruand in the 1670s at the behest of Louis XIV to house wounded, or invalid, soldiers. The 17th-century **Église St-Louis des Invalides** is the Invalides's original church. More impressive is Jules Hardouin-Mansart's **Église du Dôme,** which includes **Napoléon's Tomb.** ⊠ *Pl. des Invalides, Trocadéro/Tour Eiffel* ☏ *01–44–42–38–77 Army and Model museums* ⊕ *www.invalides.org* 🖥 *€9* ⊙ *Église du Dôme and museums Apr.–Sept., Mon. and Wed.–Sat. 10–6, Sun. 10–3:30, Tues. 10–9; Oct.–Mar., daily 10–5. Closed 1st Mon. of every month* Ⓜ *La Tour-Maubourg.*

**Fodor's Choice**
★ **Louvre.** This is the world's greatest art museum—and the largest. The number one attraction—ever more so, since Dan Brown's *The Da Vinci Code* took over best-seller lists the world over—is the Most Famous Painting in the World: Leonardo da Vinci's enigmatic *Mona Lisa* (*La Joconde*, to the French), painted in 1503–06. However, the Louvre is packed with legendary collections, which are divided into seven sections: Asian antiquities; Egyptian antiquities; Greek and Roman antiquities; sculpture; paintings, prints, and drawings; furniture; and objets d'art. ⊠ *Palais du Louvre, Louvre/Tuileries* ☎ *01–40–20–53–17* ⊕ *www.louvre.fr* ☜ *€9.50, €6 after 6* PM *Wed. and Fri. Free 1st Sun. of month; €11 for Napoléon Hall exhibitions* ⊙ *Mon., Thurs., and weekends 9–6, Wed. and Fri. 9* AM*–10* PM Ⓜ *Palais-Royal.*

★ **Musée d'Orsay.** In a spectacularly converted belle époque train station, the Orsay Museum—devoted to the arts (mainly French) spanning the period 1848–1914—is one of the city's most popular, thanks to the presence of the world's greatest collection of impressionist and postimpressionist paintings. There is a dazzling rainbow of masterpieces by Renoir, Sisley, Pissarro, Monet, Cézanne, van Gogh, Gauguin, Toulouse-Lautrec, Degas, and Matisse, to name just a few. The museum's impressionist and postimpressionist galleries are undergoing a major renovation through March 2011, so some parts will not be open. ⊠ *1 rue de la Légion d'Honneur, St-Germain-des-Prés* ☎ *01–40–49–48–14* ⊕ *www.musee-orsay.fr* ☜ *€9.50, €7 after 4:15 except Thurs. after 6; free 1st Sun. of every month* ⊙ *Tues.–Sun., 9:30–6, Thurs. 9:30* AM*–9:45* PM Ⓜ *Solférino; RER: Musée d'Orsay.*

**Fodor's Choice**
★ **Notre-Dame.** Looming above the large, pedestrian Place du Parvis is la cathédrale de Notre-Dame, the most enduring symbol of Paris. Begun in 1163, completed in 1345, and restored by Viollet-le-Duc in the 19th century, Notre-Dame may not be France's oldest or largest cathedral, but in terms of beauty and architectural harmony, it has few peers. The 387-step climb to the top of the towers is worth the effort for a close-up of the famous gargoyles—most added in the 19th century by Viollet-le-Duc. The spectacular cathedral interior, with its vast proportions, soaring nave, and soft multicolor light dimly filtering through the stained-glass windows, inspires awe. ⊠ *Pl. du Parvis, Ile de la Cité* ☎ *01–53–10–07–00* ⊕ *www.notredamedeparis.fr* ☜ *Cathedral free, towers €7.50, crypt €4, treasury €3* ⊙ *Cathedral daily 8–6:45. Towers Apr.–June and Sept., daily 10* AM*–6:30* PM*; July and Aug., weekdays 10–6:30, weekends 10* AM*–11* PM*; Oct.–Mar., daily 10–5:30. Note towers close early when overcrowded. Treasury weekdays 9:30* AM*–6* PM*, Sat. 9:30–6:30, Sun. 1:30–6:30; Crypt Tues.–Sun. 10–6* Ⓜ *Cité.*

**Fodor's Choice**
★ **Sainte-Chapelle** (*Holy Chapel*). Not to be missed and one of the most magical sights in European medieval art, this Gothic chapel was built by Louis IX (1226–70; later canonized as St. Louis) in the 1240s to house what he believed to be Christ's Crown of Thorns, purchased from Emperor Baldwin of Constantinople. A dark lower chapel is a gloomy prelude to the shimmering upper one. Here the famous beauty of Sainte-Chapelle comes alive: instead of walls, all you see are 6,458 square feet of stained glass, delicately supported by painted stonework that seems to disappear in the colorful light streaming through the

windows. It's an easy walk here from Notre Dame. ⊠ *4 bd. du Palais, Ile de la Cité* ☎ *01–53–40–60–80* ⊕ *www.monuments-nationaux.fr* ⊠ *€8, joint ticket with Conciergerie €11* ⊙ *Daily 9:30–6, entry closes at 5 Nov.–Feb.* Ⓜ *Cité.*

⟳ **Tour Eiffel** *(Eiffel Tower)*. Known to the French as La Tour Eiffel (pro-
★ nounced ef-*el*), Paris's most famous landmark was built by Gustave Eiffel for the World Exhibition of 1889. At first many Parisians hated the structure, but now the largest Tinkertoy in the world is the beloved symbol of Paris. If you're full of energy, stride up the stairs as far as the third deck. If you want to go to the top, you'll have to take the elevator. ⊠ *Quai Branly, Trocadéro/Tour Eiffel* ☎ *08–92–70–12–39 (toll call)* ⊕ *www.tour-eiffel.fr* ⊠ *By elevator: 2nd fl. €4.50, 3rd fl. €8.10, 4th fl. €13.50. Climbing: 2nd and 3rd fl. only, €3* ⊙ *June–Aug., daily 9* AM–*midnight; Sept.–May, daily 9* AM–*11* PM, *stairs close at dusk in winter* Ⓜ *Bir-Hakeim; RER: Champ de Mars.*

## SHOPPING

The French practically created ready-to-wear fashion—think Cartier, Chanel, and Lacroix. The French love quality and style—and are willing to pay for it—so prices aren't cheap. The vast department stores **Galeries Lafayette** and **Printemps** on Boulevard Haussmann stock a vast range of clothing. The districts on the Left Bank and the Marais offer excellent boutiques selling one-of-a-kind accessories for the body and the home.

Normandy specialties include heavy cotton sailor's smocks, blue-and-white-stripe T-shirts, and chunky knits; popular choices in this traditional seafaring region. Calvados (distilled apple liqueur) is unique to the area, but other foodstuffs (pure butter and creamy cheeses) aren't really suitable to take home.

Honfleur has a huge choice of art galleries, craft shops, and boutiques with one-of-a-kind items. **Galerie Arthur Boudin.** This gallery displays fine range of original paintings, specializing in Normandy landscapes. ⊠ *6 pl. de l'Hôtel de Ville, Honfleur* ☎ *02–31–89–06–66* ⊕ *www. galerieboudin.com.*

**Galerie Dassonvalle.** This shop offers prints and limited editions. ⊠ *16 quai Ste-Catherine, Honfleur* ☎ *02–31–89–94–67.*

## WHERE TO EAT

$ ✕**Casino.** You can't get closer to the action. This handsome, postwar, tri-
SEAFOOD angular-gabled stone hotel, run by the same family since it was built in the 1950s, looks directly onto Omaha Beach. The bar is made from an old lifeboat, and it's no surprise that fish, seafood, and regional cuisine with creamy sauces predominate in Bruno Clemençon's airy sea-view restaurant. ⊠ *Rue de la Percée, Vierville-sur-Mer* ☎ *02–31–22–41–02* ⊟ *AE, MC, V* ⊙ *Closed mid-Nov.–late Mar.*

$$ ✕**L'Ardoise.** This minuscule storefront, decorated with enlargements of
BISTRO old sepia postcards of Paris, is a model of the kind of contemporary
**Fodor's Choice** bistros making waves in Paris. Chef Pierre Jay's first-rate three-course
★ dinner menu for €33 tempts with such original dishes as mushroom

and foie gras ravioli with smoked duck; farmer's pork with porcini mushrooms; and red mullet with creole sauce (you can also order à la carte, but it's less of a bargain). Just as enticing are the desserts, such as a superb *feuillantine au citron*—caramelized pastry leaves filled with lemon cream and lemon slices—and a boozy baba au rhum. With friendly waiters and a small but well-chosen wine list, L'Ardoise would be perfect if it weren't often crowded and noisy. ⊠ *28 rue du Mont Thabor, Louvre/Tuileries, Paris* ☎ *01–42–96–28–18* ⊕ *www.lardoise-paris. com* ▤ *MC, V* ⊙ *Closed Mon. and Aug. No lunch Sun.* Ⓜ *Concorde.*

$$$$   ✕ **Le Fleur de Sel.** A low-beamed 16th-century fisherman's house provides

FRENCH   the cozy atmosphere for chef Vincent's Guyon's locally influenced cuisine centered on the daily catch. The ambitious menu usually includes at least five different fish dishes—presented with artistic panache—along with plenty of grilled meats, like salt-marsh lamb or pigeon. For starters, the sea trout tartare, with oyster, apple, and lime with a coriander vinaigrette, draws raves, followed by a delicately spiced fillet of dorade with split-pea puree and oyster cream. Three fixed-price menus—at €28, €38, and €58—assure a splendid meal on any budget. Be sure to save room for one of the masterful desserts or an informed cheese course. ⊠ *17 rue Haute, Honfleur* ☎ *02–31–89–01–92* ⊕ *www.lafleurdesel-honfleur. com* ▤ *AE, MC, V* ⊙ *Closed Tues. and Wed. and Jan.*

# LEIXÕES, PORTUGAL (FOR PORTO)

Lining the river that made it a trading center ever since pre-Roman times, vibrant and cosmopolitan Porto centers itself some 5 km (3 mi) inland from the Atlantic Ocean. The Moors never had the same strong foothold here that they did farther south, nor was the city substantially affected by the great earthquake of 1755; as a result, Porto's architecture shows off a baroque finery little seen in the south of Portugal. Its grandiose granite buildings were financed by the trade that made the city wealthy: wine from the upper valley of the Rio Douro (Douro River, or River of Gold) was transported to Porto, from where it was then exported around the world. Industrious Porto considers itself the north's capital and, more contentiously, the country's economic center. In the shopping centers, the stately stock exchange building, and the affluent port-wine industry, Porto oozes confidence, though the fashionable commercial heart of the city contrasts with the gritty workaday atmosphere in the old town.

## ESSENTIALS

CURRENCY   The euro (€1 to US$1.36 at this writing).

HOURS   Most shops are open weekdays 9–1 and 3–7 and Saturday 9–1; malls and supermarkets often remain open until at least 10. Some are also open on Sunday. Note that most museums are closed Monday, and that churches generally close for a couple of hours in the middle of the day.

INTERNET   **Laranja Mecanica** (⊠ *Rua da Santa Caterina 274 Loja V, Porto* ☎ *222–010576* ⊕ *www.laranja-mecanica.com* ⊙ *Mon.–Sat. 10* AM*–11* PM, *Sun. 3–8.*

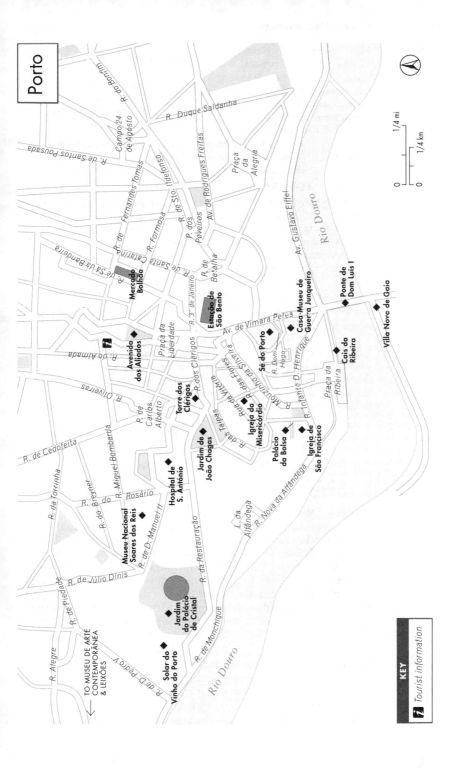

# Porto

R. do Bonfim

R. de Fernandes Tomás

Campo 24 de Agosto

R. de Santos Pousada

R. Duque Saldanha

R. de Sto. Ildefonso

R. de Rodrigues Freitas

Praça da Alegría

R. dos Poveiros

R. formosa

R. de Santa Catarina

P. de Batalha

**Mercado Bolhão**

R. 3.º de Janeiro

R. de Sá da Bandeira

**Estação de São Bento**

R. da Oliveiras

**Avenida dos Aliados**

Praça da Liberdade

Av. do Almada

P. de Carlos Alberto

**Torre dos Clérigos**

R. dos Clérigos

R. de Santa Teresa

**Igreja da Misericórdia**

R. das Flores

R. das Taipas

Rua da Vitória

R. de Cedofeita

R. da Torrinha

R. de Miguel Bombarda

R. do Breyner

R. do Rosário

**Jardim de João Chagas**

**Hospital de S. António**

R. de D. Manuel II

**Museu Nacional Soares dos Reis**

R. de Júlio Dinis

R. de Piedade

R. Alegre

TO MUSEU DE ARTE CONTEMPORÂNEA & LEIXÕES

R. de D. Pedro V

**Solar do Vinho do Porto**

**Jardim do Palácio de Cristal**

R. da Restauração

R. de Monchique

Rio Douro

Av. de Vimara Peres

**Sé do Porto**

R. Dom Hugo

**Casa-Museu de Guerra Junqueiro**

**Ponte de Dom Luís I**

R. Mouzinho da Silveira

**Palácio da Bolsa**

**Igreja de São Francisco**

R. Infante D. Henrique

**Cais da Ribeira**

Praça da Ribeira

**Villa Nova de Gaia**

Av. Gustavo Eiffel

Rio Douro

L. da Alfândega

R. Nova da Alfândega

0   1/4 mi
0   1/4 km

## KEY

*i* Tourist information

TELEPHONES Most quad- or tri-band GSM phones work in Portugal, which has a well-organized 3G compatible mobile network. You can buy prepaid phone cards at telecom shops, news vendors and tobacconists in all towns and cities. Phone cards can be used for local or international calls. Major companies include Vodafone and Optimus.

### COMING ASHORE

Vessels dock at the quays of Leixões port, just north of the mouth of the River Douro. It's a two-minute walk or a short shuttle trip to the passenger terminal (depending on the exact quay), which has few facilities, but the restaurants and shops of Leixões town are within walking distance. Taxis wait at the port entrance.

> ## PORTO BEST BETS
>
> **Sip some port.** You can try the country's famous after-dinner wine in the tasting rooms of port producers at Vila Nova de Gaia.
>
> **Climb the Torre dos Clérigos.** The panoramic views across the city are well worth the trip to the top.
>
> **Be dazzled by gold.** The exterior is undistinguished, but acres of gold leaf decorate the interior of Igreja de São Francisco.

From the port it is another 10-minute walk to the Matosinhos district, where the state-of-the-art metro will transfer you to central Porto in 30 minutes. Single tickets cost between €1 and €3.50. The single ticket from the port to downtown is €1.25. A 24-hour card is €12.15 for all zones. From the port to downtown the 24-hour ticket price is €4.30 (but this only entitles you to journey within three zones). Bus 76, which has a stop just outside the port, will also take you into Porto, but the journey time is longer.

If you intend to explore Porto on your day in port, the best option by far is to take the metro into the city. For exploration of the vineyards of the Douro River, a vehicle would be useful. Prices are expensive, at approximately €90 per day for a manual economy car.

## EXPLORING PORTO

**Avenida dos Aliados.** This imposing boulevard is lined with bright flower beds and grand buildings and is essentially the heart of the central business district. In addition to corporate businesses and banks, you'll find clothing and shoe stores, plus restaurants and coffeehouses. At one end of it is the broad Câmara Municipal (town hall). A tall bell tower sprouts from the roof of this palacelike, early-20th-century building, inside of which an impressive Portuguese wall tapestry is displayed. Praça da Liberdade—the hub from which Porto radiates—is at the other end of the avenue. Two statues adorn the square: a cast of Dom Pedro IV sitting on a horse and a modern statue of the great 19th-century Portuguese poet and novelist Almeida Garrett.

Fodor's Choice **Cais da Ribeira.** A string of fish restaurants and *tascas* (taverns) are built
★ into the street-level arcade of timeworn buildings along this pier. In the Praça da Ribeira people sit and chat around an odd, modern, cubelike sculpture; farther on, steps lead to a walkway above the river that's backed by tall houses. The pier also provides the easiest access to the

lower level of the middle bridge across the Douro. Boats docked at Cais da Ribeira offer various cruises around the bridges and up the river to Peso da Régua and Pinhão.

**Casa-Museu de Guerra Junqueiro.** This 18th-century white mansion, another of the city's buildings attributed by some to a pupil of Italian painter and architect Nicolau Nasoni and by others to Nasoni himself, was home to the poet Guerra Junqueiro (1850–1923). Although furnishings, sculptures, and paintings are labeled in Portuguese, English, and French (and there are brochures in English), the short tour of the elegant interior is less than enlightening if you don't speak Portuguese. ⊠ *Rua de Dom Hugo 32* ☎ *22/200–3689* ☒ *Tues.–Fri. €2.06, free weekends* ☉ *Tues.–Sat. 10–12:30 and 2–5:30, Sun. 2–5:30.*

FodorśChoice **Estação de São Bento.** This train station was built in the early 20th century
★ (King D. Carlos I laid the first brick himself in 1900) and inaugurated in 1915, precisely where the Convent of S. Bento de Avé-Maria was located. Therefore it inherited the convent's name—Saint Bento. The atrium is covered with 20,000 azulejos painted by Jorge Colaço (1916) depicting scenes of Portugal's history as well as ethnographic images. ⊠ *Praça Almeida Garret* ☎ *808/208208 national call center.*

**Igreja da Misericórdia.** Today's building represents a compromise between the church first built during the late 16th century and its reconstruction between 1749 and 1755 by Nicolau Nasoni. At the church museum next door you can see *Fons Vitae* (Fountain of Life), a vibrant, anonymous, Renaissance painting, depicting the founder of the church, Dom Manuel I, his queen, and their eight children kneeling before a crucified Christ. ⊠ *Rua das Flores 5* ☎ *22/207–4710* ⊕ *www.scmp.pt* ☒ *Church free, museum €1.50* ☉ *Church Tues.–Fri. 8–12:30 and 2–5:30, museum weekdays 9:30–12:30 and 2–5:30.*

**Igreja de São Francisco.** During the last days of Porto's siege by the absolutist army (the *miguelistas*) in July 1842, there was gunfire by the nearby São Francisco Convent. These shootings caused a fire that destroyed most parts of the convent, sparing only this church. The church is an undistinguished, late-14th-century Gothic building on the outside, but inside is an astounding interior: gilded carving—added in the mid-18th century—runs up the pillars, over the altar, and across the ceiling. ⊠ *Rua do Infante Dom Henrique 93* ☎ *22/206–2100* ☒ *€3.50* ☉ *Nov.–Mar., daily 9–5; Apr.–Oct., daily 9–6; May–Sept., daily 9–7.*

★ **Museu Nacional Soares dos Reis.** This art museum was the first in Portugal, founded in 1833 by King D. Pedro IV. In 1911 it was renamed after the 19th-century Portuguese sculptor whose works are contained within it. In 1940 it moved to this late-19th-century home, the Palácio dos Carrancas, which was once home to the royal family. The large art collection includes several Portuguese primitive works of the 16th century as well as superb collections of silver, ceramics, glassware, and costumes. ⊠ *Palácio dos Carrancas, Rua de Dom Manuel II* ☎ *22/339–3770* ⊕ *www.ipmuseus.pt* ☒ *Tues.–Sat. €5, free Sun.* ☉ *Tues. 2–6, Wed.–Sun. 10–6.*

FodorśChoice **Palácio da Bolsa.** Porto's 19th-century, neoclassical stock exchange takes
★ up much of the site of the former Franciscan convent at the Igreja de São Francisco. Guided tours are the only way to see the interior of this

masterpiece of 19th-century Portuguese architecture. The Arab-style ballroom, in particular, is one of the most admired chambers and was designed by civil engineer Gustavo Adolfo Gonçalves e Sousa. ⊠ *Rua Ferreira Borges* 🕾 *22/339–9000* ⊕ *www.palaciodabolsa.pt* 🖃 *Tours €6* ☾ *Apr.–Oct., daily 9–6.30; Nov.–Mar., daily 9–12:30 and 2–5:30.*

**Ponte de Dom Luís I.** This two-tier bridge, completed in 1886, leads directly to the city of Vila Nova de Gaia. Designed by Teófilo Seyrig, it affords the magnificent vistas of downtown Porto. A jumble of red-tile roofs on pastel-color buildings mixes with gray-and-white Gothic and baroque church towers, and all is reflected in the majestic Douro River; if the sun is shining just right, everything appears to be washed in gold.

**Sé do Porto.** Originally constructed in the 12th century by the parents of Afonso Henriques (Portugal's first king), Porto's granite cathedral has been rebuilt twice: first in the late 13th century and again in the 18th century, Nicolau Nasoni, was among those commissioned to work on its expansion. Despite the renovations, it remains a fortresslike structure—an uncompromising testament to medieval wealth and power. Notice a low relief on the northern tower, depicting a 14th-century vessel and symbolizing the city's nautical vocation. Size is the only exceptional thing about the interior; when you enter the two-story, 14th-century cloisters, however, the building comes to life. Decorated with gleaming azulejos, a staircase added by Nasoni leads to the second level and into a richly furnished chapter house, from which there are fine views through narrow windows. ⊠ *Terreiro da Sé* 🕾 *22/205–9028* 🖃 *Cathedral free; cloisters €3* ☾ *Apr.–Oct. Daily 8:45–12:30 and 2:30–7; Nov.–Mar, daily 8:45–12:30 and 2:30–6.*

★ **Solar do Vinho do Porto.** In a 19th-century country house called the Quinta da Macierinha, the institute offers relaxed tastings of Porto's famous wine. Tasting prices start at around €0.80 per glass. The Quinta da Macierinha is home to the **Museu Romântico da Quinta da Macierinha** (Romantic Museum), with displays of period furniture. ⊠ *Quinta da Macierinha, Rua de Entre Quintas 220* 🕾 *22/609–4749 Port Wine Institute, 22/605–7000 museum* ⊕ *www.ivp.pt* ⊘ *solarporto@ivp.pt* 🖃 *Port Wine Institute free, tasting prices vary, museum €2, free weekends* ☾ *Port Wine Institute Mon.–Sat. 4–midnight; museum Tues.–Sat. 10–12:30 and 2–5:30, Sun. 2–6.*

☾ **Torre dos Clérigos.** Designed by Italian architect Nicolau Nasoni and
**Fodor's Choice** begun in 1754, the tower of the church Igreja dos Clérigos reaches an
★ impressive height of 249 feet. There are 225 steep stone steps to the belfry, and the considerable effort required to climb them is rewarded by stunning views of the Old Town, the river, and beyond to the mouth of the Douro. The church itself, also built by Nasoni, predates the tower and is an elaborate example of Italianate baroque architecture. ⊠ *Rua S. Filipe Nery* 🕾 *22/200–1729* 🖃 *Tower €2* ☾ *Tower Sept.–May, daily 10–noon and 2–5; June and July, daily 9:30–1 and 2:30–7; Aug., daily 10–7. Church 8:45–12:30 and 3:30–7.*

☾ **Vila Nova de Gaia.** A city across the Rio Douro from central Porto, Vila
★ Nova de Gaia has been the headquarters of the port-wine trade since the late 17th century, when import bans on French wine led British

merchants to look for alternative sources. By the 18th century, the British had established companies and a regulatory association in Porto. The wine was transported from vineyards on the upper Douro to port-wine caves at Vila Nova de Gaia, where it was allowed to mature before being exported. Little has changed in the relationship between Porto and the Douro since those days, as wine is still transported to the city, matured in the warehouses, and bottled. Instead of traveling down the river on *barcos rabelos* (flat-bottom boats), however, the wine is now carried by truck. A couple of the traditional boats are moored at the quayside on the Vila Nova de Gaia side.

## SHOPPING

The Portuguese specialize in a range of handicrafts collectively known as *artesanato*. The term includes bright *azulejos* (blue-and-white-glaze tiles), pottery and ceramics, colorful textiles, olive wood, cork items, and basket wear. Gold and plated filigree is also a regional specialty, and the shoe trade is well established. You'll see port on sale throughout the city. But first taste the wine at either the Solar do Vinho do Porto or the caves at Vila Nova de Gaia. You may want to buy a bottle of the more unusual white port, drunk as an aperitif, as it's not commonly sold in North America.

The best shopping streets are those off the Praça da Liberdade, particularly Rua 31 de Janeiro, Rua dos Clérigos, Rua de Santa Catarina, Rua Sá da Bandeira, Rua Cedofeita, and Rua das Flores. Traditionally, Rua das Flores has been the street for silversmiths found along the same street and along Rua de Santa Catarina. On Rua 31 de Janeiro you'll find goldsmiths working.

Fodor'sChoice ★ **Artesanato Centro Regional de Artes Tradicionais.** The Center for Traditional Arts has an excellent selection of regional arts and crafts. ⊠ *Rua da Reboleira 37* ☎ *22/332–0201.*

**Livraria Lello e Irmão.** This is one of the most special and important bookshops in Portugal. It opened in 1906, and shelters more than 60,000 books. It is also famous for its neo-Gothic design and two-story interior with intricate carved-wood details. ⊠ *Rua das Carmelitas 144* ☎ *22/201–8170.*

## WHERE TO EAT

$ PORTUGUESE Fodor'sChoice ★ ✕**Chez Lapin.** At this Cais da Ribeira restaurant overlooking the river the service may be slow and the folksy decor may be overdone, but the food is excellent, and the outdoor terrace is attractive. The menu has such traditional but sometimes uncommon Porto dishes as bacalhau *e polvo assado no forno* (baked and with octopus) and *caldeirada de peixe* (fish stew), all served in generous portions. ⊠ *Rua Canastreiros 40–42* ☎ *22/200–6418* ⚖ *Reservations essential* ▭ *AE, DC, MC, V.*

¢–$ CAFÉ ★ ✕**Majestic Café.** Opened in 1921, this is one of Porto's grand old coffee-houses, and it serves double duty as a reasonably priced grill-restaurant. Sit surrounded by sculpted wood, carved nymphs, and mirrors and choose from a fair list of omelets, sandwiches, salads, burgers, and steaks. Or just have coffee and a pastry. ⊠ *Rua de Santa Catarina 112* ☎ *22/200–3887* ▭ *AE, DC, MC, V* ۞ *Closed Sun.*

# LISBON, PORTUGAL

Lisbon bears the mark of an incredible heritage with laid-back pride. Spread over a string of seven hills north of the Rio Tejo (Tagus River) estuary, the city also presents an intriguing variety of faces to those who negotiate its switchback streets. In the oldest neighborhoods stepped alleys are lined with pastel-color houses and crossed by laundry hung out to dry; here and there *miradouros* (vantage points) afford spectacular river or city views. In the grand 18th-century center, black-and-white mosaic cobblestone sidewalks border wide boulevards. *Elétricos* (trams) clank through the streets, and blue-and-white azulejos (painted and glazed ceramic tiles) adorn churches, restaurants, and fountains. Some modernization has improved the city. To prepare for its role as host of the World Exposition in 1998, Lisbon spruced up its public buildings, overhauled its metro system, and completed an impressive bridge across the Rio Tejo, but Lisbon's intrinsic, slightly disorganized, one-of-a-kind charm hasn't vanished in the contemporary mix.

## ESSENTIALS

CURRENCY The euro (€1 to US$1.36 at this writing).

HOURS Most shops are open weekdays 9–1 and 3–7 and Saturday 9–1; malls and supermarkets often remain open until at least 10. Some are also open on Sunday. Note that most museums are closed Monday, and that churches generally close for a couple of hours in the middle of the day.

INTERNET **Pavilhão do Conhecimento** (⊠ *Parque das Nações* ☎ *21/891–7100*) has a cybercafé with free Internet access. It's open Tuesday–Friday 10–6, weekends and holidays 11–7.

TELEPHONES You can use most tri- and quad-band GSM phones in Portugal, which has a well-organized 3G-compatible mobile network. You can buy prepaid phone cards at telecom shops, news vendors, and tobacconists in all towns and cities. Phone cards can be used for local or international calls. Major companies include Vodafone and Optimus.

## COMING ASHORE

Vessels dock at one of three quays along the River Tagus in a port area rebuilt for Expo '98 (the 1998 World's Fair). The main cruise port is the Cais de Alcántara, which has a terminal with shops, taxi ranks, and restrooms. Cais da Rocha Conde Óbidos also has a terminal with the same facilities. From both these terminals there are public transit routes into the city by bus (Buses 28, 201, 714, 727, 729, 751) or tram (Tram 15E). A suburban train also runs alongside the cruise terminal, and the Alcántara Mar station is the place to get on; the trip to Lisbon's main railway station takes about 10 minutes. Fares for all these options are €1.45 per journey. The walk into town from the cruise port takes around an hour, but is not unpleasant if you have the time. A one-day travel card for bus and metro costs €3.75.

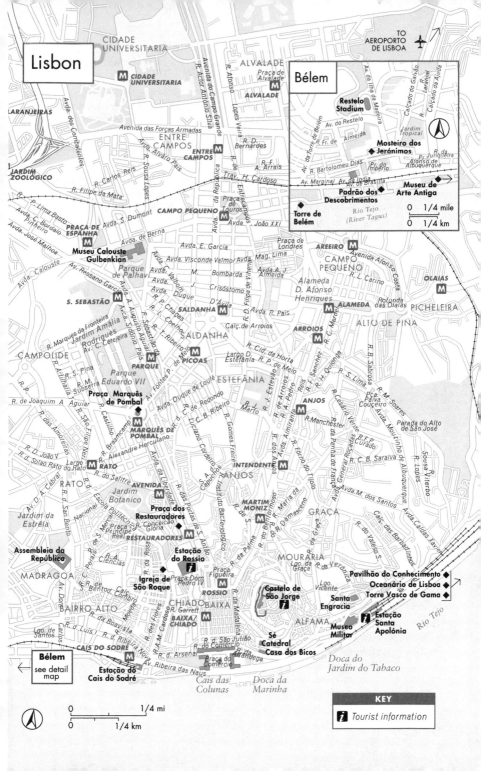

Some small and midsize ships call at a smaller terminal in Santa Apoló-
nia, which is closer to the center of the city and from where it's possible
to walk to Alfalma and central Lisbon.

There are many companies running tours of the city. Don't rent a car
if you are staying in Lisbon, where navigation and parking are almost
impossible, but if you want to explore the countryside, you'll need one.
An economy manual vehicle is about €90 per day.

## EXPLORING LISBON

The center of Lisbon stretches north from the spacious Praça do Comér-
cio—one of Europe's largest riverside squares—to the Rossío, a smaller
square lined with shops and cafés. The district in between is known
as the Baixa (lower town), an attractive grid of parallel streets built
after the 1755 earthquake and tidal wave. The Alfama, the old Moorish quarter that survived the earthquake, lies east of the Baixa. In this
part of town are the Sé (the city's cathedral) and, on the hill above, the
Castelo de São Jorge (St. George's Castle).

West of the Baixa, sprawled across another of Lisbon's hills, is the
Bairro Alto (Upper Town), an area of intricate 17th-century streets,
peeling houses, and churches. Five kilometers (3 mi) farther west is
Belém. A similar distance to the northeast is Lisbon's postmodernist
Parque das Nações.

The modern city begins at Praça dos Restauradores, adjacent to the
Rossío. From here the main Avenida da Liberdade stretches northwest
to the landmark Praça Marquês de Pombal, dominated by a column
and a towering statue of the man himself. The praça is bordered by
the green expanse of the Parque Eduardo VII, named in honor of King
Edward VII of Great Britain, who visited Lisbon in 1902.

**Fodor's** Choice ★ **Igreja de São Roque.** Filippo Terzi, the architect who designed São Vicente
on the outskirts of the Alfama, was also responsible for this Renaissance
church. He was commissioned by Jesuits and completed the church in
1574. Curb your impatience with its plain facade and venture inside.
Its eight side chapels have statuary and art dating from the early 17th
century. The last chapel on the left before the altar is the extraordinary
18th-century Capela de São João Baptista (Chapel of St. John the Baptist): designed and built in Rome, with rare stones and mosaics that
resemble oil paintings, the chapel was taken apart, shipped to Lisbon,
and reassembled here in 1747. ✉ *Largo Trindade Coelho, Bairro Alto*
☎ *21/323–5381* ✆ *Church free; museum €1.50 Mon.–Sat., free Sun.*
☉ *Church weekdays 8:30–5, weekends 9:30–5; museum daily 10–5*
Ⓜ *Baixa-Chiado.*

**Fodor's** Choice ★ **Mosteiro dos Jerónimos.** Conceived and commissioned by Dom Manuel I,
who petitioned the Holy See for permission to build it in 1496, Belém's
famous Jerónimos Monastery was financed largely by treasures brought
back from Africa, Asia, and South America. Construction began in 1502.
The monastery is a supreme example of the Manueline style of building (named after King Dom Manuel I), which represented a marked
departure from the prevailing Gothic. Much of it is characterized by

elaborate sculptural details. Inside, the remarkably spacious interior contrasts with the riot of decoration on the six nave columns, which disappear into a complex latticework ceiling. ⊠ *Praça do Império, Belém* ☎ *21/362–0034* ⊕ *www.mosteirojeronimos.pt* ⌀ *Cloister €6, free Sun. before 2. Combined ticket with Torre Belém €8* ⦿ *May–Sept., Tues.–Sun. 10–6; Oct.–Apr., Tues.–Sun. 10–5.*

**Fodor's** Choice ★ **Museu Calouste Gulbenkian.** On its own lush grounds, the museum of the celebrated Fundação Calouste Gulbenkian (Calouste Gulbenkian Foundation), a cultural trust, houses treasures collected by Armenian oil magnate Calouste Gulbenkian (1869–1955) and donated to the people of Portugal in return for tax concessions. The collection is split in two: one part is devoted to Egyptian, Greek, Roman, Islamic, and Asian art and the other to European acquisitions. Both holdings are relatively small, but the quality of the pieces on display is magnificent.

One of the highlights in the astounding Egyptian Room is a haunting gold mummy mask. Greek and Roman coins and statuary, Chinese porcelain, Japanese prints, and a set of rich 16th- and 17th-century Persian tapestries follow. The European art section has pieces from all the major schools from the 15th through the 20th century. ⊠ *Av. de Berna 45, São Sebastião* ☎ *21/782–3000* ⊕ *www.museu.gulbenkian.pt* ⌀ *€4, combined ticket with Modern Art Center €7; free Sun.* ⦿ *Tues.–Sun. 10–5:45* Ⓜ *São Sebastião or Praça de Espanha.*

**Fodor's** Choice ★ **Museu de Arte Antiga.** The only museum in Lisbon to approach the status of the Gulbenkian is the Ancient Art Museum, founded in 1884. It was the first large public museum dedicated to the arts in Portugal. In a 17th-century palace, once owned by the Counts of Alvor, and vastly enlarged in 1940 when it took over the Convent of St. Albert, it has a beautifully displayed collection of Portuguese art—mainly from the 15th through 19th century. Of all the holdings, the religious works of the Portuguese school of artists (characterized by fine portraiture with a distinct Flemish influence) stand out, especially the acknowledged masterpiece of Nuno Gonçalves, the *St. Vincent Altarpiece.* ⊠ *Rua das Janelas Verdes, Lapa* ☎ *21/391–2800* ⊕ *www.mnarteantiga-ipmuseus.pt* ⌀ *€5. Free Sun. before 2* ⦿ *Tues. 2–6, Wed.–Sun. 10–6.*

☾ ★ **Oceanário de Lisboa.** With 25,000 fish, seabirds, and mammals, this is Europe's largest aquarium and the first ever to incorporate several ocean habitats (North Atlantic, Pacific, Antarctic, and Indian) in one place. ⊠ *Esplanada D. Carlos I (Doca dos Olivais), Parque das Nações*

---

**LISBON BEST BETS**

**Take time to enjoy the exquisite decoration at the Mosteiro dos Jerónimos.** Paid for with the profits from the sale of treasures from New World colonies.

**Enjoy the first-class artifacts on display at Museu Calouste Gulbenkian.** The collection reflects the personal taste of Gulbenkian himself.

**Stroll the avenues of the Biaxa district.** An architectural whole built after the devastating earthquake of 1755 is Lisbon's most attractive neoclassical neighborhood.

☎ *21/891–7002 or 21/891–7006* ⊕ *www.oceanario.pt* 🎫 *€12* ⊙ *Apr.–Oct., daily 10–8, last admission 7; Nov.–Mar., daily 10–7, last admission 6.*

**Padrão dos Descobrimentos.** The white, monolithic Monument of the Discoveries was erected in 1960 to commemorate the 500th anniversary of the death of Prince Henry the Navigator. It was built on what was the departure point for many voyages of discovery, including those of Vasco da Gama for India and—during Spain's occupation of Portugal—of the Spanish Armada for England in 1588. Henry is at the prow of the monument, facing the water; lined up behind him are the Portuguese explorers of Brazil and Asia, as well as other national heroes. On the ground adjacent to the monument an inlaid map shows the extent of the explorations undertaken by the 15th- and 16th-century Portuguese sailors. The 25-minute movie "Discover Portugal" provides an interesting context to the highlights of the country's history. ✉ *Av. de Brasília, Belém* ☎ *21/303–1950* ⊕ *www.padraodescobrimentos.egeac.pt* 🎫 *€2.50; movie €4* ⊙ *Monument May–Sept. Daily 10–7, Oct.–Apr., Tues.–Sun 10–6 (last admission 30 mins before close throughout year). Movie Tues.–Sun 10–5.*

**Pavilhão do Conhecimento.** The white, angular, structure designed by architect Carrilho de Graça for the Expo seems the perfect place to house the Knowledge Pavilion, or Living Science Centre, as it's also known. All of the permanent and temporary exhibits here are related to math, science, and technology. ✉ *Parque das Nações* ☎ *21/891–9898* ⊕ *www.pavconhecimento.pt* 🎫 *€7* ⊙ *Tues.–Fri. 10–6, weekends and holidays 11–7.*

**Praça Marquês de Pombal.** Dominating the center of Marquês de Pombal Square is a statue of the marquês himself, the man responsible for the design of the "new" Lisbon that emerged from the ruins of the 1755 earthquake. On the statue's base are representations of both the earthquake and the tidal wave that engulfed the city; a female figure with outstretched arms signifies the joy at the emergence of the refashioned city.

**Praça dos Restauradores.** Although this square, which is adjacent to Rossío train station, marks the beginning of modern Lisbon, it's technically part of the Baixa district. Here the broad, tree-lined Avenida da Liberdade starts its northwesterly ascent. *Restauradores* means "restoration," and the square commemorates the 1640 uprising against Spanish rule that restored Portuguese independence. An obelisk (raised in 1886) commemorates the event. Note the elegant 18th-century Palácio Foz, on the square's west side. Today it houses a tourist office. The only building to rival the palace is the restored Eden building, just to the south.

★ **Torre de Belém.** The openwork balconies and domed turrets of the fanciful Belém Tower make it perhaps the country's purest Manueline structure. It was built between 1514 and 1520 on an island in the middle of the Rio Tejo, and dedicated to St. Vincent, the patron saint of Lisbon. Today the chalk-white tower stands near what has become the north bank—evidence of the river's changing course. It was originally constructed to defend the port entrance, but it has also served as a customs control point, a telegraph station, a lighthouse, and even a prison from the late-16th through the 19th centuries. ⊠ *Av. de Brasília, Belém* ☎ *21/362-0034* ⊠ *€4. Combined ticket with Mosteiro dos Jerónimos €8* ☉ *May–Sept. daily 10–6:30; Oct.–Apr. daily 10–5.*

**Torre Vasco da Gama.** Rising 480 feet, the graceful, white Vasco da Gama Tower is Portugal's tallest structure. Three glass elevators whisk you up 345 feet to the observation deck. In addition to taking in vistas across Lisbon and the Atlantic Ocean, you'll feel as if you're eye to eye with the 18-km (11-mi) Ponte Vasco da Gama (Vasco da Gama Bridge). ⊠ *Av. Pinto Ribeiro, Parque das Nações* ☎ *21/893–9550* ⊠ *€4.45* ☉ *Daily 10–6.*

# SHOPPING

Although fire destroyed much of Chiado, Lisbon's smartest shopping district, in 1988, a good portion of the area has been restored. The neighborhood has a large new shopping complex as well as many small stores with considerable cachet, particularly on and around Rua Garrett. The Baixa's grid of streets from the Rossío to the Rio Tejo have many small shops selling jewelry, shoes, clothing, and foodstuffs. The Bairro Alto is full of little crafts shops with stylish, contemporary goods. Excellent stores continue to open in the residential districts north of the city, at Praça de Londres and Avenida de Roma. Most of Lisbon's antiques shops are in the Rato and Bairro Alto districts along one long street, which changes its name four times as it runs southward from Largo do Rato: Rua Escola Politécnica, Rua Dom Pedro V, Rua da Misericórdia, and Rua do Alecrim.

Handmade goods, such as leather handbags, shoes, gloves, embroidery, ceramics, linens, and basketwork, are sold throughout the city. Apart from top designer fashions and high-end antiques, prices are moderate.

**Antiquália.** This home store is packed with furniture, chandeliers, and porcelain. ⊠ *Praça Luís de Camões 37, Chiado* ☎ *21/342–3260.*

**Atelier.** The Atelier specializes in hand-painted tiles. You can often see an artist at work here. What's more, they ship worldwide, and you can even order online. ⊠ *Rua dos Bacalhoeiros 12–A, Alfama* ☎ *21/886–5563* ⊕ *www.loja-descobrimentos.com.*

**Vista Alegre.** Portugal's most famous porcelain producer established its factory in 1824. ⊠ *Largo do Chiado 20–23, Chiado* ☎ *21/346–1401* ⊕ *www.vistaalegreatlantis.com.*

# WHERE TO EAT

$  
PORTUGUESE

✕ **Andorra.** On the renowned Baixa street of fish restaurants, the Andorra is a perfect place for a simple lunch; from the terrace you can people-watch and smell the charcoal-grilled sardines. The friendly staff serves plates of well-cooked Portuguese favorites, and you can choose from a short wine list that caters to most tastes. ⊠ *Rua Portas de Santo Antão 82, Restauradores* ☎ *21/342–6047* ▭ *MC, V.*

$  
PORTUGUESE

✕ **Solar dos Bicos.** As the name implies, this charming restaurant with stone arches and beautiful azulejos offers typical Portuguese cuisine at very reasonable prices. ⊠ *Rua dos Bacalhoeiros, 8–A, Alfama* ☎ *21/886–9447* ⊕ *www.solardosbicos.pt* ▤ *AE, MC, V* ⦵ *Closed Mon.*

# LIVORNO, ITALY (FOR FLORENCE AND PISA)

One of the biggest and grittiest ports on the northwestern Italian coast, Livorno has little to attract visitors in itself. Nevertheless, the city is one of the most popular cruise ports of call in the western Mediterranean as the gateway to some of Italy's finest attractions, the cities of Florence and Pisa, not to mention the delightful landscapes of Tuscany. Florence, the city of the lily, gave birth to the Renaissance and changed the way we see the world. For centuries it has captured the imagination of travelers, who have come seeking rooms with views and phenomenal art. Pisa is famous for one of the world's most quirky historical attractions: its leaning tower, but this structure is one part of a triumvirate that offers one of the most dramatic architectural vista's in the country. It's unlikely you'll have time to see everything during this port stop, so plan your time wisely.

## ESSENTIALS

CURRENCY  The euro (€1 to US$1.36 at this writing).

HOURS  Shops are generally open 9 to 1 and 3:30 to 7:30 and are closed Sunday and Monday morning most of the year. Summer (June to September) hours are usually 9 to 1 and 4 to 8, and some shops close Saturday afternoon instead of Monday morning.

INTERNET  **Internet Train** (⊠ *Borgo San Jacappo 30/r, Florence* ☎ *055/2657935* ⊕ *www.internettrain.it*) has views of the Ponte Vecchio, so you can sightsee and surf at the same time.

TELEPHONES  Tri-band GSM phones work in Italy. You can buy prepaid phone cards at telecom shops, news vendors, and tobacconists in all towns and cities. Phone cards can be used for local or international calls.

## COMING ASHORE

The port of Livorno has good cruise facilities, including car-rental offices, ticket and information offices, a bar, and a garden. It is near the heart of the town, just a few blocks from Livorno's central area. The railway station is 3 km (2 mi) from the port, but there is no good public transport option there, so take a taxi at a cost of about €20.

Trains from Livorno to Florence currently run once per hour throughout the day. The journey time is about 90 minutes. Prices are about €14–€20 round-trip depending on time of departure. From Livorno it is just a 15-minute train journey to Pisa, at a price of about €2.90 depending on time of departure; from Pisa Central Station take a train to San Rossore, from where it is a five-minute walk to the Leaning Tower area. If you buy tickets on Trenitalia's (Italian railways') Web site (⊕ *www.trenitalia.com*), you can print them out at self-service machines in Livorno station.

Taxis charge approximately €2.38 initially, then €0.88 per km (½-mi) with an additional €0.10 per 113 meters (370 feet) when the taxi travels at less than 20 kph (12 mph). Car rental would give you greater flexibility to explore Tuscany, but if you are going only to Florence, then a train will be better, since parking is difficult in Florence. Rentals are approximately €45 per day for a compact manual vehicle.

## EXPLORING FLORENCE AND PISA

### FLORENCE

*95 km (60 mi) east of Livorno, 82 km (51 mi) east of Pisa.*

The heart of Florence, stretching from the Piazza del Duomo south to the Arno, is as dense with artistic treasures as anyplace in the world. The churches, medieval towers, Renaissance palaces, and world-class museums and galleries contain some of the most outstanding aesthetic achievements of Western history.

★ **Bargello.** During the Renaissance, this building was headquarters for the *podestà,* or chief magistrate. Today it houses the **Museo Nazionale,** home to what is probably the finest collection of Renaissance sculpture in Italy. For Renaissance art lovers, the Bargello is to sculpture what the Uffizi is to painting. ⊠ *Via del Proconsolo 4, Bargello* ☎ *055/2388606* ⊕ *www.polomuseale.firenze.it* 🎫 *€4* ☉ *Daily 8:15–5; closed 2nd and 4th Mon. of month and 1st, 3rd, and 5th Sun. of month.*

**Battistero** *(Baptistery).* The octagonal Baptistery across from the Duomo is one of the supreme monuments of the Italian Romanesque style and one of Florence's oldest structures. The interior dome mosaics from the beginning of the 14th century are justly renowned, but—glittering beauties though they are—they could never outshine the building's famed bronze Renaissance doors decorated with panels crafted by Lorenzo Ghiberti. The doors—or at least copies of them (the originals are in the Museo dell'Opera del Duomo—are on the north and east sides of the Baptistery, and the Gothic panels on the south door were designed by Andrea Pisano (circa 1290–1348) in 1330. ⊠ *Piazza del Duomo* ☎ *055/2302885* ⊕ *www.operaduomo.firenze.it* 🎫 *€4* ☉ *Mon.–Sat. 12:15–7, Sun. 8:30–2.*

**Campanile.** The Gothic bell tower designed by Giotto (circa 1266–1337) is a soaring structure of multicolor marble originally decorated with reliefs that are now in the Museo dell'Opera del Duomo. A climb of 414 steps rewards you with a sweeping view of the city. ⊠ *Piazza del Duomo* ☎ *055/2302885* ⊕ *www.operaduomo.firenze.it* 🎫 *€6* ☉ *Daily 8:30–7:30.*

★ **Cappelle Medicee** *(Medici Chapels).* This magnificent complex includes the **Cappella dei Principi,** the Medici chapel and mausoleum that was begun in 1605 and kept marble workers busy for several hundred years, and the **Sagrestia Nuova** (New Sacristy), designed by Michelangelo and so called to distinguish it from Brunelleschi's Sagrestia Vecchia (Old Sacristy) in San Lorenzo. ⊠ *Piazza di Madonna degli Aldobrandini, San Lorenzo* ☎ *055/294883* ⊕ *www.firenzemusei.it* 🎫 *€6* ☉ *Daily 8:15–5. Closed 1st, 3rd, and 5th Mon. and 2nd and 4th Sun. of month.*

★ **Duomo** *(Cattedrale di Santa Maria del Fiore).* In 1296 Arnolfo di Cambio (circa 1245–circa 1310) was commissioned to build "the loftiest, most sumptuous edifice human invention could devise." The immense Duomo

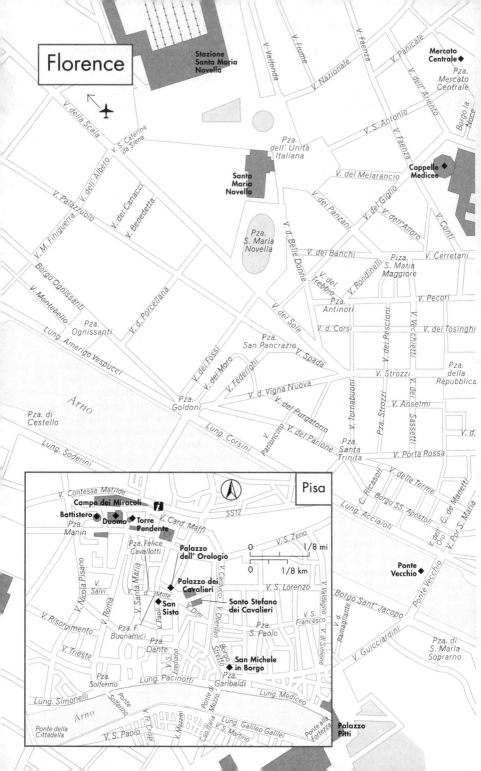

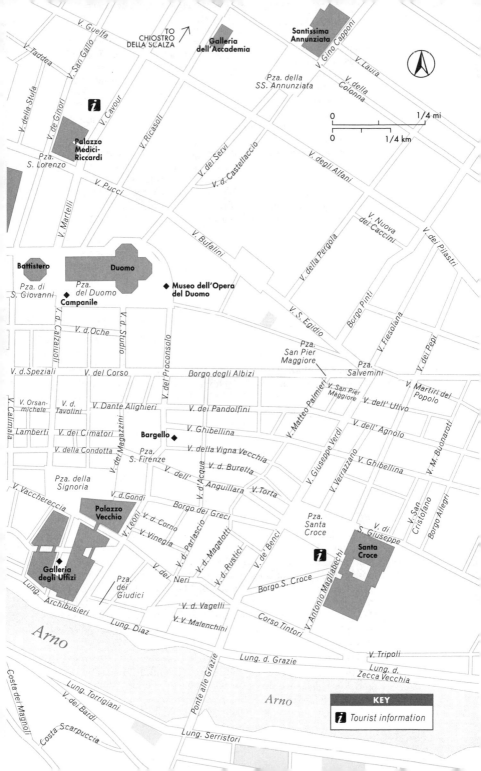

was not completed until 1436. The imposing facade dates only from the 19th century; its neo-Gothic style complements Giotto's genuine Gothic 14th-century campanile. The real glory of the Duomo, however, is Filippo Brunelleschi's dome, presiding over the cathedral with a dignity and grace that few domes to this day can match. Brunelleschi's **cupola** was an ingenious engineering feat, and today the Duomo has come to symbolize Florence in the same way that the Eiffel Tower symbolizes Paris. ✉ *Piazza del Duomo* ☎ *055/2302885* ⊕ *www. operaduomo.firenze.it* ✍ *Church free, crypt €3, cupola €8* ☉ *Church Mon.–Wed. and Fri. 10–5, Sat. 10–4:45, Sun. 1:30–4:45; Thurs.: June–Sept. 10–5, May and Oct. 10–3:30, Nov.–Apr. 10–4:30. Crypt Mon.–Wed. and Fri. 10–5, Thurs. 10–3:30, Sat. 10–5:45. Cupola weekdays 8:30–7, Sat. 8:30–5:40.*

> ## LIVORNO BEST BETS
>
> **The Uffizi.** The mother lode of Renaissance art offers priceless examples by artists including Michelangelo, Botticelli, and Raphael.
>
> **Galleria dell'Accademia.** The number one draw in this museum is Michelangelo's *David*, a sculpture that has captured human imagination, but don't miss the rest of the collection.
>
> **Torre Pendente.** Completed in 1173 Pisa's famous tower began to subside almost immediately. Intervention in the 1990s saved it from collapse and stabilized the structure.

**Fodor's**Choice **Galleria degli Uffizi.** The venerable Uffizi Gallery occupies the top floor
★ of the U-shape **Palazzo degli Uffizi** (Uffizi Palace), designed by Giorgio Vasari (1511–74) in 1560 to hold the administrative offices of the Medici grand duke Cosimo I (1519–74). Later, the Medici installed their art collections here. It's probably the greatest collection of Renaissance paintings in the world. Lines can be long, and you may wish to consider buying your tickets in advance or going on a ship-sponsored shore excursion to avoid them. A bar inside the gallery is a good place for a coffee break; for a close-up view of the Palazzo Vecchio, step out onto the terrace. ✉ *Piazzale degli Uffizi 6, Piazza Signoria* ☎ *055/2388651 advance tickets* ✉ *Consorzio ITA, Piazza Pitti 1* ☎ *055/294883* ⊕ *www. uffizi.firenze.it* ✍ *€6.50, reservation fee €4* ☉ *Tues.–Sun. 8:15–6:50.*

☿ **Galleria dell'Accademia** *(Accademia Gallery).* The collection of Florentine
★ paintings, dating from the 13th to the 18th centuries, is largely unremarkable, but the sculptures by Michelangelo are worth the price of admission. The unfinished *Slaves*, fighting their way out of their marble prisons, were meant for the tomb of Michelangelo's overly demanding patron Pope Julius II (1443–1513). But the focal point is the original *David*, moved here from Piazza della Signoria in 1873. ✉ *Via Ricasoli 60, San Marco* ☎ *055/294883 reservations, 055/2388609 gallery* ✍ *€6.50, reservation fee €4* ☉ *Tues.–Sun. 8:15–6:50.*

**Museo dell'Opera del Duomo** *(Cathedral Museum).* Ghiberti's original Baptistery door panels and the *cantorie* (choir loft) reliefs by Donatello and Luca della Robbia (1400–82) keep company with Donatello's *Mary Magdalen* and Michelangelo's *Pietà* (not to be confused with his more famous *Pietà* in St. Peter's in Rome). Renaissance sculpture is in part defined by its revolutionary realism, but in its palpable suffering Donatello's *Magdalen* goes beyond realism. ⊠ *Piazza del Duomo 9* ☎ *055/2302885* ⊕ *www.operaduomo.firenze.it* 🎟 €6 ⊗ *Mon.–Sat. 9–7:30, Sun. 9–1:45.*

**Palazzo Vecchio** *(Old Palace).* Florence's forbidding, fortresslike city hall was begun in 1299, and its massive bulk and towering campanile dominate the Piazza della Signoria. The interior courtyard is a good deal less severe, having been remodeled by Michelozzo (1396–1472) in 1453; a copy of Verrocchio's bronze *puttino* (little infant boy), topping the central fountain, softens the space. The main attraction is on the second floor: two adjoining rooms that supply one of the most startling contrasts in Florence. The first is the vast **Sala dei Cinquecento,** which contains Michelangelo's *Victory* group. The second room is the little **Studiolo,** to the right of the sala's entrance, designed by Vasari and decorated by Vasari and Bronzino (1503–72); it's intimate, civilized, and filled with complex, questioning, allegorical art. ⊠ *Piazza della Signoria* ☎ *055/2768325* ⊕ *www.museicivicifiorentini.it* 🎟 €6 ⊗ *Mon.–Wed., Fri. and Sat. 9–7, Thurs. 9–2, Sun. 9–7.*

★ **Ponte Vecchio** *(Old Bridge).*This charmingly simple bridge is to Florence what the Tower Bridge is to London. It was built in 1345, and the shops along the bridge housed first butchers, then grocers, blacksmiths, and other merchants. But in 1593 the Medici grand duke Ferdinand I (1549–1609), whose private corridor linking the Medici palace (Palazzo Pitti) with the Medici offices (the Uffizi) crossed the bridge atop the shops, decided that all this plebeian commerce under his feet was unseemly. So he threw out the butchers and blacksmiths and installed 41 goldsmiths and 8 jewelers. The bridge has been devoted solely to these two trades ever since.

Fodor's Choice **Santa Croce.** Like the Duomo, this church is Gothic, with a facade dat-
★ ing from the 19th century. As a burial place, the church probably contains more skeletons of Renaissance celebrities than any other in Italy including those of Michelangelo, Galileo, Machiavelli, and the composer Gioacchino Rossini, as well as a memorial for Dante Alighieri. The collection of art within the complex is by far the most important of any church in Florence. ⊠ *Piazza Santa Croce 16* ☎ *055/2466105* ⊕ *www.santacroce.firenze.it* 🎟 €5 *combined admission to church and museum* ⊗ *Mon.–Sat. 9:30–5:30, Sun. 1–5:30.*

## PISA

*22 km (14 mi) north of Livorno, 82 km (51 mi) west of Florence.*

All of Pisa's treasures date from a short period between the 11th and the 13th centuries, when Pisa was a leading power in the region. The three buildings set on Pisa's grassy Field of Miracles form one of the finest Romanesque ensembles in Italy.

**Battistero.** This smaller baptistery building completes the collection of Pisa's top sights. Remarkable for its ornate exterior, the interior is almost devoid of adornment. ⊠ *Piazza del Duomo* 🎟 €5 *for entry to Battistero, combined tickets €6 for entry to 2 monuments, €8 for entry into 4 monuments, €10 for entry into 5 monuments (not including the*

*Torre Pendente)* ⊙ *Daily Apr.–Sept. 8–8; Oct. 9–7; Nov.–Feb. 10–5; Mar. 10–6.*

**Duomo.** The magnificent black-and-white decoration of the exterior of the Duomo ushered in the Pisan style. The foundation was laid in 1063, a century before the tower was completed. Sadly, a fire in 1595 destroyed much of the interior decoration, though not the ornate font (1310) by Giovanni Pisano. The bronze doors at **Portale di San Renieri**, the main entrance, are also original (1180). ⊠ *Piazza del Duomo* 🖼 *€5 for entry to Duomo, combined tickets €6 for entry to 2 monuments, €8 for entry into 4 monuments, €10 for entry into 5 monuments (not including the Torre Pendente).* ⊙ *Daily Apr.–Sept. 8:30–8, Oct. 10–7, Mar. 10–6, Nov., and Feb. 10–12:45 and 2–5, Dec.–Jan. 10–12.45 and 2–5.*

**Torre Pendente.** Probably one of the most recognizable tourist attractions in the world, this funny little tower refuses to fall down. We've all seen the pictures, but nothing can prepare you for seeing it for real; it's kooky, but it's also very beautiful. The tower leans because 14.5 thousand tons of marble press down on badly formed foundations. The tower settled at an incline of 5.5 degrees to the vertical, the top being displaced by 15 feet from the base. Visitor numbers are limited to 40 per group at 30-minute intervals throughout the day. Buy a ticket as soon as you arrive at the site or book online. ⊠ *Piazza del Duomo* 🕾 *050/560547* ⊕ *www.opapisa. it* 🖼 *€15* ⊙ *Daily July and Aug. 8:30* AM*–11* PM; *Apr.–June and Sept. 8:30–8; Oct. 10–7; Mar. 9–5:30; Nov., and Feb. 9:30–5:30; Dec.–Jan. 10–4:30 (times listed are times of last admittance).*

# SHOPPING

Window-shopping in Florence is like visiting an enormous contemporary-art gallery. Many of today's greatest Italian artists are fashion designers—Prada, Gucci, Versace, to name but a few—and most keep shops in Florence. Italian leather is famed for its quality and fashioned into clothing, shoes, and accessories. True art also makes a big impact on the souvenir market, with many street artists around the town and smarter galleries in the historic center. Terra-cotta pottery, straw goods, and hand-made paper are all traditional handicrafts. Excellent olive oils and wines are also worthwhile buys in Florence.

The fanciest designer shops are mainly on **Via Tornabuoni** and **Via della Vigna Nuova.** The city's largest concentrations of antiques shops are on **Borgo Ognissanti** and the Oltrarno's **Via Maggio.** The **Ponte Vecchio** houses reputable but very expensive jewelry shops, as it has since the 16th century. The area near **Santa Croce** is the heart of the leather merchants' district.

**Pollini.** This store has beautifully crafted shoes and leather accessories for those willing to pay that little bit extra. ⊠ *Via Por Santa Maria 42r, Pedestrian zone, Florence* 🕾 *055/288672.*

**Sbigoli Terrecotte.** This store carries traditional Tuscan terra-cotta and ceramic vases, pots, and cups and saucers. ⊠ *Via Sant'Egidio 4/r, Santa Croce, Florence* 🕾 *055/2479713* ⊕ *www.sbigoliterrecotte.it.*

## WHERE TO EAT

**$$$$**
ITALIAN
✗ **Frescobaldi Wine Bar.** Frescobaldi serves lunch and dinner in a swank setting. The food is typically Tuscan with twists of fantasy, including *acciughe marinate* (marinated anchovies) and *affettati misti* (a selection of sliced, cured meats). The menu includes a range of pasta dishes and grilled meats. There's a separate wine bar within the restaurant called Frescobaldino. ⊠ *Via de'Magazzini 2–4/r, near Piazza della Signoria* ☎ *055/284724* ⊕ *www.deifrescobaldi.it* ▭ *MC, V* ⊙ *Closed Sun. No lunch Mon.*

**$$$**
ITALIAN
✗ **Il Latini.** It may be the noisiest, most crowded trattoria in Florence, but it's also one of the most delightful ones. The genial host, Torello ("little bull") Latini, presides over his four big dining rooms, and somehow it feels as if you're dining in his home. Ample portions of *ribollita*, the traditional Tuscan vegetable and bread soup, prepare the palate for the hearty meat dishes that follow. Both Florentines and tourists alike tuck into the *agnello fritto* (fried lamb) with aplomb. Though reservations are advised, there's always a wait anyway. ⊠ *Via dei Palchetti 6/r, Santa Maria Novella* ☎ *055/210916* ⊕ *www.illatini.com* ▭ *AE, DC, MC, V* ⊙ *Closed Mon. and 15 days at Christmas.*

# MÁLAGA, SPAIN (WITH MARBELLA, NERJA, AND GRANADA)

The city of Málaga and the surrounding region of eastern Andalusia creates the kind of contrast that makes travel in Spain so tantalizing. A Moorish legacy is a unifying theme and offers some of its most interesting and visually stunning historical attractions. Since the birth of mass tourism, Europeans have flocked here to the Costa del Sol or Sunshine Coast, a 70-km (43-mi) sprawl of hotels, vacation villas, golf courses, marinas, and nightclubs west of Málaga. Since the late 1950s this area has mushroomed from a group of impoverished fishing villages into an overdeveloped seaside playground and retirement haven. Despite the hubbub, you *can* unwind here. Málaga itself is a vibrant Spanish city, virtually untainted by tourism, and inland are quiet whitewashed villages just waiting to be explored.

### ESSENTIALS

CURRENCY
The euro (€1 to US$1.36 at this writing).

HOURS
Museums generally open 9 until 7 or 8, many are closed on Monday and some close in the afternoon. Most stores are open Monday through Saturday 9 to 1:30 and 5 to 8, but a few tourist shops open in the afternoon and on Sunday.

INTERNET
**Navegaweb** ⊠ *Calle Molina Lario 11, Málaga* ☎ *952/352300.*

TELEPHONES
Most tri-band and quad-band GSM phones work in Spain, where mobile services are 3G-compatible. Public kiosks accept phone cards that support international calls (cards sold in press shops, bars, and telecom shops). Major companies include Vodafone.

## COMING ASHORE

The cruise port at Málaga is coming to the end of a vast renovation, which includes a new cruise terminal. The port area will have attractions, including an aquarium, shopping, eateries, and parks that will be draws for local people and international tourists in addition to cruise passengers. Málaga is a large port with several berths, and shuttle buses carry passengers to the terminal areas. Passenger facilities will be extensive once the program is complete.

The city of Málaga awaits just beyond the gates of the port, and you can explore the Old Town on foot. Granada is 1½ hours away to the north by road. Bus services to Granada are frequent, and buses are modern and air-conditioned; the fare at this writing is €15.26 for a single leg. The main bus station is next to the railway station in the city. Taking a taxi from the cruise port is the quickest and simplest transfer. Rail travel from Málaga to Granada is a much slower option, at 3 hours, and with few trains each day this is not a realistic option for passengers in town for just a day. Renting a car would allow you to visit Granada or explore some of the resorts ot countryside surrounding Málaga. The price for an economy manual vehicle is approximately €65 per day.

# EXPLORING MÁLAGA AND VICINITY

## MÁLAGA

**Alcazaba.** Just beyond the ruins of a Roman theater on Calle Alcazabilla, this Moorish fortress is Málaga's greatest monument. It was begun in the 8th century, when Málaga was the principal port of the Moorish kingdom, though most of the present structure dates from the 11th century. The inner palace was built between 1057 and 1063, when the Moorish emirs took up residence; and Ferdinand and Isabella lived here for a while after conquering Málaga in 1487. ⊠ *Entrance on Calle Alcazabilla* 🎟 *€2.10, €3.45 combined with entry to Gibralfaro* ⊙ *Mid-Oct.–mid-Mar., Tues.–Sun. 8.30–6; mid-Mar.–mid-Oct., Tues.–Sun. 8:30–8.*

> ### MÁLAGA BEST BETS
>
> **Climb the parapets of the Alcazaba.** Málaga's Moorish fortress is the city's greatest monument.
>
> **Take a hike in the Parque Natural del Torcal de Antequera.** Walk through a surreal wind-sculpted landscape of pink granite.
>
> **Strolling through the Alhambra.** The Moorish palace in Granada is about 90 minutes from Málaga and well worth the trip.

**Cathedral.** Málaga's main cathedral, built between 1528 and 1782, is a triumph. Because it lacks one of its two towers, the building is nicknamed *La Manquita* (The One-Armed Lady). The enclosed choir, which miraculously survived the burnings of the civil war, is the work of 17th-century artist Pedro de Mena. A walk around the cathedral on Calle Cister will take you to the magnificent Gothic Puerta del Sagrario. ⊠ *C. de Molina Larios* 🕾 *952/215917* 🎟 *€4* ⊙ *Weekdays 10–6, Sat. 10–5:45.*

**Fundación Picasso.** The childhood home of Málaga's most famous native son, Pablo Picasso, has been painted and furnished in the style of the era and houses a permanent exhibition of Picasso's early sketches and sculptures, as well as memorabilia, including the artist's christening robe and family photographs. ⊠ *Pl. de la Merced 15* 🕾 *952/600215* ⊕ *www.fundacionpicasso.malaga.eu* 🎟 *€1* ⊙ *Daily 9:30–8*

**Gibralfaro.** Magnificent vistas beckon at this fort. The fortifications were built for Yusuf I in the 14th century; the Moors called them Jebelfaro, from the Arab word for "mount" and the Greek word for "lighthouse," after a beacon that stood here to guide ships into the harbor and warn of pirates. ⊠ *Gibralfaro Mountain* 🕾 *952/220043* 🎟 *€2.10, €3.45 combined entry with Alcazaba* ⊙ *Nov.–Mar., daily 9–5:45; Apr.–Oct., daily 9–7:45.*

**Mercado de Atarazanas.** From the Plaza Felix Saenz, at the southern end of Calle Nueva, turn onto Sagasta to reach the most colorful market in all of Andalusia. The typical 19th-century iron structure incorporates the original **Puerta de Atarazanas,** the exquisitely crafted 14th-century Moorish gate that once connected the city with the port.

**Fodor's Choice**
★ **Museo Picasso.** The city's most prestigious museum houses works that Pablo Picasso kept for himself or gave to his family. The holdings were largely donated by two family members—Christine and Bernard

Ruiz-Picasso, the artist's daughter-in-law and grandson. The works are displayed in chronological order according to the periods that marked his development as an artist, from blue and rose to cubism, and beyond. ⊠ *C. de San Agustín* ☎ *952/127600* ⊕ *www.museopicassomalaga.org* 🎫 *Permanent exhibition €6, combined permanent and temporary exhibition €8, last Sun. of every month free* ☉ *Tues.–Thurs. 10–8, Fri. and Sat. 10–9.*

**Palacio Episcopa** *(Bishop's Palace).* This building has one of the most stunning facades in the city. It's now a venue for temporary art exhibitions. ⊠ *Pl. Obispo 6* ☎ *952/602722* 🎫 *Free* ☉ *Tues.–Sun. 10–2 and 6–9.*

**Pasaje Chinitas.** Wander the warren of passageways and peep into the dark, vaulted bodegas, where old men down glasses of *seco añejo* or *Málaga Virgen,* local wines made from Málaga's muscatel grapes. Silversmiths and vendors of religious books and statues ply their trades in shops that have changed little since the early 1900s. Backtrack across Larios, and, in the streets leading to Calle Nueva you can see shoeshine boys, lottery-ticket vendors, Gypsy guitarists, and tapas bars with wine served from huge barrels.

## NERJA
★ *52 km (32 mi) east of Málaga.*

Nerja—the name comes from the Moorish word *narixa,* meaning "abundant springs." The village is on a headland above small beaches and rocky coves. In high season, Nerja is packed with tourists, but the rest of the year it's a pleasure to wander the Old Town's narrow streets.

**Balcón de Europa.** Nerja's highlight is the tree-lined promenade with magnificent views, on a promontory just off the central square.

☾ **Cuevas de Nerja** *(Nerja Caves).* These caverns lie between Almuñecar and Nerja on a road surrounded by giant cliffs and dramatic seascapes. The caves are floodlighted for better views of the spires and turrets created by millennia of dripping water. One suspended pinnacle, 200 feet long, is in fact the world's largest known stalactite. ☎ *952/529520* ⊕ *www.cuevanerja.com* 🎫 *€8.50* ☉ *Oct.–Apr., daily 10–2 and 4–6:30; May–Sept., daily 10–7:30.*

## MARBELLA
*52 km (32 mi) west of Málaga.*

Playground of the rich and home of movie stars, rock musicians, and dispossessed royal families, Marbella has attained the top rung on Europe's social ladder. Dip into any Spanish gossip magazine and chances are the glittering parties that fill its pages are set in Marbella. However, much of this action takes place on the fringes—grand hotels and luxury restaurants line the waterfront for 20 km (12 mi) on each side of the town center. In the town itself you may well wonder how Marbella became so famous.

**Old Village.** Marbella's appeal lies in the heart of the Old City, which remains miraculously intact. Here narrow alleys of whitewashed houses cluster around the central **Plaza de los Naranjos** (Orange square), where colorful, albeit pricey, restaurants vie for space under the orange trees.

Climb onto what remains of the old fortifications and stroll along the Calle Virgen de los Dolores to the Plaza de Santo Cristo. Wander the maze of lanes and enjoy the geranium-speckled windows and splashing fountains.

**Puerto Banús.** Marbella's wealth glitters most brightly along the Golden Mile, stretching from Marbella to Puerto Banús. Here a mosque, Arab banks, and the onetime residence of Saudi Arabia's King Fahd betray the influence of oil money in this wealthy enclave. Though now hemmed in by a belt of high-rises, Marbella's plush marina, with 915 berths, is a gem of ostentatious wealth, a Spanish answer to St-Tropez. ⊠ *About 7 km (4½ mi) west of central Marbella.*

## GRANADA
*128 km (80 mi) northeast of Málaga.*

Granada rises majestically from a plain onto three hills, dwarfed—on a clear day—by the Sierra Nevada. Atop one of these hills perches the pink-gold Alhambra palace. The stunning view from its mount takes in the sprawling medieval Moorish quarter, the caves of the Sacromonte, and, in the distance, the fertile *vega* (plain), rich in orchards, tobacco fields, and poplar groves. These days much of the Alhambra and Albaicín areas are closed to cars, because of the difficult access, but starting from the Plaza Nueva there are now minibuses—Nos. 30, 31, 32, and 34—that run frequently to these areas.

**Fodor's** Choice **Alhambra.** With about 2 million annual visitors, the Alhambra is Spain's
★ most popular attraction. Simply take one of the minibuses, Nos. 30 and 32, up from the Plaza Nueva. They run every few minutes; pay the fare of €0.90 on board. The Alhambra was begun in the 1240s by Ibn el-Ahmar, or Alhamar, the first king of the Nasrids. The great citadel once comprised a complex of houses, schools, baths, barracks, and gardens surrounded by defense towers and seemingly impregnable walls. Today only the Alcazaba and the Palacios Nazaríes, built chiefly by Yusuf I (1334–54) and his son Mohammed V (1354–91), remain. The palace is an endless, intricate conglomeration of patios, arches, and cupolas made from wood, plaster, and tile; lavishly colored and adorned with marquetry and ceramics in geometric patterns; and topped by delicate, frothy profusions of lacelike stucco and *mocárabes* (ornamental stalactites).

Entrance to the Alhambra complex of the Alcazaba, Nasrid Palaces, Mosque Baths, and Generalife is strictly controlled by quotas. There are three types of timed tickets: morning, afternoon, and evening, but the evening ticket is valid only for the Nasrid Palaces. Because the number of tickets is limited and subject to availability, try to book your tickets in advance. You can do this in several ways: via the Web (⊕ *www.alhambra-tickets.com*), or via phone (☎ *902/888001*), and tickets can then be collected at the Caixa ticket office at the entrance to the Alhambra just before you make your visit. There is a booking fee of €1.

If you wait and take your chances at the ticket office, its hours are March to October, daily from 8 to 7 and 9:30 to 10:30, and November to February, daily from 8 to 5 and 7:30 to 8:30. Be aware that tickets may be sold out, so prebooking is advised. ⊠ *Cuesta de Gómérez, Alhambra* ⊕ *www.alhambra-patronato.es* ⛦*€12.*

## SHOPPING

Málaga offers a full range of local specialties made throughout the region. Shoes and leather goods are of high quality. Handmade and mass-produced ceramics are produced in a range of colors and styles. Fans and silk shawls, along with other traditional Spanish clothing, range in price, depending on quality. Olives and olive oil will make gourmets happy, and olive oil is also used for a range of hair and beauty products. Other edibles include dried serrano ham, Manchego cheese, and *turrón* (an almond and honey sweet). *Seco añejo* sweet wine is also produced in the region.

In Málaga the main shopping street is Marqués de Larios, known locally as Larios, a traffic-free boulevard with excellent boutiques.

**Corte Inglés.** This department store offers one-stop shopping over its six vast floors. Head to the fifth floor for year-round sale items. ✉ *Av. de Andalucía 4–6* ☎ *952/076500* ⊕ *www.elcorteingles.es* ⊙ *Mon.–Sat. 10–10.*

## BEACHES

Lobster-pink sun worshippers from northern Europe pack these beaches in summer so heavily that there's little towel space on the sand. Beach chairs can be rented for around €5 a day. Beaches range from shingle and pebbles (Almuñecar, Nerja, Málaga) to fine, gritty sand (westward of Málaga). The best are those around Marbella. It's acceptable for women to go topless; if you want to take it *all* off, go to beaches designated *playa naturista*. The most popular nude beach is Maro (near Nerja).

## WHERE TO EAT

¢ ✕ **Logueno.** This traditional tapas bar has two dining spaces: the original
SPANISH well-loved bar shoehorned into a deceptively small space on a side street
**Fodor's Choice** near Calle Larios and a more recent expansion across the street. Check
★ out the original with its L-shape wooden bar crammed with a choice of more than 75 tantalizing tapas, including many Logueno originals, such as grilled oyster mushrooms with garlic, parsley, and goat cheese. There's an excellent selection of Rioja wines, and the service is fast and good, despite the lack of elbow room. ✉ *Marin Garcia s/n* ☎ *No phone* ▭ *No credit cards* ⊙ *Closed Sun.*

$ ✕ **Tintero.** Come to this sprawling, noisy restaurant for the experi-
SPANISH ence rather than the food, which is fine but not spectacular. There's no menu—waiters circle the restaurant carrying various dishes (tapas and main courses) and you choose whatever looks good. The bill is totaled up according to the number and size of the plates on the table at the end of the meal. On the El Palo seafront, Tintero specializes in catch-of-the-day seafood, such as *boquerones* (fresh anchovies), *sepia* (cuttlefish), and the all-time familiar classic, *gambas* (grilled prawns). Be warned that it's packed on Sundays with the local expat community and boisterous Spanish families (i.e., not the place for a romantic

lunch for two). ⊠ *Playa del Dedo, El Palo* ☎ *952/204464* ⊟ *No credit cards* ⊘ *No dinner.*

# MALLORCA, SPAIN

More than five times the size of its fellow Balearic islands, Mallorca is shaped roughly like a saddle. The Sierra de Tramuntana, a dramatic mountain range soaring to nearly 5,000 feet, runs the length of its northwest coast, and a ridge of hills borders the southeast shores; between the two lies a great, flat plain that in early spring becomes a sea of almond blossoms, "the snow of Mallorca." The island draws more than 10 million visitors a year, many of them bound for summer vacation packages in the coastal resorts. The beaches are beautiful, but save time for the charms of the northwest and the interior: caves, bird sanctuaries, monasteries and medieval cities, local museums, outdoor cafés, and village markets.

### ESSENTIALS

CURRENCY  The euro (€1 to US$1.36 at this writing).

HOURS  Museums generally open 9 until 7 or 8, many are closed on Monday and some close in the afternoon. Most stores are open Monday through Saturday 9 to 1:30 and 5 to 8, but tourist shops may open in the afternoon and also on Sunday between May and September.

INTERNET  **Cibertango.com** ⊠ *Calle San Cristobal 20, Palma* ☎ *971/442826.*

TELEPHONES  Most tri-band or quad-band GSM phones will work in Spain, where services are 3G-compatible. Public kiosks accept phone cards that support international calls (cards sold in press shops, bars, and telecom shops). Major companies include Vodafone.

### COMING ASHORE

Vessels dock at the port directly in front of the old town of Palma. There is no shuttle, so passengers docking at the farthest berth (south side of the harbor) have a 20-minute walk to the terminal building and the port entrance. From the port entrance you can walk into Palma town. There are few facilities at the cruise terminal or in the port.

If you only want to enjoy Palma, you won't need to worry about transportation; however, Mallorca is a small island, and you can see a great deal of it in a day with a vehicle or on public transportion. Regular and reliable bus services link the major towns, though services are fewer on Sunday. Car rentals cost around €65 per day for an economy manual vehicle, but it's much cheaper to explore by public transit.

# EXPLORING MALLORCA

### PALMA DE MALLORCA

If you look north of the cathedral (La Seu, or the "seat" of the Bishopric, to Mallorcans) on a map of the city of Palma, you can see the jumble of tiny streets around the Plaça Santa Eulalia that made up the early town. A stroll through these streets will bring you past many interesting neoclassical and modernist buildings.

**Ajuntament** *(Town Hall).* Carrer Colom brings you to the 17th-century; stop in to see the collection of *gigantes*—the huge painted and costumed mannequins paraded through the streets at festivals—on display in the lobby. The olive tree on the right side of the square is one of Mallorca's so-called *olivos milenarios*—thousand-year-old olives—and may be even older. ⊠ *Plaça Cort.*

**Castell de Bellver** *(Bellver Castle).* Overlooking the city and the bay from a hillside above the Terreno nightlife area, this castle was built at the beginning the 14th century, in Gothic style but with a circular design—the only one of its kind in Spain. The fortress houses an archeological **museum** of the history of Mallorca, and a small collection of classical sculpture. ⊠ *Camilo José Cela s/n* ☎ *971/730657* ⬚*€2.50, free Sun.* ☺ *Castle and museum Oct.– Mar., Mon.–Sat. 8:30–6:45; Apr.–Sept., Mon.–Sat. 8:30–8:30. Castle only Sun. 10–4:30.*

**Fodor'sChoice**
★ **Cathedral.** Palma's cathedral is an architectural wonder that took almost 400 years to build (1230–1601). The extraordinarily wide (63-foot) expanse of the nave is supported on 14 extraordinarily slender 70-foot-tall columns, which fan out at the top like palm trees. The nave is dominated by an immense rose window, 40 feet in diameter, from 1370. Over the main altar (consecrated in 1346) is the almost surrealistic **baldoquí** by Antoni Gaudí: an enormous canopy, lamps suspended from it like elements of a mobile, rising to a Crucifixion scene at the top. This is Gaudí's most remarkable contribution to the remodeling of the Royal Chapel—a project he worked on for six years, and completed in 1912. To the right of it, in the Chapel of the Santísima, is an equally remarkable work by the modern sculptor Miquel Barceló: a painted ceramic tableau that covers the walls of the chapel like a skin. Unveiled in 2007, the tableau is based on the New Testament account of the miracle of the loaves and fishes. ⊠ *Pl. Almoina s/n, Barrio Antiguo* ☎ *971/723130* ⊕ *www.catedraldemallorca.org* ⬚*€4* ☺ *Apr. and May, weekdays 10–5:15; June–Sept., weekdays 10–6:15; Oct.–Mar., weekdays 10–3:15; year-round, Sat. 10–2:15, Sun. for worship only, 8:30–1:45, 6:30–7:45.*

**Llotja** *(Exchange).* This commodities exchange was built in the 15th century. With its decorative turrets, battlements, fluted pillars, and Gothic stained-glass windows—part fortress, part church—it attests to the veneration of wealth Mallorca achieved in its heyday as a Mediterranean trading power. It can be visited inside only when there are special exhibitions in the Merchants Chamber. ⊠ *Pl. de la Llotja 5, La Llotja* ☎ *971/711705* ☺ *During exhibits, Tues.–Sat. 11–2 and 5–9, Sun. 11–2.*

---

**MALLORCA BEST BETS**

**The Cathedral.** Palma's cathedral has a unique circular design as well as decrations by Gaudí.

**Museu d'Es Baluard.** The museum of modern and contemporary art is an exciting convergence of old and new.

**Sóller.** One of the most beautiful towns on the island, with a large collection of moderniste buildings.

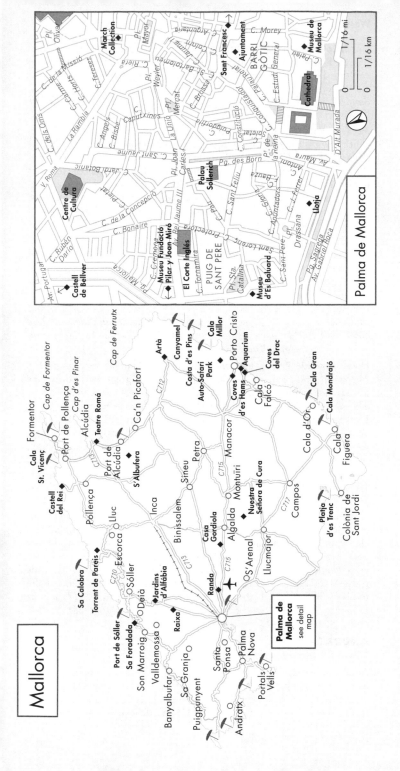

# Mallorca

Cap de Formentor
Cap d'es Pinar
Cap de Ferrutx

Formentor
Cala St. Vicenç
Port de Pollença
Alcúdia
Teatre Romà
Port de Alcúdia
Ca'n Picafort
S'Albufera

Castell del Rei
Pollença
Lluc
Escorca
Inca
Binissalem
Sineu
Petra
Manacor

Sa Calobra
Torrent de Pareis
Sóller
Jardins d'Alfàbia
Son Marroig
Deià
Raixa
Valldemossa

Port de Sóller
Sa Foradada

Banyalbufar
Sa Granja
Puigpunyent

Andratx
Portals Vells

Santa Ponsa
Palma Nova

**Palma de Mallorca**
see detail map

Casa Gordiola
Algaida
Randa
S'Arenal
Llucmajor

Montuïri
Nuestra Señora de Cura
Campos

Artà
Canyamel
Costa d'es Pins
Cala Millor
Porto Cristo
Aquarium
Auto-Safari Park
Coves d'es Hams
Coves del Drac
Cala Falcó
Cala d'Or
Cala Gran
Cala Mondrajó
Cala Figuera

Platja d'es Trenc
Colònia de Sant Jordi

C712
C713
C710
C715
C717

0        10 miles
0      15 km

---

## Palma de Mallorca

March Collection
Pl. Olivar
Pl. Mayol
C. de la Missió
C. carnal
C. dels Horts
C. Teresates
C. Terestes
La Rambla
C. dels Oms
V. Roma
Jard Botanic
C. Rubén Dario
Av. Portugal

**Castell de Bellver**

Centre de Cultura
C. de la Concepció
C. Bonaire
C. Cremona
C. Sant Jaume
C. Angels
C. Bisbe
C. Caputxines
C. Concepció
Pl. Mercat
La Unió
Pl. Pou
C. Brossa
C. Weyler
St. Bartolomeu
C. Corrin
C. Jaume II
C. Argentina

**Sant Francesc**
**Ajuntament**
C. Morey
BARRI GOTIC
**Museu de Mallorca**
Palau

**Cathedral**
C. Estudi General

Museu Fundació Pilar y Joan Miró
El Corte Inglés
PUIG DE SANT PERE
Pl. Sta. Catalina
**Museu d'Es Baluard**

**Palau Solleric**
Pg. des Born
C. Sant Feliu
C. Pau
Av. Rei Jaume III
C. Protectora
Sant Llorenç
C. Sant Pere
Drassana
Pl.
Pg. Sagrera
Av. Gabriel Roca

**Llotja**

D'Alt Murada
Av. Maura
Antoni
Bauzà
C. Ferrer
C. J. Ferrer
C. Glòria
C. Apuntadors

0        1/16 mi
0        1/16 km

★ **March Collection.** This fine little museum was established by the Joan March Foundation in a sumptuous private home dating to the 18th century. The second and third floors were redesigned to accommodate a series of small galleries with works by Picasso, Miró, and Dalí. ⊠ C. *Sant Miguel 11* ☎ *971/713515* ⊕ *www.march.es/museupalma* ✉ *Free* ⊙ *Weekdays 10–6:30, Sat. 10:30–2.*

**Museu de Mallorca.** From the Plaça Sant Francesc, take Carrer Pere Nadal south toward the bay; the street changes names as it descends. On the left as it turns to Carrer de la Portella is the 18th-century ducal palace of the Condes de Ayamans. The museum housed here exhibits the findings of all the major archaeological research on Mallorca, from prehistory to the Roman, Vandal, and Moorish occupations: pottery, bronzes, stone burial chambers, tools, and ornaments. ⊠ *Portella 5, Barrio Antiguo* ☎ *971/717540* ✉ *€2.40* ⊙ *Tues.–Sat. 10–7, Sun. 10–2.*

★ **Museu d'Es Baluard.** Inaugurated in January 2004, the Museum of Modern and Contemporary Art of Palma is an outstanding convergence of old and new: the exhibition space uses and merges into the surviving 16th-century perimeter walls of the fortified city, with a stone courtyard facing the sea and a promenade along the ramparts. The collection includes work by Miró, Picasso, Magritte, Tapiès, Calder, and other major artists. ⊠ *Plaça Porta de Santa Catalina s/n, Puig Sant Pere* ☎ *971/908200* ⊕ *www.esbaluard.org* ✉ *€6* ⊙ *Oct.–June 15, Tues.–Sun. 10–8; June 16–Sept., Tues.–Sun. 10–10.*

**Museu Fundació Pilar y Joan Miró** *(Pilar and Joan Miró Foundation Museum).* The permanent collection includes a great many drawings and studies by the Catalan artist, who spent his last years on Mallorca. The adjacent studio was built for Miró by his friend the architect Josep Lluis Sert; the artist did most of his work here from 1957 on; the rooms are filled with paintings—on easels, stacked against walls—still in progress when he died. The museum is 3 km (2 mi) west of the city center, off the Passeig Marítim. ⊠ *Carrer Joan de Saridakis 29, Cala Major, Marivent* ☎ *971/701420* ⊕ *miro.palmademallorca.es* ✉ *€6* ⊙ *Sept. 16–May 15, Tues.–Sat. 10–6, Sun. 10–3; May 16–Sept. 15, Tues.–Sat. 10–7, Sun. 10–3.*

**Sant Francesc.** From the Plaça de Sant Eulalia, take the Carrer del Convent de Sant Francesc to see the beautiful 13th-century monastery church established by Jaume II when his eldest son took monastic orders and gave up rights to the throne. Fra Junípero Serra, the missionary who founded San Francisco, California, was later educated here; his statue stands to the left of the main entrance. The basilica houses the tomb of the eminent 13th-century scholar Ramón Llull. ⊠ *Plaça Sant Francesc, Barrio Antiguo* ☎ *971/712695* ✉ *€1* ⊙ *Mon.–Sat. 9:30–1 and 3–6, Sun. 9:30–1.*

## ANDRATX

*16 km (10 mi) west of Palma.*

Andratx is a charming cluster of white-and-ocher hillside houses, rather like cliff dwellings, with the 3,363-foot Mt. Galatzó behind it. Many of the towns on Majorca are at some distance from their seafronts; from Andratx you can take a 4-km (1½-mi) drive through S'Arracó to

Sant Elm and on to the rocky shore opposite Sa Dragonera—an island shaped indeed like the long-armored back of a dragon. Local history has it that the tiny island of Pantaleu, just to the west of it, was where Jaume I chose to disembark in September 1200, on his campaign to retake Majorca from the Moors.

## VALLDEMOSSA

*18 km (11 mi) north of Palma.*

**Reial Cartuja** *(Royal Carthusian Monastery).* The monastery was founded in 1339, but when the monks were expelled in 1835 it was privatized, and the cells became apartments for travelers. The most famous lodgers were Frédéric Chopin and his lover, the Baroness Amandine Dupin— better known by her nom de plume, George Sand—who spent three difficult months here in the winter of 1838–39. The tourist office, in the plaza next to the church, sells a ticket good for all of the monastery's attractions. ⊠ *Pl. de la Cartuja s/n* ☎ *971/612106* 🖨 *971/612514* ⊕ *www.valldemossa.com* 🎫 *€8* ✆ *Dec. and Jan., Mon.–Sat. 9:30–5; Feb., Mon.–Sat. 9:30–5, Sun. 10–1; Mar. and Oct., Mon.–Sat. 9:30– 5:30, Sun. 10–1; Apr.–Sept., Mon.–Sat. 9:30–6:30, Sun. 10–1; Nov. 9:30–4:30, Sun. 10–1.*

## JARDINS D'ALFÀBIA

*17 km (10½ mi) north of Palma.*

You don't often hear in the Majorcan interior what you hear in the Alfàbia Gardens: the sound of falling water. The Moorish viceroy of the island developed the springs and hidden irrigation systems here sometime in the 12th century to create this remarkable oasis on the road to Sóller, with its 40-odd varieties of trees, climbers, and flowering shrubs. The 17th-century manor house has a collection of original documents that chronicle the history of the estate. ⊠ *Ctra. Palma–Sóller, Km. 17* ☎ *971/613123* ⊕ *www.jardinesdealfabia.com* 🎫 *€4.50* ✆ *Nov.–Mar., weekdays 9–5:30, Sat. 9–1; Apr.–Oct., Mon.–Sat. 9–6:30.*

## ★ SÓLLER

*13 km (8 ½ mi) north of Jardins d'Alfàbia, 30 km (19 mi) north of Palma.*

This is one of the most beautiful towns on the island, thick with palatial homes built in the 19th and early 20th centuries by the owners of agricultural estates in the Sierra de Tramuntana, and the merchants who thrived on the export of the region's oranges, lemons, and almonds. Many of the buildings here, like the **Church of Sant Bartomeu** and the **Bank of Sóller,** on the Plaça Constitució, and the nearby **Can Prunera,** are gems of the Moderniste style, designed by contemporaries of Antoni Gaudí. The tourist information office in the **Town Hall,** next to Sant Bartomeu, has a walking tour map of the important sites.

Travel retro to Sóller from Palma on one of the six daily trains (round-trip: €20) from Plaça d'Espanya: a string of wooden coaches with leather-covered seats, dating from 1912.

Visit the Station Building Galleries before you set out on your exploration of the town—and if you're spending the night, book early: Sóller is not overly endowed with hotels.

Return to the station to catch the charming old blue-and-brass trolly (€4) that threads its way through town, down to Port de Sóller. Spend the day at the beach. Better yet: rent a car at the port for the spectacular drive over the Sierra de Tramontana to Deià and Son Marroig, or the Monestary of Lluc.

**Station Building Galleries.** Sóller's Station Building Galleries have two small collections, one of engravings by Joan Miró, the other of ceramics by Picasso. ⊠ *Pl. Espanya 6* ☎ *971/360130* ⊕ *www.trendesoller.com* ⊠ *Free* ⊗ *Daily 10:30–6:30.*

## DEIÀ

★ *9 km (5½ mi) southwest of Sóller.*

Deià is perhaps best known as the adopted home of the English poet and writer Robert Graves, who lived here off and on from 1929 until his death in 1985. The village is still a favorite haunt of writers and artists, including Graves's son Tomás, author of *Pa amb oli (Bread and Olive Oil)*, a guide to Majorcan cooking, and British painter David Templeton. The setting is unbeatable; all around Deià rise the steep cliffs of the Sierra de Tramuntana. On warm afternoons literati gather at the beach bar in the rocky cove at Cala de Deià, 2 km (1 mi) downhill from the village. Walk up the narrow street to the village church; the small **cemetery** behind it affords views of mountains terraced with olive trees and of the coves below. It's a fitting spot for Graves's final resting place, in a quiet corner beneath a simple slab.

**Ca N'Alluny.** In 2007 the Fundació Robert Graves opened a museum dedicated to Deià's most famous resident, in the house he built in 1932, overlooking the sea. (⊠ *Ctra. Deià-Sóller s/n* ☎ *971/636185* ⊕ *www.lacasaderobertgraves.com* ⊠ *€5* ⊗ *Apr.–Oct., weekdays 10–5, Sat. 10–3; Nov., Feb., and Mar., weekdays 9–4. Sat. 9–2; Dec. and Jan., weekdays 10–3).*

# SHOPPING

Mallorca's specialties are leather shoes and clothing, porcelain, souvenirs carved from olive wood, handblown glass, artificial pearls, and espadrilles. Top-name fashion boutiques line **Avinguda Jaume III** and the nearby Plaça Joan Carles I. You can find several antiques shops on Plaça Almoina. Less-expensive shopping strips are **Carrer Sindicat** and **Carrer Sant Miquel**—both pedestrian streets running north from the Plaça Major—and the small streets south of the Plaça Major. The **Plaça Major** itself has a modest crafts market Monday, Thursday, Friday, and Saturday 10 to 2. In summer the market is open daily 10 to 2; January and February, it's open weekends only.

**Gordiola.** Visit this glassmaker, which has been in business since 1719, for a variety of original bowls, bottles, plates, and decorative objects. ⊠ *Carrer de la Victoria 2, Centro* ☎ *971/711541* ⊕ *www.gordiola.com.*

**Las Columnas.** This store has ceramics from all over the Balearic Islands. ⊠ *C. Sant Domingo 24, Barrio Antiguo.*

**2**

**Loewe.** Leather is best in the high-end branch of the famed Spanish firm founded in 1846. ☒ *Av. Jaime III 1, Centro* ☎ *971/715275* ⊕ *www. loewe.com.*

## GOLF

Mallorca has more than a score of 18-hole golf courses, among them PGA championship venues of fiendish difficulty.

**Son Vida Golf.** This club offers 18 holes. ☒ *Next to Castillo Son Vida hotel, 5 km [3 mi] from Palma, Son Vida* ☎ *971/791210* ⊕ *www. golfsonvida.com.*

## BEACHES

The closer a beach is to Palma, the more crowded it's likely to be. West of the city is **Palma Nova**; behind the lovely, narrow beach rises one of the most densely developed resorts on the island. **Paguera,** with several small beaches, is the only sizable local resort not overshadowed by high-rises. **Camp de Mar,** with a good beach of fine white sand, is small and relatively undeveloped, but is sometimes overrun with day-trippers from other resorts. **Sant Elm,** at the end of this coast, has a pretty little bay and a tree-shaded parking lot. East of Palma, a 5-km (3-mi) stretch of sand runs along the main coastal road from C'an Pastilla to Arenal, forming a package-tour nexus also known collectively as **Playa de Palma**; the crowded beach is long with fine white sand.

## WHERE TO EAT

¢   ✗ **Café la Lonja.** Both the sunny terrace in front of the Llotja—a privi-
SPANISH   leged dining spot—and the restaurant inside are excellent places for drinks, tapas, baguettes, sandwiches, and salads. The seasonal menu might include a salad of tomato, avocado, and Manchego cheese; fluffy quiche; and tapas of squid or mushrooms. It's a good rendezvous point and watering hole. ☒ *Carrer Lonja del Mar 2, La Llotja* ☎ *971/722799* ▤ *AE, MC, V* ⊗ *Closed Sun.*

¢–$   ✗ **La Bóveda.** Within hailing distance of the Llotja, with a huge front
SPANISH   window, this bustling, popular eatery serves tapas and inexpensive platters such *revuelto con setas y jamón* (scrambled eggs with mushrooms and ham). Tables are at a premium; there's additional seating at the counter, or on stools around upended wine barrels. Nothing fancy here: just ample portions of good food. ☒ *Carrer de la Botería 3, La Llotja, Palma* ☎ *971/714863* ⊕ *restaurantelaboveda.com* ▤ *AE, MC, V* ⊗ *Closed Sun. and Feb.*

# MARSEILLE, FRANCE

Marseille may sometimes be given a wide berth by travelers in search of a Provençal idyll, but it's their loss. Miss it, and you miss one of the most vibrant, exciting cities in France. With its cubist jumbles of white stone rising up over a picture-book seaport, bathed in light of blinding clarity and crowned by larger-than-life neo-Byzantine churches, the city's neighborhoods teem with multiethnic life. Its souklike African markets reek deliciously of spices and coffees, and its labyrinthine Vieille Ville is painted in broad strokes of saffron, cinnamon, and robin's-egg blue. Feisty and fond of broad gestures, Marseille is a dynamic city, as cosmopolitan now as when the Phoenicians first founded it, and with all the exoticism of the international shipping port it has been for 2,600 years. Vital to the Crusades in the Middle Ages and crucial to Louis XIV as a military port, Marseille flourished as France's market to the world—and still does today. In 2013 Marseille will be the European Capital of Culture and will host all manner of special events throughout the year.

> **MARSEILLE BEST BETS**
>
> **Order bouillabaise.** This aromatic fish stew is one of the world's most famous dishes, and originated here as a way for fishermen to use the leftover catch.
>
> **Stroll around Viuex Port and La Panier.** The Vieux Port bustles with activity, but especially during the morning fish market. Neighboring Le Panier is a maze of narrow streets and picturesque corners with pretty boutiques and good museums.
>
> **Centre de la Vieille Charite.** The museums here have important collections and artifacts from civilizations and societies from around the world.

## ESSENTIALS

CURRENCY The euro (€1 to US$1.36 at this writing).

HOURS Stores are open Monday through Saturday 9–7, but many close at lunchtime (usually noon–2 or 3) and some will open later and on Sunday during July and August. Museums are open 10–5, but most are closed on either Monday or Tuesday.

INTERNET **Info Café** (⊠ *1 Quai de Rive Neuve* ☎ *04–91–33–74–98*), at the southeast corner of the port, is convenient; it's open Monday–Saturday 9 AM–10 PM and Sunday 2:30–7:30, and charges about €4 per hour of access.

TELEPHONES Tri-band GSM phones work in France. You can buy prepaid phone cards at telecom shops, news vendors, and tobacconists in all towns and cities. Phone cards can be used for local or international calls. France Telecom and Orange are leading telecom companies.

## COMING ASHORE

The Marseille Cruise Terminal is north of the Vieux Port historic area and has recently benefited from a €90 million redevelopment. It now offers three different docking areas depending on the size of the vessel and a state-of-the-art welcome center with an ATM, shops, bars, and restaurants. Aside from this, the terminal is in an industrial area and is too distant to allow you to walk into the city. Most cruise lines offer shuttle service into town, but you should spring for a taxi if you don't take the shuttle.

A taxi from the cruise terminal into town is approximately €27 and takes around 20 minutes. Once in the Vieux Port area, most of the major attractions are reachable on foot. Taxis are plentiful and can provide tourist itineraries. Single journeys begin at €2.30 and are €0.77 per km thereafter.

Although there is no reason to drive if you're just staying in Marseille, renting a vehicle is the ideal way to explore the beautiful Provençal towns and landscapes around the city. Expect to pay around €75 per day for an economy manual vehicle.

## EXPLORING MARSEILLE

**Cathédrale de la Nouvelle Major.** A gargantuan, neo-Byzantine 19th-century fantasy, the cathedral was built under Napoléon III—but not before he'd ordered the partial destruction of the lovely 11th-century original, once a perfect example of the Provençal Romanesque style. You can view the flashy decor—marble and rich red porphyry inlay—in the newer of the two churches; the medieval one is more sedate in style. ⊠ *Pl. de la Major, Le Panier.*

★ **Centre de la Vieille Charité** *(Center of the Old Charity).* At the top of the Panier district, this superb ensemble of 17th- and 18th-century architecture was designed as a hospice for the homeless by Marseillais artist-architects Pierre and Jean Puget. Even if you don't enter the museums, walk around the inner court, studying the retreating perspective of triple arcades and admiring the baroque chapel with its novel egg-peaked dome. Of the complex's two museums, the larger is the **Musée d'Archéologie Méditerranéenne** (Museum of Mediterranean Archaeology), with a sizable collection of pottery and statuary from classical Mediterranean civilization, elementally labeled (for example, "pot"). There's also a display on the mysterious Celt-like Ligurians who first peopled the coast, cryptically presented with emphasis on the digs instead of the finds themselves. The best of the lot is the evocatively mounted Egyptian collection, the second-largest in France after the Louvre's. There are mummies, hieroglyphs, and gorgeous sarcophagi in a tomblike setting. Upstairs, the **Musée d'Arts Africains, Océaniens, et Amérindiens** (Museum of African, Oceanic, and American Indian Art) creates a theatrical foil for the works' intrinsic drama: the spectacular masks and sculptures are mounted along a pure black wall, lighted indirectly, with labels across the aisle. ⊠ *2 rue de la Charité, Le Panier* ☎ *04–91–14–58–80* ⊕ *www.vieille-charite-marseille.org* ⊠ €2 *per museum* ☉ *June–Sept., Tues.–Sun. 11–6; Oct.–May, Tues.–Sun. 10–5.*

★ **Château d'If.** François I, in the 16th century, recognized the strategic advantage of an island fortress surveying the mouth of Marseille's vast harbor, so he had one built. Its effect as a deterrent was so successful that it never saw combat, and was eventually converted into a prison. It was here that Alexandre Dumas locked up his most famous character, the Count of Monte Cristo. Though the count was fictional, the hole Dumas had him escape through is real enough, and is visible in the cells today. Video monitors playing relevant scenes from dozens of Monte Cristo films bring each tower and cell to life. On the other hand, the real-life Man in the Iron Mask, whose supposed cell is still being shown, was not actually imprisoned here. You get here by boat, and the ride plus the views from the broad terrace alone are worth the

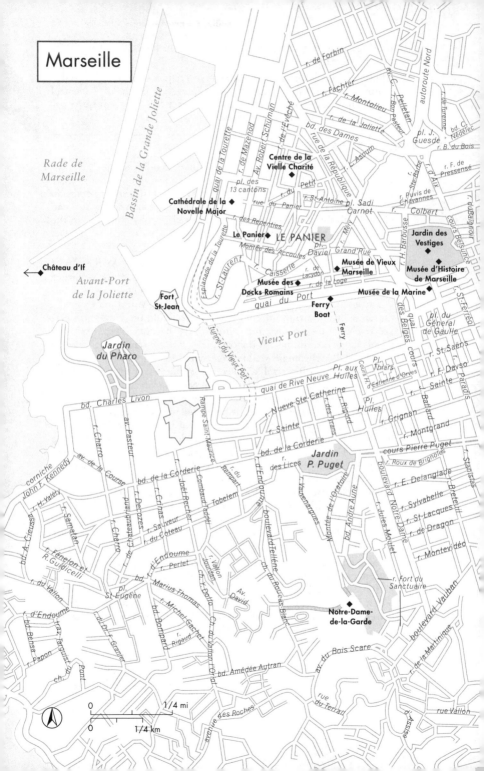

trip. ☎ *04–91–59–02–30 château, 04–91–46–54–65 boat information* ⊕ *www.frioul-if-express.com* ✉ *Château €5, boat ride from Quai des Belges €10* ☉ *Apr.–Sept. 14, daily 9–6:30; Sept. 15–Mar., Tues.–Sun. 9:30–5.*

**Fodor's Choice**
★
**Ferry Boat.** Departing from the quay below the Hôtel de Ville, the ferry is a Marseille treasure. To hear the natives pronounce "fer-ry bo-at" (they've adopted the English) is one of the joys of a visit here. You can file onto this 45-seater solar-electric barge and glide across the Vieux Port taking in the sights and sounds of this bustling fishing harbor for free. ✉ *Pl. des Huiles on Quai de Rive Neuve side and Hôtel de Ville on Quai du Port, Vieux Port* ✉ *Free.*

**Jardin des Vestiges** *(Garden of Remains).* Just behind the Marseille History Museum, this garden stands on the site of Marseille's classical waterfront, and includes remains of the Greek fortifications and loading docks. It was discovered in 1967 when roadwork was being done next to the Bourse (stock exchange). ✉ *Centre Bourse, Vieux Port* ☎ *04–91–90–42–22* ✉ *€3, includes entry to Musée d'Histoire* ☉ *Mon.–Sat. noon–7.*

★ **Le Panier.** The old heart of Marseille is a maze of high shuttered houses looming over narrow cobbled streets, *montées* (stone stairways), and tiny squares. Long decayed and neglected, it is the principal focus of the city's efforts at urban renewal. Wander this atmospheric neighborhood at will, making sure to stroll along Rue du Panier, the Montée des Accoules, Rue du Petit-Puits, and Rue des Muettes.

**Musée des Docks Romains** *(Roman Docks Museum).* In 1943 Hitler destroyed the neighborhood along the Quai du Port—some 2,000 houses—displacing 20,000 citizens. This act of brutal urban renewal, ironically, laid the ground open for new discoveries. When the rebuilding of Marseille was begun in 1947, workers dug up remains of a Roman shipping warehouse full of the terra-cotta jars and amphorae that once lay in the bellies of low-slung ships. The museum created around it demonstrates the scale of Massalia's shipping prowess. ✉ *10 pl. de Vivaux, Vieux Port* ☎ *04–91–91–24–62* ✉ *€2* ☉ *Oct.–May, Tues.–Sun. 10–5; June–Sept., Tues.–Sun. 11–6.*

★ **Musée d'Histoire de Marseille** *(Marseille History Museum).* The modern, open museum illuminates Massalia's history by mounting its treasure of archaeological finds in didactic displays and miniature models of the city as it appeared in various stages of history. There's a real Greek-era wooden boat in a hermetically sealed display case. ✉ *Centre Bourse, entrance on Rue de Bir-Hakeim, Vieux Port* ☎ *04–91–90–42–22* ✉ *€3, includes entry into Jardin des Vestiges* ☉ *June–Sept., Mon.–Sat. 10–6; Oct.–May, Tues.–Sun. 10–5.*

**Musée de la Marine et de l'Economie de Marseille** *(Marine and Economy Museum).* One of many museums devoted to Marseille's history as a shipping port was inaugurated by Napoléon III in 1860. The impressive building houses both the museum and the city's Chamber of Commerce. The front entrance and hallway are lined with medalions celebrating the ports of the world with which the city has traded, or trades still. The museum charts the maritime history of Marseille from the 17th century onward with paintings and engravings. It's a model lover's dream with hundreds of steamboats and schooners, all in miniature. ⊠ *Palais de la Bourse, 9 La Canebière, La Canebière* ☎ *04–91–39–33–33* 💬 *€2* ⊙ *Daily 10–6.*

**Musée du Vieux Marseille** *(Museum of Old Marseille).* In the 16th-century **Maison Diamantée** (diamond house)—so named for its diamond-faceted Renaissance facade—was built in 1570 by a rich merchant. Focusing on the history of Marseille, the newly reopened, painstakingly renovated museum features *santons* (figurines), crèches, and furniture offering a glimpse into 18th-century Marseille life. ⊠ *Rue de la Prison, Vieux Port* ☎ *04–91–55–28–69* 💬 *€2* ⊙ *June–Sept., Tues.–Sun. 10–6; Oct.–May, Tues.–Sun. 10–5.*

**Notre-Dame-de-la-Garde.** Towering above the city and visible for miles around, the preposterously overscaled neo-Byzantine monument was erected in 1853 by the ever-tasteful Napoléon III. Its interior is a Technicolor bonanza of red-and-beige stripes and glittering mosaics. The gargantuan *Madonna and Child* on the steeple (almost 30 feet high) is covered in real gold leaf. The boggling panoply of naive ex-votos, mostly thanking the Virgin for death-bed interventions and shipwreck survivals, makes the pilgrimage worth it. ✣ *On foot, climb up Cours Pierre Puget, cross Jardin Pierre Puget, cross bridge to Rue Vauvenargues, and hike up to Pl. Edon. Or catch Bus 60 from Cours Jean-Ballard* ☎ *04–91–13–40–80* ⊕ *www.notredamedelagarde.com* ⊙ *May–Sept., daily 7* AM*–7:15* PM*; Oct.–Apr., daily 7–6.*

# SHOPPING

Marseille offers contrasting shopping opportunities. For lovers of French haute couture there are many boutiques in the new town stocking the major designer labels—Christian Lacroix is a local boy—plus a thriving new fashion scene of young designers selling their own ready-to-wear collections from stylish galleries. Cours Julien is lined with stores, while Rue de la Tour in the Opera district is a center of modern design, known locally as "Fashion Street."

By contrast, the city, particularly Le Panier and rue St-Ferréol, also has numerous shops selling regional crafts and delicacies, including bright fabrics of blue and yellow, pottery, olive-wood items, plus delicious olives, olive oils, honey, tapenade (an olive paste), and dried herbs. **Savon de Marseille** (Marseille soap) is a household standard in France, often sold as a satisfyingly crude and hefty block in odorless olive-oil green. But its chichi offspring are dainty pastel guest soaps in almond, lemon, vanilla, and other scents.

**Four des Navettes.** The locally famous bakery, up the street from Notre-Dame-de-la-Garde, makes orange-spice, shuttle-shape *navettes*. These cookies are modeled on the little boat in which Mary Magdalene and Lazarus supposedly washed up onto Europe's shores and are a Marseille specialty. ⊠ *136 rue Sainte, Garde Hill* ☎ *04–91–33–32–12* ⊕ *www. fourdesnavettes.com.*

**La Compagnie de Provence.** This is a major producer of savon de Marseille and has an excellent range to choose from. ⊠ *1 rue Caisserie, Le Panier* 🕾 *04–91–56–20–94* ⊕ *www.compagniedeprovence.com.*

**Santons Marcel Carbonel.** This store designs and fabricates the traditional "santons" and "creches" displayed at Christmastime in Provençal churches and homes. ⊠ *49 rue Neuve Sainte Catherine, Vieux Port* 🕾 *04–91–13–61–36* ⊕ *www.santonsmarcelcarbonel.com.*

## WHERE TO EAT

**$$$$** ✘ **Chez Fonfon.** Tucked into the film-ready tiny fishing port Vallon des
SEAFOOD   Auffes, this is a Marseillais landmark. Yes, it's expensive at €46, but try classic bouillabaisse served with all the bells and whistles—broth, hot-chili rouille, and flamboyant table-side filleting—if you want a genuinely Marseille experience. ⊠ *140 rue du Vallon des Auffes, Vallon des Auffes* 🕾 *04–91–52–14–38* ⊕ *www.chez-fonfon.com* ⚓ *Reservations essential* ⊟ *AE, DC, MC, V* ☉ *Closed Sun. and 1st 2 wks in Jan. No lunch Mon.*

**$$** ✘ **Etienne.** This historic Le Panier hole-in-the-wall has more than just
FRENCH   good fresh-anchovy pizza from a wood-burning oven. There are also
★   fried squid, eggplant gratin, a slab of rare-grilled beef big enough for two, and the quintessential *pieds et paquets,* Marseille's earthy classic of sheeps' feet and stuffed tripe. Be warned: pizza is considered an appetizer here, and main courses are huge. ⊠ *43 rue de la Lorette, Le Panier* 🕾 *No phone* ⊟ *No credit cards.*

# MENORCA, SPAIN (MAHÓN)

Menorca, the northernmost Balearic island, is a knobby, cliff-bound plateau with a single central hill—El Toro—from whose 1,100-foot summit you can see the whole island. Prehistoric monuments—*taulas* (huge stone T-shapes), *talayots* (spiral stone cones), and *navetes* (stone structures shaped like overturned boats)—left by the first Neolithic settlers are everywhere on the island, rising up out of a landscape of small, tidy fields bounded by hedgerows and drystone walls. Tourism came late to Menorca, but having sat out the early Balearic boom, Menorca has avoided many of the other islands' industrialization troubles: there are no high-rise hotels, and the herringbone road system, with a single central highway, means that each resort is small and separate.

### ESSENTIALS

CURRENCY   The euro (€1 to US$1.36 at this writing).

HOURS   Museums generally open 9 until 7 or 8, many are closed on Monday and some close in the afternoon. Most stores are open Monday through Saturday 9 to 1:30 and 5 to 8, but a few tourist shops may open in the afternoon and also on Sunday between May and September.

TELEPHONES   Most tri-band or quad-band GSM phones will work in Spain, where services are 3G-compatible. Public kiosks accept phone cards that support international calls (cards sold in press shops, bars and telecom shops). Major companies include Vodafone.

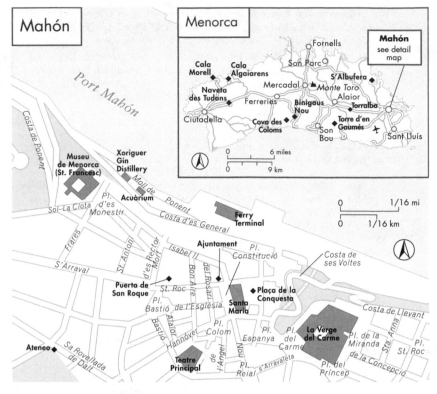

**COMING ASHORE**

Vessels dock at the commercial port in Mahón, which sits directly below the Old Town. From here it is a short but steep walk up to the heart of the Old Town. There are few facilities at the port itself, but a selection of shops and cafés line the shady street outside. Taxis wait outside the port, and drivers can be hired for the day to do tourist itineraries.

Menorca is a small island, and you can travel across it in 40 minutes by vehicle. Public bus services are modern and reliable, but services to the smaller towns may not be frequent. The bus station is at the far side of Mahón and involves a steep climb from the port area. It might be advisable to take a taxi to the station. The journey time from Mahón to Ciutadella is 1 hour. Renting a car is the ideal way to get around; expect to pay as much as €65 per day for an economy manual vehicle.

# EXPLORING MENORCA

### MAHÓN

Established as the island's capital in 1722, when the British began their nearly 80-year occupation, Mahón still bears the stamp of its former rulers. The streets nearest the port are lined with four-story Georgian town houses in various states of repair; the Mahónese still nurse a craving for Chippendale furniture, and drink gin. You'll notice as you travel around the town and island that Menorcans use both Catalan and Castillian names in signage, Catalon most often by the people themselves. So you may hear Mahón called, simply, Maó by the locals, and will also see this on signs.

**Ajuntament.** Mahón's city hall is a large Georgian building. Reach it by walking up Carrer Alfons III from the Plaça de la Conquesta. Nearby, on Carrer Isabel II, you'll find many of the more imposing Georgian homes in Menorca. ✉ *Pl. de la Constitució 1* ☎ *971/369800.*

**Ateneo** (*Ateneu*). A good place to begin your tour of Mahón is at the northwest corner of the Plaça de S'Esplanada. Stop in at No. 25; the island's cultural and literary society has displays of wildlife, seashells, seaweed, minerals, and stuffed birds. Side rooms include paintings and mementos of Menorcan writers, poets, and musicians. ✉ *Rovellada de Dalt 25* ☎ *971/360553* ⊕ *www. ateneumao.org* ⌕ *Free* ☉ *June–Sept., weekdays 10–2 and 4–10, Sat. 5–9; Oct.–May, Mon.–Sat. 10–2 and 4–10, Sat. 10–1:30.*

**La Verge del Carme.** Carrer Costa d'en Deià descends to the Plaça Reial (a bit grandiosely named, for an unimposing little rectangle dominated by a café called the American Bar), where it becomes the Carrer sa Ravaleta. Ahead is this church, which has a fine painted and gilded altarpiece. Adjoining are the cloisters, now used as a **public market,** the intervals between the massive stone arches filled with stalls selling fresh produce and a variety of local specialties such as cheeses and sausages. ✉ *Pl. del Carme* ☎ *971/362402.*

**Plaça de la Conquesta.** Behind the church of Santa María is this plaza with a statue of Alfons III of Aragón, who wrested the island from the Moors in 1287.

**Puerta de San Roque.** At the far end of Carrer Rector Mort is the massive gate of the only surviving portion of the 14th-century city walls, rebuilt in 1587 to protect Mahón from the pirate Barbarossa (Redbeard). ✉ *Carrer Rector Mort.*

**Santa María.** A few steps north from the Cloister del Carme bring you to the church of St. Mary, which dates from the 13th century but was rebuilt during the British occupation and restored after being sacked during the civil war. The church's pride is its 3,200-pipe baroque organ, imported from Austria in 1810. There are concerts (€4) here from May through October, Monday–Saturday at 11. ✉ *Pl. de la Constitució* ☎ *971/363949.*

**Teatre Principal.** From Sa Rovellada de Dalt, turn left on Carrer de ses Moreres, then right on Carrer Bastió to where it becomes Carrer Costa d'en Deià, and—if it's open—have a look at Mahón's lovely theater. It

---

**MENORCA BEST BETS**

**Explore the Gothic and Renaissance core of Ciutadella.** The island's old capital was the religious and commercial heartbeat for several hundred years.

**Tuck into a pot of** *Es Pla caldereta de langosta.* This lobster stew is always the most expensive item on the menu, but it's Menorca's pièce de résistance.

**Take to the water.** The bay at Fornells is the perfect place to take up sailing or windsurfing.

was built in 1824 as an opera house, with five tiers of boxes, red plush seats, and gilded woodwork—a La Scala in miniature. Opera companies from Italy would make this their first port of call, en route to their mainland tours; anything that went down poorly with the critical audience in Mahón would get cut from the repertoire. Fully restored in 2005, the Principal still hosts a brief opera season; if you're visiting in the first week of December or June, get tickets at all costs. ⊠ *Carrer Costa d'en Deia s/n* ☎ *971/355603* ⊕ *www.teatremao.com.*

## FORNELLS
*35 km (21 mi) northwest of Mahón.*

The first fortifications built here to defend the Bay of Fornells from pirates date to 1625. A little village (full-time population: 500) of white-washed houses with red tile roofs. The bay—Menorca's second-largest and its deepest—offers ideal conditions for windsurfing, sailing, and scuba diving. The real draw of Fornells is its restaurants. This is the best place on the island to try Menorca's specialty, *Es Pla caldereta de langosta* (lobster stew).

## CIUTADELLA
*44 km (27 mi) west of Mahón.*

Ciutadella was Menorca's capital before the British settled in Mahón, and its history is richer. As you arrive via the ME1, the main artery across the island from Mahón, turn left at the second roundabout and follow the ring road to the Passeig Maritim; at the end, near the **Castell de Sant Nicolau** watchtower (visits daily, June–October 10–1 and 5–10) is a **monument to David Glasgow Farragut,** the first admiral of the U.S. Navy, whose father emigrated from Ciutadella to the United States. From here, take Passeig de Sant Nicolau to the **Plaça de s'Esplanada,** and park near the Plaça d'es Born.

**Ajuntament.** From a passage on the left side of Ciutadella's columned and crenellated city hall, on the west side of the Born, steps lead up to the **Mirador d'es Port,** a lookout from which you can survey the harbor. ⊠ *Pl. d'es Born.*

**Cathedral.** The Carrer Major leads to the Gothic cathedral, which has some beautifully carved, intricate choir stalls. The side chapel has round Moorish arches, remnants of the mosque that once stood on this site; the bell tower is a converted minaret. ⊠ *Pl. de la Catedral at Plaça Píus XII.*

**Museu Municipal.** The local museum houses artifacts of Menorca's prehistoric, Roman, and medieval past, including records of land grants made by Alfons III to the local nobility after defeating the Moors. It's in the Bastió de Sa Font (Bastion of the Fountain), an ancient defense tower at the east end of the harbor. ☎ *971/380297* ⊕ *www.ciutadella.org/museu/castella* ⊠ *€2, free Wed.* ⊙ *Nov.–Apr., Tues.–Sat. 10–2; May–Oct., Tues.-Sat. 10–2 and 6–9.*

**Palau Torresaura.** The monument in the middle of the Plaça d'es Born commemorates the citizens' resistance to a Turkish invasion in 1588. South from the plaza along the east side of the Born is the block-long 19th-century palace, built by the Baron of Torresaura, one of the many noble families from Aragón and Catalonia that repopulated Menorca after it was captured from the Moors in the 13th century. The interesting facade faces the plaza, though the entrance is on the side street (it is not open to the public). ⊠ *Carrer Major del Born 8.*

**Palau Salort.** On the opposite side of the Carrer Major is the only noble home regularly open to the public. The coats of arms on the ceiling are those of the families Salort (a salt pit and a garden: *sal* and *ort*, or *huerta*) and Martorell (a marten). ⊠ *Carrer Major des Born* 🎟€2 ⊙ *May–Oct., Mon.–Sat. 10–2.*

**Port.** Ciutadella's port is accessible from steps that lead down from Carrer Sant Sebastià. The waterfront here is lined with seafood restaurants, some of which burrow into caverns far under the Born.

**Seminari of the 17th-century Convent and Eglésia del Socors.** Follow the arcade of Carrer de Quadrado north from the cathedral and turn right on Carrer del Seminari, lined on the west side with some of the city's most impressive historic buildings. Among them is this one, which hosts Ciutadella's summer festival of classical music. ⊠ *Carrer del Seminari at Carrer Obispo Vila.*

## SHOPPING

Menorca is known for shoes and leather, cheese, gin (introduced during British rule)—and recently, wine. The fine supple quality of the leather here serves high-class couturiers around the world, the surplus being sold in island factory shops. The streets of the compact center of Mahón are excellent for shopping.

**Jaime Mascaro.** This designer's showroom on the main highway to Cuitadella features not only shoes and bags but fine leather coats and belts for men and women. Mascaro also has a shop in Mahón, at Carrer ses Moreres. ⊠ *Poligon Industrial s/nFerreries* ☎ *971/373837* ⊕ *www.mascaro.com.*

**Marks.** In Mahón, buy leather goods here. ⊠ *S'Arravaleta 18, Mahón* ☎ *971/322660.*

**Pons Quintana.** Inland, this showroom has a full-length window overlooking the factory where they make their ultrachic women's shoes. The company also has a shop in Mahón, at Sa Ravaleta 21. Both locations are closed weekends. ⊠ *Calle San Antonio 120, Alaior* ☎ *971/371050* ⊕ *www.ponsquintana.com.*

**Xoriguer Distillery.** Visit this distillery on Mahón's quayside, near the ferry terminal, and take a guided tour, sample various types of gin, and buy some to take home. ⊠ *Anden de Poniente 91, Mahón* ☎ *971/362197.*

## ACTIVITIES

Several miles long and a mile wide, but with a narrow entrance to the sea and virtually no waves, the Bay of Fornells gives the windsurfing and sailing beginner a feeling of security and the expert plenty of excitement.

**Wind Fornells.** This company rents boards, dinghies, and catamarans, and gives windsurfing lessons in English or Spanish; they're open from

May to October. ⊠ *C. Nou 33, Es Mercadal* ☎ *971/188150* ⊕ *www. windfornells.com.*

## WHERE TO EAT

**$$** ✕**El Jàgaro.** Named for a mussel-like bivalve that has a tail to propel
SEAFOOD itself across the ocean floor, this simple waterfront restaurant is a local
favorite. The eager lunchtime crowd comes for the platter of lightly fried
mixed fish with potatoes, while in the evening you can enjoy grilled
*pescado de roca* (rockfish), *sepia* (cuttlefish), or Menorcan mussels.
The menu takes a quantum leap in price for the €71 spiny lobster, a
delicacy in its various forms. The *ortigues* (sea anemones) are a house
specialty not to be missed. The prix-fixe lunch (is a good value. ⊠ *Moll
de Llevant 334–35* ☎ *971/362390* ⊟ *AE, MC, V* ☉ *Closed Mon. and
Sun. evenings Nov.–Mar.*

**$** ✕**Itake.** On the port since 1994, Itake is an amiable clutter of 12 tables,
ECLECTIC specials of the day on a chalkboard, ceiling fans, paper place mats, and
frosted-glass lamps. This is arguably the best place in Mahón for an
inexpensive, informal meal with a different touch. Where neighboring
eateries pride themselves on fresh fish, Itake serves goat cheese and
burgers, kangaroo steaks in mushroom sauce, and ostrich breast with
strawberry coulis. That said, nothing here is made with any real elabo-
ration: orders come out of the kitchen at nearly the rate of fast food.
⊠ *Moll de Llevant 317* ☎ *971/354570* ⊟ *AE, DC, MC, V* ☉ *No dinner
Sun. Sept.–June. Closed Mon.*

# MESSINA, ITALY (FOR TAORMINA AND MT. ETNA)

Sicily has beckoned seafaring wanderers since the trials of Odysseus
were first sung in Homer's *Odyssey.* Strategically poised between
Europe and Africa, this mystical volcanic land has been a melting pot
of every great civilization on the Mediterranean: Greek and Roman;
then Arab and Norman; and finally French, Spanish, and Italian. Today
Sicily fuses the remains of sackings past: graceful Byzantine mosaics
rubbing elbows with Greek temples, Roman amphitheaters, Roman-
esque cathedrals, and baroque flights of fancy. Messina's ancient history
lists a series of disasters, but the city nevertheless managed to develop a
fine university and a thriving cultural environment. On December 28,
1908, Messina changed from a flourishing metropolis of 120,000 to a
heap of rubble, shaken to pieces by an earthquake that turned into a
tidal wave and left 80,000 dead and the city almost completely leveled.
For this reason there are few historic treasures, but the town makes a
good jumping-off point for explorations of other treasures.

### ESSENTIALS

CURRENCY The euro (€1 to US$1.36 at this writing).

HOURS Shops are generally open 9 to 1 and 3:30 to 7:30, and are closed Sunday
and Monday morning most of the year. Summer (June to September)
hours are usually 9 to 1 and 4 to 8.

## Taormina

Castello Saraceno
Porta Messina
Palazzo Corvaja
*V. Luigi Pirandello*
*V. Leonardo da Vinci*
Odeon
Sta. Catarina
*Pza. Vittorio Emanuele*
Teatro Comunale
Sanctuaria Madonna della Rocca
*Circonvallazione*
*Naumachia*
*V. Teatro Greco*
San Domenico
Teatro Greco
Torre del Orologio
San Agostino
Antiquarium
Porta Catania
*Pza. San Antonio*
*Corso Umberto I*
*Pza. San Aprile*
*V. Roma*
*V. Roma*
Archeological Area
*V. Bagnoli Croce*
Palazzo San Stefano
Duomo
*Piazzale San Domenico*
*V. Roma*
Madonna della Grazie
Taormina Mare
Villa Comunale
*Parque Duchi di Cenaro*

0        500 ft

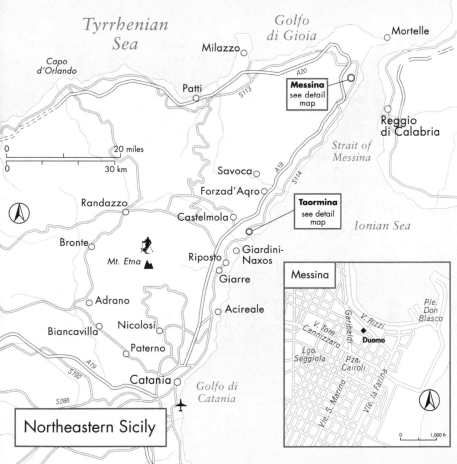

## Northeastern Sicily

*Tyrrhenian Sea*
*Golfo di Gioia*
Mortelle
Milazzo
*Capo d'Orlando*
Patti
S113
A20
Messina
**see detail map**
Reggio di Calabria
*Strait of Messina*
0        20 miles
0        30 km
Savoca
A18
S114
Forzad'Aqro
Randazzo
Castelmola
Taormina
**see detail map**
*Ionian Sea*
Bronte
Mt. Etna
Riposto
Giardini-Naxos
Adrano
Giarre
Biancavilla
Nicolosi
Acireale
Paterno
S192
A19
Catania
*Golfo di Catania*
S288
S114

## Messina

*Ple. Don Blasco*
*V. Rizzi*
*Garibaldi*
*V. Tom. Cannizzaro*
Duomo
*Lgo. Seggiola*
*Pza. Cairoli*
*Vle. S. Martino*
*Vle. la Farina*

0        1,000 ft

INTERNET **Fast Net Café** ⊠ *Via Garibaldi 72* ☎ *090/662758.*

TELEPHONES Tri-band GSM phones work in Italy. You can buy prepaid phone cards at telecom shops, news-vendors, and tobacconists in all towns and cities. Phone cards can be used for local or international calls.

### COMING ASHORE

Ships dock in the main port of Messina. Passenger facilities cater to the many commercial ferry passengers who enter Sicily here, and though there are refreshment stands, they are often busy. There is no shuttle service, but it is possible to walk into Messina. Taxis wait at the port entrance, and it's a five-minute transfer to the train station.

It is possible to reach Taormina by train from Messina followed by the cable car from the town below up to Taormina proper. Most services take around 45 minutes and cost approximately €7.50 round-trip. Taxis charge approximately €3.05 initially, then €0.80 per km with an increment of €0.13 per 140m when the taxi travels at less than 20 kph (12 mph). Mt. Etna is not easy to reach by public transport.

Taormina makes a good departure point for excursions around—but not always to the top of—Mt. Etna, with private companies offering a guiding service. A rental car would allow you to explore much of northern Sicily during your day in port. Rental costs are approximately €60 per day for a compact manual vehicle.

## EXPLORING NORTHEASTERN SICILY

### MESSINA

**Duomo.** The reconstruction of Messina's Norman and Romanesque Duomo, originally built by the Norman king Roger II in 1197, has retained much of the original plan, including a handsome crown of Norman battlements, an enormous apse, and a splendid wood-beamed ceiling. The adjoining **bell tower** contains one of the largest and most complex mechanical clocks in the world, constructed in 1933 with a host of gilded automatons, including a roaring lion, that spring into action every day at the stroke of noon. ⊠ *Piazza del Duomo* ☎ *090/774895* ⊙ *Weekdays 7:20–7, weekends 7:20–12:30 and 4–7.*

### TAORMINA

*43 km (27 mi) southwest of Messina.*

The medieval cliff-hanging town of Taormina is overrun with tourists and trinket shops, but its natural beauty is still hard to argue with. The view of the sea and Mt. Etna from its jagged cactus-covered cliffs is as close to perfection as a panorama can get, especially on clear days, when the snow-capped volcano's white puffs of smoke rise against the blue sky. Writers have extolled Taormina's beauty almost since its founding in the 6th century BC by Greeks from Naples; Goethe and D. H. Lawrence were among its more recent well-known enthusiasts. The town's boutique-lined main streets get old pretty quickly, but don't overlook the many hiking paths that wind through the beautiful hills surrounding Taormina. Nor should you miss the trip up to stunning Castelmola—whether on foot or by car.

**Castello Saraceno.** By footpath or car you can approach the medieval castle, enticingly perched on an adjoining cliff above town, but you cannot continue all the way to the castle itself. ⊠ *Monte Tauro.*

**Palazzo Corvaja.** Many of Taormina's 14th- and 15th-century palaces have been carefully preserved. Especially beautiful, the Palazzo Corvaja has characteristic black-lava and white-limestone inlays. Today it houses the tourist office and the **Museo di Arte e Storia Popolare,** which has a collection of puppets and folk art, carts, and cribs. ⊠ *Largo Santa Caterina* ☎ *0942/610274 Palazzo* 🎟 *Museum €2.60* 🕙 *Museum Tues.–Sun. 9–1 and 4–8.*

**Taormina Mare.** Down below the main city of Taormina, at sea level, is this beach near Giardini Naxos, where beachgoers hang out in summer. It's accessible by a **funivia** (gondola) that glides past incredible views on its way down. ☎ *0942/23906* 🎟 *Funivia €2.50 one way, €3.50 round-trip* 🕙 *Apr.–Oct. daily, every 15 mins 8 AM–midnight; Nov.–Mar. daily, every 15 mins 8–8.*

**Teatro Greco.** The Greeks put a premium on finding impressive locations to stage their dramas, and the site of Taormina's hillside theater is a fine one. Beyond the columns you can see the town's rooftops spilling down the hillside, the arc of the coastline, and Mt. Etna in the distance. The theater was built during the 3rd century BC and rebuilt by the Romans during the 2nd century AD. Its acoustics are exceptional: even today a stage whisper can be heard in the last rows. In summer Taormina hosts an arts festival of music and dance events and a film festival; many performances are held in the Teatro Greco. ⊠ *Via Teatro Greco* ☎ *0942/620198* 🎟 *€6* 🕙 *Daily 9–1 hr before sunset. Closed Mon. Oct.–Mar.*

★ **Villa Comunale.** Stroll down Via Bagnoli Croce from the main Corso Umberto to this oasis. Also known as the Parco Duca di Cesarò, the lovely public gardens were designed by Florence Trevelyan Cacciola, a Scottish lady "invited" to leave England following a romantic liaison with the future Edward VII (1841–1910). Arriving in Taormina in 1889, she married a local professor and devoted herself to the gardens, filling them with Mediterranean plants, ornamental pavilions (known as the beehives), and fountains. Stop by the panoramic bar, which has stunning views. ⊠ *Via Bagnoli Croce* 🕙 *Daily 9 AM–sunset.*

## CASTELMOLA

*5 km (3 mi) west of Taormina.*

You may think that Taormina has spectacular views, but tiny Castelmola, floating 1,800 feet above sea level, takes the word "scenic" to a whole new level. Along the cobblestone streets within the ancient walls, the 360-degree panoramas of mountain, sea, and sky are so ubiquitous that you almost get used to them (but not quite). Collect yourself with a sip of the sweet almond wine (best served cold) made in the local bars, or with lunch at one of the humble pizzerias or panino shops.

A 10-minute drive on a winding but well-paved road leads from Taormina to Castelmola; you must park in one of the public lots on the hillside below and climb a series of staircases to reach the center. On a nice day, hikers are in for a treat if they walk instead of driving. It's a serious uphill climb, but the 1½-km (¾-mi) path is extremely well maintained and not too challenging. You'll begin at Porta Catania in Taormina, with a walk along Via Apollo Arcageta past the Chiesa di San Francesco di Paolo on the left. The Strada Comunale della Chiusa then leads past Piazza Andromaco, revealing good views of the jagged promontory of Cocolanazzo di Mola to the north. Allow 45 minutes on the way up, a half-hour down. There's another, slightly longer— 2-km (1-mi)—path that heads up from Porta Messina past the Roman aqueduct, Convento dei Cappuccini, and the northeastern side of Monte Tauro. You could take one path up and the other down.

**Fodor's Choice** &#9733; **Castello Normanno.** The best place to take in Castelmola's views is from the old ruin, reached by a set of steep staircases rising out of the town center. In all Sicily, there may be no spot more scenic than atop the castle ruins, where you can gaze upon two coastlines, smoking Mt. Etna, and the town spilling down the mountainside. As the castle is completely open-air, you can visit at any time, but you should come to Castelmola during daylight hours for the view.

## MT. ETNA
**Fodor's Choice** &#9733; *64 km (40 mi) southwest of Taormina.*

Mt. Etna is one of the world's major active volcanoes and is the largest and highest in Europe—the cone of the crater rises to 10,902 feet above sea level. Plato sailed in just to catch a glimpse in 387 BC; in the 9th century AD the oldest gelato of all was shaved off its snowy slopes; and in the 21st century the volcano still claims annual headlines. Etna has erupted 12 times in the past 30 or so years, most spectacularly in 1971, 1983, 2001, and 2002; many of these eruptions wiped out cable-car stations. There were two eruptions in 2008 and a sizeable one in 2009. The refuge at Sapienza, however, is currently operational. Although each eruption is predictably declared a "tragedy" by the media, owing to the economic losses, Etna almost never threatens human life. Travel in the proximity of the crater depends on Mt. Etna's temperament, but you can walk up and down the enormous lava dunes and wander over its moonlike surface of dead craters. The rings of vegetation change markedly as you rise, with vineyards and pine trees gradually giving way to growths of broom and lichen. Taormina makes a good departure point for excursions around—but not always to the top of—Mt. Etna.

**Circumetnea Railroad.** Instead of going up Mt. Etna, you can circle it on this train, which runs near the volcano's base. The private railway almost circles the volcano, running 114 km (71 mi) between Catania and Riposto—the towns are 30 km (19 mi) apart by the coast road. The line is small, slow, and only single-track, but has some dramatic vistas of the volcano and goes through lava fields. The round trip takes about five hours; there are about 10 departures a day. ✉ *Via Caronda 352, Catania* ☏ *095/541250* ⊕ *www.circumetnea.it* ✍ *€11.50 round-trip* ☉ *Mon.–Sat. 6 AM–9 PM.*

## SHOPPING

Taormina is the place in eastern Sicily for shopping, especially along Corso Umberto I and the surrounding alleyways, where chic boutiques sell lace and linen, including placemats and napkins. The island as a whole is famed for its ceramics, particularly its practical folk pottery from Caltagirone, close by along the north coast. Marble and wrought iron are also fashioned into souvenir pieces, and antique shops are numerous, though prices can be high.

A marzipan devotee should not leave Taormina without trying one of the almond-based sweets—maybe in the guise of the ubiquitous *fico d'India* (prickly pear), or in more unusual *frutta martorana* varieties. Locals also swear by the cannoli, and a block of almond paste makes a good souvenir—you can bring it home to make an almond latte or granita. Local wines and spirits, including limocello are worth seeking out.

**Pasticceria Etna.** This is the place for locally made marzipan. ✉ *Corso Umberto 112, Taormina* ☏ *0942/24735* 🖷 *0942/21279.*

## ACTIVITIES

Mount Etna is a natural magnet for adventure-seekers, but because the volcano is active you should consult experts before tackling the peak. Hiking is certainly a popular choice on the lower slopes, while climbing Mt. Etna proves more challenging.

**Club Alpino Italiano.** This organization in Catania is a great resource for Mt. Etna climbing and hiking guides. If you have some experience and don't like a lot of hand-holding, these are the guides for you. ✉ *Piazza Scammacca, Catania* ☏ *095/7153515* ⊕ *www.caicatania.it.*

**Gruppo Guide Etna Nord.** If you're a beginning climber, call this company to arrange for a guide. Their service is a little more personalized—and expensive—than others. Reserve ahead. ✉ *Via Roma 93, Linguaglossa* ☏ *095/7774502* ⊕ *www.guidetnanord.com.*

**No Limits Etna Center.** For a bird's-eye view of Mt. Etna, you can try paragliding or hang gliding; contact this company, which also organizes climbing, caving, and diving expeditions. ✉ *Via Milano 6/A, Catania* ☏ *095/7213682* ⊕ *www.etnacenter.net.*

## WHERE TO EAT

**$$$$**
ITALIAN

✗ **L'Arco dei Cappuccini.** Just off the radar screen of the main tourist strip lies this clean, diminutive restaurant with white tablecloths. Outdoor seating and an upstairs kitchen help make room for a few extra tables—necessary because the locals are well aware that both the price and the quality cannot be beat elsewhere in town. Indulge in *sopressa di polipo* (steamed octopus carpaccio), gnocchi *con pistacchi* (with pistachio cream sauce), or the fresh catch of the day. ✉ *Via Cappuccini 7, off Via Costanino Patricio near Porta Messina, Taormina* ☎ *0942/24893* ⌃ *Reservations essential* ⊟ *AE, DC, MC, V* ⊘ *Closed Wed., Feb. and 1st wk in Nov.*

**$$**
**ITALIAN**  ✕ **Ristorante Pizzichella.** On the road heading down to Taormina stands this three-level terrace restaurant. The food—seafood dishes like mixed shellfish risotto, grilled prawns or swordfish, and pizzas from a wood-burning oven—is eclipsed by the memorable views from almost every table on the terraces. ✉ *Via Madonna della Scala 1* ☎ *0942/28831* ⊕ *www.pizzichella.it* ⊟ *AE, MC, V* ⊘ *Closed Wed. Oct.–Apr. and occasionally on other days in winter.*

# MONTE CARLO, MONACO

In 1297 the Grimaldi family seized this fortified town and, except for a short break under Napoléon, they have ruled here ever since. The Principality of Monaco covers 473 acres; it would fit comfortably inside New York's Central Park while its 5,000 citizens would fill only a small fraction of the seats in Yankee Stadium. The Grimaldis made money from gambling and attracted a well-heeled, monied crowd, but the whole world watched as Hollywood princess Grace Kelly wed Prince Rainier ruler of Monaco to put this place on the map. It's the very favorable tax system, not the gambling, that makes Monaco one of the most sought-after addresses in the world, and the principality bristles with gleaming high-rise apartment complexes owned by tax exiles. But at the town's great 1864 landmark Hôtel de Paris—still a veritable crossroads of the buffed and befurred Euro-gentry—at the Opéra, or the ballrooms of the Casino, you'll still be able to conjure up Monaco's belle epoque.

## ESSENTIALS

**CURRENCY**  The euro (€1 to US$1.36 at this writing).

**HOURS**  Most stores open Monday through Saturday from 9 to 7, but many close at lunchtime (usually noon to 2 or 3), and some will open later and on Sunday during July and August. Museums are usually open 10 to 5, but most are closed on either Monday or Tuesday.

**INTERNET**  **Stars n Bars** (✉ *Quai Antoine 1, west side of harbor* ☎ *377/97–97–95–95* ⊕ *www.starsnbars.com*) is a great American-style fast food restaurant that sees its fair share of celebrities. It's open Monday–Saturday until midnight. It's closed Monday between October and April.

**TELEPHONES**  Tri-band GSM phones work in Monte Carlo, as in France. You can buy prepaid phone cards at telecom shops, news vendors, and tobacconists. Phone cards can be used for local or international calls. France Telecom and Orange are leading telecom companies.

## COMING ASHORE

Cruise ships dock at Port Hercule, just below Monaco-Ville, at a state-of-the-art cruise port within a $200-million breakwater that can accommodate several ships at a time. Even still, on busy days you may be tendered to the landing dock. There are few facilities at the port itself. An elevator about 500 yards away leads up to the town, where the attractions of old Monaco are located. It is approximately 1 mi

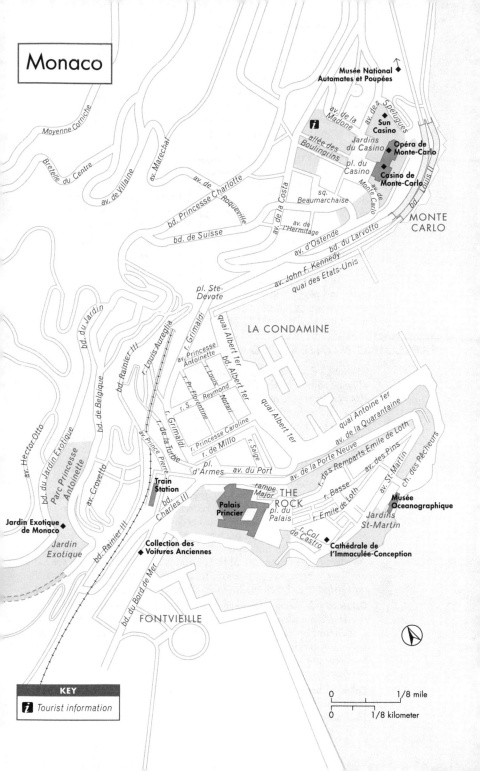

from the port to the Monte Carlo district, this is a 15- to 30-minute walk depending on your level of fitness. Although the distance is not too great, there are many hills.

If you intend to confine your explorations to the principality, there is no need to hire a car. All the attractions of the Old town are less than a 10-minute walk apart. Bus services 1 and 2 link Monaco-Ville with Monte Carlo; prices are €1 per journey. If you want to tour the stunning surrounding Provençal countryside, a vehicle would be useful. Expect to pay €75 for an economy manual vehicle for the day. Taxis wait outside the port gates and can provide tourist itineraries. For single journeys, tariffs are €2.80 initially, then €0.84 per km.

> ### MONTE CARLO BEST BETS
>
> **Watch the Changing of the Guard.** This short ceremony at exactly 11:55 AM in the palace square has been taking place for centuries.
>
> **Place your bets.** The Casino de Monte Carlo is surely the most beautiful place in the world to lose your shirt. If you don't want to bet, buy a chip as a souvenir.
>
> **Have an aperitif at the café in the place de Casino.** This is the place to watch the beautiful and megarich come and go and to enjoy the genteel atmosphere.

## EXPLORING MONTE CARLO

Monte Carlo or Monaco? Many people use the names interchangeably, but officially, the Old Town or Vieille Ville is **Monaco-Ville** (or Le Rocher because it sits on a rocky plateau). This is where the Grimaldis live and the business of government is done. The "new" town, built in the 18th and 19th centuries and expanding upward rapidly even today, is called **Monte Carlo,** while the harbor area, or **La Condamine,** connects the two.

★ **Casino de Monte Carlo.** The Place du Casino is the center of Monte Carlo, and the Casino itself is a must-see, even if you don't bet a *sou*. Into the gold-leaf splendor of the Casino, the hopeful traipse from tour buses to tempt fate beneath the gilt-edge rococo ceiling. (But do remember the fate of Sarah Bernhardt, who lost her last 100,000 francs here.) Jacket and tie are required in the back rooms, which open at 3 PM. Bring your passport (under-18 not admitted). Note that there are special admission fees to get into many of the period gaming rooms—only the Salle des Jeux Americains (where you'll find the slot machines) is free. ⊠ *Pl. du Casino* ☎ *377/98–16–20–00* ⊕ *www.sbm.mc* ☉ *Daily 2 PM–4 AM.*

**Cathédrale de l'Immaculée-Conception.** Follow the flow of crowds down the last remaining streets of medieval Monaco to the principality's cathedral, an uninspired 19th-century version of the Romanesque style. Nonetheless, it harbors a magnificent altarpiece, painted in 1500 by Bréa, and the tombs of Princess Grace and Prince Rainier. ⊠ *Av. St-Martin.*

**Collection des Voitures Anciennes.** On the Terrasses de Fontvieille are two remarkable sights: the vintage car collection and the **Jardin Animalier** (Animal Garden). The former is a collection of Prince Rainier's vintage vehicles from a De Dion Bouton to a Lamborghini Countach; the latter, a mini-zoo housing the Rainier family's animal collection, an astonishing array of wild beasts including monkeys and exotic birds. ☒ *Terrasses de Fontvieille* ☎ *377/92–05–28–56 or 377/93–25–18–31* ⊕ *www.mtcc. mc* ☒ *Collection des Voitures €6, Jardin Animalier €4* ۞ *June–Sept., daily 9–noon and 2–7; Oct.–Feb., daily 10–noon and 2–5; Mar.–May, daily 10–noon and 2–6.*

**Fodor's Choice**  **Jardin Exotique de Monaco.** Carved out of the rock face—and one of
★ Monte Carlo's most stunning escape hatches—the "exotic" garden is studded with thousands of succulents and cacti, all set along promenades and belvederes over the sea, and even framing faux boulders (actually hollow sculptures). There are rare plants from Mexico and Africa, and the hillside plot, threaded with bridges and grottoes, can't be beat for coastal splendor. Thanks go to Prince Albert I, who started it all. Also on the grounds, or actually under them, are the **Grottes de l'Observatoire**—spectacular grottoes and caves a-drip with stalagmites and spotlit with fairy lights. The largest cavern is called La Grande Salle (the big room) and looks like a Romanesque rock cathedral. Traces of Cro-Magnon civilization have been found here, so the grottoes now bear the official name of the **Musée d'Anthropologie Préhistorique.** ☒ *Bd. du Jardin Exotique* ☎ *377/93–15–29–80* ☒ *€6.90* ۞ *Mid-May–mid-Sept., daily 9–7; mid-Sept.–mid-May, daily 9–6* ۞ *Closed mid-Nov.–mid-Dec.*

**Musée National Automates et Poupées.** From Place des Moulins an elevator descends to the Larvotto Beach complex, artfully created with imported sand, and this museum housed in a Garnier villa within a rose garden. It has a beguiling collection of 18th- and 19th-century dolls and automatons. ☒ *17 av. Princesse Grace* ☎ *377/93–30–91–26* ☒ *€6* ۞ *Daily 10–6.*

۞ **Musée Océanographique.** At the prow of the Rock, the grand oceanog-
★ raphy museum perches dramatically on a cliff. It's a splendid Edwardian structure, built under Prince Albert I to house specimens collected on amateur explorations. Jacques Cousteau (1910–97) led its missions from 1957 to 1988. The main floor displays skeletons and taxidermy of enormous sea creatures; early submarines and diving gear dating from the Middle Ages; and a few interactive science displays. The main draw is the famous **aquarium,** a vast complex of backlighted tanks containing every imaginable species of fish, crab, and eel. ☒ *Av. St-Martin* ☎ *377/93–15–36–00* ⊕ *www.oceano.mc* ☒ *€11* ۞ *July and Aug., daily 9:30–7:30; Apr.–June, daily 8:30–7; Sept., daily 9:30–7; Oct.–Mar., daily 10–6.*

**Azur Express Tourist Train.** This little train takes a tour around Monaco and Monte Carlo, passing all the major sites and with accompanying audio guide in English. The trip lasts 30 minutes, offers a useful overview of the principality, and saves those tired feet. ☒ *Oceanographic Museum, av. Saint Martin* ☎ *377/92–05–64–38* ☒ *€7* ۞ *Winter daily 10:30–5, summer daily 10–5. Closed mid-Nov.–late Jan.*

**Opéra de Monte-Carlo.** In the true spirit of the town, it seems that the opera house, with its 18-ton gilt-bronze chandelier and extravagant frescoes, is part of the casino complex. The grand theater was designed by Charles Garnier, who also built the Paris Opéra. Its main auditorium, the Salle Garnier, was inaugurated by Sarah Bernhardt in 1879. ⊠ *Pl. du Casino* ☎ *377/98–06–28–00* ⊕ *www.opera.mc.*

**Palais Princier.** West of Monte Carlo stands the famous Rock, crowned by the palace where the royal family resides. A 40-minute guided tour (summer only) of this sumptuous chunk of history, first built in the 13th century and expanded and enhanced over the centuries, reveals an extravagance of 16th- and 17th-century frescoes, as well as tapestries, gilt furniture, and paintings on a grand scale. Note that the **Relève de la Garde** (Changing of the Guard) is held outside the front entrance of the palace most days at 11:55 AM.

One wing of the Palais Princier, open throughout the year, is the **Musée Napoléon** (☎ *377/93–25–18–31*), filled with Napoleonic souvenirs—including that hat and a tricolor scarf—and genealogical charts of France's famous emperor. ⊠ *Pl. du Palais* ☎ *377/93–25–18–31* ⊕ *www. palais.mc* ⌸ *Palace €6, museum €4.50, joint ticket €9* ☯ *Palais Princier: Apr.–Oct., daily 10–6:15; Musée Napoléon: Apr.–Oct., daily 10–6:15; Dec.–Mar., daily 10:30–5.*

**Sun Casino.** Some say the most serious gamblers play at in the Monte Carlo Grand Hotel, which is near the vast convention center that juts over the water. ⊠ *12 av. des Spélugues* ☎ *377/98–06–12–12* ⊕ *www. montecarlosuncasino.com* ☯ *Tables open weekdays at 5 PM and weekends at 4 PM; slot machines open daily at noon.*

## SHOPPING

The wealthy live in Monaco, and the wealthy visit Monaco, so it should not be a surprise that you can buy the finest designer clothing and accessories from very smart boutiques on the streets radiating out from the **place du Casino. Monaco Ville,** on the hill, has a range of souvenir emporia with a predominance of Princess Grace memorabilia, from the tacky to the tasteful. **La Condamine** has a range of shopping for those without sky-high credit card limits. Look out also for Formula 1 motor racing souvenirs; this race around the streets takes place in late May and is one of the highlights of the social season.

**Bijoux Marlene.** This boutique sells high-class costume jewelry based on Cartier and Van Arpels, usually made of silver. ⊠ *Les Galereries du Métropole* ☎ *377/93–50–17–57.*

**Boutique du Rocher.** This company was set up by Princess Grace to promote Monagasque handicrafts. Everything here is locally made. ⊠ *1 av. de la Madone* ☎ *377/93–30–91–97.*

**Formule 1.** This store handles official race merchandise. ⊠ *15 rue Grimaldi* ☎ *377/93–15–92–44.*

**Jeunemaitre Haute Fourrures.** This store supplies furs to the royal family and others. ⊠ *2 rue des Iris* ☎ *377/93–30–00–87.*

**Lanvin.** The designer shop offers bespoke tailoring for men who want to look elegant at the casino or the opera. ⊠ *pl. du Casino* ☎ *377/93–25–01–79* ⊕ *www.lanvin.com.*

**Stock Griffe.** This upscale outlet has up to 90% reductions on designer labels. ⊠ *5 bis av. St-Michel* ☎ *377/93–51–86–06.*

## ACTIVITIES

**Société des Bains de Mer.** Monte Carlo Golf Club has a highly rated course just outside the principality, and the Monte Carlo Country Club offers a range of provision but is most renowned for its tennis. This is the club that hosts the prestigious Monte Carlo Tennis Masters tournament. Admission to the clubs is €38 per day, plus greens fees for golf. Both clubs are run by the Société des Bains de Mer. ⊠ *Pl. du Casino* ☎ *377/98–06–30–00* ⊕ *www.montecarloresort.com.*

## BEACHES

Larvotto is the public beach of the principality, but many people choose to buy a temporary membership in a private beach club, which also has facilities such as changing cabins, showers, and restaurants.

**Monte Carlo Beach Club.** Access here is €50 per day weekdays, and €75 per day weekends. ⊠ *Larvotto, Monte Carlo* ☎ *377/98–06–52–46.*

## WHERE TO EAT

$$$$
FRENCH

✕ **Bar Boeuf & Co.** For those wanting to try Alain Ducasse cuisine without having to pay Louis XVI prices, this bar (sea bass) and boeuf (beef) concept restaurant is a treat. The sea views are gorgeous for those seated on the terrace, and the up-to-the-minute service is actually laid-back enough for you to relax and simply enjoy. ⊠ *Le Sporting, av Princesse Grace* ☎ *377/98–06–71–71* ⊕ *www.alain-ducasse.com* ⊟ *AE, DC, MC, V* ⊗ *Closed Oct.–Apr.*

$$$
FRENCH

✕ **Café de Paris.** This landmark belle époque brasserie, across from the casino, offers the usual classics (shellfish, steak tartare, matchstick frites, and fish boned table-side). Supercilious, super-pro waiters fawn gracefully over titled preeners, gentlemen, jet-setters, and tourists alike. ⊠ *Pl. du Casino* ☎ *377/92–16–20–20* ⊟ *AE, DC, MC, V.*

# NAPLES, ITALY (WITH HERCULANEUM, POMPEII, AND CAPRI)

Campania is a region of evocative names—Capri, Sorrento, Pompeii, Herculaneum—that conjure up visions of cliff-shaded coves, sun-dappled waters, and mighty ruins. The area's unique geology is responsible for its gorgeous landscape. A languid coastline stretches out along a deep blue sea, punctuated by rocky islands. Heading inland, the hills at first roll gently, then transform into mountains. Campania's complex identity is most intensely felt in its major city, Naples, which sprawls around its bay as though attempting to embrace the island of Capri, while behind it Mt. Vesuvius glowers. It's one of those few cities in the world that is instantly recognizable: lush, chaotic, scary, funny, confounding, intoxicating, and very beautiful. Few who visit remain ambivalent. You needn't participate in the mad whirl of the city, however. The best pastime in Campania is simply finding a spot with a stunning view and indulging in *il dolce far niente* (the sweetness of doing nothing).

## ESSENTIALS

CURRENCY The euro (€1 to US$1.36 at this writing).

HOURS Shops are open 9:30 until 1, then 4:30 until 8. Most are closed on Sunday and also on Monday morning.

INTERNET **Opus Informatica** (✉ *Piazza Cavour 146, Naples* ☎ *081/298877* ⊕ *www. internetnapoli.it*).

SAFETY Naples has a reputation for active pickpocketing and bag-snatching, especially in the historic Old Town and on public transportation. It always pays to be vigilant to avoid becoming a victim. Keep bags and purses closed and carry them across the front of your body; thieves do cut bag straps to steal your belongings. Bag-snatchers often ride on scooters, grabbing your bag on the streetside as they whiz by. Crowded trams and trains are popular with pickpockets. Certainly never carry any cash or valuables that you don't need.

Generally, you can avoid problems by acting with confidence; thieves are more likely to target travelers who seem confused or lost. And you should try to blend in by dressing smartly. Locals in Naples rarely wear shorts and T-shirts.

TELEPHONES Tri-band GSM phones work in Italy. You can buy prepaid phone cards at telecom shops, news vendors, and tobacconists in all towns and cities. Phone cards can be used for local or international calls.

## COMING ASHORE

The Stazione Maritima is on the city's seafront; passenger facilities include a tourist information office, shops, and cafés.

Buses 3S, 152, Sepsa, and CTP run to the train station along with tram routes 1 to 4. By the Circumvesuviana line from Piazza Garibaldi, you can reach Pompeii, Ercolano (Herculanium), and Castellammare (for the funicular up to Mount Vesuvius). There are at least four hourly trains, and fares begin at €1.80 to Pompeii (one way); a one-day ticket from the center on Naples to the public transport zone for Pompei and Herculanium sites (Zone 2) is €3.70 on weekdays, €2.90 on weekends.

The EAVBUS route also links central Naples with Vesuvius and Pompeii with Vesuvius. Departing from Piazza Piedigrotta in Naples at 9 AM or 10:15. A one-day ticket costs €12.30.

Ferries to Capri depart from the same port where cruise ships disembark, and you can just walk on the ferry after buying a ticket. Fast-ferry prices are €14.50, and hydrofoils (the quickest crossing) are €17. Once on the island, the funicular railway from the port up to Capri Town is €1.40 round-trip.

Taxis charge approximately €2.33 initially, then €0.78 per km (½-mi) with an increment of €0.11 per 140 meters (260 feet) in slow traffic. A car rental could be useful if you want to explore the Amalfi coast, but it imperative that you return to Naples with time to spare, because traffic along the coast can be very heavy and slow-moving. Expect to pay €55 per day for a compact manual vehicle.

# EXPLORING NAPLES AND VICINITY

## NAPLES

**Castel Nuovo.** Also known as the Maschio Angioino, this massive fortress was built by the Angevins in the 13th century and completely rebuilt by the Aragonese rulers who succeeded them. The decorative marble triumphal arch that forms the entrance was erected during the Renaissance in honor of King Alfonso V of Aragon (1396–1458). Within the castle are the city's **Museo Civico** and the **Sala dell'Armeria,** the Armory with the remains of a Roman villa and a medieval necropolis. ⊠ *Piazza Municipio, Toledo* ☎ *081/7952003* ▣ *€5* ⊙ *Mon.–Sat. 9–6, Sun. courtyard only 9–1.*

**Castel Sant'Elmo.** Perched on Vomero hill, this castle was built by the Angevins in the 14th century to dominate the port and the Old City and remodeled by the Spanish in 1537. The stout fortifications are still in use today by the military, and occasionally there are performances, exhibitions, and fairs. You get in free if you have a ticket to the adjoining Certosa di San Martino. ⊠ *Largo San Martino, Vomero* ☎ *081/5784030* ▣ *€3* ⊙ *Thurs.–Tues. 8:30–7:30.*

**Duomo.** Though the Duomo was established in the 1200s, the building you see was erected a century later and has since undergone radical changes, especially during the baroque age. Inside the cathedral are 110 ancient columns salvaged from pagan buildings. Off the left aisle you step down into the 4th-century church of **Santa Restituta,** which was incorporated into the cathedral.

On the right aisle of the cathedral is the **Cappella di San Gennaro,** honoring St. Januarius, miracle-working patron saint of Naples. Three times a year—on September 19; on the Saturday preceding the first Sunday in May; and on December 16—his dried blood, contained in two sealed vials, is believed to liquefy during rites in his honor. The **Museo del tesoro di San Gennaro** houses a rich collection of treasures associated with the saint. ⊠ *Via Duomo 147, Spaccanapoli* ☎ *081/449097 Duomo, 081/294980 museum* ⊕ *www.museosangennaro.com* ▣ *€6* ⊙ *Duomo daily 7:30–noon and 4–7. Museum Tues.–Sat. 9–4:30, Sun. 9–2.*

**Fodor's Choice** **Museo Archeologico Nazionale.** The National Archaeological Museum
★ holds one of the world's great collections of Greek and Roman antiquities, including such extraordinary sculptures as the *Hercules Farnese,* an exquisite Aphrodite attributed to the 4th-century BC Greek sculptor Praxiteles. Countless objects from Pompeii and Herculaneum provide insight into life in ancient Rome. ⊠ *Piazza Museo 19, Spaccanapoli* ☎ *081/440166* ⊕ *marcheo.napolibeniculturali.it* ▣ *€6.50, €10 for special exhibits* ⊙ *Wed.–Mon. 9–7:30 (last ticket sold at 7).*

★ **Museo di Capodimonte.** The grandiose 18th-century neoclassical Bourbon royal palace houses an impressive collection of fine and decorative art. Capodimonte's greatest treasure is the excellent collection of paintings well-displayed in the **Galleria Nazionale,** on the palace's first and second

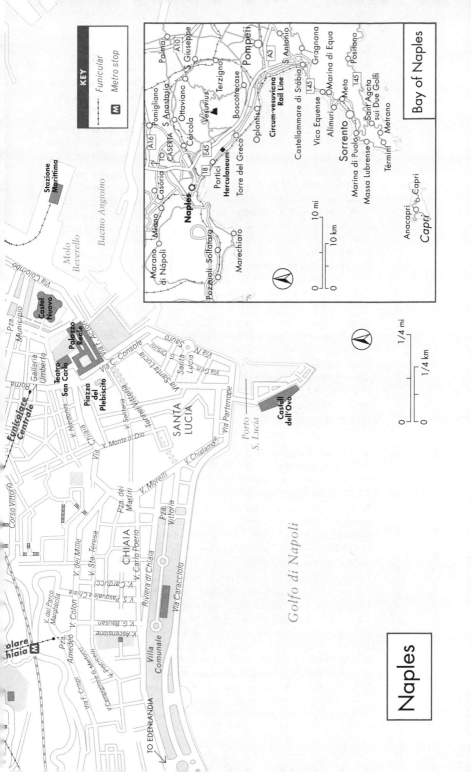

Naples

Bay of Naples

floors. Part of the **royal apartments** still has a complement of beautiful antique furniture. ⊠ *Via Miano 2, Porta Piccola, Via Capodimonte* ☏ *081/7499111* ⊕ *www.museocapodimonte.it* ⚏ *€7.50, €6.50 after 2* PM ☉ *Thurs.–Tues. 8:30–7:30; ticket office closes at 6:30.*

**Palazzo Reale.** Dominating Piazza del Plebiscito, the huge palace dates from the early 1600s. It was renovated and redecorated by successive rulers, including Napoléon's sister Caroline and her husband, Joachim Murat (1767–1815), who reigned briefly in Naples. Don't miss seeing the **royal apartments**, sumptuously furnished and full of precious paintings, tapestries, porcelains, and other objets d'art. ⊠ *Piazza del Plebiscito* ☏ *081/400547* ⊕ *www.palazzorealenapoli.it* ⚏ *€4* ☉ *Thurs.–Tues. 9–7.*

**Santa Chiara.** This monastery church is a Neapolitan landmark and the subject of a famous old song. It was built in the 1300s in Provençal Gothic style, and it's best known for the quiet charm of its cloister garden. ⊠ *Piazza Gesù Nuovo, Spaccanapoli* ☏ *081/7971231* ⊕ *www.santachiara.info* ⚏ *Museum and cloister €5* ☉ *Church daily 7–12:30 and 4:30–6:30; museum and cloister Mon.–Sat. 9:30–5:30, Sun. 10–2:30.*

### HERCULANEUM

❀ *10 km (6 mi) southeast of Naples.*

About 5,000 people lived in Herculaneum when it was destroyed. In AD 79 the gigantic eruption of Vesuvius buried the town under a tide of volcanic mud. The semiliquid mass seeped into the crevices of every building, sealing all in a compact, airtight tomb.

Much excitement is presently focused on one excavation in a corner of the site, the Villa dei Papiri, built by Julius Caesar's father-in-law. The building is named for the 1,800 carbonized papyrus scrolls dug up here in the 18th century, leading scholars to believe that this may have been a study center or library.

Domestic, commercial, and civic buildings are accessible. Decorations are especially delicate in the **Casa del Nettuno ed Anfitrite** (House of Neptune and Amphitrite), and in the **Terme Femminili** (Women's Baths). On the other side of the house is the **Casa del Bel Cortile** (House of the Beautiful Courtyard). In one of its inner rooms is the temporary display of a cast taken of some skeletons found in the storerooms down at the old seafront, where almost 300 inhabitants were encapsulated for posterity. The sumptuously decorated **Terme Suburbane** (Suburban Baths)—open only mornings—and the **Casa dei Cervi** (House of the Stags), are all evocative relics of a lively and luxurious way of life. ⊠ *Corso Ercolano, a 5-min walk downhill from Ercolano*

*Circumvesuviana station* 🏛 *081/8575347* ⊕ *www.pompeiisites.org* 🎫*€11; €20 includes Pompeii and 3 other sites for 3 days* ⊙ *Apr.– Oct., daily 8:30–7:30 (ticket office closes at 6); Nov.–Mar., daily 8:30–5 (ticket office closes at 3:30).*

### POMPEII

Fodor'sChoice ★ *11 km (7 mi) southeast of Herculaneum, 24 km (15 mi) southeast of Naples.*

The Scavi di Pompeii, petrified memorial to Vesuvius's eruption on the morning of August 23, AD 79, is the largest and most accessible of excavations anywhere. A busy commercial center with a population of 10,000 to 20,000, ancient Pompeii covered about 160 acres on the seaward end of the fertile Sarno Plain.

As you enter the ruins at Porta Marina, make your way to the **Foro** (Forum), which served as Pompeii's cultural, political, and religious center. The **Anfiteatro** (Amphitheater) was the ultimate in entertainment for local Pompeians, but quite small by Roman standards (seating 20,000). Built in about 80 BC, it was oval and divided into three seating areas like a theater. The **Terme Suburbane** (Suburban Baths) have eyebrow-raising frescoes in the *apodyterium* (changing room). On the walls of the **Lupanare** (brothel) are scenes of erotic games in which clients could engage.

Several homes were captured in various states by the eruption of Vesuvius. The **Casa del Poeta Tragico** (House of the Tragic Poet) is a typical middle-class house. On the floor is a mosaic of a chained dog and the inscription CAVE CANEM (beware of the dog). The **Casa degli Amorini Dorati** (House of the Gilded Cupids) is an elegant, well-preserved home with original marble decorations in the garden. Many paintings and mosaics were executed at **Casa del Menandro** (House of Menander), a patrician's villa named for a fresco of the Greek playwright.

The House of the Vettii is the best example of a house owned by wealthy *mercatores* (merchants). It contains vivid murals, but there are also magnificently memorable frescoes on view at the **Villa dei Misteri** (Villa of the Mysteries). This villa had more than 60 rooms painted with frescoes; the finest are in the triclinium. ⊠ *Porta Marina, a 5-min walk from Pompeii-Villa dei Misteri station* 🏛 *081/8575347* ⊕ *www.pompeiisites. org* 🎫*€11; €20 includes Herculaneum and 3 other sites for 3 days* ⊙ *Apr.–Oct., daily 8:30–7:30 (ticket office closes at 6); Nov.–Mar., daily 8:30–5 (ticket office closes at 3:30).*

### CAPRI

*75 min by boat, 40 min by hydrofoil from Naples.*

Once a pleasure dome to Roman emperors and now Italy's most glamorous seaside getaway, Capri (pronounced with an accent on the first syllable) is a craggy island at the southern end to the bay of Naples.

### CAPRI TOWN

The town is perched some 450 feet above the harbor. Piazza Umberto I, much better known as the Piazzetta, is the island's social hub.

**Certosa di San Giacomo.** You can window-shop along Via Vittorio Emanuele, which leads south toward this many-domed monastery. You can visit the church and cloister of this much-restored monastery and also pause long enough to enjoy the breathtaking view of Punta Tragara and the Faraglioni, three towering crags, from the viewing point at the edge of the cliff. ⊠ *Via Certosa, Capri Town* ☏ *081/8376218* ⊙ *Tues., Wed., Fri.–Sun. 9–2, Thurs. 3–7.*

**Giardini di Augusto** *(Gardens of Augustus).* Terraces of this beautifully planted public garden offer excellent views. You can see the village of Marina Piccola below and admire the steep and winding Via Krupp, actually a staircase cut into the rock. ⊠ *Via Matteotti, beyond monastery of San Giacomo, Capri Town* ⊙ *Daily dawn–dusk.*

### ANACAPRI

A tortuous road leads up to Anacapri, the island's "second city," about 3 km (2 mi) from Capri Town. Crowds are thick down Via Capodimonte leading to Villa San Michele and around the square, Piazza Vittoria, which is the starting point of the chairlift to the top of Monte Solaro. Elsewhere, Anacapri is quietly appealing.

**Monte Solaro.** An impressive limestone formation and the highest point on Capri (1,932 feet), Monte Solaro, which looms above the town of Anacapri, affords gasp-inducing views toward the bays of both Naples and Salerno. A 12-minute chairlift ride from the heart of town will take you right to the top. ⊠ *Piazza Vittoria, Anacapri* ☏ *081/8371428* ⊠ *€7 one way, €9 round-trip* ⊙ *Mar.–Oct., daily 9:30–4:30; Nov.–Feb., daily 10:30–3:30.*

**San Michele.** In the heart of Anacapri, the octagonal baroque church, finished in 1719, is best known for its exquisite majolica pavement designed by Solimena. ⊠ *Piazza San Nicola, Anacapri* ☏ *081/8372396* ⊕ *www.chiesa-san-michele.com* ⊠ *€3* ⊙ *Apr.–Sept., daily 9–7; Oct.–Mar., daily 10–3. Closed Nov. 27–Dec. 8.*

### ELSEWHERE ON THE ISLAND

**Grotta Azzurra.** Only when the famous Blue Grotto was "discovered" in 1826 by the Polish poet August Kopisch and Swiss artist Ernest Fries did Capri become a tourist haven. The water's extraordinary sapphire color is caused by a hidden opening in the rock that refracts the light. ⊠ *Marina Grande* ⊠ *€21, including admission to grotto* ⊙ *Daily 9–1 hr before sunset; closed if sea is even minimally rough.*

# SHOPPING

Leather goods, jewelry, and cameos are some of the best items to buy in Campania. In Naples you'll generally find good deals on handbags, shoes, and clothing. If you want the real thing, make your purchases in shops, but if you don't mind imitations, rummage around at the various street-vendor *bancherelle* (stalls).

In Naples the immediate area around **Piazza dei Martiri,** in the center of Chiaia, has the densest concentration of luxury shopping, with perfume shops, fashion outlets, and antiques on display. **Via dei Mille** and **Via Filangieri,** which lead off Piazza dei Martiri, are home to Bulgari, Mont Blanc, and Hermes stores. The small, pedestrian-only **Via Calabritto,** which leads down from Piazza dei Martiri toward the sea, is where you'll find high-end retailers such as Prada, Gucci, Versace, Vuitton, Cacharel, Damiani, and Cartier. **Via Chiaia** and **Via Toledo** are the two busiest shopping streets for most Neapolitans; there you'll find reasonably priced clothes and shoes. The **Vomero** district yields more shops, especially along Via Scarlatti and Via Luca Giordano. **Via Santa Maria di Costantinopoli,** which runs from Piazza Bellini to the Archaeological Museum, is the street for antiques shops.

**Melinoi.** This store stands out from the many small boutiques in Naples for its originality; it stocks clothes and accessories by Romeo Gigli as well as a number of French designers. ⊠ *Via Benedetto Croce 34, Spaccanapoli, Naples* ☎ *081/5521204.*

**Nel Regno di Pulcinella.** This is the workshop of Lello Esposito, renowned maker of Neapolitan puppets. ⊠ *Vico San Domenico Maggiore 9, Spaccanapoli, Naples* ☎ *081/5514171.*

## WHERE TO EAT

**$$$**
ITALIAN

✕**Ristorante Pizzeria Aurora.** Though often frequented by celebrities— their photographs adorn the walls—this restaurant offers *simpatia* to all its patrons. The cognoscenti start off by sharing a pizza *all'acqua,* a thin pizza with mozzarella and a sprinkling of *peperoncino* (dried chili peppers). ⊠ *Via Fuorlovado 18–20, Capri Town* ☎ *081/8370181* ⊕ *www.auroracapri.com* ▭ *AE, DC, MC, V* ⊘ *Closed Jan.–mid-Mar.*

**$$$$**
NEAPOLITAN

✕**Umberto.** Run by the Di Porzio family since 1916, Umberto is one of the city's classic restaurants. It combines the classiness of the Chiaia neighborhood and the friendliness of other parts of the city. Try the *tubettini 'do tre dita* ("three-finger" pasta with a mixture of seafood), which bears the nickname of the original Umberto. Owner Massimo and sister Lorella (Umberto's grandchildren) are both wine experts and oversee a fantastic cellar. Umberto is also one of the few restaurants in the city that cater to those who have a gluten allergy. ⊠ *Via Alabardieri 30–31, Chiaia* ☎ *081/418555* ⊕ *www.umberto.it* ▭ *AE, DC, MC, V* ⊘ *Closed Mon. and 3 wks in Aug.*

# NICE, FRANCE

The fifth-largest city in France, Nice is also one of the noblest. The city is capped by a dramatic hilltop château, at whose base a bewitching warren of ancient Mediterranean streets unfolds. Although now French to the core, the town was allied with a Latin Duchy until 1860, and this almost 500 years of history adds a rich Italian flavor to the city's culture, architecture, and dialect. In the late 19th century, Nice saw the birth of tourism, as English and Russian aristocrats began to winter in the temperate climate along the famed waterfront, Promenade des Anglais, which is now lined with grand hotels, a part of their legacy. Nowadays Nice strikes an engaging balance between historic Provençal grace, port-town exotica, urban energy, whimsy, and high culture. Its museums—particularly its art collections—are excellent, and the atmosphere is langourous yet urbane.

## ESSENTIALS

CURRENCY  The euro (€1 to US$1.36 at this writing).

HOURS  Most stores open Monday through Saturday from 9 to 7, but many close at lunchtime (usually noon to 2 or 3), and some will open later and on Sunday during July and August. Museums are usually open 10 to 5, but most are closed on either Monday or Tuesday.

INTERNET  **Cyberpoint** (✉ *10 av. Félix Faure, Nice* ☎ *04–93–92–70–63* ⊕ *www. cyberpoint-nice.com*) is open weekdays 10–8, Saturday noon–7.

TELEPHONES  Tri-band GSM phones work in France. You can buy prepaid phone cards at telecom shops, news vendors, and tobacconists in all towns and cities. Phone cards can be used for local or international calls. France Telecom and Orange are leading telecom companies.

## COMING ASHORE

Ships dock at Nice Port, east of the city center and a 30- to 40-minute walk from the city's attractions. The port facilities include a tourist office and currency exchange desk. There is a free shuttle service into the downtown core in high season, and taxis are also available.

Don't rent a car if you intend to explore in the city, but it is a sensible option if you want to tour the spectacular Provençal countryside. Expect to pay approximately €75 per day for an economy manual vehicle. Taxis are plentiful and can provide tourist itineraries. For single journeys, fares begin at €2.80 and then €0.87 per km.

Public transport is reliable and comprehensive,, with Ligne d'Azur (⊕ *www.lignedazur.com*) providing services within the city and suburbs. Route 15 heads to Cimiez and offers a free transfer between the Chagall and Matisse museums. Single tickets are €1 at this writing, and allow you to ride for for 74 minutes. A one-day pass is €4. There is fast and reliable train service between Nice and Cannes, Monte Carlo, Antibes, and other coastal towns if you want to explore farther afield without a car.

# EXPLORING NICE

## VIEUX NICE

Framed by the "château"—really a rocky promontory—and Cours Saleya, Nice's Vieille Ville is its strongest drawing point and the best place to capture the city's historic atmosphere. Its grid of narrow streets, darkened by houses five and six stories high with bright splashes of laundry fluttering overhead and jewel-box baroque churches on every other corner, creates a magic that seems utterly removed from the French Riviera fast lane.

**Colline de Château** *(Château Hill).* Though nothing remains of the once-massive medieval stronghold but a few ruins left after its 1706 dismantling, this park still bears its name. From here, take in extraordinary views of the Baie des Anges, the length of the Promenade des Anglais, and the red-ocher roofs of the Vieille Ville. ⊙ *Daily 7–7.*

★  **Cours Saleya.** This long pedestrian thoroughfare, half street, half square, is the nerve center of Old Nice, the heart of the Vieille Ville and the stage

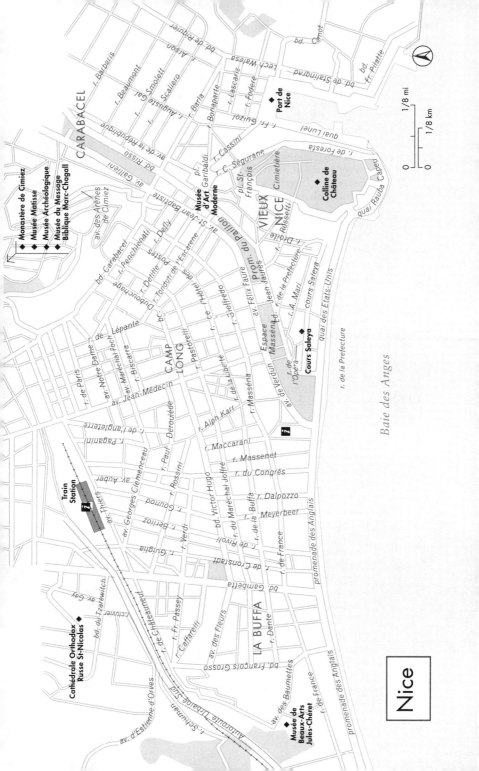

Nice

set for the daily dramas of market-place and café life. Framed with 18th-century houses and shaded by plane trees, the long, narrow square bursts into a fireworks show of color Tuesday through Sunday, when flower-market vendors roll armloads of mimosas, irises, roses, and orange blossoms into *cornets* (paper cones) and thrust them into the arms of shoppers. Cafés and restaurants, all more or less touristy, fill outdoor tables with onlookers who bask in the sun. At the far east end, antiques and *brocantes* (collectibles) draw avid junk-hounds every Monday morning.

**Musée d'Art Moderne.** The assertive contemporary architecture of the Modern Art Museum makes a bold and emphatic statement regarding Nice's presence in the modern world. The art collection inside focuses intently and thoroughly on contemporary art from the late 1950s onward, but pride of place is given to sculptor Nikki de Saint Phalle's recent donation of over 170 exceptional pieces. ✉ *Promenade des Arts, Vieux Nice* ☎ *04–97–13–42–01* ⊕ *www.mamac-nice.org* ✆ *Free* ☉ *Tues.–Sun. 10–6.*

★ **Musée des Beaux-Arts Jules-Chéret** *(Jules-Chéret Fine Arts Museum).* While the collection here is impressive, it is the 19th-century Italianate mansion that houses it that remains the showstopper. Originally built for a member of Nice's Old Russian community, the Princess Kotschoubey, this was a belle époque wedding cake, replete with one of the grandest staircases on the coast, salons decorated with Neo-Pompéienne frescoes, an English-style garden, and white columns and balustrades by the dozen. After the *richissime* American James Thompson took over and the last glittering ball was held here, the villa was bought by the municipality as a museum in the 1920s. Unfortunately, much of the period decor was sold, but in its place now hang paintings by Degas, Boudin, Monet, Sisley, Dufy, and Jules Chéret, whose posters of winking *damselles* distill the *joie* of the belle époque. From the Negresco Hotel area the museum is about a 15-minute walk up a gentle hill. ✉ *33 av. des Baumettes, Centre Ville* ☎ *04–92–15–28–25* ⊕ *www.musee-beaux-arts-nice.org* ✆ *Free* ☉ *Tues.–Sun. 10–6.*

## CIMIEZ

Once the site of the powerful Roman settlement Cemenelum, the hilltop neighborhood of Cimiez—4 km (2½ mi) north of Cours Saleya—is Nice's most luxurious quarter (use Bus 15 from Place Masséna or Avenue Jean-Médecin to visit its sights).

---

### NICE BEST BETS

**Musée Matisse.** Nice, where the artist made his home from 1917 until his death in 1954, has the finest collection of his work.

**Musée du Message Biblique Marc-Chagall.** Specially designed galleries house the 17 canvases making up "Biblical Message," one of the Postimpressionist's most charismatic works.

**Strolling through the alleyways of Vieux Nice.** The pastel facades of the lively Old Town have inspired generations of artists. Enjoy the cafés, the quaint boutiques, and the flower market on Cours Saleya.

**Monastère de Cimiez.** This fully functioning monastery is worth the pilgrimage. You'll find a lovely **garden,** replanted along the lines of the original 16th-century layout; the **Musée Franciscain,** a didactic museum tracing the history of the Franciscan order; and a 15th-century **church** containing three works of remarkable power and elegance by Bréa. ⊠ *Pl. du Monastère, Cimiez* ☎ *04–93–81–00–04* ⌧ *Free* ⊘ *Mon.–Sat. 10–noon and 3–6.*

**Musée Archéologique** *(Archaeology Museum).* This museum, next to the Matisse Museum, has a dense and intriguing collection of objects extracted from the digs around the Roman city of Cemenelum, which flourished from the 1st to the 5th centuries. ⊠ *160 av. des Arènes-de-Cimiez, Cimiez* ☎ *04–93–81–59–57* ⊕ *www.musee-archeologique-nice. org* ⌧ *€3* ⊘ *Wed.–Mon. 10–6.*

★ **Musée du Message Biblique Marc-Chagall** *(Marc Chagall Museum of Biblical Themes).* This museum has one of the finest permanent collections of Chagall's (1887–1985) late works. Superbly displayed, 17 vast canvases depict biblical themes, each in emphatic, joyous colors. ⊠ *Av. du Dr-Ménard, head up Av. Thiers, then take a left onto Av. Malausséna, cross railway tracks, and take first right up Av. de l'Olivetto, Cimiez* ☎ *04–93–53–87–20* ⊕ *www.musee-chagall.fr* ⌧ *€7.50* ⊘ *May.–Oct., Wed.–Mon. 10–6; Nov.–Apr., Wed.–Mon. 10–5.*

Fodor's Choice
★ **Musée Matisse.** In the '60s the city of Nice bought this lovely, light-bathed 17th-century villa, surrounded by the ruins of Roman civilization, and restored it to house a large collection of Henri Matisse's works. Matisse settled in Nice in 1917, seeking a sun cure after a bout with pneumonia, and remained here until his death in 1954. During his years on the French Riviera, Matisse maintained intense friendships and artistic liaisons with Renoir, who lived in Cagnes, and with Picasso, who lived in Mougins and Antibes. Settling first along the waterfront, he eventually moved up to the rarefied isolation of Cimiez and took an apartment in the Hôtel Regina (now an apartment building), where he lived out the rest of his life. Matisse walked often in the parklands around the Roman remains and was buried in an olive grove outside the Cimiez cemetery. The collection of artworks includes several pieces the artist donated to the city before his death; the rest were donated by his family. In every medium and context—paintings, gouache cutouts, engravings, and book illustrations—it represents the evolution of his art, from Cézanne-like still lifes to exuberant dancing paper dolls. Even the furniture and accessories speak of Matisse, from the Chinese vases to the bold-printed fabrics with which he surrounded himself. A series of black-and-white photographs captures the artist at work, surrounded by personal—and telling—details. ⊠ *164 av. des Arènes-de-Cimiez, Cimiez* ☎ *04–93–81–08–08* ⊕ *www.musee-matisse-nice.org* ⌧ *€5* ⊘ *Wed.–Mon. 10–6.*

# SHOPPING

As the largest city in Provence, Nice is a trove of regional crafts and delicacies, including basketware, bright fabrics, perfumes, lavender soaps, olive-wood items, plus delicious olives, olive oils, honey, dried herbs, and quaffable local wines. The city is particularly renowned for its delicious crystallized fruit. The best place to find crafts is in the Old Town, while French couture can be found on the elegant boulevards of the new town.

**Alziari.** Olive oil by the gallon in cans with colorful, old-fashioned labels is sold at this tiny store. ⊠ *14 rue St-François-de-Paule, Vieux Nice.*

**Boutique 3.** For fragrances, linens, and pickled-wood furniture, head to this shop. ⊠ *3 rue Longchamp, Vieux Nice.*

**Confiserie du Vieux Nice.** A good source for crystallized fruit, this store is on the west side of the port. ⊠ *14 quai Papacino, Vieux Nice.*

**Henri Auer.** This chocolatier and candy mainstay has been open since 1820. ⊠ *7 rue St-François-de-Paule, Vieux Nice.*

## BEACHES

Nice's pebble beaches extend all along the Baie des Anges, backed full-length by the Promenade des Anglais. Public stretches alternate with posh private beaches that have restaurants—and bar service, mattresses and parasols, waterskiing, parasailing, windsurfing, and jet-skiing.

**Beau Rivage.** One of the handiest private beaches is just across from the Opera. ⊠ *Promenade des Anglais* ☎ *04–92–47–82–82* ⊕ *www. hotelnicebeaurivage.com.*

**Ruhl.** The sun can also be yours for the basking at this beach across from the casino. ⊠ *Promenade des Anglais* ☎ *04–93–87–09–70* ⊕ *www. ruhl-plage.com.*

## WHERE TO EAT

¢    ✕ **Chez René/Socca.** This back-alley landmark is the most popular dive in
FRENCH    town for *socca,* the chickpea-pancake snack food unique to Nice. Rustic olive-wood tables line the street, and curt waiters splash down your drink order. For the food, you get in line at the Socca, choose your €3 plate (or plates), and carry it steaming to the table yourself. It's off Place Garibaldi on the edge of the Vieille Ville, across from the *gare routière* (bus station). ⊠ *2 rue Miralheti, Vieux Nice* ☎ *04–93–92–05–73* ⊟ *No credit cards* ☉ *Closed Mon.*

$$$$    ✕ **Grand Café de Turin.** Whether you squeeze onto a banquette in the
SEAFOOD    dark, low-ceiling bar or win a coveted table under the arcaded porticoes on place Garibaldi, this is *the* place to go for shellfish in Nice: sea snails, clams, plump *fines de claires* and salty *bleue* oysters, and urchins by the dozen. It's packed noon and night, so don't be too put off by the sometimes brusque reception of the waiters. ⊠ *5 pl. Garibaldi, Vieux Nice* ☎ *04–93–62–29–52* ⊟ *AE, DC, MC, V.*

# PALERMO, ITALY

Once the intellectual capital of southern Europe, Palermo has always been at the crossroads of civilization. Favorably situated on a crescent-shaped bay at the foot of Monte Pellegrino, it has attracted almost every

2

culture touching the Mediterranean world. To Palermo's credit, it has absorbed these diverse cultures into a unique personality that is at once Arab and Christian, Byzantine and Roman, Norman and Italian. The city's heritage encompasses all of Sicily's varied ages, but its distinctive aspect is its Arab-Norman identity, an improbable marriage that, mixed in with Byzantine and Jewish elements, created some resplendent works of art. No less noteworthy than the architecture is Palermo's chaotic vitality, on display at some of Italy's most vibrant outdoor markets, public squares, street bazaars, and food vendors, and above all in its grand climax of Italy's most spectacular *passeggiata* (the leisurely social stroll along the principal thoroughfare).

### ESSENTIALS

CURRENCY   The euro (€1 to US$1.36 at this writing).

HOURS   Most shops are open 9 to 1 and 4 or 4:30 to 7:30 or 8 and closed Sunday; in addition, most food shops close Wednesday afternoon, and other shops normally close Monday morning. Most museums/attractions open throughout the day, though some, particularly churches, close in the afternoon.

INTERNET   There is Internet access in the port terminal building at the Western Union desk.

TELEPHONES   Tri-band GSM phones work in Italy. You can buy prepaid phone cards at telecom shops, news vendors, and tobacconists in all towns and cities. Phone cards can be used for local or international calls.

### COMING ASHORE

Palermo's cruise port has recently been expanded to accommodate larger vessels. The terminal building has a café and a shop. Just outside the gates are taxis and horse-drawn carriages. It is possible to walk directly from the ship into the city; however, the port area has a reputation for pickpockets and scam artists, so be aware.

Three bus routes (Gialla, Rossa, and Verde) ply the streets of the old town, but none links with the port; tickets cost €1. Taxis charge approximately €2.33 initially, then €0.78 per km (½-mi) with an increment of €0.11 per 140 meters (460 feet) when traffic is slow. Renting a car would open up much of the island to you. Expect to pay about €60 per day for a compact manual vehicle.

## EXPLORING PALERMO

**Catacombe dei Cappuccini.** The spookiest sight in all of Sicily, this 16th-century catacomb houses more than 8,000 corpses of men, women, and young children, some in tombs but many mummified and preserved, hanging in rows on the walls. Many of the fully clothed corpses wear priests' smocks (most of the dead were Capuchin monks). The Capuchins were founders and proprietors of the bizarre establishment from 1559 to 1880. ⊠ *Piazza Cappuccini off Via Cappuccini, near Palazzo Reale* ☎ *091/212117* 🔅 *€3* ⊙ *Late Oct.–Mar., daily 9–12:30 and 3–5:30; Apr.–late Oct., daily 8:30–1 and 2:30–6.*

★ **Cattedrale.** This church is a lesson in Palermitan eclecticism—originally Norman (1182), then Catalan Gothic (14th–15th century), then fitted

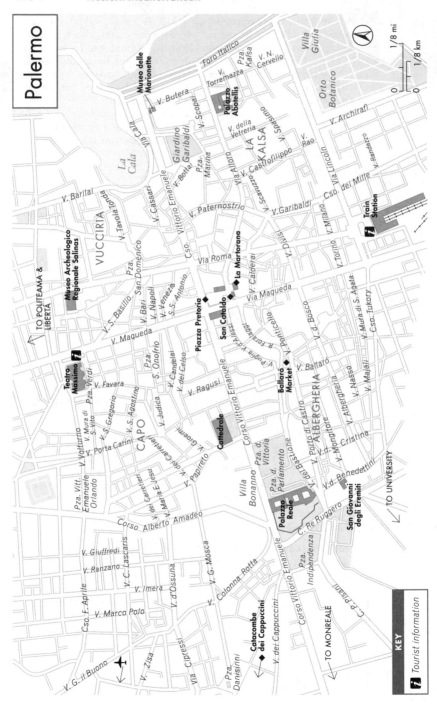

# Palermo

TO POLITEAMA & LIBERTÀ

TO UNIVERSITY

TO MONREALE

Foro Italico

**Museo delle Marionette**

V. Butera

Villa Giulia

Orto Botanico

V. Archirafi

V. Randazzo

Cso. Via Lincoln

Cso. dei Mille

V. N. Cervello

Pza. Kalsa

V. Torremazza

V. Scopari

**Palazzo Abatellis**

V. della Vetreria

V. Spasimo

V. Rao

**LA KALSA**

V. Alloro

V. Castrofilippo

Scavuzzo

La Cala

Giardino Garibaldi

V. Cala

V. Bottai

V. Cassari

Marina

V. Paternostrio

V. Garibaldi

V. Milano

V. Torino

**Train Station**

V. Barilai

V. Tavola Tonda

Pza. San Domenico

Corso Vittorio Emanuele

**VUCCIRIA**

**Museo Archeologico Regionale Salinas**

Via Roma

**La Martorana**

V. Calderai

Via Maqueda

V. Divisi

V. d. Agata

Cso. Via di S. Agata

V. Mura di S. Agata

Cso. Tukory

V. S. Basilio

V. Bari

V. Napoli

V. Venezia

S. S. Antonio

V. Maqueda

Pza. S. Onofrio

V. Candelai

V. del Celso

**Piazza Pretoria**

**San Cataldo**

V. Alessi

V. Ponticello

V. d. Bosco

**ALBERGHERIA**

V. Nasso

V. Majali

**Teatro Massimo**

Pza. Verdi

V. Favara

V. S. Agostino

V. S. Gregorio

V. Judica

V. Ragusi

**Ballarò Market**

V. Ballarò

V. Puglia

V. d. Foraglia

V. Alberghria

V. Majali

**CAPO**

V. Volturno

V. Mura di S. Vito

V. Porta Carini

V. Giovni

Corso Vittorio Emanuele

**Cattedrale**

V. del Castro

V. Porto di Castro

V. Mongitore

V. d. Cristina

Pza. Vitt. Emanuele Orlando

V. d. Carrieri

V. Maria E. Gesu

V. Papireto

Villa Bonanno

Pza. d. Vittoria

Pza. d. Parlamento

V. del Bastione

V. d. Benedettini

**San Giovanni degli Eremii**

**Palazzo Reale**

C. Re Ruggero

Corso Alberto Amadeo

V. Giuffredi

V. Ranzano

V. C. Lascaris

V. d'Ossuna

V. G. Mosca

V. Colonna Rotta

Pza. Indipendenza

Corso Vittorio Emanuele

C. Pisani

Cso. F. Aprile

V. Imera

V. Marco Polo

V. Zisa

Via Cipressi

**Catacombe dei Cappuccini**

V. dei Cappuccini

Pza. Danisinni

V. G. il Buono

1/8 mi

1/8 km

0

**KEY**

🛈 *Tourist information*

🛈 *Tourist information*

out with a baroque and neoclassical interior (18th century). Its turrets, towers, dome, and arches come together in the kind of meeting of diverse elements that King Roger II (1095–1154), whose tomb is inside along with that of Frederick II, fostered during his reign. The back of the apse is gracefully decorated with interlacing Arab arches inlaid with limestone and black volcanic tufa. ⊠ *Corso Vittorio Emanuele, Capo* ☎ *091/334373* ⊕ *www. cattedrale.palermo.it* ⊠ *Church free, crypt €2.50* ☉ *Church free, crypt €2.50* ☉ *Mar.–Oct., Mon.– Sat. 9:30–5:30; Nov.–Feb., Mon.– Sat. 9:30–1:30.*

**La Martorana.** Distinguished by an elegant Norman campanile, this church was erected in 1143 but had its interior altered considerably during the baroque period. High along the western wall, however, is some of the oldest and best-preserved mosaic artwork of the Norman period. Near the entrance is an interesting mosaic of King Roger II being crowned by Christ. ⊠ *Piazza Bellini 3, Quattro Canti* ☎ *091/6161692* ☉ *Mon.–Sat. 9:15–1 and 3:30–6:30, Sun. 8:30–1.*

**Museo Archeologico Regionale Salinas.** Especially interesting pieces in this small but excellent collection are the examples of prehistoric cave drawings and a marvelously reconstructed Doric frieze from the Greek temple at Selinunte created some 2,500 years ago. The museum is closed at this writing, but is scheduled to reopen gradually (with temporarily reduced ticket prices) over the course of 2011. ⊠ *Piazza Olivella 24, Via Roma, Olivella* ☎ *091/6116806* ⊠ *€6* ☉ *Tues.–Fri. 8:30–2 and 2:30–6:45, Sat.–Mon. 8:30–1:45.*

☺ **Museo delle Marionette.** The traditional Sicilian *pupi* (puppets), with their glittering armor and fierce expressions, have become a symbol of Norman Sicily. Plots of the weekly performances center on the chivalric legends of the troubadours, who, before the puppet theater, kept alive tales of Norman heroes in Sicily. ⊠ *Piazzetta Niscemi 1, at Via Butera, Kalsa* ☎ *091/328060* ⊕ *www.museomarionettepalermo.it* ⊠ *€5* ☉ *Weekdays 9–1 and 3:30–6:30, Sat. 9–1.*

**Palazzo Abatellis.** Housed in this late-15th-century Catalan Gothic palace with Renaissance elements is the **Galleria Regionale**. Among its treasures are an *Annunciation* (1474) by Sicily's prominent Renaissance master Antonello da Messina (1430–79) and an arresting fresco by an unknown painter, titled *The Triumph of Death*, a macabre depiction of the plague years. ⊠ *Via Alloro 4, Kalsa* ☎ *091/6230011* ⊠ *€8, guided tour an additional €3.50* ☉ *Tues. and Thurs. 9–1 and 2:30–6, Wed. and Fri.–Sun. 9–1 (temporary exhibitions may have shorter hrs).*

**Palazzo Reale.** The historic royal palace, also called Palazzo dei Normanni (Norman Palace), was for centuries the seat of Sicily's semi-autonomous rulers. The building is an interesting mesh of abutting 10th-century Norman and 17th-century Spanish structures. Because it now houses the Sicilian Parliament, little is accessible to the public. The **Cappella Palatina** (Palatine Chapel) remains open. Built by Roger II in 1132, it's a dazzling example of the harmony of artistic elements produced under the Normans. Here the skill of French and Sicilian masons was brought to bear on the decorative purity of Arab ornamentation and the splendor of 11th-century Greek Byzantine mosaics.

Upstairs are the royal apartments, including the **Sala di Re Ruggero** (King Roger's Hall), decorated with medieval murals of hunting scenes—an earlier (1120) secular counterpoint to the religious themes seen elsewhere. To see this area of the palace, ask one of the tour guides (free) to escort you around the halls once used by one of the most splendid courts in Europe. ⊠ *Piazza Indipendenza, Albergheria* 🏛 *091/7051111* 🎫 *€7 to Cappella Palatina or Palazzo Reale, or €8.50 for both attractions* ⊙ *Palazzo Reale: Mon., Fri., and Sat. 8:30–noon and 2–5, Sun. 8:30–12:30. Cappella Palatina: Mon.–Sat. 8:30–noon and 2–5, Sun. 8:30–12:30.*

**Piazza Pretoria.** The square's centerpiece, a lavishly decorated fountain with 500 separate pieces of sculpture and an abundance of nude figures, so shocked some Palermitans when it was unveiled in 1575 that it got the nickname "Fountain of Shame."

★ **San Cataldo.** Three striking Saracenic scarlet domes mark this church, built in 1154 during the Norman occupation of Palermo. The church now belongs to the Knights of the Holy Sepulchre, and the spare but intense stone interior is rarely open to the public. If the church is closed, inquire next door at La Martorana. ⊠ *Piazza Bellini 3, Kalsa* 🏛 *3483394617* 🎫 *€1* ⊙ *Mar.–Oct., Mon.–Sat. 9–2 and 3:30–7, Sun. 9–2; Nov.–Feb., Mon.–Sun. 9–2.*

**San Giovanni degli Eremiti.** Distinguished by its five reddish-orange domes and stripped-clean interior, this 12th-century church was built by the Normans on the site of an earlier mosque—one of 200 that once stood in Palermo. The emirs ruled Palermo for nearly two centuries and brought to it their passion for lush gardens and fountains. One is reminded of this while sitting in San Giovanni's delightful cloister of twin half columns, surrounded by palm trees, jasmine, oleander, and citrus trees. The last tickets are sold a half-hour before closing. At this writing, the cloister was under construction and half the church was not viewable. ⊠ *Via dei Benedettini, Albergheria* 🏛 *091/6515019* 🎫 *€6* ⊙ *Tues.–Sat. 9–5.*

**Teatro Massimo.** Construction of this formidable neoclassical theater was started in 1875 by Giovanni Battista Basile and completed by his son Ernesto in 1897. A fire in 1974 rendered the theater inoperable but it reopened with great fanfare in 1997, its interior as glorious as ever. *The Godfather Part III* ended with a famous shooting scene on the theater's steps. Visits are by 25-minute guided tour only; English-speaking guides are available 10–2 and 3–4. ⊠ *Piazza Verdi 9, at top of Via Maqueda,*

*Olivella* ☎ *091/6053111 or booking for guided tours 091/6090831*
⊕ *www.teatromassimo.it* 🎫 *€5* ⊙ *Tues.–Sun. 10–3 for guided visits,*
*except during rehearsals. Last tour leaves at 2:30.*

**MONREALE**

*10 km (6 mi) southwest of Palermo.*

**Cloister.** The lovely cloister of the abbey adjacent to the Duomo was
built at the same time as the church but enlarged in the 14th century.
The beautiful enclosure is surrounded by 216 intricately carved double
columns, every other one decorated in a unique glass mosaic pattern.
Afterward, don't forget to walk behind the cloister to the **belvedere,**
with stunning panoramic views over the Conca d'Oro (Golden Conch)
valley toward Palermo. ⊠ *Piazza del Duomo* ☎ *091/6404403* 🎫 *€6*
⊙ *Daily 9–6:30.*

★ **Duomo.** Monreale's splendid cathedral is lavishly covered with mosaics
depicting events from the Old and New Testaments. After the Norman
conquest of Sicily the new princes showcased their ambitions through
monumental building projects. William II (1154–89) built the church
complex with a cloister and palace between 1174 and 1185, employing
Byzantine craftsmen. The result was a glorious fusion of Eastern and
Western influences, widely regarded as the finest example of Norman
architecture in Sicily.

The major attraction is the 68,220 square feet of glittering gold mosaics
decorating the cathedral interior. *Christ Pantocrator* dominates the apse
area; the nave contains narratives of the Creation; and scenes from the
life of Christ adorn the walls of the aisles and the transept. The painted
wooden ceiling dates from 1816–37. The roof commands a great view
(a reward for climbing 172 stairs).

Bonnano Pisano's **bronze doors,** completed in 1186, depict 42 biblical
scenes and are considered among the most important of medieval artifacts. Barisano da Trani's 42 panels on the north door, dating from 1179,
present saints and evangelists. ⊠ *Piazza del Duomo* ☎ *091/6404413*
⊙ *Mid-Apr.–mid-Oct., daily 8:30–1 and 2:30–6:30; mid-Oct.–mid-*
*Apr., daily 8–12:30 and 2:30–6:30.*

## SHOPPING

Sicilian specialties include lace and linen, including place mats and napkins, and ceramics, particularly its practical folk pottery from Caltagirone, on the north coast. Marble and wrought iron are also fashioned
into souvenir pieces and antiques shops are numerous, though prices
can be high. Edibles include an excellent range of wines and olive oils,
jams, and tasty sweets.

In Palermo, north of Piazza Castelnuovo, **Via della Libertà** and the streets
around it represent the luxury end of the shopping scale, with some
of Palermo's best-known stores. A second nerve center for shoppers is
the pair of parallel streets connecting modern Palermo with the train
station, **Via Roma,** and **Via Maqueda,** where boutiques and shoe shops
become increasingly upmarket as you move from the Quattro Canti past

Teatro Massimo to Via Ruggero Settimo, but are still a serious notch below their counterparts in the Libertà area.

If you're interested in truly connecting with local life while searching for souvenirs, a visit to one of Palermo's many bustling markets is essential. Between Via Roma and Via Maqueda the many **bancherelle** *(market stalls)* on Via Bandiera sell everything from socks to imitation designer handbags.

**Enoteca Picone.** This is the best wine shop in town, with a fantastic selection of Sicilian and national wines. ⊠ *Via Marconi 36, Libertà* ☎ *091/331300* ⊕ *www.enotecapicone.it* ⊠ *Viale Strasburgo 235 Libertà.*

**Giuseppe Gramuglia.** Seekers of fringes, tassels, and heavy fabrics should stop in here. ⊠ *Via Roma 412–414, at Via Principe di Belmonte, Vucciria* ☎ *091/583262.*

## WHERE TO EAT

$ ✕ **Pizzeria Ai Comparucci.** One of Palermo's best pizzerias doubles as an PIZZA informal modern art gallery, with colorful modern paintings on the walls, giving it a fun, casual vibe that draws in local crowds on the spur of the moment. Better yet are the delicious Neapolitan pizzas coming out of the big oven in the open kitchen. The genius is in the crust, which is seared in the oven in a matter of seconds (so don't expect a long, leisurely meal). The place serves until 11 PM or midnight—later than almost any other restaurant in the neighborhood. ⊠ *Messina 36, between Yarzili and Libertà, Libertà* ☎ *091/6090467* ☰ *AE, MC, V* ☺ *Closed Mon.*

$$ ✕ **Trattoria Altri Tempi.** The "Olden Days" restaurant is a favorite among ITALIAN locals searching for the true rustic cooking of their Sicilian ancestors. ★ Knickknacks fill the walls of the small, friendly space. A meal begins with a carafe of the house red set down without asking and a superb spread of traditional antipasti. Dishes have old Palermitan names: *fave a cunigghiu* is fava beans prepared with olive oil, garlic, and remarkably flavorful oregano; and *vampaciucia c'anciova* is a lasagna-like pasta dish with a concentrated sauce of tomatoes, anchovies, and grapes. The meal ends well, too, with free house-made herb or fruit liquors and excellent cannoli. ⊠ *Via Sammartino 65/67, Libertà* ☎ *091/323480* ☰ *AE. DC, MC, V* ☺ *Closed mid-Aug.–mid-Sept. and Sun. June–Aug. No dinner Sun.*

# POLTU QUATU, SARDINIA, ITALY

An uncut jewel of an island, Sardinia remains unique and enigmatic. Would-be conquerors have left their marks, but inland, a proud Sard culture and language flourish. Sardinia has some of Europe's most expensive resort destinations, but it's also home to areas as rugged and undeveloped as anywhere on the continent. Fine sand and clean waters draw sun seekers to beaches that are unquestionably among the best in the Mediterranean. Best known are those along the Costa Smeralda (Emerald Coast), where the superrich have anchored their

**Northern Sardinia**

0  20 miles
0  30 km

Isola Asinara
Golfo dell' Asinara
Stintino
Porto Torres
Castelsardo
Santa Teresa di Gallura
La Maddalena
Caprera
Palau
Poltu Quatu
Arzachena
Porto Cervo
Porto Rotondo
Golfo Aranci
Olbia
COSTA SMERALDA
SS200
SS133
Anghelu Ruiu
Sassari
Oschiri
SS127
SS199
SS125
Capo Caccia
Alghero
Grotta di Nettuno
Ozieri
Siniscola
S A R D I N I A
SS131
SS129
Macomer
Nuoro
Lago Omodeo
Oliena
Cala Gonone
Golfo di Orosei

**Porto Cervo**
Yacht Club
Baia di Porto Cervo
Vecchio Molo
MARINA
VILLAGE

yachts since the 1960s. But most of the coast is unsettled, a jagged series of wildly beautiful inlets accessible only by sea. And inland, Sardinia remains shepherd's country, silent and stark. Spaghetti Westerns were once filmed here, and it's not hard to imagine why: the desolate mountainous terrain seems the perfect frontier set. Against this landscape are the striking and mysterious stone *nuraghi* (ancient defensive structures), which provide clues to the lifestyles of the island's prehistoric peoples.

## ESSENTIALS

CURRENCY   The euro (€1 to US$1.36 at this writing).

HOURS   Stores are generally open from 9 or 9:30 to 1 and from 3:30 or 4 to 7 or 7:30. Many shops close Sunday. Many national museums are closed on Monday and may have shorter hours on Sunday.

INTERNET   **Libreria Il Labirinto** (✉ *Via Carlo Alberto 119, Alghero* ☎ *079/980496* ⊕ *nuke.librerialabirinto.it*) is a well-stocked book and press store that has four Internet ports.

TELEPHONES   Tri-band GSM phones work in Sardinia, which is a part of Italy. You can buy prepaid phone cards at telecom shops, news vendors, and tobacconists in all towns and cities. Phone cards can be used for local or international calls.

### COMING ASHORE

Poltu Quatu means "hidden port" in the Sardinian dialect, and it is hidden at the head of a narrow inlet. Small cruise ships can dock at the port, but larger ships dock beyond the mouth of the inlet and tender passengers ashore. The port is one element in an extended tourist "village"; other facilities include a selection of cafés, sports outfitters, and shops. You can rent a boat for the day directly from the harbor to cruise the coast. There is no public transport to the port.

Although prices are steep, renting a car gives you a great opportunity to explore the northern half of the island and still have time to relax. Europcar has an office in the port. Other car-rental companies will deliver to the port for an extra charge. Rental prices for a compact manual vehicle start at €80 per day. There is a taxi stand within the resort village. Taxis will meet boats at the port but must be prebooked. Taxi fares are €20 into Puerto Cervo, which is just around the headland.

## EXPLORING NORTHERN SARDINIA

### PORTO CERVO

★ *35 km (22 mi) southeast of La Maddalena, 30 km (19 mi) north of Olbia.*

Sardinia's northeastern coast is fringed with low cliffs, inlets, and small bays. This has become an upscale vacationland, with glossy resorts such as Baia Sardinia and Porto Rotondo just outside the confines of the famed Costa Smeralda, developed by the Aga Khan (born 1936), who in 1965 accidentally discovered the coast's charms—and potential— when his yacht took shelter here from a storm. In the late 1960s and '70s the Costa Smeralda, with its heart in Porto Cervo, was *the* place to summer. The attractions remain geared to those who can measure themselves by the yardstick of Khan's fabled riches. Italy's most expensive hotels are here, and the world's most magnificent yachts anchor in the waters of Porto Cervo.

All along the coast, carefully tended lush vegetation surrounds vacation villages and discreet villas that have sprung up over the past decade in spurious architectural styles best described as "bogus Mediterranean." The trend has been to keep this an enclave of the very rich. Outside the peak season, however, prices plunge and the majesty of the natural surroundings shines through, justifying all the hype and the Emerald Coast's fame as one of the truly romantic corners of the Mediterranean.

### LA MADDALENA

*30 km (19 mi) east of Santa Teresa di Gallura, 45 km (20 mi) northwest of Olbia.*

From the port of Palau you can visit the archipelago of La Maddalena, seven granite islands embellished with lush green scrub and wind-bent pines. Car ferries make the 3-km (2-mi) trip about every half hour.

**Giuseppe Garibaldi's tomb.** Pilgrims pay homage to the national hero, who is buried on the grounds of his farm on Isola Caprera. The patriot, who laid the groundwork for the first unification of Italy, lived from 1807 to 1882, and at one point owned half of Isola Caprera. Take the ferry to Isola Maddalena and then the bridge to Isola Caprera. ⊕ *7 km (4½ mi) east of Isola Maddalena* ☎ *0789/727162* ⊕ *www.compendiogaribaldino.it* ☎ *€4* ⊗ *Oct.–Apr., Tues.–Sun. 9–1:30; May–Sept., Tues.–Sun. 9–6:30.*

### SANTA TERESA DI GALLURA
*55 km (34 mi) west of Porto Cervo.*

At the northern tip of Sardinia, Santa Teresa di Gallura retains the relaxed, carefree air of a former fishing village. Nearby beaches rival those farther down the coast, but manage not to seem over-touristed.

### GOLFO ARANCI
*47 km (29 mi) southeast of Puerto Cervo.*

At the mouth of the Gulf of Olbia, Golfo Aranci is a small-scale resort and major arrival point for ferries from the mainland. The craggy headland west of town has been left undeveloped as a nature reserve, and there are some inviting beaches within an easy drive.

### OLBIA
*30 km (19 mi) south of Porto Cervo, 19 km (12 mi) southwest of Golfo Aranci, 65 km (41 mi) southeast of Santa Teresa di Gallura.*

Amid the resorts of Sardinia's northeastern coast, Olbia is a lively little seaport and port of call for mainland ferries at the head of a long, wide bay.

**San Simplicio.** The little basilica, a short walk behind the main Corso Umberto, is worth searching out if you have any spare time in Olbia. The simple granite structure dates from the 11th century, part of the great Pisan church-building program, using pillars and columns recycled from Roman buildings. ⊠ *Via San Simplicio* ☎ *0789/23358* ⊗ *Daily 7:30–12:30 and 4–7.*

### SASSARI
*100 km (62 mi) southwest of Santa Teresa di Gallura.*

Inland Sassari is an important university town and administrative center, notable for its history of intellectualism and bohemian student culture, an ornate old cathedral, and a good archaeological museum. Look for downtown vendors of *fainè*, a pizzalike chickpea-flour pancake glistening with olive oil, which is a Genoese and Sassarese specialty. Sassari is the hub of several highways and secondary roads leading to various coastal resorts, among them Stintino and Castelsardo.

**Duomo.** It took just under 600 years to build Sassari's Duomo, dedicated to Saint Nicolas of Bari. The foundations were laid in the 12th century and the facade, in Spanish colonial style, was finished in the 18th. Of particular interest in the interior are the ribbed Gothic vaults, the

---

### SARDINIA BEST BETS

**Take an espresso in the harbor at Porto Cervo.** Most of Europe's royalty spends at least some time here every summer, as does a sprinkling of celebrities. This is a prime place for people-watching.

**Take a dip on the Costa Smeralda.** The setting of golden sand, russet rocks, and limpid waters is sublime.

**Take a stroll around Alghero.** Built by the Spanish as their capital in medievel times, Alghero is still a little piece of Spain in modern Italy.

14th-century painting of the Maddona del Bosco on the high alter, and the early-19th-century tomb of Placido Benedetto di Savoia, the uncle of united Italy's first king. ⊠ *Piazza Duomo 3* ☏ *079/233185* 🎫 *Free* ⊘ *Apr.–Oct., daily 9–noon and 5–7; Nov.–Mar., daily 9–12:30 and 4–6.*

**Museo Sanna.** Sassari's excellent museum has the best archaeological collection outside Cagliari, spanning nuraghic, Carthaginian, and Roman histories, including well-preserved bronze statues and household objects from the 2nd millennium BC. Summer hours vary from one year to the next. ⊠ *Via Roma 64* ☏ *079/272203* 🎫 *€4* ⊘ *Tues.–Sun. 9–8.*

## ALGHERO
*34 km (21 mi) southwest of Sassari, 137 km (85 mi) southwest of Olbia.*

A tourist-friendly town with a distinctly Spanish flavor, Alghero is also known as "Barcelonetta" (little Barcelona). Rich wrought-iron scrollwork decorates balconies and screened windows; a Spanish motif appears in stone portals and in bell towers. The town was built and inhabited in the 14th century by the Aragonese and Catalans, who constructed seaside ramparts and sturdy towers encompassing an inviting nucleus of narrow, winding streets with whitewashed palazzi. The native language spoken here is a version of Catalan, not Italian, although you probably have to attend one of the Masses conducted in Algherese (or listen in on stories swapped by older fishermen) to hear it.

**Capo Caccia.** West of Alghero are broad sandy beaches and the spectacular heights of an imposing limestone headland.

☾ **Grotta di Nettuno** *(Neptune's Caves).* At the base of a sheer cliff, the
★ pounding sea has carved an entrance to the vast fantastic cavern filled with water pools, stalactites, and stalagmites. You must visit with a guide; tours start on the hour. It's possible to reach the caves by boat or by land. ✛ *13 km (8 mi) west of Alghero* ☏ *079/946540* 🎫 *€12* ⊘ *Apr.–Sept., daily 9–7; Oct., daily 9–5; Nov.–Mar., daily 9–4.*

**Escala del Cabirol** *(Mountain Goat's Stairway).* By land, you can reach the entrance to the Grotta di Nettuno by descending the 654 dizzying steps of the aptly named stairway. The trip to the top of the stairway takes about 50 minutes by public bus. ⊠ *Via Catalogna* ☏ *079/950179* 🎫 *€5 round-trip* ⊘ *From Alghero: 9:15 year-round and 3:10 and 5:10 June–Sept. From Capo Caccia: noon year-round and 4:05 and 6:05 June–Sept.*

**Museo Diocesano d'Arte Sacra** *(Diocesan Museum of Sacred Art).* This museum is housed in a 13th-century church. The usual assortment of religious treasures—paintings, wooden sculptures, and bronzes—is on display; look for the masterful 16th-century Catalan silverware. ⊠ *Via Maiorca 1* ☏ *079/9733041* 🎫 *€3* ⊘ *Jan.–Mar., Thurs.–Tues. by appointment; Apr., May, and Oct., Thurs.–Tues. 10–1 and 5–8; June and Sept., Thurs.–Tues. 10–1 and 5–9; July and Aug., Thurs.–Tues. 10–1 and 6–11; Dec., Thurs.–Tues. 10–1 by appointment and 4–7; the museum is closed Nov.*

**Torre San Giovanni.** This old tower fortress can be climbed for good views from the terrace. Stop at the interesting city history display on the computer terminals inside the tower. There's also a rotating set of exhibits and a miniature model of Alghero's Old Town. ⊠ *Via Mateotti 12*☎ *079/9734045* 🎫 *Free* 🕑 *Varies with exhibits.*

## CASTELSARDO
*32 km (20 mi) northeast of Sassari.*

The walled seaside citadel of Castelsardo is a delight for craft lovers, with tiny shops crammed with all kinds of souvenirs, particularly woven baskets. The appropriately shaped **Roccia dell'Elefante** *(Elephant Rock)* on the road into Castelsardo was hollowed out by primitive man to become a *domus de janas* (literally, "fairy house," in fact a Neolithic burial chamber).

# SHOPPING

The Sard are very adept craftsmen and -women. For many generations the people in the mountains had to be self-sufficient and worked with bone, wood, and clay to produce practical yet beautiful items, including fine knives, the must-have tool of the shepherd. The women were traditionally weavers—in wool and straw—or lace-makers. Red coral and filigree jewelry also have a long tradition here. If you are looking for some comestibles to take home, Sardinian wine and honey are highly prized. The narrow streets of Alghero and Castelsardo are the best places to shop for locally made crafts. Porto Cervo has fewer craft shops, but designer names line the shopping streets with top-quality haute couture and jewelry stores plus independent boutiques selling gifts and collectibles.

The walled seaside citadel of **Castelsardo**, 32 km (20 mi) northeast of Sassari, is a delight for basket lovers. Roadside stands and shops in the Old Town sell woven baskets, as well as rugs and wrought iron.

**ISOLA.** ISOLA is an organization set up to promote Sardinian crafts. Sassari has Sardinia's main craft exhibition center in the public gardens next to Viale Mancini, built specifically as a showcase for gifts and souvenirs. ⊠ *Giardini Pubblici, Sassari* ☎ *079/230101.*

# ACTIVITIES

The Costa Smeralda has world-class water-sports facilities and boat rentals from the harbor.

**Pevero Golf Course.** The world-class, 18-hole golf course was designed by Robert Trent Jones. Green fees run €125. ⊠ *Bay of Pevero* ☎ *0789/96210* 🌐 *www.golfclubpevero.com.*

**Yacht Club Costa Smeralda.** The club provides use of its pool, restaurant, bar, and guest rooms to those with memberships at other yacht clubs. ⊠ *Via della Marina, Port Cervo* ☎ *0789/902200* 🌐 *www.yccs.it.*

# BEACHES

The beaches around the Costa Smeralda are some of the most exclusive in Europe, but they don't disappoint, with fine golden sand sheltered by red cliffs and fronting azure waters. Most can only be reached by boat, and there are regular small ferries from Porto Cervo. Rentals of sunbeds and towels are reassuringly expensive.

## WHERE TO EAT

**$$**
ITALIAN

✗ **Da Pietro.** A menu that includes *bucatini all'algherese* (hollow, spaghetti-like pasta with a sauce of clams, capers, tomatoes, and olives) and baked fish with a white-wine sauce keeps this seafood restaurant bustling below its vaulted ceilings. This is a great place to sample sebadas, ravioli stuffed with mascarpone cheese and topped with honey. Look for Da Pietro in the Old Town near Largo San Francesco. ⊠ *Via Ambrogio Machin 20, Alghero* ☎ *079/979645* ▭ *AE, MC, V* ☺ *Closed Wed. and 2 wks in Dec.*

**¢–$**
ITALIAN

✗ **L'Assassino.** Get a true taste of great local Sassarese cooking—and many of the other obscure Sardinian specialties you might have been looking for but not yet found. Horse, donkey, and roast pig figure prominently on the menu; best of all is a *cena sarda,* a 10-dish tasting menu with *porcetto* (roast suckling pig), also spelled porcheddu. The service is friendly, and the room is warm and cozy. Food is served all afternoon long. ⊠ *Vicolo Ospizio Cappuccini 1, near Via Rosello, Sassari* ☎ *079/235041* ▭ *AE, DC, MC, V* ☺ *Closed Sun.*

# PORTOFERRAIO, ITALY (ELBA)

Elba is the Tuscan archipelago's largest island, but it resembles nearby verdant Corsica more than it does its rocky Italian sisters, thanks to a network of underground springs that keep the island lush and green. It's this combination of semitropical vegetation and dramatic mountain scenery—unusual in the Mediterranean—that has made Elba so prized for so long, and the island's uniqueness continues to draw boatloads of visitors throughout the warm months. Lively Portoferraio, the main port, makes a good base for exploring the island.

## ESSENTIALS

CURRENCY  The euro (€1 to US$1.36 at this writing).

HOURS  Many shops are open 9–1 and 3:30–7:30 Monday through Saturday. Banks are open weekdays 8:30–1:30 and 2:45–3:45.

INTERNET  **Ristorante da Ciro** (⊠ *Via Vittorio II, 14, Portoferraio* ☎ *0565/919000* has a small internet area.

TELEPHONES  Prepaid *carte telefoniche* (calling cards) are available at post offices, tobacconists, and newsstands. Tear off the corner of the card and insert it in the slot. The cards may be used in almost every public pay phone. There are pay phones near the cruise ship port.

## COMING ASHORE

The cruise-ship dock is just a stone's throw from the historic center of Portoferraio, so most passengers just walk to town. If you want to get around the island, public buses operated by ATL (⊕ *www.atl.livorno.it*) stop at most towns several times a day; the tourist office has timetables. Sixty-minute tickets cost €0.90 and day tickets €3.40. There are numerous places to rent bikes, scooters, motorcycles, or cars. Expect

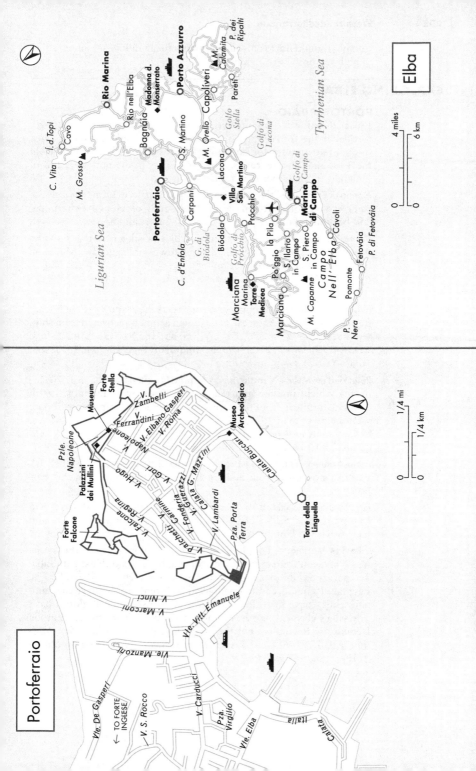

## Portoferraio

- Forte Falcone
- Palazzini dei Mullini
- Pzle. Napoleone
- Museum
- Forte Stella
- V. Zambelli
- V. Ferrandini
- V. Napoleone
- V. Elbano Gasperi
- V. Roma
- V. Hugo
- V. Gori
- V. Falcone
- V. Regina
- V. Parchetti
- V. Fonderia
- V. Carmine
- V. Guerrazzi
- Cala G. Mazzini
- V. Lambardi
- Pza. Porta Terra
- Museo Archeologico
- Calata Buccari
- Torre della Linguella
- V. Marconi
- V. Ninci
- Vle. Vitt. Emanuele
- Vle. Manzoni
- Vle. De Gasperi
- → TO FORTE INGLESE
- V. S. Rocco
- V. Carducci
- Pza. Virgilio
- Vle. Elba
- Cala Italia

0    1/4 mi
0    1/4 km

## Elba

- Ligurian Sea
- C. Vita
- I. d. Topi
- Cavo
- M. Grosso
- Rio Marina
- Rio nell'Elba
- Bagnaia
- Madonna d. Monserrato
- Porto Azzurro
- P. dei Ripalti
- S. Martino
- M. Orello
- Capoliveri
- M. Calamita
- Paréti
- Golfo Stella
- Golfo di Lacona
- Portoferráio
- Carpani
- Iacona
- Villa San Martino
- M. Orello
- Prócchio
- Golfo di Prócchio
- C. d'Enfola
- G. di Biódola
- Biódola
- la Pila
- Poggio
- S. Ilario in Campo
- S. Piero in Campo
- Marina di Campo
- Golfo di Campo
- Cavoli
- Marciana Marina
- Torre Medicea
- Marciana
- M. Capanne
- Campo Nell'Elba
- Pomonte
- Fetováia
- P. di Fetováia
- P. Nera
- Tyrrhenian Sea

0    4 miles
0    6 km

to pay around €45 for a compact manual car in low season and €75 in high season.

## EXPLORING ELBA

### PORTOFERRAIO

Especially enjoyable in Portoferraio is a stroll around the *centro storico*, fortified in the 16th century by the Medici grand duke Cosimo I. Most of the pretty, multicolor buildings that line the old harbor date from the 18th and 19th centuries, when the boats in the port were full of mineral exports rather than tourists.

**Marina di Campo.** On the south side of Elba, Marina di Campo is a classic summer vacationers' town, with a long sandy beach and a charming, laid-back marina full of bars, boutiques, and restaurants.

**Monte Capanne.** These slopes are crossed by a twisting road that provides magnificent vistas at every turn; the tiny towns of **Poggio** and **Marciana** have enchanting little piazzas full of flowers and trees. You can hike to the top of Monte Capanne, or take an unusual open-basket cable car from just above Poggio.

**Museo Archeologico.** The museum reconstructs the island's ancient history through a display of Etruscan and Roman artifacts recovered from ship-wrecks. ⊠ *Calata Buccari, Portoferraio* ☎ *0565/917338* ⊒ *€2* ☉ *June 15–Sept. 15, daily 9:30–2:30 and 5–midnight; Sept. 16–June 14, Thurs. 10:30–1:30 and 4–8.*

**Palazzina dei Mulini.** Napoléon was famously exiled on Elba in 1814–15, during which time he built this home out of two windmills. It still contains furniture from the period and Napoléon's impressive library, with the more than 2,000 volumes that he brought here from France. ⊠ *Piazzale Napoleone 1, Portoferraio* ☎ *0565/915846* ⊒ *€3, €5 with admission to Villa San Martino* ☉ *Mon. and Wed.–Sat. 9–7, Sun. 9–1.*

**Porto Azzurro.** The waters here are noticeably *azzurro* (sky-blue). It's worth a stop for a walk and a gelato along the rows of yachts harbored here.

**Rio Marina.** The island of Elba's quietest town is old-fashioned Rio Marina, with a pebble beach, an old mine, a leafy public park, and ferry service to Piombino.

**Villa San Martino.** A couple of miles outside Portoferraio, this home was Napoléon's summer residence during his 10-month exile on Elba. Temporary exhibitions are held in a gallery attached to the villa. The Egyptian Room, decorated with idealized scenes of the Egyptian campaign, may have provided Napoléon the consolation of glories past. The villa's classical facade was added by a Russian prince, Anatolia Demidoff, after he bought the house in 1852. ⊠ *Località San Martino* ☎ *0565/914688* ⊒ *€3, €5 with admission to Palazzina dei Mulini* ☉ *Tues.–Sat. 9–7 and Sun. 9–1.*

## BEACHES

Elba's most celebrated beaches are the sandy stretches at **Biodola, Procchio,** and **Marina di Campo,** but the entire island—and particularly the westernmost section, encircling Monte Capanne—is ringed with beautiful coastline. Indeed, it seems that every sleepy town has its own perfect tiny beach. Try **Cavoli** and **Fetovaia** anytime but July and August, when all the car-accessible beaches on the island are packed (there are also some accessible only by boat, such as the black-sand beach of **Punta Nera**).

## ACTIVITIES

### WATER SPORTS

**Il Viottolo.** Adventurous types can rent sea kayaks and mountain bikes from this outfitter, which also organizes three-day guided excursions on land and sea. ✉ *Via Pietri 6, Marina di Campo* ☎ *0565/978005* ⊕ *www.ilviottolo.it.*

**Spaziomare.** This company has motorboats available for half- and full-day rentals and sailboats to rent by the week. ✉ *Via Vittorio Veneto, Porto Azzurro* ☎ *0565/95112 or 348/6017862* ⊕ *www.spaziomare.it.*

**Subnow.** This outfitter organizes daily diving excursions, for experts and beginners, into the waters of Elba's National Marine Park. ✉ *Ville degli Ulivi Camping, Località La Foce, Marina di Campo* ☎ *0565/976048* ⊕ *www.subnow.it.*

# WHERE TO EAT

$ ✕ **Il Mare.** Homemade pastas and fresh seafood are served here with a
ITALIAN dash of style. The young chef puts a creative spin on the classics, coming
★ up with such delights as homemade vegetable gnocchi with scampi in a butter and saffron sauce. The *semifreddi* (literally, "half cold"; chilled or partially frozen desserts) are particularly good. Just a few steps from Rio Marina's pretty port, this is an easy stop on your way to or from the ferry. ✉ *Via del Pozzo 16, Rio Marina* ☎ *0565/962117* ▭ *V.*

$$$$ ✕ **Trattoria da Lido.** Come here for commendable *gnocchetti di pesce*
ITALIAN (bite-size potato-and-fish dumplings) with a white cream sauce and fresh *pesce all'elbana* (whitefish baked with vegetables and potatoes). The bustling, casual trattoria is in the old center of Portoferraio, at the beginning of the road to the old Medici walls. ✉ *Salita del Falcone 2, Portoferraio* ☎ *0565/914650* ▭ *AE, DC, MC, V* ⊗ *Closed mid-Dec.–mid-Feb.*

# PORTOFINO, ITALY

Like the family jewels that bedeck its habitual visitors, the Italian Riviera is glamorous, but in an old-fashioned way. The rustic and elegant, the provincial and chic, the cosmopolitan and the small-town are blended together here in a sun-drenched pastiche that defines the Italian side of the Riviera. Although the region bearing the name Liguria extends inland, its greatest charms are found on the coast, which has inspired poets and artists for centuries. One of the most photographed villages along the Ligurian coast, with a decidedly romantic and affluent aura, Portofino has long been a popular destination for foreigners. Once an ancient Roman colony and taken by the Republic of Genoa in 1229, it has also been ruled by the French, English, Spanish, and Austrians, as well as by marauding bands of 16th-century pirates. Elite British tourists first flocked to the lush harbor in the mid-1800s, and today some of Europe's wealthiest lay anchor in Portofino in summer.

### ESSENTIALS

CURRENCY   The euro (€1 to US$1.36 at this writing).

HOURS   Stores are generally open from 9 or 9:30 to 1 and from 3:30 or 4 to 7 or 7:30. Many shops close Sunday. Many national museums are closed Monday and may have shorter hours on Sunday.

TELEPHONES   Tri-band GSM phones work in Italy. You can buy prepaid phone cards at telecom shops, news vendors, and tobacconists in all towns and cities. Phone cards can be used for local or international calls.

### COMING ASHORE

Ships must tender passengers ashore in the heart of the picturesque port. There is no train station in Portofino: You must take the bus to Santa Margherita (€1) and pick up train services from there. An alternative is to take a boat around the bay to Santa Margherita Ligure. The journey time to Genoa (⇨ *above*) is between 40 and 60 minutes and costs €2.10.

Taxis charge €2.33 initially, then €0.78 per km (½-mi), €0.11 per 140 meters (260 feet) in slow traffic. A rental car is useful to explore the Ligurian coast, but allow plenty of time to return your rental car as roads become extremely busy during the summer, and journey times may be longer than the distance suggests. Expect to pay about €45 for a compact manual vehicle. Delivery to the portside is an additional cost.

## EXPLORING PORTOFINO AND VICINITY

### PORTOFINO

**Abbazia di San Fruttuoso** (*Abbey of San Fruttuoso*). On the sea at the foot of Monte Portofino, the medieval abbey—built by the Benedictines of Monte Cassino—protects a minuscule fishing village that can be reached only on foot or by water (a 20-minute boat ride from Portofino and also reachable from Camogli, Santa Margherita Ligure, and Rapallo). The restored abbey is now the property of a national conservation fund (FAI) and occasionally hosts temporary exhibitions. The church contains the tombs of some illustrious members of the Doria family, an influential dynasty during Liguria's medieval heyday. The old abbey and its grounds are a delightful place to spend a few hours, perhaps lunching at one of the modest beachfront trattorias nearby (open only in summer). Boatloads of visitors can make it very crowded very fast; you might appreciate it most off-season. The last entry is 30 minutes before closing time. ⊠ *15-min boat ride or 2-hr walk northwest of Portofino* ☎ *0185/772703* ⊠ *€7 Apr.–Sept., €5 Oct.–Mar.* ⊗ *Mar., Apr., and Oct., Tues.–Sun. 10–3:45; May–Sept., daily 10:45–6; Nov.–Feb.,*

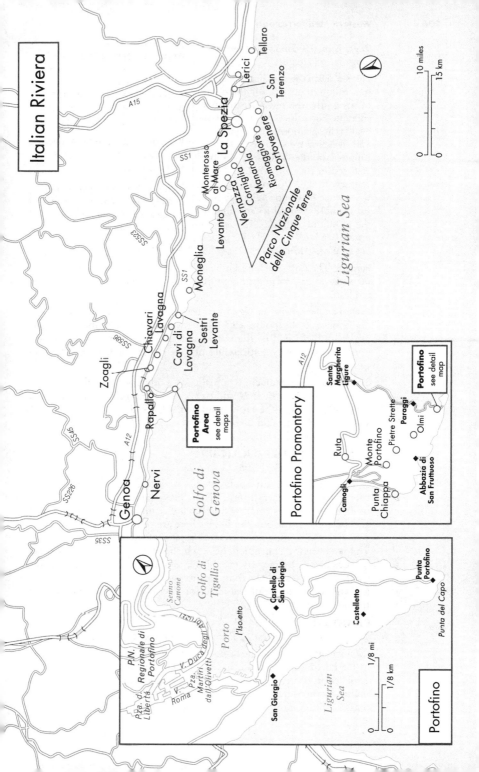

*Tues.–Sun. 10–3:45. Last entry 45 mins before closing.*

**Castello di San Giorgio.** From the harbor, follow the signs for the climb to the castle, the most worthwhile sight in Portofino, with its medieval relics, impeccable gardens, and sweeping views. The castle was founded in the Middle Ages but restored in the 16th through 18th century. In true Portofino form, it was owned by Genoa's English consul from 1870 until its opening to the public in 1961. ⊠ *Above harbor* ☎ *0185/269046* 🖵 *€3* ⊗ *Apr.–Sept., Wed.–Mon. 10–6; Oct.–Mar., Wed.–Mon. 10–5.*

> **PORTOFINO BEST BETS**
>
> **Linger over an espresso at a waterfront café.** Portofino is a place to see and be seen, so relax and survey your surroundings.
>
> **Walk the hillside paths above the town.** The views along the Riviera are delightful.
>
> **Visit Camogli.** You'll get a touch of gritty reality contrasting with the glitz of Portofino itself.

**Paraggi.** The only sand beach near Portofino is at a cove on the road between Santa Margherita and Portofino. The bus will stop there on request.

**Punta Portofino.** Pristine views can be had from the deteriorating *faro* (lighthouse) at this point, a 15-minute walk along the point that begins at the southern end of the port. Along the seaside path you can see numerous impressive, sprawling private residences behind high iron gates.

**San Giorgio.** This small church, sitting on a ridge, was rebuilt four times during World War II. It is said to contain the relics of its namesake, brought back from the Holy Land by the Crusaders. Portofino enthusiastically celebrates St. George's Day every April 23. ⊠ *Above harbor* ☎ *0185/269337* ⊗ *Daily 7–6.*

## SANTA MARGHERITA LIGURE
*5 km (3 mi) from Portofino.*

A beautiful old resort town favored by well-to-do Italians, Santa Margherita Ligure has everything a Riviera playground should have—plenty of palm trees and attractive hotels, cafés, and a marina packed with yachts. Some of the older buildings here are still decorated on the outside with the trompe-l'oeil frescoes typical of this part of the Riviera. This is a pleasant, convenient base, which for many represents a perfect balance on the Italian Riviera: bigger and less Americanized than the Cinque Terre; less glitzy than San Remo; more relaxing than Genoa and environs; and ideally situated for day trips, such as an excursion to Portofino.

## CAMOGLI
★ *15 km (9 mi) northwest of Portofino, 20 km (12 mi) east of Genoa.*

Camogli, at the edge of the large promontory and nature reserve known as the Portofino Peninsula, has always been a town of sailors. By the 19th century it was leasing its ships throughout the continent. Today multicolor houses, remarkably deceptive trompe-l'oeil frescoes, and a massive 17th-century seawall mark this appealing harbor community, perhaps as beautiful as Portofino but without the glamour. When exploring on foot, don't miss the boat-filled second harbor, which is reached by ducking under a narrow archway at the northern end of the first one.

**Acquario** *(Aquarium)*. The Castello Dragone, built onto the sheer rock face near the harbor, is home to this aquarium, which has tanks filled with local marine life built into the ramparts. ⊠ *Via Isola* ☎ *0185/773375* 🖾 *€3* ☉ *May–Sept., daily 10–noon and 3–7; Oct.–Apr., Fri.–Sun. 10–noon and 2:30–6, Tues.–Thurs. 10–noon.*

## RAPALLO

*8 km (5 mi) north of Portofino, 3 km (2 mi) north of Santa Margherita, 28 km (17 mi) east of Genoa.*

Rapallo was once one of Europe's most fashionable resorts, but it passed its heyday before World War II and has suffered from the building boom brought on by tourism. Ezra Pound and D.H. Lawrence lived here, and many other writers, poets, and artists have been drawn to it. Today the town's harbor is filled with yachts. A single-span bridge on the eastern side of the bay is named after Hannibal, who is said to have passed through the area after crossing the Alps.

**Il Museo del Merlatto.** This museum, in a 19th-century mansion, has a collection of antique lace, a dying art for which Rapallo was once renowned. ⊠ *Villa Tigullio* ☎ *0185/63305* 🖾 *€3* ☉ *Oct.–Aug., Tues., Wed., Fri., and Sat. 3–6, Thurs. 10–11:30* AM.

**Santi Gervasio e Protasio.** The highlight of the town center, the cathedral at the western end of Via Mazzini was founded in the 6th century. ⊠ *Via Mazzini* ☎ *0185/52375* ⊕ *www.provarapallo.altervista.org* 🖾 *Free* ☉ *Daily 6:30–noon and 3–6:30.*

# SHOPPING

In addition to the fine leather and haute couture for which Italy is known, Liguria is famous for its fine laces, silver-and-gold filigree work, and ceramics. Look for bargains in velvet, macramé, olive wood, and marble. Don't forget the excellent wines, cheeses, dried meats, and olive oils.

Portofino is awash with small boutiques selling fashion and gift items, but it's also one of the most expensive places to shop along the coast, catering to the wealthy yacht owners who call in during the summer. However, all the coastal villages have pretty shops to explore.

The attractive coastal village of **Zoagli** on the S1, 4 km (2½ mi) east of Rapallo, has been famous for silk, velvet, and damask since the Middle Ages.

**Bottega dei Sestieri.** Guido Porati's aromatic shop sells Ligurian cheeses, wines, and other delicacies. For something truly regional, try the *trarcantu,* a cow's-milk cheese aged in grape skins. The store is on a narrow lane that runs parallel to Rapallo's waterfront. ⊠ *Via Mazzini 44, Rapallo* ☎ *0185/230530.*

## ACTIVITIES

If you have the stamina, you can hike to the **Abbazia di San Fruttuoso** from Portofino. It's a steep climb at first, and the walk takes about 2½ hours one way. If you're extremely ambitious and want to make a day of it, you can hike another 2½ hours all the way to Camogli. Much more modest hikes from Portofino include a 1-hour uphill walk to Cappella delle Gave, a bit inland in the hills, from where you can continue downhill to Santa Margherita Ligure (another 1½ hours) and a gently undulating paved trail leading to the beach at Paraggi (½ hour). Finally, there's a 2½-hour hike from Portofino that heads farther inland to Ruta, through Olmi and Pietre Strette. The trails are well marked, and maps are available at the tourist information offices in Rapallo, Santa Margherita, Portofino, and Camogli.

## BEACHES

The Ligurian coast is known for its rocky vistas, but the Portofino promontory has one sandy beach, on the east side, at **Paraggi.**

## WHERE TO EAT

¢   ✕ **Canale.** If the staggering prices of virtually all of Portofino's restau-
ITALIAN   rants put you off, the long line outside this family-run bakery indicates that you're not alone, and that something special is in store. Here all the focaccia is baked on the spot and served fresh from the oven, along with all kinds of sandwiches, pastries, and other refreshments. The only problem is there's nowhere to sit—time for a picnic! ⊠ *Via Roma 30* ☎ *0185/269248* ⊟ *No credit cards* ☉ *Closed Nov. and Dec. No lunch Jan.–Apr. and Oct.*

$$   ✕ **Vento Ariel.** This small, friendly restaurant serves some of the best
LIGURIAN   seafood in town. Dine on the shaded terrace in summer months and watch the bustling activity in the nearby port. Only the freshest of seafood is served; try the spaghetti *alle vongole* (with clams) or the mixed grilled fish. ⊠ *Calata Porto* ☎ *0185/771080* ⊟ *AE, DC, MC, V* ☉ *Closed Wed., 1st half of Dec., and Jan.*

# ST-TROPEZ, FRANCE

Brigitte Bardot kick-started the rush in the early 1960s, and she was followed by the likes of Liz Taylor and Sophia Loren. People still flock to St-Tropez for the sun, the sea, and, the celebrities. The new generation includes Elton, Barbra, Oprah, Jack, and Uma, though they stay hidden in villas, and the people you'll see on the streets are mere mortals, lots of them, many intent on displaying the best—and often the most—of their youth, beauty, and wealth. Still, if you take an early-morning stroll around the pretty port or down the narrow medieval streets with their candied-almond hues, you'll see just how charming St-Tropez can be. There's a weekend's worth of boutiques to explore and many cute cafés where you can sit under colored awnings and watch the spectacle that

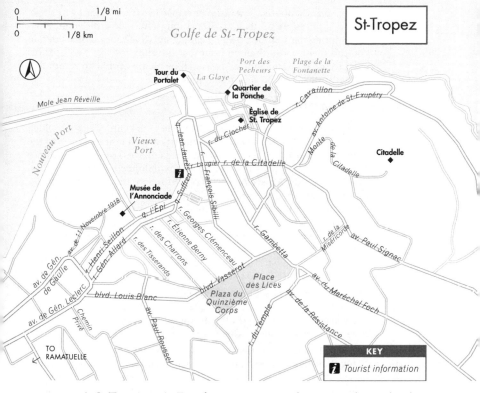

is St-Trop (*trop* in French means "too much") saunter by. Or head to the beaches, which are some of the most fashionable in Europe.

## ESSENTIALS

CURRENCY  The euro (€1 to US$1.36 at this writing).

HOURS  Most stores are open Monday–Saturday 9–7, but many close at lunchtime (usually from noon to 2 or 3), and some open on Sunday during July and August. Museums are generally open 10–5, but most are closed either Monday or Tuesday.

TELEPHONES  Tri-band GSM phones work in France. You can buy prepaid phone cards at telecom shops, news vendors, and tobacconists in all towns and cities. Phone cards can be used for local or international calls. France Telecom and Orange are leading telecom companies.

## COMING ASHORE

The port at St-Tropez is too small to accept commercial cruise vessels, so passengers are tendered to a landing dock, which is about a five-minute walk from town. There are no passenger facilities portside. Taxis and tour buses are not allowed into the staging area, which means a walk from the landing stage to transport connections is unavoidable.

Car-rental offices can be found in the town; expect to pay about €75 for an economy manual vehicle. Taxis are available at the port entrance and can provide tourist itineraries or transfers to the beaches. For single journeys, prices are €3 then €0.80 per km (½-mi). Be aware that, especially during the summer, traffic heading into St-Tropez builds up, and you can spend more than an hour just traveling the last two or three miles to the port and town. Always allow plenty of time to return any rental car or make the return taxi journey.

## EXPLORING ST-TROPEZ

**Citadelle.** Head up Rue de la Citadelle to the 16th-century citadel, which stands in a lovely hilltop park; its ramparts offer a fantastic view of the town and the sea. Although it's hard to imagine St-Tropez as a military outpost amidst today's bikini-clad sun worshippers, inside the Citadelle's donjon the **Musée Naval** (Naval Museum) displays ship models, cannons, maps, and pictures of St-Tropez from its days as a naval port. At this writing, the museum is closed for renovations, but is expected to reopen in late 2011. It is likely that the theme of the museum will change, but until that decision is made you can still see some of the navy models in the Citadelle, as well as a series of temporary art exhibitions. ⊠ *Rue de la Citadelle* 📷 *04–94–97–59–43* 🖾 *€2.50* ۞ *Oct.–Mar., daily 10–noon and 1:30–5; Apr.–Sept., daily 10–12:30 and 1–6:30.*

**Église de St-Tropez.** Head up rue Guichard to this baroque church to pay your respects to the bust and barque of St. Torpes every day but May 17, when they are carried aloft in the Bravade parade honoring the town's namesake saint. ⊠ *Rue Guichard.*

★ **Musée de l'Annonciade.** Just inland from the southwest corner of the Vieux Port stands the extraordinary Annunciation Museum, where the legacy of the artists who loved St-Tropez has been lovingly preserved. This 14th-century chapel, converted to an art museum, alone merits a visit to St-Tropez. Cutting-edge temporary exhibitions keep visitors on their toes, while works stretching from pointillists to fauves to cubists line the walls of the permanent collection. Signac, Matisse, Signard, Braque, Dufy, Vuillard, Rouault—many of them painted in (and about) St-Tropez, tracing the evolution of painting from impressionism to expressionism. The museum also hosts temporary exhibitions every summer, from local talent to up-and-coming international artists. ⊠ *Quai de l'Épi/Pl. Georges Grammont* 📷 *04–94–17–84–10* 🖾 *€5, €6 special exhibits* ۞ *June–Sept., Wed.–Mon. 10–1 and 3–7; Oct.–May, Wed.–Mon. 10–noon and 2–6.*

**Place des Lices.** This square, also called the Place Carnot, is the social center of the Old Town. Here you'll hear *pétanque* balls clicking in the sand square. (Pétanque is a a southern version of *boules,* a French lawn-bowling game similar to boccie.) The square's symmetrical forest of plane trees (what's left of them) provides shade to rows of cafés and restaurants, skateboarders, children, and the grandfatherly pétanque players. Enjoy a time-out in the town "living room," Le Café (not to be confused with the nearby Café des Arts). The square becomes a moveable feast (for both eyes and palate) on market days—Tuesday and Saturday.

**Quartier de la Ponche.** The old fisherman's quarter is just east of the Quai Jean-Jaurès. Complete with gulf-side harbor, this old-town maze of backstreets and old ramparts is daubed in shades of gold, pink, ocher, and sky-blue. Trellised jasmine and wrought-iron birdcages hang from the shuttered windows, and many of the tiny streets dead-end at the sea. Here you'll find the **Port des Pécheurs** (Fishermen's Port), on whose beach Bardot did a star-turn in *And God Created Woman.* Twisting, narrow streets, designed to break the impact of the mistral, open to tiny squares with fountains. The main drag here, Rue de la Ponche, leads into Place l'Hôtel de Ville, landmarked by a mairie (town hall) marked out in typical Tropezienne hues of pink and green.

> ## ST-TROPEZ BEST BETS
>
> **Stroll around the Port.** This is the place to see and be seen; to dress and strut whether you are 17 or 70. Yes, the celebrities flock here, but so do Europe's fashion peacocks.
>
> **Sip an aperitif in the Place des Lices.** Sit in the shade of an ancient plane tree, soak in the Provençal atmosphere, and watch the southern French *joie-de-vivre.*
>
> **Browse the boutiques.** This is stylish shopping at its best, with myriad small and exclusive and upscale shops.

**Vieux Port.** Bordered by the Quai de l'Epi, the Quai Bouchard, the Quai Peri, the Quai Suffren, and the Quai Jean-Jaurès, Old Port is the nerve center of this famous yachting spot, a place for strolling and looking over the shoulders of artists daubing their versions of the view on easels set up along the water's edge, surreptitiously looking out for any off-duty celebs. For it is here, from folding director's chairs at the famous port-side cafés Le Gorille (named for its late exceptionally hirsute manager), Café de Paris, and Sénéquier's—which line Quai Suffren and Quai Jean-Jaurès—that the cast of St-Tropez's living theater plays out its colorful roles. Head beyond the 15th-century Tour du Portalet to the Mole Jean Réveille, the harbor wall, for a good view of Ste-Maxime across the sparkling bay, the hills of Estérel and, on a clear day, the distant Alps.

## RAMATUELLE
*12 km (7 mi) southwest of St-Tropez.*

A typical hilltop whorl of red-clay roofs and dense inner streets topped with arches and lined with arcades, this ancient market town was destroyed in the Wars of Religion and rebuilt as a harmonious whole in 1620, complete with venerable archways and vaulted passages. Now its souvenir shops and galleries attract day-trippers out of St-Tropez, who enjoy the pretty drive through the vineyards as much as the village itself. At the top of the village you can visit the Moulin de Paillas, on Route du Moulin de Paillas, a windmill recently restored in the old style with a mechanism made entirely of wood; the site offers a panoramic view of the coastline. Free guided tours of the windmill are held every Tuesday from 10 to noon. Ramatuelle is also just a heartbeat away from the **Plage de Pamplonne**—a destination location among hippies and starlets alike.

**Club 55.** The ever famous club is located in Ramatuelle; it's one of the places where the area's rich and famous are known to play. ⊠ *Plage de Pamplonne* ☎ *04-94-55-55-55* ⊕ *www.leclub55.com.*

## SHOPPING

This high-fashion town abounds in boutiques full of the latest modes and chic accessories plus stylish items for the home you'll find in the pages of design magazines. The must-have souvenirs are the handmade strappy leather sandals, called Tropéziennes, or the delicious Tarte Tropézienne (a cream-filled cake) invented by a local confectioner and enjoyed by Brigitte Bardot during the filming of *And God Created Woman* in 1955.

Designer boutiques may be spreading like wild mushrooms all over St-Tropez, but the main fashionista-strutting runways are still along **Rue Gambetta** or **Rue Allard. Rue Sibilli,** behind the Quai Suffren, is lined with all kinds of trendy boutiques. The **Place des Lices** overflows with produce, regional foods, clothing, and *brocantes* (collectibles) on Tuesday and Saturday mornings. Don't miss the picturesque little fish market that fills up **Place aux Herbes** every morning.

Artists have long found the colors of the town inspirational, as witnessed at the Musée de l'Annonciade. Today a new generation of artists crowds the port, setting up impromptu stalls around their easels. Simply choose a style you like.

**La Tarte Tropézienne.** This is the place to buy the famous cakes. ⊠ *36 rue Clemenceau* ☎ *04-94-97-71-42* ⊕ *www.tarte-tropezienne.com.*

**Rondini.** For Tropéziennes, head to this family-run store where the owners have been hand-crafting sandals since 1927. ⊠ *16 rue Clemenceau* ☎ *04-94-97-19-55* ⊕ *www.rondini.fr.*

## BEACHES

The famous beaches of St-Tropez lie southeast of the town on a small peninsula.

**Pampelonne.** The long stretch of fine sand is now divided into a number of sections, each served by a trendy restaurant and beach club, where the glitterati head to lunch and the paparazzi are kept at a discreet distance. Rent a beach bed and soak in the sun for a few hours. Be aware that topless sunbathing is accepted practice here, so there will be bare breasts on view. ⊠ *Along route des Plages, Ramatuelle Peninsula, 5 mi from St-Tropez.*

## WHERE TO EAT

**$$-$$$$**  ✕ **La Table du Marché.** With an afternoon tearoom and a summer deli/
FRENCH  sushi bar, this charming bistro from celebrity chef Christophe Leroy offers up a mouthwatering spread of regional specialties in a surprisingly casual atmosphere. Sink into one of the overstuffed armchairs in the upstairs dining room, cozy with chic Provençal accents and antique bookshelves, and, for a light snack, try the tomato *pistou* tart. Hungry

guests can happily dive into a nicely balanced €18 or €26 set lunch menu while perusing the good wine list. ⊠ *38 rue Georges Clemenceau* ☎ *04–94–97–85–20* ⊕ *www.christophe-leroy.com* ⊟ *AE, D, MC, V.*

**$$–$$$$**
FRENCH

✕ **Le Café.** The busy terrace here often doubles as a stadium for different factions cheering on favorite local pétanque players in the Place des Lices. You, too, can play—borrow some boules from the friendly bar staff (and get your pastis bottle at the ready: you'll need it to properly appreciate the full pétanque experience). Note that hilarious "beginner" pétanque soirees are on tap Saturday nights in spring and summer. A great way to really sink into the local culture, it's an even bigger bonus that the food is as good as the setting. Try the Provençal beef stew and traditional fish soup. It's always busy, so reservations are strongly recommended. ⊠ *5 pl. des Lices* ☎ *04–94–97–44–69* ⊕ *www.lecafe.fr* ⊟ *AE, MC, V.*

# VALENCIA, SPAIN

Despite its proximity to the Mediterranean, Valencia's history and geography have been defined most significantly by the River Turia and the fertile floodplain (*huerta*) that surrounds it. Modern Valencia was best known for its flooding disasters until the River Turia was diverted to the south in the late 1950s. Since then, the city has been on a steady course of urban beautification. The lovely *puentes* (bridges) that once spanned the Turia look equally graceful spanning a wandering municipal park, and the spectacular futuristic Ciudad de las Artes y de las Sciencias (City of Arts and Sciences), designed by Valencian-born architect Santaigo Clalatrava, has at long last created an exciting architectural link between this river town and the Mediterranean. Valencia's port, and parts of the city itself, underwent major structural refurbishment for the 2007 America's Cup sailing classic held here in June 2007.

## ESSENTIALS

CURRENCY The euro (€1 to US$1.36 at this writing).

HOURS Museums are generally open from 9 until 7 or 8, but many are closed on Monday and some close in the afternoon. Most stores are open Monday–Saturday 9–1:30 and 5–8, but tourist shops may open in the afternoon and also on Sunday between May and September.

INTERNET **Work Center.** ⊠ *Colón 84, Valencia* ☎ *96/3536919* ⊕ *www.workcenter. es.*

TELEPHONES Most tri-band and quad-band GSM phones will work in Spain, where mobile services are 3G-compatible. Public kiosks accept phone cards that support international calls (cards sold in press shops, bars, and telecom shops). Major companies include Vodafone.

## COMING ASHORE

Valencia's port area received a facelift to coincide with the arrival of the America's Cup competition in June 2007. Though the terminal itself has limited facilities, the public interface areas, where the port and waterfront meet the city, has lots of restaurants, cafés, and shops.

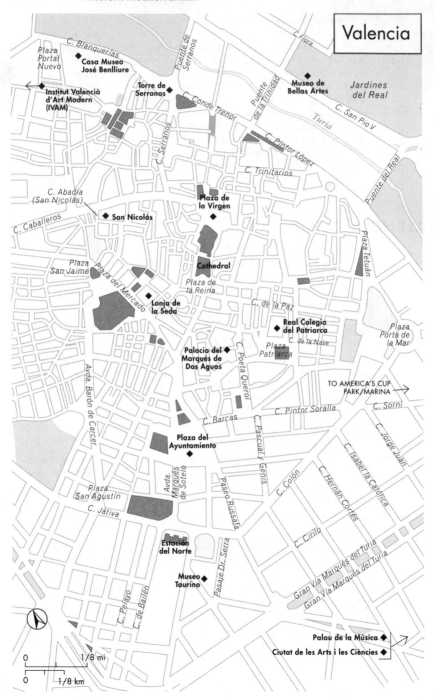

**Valencia**

Plaza Portal Nuevo

C. Blanquerías

Casa Museo José Benlliure

Institut Valencià d'Art Modern (IVAM)

Torre de Serranos

Puente de Serranos

C. Flora

C. Conde Trenor

Puente de la Trinidad

Museo de Bellas Artes

Jardines del Real

C. San Pio V

Turia

C. Serranos

C. Pintor López

C. Trinitarios

Puente del Real

C. Abadía (San Nicolás)

Plaza de la Virgen

C. Caballeros

San Nicolás

Plaza Tetuán

Cathedral

Plaza San Jaime

Plaza del Mercado

Plaza de la Reina

C. de la Paz

Real Colegio del Patriarca

Plaza Porta de la Mar

Lonja de la Seda

C. de la Nave

Palacio del Marqués de Dos Aguas

Plaza Patriarca

C. Poeta Querol

TO AMERICA'S CUP PARK/MARINA →

Avda. Barón de Cárcer

C. Barcas

C. Pintor Sorolla

C. Sorni

Plaza del Ayuntamiento

C. Pascual y Genís

Paseo Russafa

C. Colón

C. Hernán Cortés

C. Isabel la Católica

C. Jorge Juan

Plaza San Agustín

Avda. Marqués de Sotelo

C. Játiva

C. Cirilo

Estación del Norte

Pasaje Dr. Serra

Museo Taurino

Gran Vía Marqués del Turia

Gran Vía Marqués del Turia

C. Pelayo

C. de Bailén

Palau de la Música →

Ciutat de les Arts i les Ciències

0        1/8 mi

0        1/8 km

It is a long walk from the port to the historic downtown district, but the trip is enjoyable if you want to take the time. Two buses are useful for exploring the city. Route 5 plies a circular route through the Old Town, while route 19 leads past the port into the Old Town. The city has an excellent public transport system, so reaching all parts of the city by bus or metro is a cinch. A single journey is €2.15, and a one-day ticket is €3.50 within the downtown zone, €10 for all zones. Renting a car won't be an advantage when exploring the city, but it will allow you to head out along the coast or inland to explore the countryside. For an economy manual vehicle, expect to pay about €70 per day.

---

**VALENCIA BEST BETS**

**Go straight to the top.** The view of Valencia from the Miguelete Tower is magnficient.

**Cast an eye over Ciutat de les Arts i les Ciències.** One of Spain's most imaginative Modern-iste developments is in Valencia.

**Leave the bull at home.** Tread carefully in the Museo Nacional de Cerámica, which showcases porcelain, one of the city's most famous exports.

---

## EXPLORING VALENCIA

**Casa Museo José Benlliure.** The modern Valencian painter-sculptor Jose Benlliure is known for his portraits and large-scale historical and religious paintings, many of which hang in Valencia's Museo de Bellas Artes (Museum of Fine Arts). Here in his elegant house and studio are 50 of his works. On display are also works by his son, Pepino, and iconographic sculptures by Benlliure's brother, the well-known sculptor Mariano Benlliure. ⊠ *Calle Blanquerías 23* ☏ *963/919103* ☑ *€2 for museum, €6 card for all municipal museums* ☉ *Tues.–Sat. 10–2 and 4:30–8.30, Sun. 10–3.*

**Cathedral.** Valencia's 13th- to 15th-century cathedral is the heart of the city. The building has three portals—Romanesque, Gothic, and rococo respectively. Inside, Renaissance and baroque marble were removed in a successful restoration of the original Gothic style, as is now the trend in Spanish churches. The Capilla del Santo Cáliz (Chapel of the Holy Chalice) displays a purple agate vessel once said to be the Holy Grail (Christ's cup at the Last Supper) and thought to have been brought to Spain in the 4th century. Behind the altar you can see the left arm of **St. Vincent,** who was martyred in Valencia in 304. Stars of the cathedral **museum** are Goya's two famous paintings of St. Francis de Borja, Duke of Gandia. To the left of the cathedral entrance is the octagonal tower **El Miguelete,** which you can climb: the roofs of the Old Town create a kaleidoscope of orange and brown terra-cotta, and the sea appears in the background. It's said that you can see 300 belfries from here, including bright-blue cupolas made of ceramic tiles from nearby Manises. The tower was built in 1381, and the final spire added in 1736. ⊠ *Pl. de la Reina* ☏ *963/918127* ⊕ *www.catedraldevalencia.es* ☑ *Cathedral free, museum €1.20, tower €1.20* ☉ *Cathedral Mar. 20–Oct., Mon–Sat. 10–6:30, Sun. 2–6:30; Nov–Mar. 19, Mon.–Sat. 10–5:30, Sun. 2–5.*

*Museum and chapel Mar. 20–Oct., weekdays 10–6:30, Sat. 10–5:30, Sun. 2–5:30; Nov.– Mar. 19, Mon.–Sat. 10–5:30, Sun. 10–2. Tower weekdays 10–12:30 and 4:30–6:30, weekends 10–1:30 and 5–6:30.*

Ⓒ **Ciutat de les Arts i les Ciències.** Designed by native son Santiago Calatrava,
**Fodor's**Choice this sprawling futuristic complex is the home of Valencia's **Museu de les**
★ **Ciències Príncipe Felipe** (Prince Philip Science Museum), **L'Hemisfèric** (Hemispheric Planetarium), **L'Oceanogràfic** (Oceanographic Park), and **Palau de les Arts** (Palace of the Arts). With resplendent buildings resembling combs and crustaceans, the Ciutat is a favorite of architecture buffs and curious kids. The Science Museum has soaring platforms filled with lasers, holograms, simulators, and hands-on lab experiments. The eye-shape planetarium projects 3-D virtual voyages on its huge IMAX screen. At the Oceanographic Park you can take a submarine ride through a coastal marine habitat. ⊠ *Av. Autovía del Saler 7* ☎ *902/100031* 📠 *961/974505* ⊕ *www.cac.es* 💷 *Museu de les Ciències €7.50, L'Hemisfèric €7.50, €11.50 for admission to both, L'Oceanogràfic €23.90, €31.60 for admission to all 3* ۞ *Mid-Sept.– June, daily 10–7; July–mid-Sept., daily 10–9. L'Oceanogràfic mid-Sept.– mid-June, Sun.–Fri. 10–6, Sat. 10–8; mid-June–mid-July and early Sept., daily 10–8; mid-July–late Aug. 10–midnight. L'Hemisfèric daily shows generally every hr on the hr 10–9* PM.

**Estación del Norte.** Designed by Demetrio Ribes Mano in 1917, the train station is a splendid Moderniste structure replete with citrus motifs. ⊠ *C. Játiva s/n* ☎ *963/106253.*

**Institut Valèncià d'Art Modern (IVAM).** Dedicated to modern and contemporary pieces, the art institute has a permanent collection of 20th-century avant-garde works, European Informalism (including the Spanish artists Antonio Saura, Antoni Tàpies, and Eduardo Chillida), pop art, and photography. The museum is out near the Turia riverbed's elbow. ⊠ *Guillem de Castro 118* ☎ *963/863000* ⊕ *www.ivam.es* 💷 *€2, free Sun.* ۞ *July and Aug., Tues.–Sun. 10–10; Sept.–June, Tues.–Sun. 10–8.*

**Lonja de la Seda** *(Silk Exchange).* Downhill from San Nicolás, on the Plaza del Mercado, is the 15th-century Lonja, a product of Valencia's golden age, when the city's prosperity as one of the capitals of the Corona de Aragón made it a leading European commercial and artistic center. Widely regarded as one of Spain's finest civil Gothic buildings, its facade is decorated with ghoulish gargoyles, complemented inside by high vaulting and slender helicoidal (twisted) columns. Opposite the Lonja stands the **Iglesia de los Santos Juanes** (Church of the St. Johns), whose interior was destroyed during the 1936–39 Spanish civil war, and, next door, the Moderniste **Mercado Central** (Central Market), built entirely of iron and glass. ⊠ *Pl. del Mercado s/n* ☎ *963/917395* ⊕ *www.lonjadevalencia.com* 💷 *Free* ۞ *Tues.–Sat. 10–2 and 4:30–8:30, Sun. 10–3.*

Ⓒ **Museo de Bellas Artes.** Valencia was a thriving center of artistic activity in
★ the 15th century, and the city's Museum of Fine Arts is one of the best in Spain. Many of the best paintings by Jacomart and Juan Reixach, two of several artists known as the Valencian Primitives, are here, as is work by Hieronymus Bosch—or El Bosco, as they call him here. The ground

floor has a room devoted to Goya. ⊠ *C. San Pío V 9* ☎ *963/870300* ⊕ *www.museobellasartesvalencia.gva.es* ▧ *Free* ☼ *Tues.–Sun. 10–8.*

**Museo Taurino** *(Bullfighting Museum).* Just beyond Valencia's bull ring, one of the oldest in Spain, the museum displays bullfighting memorabilia, including bulls' heads and matadors' swords. ⊠ *Pasaje Doctor Serra 10* ⊕ *www.museotaurinovalencia.es* ▧ *Free* ☼ *Bullring Feb.–Oct., Tues.–Sun., 10–8; Museum Tues.–Sun. 10–8.*

★ **Palacio del Marqués de Dos Aguas.** This building has a fascinating baroque alabaster facade. Embellished with fruits and vegetables, it centers on the figures of the *Dos Aguas* (*Two Waters*), carved by Ignacio Vergara in the 18th century. The palace contains the **Museo Nacional de Cerámica**, with a magnificent collection of mostly local ceramics. ⊠ *C. Poeta Querol 2* ☎ *963/516392* ▧ *Palace and museum €3, free Sat. afternoon and Sun. morning* ☼ *Tues.–Sat. 10–2 and 4–8, Sun. 10–2.*

**Palau de la Música.** On one of the nicest stretches of the Turia riverbed, a pond is backed by a huge glass vault: Valencia's Palace of Music. Supported by 10 porticoed pillars, the dome gives the illusion of a greenhouse, both from the street and from within its sun-filled, tree-landscaped interior. Home of the Orquesta de Valencia, the main hall also hosts performers on tour from around the world, including chamber and youth orchestras, opera, and an excellent concert series featuring early, baroque, and classical music. To see the building without concert tickets, pop into the **art gallery,** which is host to free changing exhibits. ⊠ *Paseo de la Alameda 30* ☎ *963/375020* ☼ *Gallery daily 10:30–1:30 and 5:30–9.*

**Plaza del Ayuntamiento.** Down Avenida María Cristina from the market, this plaza is the hub of city life, a fact well conveyed by the massiveness of its baroque facades. The **ayuntamiento** itself contains the city tourist office and a museum on the history of Valencia. ☼ *Ayuntamiento weekdays 8:30–2:30.*

**Plaza de la Virgen.** From the cathedral's Gothic Puerta de los Apóstoles (Apostle Door), emerge on this pedestrian plaza, a lovely place for a refreshing *horchata* (tiger-nut milk) in the late afternoon. Next to its portal, market gardeners from the huerta bring their irrigation disputes before the Water Tribunal, which has met every Thursday at noon since 1350. It is said that it is the oldest surviving legal system in the world. Verdicts are given on the spot, and sentences have ranged from fines to deprivation of water.

**Real Colegio del Patriarca.** The Royal College of the Patriarch stands on the far side of Plaza Patriarca, toward the center of town. Founded by San Juan de Ribera in the 16th century, it has a lovely Renaissance patio and an ornate church, and its museum holds works by Juan de Juanes, Francisco Ribalta, and El Greco. ⊠ *C. de la Nave 1* ☎ *963/514176* ▧ *€1.20* ☼ *Daily 11–1:30.*

**San Nicolás.** A small plaza contains Valencia's oldest church, once the parish of the Borgia Pope Calixtus III. The first portal you come to, with a tacked-on, rococo bas-relief of the Virgin Mary with cherubs, hints well at what's inside: every inch of the originally Gothic church is covered with Churrigueresque embellishments. ⊠ *C. Caballeros 35*

☎ *963/913317* ✉ *Free* ⊙ *Open for mass daily 8–9* AM *and 7–8* PM, *Sat. 6:30–8:30* PM, *Sun. various masses 8–1:15.*

## SHOPPING

Shoes and leather goods are among Valencia's main products. Both handmade and mass-produced ceramics are created in a range of colors and styles. Fans and silk shawls, along with other traditional Spanish dress, are priced according to quality. Olives and olive oil will make gourmets happy, and olive oil is also used for a range of hair and beauty products.

The town of Manises, 9 km (5 ½ mi) west of Valencia, is a center for Valencian ceramics, known particularly for its azulejos.

**Lladró.** The maker of porcelain figurines has its world headquarters, including a factory shop and museum, on the city outskirts to the northeast. ✉ *Ctra de Alboraya, Tavernes Blanqués* ☎ *96/3187001* ⊕ *www. lladro.com.*

**Lladró.** The retail outlet of the famous porcelain figurine maker is in the center of the city. ✉ *Poeta Querol 9, Valencia* ☎ *96/3511625.*

**Nöel Ribes.** This shop has top-quality antiques with correspondingly daunting price tags. For better deals, try stores on Calle Avellanas near the cathedral. ✉ *Vilaragut 7, Valencia.*

## GOLF

Mild conditions year-round mean the countryside around Valencia is dotted with golf courses, and most don't need membership to play a round.

**El Bosque.** This is a Robert Trent Jones–designed course. ✉ *Godelleta, Km. 4.1, Chiva* ☎ *96/1808009* ⊕ *www.elbosquegolf.com.*

**El Saler.** The most famous course in the region is well regarded by both professionals and amateurs. ✉ *Av. de los Pinares, El Saler* ☎ *96/ 1611186.*

## WHERE TO EAT

**$-$$**
SPANISH
✗ **La Riuà.** This local secret, which serves Valencian food, is decorated with beautiful ceramic tiles. House specialties include *anguilas* (eels) prepared with *all i pebre* (garlic and pepper), *pulpitos guisados* (stewed baby octopus), and traditional rice dishes. Wash it down with a cold bottle of *Llanos de Titaguas,* a dry yet snappy white Valencian table wine. The restaurant is just off Plaza de la Reina. ✉ *C. del Mar 27* ☎ *963/914571* ▤ *AE, DC, MC, V* ⊙ *Closed Sun., Easter wk, and Aug. No dinner Mon.*

**$$**
SPANISH
✗ **Patos.** Small, cozy, and very popular with locals, this restored 18th-century town house has an earthy look, thanks to the terra-cotta tiles, wood-panel walls, and overhead beams. On weekdays the set lunch menu is a real bargain at €13, and usually includes *ternera* (veal) and *lomo* (pork loin). The set dinner (and weekend) menu is €22, and sometimes includes *cordero* (lamb) and *solomillo* (pork sirloin). Get here

by 9:30 PM to snag a table; you can also dine outside in summer. The restaurant is just north of Calle de la Paz, in the Old Quarter. ⊠ C. del Mar 28 ☎ 963/921522 ⊟ MC, V ⊘ No dinner Sun. and Mon.

# VALLETTA, MALTA

**2**

Hulking megalithic temples, ornate baroque churches, narrow Old World streets, and hilltop citadels are Malta's human legacy. Dizzying limestone cliffs, sparkling seas, and charming rural landscapes make up its natural beauty. In its 7,000 years of human habitation, Malta has been overrun by every major Mediterranean power: Phoenicians, Carthaginians, Romans, Byzantines, and Arabs; Normans, Swabians, Angevins, Aragonese, and the Knights of the Order of St. John of Jerusalem; the French, the British, and now tourists. The Germans and Italians tried to take it in World War II—their air raids were devastating—but could not. The islands' history with the Knights of the Order of St. John has given them their lasting character. In 1565, when the forces of Süleyman the Magnificent laid siege here, it was the Knights' turn, with the faithful backing of the Maltese, to send the Turks packing. The handsome limestone buildings and fortifications that the wealthy Knights left behind are all around the islands.

## ESSENTIALS

CURRENCY The euro (€1 to US$1.36 at this writing).

HOURS Government museums are open daily 10–4 and are closed on Thursday. All sites are closed on January 1, Good Friday, December 24, 25, and 31. Some archaeological sites are open by appointment only. Shops are open Monday–Saturday 9–1 and 4–7.

INTERNET **YMCA** (⊠ 178 Merchant St. ☎ 356/2124–0680) has several Internet-connected computers.

LANGUAGE The official languages of Malta are English and Maltese, a Semitic language combining elements of French, Italian, and English.

TELEPHONES Malta's mobile services operate on a single GSM-band system. The system supports text and data but not 3G technology. Public phones operate by means of telecards with smartchip technology. They can be used to make international calls. GO and Vodafone are the main providers.

## COMING ASHORE

Cruise ships dock at the Valletta Waterfront Facility in the heart of the historic Grand Harbour. The facility is extensive, and houses modern, high-quality shops, eight restaurants, and exhibition spaces. Taxi fare to the town of Valetta is €10 and the trip takes only five minutes. It's a steep walk up to the Valletta citadel on foot, but it's an easy route. Malta has a well-organized public bus service, but there are also car rentals and taxis.

Most bus routes across the island start at Valletta Terminal just outside the entrance to the Citadel, and run daily from 5:30 AM to 11 PM. A day ticket is available for €3.50. Bus routes are marked on the maps distributed by the tourist office.

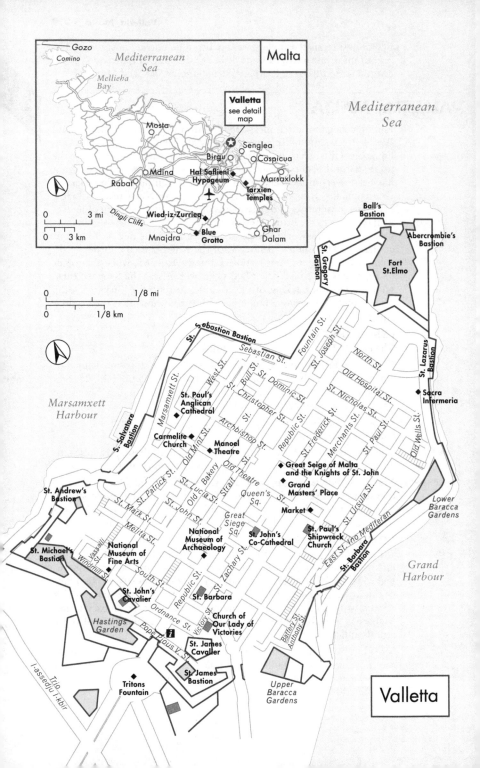

Renting a car would allow you to visit many of Malta's attractions during a day. Prices for a compact manual vehicle are about €35 per day. Driving is on the left. Void of highways, Malta is traversed by country roads with speed limits ranging between 24 and 40 MPH. Seatbelt laws are strictly enforced.

Taxis operate on a fixed-fee basis from the port. Sample fares are (€20) to Marsaxlokk and (€23.29) to Mdina. Taxi tours can be organized on a per-hour basis; for example, the fare for five hours is about €70. Some taxis have meters, but it is best to ask approximate rates before the ride begins.

**Supreme Travel** (✉ *Castellana Rd., Zejtun* ☎ *356/2169–4967* ⊕ *www. maltasightseeing.com* ⊗ *Tours depart every hr 9–3*) offers hop-on hop-off buses that depart hourly from Sliema Ferries. The cost is €15.

# EXPLORING MALTA

## VALLETTA

Malta's capital, the minicity of Valletta, has ornate palaces and museums protected by massive fortifications of honey-color limestone. Houses along the narrow streets have overhanging wooden balconies for people-watching from indoors. The main entrance to town is through the City Gate (where all bus routes end), which leads onto Triq Repubblika (Republic Street), the spine of the grid-pattern city and the main shopping street. Triq Mercante (Merchant Street) parallels Repubblika to the east and is also good for strolling. From these two streets, cross streets descend toward the water; some are stepped. Valletta's compactness makes it ideal to explore on foot. Before setting out along Republic Street, stop at the tourist information office (just inside the city gate) for maps and brochures.

**Fort St. Elmo.** Built in 1552 by the Knights to defend the harbor, the fort was completely destroyed during the siege of 1565 and rebuilt by succeeding military leaders. Today part of the fort houses the War Museum, with its collection of military objects related to World War II. ✉ *St. Elmo Pl.* ☎ *356/2122–2430* 🎫 *€7* ⊗ *Daily 9–5.*

★ **Grand Masters' Palace.** The palace houses the president's office, and Malta's parliament meets here. Completed in 1574, the palace has a unique collection of Gobelin tapestries; the main hall is decorated with frescoes depicting the history of the Knights and the Great Siege. On view are works by Ribera, Van Loo, and Batoni. At the back of the building is the Armoury of the Knights, with exhibits of arms and armor through the ages. ✉ *Merchants St.* ☎ *356/2124–9349* 🎫 *€10, includes entrance to Armoury and State Rooms* ⊗ *Daily 9–5.*

★ **Great Siege of Malta and the Knights of St. John.** A walk-through presentation traces the order's history from its founding in 1099 in the Holy Land and its journeys from Jerusalem to Cyprus, Rhodes, and Malta. Also depicted are epic scenes from the Great Siege of 1565, the naval Battle of Lepanto, and the order's eviction from Malta by the French. ✉ *Cafe Premier Complex, 34 Republic Sq., Republic St.* ☎ *356/2248–9300* ⊕ *www.greatsiege.com.mt* 🎫 *€7.50* ⊗ *Daily 10–6.*

★ **National Museum of Archaeology.** Housed in the Auberge de Provence (the hostel of the Knights from Provence), the museum has an excellent collection of finds dating back to 5200 BC from Malta's many prehistoric sites. ⊠ *Triq Repubblika* ☎ *356/2122–1623* ⊕ *www.maltavoyager.com/moa/* ⊡ *€5* ☉ *Mon.–Wed. 10–5:30, Thurs.-Sat. 11:30–7, Sun. noon–5:30.*

**Sacra Infermeria** (*Hospital of the Knights*). This gracious building near the seawall has been converted into the Mediterranean Conference Center. For an introduction to the island, see "The Malta Experience," here, a multimedia presentation on the history of Malta. ⊠ *Mediterranean St.* ☎ *356/2559–5215* ⊕ *www.themaltaexperience.com* ⊡ *€9.50* ☉ *Shows July–Sept., weekdays 11, noon, 1, 2, 3, 4, weekends 11, noon, 1, 2; Oct.–June, daily 2.*

★ **St. John's co-Cathedral.** Functional in design but lavishly decorated, the Order of St. John's own church (1578) is Malta's most important treasure. Many of the paintings and the decoration scheme are by the island's beloved 17th-century painter Mattia Preti (b. 1613). The artistic tour de force, however is Caravaggio's *The Beheading of St. John the Baptist,* commissioned by the Knights and the only painting the artist ever signed. The cathedral museum has illuminated manuscripts, Caravaggio's *St. Jerome,* tombstones of noblemen from the 16th to 18th centuries, and a rich collection of Flemish tapestries. ⊠ *Pjazza San Gwann.* ☎ *356/2122–0536* ⊕ *stjohnscocathedral.com* ⊡ *€6* ☉ *Weekdays 9:30–4:30, Sat. 9:30–12:30*

★ **St. Paul's Shipwreck Church.** The importance of St. Paul to the Maltese explains the work lavished on this baroque marvel. The *os brachii* (arm bone) relic of the saint and column on which he was beheaded are housed in a chapel on the right, a splendid gated chapel is on the left, and a baptismal font stands by the entrance. ⊠ *Triq San Pawl* ☉ *Mon.–Sat. 11–6.*

**THE THREE CITIES**

*Birgu is 8 km (5 mi) east of Valletta.*

East across the Grand Harbor from Valletta, the three cities of **il-Birgu** (aka Vittoriosa), **i-Isla** (aka Senglea), and **Bormla** (aka Cospicua) are where the Knights of the Order of St. John first settled—and where crucial fighting took place in the Great Siege of the Turks in 1565. Vittoriosa is named for the victory over the Turks. The great walls around the cities are the Cottonera Lines, built in the 1670s. On the narrow streets north of the main square you can loop from the Triq La Vallette to the Triq Majjistral on the right. Triq It-Tramuntana takes you past baroque doorways, the Knights' Auberge d'Angleterre ("Inn of England," and headquarters of the English branch of knights of St. John), and a Saracen-style house that is thought to date from the 1200s. The best days to visit the Three Cities are during Good Friday and Easter, when communities carry statues of the "Risen Christ" through the streets.

**Church of St. Lawrenz.** Below Birgu's main square is the city's finest church, with the 17th-century painter Mattia Preti's *Martyrdom of San Lawrenz.* Designed by baroque architect Lorenzo Gafa, the church was built between 1681 and 1697. ⊠ *Triq San Lawrenz, Birgu* ☎ *356/2155–6073.*

**Gardjola Garden.** At the tip of Senglea, this garden, once a guard post, has panoramic views and a turret carved with a vigilant eye and ear.

**Inquisitor's Palace.** The displays in Birgu's palace reveal less discussed aspects of less tolerant times in Malta. ⊠ *Triq Il-Mina Il-Kbira, Birgu* ☎ *356/2182–7006* ⊠ *€6* ⊙ *Daily 9–5.*

## PAOLA AND TARXIEN
*Paola 4.8 km (3 mi) south of Valletta.*

★ **Hal Saflieni Hypogeum.** This massive labyrinth of underground chambers was used for burials more than 4,000 years ago. Reservations must be made in advance through Heritage Malta. ⊠ *On road to Santa Lucija.* ☎ *356/2180–5018* ⊠ *€20* ⊙ *Daily; tours on the hr 9–4.*

**Tarxien Temples.** The three interconnecting temples have curious carvings, oracular chambers, and altars, all dating from about 2800 BC. Nearby are remains of an earlier temple from about 4000 BC. ⊠ *Neolithic Temples St., behind Paola's Church of Christ the King Tarxie* ☎ *356/2169–5578* ⊠ *€6* ⊙ *Daily 9–5.*

## MARSAXLOKK
*8 km (5 mi) southeast of Valletta.*

At the pretty fishing and resort town Marsaxlokk, on the southeast coast, you can see the *luzzu,* Malta's multicolor, traditional fishing boat, a symbol of the island. Its vertical prow has Phoenician ancestry.

## GHAR DALAM
*9 km (6 mi) southeast of Valletta.*

**Ghar Dalam Museum.** The semifossilized remains of long-extinct species of dwarf elephants and hippopotamuses that roamed the island some 125,000 years ago were found in a cave in Ghar Dalam. The fossils are now on display in the small museum. ⊠ *Ghar Dalam* ☎ *356/2165–7419* ⊠ *€5* ⊙ *Daily 9–5.*

## ZURRIEQ
*11km (7 mi) south of Valletta.*

On the way to Zurrieq from Valletta you will pass limestone quarries, where orchards are planted, protected from the wind, after the limestone is exhausted.

★ **Blue Grotto.** The turnoff for the grotto is 1 km (½ mi) beyond the lookout. A steep road takes you to the rocky inlet where noisy boats leave for the grottoes (there are many) and the stained-glass-blue waters that splash their walls. Bring a bathing suit in case the water is calm enough for swimming. ⊠ *Coast Rd.*

★ **Mnajdra.** Views are superb from this temple, which is prounced *"mna-EE-dra"* and stands on the edge of a hill by the sea. The temple is encircled by hard coralline limestone walls and has the typical, clover-like trefoil plan. ⊠ *Coast Rd.*☎ *356/2142–4231* ✉ *€9* ⊙ *Daily 9–5.*

**Wied-iz-Zurrieq** *(Zurrieq Valley).* On the far side of town, the valley runs along the road to a lookout over the towering walls of the Blue Grotto's bay.

## MDINA
★ *12 km (7 mi) southwest of Valletta.*

In Mdina, Malta's ancient, walled capital—the longtime stronghold of Malta's nobility—traffic is limited to residents' cars, and the noise of the world outside doesn't penetrate the thick, golden walls. The quiet streets are lined with sometimes block-long, still-occupied noble palaces.

**Carmelite Priory Museum.** As the only monastery in Malta open to the public, the museum offers daily tours at 11 and 3, as well as concerts every Saturday at noon. ⊠ *Villegaignon St., Mdina* ☎ *356/2702–0404* ⊕ *www.carmelitepriorymuseum.com* ✉ *€4* ⊙ *Daily 10–5.*

**Mdina Dungeons.** Beneath the magisterial Vilhena Palace, these underground passageways feature re-creations of Maltese history in a medieval dungeon-like setting. ⊠ *St. Publius Sq., Mdina* ☎ *356/2145–0267* ⊕ *www.dungeonsmalta.com* ⊙ *Daily 10–4:30.*

**Mdina Cathedral.** The serene baroque cathedral dedicated to St. Peter and St. Paul contains Mattia Preti's 17th-century painting *The Shipwreck of St. Paul.* In the cathedral museum are Dürer woodcuts and illuminated manuscripts. ⊠ *Archbishop Sq.* ☎ *356/2145–6620.*

**Palazzo Falson.** The former home of Capt. Olof Frederick Gollcher, this historic museum houses a collection of paintings, silver, furniture, jewelry, and armor, and a library containing more than 4,500 books and manuscripts. ⊠ *Villegaignon St., Mdina* ☎ *356/2145–4512* ⊕ *www.palazzofalson.com* ✉ *€10* ⊙ *Tues.–Sun. 10–5.*

## RABAT
*13km (8 mi) southwest of Valletta.*

Rabat means "suburb"—in this case of Mdina.

**Catacombs.** Catacombs run under much of Rabat. Up Triq Santa Agatha from Parish Square, the Catacombs of St. Paul are devoid of bones but full of carved-out burial troughs. Don't forget the way out when you set off to explore. St. Agatha's Crypt and Catacombs, farther up the street, were beautifully frescoed between 1200 and 1480, then defaced by Turks in 1551. ⊠ *St. Agatha St.* ☎ *356/2145–4562* ✉ *€5* ⊙ *Daily 9–5.*

**St. Paul's Church.** The beautiful church stands above a grotto where St. Paul reputedly took refuge after his shipwreck on Malta. ⊠ *Parish Sq.* ☎ *356/454–467* ⊙ *Daily 9:30–1:30 and 2:30–5.*

### MOSTA
*10 km (6 mi) west of Valletta.*

**Rotunda.** This church, *which is dedicated to the Assumption of Our Lady,* has the third-largest unsupported dome in Europe, after St. Peter's in Rome and Hagia Sophia in Istanbul. A German bomb fell through the roof during World War II—without detonating. ⊠ *Rotunda Sq.*☎ *356/2143–3826* ⊙ *Daily 9–noon and 3–6.*

## SHOPPING

Most shops in Malta are open from 9 to 7, except in commercial areas where they stay open until 10 PM. Generally stores are closed on Sunday and public holidays. Malta has several crafts that make excellent souvenirs. Blown glass is a modern phenomenon, but is now a signature gift of the island. More traditional are bizzilla (hand-woven lace), silver filigree, globigerina limestone, and coralline limestone. Valletta's main shopping street, **Triq Repubblika,** is lined with touristy shops—pick up postcards and film here, and then venture onto side streets for a look at everyday Maltese wares. At the **open-air market** *(Triq Mercante),* with some haggling you may snap up a good bargain

**Centru tas-Snajja'.** This craft center in St. John's Square showcases various artisans registered with the Malta Cafts Council. (⊠ *St. John's Sq.*☎ *356/2569–0332* ⊕ *www.mcc.gov.mt*).

**Government Craft Center.** You can buy any number of traditional handmade goods at this government-sponsored market. ⊠ *Pjazza San Gwann, Valletta.*

## ACTIVITIES

Water sports are well organized, and all the major beaches have watersports centers offering windsurfing, wakeboarding, and paragliding. Scuba diving is particularly well organized with exciting wreck and cave dives.

**Divewise.** This is one of the oldest dive schools on the island, with almost 30 years experience. ⊠ *Westin Dragonara Hotel, St Julian's* ☎ *356/2135–6411* ⊕ *www.divewise.com.mt.*

## BEACHES

Malta has many lovely beaches, which range from small rock-flanked coves to vast strands. Many beaches see lots of European (mainly British) tourists during the summer season, so they may be busy.

**Ghajn Tuffieha Bay.** This sandy bay on the northwestern coast is wonderful for an afternoon by the sea. The sometimes bumpy bus (Route 47) ride takes you through the rolling countryside, which is patchworked with ancient stone walls and occasional fields of root crops. ⊠ *Ghajn Tuffieha.*

**Mellieha Bay.** This is the island's largest beach, with a range of water sports and eateries. It's popular with families. ⊠ *Mellieha.*

**Paradise Bay.** This is the most attractive beach on the island, set in a natural cove. ⊠ *Cirkewwa.*

## WHERE TO EAT

¢  ✕ **Caffe Cordina.** On the ground floor of the original treasury of the
CAFÉS  Knights is Valletta's oldest café. Since 1837 this ornate, vaulted con-
★  fectionery has produced hot, savory breakfast pastries and *qaghaq ta'*
*l-ghasel* (honey rings). ⊠ *244–45 Triq Repubblika, Valletta* ☎ *356/2123–*
*4385* ⊕ *www.caffecordina.com* ⊟ *AE, DC, MC, V.*

$–$$  ✕ **Ix-Xlukkajr.** Seafood is the draw at this harborside restaurant. Octopus
SEAFOOD  marinated in garlic sauce is a wonderful cold starter. Try the whole-fish
specials and, for dessert, homemade prickly-pear and kiwi ice creams.
⊠ *Xatt Is-Sajjieda., Marsaxlokk* ☎ *356/2165–2109* ⊕ *www.xlukkajr.*
*com* ⊟ *MC, V* ☉ *Closed Mon.*

# VENICE, ITALY

It's called La Serenissima, "the most serene," a reference to the majesty, wisdom, and monstrous power of this city that was for centuries the unrivaled mistress of trade between Europe and the Orient and the bulwark of Christendom against the tides of Ottoman expansion. Built entirely on water by men who defied the sea, Venice is unlike any other town. No matter how many times you've seen it in movies or on TV, the real thing is more dreamlike than you could ever imagine. Its landmarks, the Basilica di San Marco and the Palazzo Ducale, are exotic mixes of Byzantine, Gothic, and Renaissance styles. Shimmering sunlight and silvery mist soften every perspective here, and you understand how the city became renowned in the Renaissance for its artists' rendering of color. It's full of secrets, inexpressibly romantic, and at times given over entirely to pleasure.

### ESSENTIALS

CURRENCY  The euro (€1 to US$1.36 at this writing).

HOURS  Shops are generally open 9–1 and 3:30–7:30, and are closed Sunday and Monday morning most of the year, however tourist shops in the city will remain open throughout the day and into the evening.

INTERNET  **OFFicina** (⊠ *2799 Dorsoduro* ☎ *041/7241214*).

TELEPHONES  Tri-band GSM phones work in Italy. You can buy prepaid phone cards at telecom shops, news vendors, and tobacconists in all towns and cities. Phone cards can be used for local or international calls.

### COMING ASHORE

Venice is a huge port handling vast numbers of cruise ships and much of commercial traffic as well. The cruise terminal sits at the southwestern corner of city, and has two main docking areas, the Marittima area for large ships and the San Basilio for smaller ones.

Marittima has duty-free shops and information desks but no refreshment facilities. From here there is a shuttle bus to Piazzale Roma at the western edge of the city, just outside the port, or you can take Bus 6 from the port entrance. You can also take a boat. Among the seafaring

2

options are the Alilaguna M Line (Linea M) boat, which travels direct from Marittima to Piazza San Marco. You could also take Linea Blu or Linea Rosso from Tronchetto to San Marco, though this service has more stops enroute. Vaporetto services 41, 42, 51, 52, 61, 62 operate along the same route. The journey takes around 20 minutes.

At San Basilio there are fewer passenger facilities, but the quay has a vaporetto stop, from which services 61, 62, and 82 take you into the heart of Venice. The current fare is €6.50.

Taxis charge approximately €2.33 initially, then €0.78 per km (½ mi) and €0.11 per 140 meters (460 feet) in slow traffic, but taxis can't take you into the heart of the city, just to its edge, so it seems a needless expense to us. Vaporetto services are much more useful once you reach the city, because they can take you right to St. Mark's Square. Cars aren't allowed into Venice proper, so there is no point to renting a car unless you want to explore the Veneto region. Expect to pay about €45 for a compact manual vehicle.

### GETTING TO THE AIRPORT

If you do not purchase airport transfers from your cruise line, the simplest transfer would be to hire a taxi or private transfer company to whisk you from the port to the airport, or vice versa. If you want to use public transport, the options are inexpensive, but the journey involves traveling through the downtown area and transfering with your luggage at some point in the journey.

A private motoscafo (water taxi) transfer direct from the airport dock to the cruise port will cost around €110 for four people. Alilaguna ⊕ *www.venicelink.com* is one company that offers this service. Aligaluna also offers shared transfers from the airport for a minimum of two people. Prices start at €27 per person one way, €50 round-trip.

The quickest transfer on public transport is to take the airport shuttle bus overland to Piazzale Roma and then transfer from Piazzale Roma to the cruise port. Blue buses run by **ATVO** (☎ *0421/383672* ⊕ *www.atvo. it*) make a 20-minute trip from the airport to Piazzale Roma (tickets €3). Tickets are sold from machines and at the airport booth in Ground Transportation (open daily 9–7:30), and on the bus when tickets are otherwise unavailable. A land taxi to Piazzale Roma costs about €35. From Piazzale Roma there are shuttle buses to the cruise terminal.

## EXPLORING VENICE

There's no better introduction to Venice than a trip down the Grand Canal, or as Venetians refer to it, Canalazzo. It is, without a doubt, one of the world's great "avenues." For 4 km (2½ mi) it winds its way in a backward "S," past 12th- to 18th-century palaces built by the city's richest families. There is a definite theatrical quality to the Grand Canal; it's as if each facade had been designed to steal your attention from its rival across the way. The most romantic—albeit expensive—way to see the canal is from a gondola. The next best thing—at a fraction of the cost—is to take in the view from vaporetto Line 1.

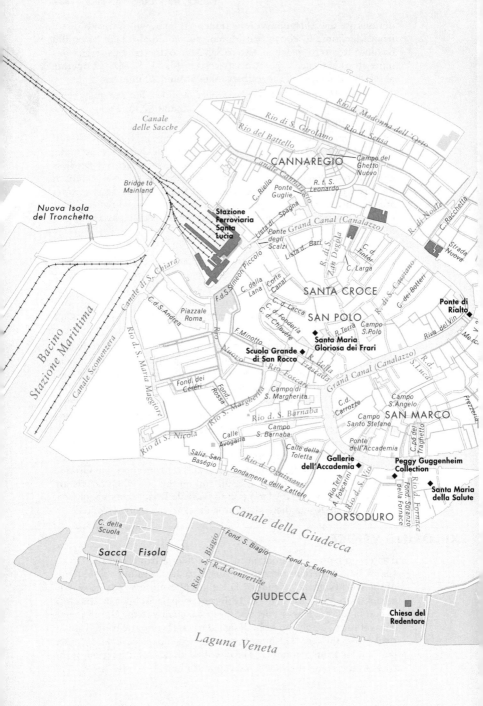

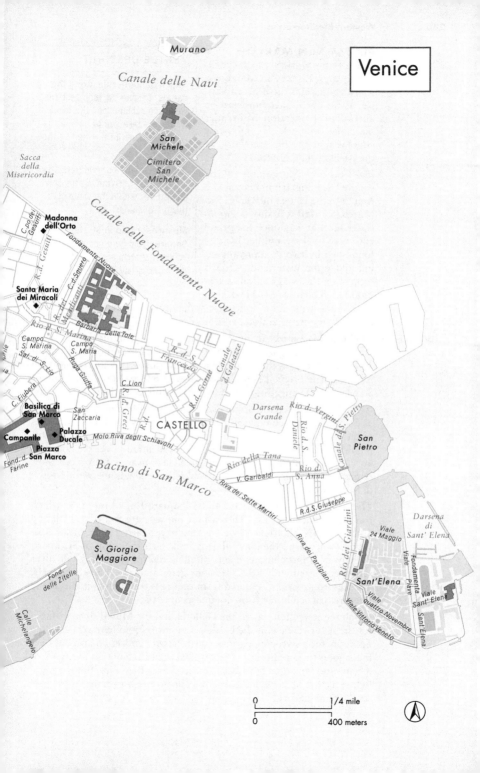

## PIAZZA SAN MARCO

One of the world's most evocative squares, Piazza San Marco (St. Mark's Square) is the heart of Venice, a vast open space bordered by an orderly procession of arcades marching toward the fairy-tale cupolas and marble lacework of the Basilica di San Marco.

Piazzetta San Marco, the "little square" leading from Piazza San Marco to the waters of Bacino San Marco (St. Mark's Basin), is a *molo* (landing) that was once the grand entryway to the republic. It's distinguished by two columns towering above the waterfront. One is topped by the winged lion, a traditional emblem of St. Mark that became the symbol of Venice itself; the other supports St. Theodore, the city's first patron, along with his dragon.

**Fodor's Choice** **Basilica di San Marco.** An opulent synthesis of Byzantine and Romanesque styles, Venice's gem didn't become the cathedral of Venice until 1807, but its role as the Chiesa Ducale (the duke's private chapel) gave it kudos. The original church was built in 828 to house the body of St. Mark the Evangelist, filched from Alexandria by the duke's agents.

A 976 fire destroyed the original church. The replacement would serve as a symbol of Venetian wealth and power, endowed with all the riches of the Orient, to the point where it earned the nickname Chiesa d'Oro (golden church). The four bronze horses that prance over the doorway are copies of sculptures that victorious Venetians took from Constantinople in 1204 after the Fourth Crusade (the originals are in the Museo di San Marco).

The basilica is famous for its 43,055 square feet of mosaics, which run from floor to ceiling. The earliest mosaics are from the 11th and 12th centuries, and the last were added in the early 1700s. In the **Santuario** (sanctuary), the main altar is built over the tomb of St. Mark. Perhaps even more impressive is the **Pala d'Oro**, a dazzling gilt silver screen encrusted with 1,927 precious gems and 255 enameled panels. The **Tesoro** (treasury), entered from the right transept, contains many treasures carried home from conquests abroad.

Climb the steep stairway to the **Galleria** and the **Museo di San Marco** for the best overview of the basilica's interior. From here you can step outdoors for a sweeping panorama of Piazza San Marco and out over the lagoon to San Giorgio. The displays focus mainly on the types of mosaic and how they have been restored over the years. But the highlight is a close-up view of the original gilt-bronze horses that were once on the outer gallery.

Be aware that guards at the basilica door turn away anyone with bare shoulders or knees; no shorts, short skirts, or tank tops are allowed. ■TIP➔ **To skip the line at the Basilica entrance, reserve your arrival—at no extra cost—on the Basilica Web site** ⊠ *Piazza San Marco* 🕿 *041/2708311 basilica, 041/2413817 (10–noon weekdays) tour info* ⊕ *www.basilicasanmarco.it* ▣ *Basilica free, Tesoro €2, Santuario and Pala d'Oro €1.50, Galleria and Museo di San Marco €3* ☉ *May–Sept., Mon.–Sat. 9:45–5, Sun. 2–5; Oct.–Apr., Mon.–Sat. 9:45–5, Sun. 2–4; last entry ½ hr before closing* Ⓜ *Vallaresso/San Zaccaria.*

Ⓒ ★ **Campanile.** Venice's famous brick bell tower (325 feet tall, plus the angel) had been standing nearly 1,000 years when in 1902, practically without warning, it collapsed. The new tower, rebuilt to the old plan, reopened in 1912. The stunning view from the tower on a clear day includes the Lido, the lagoon, and the mainland as far as the Alps, but, strangely enough, none of the myriad Venetian canals. ⊠ *Piazza San Marco* 🕿 *041/5224064* ▣ *€8* ☉ *Easter–June, Oct., and Nov., daily 9–7; July–Sept., daily 9–9; Nov.–Easter, daily 9–3:45. Last entry 1 hr before closing* Ⓜ *Vallaresso/San Zaccaria.*

★ **Palazzo Ducale** *(Doge's Palace).* Rising above the Piazzetta San Marco, this Gothic-Renaissance fantasia of pink-and-white marble is a majestic expression of the prosperity and power attained during Venice's most glorious period. Always much more than a residence, the palace was Venice's White House, senate, torture chamber, and prison rolled into one. The palace's sumptuous chambers have walls and ceilings covered with works by Venice's greatest artists including Veronese and Tintoretto. The ceiling of the **Sala del Senato** (senate chamber), featuring *The Triumph of Venice* by Tintoretto, is magnificent, but it's dwarfed by his masterpiece *Paradise* in the **Sala del Maggiore Consiglio** (Great Council Hall). ⊠ *Piazzetta San Marco* 🕿 *041/2715911* ⊕ *www. museicivicivenezuani.it* ▣ *Museums of San Marco pass €12 (Nov.– Mar.) or €13 (Apr.–Oct.), Musei Civici museum pass €18* ☉ *Apr.–Oct., daily 9–7; Nov.–Mar., daily 9–5; last tickets sold 1 hr before closing* Ⓜ *Vallaresso/San Zaccaria.*

## ELSEWHERE IN VENICE

★ **Gallerie dell'Accademia.** Napoléon founded these galleries in 1807 on the site of a religious complex he'd suppressed, and what he initiated now amounts to the world's most extraordinary collection of Venetian art, with works by father and son Jacopo and Giovanni Bellini, Cima da Conegliano (circa 1459–1517), Vittore Carpaccio (circa 1455–1525), Veronese, and Titian, among many others. ⊠ *Campo della Carità, Dorsoduro 1050* 🕿 *041/5222247, 041/5200345 reservations* ⊕ *www. gallerieaccademia.org* ▣ *€6.50, €11 includes Ca' d'Oro and Museo Orientale* ☉ *Tues.–Sun. 8:15–7:15, Mon. 8:15–2* Ⓜ *Accademia.*

★ **Madonna dell'Orto.** From a campo elegantly parqueted in red brick and white Istrian stone rises an Oriental-style campanile complete with its own cupola. There, captured between earth and sky, are the 12 apostles, hovering upon the facade of this 14th-century church. Madonna dell'Orto remains one of the most typical Gothic churches in Venice.

Named for a miraculous statue found in the nearby *orto* (garden) now displayed inside the **Cappella di San Mauro.**

Tintoretto lived nearby, and this, his parish church, contains some of his most powerful work. Lining the chancel are two huge (45 feet by 20 feet) canvases, *Adoration of the Golden Calf* and *Last Judgment,* in contrast to Tintoretto's *Presentation at the Temple* and the simple chapel where Tintoretto and his children, Marietta and Domenico, are buried. ⊠ *Campo della Madonna dell'Orto, Cannaregio* ☏ *041/2750462 Chorus Foundation* ⊕ *www.chorusvenezia.org* ▧ *€3, Chorus Pass €10* ⊗ *Mon.–Sat. 10–5, Sun. 1–5* Ⓜ *Orto.*

ⓒ **Peggy Guggenheim Collection.** A small but choice selection of 20th-century painting and sculpture is on display at this gallery in the heiress Guggenheim's former Grand Canal home. Her collection here in Palazzo Venier dei Leoni includes works by Picasso, Kandinsky, Pollock, Motherwell, and Ernst (at one time her husband). ⊠ *Fondamenta Venier dei Leoni, Dorsoduro 701* ☏ *041/2405411* ⊕ *www.guggenheim-venice.it* ▧ *€10* ⊗ *Wed.–Mon. 10–6* Ⓜ *Accademia.*

★ **Ponte di Rialto** *(Rialto Bridge).* One of Venice's most famous sights, the bridge was built in the late 16th century. Along the railing you'll enjoy one of the city's most famous views: the Grand Canal vibrant with boat traffic. Ⓜ *Rialto.*

★ **Santa Maria dei Miracoli.** Tiny yet perfectly proportioned, this early Renaissance gem is sheathed in marble and decorated inside with exquisite marble reliefs. The church was built in the 1480s to house *I Miracoli,* an image of the Virgin Mary that is said to perform miracles—look for it on the high altar. ⊠ *Campo Santa Maria Nova, Cannaregio* ☏ *041/2750462 Chorus Foundation* ⊕ *www.chorusvenezia.org* ▧ *€3, Chorus Pass €10* ⊗ *Mon.–Sat. 10–5* Ⓜ *Rialto.*

**Santa Maria della Salute.** Built to honor the Virgin Mary for saving Venice from a plague that killed 47,000 residents, this simple white octagon is adorned with a colossal cupola flanked by snail-like buttresses and a Palladian-style facade. The Byzantine icon above the main altar has been venerated as the Madonna della Salute (of health) since 1670, when Francesco Morosini brought it here from Crete. The **Sacrestia Maggiore** contains a dozen works by Titian. You'll also see Tintoretto's *The Wedding at Cana.* ⊠ *Punta della Dogana, Dorsoduro* ☏ *041/2743928* ▧ *Church free, sacristy €2* ⊗ *Apr.–Sept., daily 9–noon and 3–6:30; Oct.–Mar., daily 9–noon and 3–5:30* Ⓜ *Salute.*

Fodor's Choice **Santa Maria Gloriosa dei Frari.** This immense Gothic church, completed
★ in the 1400s, is deliberately austere, befitting the Franciscan brothers' insistence on spirituality and poverty. However, *I Frari* (as it's known locally) contains some of the most brilliant paintings in any Venetian church, including works by Titian and Giovanni Bellini, and sculptures by Antonion Canova and Jacopo Sansovino. ⊠ *Campo dei Frari, San Polo* ☏ *041/2728618, 041/2750462 Chorus Foundation* ⊕ *www. chorusvenezia.org* ▧ *€3, Chorus Pass €10* ⊗ *Mon.–Sat. 9–6, Sun. 1–6* Ⓜ *San Tomà.*

**Scuola Grande di San Rocco.** St. Rocco's popularity stemmed from his miraculous recovery from the plague and his care for fellow sufferers.

Followers and donations abounded, including a series of more than 60 paintings by Tintoretto. ⊠ *Campo San Rocco, San Polo 3052* ☎ *041/5234864* ⊕ *www.scuolagrandesanrocco.it* 🖃 *€7* ⊙ *Daily 9–5:30. Last entry ½ hr before closing* Ⓜ *San Tomà.*

## SHOPPING

Glass, most of it made on the separate island of Murano, is Venice's number-one product, and you'll be confronted by mind-boggling displays of traditional and contemporary glassware, much of it kitsch. Carnival masks also make a unique souvenir. The finest ones are handcrafted to fit the wearer, but inexpensive alternatives abound. The city also has a long history of supplying lace and luxury materials, though many of the cheaper items on sale are now imported. Don't forget classic Italian design in clothing, shoes, and leather accessories such as purses and belts. All these can be found in the streets radiating out from St Mark's Square.

**Il Merletto.** This shop sells authentic, handmade lace kept in the drawers behind the counter. ⊠ *Sotoportego del Cavalletto, under the Procuratie Vecchie, Piazza San Marco 95* ☎ *041/5208406.*

**L'Isola.** For chic, contemporary glassware, Carlo Moretti is a good choice; his designs are on display at this store. ⊠ *Campo San Moisè, San Marco 1468* ☎ *041/5231973* ⊕ *www.carlomoretti.com.*

**Lorenzo Rubelli.** Go to this boutique for the same brocades, damasks, and cut velvets used by the world's most prestigious decorators. ⊠ *Palazzo Corner Spinelli, San Marco 3877* ☎ *041/5236110* ⊕ *www.rubelli.it.*

**Mondonovo.** Guerrino Lovato, the proprietor here, is one of the most respected mask-makers in town, but genuine Carnival masks (unlike the tourist-trade clones), are quite expensive. ⊠ *Rio Terà Canal, Dorsoduro 3063* ☎ *041/5287344* ⊕ *www.mondonovomaschere.it.*

## WHERE TO EAT

$$$$
VENETIAN

✕**Alla Madonna.** Locals relax at Alla Madonna, which prides itself on the freshness, abundance, and caliber of their fish. In business since 1954 (Rado Fluvio still runs the place), it is a classic in service, atmosphere, and cuisine. The quality of *la materia prima* (the principal ingredients) is of paramount importance here, and impeccable preparation ensures its characteristics are always accentuated, never overwhelmed. Get your server's recommendation for the day. There are a variety of meat dishes, a fine wine list, and space for groups. It's a popular spot, so expect a lively and bustling atmosphere. ⊠ *Calle della Madonna, San Polo 594* ☎ *041/5223824* ⊕ *www.ristoranteallamadonna.com* ⌕ *Reservations essential* ▤ *AE, MC, V* ⊙ *Closed Sun., Jan., and 2 wks in Aug.* Ⓥ *San Silvestro.*

$$
VENETIAN
**Fodor's**Choice
★

✕**Vini da Gigio.** Paolo and Laura, a brother-sister team, run this refined trattoria as if they've invited you to dinner in their home, while keeping the service professional. Deservedly popular with Venetians and visitors alike, it's one of the best values in the city. Indulge in homemade pastas such as rigatoni with duck sauce and arugula-stuffed ravioli. Fish is well represented—try the sesame-encrusted tuna—but the meat dishes steal the show. The *anatra* (duck) is a flavorful fricassee; the steak with red-pepper sauce and the *tagliata di agnello* (sautéed lamb fillet with a light, crusty coating) are both superb, and you'll never enjoy a better *fegato alla veneziana* (Venetian-style liver with onions). It's a shame to order the house wine here: just let Paolo know your budget and he'll choose for you from his more than 3,000 labels. ⊠ *Fondamenta San Felice, Cannaregio 3628/A* ☏ *041/5285140* ⊕ *www.vinidagigio.com* ⚐ *Reservations essential* ⊟ *MC, V* ⊘ *Closed Mon. and Tues., 2 wks in Jan., and 3 wks in Aug.* Ⓥ *Ca' d'Oro.*

## WHERE TO STAY

**$$$**
**Fodor's Choice**
**★**

⊡ **Locanda Orseolo.** This cozy, elegant hotel offers a welcome respite from the throngs churning around Piazza San Marco. Family owned, it has an attentive staff and comfortable, well-appointed rooms. Classic Venetian designs are given a Carnevale theme, with each room's decor dedicated to one of the traditional masks. The relaxed atmosphere pervades at breakfast, where it's common to get engrossed in conversation with the other guests. **Pros:** intimate and romantic; extraordinarily friendly staff; Wi-Fi is free. **Cons:** in the one of the busiest and most commercial areas of the city. ⊠ *Corte Zorzi, off Campo San Gallo, San Marco 1083* ☏ *041/5204827* ⊕ *www.locandaorseolo.com* ⤵ *12 rooms* ⚐ *In-room: safe, refrigerator, Wi-Fi. In-hotel: room service, laundry facilities, laundry service, Internet terminal, Wi-Fi hotspot* ⊟ *AE, DC, MC, V* ⊘ *Closed Jan.* ⓇⒷ⒫ Ⓥ *Rialto/Vallaresso.*

**$$$$**

⊡ **Palazzo Sant'Angelo sul Canal Grande.** There's a distinguished yet comfortable feel to this elegant palazzo, which is large enough to deliver expected facilities and services but small enough to pamper its guests. Rooms have tapestry-adorned walls and Carrara and Alpine marble in the bath; those facing the Grand Canal have balconies that practically bring the canal to you. Common areas include an entrance hall with original Palladian flooring, a bright front lounge, and an intimate bar that puts the canal almost at arm's length. Ask ahead for a room with a view. **Pros:** convenient to vaporetto stop. **Cons:** some rooms have no special view; fee for Wi-Fi. ⊠ *Campo Sant'Angelo, San Marco 3488* ☏ *041/2411452* ⊕ *www.palazzosantangelo.com* ⤵ *14 rooms* ⚐ *In-room: safe, refrigerator, Internet, Wi-Fi. In-hotel: bar, laundry service, Wi-Fi hotspot, some pets allowed* ⊟ *AE, DC, MC, V* ⓇⒺⓅ Ⓥ *Sant'Angelo.*

**$$$–$$$$**
**★**

⊡ **Palazzo Stern.** The gracious terrace that eases onto the Grand Canal is almost reason alone to stay here. An opulent refurbishment of this early-15th-century neo-Gothic palace, carried out by the Stern family in the early 20th century, incorporated marble-columned arches, terrazzo floors, frescoed ceilings, mosaics, and a majestic carved staircase (copied from the Ca' d'Oro). It's also one of a limited number of palaces in the city that have not one, but two exposed sides decorated, one facing the Canal Grand, the other Rio Malpaga. Inside, some rooms have tufted walls, parquet flooring, and 42-inch, flat-screen TVs. From the rooftop terrace—which has a Jacuzzi—you get a classic Venetian view: over the city's roofs to the Campanile, and even to the Dolomites on a clear day.

Lodgings range from standard rooms to junior suites to an eclectic attic suite. **Pros:** excellent service; lovely views from many rooms; modern renovation retains historic ambience. **Cons:** no in-house restaurant (at this writing). ✉ *Calle del Traghetto, Dorsoduro 2792* ☎ *041/2770869* 🌐 *www.palazzostern.com* ⇒ *21 rooms, 3 suites* ♨ *In-room: safe, refrigerator, Wi-Fi. In-hotel: room service, bar, laundry service* ▭ *AE, MC, V* 🍴 *EP* Ⓥ *Ca' Rezzonico.*



# VIGO, SPAIN (FOR SANTIAGO DE COMPOSTELA)

Spain's most Atlantic region is en route to nowhere, an end in itself. Northwestern Spain is a series of rainy landscapes, stretching from your feet to the horizon and the country's wildest mountains, the Picos de Europa. Ancient granite buildings wear a blanket of moss, and even the stone *horreos* (granaries) are built on stilts above the damp ground.

Santiago de Compostela, where a cathedral holds the remains of the apostle James, has drawn pilgrims over the same roads for 900 years, leaving northwestern Spain covered with churches, shrines, and former hospitals. Asturias, north of the main pilgrim trail, has always maintained a separate identity, isolated by the rocky Picos de Europa. This and the Basque Country are the only parts of Spain never conquered by the Moors, so regional architecture shows little Moorish influence.

## ESSENTIALS

CURRENCY The euro (€1 to US$1.36 at this writing).

HOURS Museums generally open from 9 until 7 or 8; many are closed on Mondays and some close in the afternoons. Most stores are open Monday–Saturday 9–1:30 and 5–8, but tourist shops may open in the afternoon and also on Sunday between May and September.

INTERNET **Cibernova Street** (✉ *Rúa Nova 50, Santiago de Compostela* ☎ *981/560100*). **Ciber Vigo Copicentro** (✉ *Principe 22, Vigo* ☎ *No 986/222869*).

TELEPHONES Spain has good land and mobile services. Public kiosks accept phone cards that support international calls (cards sold in press shops, bars, and telecom shops). Mobile services are 3G compatible. Major companies include Vodafone.

## COMING ASHORE

The cruise terminal sits on the waterfront directly off the Old Town. It's possible to walk from the ship and explore on foot with shops and restaurants close by. Facilities are basic at the terminal, but there are plans to expand and add a hotel, spa, and leisure area.

In Vigo a tourist bus operates a continuous hop-on, hop-off service during the summer (April–September) and on cruise-ship days during the rest of the year. Tickets cost €7.50. The bus passes the port when cruise ships are in dock.

There is at least one train per hour to Santiago de Compostela. Journey time is 1½ hours, and tickets cost approximately €8.50 one way. It's a 30-minute walk from the port to the railway station or a 10-minute taxi trip.

Renting a vehicle would allow you to explore Santiago de Compostela and the rugged countryside of this wild corner of Spain. Rental price for an economy manual vehicle is approximately €75.

# EXPLORING VIGO AND SANTIAGO DE COMPOSTELA

## VIGO

Vigo's formidable port is choked with trawlers and fishing boats and lined with clanging shipbuilding yards. Its sights (or lack thereof) fall far short of its commercial swagger. The city's casual appeal lies a few blocks inland, where the port commotion gives way to the narrow, dilapidated streets of the Old Town. From 8:30 to 3:30 daily on **Rúa Pescadería**, in the barrio called La Piedra, Vigo's famed *ostreras*—a group of rubber-glove fisherwomen who have been peddling fresh oysters to passersby for more than 50 years.

**Parque del Castro.** South of Vigo's Old Town is the hilltop park with sandy paths, palm trees, mossy embankments, and stone benches. Atop a series of steps are the remains of an old fort and a *mirador* (lookout) with fetching views of Vigo's coastline and the Islas Cíes. (⊠ *Between Praza de España and Praza do Rei, beside Av. Marqués de Alcedo*).

## SANTIAGO DE COMPOSTELA
*80 km (50 mi) north of Vigo, 77 km (48 mi) southwest of À Coruña.*

A large, lively university makes Santiago one of the most exciting cities in Spain, but its cathedral makes it one of the most impressive. The building is opulent and awesome, yet its towers create a sense of harmony as a benign St. James, dressed in pilgrim's costume, looks down from his perch.

**Casco Antiguo** *(Old Town).* Walk around Santiago do Campostela's Old Quarter, losing yourself in its maze of stone-paved narrow streets and little plazas. The most beautiful pedestrian thoroughfares are Rúa do Vilar, Rúa do Franco, and Rúa Nova—portions of which are covered by arcaded walkways called *soportales,* designed to keep walkers out of the rain.

**Cathedral.** From the **Praza do Obradoiro,** climb the two flights of stairs to the main entrance to Santiago's cathedral. Although the facade is baroque, the interior holds one of the finest Romanesque sculptures in the world, the **Pórtico de la Gloria.** Completed in 1188 by Maestro Mateo (Master Mateo), this is the cathedral's original entrance, its three arches carved with biblical figures from the Apocalypse, the Last Judgment, and purgatory. On the left are the prophets; in the center, Jesus is flanked by the four evangelists (Matthew, Mark, Luke, and John) and, above them, the 24 elders of the Apocalypse playing celestial instruments. Just below Jesus is a serene St. James, poised on a carved column. Look carefully, and you can see five smooth grooves, formed by the millions of pilgrims who have placed their hands here over the centuries. St. James presides over the **high altar.** The stairs behind it are the cathedral's focal point, surrounded by dazzling baroque decoration,

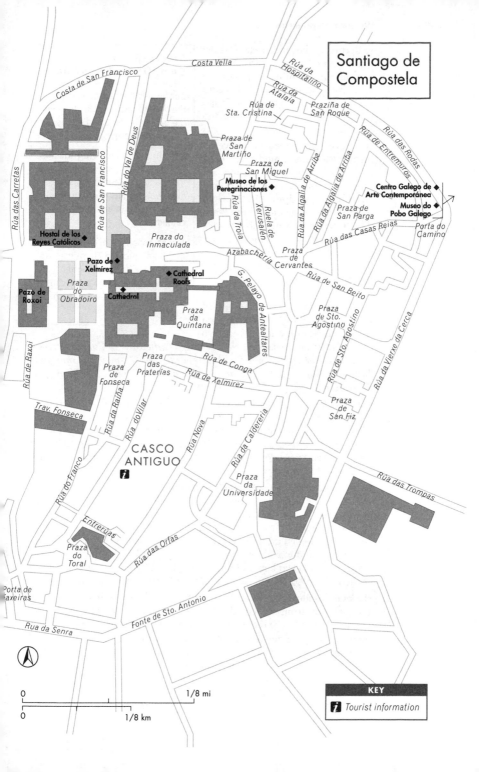

sculpture, and drapery. Here, as the grand finale of their spiritual journey, pilgrims embrace St. James and kiss his cloak. In the crypt beneath the altar lie the remains of St. James and his disciples, St. Theodore and St. Athenasius.

A huge *botafumeiro* (incense burner used since medieval times) and other cathedral treasures are on display in the **museums** downstairs and next door. On the right (south) side of the nave is the **Porta das Praterías** (Silversmiths' Door), the only purely Romanesque part of the cathedral's facade. The statues on the portal were cobbled together from parts of the cathedral. The double doorway opens onto the **Praza das Praterías**, named for the silversmiths' shops that used to line it. ⊠ *Praza do Obradoiro*

> ### SANTIAGO DE CAMPOSTELA BEST BETS
>
> **Santiago's Cathedral.** One of the holiest places in Christendom; the quality of the Romanesque stonework is exquisite.
>
> **The Museo de las Peregrinaciones.** Learn about the triumphs, trials, and tribulations of the medieval pilgrims who journeyed across Europe to worship at the cathedral.
>
> **The atmosphere of Santiago's medieval quarter.** These narrow streets have been serving the needs of travelers since the cathedral was completed in the 12th century.

☎ *981/560527 museums, 981/569327 cathedral* 🖾 *Cathedral free, combined museum ticket €5* ☉ *Cathedral daily 7 AM–9 PM; museums June–Oct., Mon.–Sat. 10–2 and 4–8, Sun. 10–2; Nov.–May, Mon.–Sat. 10–1:30 and 4–6:30, Sun. 10–1:30.*

**Cathedral Roofs.** For excellent views of the city and the plazas surrounding the cathedral, join a tour across the granite steps of cathedral roofs. Pilgrims made the same 100-foot climb in medieval times to burn their travel-worn clothes below the Cruz dos Farrapos (cross of rags). ⊠ *Pazo de Xelmírez, Praza do Obradoiro* ☎ *981/552985* 🖾 *€10* ☉ *Tues.–Sun. 10–2 and 4–8.*

**Centro Galego de Arte Contemporánea** *(Galician Center for Contemporary Art).* On the north side of town off the Porta do Camino, the contemporary art center is a stark but elegant modern building that offsets Santiago's ancient feel. Portuguese designer Álvaro Siza built the museum of smooth, angled granite, which mirrors the medieval convent of San Domingos de Bonaval next door. The museum has a good permanent collection and even better changing exhibits. ⊠ *Rúa de Valle Inclán s/n* ☎ *981/546619* ⊕ *www.cgac.org* 🖾 *Free* ☉ *Tues.–Sun. 11–8.*

**Hostal de los Reyes Católicos** *(Hostel of the Catholic Monarchs).* Facing the cathedral from the left, this hostel was built in 1499 by Ferdinand and Isabella to house the pilgrims who slept on Santiago's streets every night. Having lodged and revived travelers for nearly 500 years, it's the oldest refuge in the world, and was converted from a hospital to a luxury parador in 1953. The facade bears a Castilian coat of arms along with Adam, Eve, and various saints. Walk-in spectators without room keys risk being asked to leave, but for a negotiable cost, as part of a city tour, you can visit in the company of an official guide from the

tourist office. ⊠ *Praza do Obradoiro 1* ☎ *981/582200 hostel* ⊕ *www.*
*parador.es* ⊘ *Daily 10–1 and 4–6.*

**Museo de las Peregrinaciones** *(Pilgrimage Museum).* North of Azabachería
(follow Ruela de Xerusalén) is this museum, which contains Camino de
Santiago iconography from sculptures and carvings to *azabache* (compact black coal, or jet) talismans. For an overview of the history of the
pilgrimage and the role of the *camino* in the development of the city
itself, this is a key visit. ⊠ *Rúa de San Miguel 4* ☎ *981/581558* ⊠ *€2.50*
⊘ *Tues.–Fri. 10–8, Sat. 10:30–1:30 and 5–8, Sun. 10:30–1:30.*

**Museo do Pobo Galego** *(Galician Folk Museum).* Next door to the Center
for Contemporary Art is this museum, in the medieval convent of Santo
Domingo de Bonaval. The star attraction is the 13th-century self-sup-
porting spiral granite staircase that still connects three floors. ⊠ *Calle*
*San Domingos de Bonaval* ☎ *981/583620* ⊕ *www.museodopobo.es*
⊠ *Free* ⊘ *Tues.–Sat. 10–2 and 4–8, Sun. 11–2.*

**Pazo de Xelmírez** *(Palace of Archbishop Xelmírez).* On the wide Praza da
Quintana, stop into this rich 12th-century palace, an unusual example
of Romanesque civic architecture with a cool, clean, vaulted dining
hall. ⊠ *Praza do Obradoiro* ⊠ *Included in combined museum (€5)*
⊘ *Tues.–Sun. 10–2 and 4–8.*

# SHOPPING

Souvenirs of Galicia include authentic *zuecos* (hand-painted wooden
clogs) still worn in some villages to navigate mud, jewelry and trinkets carved from azabache (jet, or compact black coal), ceramics, and
excellent leatherwear of all kinds. Santiago has an excellent selection
of religious items in all price ranges.

**Sargadelos.** Galicia is known throughout Spain for its distinctive blue-
and-white ceramics with bold modern designs, made in Sargadelos and
O Castro. There is a wide selection at Sargadelos. ⊠ *Rúa Nova 16*
☎ *981/581905.*

# WHERE TO EAT

**$–$$$** ✕ **A Barrola.** Polished wooden floors, a niche with wine and travel
SPANISH   books, and a lively terrace make this tavern a favorite with univer-
sity faculty. The house salads, mussels with *santiaguiños* (crabmeat),
*arroz con bogavante* (rice with lobster), and seafood empanadas are
superb. ⊠ *Rúa do Franco 29, Santiago de Campostela* ☎ *981/577999*
⊕ *www.restaurantesgrupobarrola.com* ⊟ *AE, MC, V* ⊘ *Closed Mon.*
*and Jan.–Mar.*

**$–$$** ✕ **Carretas.** This casual spot for fresh Galician seafood is around the
SEAFOOD   corner from the Hostal de los Reyes Católicos. Fish dishes abound, but
the specialty here is shellfish. For the full experience, order the labor-
intensive *variado de mariscos,* a comprehensive platter of langostinos,
king prawns, crab, and goose barnacles that comes with a shell-cracker.
*Salpicón de mariscos* presents the same creatures preshelled. ⊠ *Rúa de*
*Carretas 21, Santiago de Campostela* ☎ *981/563111* ⊟ *AE, DC, MC,*
*V* ⊘ *Closed Sun.*

# VILLEFRANCHE-SUR-MER

Nestled discreetly along the deep scoop of harbor between Nice and Cap Ferrat, this pretty watercolor of a fishing port is a stage set of brightly colored houses—the sort of place where Pagnol's *Fanny* could have been filmed. Genuine fishermen actually skim up to the docks here in weathered blue *barques*, and the streets of the Vieille Ville flow directly to the waterfront, much as they did in the 13th century. The deep harbor, in the caldera of a volcano, was once preferred by the likes of Onassis and Niarchos and royals on their yachts. The character of Villefranche was subtly shaped by the artists and authors who gathered at the Hôtel Welcome, and above all, Jean Cocteau, who came here to recover from the excesses of Paris life. Villefranche is also the gateway to other treasures along this most select part of the Riviera.

## ESSENTIALS

CURRENCY   The euro (€1 to US$1.36 at this writing).

HOURS   Stores open Monday–Saturday 9–7, but many close at lunchtime (usually noon to 2 or 3) and some will open later and on Sunday during July and August. Museums open 10–5, but most are closed on either Monday or Tuesday.

INTERNET   **L'X Cafe** (✉ *5 pl. de la Marché* ☎ *04–93–53–27–99*) is a stylish spot offering drinks and snacks as well as computer terminals and Wi-Fi.

TELEPHONES   Tri-band GSM phones work in France. You can buy prepaid phone cards at telecom shops, news vendors, and tobacconists in all towns and cities. Phone cards can be used for local or international calls. France Telecom and Orange are leading telecom companies.

## COMING ASHORE

Cruise ships dock offshore in the bay of Villefranche-sur-Mer and passengers are tendered to the quayside in the heart of the town. The terminal is small, but has an information center, restrooms, and car-rental kiosks. You can tour Villefranche-sur-Mer itself on foot from here, but to visit surrounding attractions you'll need transport. The train station is a five-minute walk from the cruise port and the service along the coast to Beaulieu and Èze-sur-Mer is frequent (at least two trains per hour), fast (less than 10 minutes travel time), and reliable. Tickets cost around €2 for the short hop between Villefranche-sur-Mer and Beaulieu-sur-Mer. From the train station at Èze-sur-Mer there are frequent shuttle buses to Èze village (15 minutes, Route 83). By train both Nice and Monte Carlo are also within 15-minutes journey time. Frequent bus services by Ligne d'Azur (⊕ *www.lignedazur.com*) link Villefranche-sur-Mer with Beaulieu-sur-Mer, Cap Ferrat, Èze, Nice, and Monte Carlo. One ride is €1.10, and a day pass is €4. Route 81 links Villefranche-sur-Mer with Beaulieu-sur-Mer and St-Jean-Cap-Ferrat (also with Nice). Line 100 links Villefranche-sur-Mer with Nice and Èze-sur-Mer (and on to Monte Carlo).

The cost of car rental is approximately €75 for an economy manual vehicle. However, there are no car-rental options in town so vehicles have to be prebooked and there are fees for delivery and return.

Taxis are plentiful, and can provide tourist itineraries. For a single journey, fares are €2.80 for pick-up followed by a day fare of €0.84 per km (½-mi) plus a fee for any waiting time. Taxis can be pre-booked for return journeys, making them a good option for transfer to local attractions.

2

## EXPLORING VILLEFRANCHE-SUR-MER AND VICINITY

### VILLEFRANCHE-SUR-MER

**Chapelle St-Pierre.** So enamored was Jean Cocteau of this painterly fishing port that he decorated the 14th-century chapel with images from the life of St. Peter and dedicated it to the village's fishermen. ⊠ *Pl. Pollanai Quai Courbet* ☎ *04–93–76–90–70* ⊠ *€2.50* ☉ *Closed Mon. mid-Mar.–mid-Sept., 10–noon and 3–7; mid-Sept.–mid-Mar., 10–noon and 2–6.*

**Citadelle St-Elme.** The stalwart 16th-century fortress, restored to perfect condition, anchors the harbor with its broad, sloping stone walls. Beyond its drawbridge lie the city's administrative offices and a group of minor gallery-museums, with a scattering of works by Picasso and Miró. Whether or not you stop into these private collections of local art (all free of charge), you are welcome to stroll around the inner grounds and to circle the imposing exterior.

**Rue Obscure.** Running parallel to the waterfront, the extraordinary 13th-century "dark street" is entirely covered by vaulted arcades; it sheltered the people of Villefranche when the Germans fired their parting shots—an artillery bombardment—near the end of World War II.

### BEAULIEU-SUR-MER
*4 km (2½ mi) east of Villefranche.*

With its back pressed hard against the cliffs of the corniche and sheltered between the peninsulas of Cap Ferrat and Cap Roux, this once-grand resort basks in a tropical microclimate that earned its central neighborhood the name *Petite Afrique* (little Africa). The town was the pet of 19th-century society, and its grand hotels welcomed Empress Eugénie, the Prince of Wales, and Russian nobility. Today it's still a posh address.

Fodor's Choice
★ **Villa Kerylos.** One manifestation of Beaulieu's belle époque excess is the eye-knocking mansion built in 1902 in the style of classical Greece (to be exact, of the villas that existed on the island of Delos in the 2nd century BC). It was the dream house of the amateur archaeologist Théodore Reinach, who originally hailed from a super-rich family from Frankfurt, helped the French in their excavations at Delphi, and became an authority on ancient Greek music. He commissioned an Italian architect from Nice, Emmanuel Pontremoli, to surround him with Grecian delights: cool Carrara marble, rare fruitwoods, and a dining salon where guests reclined to eat *à la Greque*. Don't miss this—it's one of the most unusual houses in the south of France. ⊠ *Rue Gustave-Eiffel* ☎ *04–93–01–01–44* ⊕ *www.villa-kerylos.com* ⊠ *€8.50, joint ticket with Villa Ephrussi de Rothschild (must be used in same wk)* €15 ☉ *Mid-Feb.–June, Sept., and Oct., daily 10–6; July and Aug., daily 10–7; Nov.–mid-Feb., weekdays 2–6, weekends 10–6.*

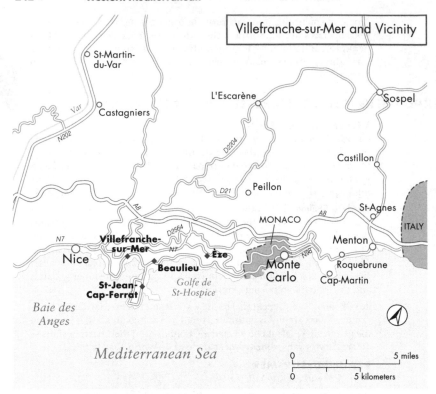

Villefranche-sur-Mer and Vicinity

*Mediterranean Sea*

*Baie des Anges*

## ST-JEAN-CAP-FERRAT
*2 km (1 mi) south of Beaulieu on D25.*

This luxuriously sited pleasure port moors the peninsula of Cap Ferrat; from its port-side walkways and crescent of beach you can look over the sparkling blue harbor to the graceful green bulk of the corniches. Yachts purr in and out of port, and their passengers scuttle into cafés for take-out drinks to enjoy on their private decks. Unfortunately, Cap Ferrat is a vast peninsula and hides its secrets—except for the Villa Ephrussi, most fabled estates are hidden behind iron gates and towering hedges—particularly well.

★ **Villa Ephrussi de Rothschild.** Between the port and the mainland, the floridly beautiful villa stands as witness to the wealth and worldly flair of the baroness who had it built. Constructed in 1905 in neo-Venetian style (its flamingo-pink facade was thought not to be in the best of taste by the local gentry), the house was baptized "Ile-de-France" in homage to the Baroness Bétrice de Rothschild's favorite ocean liner (her staff used to wear sailing costumes and her ship travel-kit is on view in her bedroom). Precious artworks, tapestries, and furniture adorn the salons—in typical Rothschildian fashion, each room is given over to a different 18th-century "époque." Upstairs are the private apartments of Madame la Baronne, which can only be seen on a guided tour offered around noon. The grounds are landscaped with no fewer than seven theme gardens and topped off with a Temple of Diana (no less); be sure to allow yourself time to wander here, as this is one of the few places on the coast where you'll be allowed to experience the lavish pleasures characteristic of the belle époque Côte d'Azur. Tea and light lunches are served in a glassed-in porch overlooking the grounds and spectacular views of the coastline. ⊠ *Av. Ephrussi* ☎ *04–93–01–33–09* ⊕ *www.villa-ephrussi.com* ⊠ *Access to ground floor and gardens €10, joint ticket with Villa Kerylos (must be used in same wk) €15, guided tour upstairs €3* ☉ *Mid-Feb.–June, Sept., and Oct., daily 10–6; July and Aug., daily 10–7; Nov.–mid-Feb., weekdays 2–6, weekends 10–6.*

**VILLEFRANCHE-SUR-MER BEST BETS**

**Èze.** One of the most charming of France's *villages perchés*, or perched villages, is built high on a rocky parapet. Views down the Riviera coast are spectacular.

**Villa Kerylos.** The splendors of ancient Greek art and architecture are beautifully re-created here in the south of France at the home of a wealthy amateur archaeologist.

**Villa Ephrussi de Rothschild.** This magnificent century-old mansion surrounded by glorious gardens is stuffed with the finest furniture and decoration its baroness owner could afford.

## ÈZE

**Fodor's Choice** ★

*2 km (1 mi) east of Beaulieu.*

Towering like an eagle's nest above the coast and crowned with ramparts and the ruins of a medieval château, preposterously beautiful Èze (pronounced *ehz*) is the most accessible of all the perched villages—this means crowds, many of whom head here to shop in the boutique-lined staircase-streets. (Happily, most shops here are quite stylish, and there is a nice preponderance of bric-a-brac and vintage fabric dealers.) But most come here to drink in the views, for no one can deny that this is the most spectacularly sited of all coastal promontories; if you can manage to shake the crowds and duck off to a quiet overlook, the village commands splendid views up and down the coast, one of the draws that once lured fabled visitors—lots of crowned heads, Georges Sand, Friedrich Nietzsche—and residents: Consuelo Vanderbilt, when she was tired of being duchess of Marlborough, traded in Blenheim Palace for a custom-built house here.

**Jardin Exotique** *(Tropical Garden)*. From the crest-top garden, full of rare succulents, you can pan your videocam all the way around the hills and waterfront. But if you want a prayer of a chance of enjoying the magnificence of the village's arched passages, stone alleyways, and ancient fountains, come at dawn or after sunset—or (if you have the means) stay the night—but spend the midday elsewhere to avoid the searing afternoon sun. ⊠ *Èze* ☎ *No phone* ⊠ *€5* ☉ *July and Aug., daily 9–8; Sept.–June, daily 9–5:30.*

**Notre-Dame.** This church consecrated in 1772 glitters inside with baroque retables and altarpieces.

**Sentier Friedrich Nietzsche.** Èze's tourist office, on Place du Général-de-Gaulle, can direct you to the numerous footpaths—the most famous being the Sentier Friedrich Nietzsche—that thread Èze with the coast's three corniche highways. The views from the 1,001 switchbacks leading to and from the village are breathtaking.

## SHOPPING

This part of the Riviera coastline has some of the most expensive addresses, and thus some of the finest shopping, with excusive boutiques selling very high-class fashion and decorative goods. In the shops of Cap Ferrat and Beaulieu you'll shop among France's more mature lunching ladies, while Villefranche-sur-Mer has a good selection of characterful boutiques with more down-to-earth prices. The streets of Èze are replete with artists' studios selling excellent art and ceramics, plus cute collectibles. In every town you'll find local Provençal specialties such as excellent olive oil, soaps, dried herbs, colorful fabrics, pottery, and basketware.

**Art dessin JMB Studio.** This gallery is full of oil and watercolor images of wonderful Provençal landscapes in a variety of sizes. ⊠ *8 rue de la Paix, Èze* ☎ *06–89–80–34–94.*

**Feux et Flammes.** This small shop carries genuinely local arts and handicrafts. ⊠ *Av. du Jardin Exotique, Èze* ☎ *04–93–41–06–33.*

**Terres Dorees.** This store sells a range of fragrant handmade soaps. ⊠ *10 av. Sadi Carnot, Villefranche-sur-Mer* ☎ *04–93–76–66–75* ⊕ *www. terres-dorees.com.*

## WHERE TO EAT

**$**
FRENCH
✕ **La Grignotière.** Tucked down a narrow side street just a few steps away from the marketplace, this small and friendly local restaurant offers up top-quality, inexpensive dishes. The homemade lasagna is excellent, as is the spaghetti pistou. ⊠ *3 rue du Poilu Villefranche-sur-Mer* ☎ *04–93–76–79–83* ▤ *AE, MC, V* ☯ *Apr.–mid-Nov., daily lunch and dinner; mid-Nov.–Mar. No lunch.*

**¢–$**
FRENCH
✕ **Loumiri.** Classic Provençal and regional seafood dishes are tastily prepared and married with decent, inexpensive wines at this cute little bistro near the entrance to the Vieille Ville. The best bet is to order *à l'ardoise*—that is, from the blackboard listing of daily specials. The lunch menu prix-fixe (€15) is the best deal in town. Prix-fixe dinner menus start at €23. ⊠ *Av. Jardin Exotique, Èze* ☎ *04–93–41–16–42* ▤ *MC, V* ☯ *Closed Mon. and mid-Dec.–mid-Jan. No dinner Wed.*

# Eastern Mediterranean & Aegean

PORTS IN CROATIA, CYPRUS,
EGYPT, GREECE & TURKEY

## WORD OF MOUTH

"Ephesus is probably one of the most incredible sights you will ever see. Even better than Pompeii, IMHO! You will enjoy it more if you're not in a group of 50 or 100. If you stop in Istanbul, you're in for a treat. . . . There is no place like Istanbul."

—zwho

Lindsay
Bennett

Eastern Mediterranean cruises are especially good for travelers who want to see the archaeological ruins of Europe's two great classical civilizations, Rome and Greece. These ports are rich in history, and some are even rich in natural beauty. There are few ports of call more breathtaking than Santorini or the island of Hvar.

Many Eastern Mediterranean itineraries begin in Piraeus, the seaport of Athens, or Istanbul, and visit ports in Greece and Turkey. Some may cross the Mediterranean to call in Alexandria or Port Said (for an exhausting, daylong visit to Cairo). Other cruises begin in Italy, often in Rome or Venice. These cruises may take in ports in Sicily and southern Italy (if they leave from Rome) or even Malta before heading toward Greece. Cruises beginning in Venice may call at one or more ports along Croatia's breathtaking Adriatic coast, and these port calls are highlights of any voyage.

### ABOUT THE RESTAURANTS

All the restaurants we recommend serve lunch; they may also serve dinner if your cruise ship stays late in port and you choose to dine off the ship. Cuisine in Europe is varied, but Europeans tend to eat a leisurely meal at lunch, but in most ports there are quicker and simpler alternatives for those who just want to grab a quick bite before returning to the ship. Note that several Eastern Mediterranean countries do not use the euro, including Croatia, Cyprus, Egypt, and Turkey. Price categories in those countries are based on the euro-equivalent costs of eating in restaurants.

| WHAT IT COSTS IN EUROS | | | | |
|---|---|---|---|---|
| ¢ | $ | $$ | $$$ | $$$$ |
| Restaurants | under €11 | €11–€17 | €17–€23 | €23–€30 | over €30 |

Restaurant prices are per person for a main course at dinner, including tax.

# ALEXANDRIA, EGYPT

Ancient Egypt's gateway to the Mediterranean was founded by Alexander the Great in 331 BC, but its name is inextricably linked with Cleopatra. She inhabited vast palaces and worshipped at monumental temples. The city's great library was also under her control, and her city was protected by one of the Seven Wonders of the Ancient World, the great Pharos of Alexandria, a lighthouse. Sadly, all of these great treasures are lost or buried underneath the modernity. That doesn't mean Alexandria is bereft of history; in a second incarnation it became a decadent, early-20th-century mercantile and colonial enclave with a multicultural mix. It seduced novelist E. M. Forster during World

War I and gave birth to Lawrence Durrell's *Alexandria Quartet,* which captivated a generation of American readers in the late 1950s. At the same time, its reputation as an Arabic seat of learning has stayed in the ascendant. With lively streets and graceful cafés, Alexandria is still a great city and remains an utterly charming place to visit.

### ESSENTIALS

CURRENCY The Egyptian pound (£E5.69 to US$1; £E7.31 to €1 at this writing). U.S. currency is accepted for high-value items in shops but not in restaurants or markets. ATMs can be found in Alexandria and other major destinations in Egypt

HOURS Museums are usually open from 9 to 5. Many museums are closed on Monday. Shops open from 8 until 7. During Ramadan (the Muslim month of fasting) opening times vary; during this period shops close during the day but stay open late into the evening.

TELEPHONES GSM phones work in Egypt, where mobile systems are single-band and are not 3G-compatible. Telecom Egypt runs the fixed line system. Public phones accept calling cards available from retail outlets; however, connections are not always smooth. Major companies are MobiNil and Vodafone.

### COMING ASHORE

Alexandria's cruise terminal is in the commercial port in the western harbor, and ships dock right alongside busy commercial ships; it's a frenetic environment. The terminal has shopping facilities and a taxi stand.

From the port, it is an easy 20-minute walk along the corniche to the heart of town, but navigating your way to the various attractions can be a challenge, and taxis are the best way to get around. They are inexpensive, and you can flag them down almost anywhere. The driver might try to pick up another passenger en route—it's standard practice, so don't be surprised. Drivers don't use their meters, so you have to guess at the appropriate fare or try to negotiate one in advance. A ride from the cruise port to downtown should be around £E10–£E15. If you look rich, expect to pay a bit more.

Though they're picturesque and cheap, trams are likely to take four to five times longer to get where you're going than a taxi would. The main tram station is Raml, near Maydan Sa'd Zaghlul. Buy tickets on board. Horse-drawn *caleches* (carriages) offer an alternative way to tour the town, but agree on a price before you get aboard.

**Avis.** We do not recommend car rentals in Egypt because of the difficulty of driving here, but Avis has an office at the Cecil Hotel, and has prices starting at $55 for an economy manual vehicle. ⊠ *16 Sa'd Zaghlul Sq.* ☎ *03/485-7400* ⊕ *www.avis.com.*

## EXPLORING ALEXANDRIA

**Abu al-Abbas al-Mursi Mosque.** This attractive mosque was built during World War II over the tomb of a 13th-century holy man, who is the patron saint of the city's fishermen. The area surrounding it has been turned into Egypt's largest and most bizarre religious/retail complex, with a cluster of mosques sharing a terrace that hides an underground

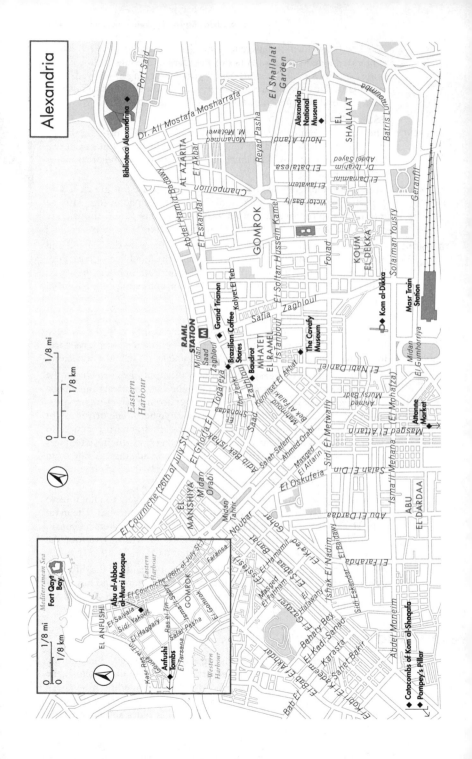

Alexandria

Eastern Harbour

Mediterranean Sea

Port Said

Biblioteca Alexandrina ◆

Dr. Ali Mostafa Mosharrafa

AT AZARITA

Abdel Ham'd Badawi

El Eskandar

El Akbar

Champollion

Reyad Pasha

Mohammed N. Motawei

Nouh Afandi

Alexandria National Museum ◆

El'Shallalat Garden

El balatesa

EL SHALLALAT

Batris Lioumoumbe

Dr. Ibrahim Abdel Sayed

El Damamini

Victor Basily

El Iawatem

GOMROK

El Soltan Hussein Kamel

Fouad

Geranfil

Solaiman Yousry

KOUM EL-DEKKA

Zaghloul

RAML STATION M

Midan Saad Zaghloul

Grand Trianon ◆

kolyet El Teb

Safia

Brazilian Coffee Stores ◆

Baudrot ◆

Ibn Zenki

Saad Zaghloul

Kennieset El Akbat

El Shohdaa

El Ghorfa El

Togareya

Adib Bek Ishak

Bek Al Falaki

Is Tambol

MHATET EL RAMEL

The Cavafy Museum ◆

El Nabi Daniel

Kom al-Dikka ◆

Midan El Gumhoriyya

Masr Train Station

EL MANSHIYA

Midan Orabi

Salah Salem

Ahmed Orabi

Noubar

Midan Tahir

Mahmoud

Masged El Attarin

El Oskufeia

Sidi El Metwally

Ismail Mehana

Salah El Din

Ahmed Mursy Badr

El Nabi Daniel

El Mohafza

Masged Mursy Badr

Masged El Attarin

El Mohafza

Athonne Market →

ABU EL DARDAA

Abu El Dardaa

El Farahda

El Baldawy

Ishak El Nadim

El Ka'bed Hamamil

El Saba'a Banat

Gohar

El Kobti E lAademi

E l Bab El Akbari

Abdel Moneim

Sidi Eskandar

Bahary Bey

El Kadi Sanad

Karasta

Sahel Bakir

El Gazyer

El Halawany

El Fahham

Masged El Fahham

Faransa

E l Saba El Banat

Catacombs of Kom al-Shaqafa ◆

Pompey's Pillar ◆

EL ANFUSHI

Fort Qayt Bay

Abu al-Abbas al-Mursi Mosque ◆

El Saiyala

Sidi Yakout

El Haggary

El Tarsana

Ras El Tin Sft (26th of July St.)

El Courniche (26th of July St.)

Eastern Harbour

GOMROK

El Gomrok

Safat Pasha

Ismail Sri

Anfushi Tombs ◆

Kasr Reselfa

Western Harbour

El Courniche (26th of July St.)

1/8 mi

1/8 km

shopping center. Intruding on the space is a horrific modernism-on-the-cheap office building (with yet more shops) that is as pointed and angular as the mosques are smooth and curved. If you are dressed modestly and the mosque is open, you should be able to get inside. If so, remove your shoes and refrain from taking photos. ⊠ *Corniche, al-Anfushi, El Anfushi.*

**Alexandria National Museum.** A small but high-quality collection of artifacts includes items found under the waters of the Western Harbor during recent marine archaeological projects. The display galleries cover every era of the city's long history, and include Christian pieces, Islamic arts and crafts, and more recent information about Alexandria's colonial era. The early 20th-century Italianate palace that houses the museum, designed by a French architect, is a prime example of this colonial past. ⊠ *110 Shar'a el Horreya, El Shallalat* ☏ *03/483–5519* ☐ *£E30* ☉ *Daily 9–4.*

**Bibliotheca Alexandrina.** This monumental, $190 million, UNESCO-sponsored project began with an instinctively appealing idea: to resurrect the Great Library of ancient Alexandria, once one of the world's major centers of learning. Its location near the Silsileh Peninsula on the edge of the Eastern Harbor has tremendous symbolic resonance, having been the royal quarters in ancient times and one of several possible locations of the original library. The modernist Norwegian-designed building is in the form of an enormous multitiered cylinder tilted to face the sea, with a roof of diamond-shape windows that allow controlled light into the seven cascading interior floors. The most impressive feature, however, is the curving exterior wall covered in rough-hewn granite blocks from Aswan that have been engraved with letters from ancient languages.

Once you've enjoyed the view of the vast interior from the mezzanine gallery, there's little to hold you in the main hall, but the library has several small museums and exhibitions that are of more interest. The **Manuscripts Museum** has a large collection of rare documents, parchments, and early printed books. The **Impressions of Alexandria** exhibition features paintings and sketches of the city dating from the 15th to the 19th centuries and photographs taken in the late 19th and early 20th centuries. The **Antiquities Museum** on the basement level has a collection of finds from Pharaonic, Roman, and Islamic Alexandria. Examples of monumental Roman statuary include *Huge Forearm Holding a Ball* (nothing else remains of the immense piece), and a finely chiseled bust of the Emperor Octavian (Augustus). Egypto-Roman artifacts include

---

## ALEXANDRIA BEST BETS

**Explore the Alexandria National Museum.** A collection of artifacts found under the shallow waters of Alexandria Bay plus galleries explaining the city's different eras help to clarify Egypt's history.

**Fort in Quayt Bay.** The site of Alexandria's famous ancient *pharos* or lighthouse, the fort protected Alexandria harbor throughout the Crusader and colonial eras.

**Catacombs of Kom al-Shoqafa.** These Roman catacombs are the most completely excavated ancient site in the city.

**3**

the mummy of Anhk Hor, governor of Upper Egypt, and several 2nd-century funerary masks showing the prevalent cross-styling between the classical Egyptian and Roman Egyptian styles. A planetarium and IMAX theater are the latest additions to the complex, offering a range of science- and astronomy-based activities including star gazing and constellation identification and interactive museum displays. ⊠ 63 *Shar'a Soter, Chatby* ☎ *03/483–9999* ⊕ *www.bibalex.org* ✉ *Library £E10, Antiquities Museum £E20, Manuscripts Museum £E20 Planetarium and IMAX shows £E25* ⊘ *Sat.–Thurs. 11–7, Fri. 3–7.*

★ **Catacombs of Kom al-Shoqafa.** This is the most impressive of Alexandria's ancient remains, dating from the 2nd century AD. Excavation started in 1892, and the catacombs were discovered accidentally eight years later when a donkey fell through a chamber ceiling. A long spiral staircase leads to the main hall. The stairs run down the outside of a shaft, which excavators used to transport the bodies of the dead. The staircase leads to the rotunda, which, like all but the lowest chamber, is undecorated but striking for the sheer scale of the underground space, supported by giant columns carved out of the bedrock.

A few rooms branch off from the rotunda: The Triclinium was a banquet hall where relatives and friends toasted the deceased, and the Caracalla Hall has four lightly painted tombs and a case of bones. The next level down contains a labyrinth of smaller nooks for storing bodies and leads to the lowest excavated room, which is framed by columns and sculpted snakes. Casts of two statues stand here—the originals are in the Greco-Roman Museum—and three tombs are of interest for their mix of pharaonic and Greek imagery. ⊠ *Shar' El Shenity Abu Mandour, Karmouz* ☎ *03/482–5800* ✉ *£E35* ⊘ *Daily 9–4:30.*

**The Cavafy Museum.** The Greek writer Constantine Cavafy was ignored during his lifetime but has received international recognition since his death in 1933. The small flat where Cavafy spent the last years of his life has been turned into a museum. Half of it is given over to a re-creation of his home. The other half of the museum houses newspaper clippings about the poet's life and a library of his works. ⊠ *4 Shar'a CP Cavafy, (formerly Shar'a Sharm El-Sheikh), Mahatet El Raml* ☎ *03/468–1598* ✉ *£E20* ⊘ *Tues.–Sun. 10–3.*

**Fort Qayt Bay.** This sandstone fort lies on the very tip of the Corniche, dominating the view of the Eastern Harbor. It was built on the site of Alexandria's Pharos lighthouse, one of the seven wonders of the ancient world and incorporates its remains—much of which is still visible—into the foundation. A Greek named Sostratus in the 3rd century BC constructed the lighthouse under the Ptolemies. Standing about 400 feet high and capable of projecting a light that could be seen 53 km (35 mi) out to sea, it was one of the most awesome structures created by the ancients. The base of the four-tiered Pharos was thought to have contained some 300 rooms, as well as a hydraulic system for lifting fuel to the top of the tower. In the centuries that followed, the Pharos was damaged and rebuilt several times, until it was finally destroyed in the great earthquake of 1307. It lay in ruins for two centuries until the Mamluk Sultan Qayt Bay had the current fortress constructed in

1479. Recently, a French team found what are thought to be parts of the Pharos in shallow waters just offshore, rekindling local interest in the ancient monument—there is even talk of an underwater museum, although that is unlikely to materialize anytime soon. ⊠ *Corniche (far western end), El Anfushi* ☏ *03/480–9144* ⊟ *£E25* ⊙ *Daily 9–5:30.*

**Kom al-Dikka** *(Roman Theater).* The focal point of this excavated section of the ancient city is a well-preserved amphitheater—the only one of its kind in Egypt—originally constructed in the 4th century AD, then rebuilt in the 6th century, following an earthquake. The other half of the site is the ancient baths and living quarters, although much of this area is, in fact, best seen through the fence from the side near Pastroudis Café, where the cisterns and walls are clearly visible. One noteworthy site in the residential section is a Roman house known as the **Villa of the Birds**, so named for its colorful floor mosaics depicting birds in several forms. ⊠ *Off Maydan El Shohada, opposite Misr train station, Kom al-Dikka* ☏ *03/490–2904* ⊟ *£E20, £E15 for Villa of the Birds* ⊙ *Daily 9–4:30.*

**Pompey's Pillar** *(Serapium Oracle).* Despite being Alexandria's most famous tourist sight, Pompey's Pillar is a disappointment. After all, it's just a granite pillar—albeit at 88 feet, a tall one—placed on a hill surrounded by ruins. Known in Arabic as *al-'Amud al-Sawiri* (Column of the Horseman), the pillar was misnamed after Pompeius (106–48 BC) by the Crusaders. In fact, it dates to the 3rd century AD, when it was erected in honor of the emperor Diocletian on the site of a Ptolemaic temple to Serapis. The late-model sphinxes lying around on pedestals add a little character. The most interesting element, ironically, is that from the hill you can get a glimpse inside the walled cemetery next door, as well as a view of a long and busy market street. ⊠ *Corner of Amoud El Sawary and El Shenity Abou Mandour, Karmouz* ☏ *03/482–5800* ⊟ *£E20* ⊙ *Daily 9–4.*

## SHOPPING

Egyptians are shrewd businessmen and retailers, and Alexandria has long been a trading city. You'll find an amazing array of crafts, but quality varies from first-class to dreadful, so do check items carefully.

Egyptians specialize in worked brass and copper articles, wood inlay on jewelry boxes and chess sets, and leather. The hookah or hubble-bubble pipe is also an interesting remembrance of the country. Egyptian cotton is a byword for quality, and the shops of Alexandria are the place to buy items like bedding and towels. The long flowing *jellabas* worn by the men are cool and comfortable, and there's a never-ending supply of cut-price T-shirts.

If you want to purchase genuine antiques and antiquities, you'll need to have a certificate of approval from the Egyptian authorities to export your purchase, but copies are on sale everywhere. These items needn't be expensive: you can buy a lucky alabaster scarab beetle for a few Egyptian pounds (it's almost a compulsory souvenir of your trip to Egypt).

Whatever you buy, you'll need to haggle. In Egypt very few items have a set price. Some visitors find this stressful, but try to remember that bartering isn't meant to be a argument; it's a discussion to reach a mutually suitable price. Start at around 40% of the first asking price and rise little by little, but walk away if the offer price seems too high. Once you've agreed on a price, it's very bad form to walk away from a transaction.

For cottons, visit the shops on the streets radiating from Sa'd Zaghlul Square. The new cruise terminal promises upmarket shopping opportunities just a short distance from the ship.

**Attarine Market.** This area acquired its reputation in the 1960s as the place where the high-quality antiques sold by fleeing foreigners resurfaced. Those days are long gone. There are now only a few true antiques stores left in the area, but it's fascinating nonetheless to see the tiny workshops where the reproduction French-style furniture so popular in Egypt originates. The market actually consists of a series of alleyways, the sum of which feels less established—and far less touristy—than Cairo's Khan al-Khalili. ✛ *To find the market, walk one block west of Attarine Mosque and cross Shar'a al-Horreya to alley between café and parts store, El Attarine.*

## WHERE TO EAT

**$$** ✕ **Grand Trianon.** This is Alexandria's most gorgeous restaurant, with
CONTINENTAL  high ceilings, elaborate carved wooden chandeliers, and swirling art nouveau murals decorating the walls. People have always said that someday the kitchen will be taken over by a chef equal to the decor, but for now the food remains enjoyable but unspectacular. If you stick close to the Egyptian or French basics, you'll play to their strengths. As appetizers the *sambousik* (phyllo pastries stuffed with cheese or meat) and French onion soup are quite good, and the entrecôte of beef makes an excellent main course. For dessert, you can linger at your table or relocate to the adjoining café. ⊠ *Maydan Sa'd Zaghlul, Raml Station* ☎ *03/482–0986* ▤ *AE, MC, V.*

# ASHDOD, ISRAEL

Busy Ashdod is not only one of Israel's fastest-growing cities, it's also the country's largest port. Perched on the Mediterranean, it processes more than 60% of the goods imported into Israel. Home to many ancient peoples over the centuries, Ashdod today is a modern, planned city. It's also a convenient jumping-off point for exploring several of Israel's most interesting cities, including Jerusalem and Bethlehem.

### ESSENTIALS
CURRENCY  The shekel (NIS 3.77 to US$1). U.S. currency is accepted for high-value items in some shops, but not in restaurants or markets. ATMs are common.

HOURS  Shops are generally open Sunday through Thursday from 9 to 7, though some close in the afternoons. Museums vary in hours, being open Monday through Thursday from around 10 to 6, but most have shorter

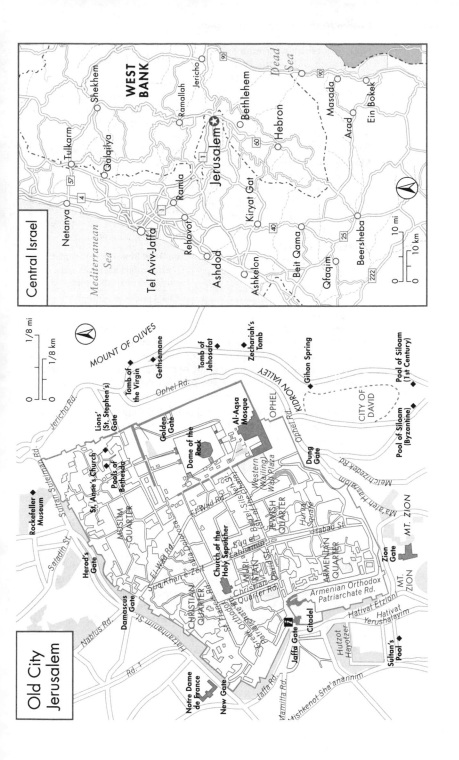

## Old City Jerusalem

0    1/8 mi
0    1/8 km

MOUNT OF OLIVES

Tomb of the Virgin ◆
Gethsemane ◆
Tomb of Jehosafat ◆
Zechariah's Tomb ◆

Jericho Rd.
Ophel Rd.

Rockefeller Museum ◆

Sultan Suleiman Rd.
Saladin St.

Herod's Gate

Damascus Gate

Nablus Rd.
Rd. 1
Hatzanhanim St.

Lions' (St. Stephen's) Gate

St. Anne's Church ◆
Pools of Bethesda ◆

MUSLIM QUARTER

Golden Gate

Dome of the Rock

Al-Aqsa Mosque

OPHEL

Gihon Spring ◆

KIDRON VALLEY

Ophel Rd.

CITY OF DAVID

Pool of Siloam (1st Century) ◆
Pool of Siloam (Byzantine) ◆

El-Wad Rd.
Suq Khan e-Zeit St.
HaGai St.
Tariq Bab es-Silsileh

Western (Wailing) Wall Plaza

Dung Gate

Melchizedek Rd.

Ma'arei HaShalom

MT. ZION

Church of the Holy Sepulcher ◆

CHRISTIAN QUARTER

St. Franciscan
Greek Orthodox Patriarchate Rd.
Christian Quarter Rd.
Souq el-Dabbagha
Muristan Rd.
David St.

JEWISH QUARTER

Hurva Square

Habad St.

ARMENIAN QUARTER

Armenian Orthodox Patriarchate Rd.

Zion Gate

MT. ZION

Hativat Etzion
Hativat Yerushalayim

Citadel ◆

Jaffa Gate

New Gate

Notre Dame de France ◆

Mamilla Rd.
Jaffa Rd.
Mishkenot Sha'anannim

Hutzot Hayotzer

Sultan's Pool ◆

ℹ️

## Central Israel

Mediterranean Sea

Netanya
Tel Aviv-Jaffa
Rehovot
Ashdod
Ashkelon

Tulkarm
Qalqiliya
Ramla
Kiryat Gat
Beit Qama
Qfaqim

Shekhem
Ramallah
Jericho

**WEST BANK**

⭐ Jerusalem

Bethlehem
Hebron
Masada
Arad
Ein Bokek
Beersheba

Dead Sea

57
4
1
6
40
25
222
90
1

0    10 mi
0    10 km

INTERNET hours from Friday through Sunday (often open only from 10 to 2 or 3). Some museums close on Fridays. **Nat Café** (✉ *232 Jaffa Rd., Downtown* ☎ *02/537–9192* ⊕ *www. cafenet.co.il*) sits in the new Central Bus Station on one of the main thoroughfares in the city.

TELEPHONES Most multiband mobile phones will work in Israel, and GSM and 3G systems are well established in the urban areas. Major providers are Cellcom Israel, Parner Communication (Orange), and Pelephone.

## COMING ASHORE

Ashdod, 43 mi west of Jerusalem, is Israel's largest port, and is therefore always busy with commercial traffic. The modern passenger terminal has a café, currency exchange desk,

## ASHDOD BEST BETS

**Dome of the Rock, Jeruslaem.** Holy to both Jews and Muslims, it is here that the lost Jewish Temple constructed by Solomon stood and also the place from where Mohammed was carried up to heaven to receive the wisdom of God.

**Church of the Holy Sepulchre, Jerusalem.** The holiest Christian site in Jerusalem is the supposed site of the crucifixion.

**The Dead Sea.** The lowest place on earth is famous for its salty waters and mud with (supposedly) healing properties.

and duty-free shops. Taxi drivers who wait at the terminal building have been security-cleared to work there; reports suggest that they charge a premium above other taxis. Other taxi drivers may not be allowed access into the port if they have not been approved, so for a cheaper alternative you can try outside the port entrance. Security is tight, so always carry ID and boarding passes.

Route 448 is a direct bus service from Ashdod Central Station to Jerusalem. Buses depart every 30 minutes at peak times, but are less frequent in the middle of the day. The journey takes around 90 minutes, and one-way fare is NIS19.70. To get to the central station in Ashdod, you'll need to take a taxi from the port if your ship doesn't provide a shuttle bus into town.

Currently it is possible to travel by bus between Jerusalem and Bethlehem, but your journey may be interrupted by security checks, which can be lengthy and may cause havoc with your scheduling. It's probably better to visit Bethlehem on a guided tour if you have limited time.

There are no car-rental offices at the cruise terminal, so you'll be charged a premium for delivery—or have to take a taxi ride to the rental office. Prices start around $70 for a compact vehicle, but mileage is usually charged on top of that. If you want to combine Jerusalem and Bethlehem with the Dead Sea (doable, albeit as a rather long day of touring), it may be worth engaging a tour company that knows the routes and locations, because this will save you time.

As the security situation in Israel is subject to change, always check whether independent travel is advised before you decide not to book your excursions through your ship, particularly if you wish to visit Bethlehem.

# Visiting Bethlehem

Although Bethlehem (approximately 70 km [43 mi] from Ashdod) is within the boundaries of the Palestinian Authority, tourists with a foreign passport will have no difficulty visiting; allow 90 minutes for travel. Although security may seem daunting at the heavily fortified border post, you simply show the cover of your passport to be whisked through. Israeli guides are not allowed to take you to the sights, but Israeli tour companies can help arrange for Palestinian guides to meet you at the border. If you're a more independent traveler, you can take one of the Palestinian taxis at the border. If taking a taxi, *sherut* (shared taxi), or bus from East Jerusalem, you must take a local bus or taxi from the Bethlehem side of the terminal to Manger Square. Driving is not recommended. Taxis will offer day-tour services, and this could be a sensible way to link the sites you want to see. Prices run around NIS 200 per hour, but may be inflated by taxi drivers with approval to wait at the cruise pier; you'll have to arrange to have your Israeli taxi driver wait while you visit the sights in Bethlehem and then return you to the pier; be sure to negotiate the price for this waiting time in advance.

**Tour Information Eshcolot Tours** (✉ *36 Keren Hayesod St., Talbieh, Jerusalem* ☎ *02/563-5555*).

## EXPLORING ISRAEL FROM ASHDOD

### BETHLEHEM

Today the great majority of Bethlehem's residents, as elsewhere in the West Bank, are Muslim. But for Christians the world over, the city is synonymous with the birth of Jesus, and the many shrines that celebrate that event. As well, Bethlehem is the site of the Tomb of Rachel, the only one of the biblical patriarchs and matriarchs not buried in Hebron.

★ **Church of the Nativity.** The stone exterior of this church is crowned by the crosses of the three denominations sharing it: the Greek Orthodox, the Latins (Roman Catholic, represented by the Franciscan order), and the Armenian Orthodox. From the right transept at the front of the church, descend to the **Grotto of the Nativity.** Immediately on the right is a small altar, and on the floor below it is the focal point of the entire site: a 14-point **silver star** with the Latin inscription HIC DE VIRGINE MARIA JESUS CHRISTUS NATUS EST (Here of the Virgin Mary, Jesus Christ was born). The little alcove a few steps down on the left at the entrance to the grotto is said to be the manger where the infant Jesus was laid. ✉ *Manger Sq.* ☎ *02/274-1020* 🎟 *Free* ☉ *Church: Apr.–Sept., daily 6:30 AM–7:30 PM; Oct.–Mar., daily 5:30–5:30. Grotto: Apr.–Sept., Mon.–Sat. 9–7:30, Sun. noon–7:30; Oct.–Mar., Mon.–Sat. 9–5:30, Sun. noon–5:30.*

**Church of St. Catherine.** This is Bethlehem's Roman Catholic parish church. From this church the midnight Catholic Christmas mass is broadcast around the world. A small wooden door (kept locked) connects the complex with the Grotto of the Nativity. ⊠ *Manger Sq.* ☎ *02/274–2425* ⊙ *Apr.–Sept., daily 6–noon and 2–7; Oct.–Mar., daily 5:30–5:30.*

**Manger Square.** Bethlehem's central plaza and the site of the Church of the Nativity, Manger Square is built over the grotto thought to be the birthplace of Jesus. The square has a tourist-information office, a few restaurants, and some shops.

**Rachel's Tomb.** The Bible relates that the matriarch Rachel, second and favorite wife of Jacob, died in childbirth on the outskirts of Bethlehem, "and Jacob set up a pillar upon her grave" (Genesis 35:19–20). There is no vestige of Jacob's original pillar, but the velvet-draped cenotaph inside the building has been hallowed by observant Jews for centuries as the site of Rachel's tomb. ⊠ *Rte. 60* ▭ *Free* ⊙ *Sun.–Thurs. 8–5, Fri. 8–1.*

**Shepherds' Fields.** The fields of the adjacent town of Bet Sahur are traditionally identified with the biblical story of Ruth the Moabite, daughter-in-law of Naomi, who "gleaned in the field" of Boaz, Naomi's kinsman. Boaz eventually "took Ruth and she became his wife" (Ruth 4:13). The same fields are identified by Christian tradition as those where shepherds "keeping watch over their flock by night" received word of the birth of Jesus in Bethlehem (Luke 2).

## DEAD SEA

The sudden and startling sight, in this bare landscape, of gleaming, ultramodern hotels surrounded by waving palm trees signals your arrival at the spa-resort area of Ein Bokek, near the southern tip of the Dead Sea. According to the Bible, it was along these shores that the Lord rained fire and brimstone on the people of Sodom and Gomorrah (Genesis 19:24) and turned Lot's wife into a pillar of salt (Genesis 26). Here, at the lowest point on Earth—the bottom of the world: 1,292 feet below sea level—the hot, sulfur-pungent air hangs heavy, and a haze often shimmers over the water. You can float, but you cannot sink, in the warm, salty water.

### MASADA

**Fodor's Choice** Isolated Masada was one of the opulent desert escape palaces of Herod
★ the Great and the last stand of the less than 1,000 Jewish rebels in the Great Revolt against Rome in AD 73. In recognition of its historical significance, it was the first site in Israel to be added to the UNESCO World Heritage List in 2001. Most visitors take the speedy **cable car** up Masada to the 20-acre site. Starting at 8 AM, it runs every half hour, with intermediate runs depending on demand. The last car up leaves an hour before closing. Among the more important buildings atop the rock are the **Northern Palace,** a three-tier structure that seems to hang off the highest and most northerly point of the mountain; the **bathhouse,** a state-of-the-art facility in Herod's time; two **mikvahs** (Jewish ritual baths) from the time of the revolt; and the **synagogue,** one of only four that have been uncovered from the Second Temple period. It was likely here, in the community's spiritual center, that the leaders of the revolt against Rome made their fateful decision. Adjoining the lower cable-car station is the **Masada Museum,** which opened to the

public in 2007. Hundreds of artifacts from the site that were previously stored in a basement are now are display. Especially moving is a set of 12 pottery shards, each bearing a single name. Archaeologists believe these might have been lots drawn to decide the order in which the last remaining rebels would die. All the artifacts are placed within scenes of daily life, so that visitors will get a sense of how they were used. ⊠ *Off Rte. 3199* ☎ *08/658–4207* ⊕ *www.parks.org.il* ⊠ *Site NIS 23; site and cable car NIS 61* ◷ *Apr.–Sept., Sat.–Thurs. 8–5, Fri. and Jewish holiday eves 8–3; Oct.–Mar., Sat.–Thurs. 8–4, Fri. and Jewish holiday eves 8–2.*

## MOUNT OF OLIVES AND EAST JERUSALEM

The sights in this area are for the most part distinctly Christian. A few are a little off the beaten path, and the best way to explore them is on foot.
**Garden of Gethsemane.** After the Last Supper, the New Testament relates, Jesus and his disciples came to a "place" called Gethsemane. There he agonized and prayed, and there, in the end, he was betrayed and arrested. In the **Church of All Nations,** built in the garden in 1924, is the so-called Rock of the Agony, where Jesus is said to have endured his Passion. ⊠ *Jericho Rd., Kidron Valley* ☎ *02/626–6444* ⊠ *Free* ◷ *Apr.– Sept., daily 8–noon and 2–6; Oct.–Mar., daily 8–noon and 2–5.*

★ **Mount of Olives Observation Point.** The Mount of Olives has been bathed in sanctity for millennia. The vast **Jewish cemetery** is reputedly the oldest still in use anywhere in the world. For more than 2,000 years, Jews have been buried here to await the coming of the Messiah and the resurrection to follow. In the Old City wall facing you is the Gate of Mercy, or Golden Gate. Jewish tradition holds that the Messiah will enter Jerusalem this way; Christian tradition says he already did, on Palm Sunday. ⊠ *E-Sheikh St., opposite Seven Arches Hotel, Mt. of Olives.*

## OLD CITY JERUSALEM

Drink in the very essence of Jerusalem as you explore the city's primary religious sites in the Muslim and Christian quarters, and at the Western Wall, and touch the different cultures that share it.
**Church of the Holy Sepulcher.** Vast numbers of Christians believe this to be the place where Jesus was crucified by the Romans, was buried, and rose from the dead. On the floor just inside the entrance of the church is the rectangular pink **Stone of Unction,** where, it is said, the body of Jesus was cleansed and prepared for burial. Steep steps take you up to **Golgotha,** or Calvary, meaning "the place of the skull," as the site is described in the New Testament. Under the altar in the central chapel is a silver disc with a hole, purportedly the place where the cross actually stood. The tomb itself is in the rotunda to the left of the main entrance of the church. ⊠ *Between Suq Khan e-Zeit and Christian Quarter Rd., Christian Quarter* ☎ *02/627–3314* ⊠ *Free* ◷ *Apr.–Sept., daily 5 AM–9 PM; Oct.–Mar., daily 4 AM–8 PM.*

**Dome of the Rock and Temple Mount.** The magnificent golden **Dome of the Rock** dominates the vast 35-acre Temple Mount, the area known to Muslims as Haram esh-Sharif (the Noble Sanctuary). At its southern end is the black-domed **Al-Aqsa Mosque,** the third most holy site for Muslims. Built in the late 1st century BC by Herod, the Temple Mount was one of the greatest religious enclosures of the ancient world. At the center of the plaza stood Herod's splendidly rebuilt Second Temple, the one Jesus knew. The Romans reduced it to smoldering ruins in the summer of AD 70. Jewish tradition identifies the great **rock** at the summit of the hill—now under the gold dome—as the foundation stone of the world, and the place where Abraham bound and almost sacrificed his son Isaac (Genesis 22). Today the Haram is a Muslim preserve. According to Muslim beliefs, the great rock is the very spot from which Muhammad ascended to receive the teachings of Islam from God. Security check lines to enter the area are often long; it's best to come early. Note: The Muslim attendants prohibit Bibles in the area. ✉ *Access between Western Wall and Dung Gate, Temple Mount* ☎ *02/628–3292 or 02/628–3313* ☉ *Apr.–Sept., Sun.–Thurs. 7:30 AM–11 AM and 1:30 PM–2:30 PM; Oct.–Mar., Sun.–Thurs. 8 AM–10 AM and 12:30 PM–2 PM, subject to change. Last entry 1 hr before closing.*

**Jerusalem Archaeological Park.** This site includes finds from the Herodian period, the late 1st century BC. Of note is the white pavement of an impressive main street and commercial area from the Second Temple period and the protrusion known as **Robinson's Arch,** a remnant of a monumental bridge to the Temple Mount. ✉ *Dung Gate, Western Wall* ☎ *02/627–7550* ⊕ *www.archpark.org.il* 🏷 *NIS 30* ☉ *Sun.–Thurs. 8–5, Fri. and Jewish holiday eves 8–2.*

**Via Dolorosa.** The Way of Suffering—or Way of the Cross, as it's more commonly called in English—is venerated as the route Jesus walked, carrying his cross, from the place of his trial and condemnation by Pontius Pilate to the site of his crucifixion and burial. Fourteen stations on the Via Dolorosa mark Jesus's route. The present tradition is essentially medieval or later, but it draws on older beliefs. ✉ *Muslim and Christian quarters.*

**Western Wall.** The 2,000-year-old Western Wall derives its status from its connection with the ancient Temple, the House of God. It was not itself part of the Temple edifice, but of the massive retaining wall King Herod built to create the vast plaza now known as the Temple Mount. After the destruction of Jerusalem by the Romans in AD 70, and especially after the dedication of a pagan town in its place 65 years later, the city became off-limits to Jews for generations. The memory of the precise location of the Temple—in the vicinity of today's Dome of the Rock—was lost. With time, the closest remnant of the period took on the aura of the temple itself, making the Western Wall a kind of holy place by proxy. Modest dress is required (men must cover their heads in the prayer area), there is segregation of men and women in prayer, and smoking and photography on the Sabbath and religious holidays are prohibited. ✉ *Near Dung Gate, Western Wall* ⊕ *english.thekotel. org* ☉ *Daily 24 hrs.*

**Western Wall Tunnel.** The long tunnel beyond the men's side (north of the plaza) was dug in recent years to expose a strip of the Western Wall along its entire length. Visits are by guided tour only. These must be booked in advance. This can be done on the Web site. ✉ *Western Wall* ☎ *02/627–1333* ⊕ *english.thekotel.org* 🏷 *NIS 25* ☉ *Sun.–Thurs. 7 AM– late evening (changing schedules), Fri. and Jewish holiday eves 7–noon. Call ahead for exact times.*

## WEST JERUSALEM

Visitors tend to focus, naturally enough, on the historic and religious sights on the eastern side of town, especially in the Old City; but West Jerusalem houses the nation's institutions, is the repository for its collective memory, and—together with the downtown—gives more insight into contemporary life in Israel's largest city. The world-class Israel Museum and Yad Vashem are located here.

Ⓒ **Israel Museum.** An eclectic treasure trove, the museum is a world-class
**Fodor's Choice** don't-miss, and reopened in July 2010 after an $80 million "renewal."
★ The galleries concentrate on three main specialties of art, archaeology, and Judaica.

The **Dead Sea Scrolls** are certainly the Israel Museum's most famous—and most important—collection. The first of the 2,000-year-old scrolls were discovered by a Bedouin boy in 1947 in a Judean Desert cave, overlooking the Dead Sea. The adventures of these priceless artifacts before they found a permanent home here are the stuff of which Indiana Jones movies are made. ⊠ *Ruppin Rd., Givat Ram* ☎ *02/670–8811* ⊕ *www.imj.org.il* ✉ *NIS 48 (includes audioguide)* ☉ *Sun., Mon., Wed., Thurs., Sat., and Jewish holidays 10–5, Tues. 4–9, Fri. and Jewish holiday eves 10–2.*

★ **Yad Vashem.** The experience of the Holocaust—the annihilation of 6 million Jews by the Nazis during World War II—is so deeply seared into the Jewish national psyche that understanding it goes a long way toward understanding Israelis themselves. The institution of Yad Vashem preserves a record of those times. The name "Yad Vashem"—"a memorial and a name (a memory)"—comes from the biblical book of Isaiah (56:5).

The riveting **Holocaust History Museum**—a 200-yard-long triangular concrete prism—is the centerpiece of the site. Powerful visual and audiovisual techniques in a series of galleries document Jewish life in Europe. ⊠ *Hazikaron St., near Herzl Blvd., Mt. Herzl* ☎ *02/644–3565* ⊕ *www.yadvashem.org* ✉ *Free* ☉ *Sun.–Wed. 9–5, Thurs. 9–8 (late closing for History Museum, Art Pavilion, and Synagogue only), Fri. and Jewish holiday eves 9–2. Last entrance 1 hr before closing.*

# WHERE TO EAT

¢ ✗ **Abu Shukri.** In the heart of the Old City, right at Station V on the Via
MIDDLE EASTERN Dolorosa, this place has an extraordinary and well-deserved reputation for the best hummus in town. Don't expect decor. This is a neighborhood eatery, and a look at the clientele—Palestinian Arabs and Jewish Israeli insiders—confirms that you have gone local. Enjoy the excellent fresh falafel balls, *labaneh* (a dairy item somewhere between tart yogurt and cream cheese), baba ghanoush, tahini, and fresh vegetable salad; no meat is served. Eat family-style, and don't over-order: you can get additional portions on the spot. ⊠ *63 El-Wad (Hagai) St., Muslim Quarter* ☎ *02/627–1538* ⚖ *Reservations not accepted* ☰ *No credit cards* ☉ *No dinner.*

$$ ✗ **Nafoura.** Just inside the Jaffa Gate (up the first street on the left),
MIDDLE EASTERN Nafoura offers an attractive tranquil courtyard for alfresco lunchtime
Ⓒ dining, where your table might lean against the Old City's 16th-century

wall. The pleasant if unremarkable interior is a comfortable refuge in inclement weather. Start with the traditional meze, an array of salads: the smaller version is enough for two people. Insist on the excellent local dishes only (hummus, eggplant dip, tahini, carrots, and so on) and skip the mushrooms and corn. Ask particularly for the *kibbeh,* delicacies of cracked wheat and ground beef, or the *lahmajun,* the meat-topped "Armenian pizza." From the typical selection of entrées, try the lamb cutlets or the sea bream (called "denise"). Smaller portions are available for many items. The NIS 50 buffet (chicken, kebab, side dishes, and fruit) is an excellent value. ⊠ *18 Latin Patriarch Rd., Christian Quarter* ☎ *02/626–0034* ⊟ *AE, DC, MC, V* ⊙ *No dinner.*

# CORFU, GREECE

Kerkyra (Corfu) is the greenest and, quite possibly, the prettiest of all Greek islands—emerald mountains, ocher-and-pink buildings, shimmering silver olive leaves. The turquoise waters lap rocky coves and bougainvillea, scarlet roses, and wisteria spread over cottages. This northernmost of the major Ionian islands has, through the centuries, inspired artists, conquerors, royalty, and, of course, tourists. Indeed, when you look at Corfu in total, it's hard to believe that any island so small could generate a history so large. Classical remains vie with architecture from the centuries of Venetian, French, and British rule, leaving Corfu with a pleasant combination of contrasting design elements. The town of Corfu remains one of the loveliest in all of Greece, every nook and cranny tells a story, every street meanders to a myth, even during the busiest summer day. Corfu today is a vivid tapestry of cultures; a sophisticated weave, where charm, history, and natural beauty blend.

## ESSENTIALS

CURRENCY  The euro (€1 to US$1.36 at this writing). ATMs are common.

HOURS  Store hours are typically 9 to 9 on weekdays and 9 to 6 on Saturday. Museums are generally from open 9 to 5, but many are closed on Monday. Some shops, restaurants, and museums close between October and April.

INTERNET  Have a drink from the bar at **Internet Cafe Netikos** (⊠ *Kalokeretou 12–14* ☎ *26610/47479*) while you do business online from 10 AM to midnight every day except Sunday, when the place opens at 6 PM.

TELEPHONES  Tri-band GSM phones work in Greece. You can buy prepaid phone cards at telecom shops, news-vendors, and tobacconists in all towns and cities. Phone cards can be used for local or international calls. Vodafone is the leading mobile telecom company. OTE is the national domestic provider. Calls can be made at OTE offices and paid for after completion.

## COMING ASHORE

Boats dock at Corfu's purpose-built cruise port, which has a welcome center with an information desk, car-rental desks, and a taxi stand. A 10-minute ride into the Old Town costs around €15. Alternatively, you can walk along the seafront in about 30 minutes.

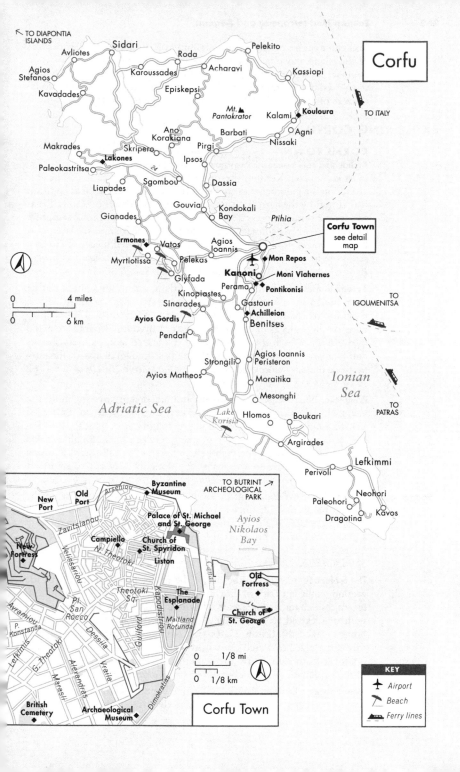

You can explore the town on foot, but you need a car to get to some of the island's loveliest places. Prices can range from €35 a day for a compact vehicle (where you pay an additional fee for each km driving) to €80 a day for a four-wheel-drive jeep with extras. Expect additional charges of around €15 for insurance, delivery, and so forth.

# EXPLORING CORFU

## CORFU TOWN

**Archaeological Museum.** Examine finds from ongoing island excavations; most come from Kanoni, the site of Corfu's ancient capital. The star attraction is a giant relief of snake-coiffed Medusa, depicted as her head was cut off by the hero Perseus—at which moment her two sons, Pegasus and Chrysaor, emerged from her body. The 56-foot-long sculpture once adorned the pediment of the 6th-century BC Temple of Artemis at Kanoni, and is one of the largest and best-preserved pieces of Archaic sculpture in Greece. ⊠ *Vraila 1, off Leoforos Dimokratias, past Corfu Palace hotel* ☎ *26610/30680* ⌦ *€3* ⊙ *Tues.–Sun. 8:30–3.*

**Byzantine Museum.** Panagia Antivouniotissa, an ornate church dating from the 16th century, houses an outstanding collection of Byzantine religious art. More than 85 icons from the 13th to the 17th century hang on the walls as the ethereal sounds of Byzantine chants are piped in overhead. Watch for works by the celebrated icon painters Tzanes and Damaskinos; they are perhaps the best-known artists of the Cretan style of icon painting. ⊠ *Arseniou Mourayio* ☎ *26610/38313* ⌦ *€2* ⊙ *Tues.–Sun. 8:30–3.*

**Campiello.** Narrow, winding streets and steep stairways make up the Campiello, the large, traffic-free medieval area of the town. Balconied Venetian buildings are mixed among multistory, neoclassical 19th-century structures, with laundry festooned between them. Small cobbled squares centered with wells, high-belfry churches, and alleyways that lead nowhere and back, with artisans' shops along the way, add to an utterly lovely urban space. ⊠ *West of Esplanade, northeast of New Fortress.*

**Fodor's**Choice  **Church of St. Spyridon.** Built in 1596, this church is the tallest on the
★  island, thanks to its distinctive red-domed bell tower, and is filled with silver treasures. The patron saint's mummified body can be seen through a glass panel, while his internal remains are contained in a silver reliquary. His miracles are said to have saved the island four times. ⊠ *Agiou Spyridon* ☎ *No phone.*

**The Esplanade.** Central to the life of the town, this huge, open parade ground on the land side of the canal is, many say, the most beautiful *spianada* (esplanade) in Greece. It is bordered on the west by a street lined with arcades and seven- and eight-story Venetian and English Georgian houses, called the **Liston.** Cafés spill out onto the passing scene, and this is the place to watch the world go by. Sunday cricket matches, a holdover from British rule, are sometimes played on the northern half of the Esplanade. ⊠ *Between Old Fortress and old town.*

**New Fortress.** Built in 1577–78 by the Venetians, the New Fortress was constructed to strengthen town defenses only three decades after the "old" fortress was built. The French and the British subsequently expanded the complex to protect Corfu Town from a possible Turkish invasion. You can wander through the maze of tunnels, moats, and fortifications. The moat (dry now) is the site of the town's marketplace. A classic British citadel stands at its heart. ⊠ *Solomou on promontory overlooking New Port* ☎ *26610/27370* ⊞ *€2* ⊗ *June–Oct., daily 9* AM*–9:30* PM.

★ **Old Fortress.** Corfu's entire population once lived within the walls of the Old Fortress, or Citadel, built by the Venetians in 1546 on the site of a Byzantine castle. Separated from the rest of the town by a moat, the fort is on a promontory mentioned by Thucydides. Its two hills, or *korypha* (known as the "bosom"), gave the island its Western name. Inside the fortress, many Venetian fortifications were destroyed by the British, who replaced them with their own structures. The most notable of these is the quirky **Church of St. George,** built like an ancient Doric temple on the outside and set up like a Greek Orthodox church on the inside. ⊠ *On eastern point of Corfu town peninsula* ☎ *26610/48310* ⊞ *€4* ⊗ *Daily 8–7.*

Fodor'sChoice **Palace of St. Michael & St. George.** Admire Ming pottery in an ornate
★ colonial palace as Homer's Ionian sea shimmers outside the windows. This elegant, colonnaded 19th-century Regency structure houses the **Museum of Asiatic Art,** a notable collection of Asian porcelains and Sino-Japanese art. ⊠ *Palaia Anaktora, at north end of Esplanade* ☎ *26610/81930* ⊞ *€3* ⊗ *Tues.–Sun. 8:30–3.*

## KANONI
*5 km (3 mi) southwest of Corfu Town.*

At Kanoni, 5 km (3 mi) south of Corfu town, the site of the ancient capital, you may behold Corfu's most famous view, which looks out over two beautiful islets.

♻ **Mon Repos.** The royal palace here was built in 1831. After Greece won independence, it was used as a summer palace for the royal family of Greece. Prince Philip, the duke of Edinburgh, was born here. After touring the palace, wander around the extensive grounds, which include ruins of temples from the 7th and 6th centuries BC. Opposite Mon Repos are ruins of Ayia Kerkyra, the 5th-century church of the Old City. ✤ *1 km (½ mi) south of Old Fortress, following oceanfront walk* ☎ *26610/41369* ⊞ *€3, gardens free* ⊗ *Tues.–Sun. 8:30–7.*

**Moni Viahernes.** The little island is reached by causeway, and has a tiny, pretty convent.

---

**CORFU BEST BETS**

**Relax over a coffee at the Liston.** This is a wonderful place to immerse yourself in modern Greek life.

**Take pictures of Pontikonisi.** Mouse Island, as this tiny islet is also known, is one of the iconic Greek landscape views. Shimmering waters and verdant foliage contrast dramatically with the modest whitewashed chapel.

**Explore Paleokastritsa.** A breathtaking landscape of tiny rocky coves, azure waters, and fragrant woodland offers exceptional vistas surrounded by the sound of buzzing cicadas.

**3**

**Pontikonisi.** Also known as Mouse Island, Pontikonisi has tall cypresses guarding a 13th-century chapel. Legend has it that the island is really Odysseus's ship, which Poseidon turned to stone here: the reason why Homer's much-traveled hero was shipwrecked on Phaeacia (Corfu) in the *Odyssey*. June to August a little motorboat runs out to Pontikonisi every 20 minutes.

## GASTOURI
*19 km (12 mi) southwest of Corfu Town.*

**Achilleion.** The village of Gastouri, still lovely despite the summer onrush of day-trippers, is the site of the Achilleion. Although in remarkably eclectic taste, the palace is redeemed by lovely gardens stretching to the sea. Built in the late 19th century by the Italian architect Rafael Carita for Empress Elizabeth of Austria, the palace was named by the empress after her favorite hero, Achilles. After Elizabeth was assassinated, Kaiser Wilhelm II bought it and lived here until the outbreak of World War I. After the armistice, the Greek government received it as a spoil of war.

The interior contains a pseudo-Byzantine chapel, a pseudo-Pompeian room, and a pseudo-Renaissance dining hall, culminating in a vulgar fresco called *Achilles in His Chariot*. One of the more interesting furnishings is Kaiser Wilhelm II's saddle seat, used at his desk. In 1962 the palace was restored, leased as a gambling casino, and later was the set for the casino scene in the James Bond film *For Your Eyes Only*. The casino has since moved to the Corfu Holiday Palace. ⊠ *Main street* ☎ *26610/56245* ⌸ *€6* ☉ *Apr.–Oct., daily 8–7; Nov.–Mar., daily 8:30–3:30.*

## PALEOKASTRITSA
*25 km (16 mi) northwest of Corfu Town.*

This spectacular territory of grottoes, cliffs, and turquoise waters is breathtaking.

**Lakones.** The village is on the steep mountain behind the Paleokastritsa Monastery. Most of the current town was constructed in modern times, but the ruins of the 13th-century **Angelokastro** also loom over the landscape. ⊠ *5 km (3 mi) northeast of Paleokastritsa.*

**Paleokastritsa Monastery.** This 17th-century structure is built on the site of an earlier monastery, among terraced gardens overlooking the Adriatic Sea. Its treasure is a 12th-century icon of the Virgin Mary, and there's a small museum with some other early icons. ⊠ *On northern headland* ☎ *No phone* ⌸ *Donations accepted* ☉ *Daily 7–1 and 3–8.*

# SHOPPING

Corfu Town has myriad tiny shops. For traditional goods, head for the narrow streets of the Campiello where olive-wood, ceramics, lace, jewelry, and wine shops abound. Kumquat liqueur is a specialty of the island.

**Alexis Traditional Products.** This company sells locally made wines and spirits, including kumquat liqueur and marmalade, traditional sweets, local olive oil, olives, and olive-oil soap—as well as honey, herbs, and spices. ⊠ *Solomou 10–12, Spilia* ☎ *26610/21831.*

**Mironis Olive Wood.** This company deals in bowls, sculptures, wooden jewelry, and much more in its two tiny family-run shops in Corfu. ⊠ *Filarmonikis 27* ☎ *26610/40621* ⊠ *Agiou Spyridon 65* ☎ *26610/40364.*

**Nikos Sculpture and Jewellery.** This jeweler makes original gold and silver designs, as well as sculptures in cast bronze; they're expensive but worth it. ⊠ *Paleologou 50* ☎ *26610/31107* ⊠ *N. Theotoki 54* ☎ *26610/32009* ⊕ *www.nikosjewellery.gr.*

**Rolandos.** This talented artist produces paintings and handmade pottery in his studio. ⊠ *N. Theotoki 99* ☎ *26610/45004*

## ACTIVITIES

Snorkeling and diving are best in the many rocky inlets and grottos on the northwest coast, and Paleokastritsa and Ermones have diving schools where you can take lessons and rent equipment. The winds on the west coast are best for windsurfing, although the water on the east coast is calmer. Sailboards are available, and paddleboats and rowboats can be rented at many beaches. Waterskiing, water polo, parasailing, jet skiing, and other water activities are sponsored by resorts throughout the island. Motorboats and sailboats can be rented at the Old Port in Corfu Town; in Paleokastritsa, Kondokali, and Kassiopi; and on the northeast coast. To charter a yacht or sailboat without a crew, you need a proficiency certificate from a certified yacht club.

**Archilleon Diving Center.** This shop offers dive tuition and equipment rental for qualified divers. ⊠ *Akrotiri Beach Hotel, Paleokastritsa* ☎ *26610/95350* ⊕ *www.achilleondivingcenter.gr.*

**Pinnacle Yachts.** This outfitter has yachts for rent and provides cruising flotillas. ⊠ *Gouvia Marina, Gouvia* ⊠ *Box 114, Tzavros* ☎ *26610/90411* ⊕ *www.pinnacleyachts.co.uk.*

## BEACHES

**Glyfada.** The large, golden beaches are the most famous on the island and the sands are inevitably packed with sunbathers. Sunbeds, umbrellas, and water-sports equipment are available for rent and there are several tourist resorts. ⊠ *2 km [1 mi] south of Pelekas.*

**Myrtiotissa.** The isolated beach, between sheer cliffs, is noted for its good snorkeling (and nude sunbathing). This sandy stretch was called by Lawrence Durrell in *Prospero's Cell* "perhaps the loveliest beach in the world," but summer crowds are the norm. ⊠ *3 km [2 mi] north of Pelekas.*

**Pelekas.** The beach here has soft, golden sand and clear water, but is developed and tends to be crowded. Free minibuses regularly transport people to the beach from the village, which is a long and steep walk otherwise.

## WHERE TO EAT

$ ✕ **Gerekos.** One of the island's most famous seafood tavernas, Gerekos SEAFOOD always has fresh fish. Opt for a table on the terrace and try the whitefish *me ladi* (cooked in olive oil, garlic, and pepper). ⊠ *Kondokali Bay,*

*6 km (4 mi) north of Corfu Town* ☎ *26610/91281* ⌁ *Reservations essential* ⊟ *AE, V.*

**$** ✕ **Rex Restaurant.** A friendly Corfiot restaurant in a 19th-century town
GREEK house, Rex has been a favorite for nearly 100 years. Classic local spe-
★ cialties are reliably delicious. Dishes such as rabbit stewed with fresh figs
and chicken with kumquats are successful twists on the regional fare.
Outside tables are perfect for people-watching on the Liston. ⊠ *Kapo-
distriou 66, west of Liston* ☎ *26610/39649* ⊕ *www.restaurantrex.gr*
⊟ *AE, D, MC, V.*

# DUBROVNIK, CROATIA

Commanding a splendid coastal location, Dubrovnik is one of the
world's most beautiful fortified cities. Its massive stone ramparts and
splendid fortress towers curve around a tiny harbor, enclosing grad-
uated ridges of sun-bleached orange-tiled roofs, copper domes, and
elegant bell towers. In the 7th century AD, residents of the Roman city
Epidaurum (now Cavtat) fled the Avars and Slavs of the north and
founded a new settlement on a small rocky island, which they named
Laus, and later Ragusa. On the mainland hillside opposite the island,
the Slav settlement called Dubrovnik grew up. In the 12th century the
narrow channel separating the two settlements was filled in, and Ragusa
and Dubrovnik became one. The city was surrounded by defensive
walls during the 13th century, and these were reinforced with towers
and bastions during the late 15th century. The city became a UNESCO
World Heritage Site in 1979. During the war for independence, it came
under heavy siege, though thanks to careful restoration work few traces
of damage remain. Today Dubrovnik is once again a fashionable, high-
class destination; Eva Longoria Parker, Beyonce, John Malkovich, and
Sir Roger Moore have been recent visitors. New in July 2010 is a cable
car, which takes visitors up to the top of Mount Srdj for fantastic views
down onto the Old Town and out to sea.

## ESSENTIALS

CURRENCY The Croatian kuna (5.3 Kn to US$1 at this writing). ATMs are easy to
find, and it is also possible to exchange currency in banks and also in
most local travel agencies. Credit cards are accepted at many restaurants and shops.

HOURS Offices are open weekdays from 8:30 to 4. Shops often close for lunch
around 1, and may close for as long as three hours; banks also sometimes close for lunch. Post offices are open on Saturday during the main
summer season, from June through September.

INTERNET In summer, small temporary Internet cafés spring up in the seaside resort
towns, so even on the islands you can find somewhere to check e-mail.
However, many are nothing more than a regular café with a PC in the
corner. **Netcafe** (⊠ *Prijeko 21, Stari Grad* ☎ *020/321–025*).

TELEPHONES Most tri- and quad-band GSM phones will work in Croatia. Public
phones use calling cards, which can be purchased at the post office,
newsstands, and hotels. Major mobile phone companies include TMobile and VIPNet.

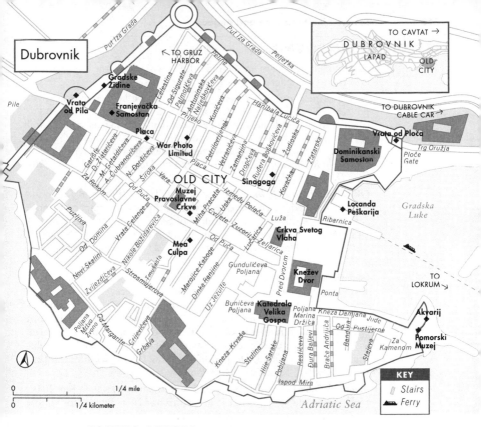

## COMING ASHORE

In Dubrovnik almost all ships dock at Gruž Harbor, which is 4 km (2½ mi) from Stari Grad (Old Town). Some ships will provide a free shuttle. The trip to Dubrovnik's Old Town takes about 10 minutes by taxi or 30 to 40 minutes on foot. You can also take a public bus. There's a taxi stand at the harbor.

A few smaller ships might still tender passengers ashore in the Old Town, where you're just steps from everything that Dubrovnik has to offer.

Since the Old Town is compact and pedestrian-friendly, we recommend that you not rent a car in Dubrovnik. It's easy to reach Cavtat by bus or ferry, and unless you want to explore the countryside away from Dubrovnik, a car will not help you. If you choose to rent, expect to pay about €55 for a manual compact vehicle, though you can rent a semiautomatic Smart car at some outlets for about €50. Note, however, that during high season it can be very difficult to find a company that is willing to rent just for one day.

# EXPLORING DUBROVNIK

All the main sites lie in Stari Grad (Old Town) within the city walls, an area that is compact and car-free.

**Akvarij** *(Aquarium).* This dark, cavernous space houses several small pools and 27 well-lighted tanks containing a variety of fish from rays to small sharks, as well as other underwater denizens such as sponges and sea urchins. Children will find the octopus, in his glass tank, either very amusing or horribly scary. ⊠ *Damjana Jude 2, Stari Grad* ☎ *020/323–978* ⌨ *40 Kn* ☉ *June–Sept., daily 9–9; Apr., May, Oct., and Nov., daily 9–6; Dec.–Mar., daily 9–1.*

**Crkva Svetog Vlaha** *(Church of St. Blaise).* This 18th-century baroque church replaced an earlier one destroyed by fire. Of particular note is the silver statue on the high altar of St. Blaise holding a model of Dubrovnik, which is paraded around town each year on February 3, the Day of St. Blaise. ⊠ *Luza, Stari Grad* ⌨ *Free* ☉ *Daily 8–noon and 4:30–7.*

**Dominikanski Samostan** *(Dominican Monastery).* With a splendid, late-15th-century floral Gothic cloister as its centerpiece, the monastery is best known for its museum, which houses a rich collection of religious paintings by the so-called Dubrovnik School from the 15th and 16th centuries. Look out for works by Bozidarevic, Hamzic, and Dobričevic, as well as gold and silver ecclesiastical artifacts crafted by local goldsmiths. ⊠ *Sv Domina 4, Stari Grad* ☎ *020/321–423* ⌨ *20 Kn* ☉ *May–Oct., daily 9–6; Nov.–Apr., daily 9–5.*

**Dubrovnik Cable Car.** Dubrovnik's cable car began operating in July 2010, replacing an old system from 1969, which had been defunct for almost two decades. Consisting of two carriages carrying 30 persons each, it takes visitors to the top of Mt. Srdj (405 m), which rises behind the medieval walled city, in just three minutes. The upper station has a viewing platform with telescopes and a café, which afford stunning views over the Old Town and out to sea. The entrance station is just outside the Ploče Gate. ⊠ *Frana Supila 35a, Old Town* ☎ *020/414–355* ⊕ *www. dubrovnikcablecar.com* ⌨ *44 Kn one way, 73 Kn return* ☉ *Daily 9–9.*

**Franjevačka Samostan** *(Franciscan Monastery).* The monastery's chief claim to fame is its pharmacy, which was founded in 1318 and is still in existence today; it's said to be the oldest in Europe. There's also a delightful cloistered garden framed by Romanesque arcades supported by double columns, each crowned with a set of grotesque figures. In the Treasury a painting shows what Dubrovnik looked like before the disastrous earthquake of 1667. ⊠ *Placa 2, Stari Grad* ☎ *020/321–410* ⌨ *30 Kn* ☉ *May–Oct., daily 9–6; Nov.–Apr., daily 9–5.*

★ **Gradske Zidine** *(City Walls).* Most of the original construction took place during the 13th century, though the walls were further reinforced with towers and bastions during the following 400 years. On average they are 80 feet high and up to 10 feet thick on the seaward side, 20 feet on the inland side. ⊠ *Placa, Stari Grad* ☎ *020/324–641* ⌨ *70 Kn* ☉ *May–Sept., daily 8–7; Oct.–Apr., daily 9–3.*

**Katedrala Velika Gospa** *(Cathedral of Our Lady).* The present structure was built in baroque style after the original was destroyed in the 1667 earthquake. The interior contains a number of notable paintings, including a large polyptych above the main altar depicting the *Assumption of Our Lady,* attributed to Titian. The Treasury displays 138 gold and silver reliquaries, including the skull of St. Blaise in the form of a bejeweled Byzantine crown and also an arm and a leg of the saint, likewise encased in decorated golden plating. ⊠ *Buniceva Poljana, Stari Grad* ☎ *020/323–459* 🖰 *Cathedral free, Treasury 15 Kn* ⊙ *Mon.–Sat. 9–5, Sun. 11–5.*

**Knežev Dvor** *(Bishop's Palace).* Originally created in the 15th century but reconstructed several times through the following years, this exquisite building with an arcaded loggia and an internal courtyard shows a combination of late-Gothic and early Renaissance styles. On the ground floor there are large rooms where, in the days of the republic, the Great Council and Senate held their meetings. Over the entrance to the meeting halls a plaque reads: OBLITI PRIVATORUM PUBLICA CURATE (Forget private affairs, and get on with public matters). Upstairs, the rector's living quarters now accommodate the Gradski Muzej (City Museum), containing exhibits that give a picture of life in Dubrovnik from early days until the fall of the republic. ⊠ *Pred Dvorom 3, Stari Grad* ☎ *020/321–497* 🖰 *40 Kn* ⊙ *May–Oct., daily 9–6; Nov.–Apr., daily 9–4.*

**Muzej Pravoslavne Crkve** *(Orthodox Church Museum).* Next door to the Orthodox Church, this small museum displays religious icons from the Balkan region and Russia, as well as several portraits of eminent early-20th-century Dubrovnik personalities by local artist Vlaho Bukovac. ⊠ *Od Puca 8, Stari Grad* ☎ *020/323–823* 🖰 *10 Kn* ⊙ *May–Oct., daily 9–2; Nov.–Apr., Mon.–Sat. 9–2.*

**Placa.** This was once the shallow sea channel separating the island of Laus from the mainland. Although it was filled in during the 12th century, it continued to divide the city socially for several centuries, with the nobility living in the area south of Placa and the commoners living on the hillside to the north. Today it forms the venue for the *korzo,* an evening promenade where locals meet to chat, maybe have a drink, and generally size one another up. ⊠ *Stari Grad.*

**Pomorski Muzej** *(Maritime Museum).* Above the Aquarium, on the first floor of St. John's Fortress, this museum's exhibits illustrate how rich and powerful Dubrovnik became as one of the world's most important seafaring nations. On display are intricately detailed models of ships as well as engine-room equipment, sailors' uniforms, paintings, and maps. ✉ *Damjana Jude 2, Stari Grad* ☎ *020/323–904* 🖻 *40 Kn* ☉ *May–Oct., Tues.–Sun. 9–6; Nov.–Apr., Tues.–Sun. 9–4.*

**Sinagoga** *(Synagogue).* This tiny 15th-century synagogue, the second-oldest in Europe (after Prague's), bears testament to Dubrovnik's once thriving Jewish community, made up largely of Jews who were expelled from Spain and Italy during the medieval period. ✉ *Zudioska 5, Stari Grad* ☎ *020/321–028* 🖻 *15 Kn* ☉ *May–Sept., daily 10–8.*

**Vrata od Pila** *(Pile Gate).* Built in 1537 and combining a Renaissance arch with a wooden drawbridge on chains, this has always been the main entrance to the city walls. A niche above the portal contains a statue of Sveti Vlah (St. Blaise), the city's patron saint, holding a replica of Dubrovnik in his left hand. From May to October, guards in deep-red period-costume uniforms stand vigilant by the gate through daylight hours, just as they would have done when the city was a republic. ✉ *Pile, Stari Grad.*

**Vrata od Ploča** *(Ploče Gate).* One of two entrances into the town walls, Ploče comprises a stone bridge and wooden drawbridge plus a 15th-century stone arch bearing a statue of Sveti Vlah (St. Blaise). As at Pile Gate, guards in period costume stand vigilant here through the summer season. ✉ *Ploče, Stari Grad.*

Fodor'sChoice
★ **War Photo Limited.** Shocking but impressive, this modern gallery devotes two entire floors to war photojournalism. Past exhibitions have featured images from conflicts in Afghanistan, Iraq, former-Yugoslavia, Israel, and Palestine. Refreshingly impartial by Croatian standards, the message—that war is physically and emotionally destructive whichever side you are on—comes through loudly and clearly. You'll find it in a narrow side street running between Placa and Prijeko. ✉ *Antuninska 6, Stari Grad* ☎ *020/322–166* ⊕ *www.warphotoltd.com* 🖻 *30 Kn* ☉ *June–Sept., daily 9–9; May and Oct., Tues.–Sat. 9–3, Sun. 9–1.*

## CAVTAT
*17 km (10½ mi) southeast of Dubrovnik.*

Founded by the ancient Greeks, then taken by the Romans, the original settlement on the site of Cavtat, which is 17 km (10½ mi) southeast of Dubrovnik, was subsequently destroyed by tribes of Avars and Slavs in the early 7th century. Today's town, which developed during the 15th century under the Republic of Dubrovnik, is an easygoing fishing town and small-scale seaside resort. The medieval stone buildings of the Old Town occupy a small peninsula with a natural bay to each side. A palm-lined seaside promenade with open-air cafés and restaurants curves around the main bay. Cavtat can be visited easily as a half-day trip from Dubrovnik. If you're going on your own, the easiest way to get there is by bus or taxi-boat ride; the trip takes about an hour.

**Galerija Vlaho Bukovac** *(Vlaho Bukovac Gallery).* The former home of local artist Vlaho Bukovac (1855–1922) has been renovated to provide a gallery for contemporary exhibitions on the ground floor. Upstairs, around 30 of Bukovac's oil paintings, tracing the periods he spent in Paris, Prague, and Cavtat, are on display in his former studio, along with pieces of period furniture. ⊠ *Bukovčeva* ☎ *020/478–646* ☜ *20 Kn* ☾ *May–Oct., Tues.–Sat. 9–1 and 4–8, Sun. 4–8; Nov.–Apr., Tues.–Sat. 9–1 and 2–5, Sun. 2–5.*

## BEACHES

**Eastwest Beach Club.** Just a short distance from the Ploče Gate, this fashionable spot has a small pebble beach complete with chaise longues and parasols, waterskiing and jet-skiing facilities, and a chic cocktail bar and restaurant. ⊠ *Frana Supila, Banje Beach* ☎ *020/412–220.*

The more upmarket hotels, such as the Excelsior and Villa Dubrovnik, have their own beaches that are exclusively for the use of hotel guests. The most natural and peaceful beaches lie on the tiny island of **Lokrum**, a short distance south of the Old Town. Through high season, boats leave from the Old Harbor, ferrying visitors back and forth from morning to early evening (9 AM to 8 PM, every 30 minutes). Return tickets cost 40 Kn.

## SHOPPING

Despite its role as an important tourist destination, Dubrovnik offers little in the way of shopping or souvenir hunting. If you're in search of gifts, your best bet is a bottle of good Dalmatian wine or *rakija* (a fruit brandy popular throughout much of eastern Europe).

**Croata.** This small boutique near the Bishop's Palace specializes in "original Croatian ties" in presentation boxes. ⊠ *Pred Dvorom 2, Ploče* ☎ *020/323–526.*

**Dubrovačka Kuća.** This tastefully decorated wine shop stocks a fine selection of regional Croatian wines, rakija, olive oil, and truffle products, plus works of art by contemporary artists on the upper two levels; it's close to the Ploče Gate. ⊠ *Svetog Dominika, Stari Grad* ☎ *020/322–092.*

**Medusa.** Medusa stocks a range of authentic and amusing handmade souvenirs, including wooden toys for kids, Dubrovnik stone faces, tablecloths decorated with traditional embroidery, and dolls in Dalmatian dress. ⊠ *Prijeko 18, Stari Grad* ☎ *020/322–004.*

## WHERE TO EAT

$   ✕ **Proto.** In the Old Town, just off Stradun, Proto dates back to 1886.
SEAFOOD   Come here for Dalmatian seafood specialties such as oysters from nearby Ston, seafood risotto, and fresh fish, served on a romantic second-floor stone terrace draped with vines. ⊠ *Široka 1, Stari Grad* ☎ *020/323–234* ⊟ *AE, DC, MC, V.*

¢–$   ✕ **Taj Mahal.** For a change from omnipresent seafood, try this small,
EASTERN   informal eatery serving Bosnian meat specialties such as čevapčići (shish
EUROPEAN   kebabs) and ražnjići (tiny pieces of pork cooked on a skewer), and round off with a syrupy slice of baklava. ⊠ *Gučetića 2, Stari Grad* ☎ *020/323–221* ⊟ *AE, DC, MC, V.*

# HAIFA, ISRAEL

Israel's largest port city (and third-largest city overall), Haifa was ruled for four centuries by the Ottomans and gradually grew up the mountainside into a cosmopolitan city whose port served the entire Middle East. In 1902 Theodor Herzl enthusiastically dubbed it "the city of the future." The city is the world center for the Baha'i faith, and the most striking landmark on the city's mountainside is the gleaming golden dome of the Baha'i Shrine, set amid utterly beautiful circular grass terraces that fill the slope from top to bottom.

## ESSENTIALS

CURRENCY  The shekel (NIS 3.77 to US$1). U.S. currency is accepted for high-value items in shops but not in restaurants or markets. ATMs are common.

HOURS  Shops are generally open Sunday through Thursday from 9 to 7, though some close in the afternoon. Museums vary in hours, but most are open Monday through Thursday from 10 to 6 with shorter hours on Friday through Sunday, often from 10 to 2 or 3. Some museums close on Friday.

INTERNET  **Tambayan** (✉ *Balfour 2, Hadar HaCarmel* ☏ *04/866–9996*).

TELEPHONES  Most multiband mobile phones work in Israel, and GSM and 3G systems are well established in the urban areas. Major providers are Cellcom Israel, Parner Communication (Orange), and Pelephone.

## COMING ASHORE

The cruise port sits directly on the Haifa waterfront. The cruise terminal has some shops, a café, currency exchange desk, and a tax-refund kiosk, and the waterfront area is slowly being improved with new restaurants and shops opening their doors. From the port it's an easy walk into downtown, but the city is built on hills, so if you intend to explore on foot, wear comfortable shoes.

The Egged bus cooperative provides regular service from Haifa to Nazareth, and to Tiberias on the Sea of Galilee. To get from Haifa to Tiberias, take the slow Bus 430 (about an hour), which leaves hourly from Merkazit Hamifratz.

Driving is the best way to explore the Lower Galilee, and you can easily link several excursions and take your time enjoying the panoramic views, since Nazareth is only 56 km (35 mi) east of Haifa and the Golan Heights around two hours' drive away. Some newer four-lane highways are excellent, but some secondary roads may be in need of repair. Signposting is clear (and usually in English), with route numbers clearly marked. Prices for a subcompact car are around $80 a day and a compact $100 per day, though many companies charge for mileage.

# EXPLORING ISRAEL FROM HAIFA

## HAIFA

The metropolis is divided into three main levels, each crisscrossed by parks and gardens: the port down below; Hadar HaCarmel, a commercial shopping area in the middle; and Merkaz HaCarmel, with the posher hotels and many restaurants, on top.

Fodor'sChoice ★ **Baha'i Shrine and Gardens.** At the center of the shrine is the mausoleum built for the Bab (literally, the "Gate"), who heralded the coming of the Baha'i faith and was martyred by the Persian authorities in 1850. The building gracefully combines the canons of classical European architecture with elements of Eastern design. The dome glistens with some 12,000 gilded tiles imported from the Netherlands. The magnificent gardens are one of Israel's 11 UNESCO World Heritage sites. Visitors to the shrine are asked to dress modestly (no shorts).

> **HAIFA BEST BETS**
>
> **Basilica of the Annunciation.** Built on a spot thought to be central to the life of Jesus and his family.
>
> **Bahia Shrine and Gardens.** A stunning World Heritage site with terraced gardens cascading down a hillside.
>
> **The Golan Heights.** Israel's Little Tuscany has breathtaking countryside.

✉ *65 Sderot Hatziyonut, Merkaz Carmel* ☎ *04/835–8358, 04/831–3131 for garden tour* ⊕ *www.bahai.org* 🎟 *Free* ⊙ *Shrine daily 9–noon; gardens daily 9–5.*

Fodor'sChoice ★ **German Colony.** Ruler-straight Ben Gurion Boulevard was the heart of a late-19th-century colony, one of five in the Holy Land, established by the German Templer religious reform movement. The early settlers formed a self-sufficient community, and it was under their influence that Haifa began to resemble a modern city, with well-laid-out streets, gardens, and attractive homes. Neglected for years, the German Colony is now one of the city's loveliest (and flattest) strolls. ✉ *German Colony.*

★ **Tikotin Museum of Japanese Art.** This graceful venue displays scrolls, screens, pottery and porcelain, lacquer and metalwork, paintings from several schools, and flower arrangements. ✉ *88 Hanassi Blvd., Merkaz Carmel* ☎ *04/838-3554* ⊕ *www.tmja.org.il* 🎟 *NIS 24* ⊙ *Mon., Wed., Thurs. 10–4, Tues. 4–8, Fri. 10–1, Sat. and Jewish holidays 10–3.*

## NAZARETH

The Nazareth where Jesus grew up was an insignificant village nestled in a hollow in the Galilean hills. Today's city of 65,000 is pulsing with energy. Apart from the occasional donkey plying traffic-clogged Paulus VI Street, there's little that evokes the Bible in contemporary Nazareth.

**Baptist Church.** Christianity speaks with many voices in Nazareth. The Baptist Church, a few hundred yards north of the Church of St. Gabriel, is affiliated with the Southern Baptist Convention of the United States. Call to arrange a visit. ✉ *Paulus VI St.* ☎ *04/657–6946 or 04/657–4370.*

★ **Basilica of the Annunciation.** Consecrated in 1969, the Roman Catholic Basilica of the Annunciation is the largest church in the Middle East. It enshrines a small ancient cave dwelling or grotto, identified by many Catholics as the home of Mary. Here, they believe, the angel Gabriel appeared to her and announced (hence "Annunciation") that she would conceive "and bear a son" and "call his name Jesus" (Luke 1). Pilgrim devotions suffuse the site throughout the day. Crusader-era walls and some restored Byzantine mosaics near the grotto bear witness to the antiquity of the tradition. The grotto is in the so-called "lower church." Look up through the "well" or opening over the grotto that connects with the "upper church" to the grand cupola, soaring 195 feet above you. The vast upper church is the parish church of Nazareth's Roman Catholic community. Beautiful Italian ceramic reliefs on the huge concrete pillars represent the Stations of the Cross, captioned in the Arabic vernacular. You now have a closer view of the cupola, its ribs representing the petals of an upside-down lily—a symbol of Mary's purity—rooted in heaven. It is repeatedly inscribed with the letter *M* for her name. The huge mosaic behind the altar shows Jesus and Peter at the center and an enthroned Mary behind them, flanked by figures of the hierarchical church (to your right) and the charismatic church (to your left). In the exit courtyard, a glass-enclosed baptistery is built over what is thought to have been an ancient mikvah, a Jewish ritual immersion bath. The adjacent small Church of St. Joseph, just past Terra Sancta College, is built over a complex of rock-hewn chambers traditionally identified as the workshop of Joseph the Carpenter. ⊠ *Casa Nova St.* ☎ *04/657–2501* ⊒ *Free* ☉ *Apr.–Sept., Mon.–Sat. 8–6, Sun. 2–6; Oct.–Mar., Mon.–Sat. 8–6, Sun. 2–5.*

**Church of St. Gabriel.** The Greek Orthodox Church of St. Gabriel is built over Nazareth's only natural water source, a spring dubbed Mary's Well. The Greek Orthodox, citing the noncanonical Gospel of St. James, believe it to be the place where the angel Gabriel appeared to Mary to announce the coming birth of Jesus. The ornate church was built in 1750, and contains a carved-wood pulpit and iconostasis (chancel screen), with painted New Testament scenes and silver-haloed saints. The walls are adorned with frescoes of figures from the Bible and the Greek Orthodox hagiography. A tiny "well" stands over the running water, and a modern aluminum cup gives a satisfying plop as it drops in. (The water is clean; the cup is more suspect.) ⊠ *Off Paulus VI St.* ☎ *04/657–6437* ⊒ *Donation expected* ☉ *Mon.–Sat. 8–5, Sun. after services–5.*

**Nazareth Village.** Using information gained from archaeological work done in the area, this attraction aims to reconstruct Jewish rural community life as Jesus would have known it more than 2,000 years ago. Workshops, farms, and houses have been created with techniques that would have been used at the time. Interpreters in period costume cook, weave, and work at wine presses, giving a sense of daily life. ⊠ *5105 St., by Nazareth YMCA downtown* ☎ *04/645–6042* ⊕ *www. nazarethvillage.com* ⊒ *NIS 50* ☉ *Mon.–Sat. 9–5.*

**Souk.** Nazareth's market, in the Old City, may have something for everyone, from coffee sets to pastries to T-shirts; antiques can also be found. The old lanes are narrow and shops are tiny, with goods spilling into the street. ⊠ *Casa Nova St. and vicinity.*

## THE GOLAN HEIGHTS

Considered the most fertile land in Israel, the Golan Heights is known for its many fine wineries. As you drive through these verdant hills, covered with wildflowers in the spring, you'll also see abundant olive groves and apple and cherry orchards. The whole region was once volcanic, and many symmetrical volcanic cones and pronounced reliefs still dominate the landscape, particularly in the upper Golan. The gentle terrain and climate of the rest of the region have historically attracted far more settlement than the less hospitable northern Upper Galilee. Today it's home to Jewish, Druze, and Alawite communities.

★ **Hermon River (Banias) Nature Reserve.** One of the most stunning parts of Israel, this reserve contains gushing waterfalls, dense foliage along riverbanks, and the remains of a temple dedicated to the god Pan. The **Banias Spring** emerges at the foot of mostly limestone Mt. Hermon, just where it meets the basalt layers of the Golan Heights. The most popular short route in the reserve is up to the **Banias Cave,** via the path that crosses the spring. Excavations have revealed the five niches hewed out of the rock to the right of the cave; these are what remains of Hellenistic and Roman temples, depicted in interesting artist's renderings. Three of the niches bear inscriptions in Greek mentioning Pan, the lover of tunes; Echo, the mountain nymph; and Galerius, one of Pan's priests. All early references to the cave identify it as the source of the spring, but earthquakes over the years have changed the landscape, and the water now emerges at the foot of the cave rather than from within it. ⊠ *Off Rte. 99* ☏ *04/695-0272* ⌖ *NIS 23* ⊙ *Apr.–Sept., Sat.–Thurs. 8–5, Fri. 8–4; Oct.–Mar., Sat.–Thurs. 8–4, Fri. 8–3; last entrance 1 hr before closing.*

⟳ **Nimrod's Fortress.** This fortress was built in 1218 by the Mameluke war-
★ lord al-Malik al-Aziz Othman to guard the vital route from Damascus via the Golan and Banias to Lebanon and to the Mediterranean coast against a Crusader *reconquista* after their 1187 defeat. It changed hands between Muslims and Christians in the succeeding centuries as both vied for control of the region. During one of its more interesting periods, from 1126 to 1129, Nimrod's Fortress was occupied by a fanatic sect of Muslims infamous for their murderous violence. Before heading out to track down their enemies, the cutthroats are said to have indulged in hashish, thus earning the nickname *hashashin* (hashish users), from which the word *assassin* is derived. ⊠ *Nimrod's Fortress National Park, Rte. 989 (off Rte. 99)* ☏ *04/694-9277* ⌖ *NIS 18* ⊙ *Apr.–Sept., Sat.–Thurs. 8–5, Fri. 8–4; Oct.–Mar., Sat.–Thurs. 8–4, Fri. 8–3; last entrance 1 hr before closing.*

### SEA OF GALILEE

The Sea of Galilee is, in fact, a freshwater lake, measuring 21 km (13 mi) long from north to south and 11 km (7 mi) wide from east to west. Almost completely ringed by cliffs and steep hills, the lake lies in a hollow about 700 feet below sea level, which accounts for its warm climate and subtropical vegetation. This is Israel's Riviera-on-a-lake, filled with beaches and outdoor recreation facilities. Its shores are also dotted with sites hallowed by Christian tradition (note that several of these sites demand modest dress) as well as some important ancient synagogues. Tiberias itself is one of Judaism's four holy cities, along with Jerusalem, Hebron, and Tzfat (Safed).

## BEACHES

Haifa's coastline is one fine, sandy public beach after another.

**Dado, Zamir, Carmel, and Bat Galim Beaches.** From south to north, these cover 5 km (3 mi) of coast, with many lifeguard stations among them.

To be on the safe side, never swim when a lifeguard is not on duty. The beaches have sports areas with paragliding and jet-skiing, changing rooms, showers, toilets, refreshment stands, restaurants, and a winding stone promenade. On Saturday afternoon (morning in winter) at Dado Beach (near the Hof HaCarmel bus and train station at the city's entrance), Israelis of all ages come and folk dance, to the delight of onlookers. ☎ 04/852–4231.

**Hof HaShaket.** Just north of Aliya Street, this beach offers separate-gender days: Sunday, Tuesday, and Thursday for women; Monday, Wednesday, and Friday for men; Saturday for whoever.

## WHERE TO EAT

$$
MEDITERRANEAN

✕ **Douzan.** Inside this old German Templer building with a pleasant outdoor terrace, a huge metal lamp studded with colored glass casts lacy designs on the walls. The food, much of it prepared by the owner's mother, is an intriguing combination of French and local Arabic cuisines. Her specialty is *kibbeh,* deep-fried torpedoes of cracked wheat kneaded with minced beef, pine nuts, onions, and exotic spices. A variation on it is *sfeeha,* puff pastry topped with delicately spiced beef, onions, and pine nuts. Among the French dishes are chicken cordon bleu with mustard cream sauce, and an onion, bacon, and thyme quiche. ⊠ *35 Ben Gurion Blvd., German Colony* ☎ *04/852–5444* ▤ *AE, DC, MC, V.*

$$$
MODERN ISRAELI

✕ **Ha Namal.** Careful renovations have transformed this old wheat and corn warehouse in Haifa's rather rundown port into a Tuscan country inn. Climbing the stairs, you arrive at five different rooms (one's the bar, with leather sofas) with original stone floors, brick walls, and lofty ceilings. The inventive chef offers starters such as salmon fillet covered in herbs and coriander seeds and entrées such as lamb sirloin in a cashew-pesto crust, smoked shrimp in a pastry shell, and Swiss chard and ricotta tortellini with white-truffle cream. There's a fixed-price lunch and a children's menu. ⊠ *24 Hanamal St., off Sha'ar Palmer St., the Port* ☎ *04/862–8899* ▤ *AE, MC, V* ✿ *Closed Sun.*

# HVAR, CROATIA

The island of Hvar bills itself as the "sunniest island in the Adriatic." Not only does it have the figures to back up this claim—an annual average of 2,724 hours of sunshine with a maximum of two foggy days a year—but it also makes visitors a sporting proposition, offering them a money-back guarantee if there is ever a foggy day. While fog has been known to happen, hotels don't ordinarily have to give much of their income back. All this sun is good for the island's fields of lavender, rosemary, and grapes. Hvar is also probably Croatia's hippest island, attracting gossip column–worthy celebrities, would-be artists, politicians, and nudists. Visitors have included King Abdullah and Queen Rania of Jordan, Nicky Hilton (Paris's sister), and local tennis champion Goran Ivanišević.

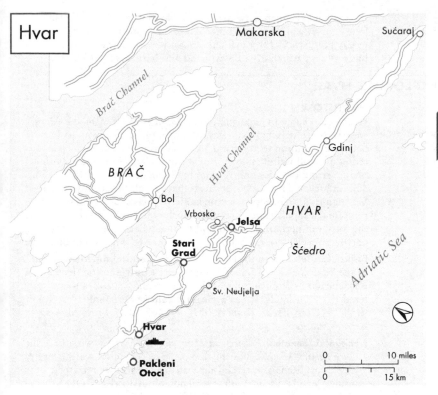

## ESSENTIALS

CURRENCY The Croatian kuna (5.3 Kn to US$1 at this writing). ATMs are easy to find, and it is also possible to exchange currency in banks and also in most local travel agencies. Credit cards are accepted at many restaurants and shops.

HOURS Offices are open weekdays from 8:30 to 4. Shops often close for lunch around 1 and may close for as long as three hours; banks also sometimes close for lunch. Post offices are open Saturday during the main summer season, from June through September.

INTERNET In summer small temporary Internet cafés spring up in the islands, so you will certainly be able to find somewhere to check e-mail. However, many are nothing more than a regular café with a PC in the corner.

TELEPHONES Most tri- and quad-band GSM phones will work in Croatia. Public phones use calling cards, which can be purchased at the post office, newsstands, and hotels. Major mobile phone companies include TMobile and VIPNet.

## COMING ASHORE

Ships can't dock in Hvar, so you'll be brought into Hvar Town from the ship by tender, which docks right in town. Most of the town is closed to cars, so the town is best seen on foot, and since many ships make Hvar a short port call (sometimes staying as few as four hours), it doesn't make much sense to set out to do too much. If you are in port long enough, you'll need to rent a car to see more of the island. Expect to pay at least €55 for a manual economy vehicle. The island also has bus service, particularly to Stari Grad and Jelsa, several times a day.

# EXPLORING HVAR

## HVAR TOWN

Hvar is the name of both the island and its capital, near the island's western tip. The little town rises like an amphitheater from its harbor, backed by a hilltop fortress and protected from the open sea by a scattering of small islands known as Pakleni Otoci. Along the palm-lined quay a string of cafés and restaurants is shaded by colorful awnings and umbrellas. Hvar Town seems to have it all: beautifully preserved Venetian-style architecture, stylish modern hotels, classy seafood restaurants, and a sophisticated nightlife. Much of the town was built during the medieval period, so you'll find Gothic palaces amid the twisting, narrow streets just away from the shoreline. And what a shoreline it is.

**Fortica** *(Castle).* Behind the town rises the majestic hilltop fortress. Built by the Venetians in 1557, its stone ramparts afford fantastic views down onto the terra-cotta rooftops of Hvar Town and out to sea to the scattered Pakleni islands. It has a pleasant café and a couple of souvenir shops. ⊠ *Grad, Hvar Town* ☎ *021/741–608* ⌑ *25 Kn* ⊙ *May–Oct., daily 8–midnight.*

**Franjevački Samostan** *(Franciscan Monastery).* East of town, along the quay past the Arsenal, lies this monastery. Within its walls a pretty 15th-century Renaissance cloister leads to the former refectory, now housing a small museum with several notable artworks. ⊠ *Obala Ivana Lučica Lavčevica, Hvar Town* ☎ *021/741–193* ⌑ *20 Kn* ⊙ *May–Oct., daily 10–noon and 5–7.*

**Kazalište** *(Theater).* On the upper floor of the Arsenal, Hvar's theater opened in 1612, making it the oldest institution of its kind in Croatia and one of the first in Europe. The Arsenal building, where Venetian ships en route to the Orient once docked for repairs, dates back to the 13th century, but was reconstructed after damage during a Turkish invasion in 1571. It reopened in summer 2010 following a restoration. ⊠ *Trg Sv Stjepana, Hvar Town* ⌑ *10 Kn* ⊙ *May–Oct., daily 9–1.*

**Promenade.** You can walk far along Hvar's seaside promenade, looking out over the Adriatic and the Pakleni Islands, the largest of which—Sveti Klementi—holds the island's yacht harbor. The town itself remains traffic-free, because there are no through streets for driving.

**Trg Sveti Stjepan.** A few steps away from the shorefront promenade, the magnificent main square, the largest piazza in Dalmatia, is backed by the 16th-century **Katedrala Sveti Stjepanp** (Cathedral of St. Stephen). Other notable sights include the *kazalište* (theater) and the Franjevački Samostan (Franciscan Monastery).

## PAKLENI OTOCI

*Sveti Klement is approximately 20 minutes by boat from Hvar Town.*

The 20 small islets that make up the Pakleni Islands are directly southwest of Hvar Town's harbor. Their name derives from the Croatian word *paklina*, which is what melted pine resin is called (the resin from the island's many pine trees was melted down to make ships watertight). The largest of the islands, Sveti Klement, is where Hvar's main yacht harbor is located; a church here is dedicated to the saint. Summer restaurants and beach bars are built on many of the islands, some of which have excellent beaches that are reachable only by boat. Jerolim, the closest of the islands to Hvar Town, has a famous nude beach.

---

### HVAR BEST BETS

**See the Tvrdalj.** This oddly interesting house in Stari Grad is worth a trip.

**Visit the Pakleni Otoci.** The small islands off Hvar's southwest coast have Hvar's best beaches, and are scenic enough to be worth a trip in their own right.

**Wander the pedestrian-only alleys of Hvar Town.** If you have just a few hours in port, spend them wandering the car-free streets of Hvar's picturesque Old Town, stopping at a café or two.

---

## JELSA

*10 km (6 mi) east of Stari Grad, 27 km (17 mi) east of Hvar Town.*

In this village on the northern coast of the island you'll see many structures from the Renaissance and baroque periods, though St. Mary's Church dates back to the early 1300s. A tower built by the ancient Greeks overlooks the harbor; it dates to the 3rd or 4th century BC. About 1 km (½ mi) east of the modern town is the older Grad, the original fortified area that was protected by the fortress called Galesink, which now stands in ruins. The small town is an alternative to the busier Hvar Town and is surrounded by swimmable beaches—including the island's most popular nude beaches—and some resorts. It's surrounded by thick forests of pine trees.

## STARI GRAD

*17 km (11 mi) east of Hvar Town.*

The site of the original Greek settlement on Hvar, called Pharos by the Greeks, Stari Grad is a conglomeration of smaller communities; it's also the entry point to the island for bus transportation from the mainland, as well as most passenger ferries.

**Tvrdalj.** The main sight in Stari Grad is the fortified Renaissance villa of the 16th-century poet Petar Hektorovic. The home has been renovated twice over the centuries, first in the 18th-century baroque style; a partial restoration was done in the 19th century. Hektorovic attempted to create a "model universe" to be embodied in his home. To that end, a large fish pond is stocked with gray mullet, as they were in the poet's own time, representing the sea; above the fish pond in a tower is a dovecote, representing the air. Ivy was allowed to cover the walls to tie the home to the land. Quotations from Hektorovic's poetry are inscribed on many walls. ⊠ *Trg Tvrdalj* ☎ *021/765–068* 🖼 *15 Kn* ☉ *July and Aug.,* *daily 10–1 and 5–8; May, June, Sept., and Oct., daily 10–1; Nov.–Apr. by appointment only.*

## SPORTS AND ACTIVITIES

### DIVING

**Diving Center Viking.** Those with a taste for underwater adventure might have a go at scuba diving. The seabed is scattered with pieces of broken Greek amphorae, while the area's biggest underwater attraction is the Stambedar sea wall, home to red and violet gorgonians (a type of coral), which is close to the Pakleni Islands. This company offers both courses and trips for divers at all levels. ⊠ *Podstine, Hvar Town* ☎ *021/742–529* ⊕ *www.viking-diving.com.*

### SAILING

Hvar Town is a popular port of call for those sailing on the Adriatic; the town harbor is packed out with flashy yachts through peak season. **ACI Marina.** The marina in Palmižana Bay on the island of Sveti Klement, one of the Pakleni Otoci, lies 2.4 nautical mi from Hvar Town. This 160-berth marina is open from mid-April through October, and is served by regular taxi boats from Hvar Town through peak season. ⊠ *Palmizana Bay, Sveti Klement* ☎ *021/744–995* ⊕ *www.aci-club.hr.*

## BEACHES

There are several decent beaches within walking distance of town—the best-equipped being the Hotel Amfora's **Bonj les Bains** beach, a pebbled cove rimmed by a 1930s stone colonnade housing private stone cabanas, 10 minutes west of the main square. However, sun worshippers in search of a more back-to-nature experience head for the nearby Pakleni Otoci (Pakleni Islands), which can be reached by taxi boats that depart regularly (in peak season, every hour, from 8 to 8) from in front of the Arsenal in the town harbor. The best-known and best-served are **Sveti Jerolim** (on the island of the same name, predominantly a nudist beach), **Stipanska** (on the island of Marinkovac, home to trendy Carpe Diem Stipanska, complete with a restaurant, lounge-bar, pool, and two beaches with palapas and wooden sun beds for hire), and **Palmižana** (on the island of Sveti Klement, also clothing-optional).

## WHERE TO EAT

¢ ✕ **Konoba Menego.** In an old stone building on the steps leading up to
EASTERN
EUROPEAN the castle, this traditional Dalmatian wine bar serves small platters of local specialties such as *kožji sir* (goat cheese) and *pršut* (prosciutto), plus big chunks of crusty homemade bread and carafes of the family's own wine. ⊠ *Groda, Hvar Town* ☎ *021/742–036* ▭ *AE, DC, MC, V* ⊗ *Closed Nov.–Mar.*

¢–$ ✕ **Restoran Palmižana.** On the tiny island of Sveti Klement, a 20-minute
SEAFOOD taxi boat ride from Hvar Town, this restaurant is backed by a romantic wilderness of Mediterranean flora and offers stunning views over the open sea. The interior is painted a deep crimson red and decorated with

modern Croatian art, and there are classical-music recitals on Sunday morning. Besides fresh seafood, goodies include *kozji sir sa rukolom* (goat cheese with arugula), and *pašticada* (beef stewed in sweet wine and prunes). ⌧ *Vinogradišce Uvala, Sveti Klement* ☎ *021/717–270* ▭ *AE, DC, MC, V* ☻ *Closed Nov.–Mar.*

# ISTANBUL, TURKEY

Though it is often remarked that Turkey straddles Europe and Asia, it's really the city of Istanbul that does the straddling. European Istanbul is separated from its Asian suburbs by the Bosphorus, the narrow channel of water that connects the Black Sea, north of the city, to the Sea of Marmara in the south. What will strike you more than the meeting of East and West in Istanbul, though, is the juxtaposition of the old and the new, of tradition and modernity. Office towers creep up behind historic old palaces; women in jeans or elegant designer outfits pass others wearing long skirts and head coverings; donkey-drawn carts vie with shiny BMWs for dominance of the streets; and the Grand Bazaar competes with Western-style boutiques and shopping malls. At dawn, when the muezzin's call to prayer rebounds from ancient minarets, there are inevitably a few hearty revelers still making their way home from nightclubs while other residents kneel in prayer.

### ESSENTIALS

CURRENCY The New Turkish Lira (YTL1.50 to US$1 and YTL 1.92 to €1 at this writing). U.S. dollars are accepted in shops and in some restaurants. ATMs and currency exchange kiosks are common.

HOURS Shops open daily from 9 to 9, though some will close for an hour or so on Friday lunchtime for prayers. Attractions are usually open daily from 8 until 5 or 6, though some are closed on Monday.

INTERNET **Istanbul Cyber Café** (⌧ *Kucuk Ayasofya Mah. Sokak 9, Sultanahmet* ☎ *212/516–5528*).

TELEPHONES Most tri- and quad-band GSM phones will work in Turkey. The Turkish mobile system is not 3G-compatible, and handsets are single band. Public phones accept tokens or telephone cards (which can be purchased at newsstands and telecom shops); phones accepting cards will also accept credit cards in payment for calls. Turk Telekom, Turkcell, and Telcim are the major telecom companies.

### COMING ASHORE

Ships dock at Karakoy, in the shadow of the famous Galata Tower. It's possible to walk from the pier to the Sultanahmet (the historic quarter) in about 45 minutes, but the immediate and pervasive bustle of the city might be off-putting (though it's not intrinsically dangerous). Taxis wait at the pier for the 10-minute ride into Sultanahmet.

We strongly advise against renting a car in Istanbul. The public transport system is also quite chaotic, so we recommend you take taxis. Once you reach Sultanahmet, many of the most important sights are all within walking distance of each other. Private tours with a guide are useful and popular. Guides will also help you shop at the Grand

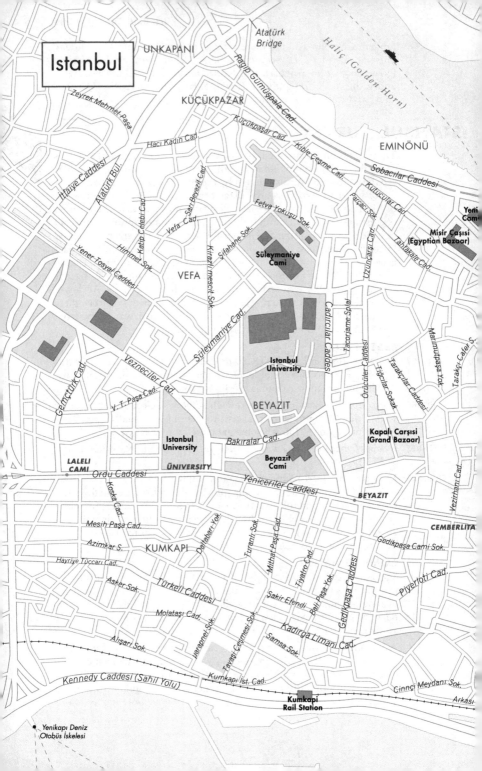

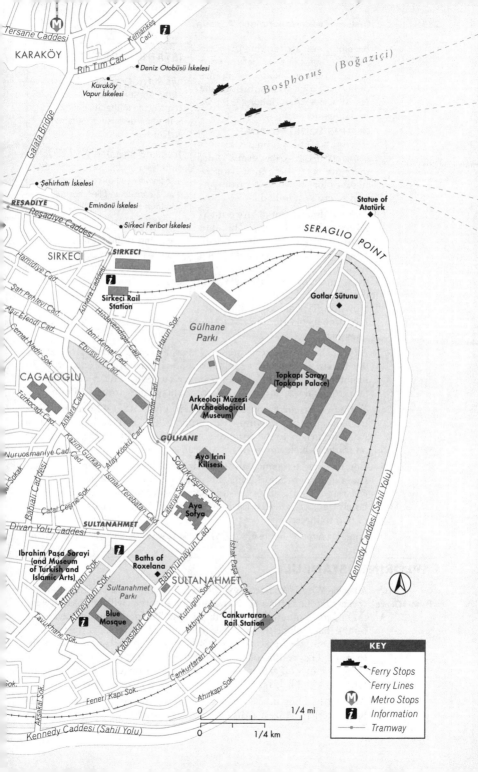

Bazaar. If you are looking to set up a private guided tour before your cruise, you can locate the names of licensed tour guides through the **Turkish Guides Association** (⊕ *www. turkishguides.org*).

### GETTING TO THE AIRPORT

If you do not purchase airport transfers from your cruise line, there are several inexpensive possibilities for your transfer from airport to cruise terminal.

Ataturk International Airport is 28 km outside the city. The light metro line links the airport with downtown at Koça Mustafa Pasha station. Trains run from around 6 AM to midnight, but the service is not high-speed and trains can be crowded. Tickets cost TRY 1.30. From the metro station a 10-minute taxi ride takes you to the cruise quayside.

| ISTANBUL BEST BETS |
| --- |

**Aya Sofya.** Once the epicenter of the Christian world, this church constructed in the 6th century is the tour de force of Byzantine architecture.

**Topkapı Sarayı.** This giant palace provides a behind-the-scenes look at daily life, sultan-style, from how a concubine filled her day to where the ruler kept his stash of jewels.

**Shopping at the Grand Bazaar.** Istanbul's giant bazaar has been providing retail therapy since the mid-15th century!

Airport shuttle buses operated by Havaş leave the arrivals terminal for the Turkish Airlines office in Taksim Square. Departures are every 30 minutes during the day, and prices are currently TRY 9 per ticket. A taxi from Taksim Square to the cruise quay takes around 15 minutes.

Taxi fares are currently set at TRY 2.50 plus TRY 1.40 per km. Fares from the airport to downtown are around TRY 20–TRY 30, and the trip from the airport to the cruise pier takes around 40 minutes depending on traffic (which can be heavy at peak times).

Commercial companies also offer inexpensive door-to-door services. Istanbul Airport Shuttle runs a transfer every couple of hours between 6 AM and 9 PM, and prices for airport to cruise port (or downtown hotel) transfers are €10 for individuals and €6 per person for a group of two to three.

Contacts **Airport Shuttle** (☎ 212/518–0354 ⊕ www.istanbulairportshuttle.com).

## EXPLORING ISTANBUL

☾
Fodor'sChoice
★

**Arkeoloji Müzesi** *(Archaeology Museum)*. Step into this vast repository of spectacular finds for a head-spinning look at the civilizations that have thrived for thousands of years in Turkey. The most stunning pieces are tombs that include the so-called Alexander Sarcophagus, carved with scenes from Alexander the Great's battles and once believed, wrongly, to be his final resting place. An excellent exhibit on Istanbul through the ages shows off artifacts from prehistory through the Byzantines and Ottomans and helps put the city's complex past in context.

Another building in the courtyard of Topkapı Sarayı houses the **Eski Şark Eserleri Müzesi** *(Museum of the Ancient Orient)*, where the mosaics, obelisks, and other artifacts are from Anatolia, Mesopotamia, and elsewhere in the Arab world, and date from the pre-Christian centuries. A particularly intricate tablet is the Treaty of Kadesh from the 13th century BC, perhaps the world's earliest known peace treaty, recording an accord between the Hittite king Hattusilis III and the Egyptian pharoah Ramses II. The **Çinili KÚşkü** *(Tiled Pavilion)* is a bright profusion of colored tiles. Inside are ceramics from the early Seljuk and Ottoman empires, as well as tiles from Iznik, the city that produced perhaps the finest ceramics in the world during the 17th and 18th centuries. ⊠ *Gülhane Park, next to Topkapı Sarayı* ☎ *212/520–7740* ⊕ *www.istanbularkeoloji.gov.tr* ⊠ *$10 (total) for the 3 museums* ☉ *Archaeology Museum: Tues.–Sun. 9–6, ticket sales until 4:30.*

**Fodor's Choice** **Aya Sofya** *(Hagia Sophia, Church of the Holy Wisdom).* This soaring
★ edifice is perhaps the greatest work of Byzantine architecture, and for almost a thousand years, starting from its completion in 537, was the world's largest and most important religious monument. Only Saint Peter's in Rome, not completed until the 17th century, surpassed Aya Sofya in size and grandeur. The Emperor Justinian commissioned the church, and in response to his dictum that Aya Sofya be the grandest place of worship ever built, craftsmen devised the magnificent dome.

Mehmet converted the church into a mosque when he took the city in 1453, and succeeding sultans added its four minarets. In the 16th century Süleyman the Magnificent ordered the church's Byzantine mosaics to be plastered over in accordance with the Islamic proscription against the portrayal of the human figure in a place of worship. The multicolor tiles that cover parts of the cavernous interior weren't rediscovered until after Atatürk made the Aya Sofya into a museum in 1936. Today, mosaics and frescoes of saints, emperors, and Christ enliven the vast space. ⊠ *Aya Sofya Sq.* ☎ *212/522–1750* ⊠ *$16* ☉ *Tues.–Sun. 9–7, ticket sales until 6:30.*

**Fodor's Choice** **Blue Mosque** *(Sultan Ahmet Cami).* Only after you enter the Blue Mosque
★ do you understand why it is so named. Inside, 20,000 shimmering blue-green Iznik tiles are interspersed with 260 stained-glass windows; an airy arabesque pattern is painted on the ceiling. After the dark corners and somber faces of the Byzantine mosaics in Aya Sofya, this light-filled mosque is positively uplifting. Such a favorable comparison was the intention of architect Mehmet Aga, known as Sedefkar (Worker of Mother-of-Pearl), whose goal was to surpass Justinian's crowning achievement. At the bequest of Sultan Ahmet I (ruled 1603–17), he spent just eight years creating this masterpiece of Ottoman craftsmanship, beginning in 1609. ⊠ *Sultanahmet Sq.* ☎ *Mosque free* ☉ *Blue Mosque: daily 9–5, access restricted during prayer times, particularly at midday on Fri.*

★ **Grand Bazaar** *(Kapalı Çarşısı).* Take a deep breath and plunge into this maze of 65 winding, covered streets crammed with 4,000 tiny shops, cafés, restaurants, mosques, and courtyards. It's said that this early version of a shopping mall is the largest concentration of stores under one roof anywhere in the world, and that's easy to believe; it's also easy to believe that some of the most aggressive salesmanship in the world takes place here. Oddly enough, though, the sales pitches, the crowds, the sheer volume of junky trinkets on offer can be hypnotizing. Originally built by Mehmet II (the Conqueror) in the 1450s, the Grand Bazaar was ravaged twice by fire in relatively recent years—once in 1954 and once in 1974. In both cases, the bazaar was quickly rebuilt into something resembling the original style, with its arched passageways and brass-and-tile fountains at regular intervals.

The amazingly polylingual sellers are all anxious to reassure you that you do not have to buy . . . just drink a glass of tea while you browse. A sizable share of the goods are trinkets tailored for the tourist trade, but a separate section for antiques at the very center of the bazaar, called the *bedestan,* always has some beautiful items on offer. ⊠ *Yeniçeriler Cad. and Fuatpaşa Cad.* 🖾 *Free* ☉ *Apr.–Oct., Mon.–Sat. 8:30–7; Nov.–Mar., Mon.–Sat. 8:30–6:30.*

**Ibrahim Paşa Sarayı** *(Ibrahim Paşa Palace).* Süleyman the Magnificent commissioned the great architect Sinan to build this stone palace, the most grandiose residence in Istanbul. The palace now houses the **Türk Ve Islâm Eserleri Müzesi** (Museum of Turkish and Islamic Arts), where you can learn about the lifestyles of Turks at every level of society, from the 8th century to the present. ⊠ *Atmeydanı 46, Sultanahmet* 🖾 *212/518–1385* 🖾 *$8* ☉ *Tues.–Sun. 9–4:30.*

★  **Süleymaniye Cami** *(Mosque of Süleyman).* Perched on a hilltop near Istanbul University, the largest mosque in Istanbul is a masterful achievement and a grand presence. This mosque houses Sinan's tomb, along with that of his patron, Süleyman the Magnificent, and the sultan's wife, Roxelana. The architectural thrill here is the enormous dome. The soaring space gives the impression that it's held up principally by divine cooperation. The complex still incorporates a hospital, a *kervansaray* (roadside inn), a kitchen, several schools, and other charitable institutions that mosques traditionally operate. ⊠ *Süleymaniye Cad., near Istanbul University's north gate* ☉ *Daily.*

Fodor'sChoice **Topkapı Sarayı** *(Topkapı Palace).* This vast palace on Seraglio Point,
★  above the confluence of the Bosphorus and the Golden Horn, was the residence of sultans as well as the seat of Ottoman rule from the 1450s until the middle of the 19th century. Few other royal residences can match this hilltop compound when it comes to the lavishly exotic intricacies of court life.

Sultan Mehmet II built the original Topkapı Palace in the 1450s, shortly after his conquest of Constantinople. Over the centuries sultan after sultan expanded the palace until some 5,000 full-time residents lived here, including slaves, concubines, and eunuchs. Topkapı was finally abandoned in 1853, when Sultan Abdül Mecit I moved his court to the palace at Dolmabahçe on the Bosphorus.

The main entrance, or Imperial Gate, leads to the **Court of the Janissaries,** also known as the First Courtyard, today converted into a parking lot. You will begin to experience the grandeur of the palace when you pass through **Bab-ı-Selam** (Gate of Salutation).

The **Second Courtyard** is filled with a series of ornate *kUşks,* pavilions once used for the business of state. To one side are the palace's kitchens, where more than 1,000 cooks once toiled at the rows of immense ovens to feed the palace residents, whose numbers sometimes swelled to 15,000 during special occasions. The space now displays one of the world's best collections of porcelain, much of it amassed over years of Ottoman rule as powers from China, Persia, and Europe bestowed gifts on the sultans; the thousands of Ming blue-and-white pieces were made to order for the palace in the 18th century. Straight ahead is the **Divan-ı-Humayun** (Assembly Room of the Council of State), once presided over by the grand vizier. The sultan would sit behind a latticed window here, hidden by a curtain, so no one would know when he was listening.

The **Harem,** a maze of 400 halls, terraces, rooms, wings, and apartments grouped around the sultan's private quarters, evokes all the exoticism and mysterious ways of the Ottoman Empire. The first Harem compound housed about 200 lesser concubines and the palace eunuchs. As you move into the Harem, the rooms become larger and more opulent. The chief wives of the sultan lived in private apartments around a shared courtyard. Beyond are the lavish apartments of the *valide* sultan (queen mother), the absolute ruler of the Harem, and finally, the sultan's private rooms—a riot of brocades, murals, colored marble, wildly ornate furniture, gold leaf, and fine carving.

Beyond the Harem, access was restricted to the **Third Courtyard,** in part because it housed the **Treasury,** filled with imperial thrones, lavish gifts bestowed to sultans, and the spoils of war. Two uncut emeralds, each weighing about 8 pounds (!), once hung from the ceiling, but are now displayed behind glass. Other pavilions show off a curious assortment of treasures—Turkish and Persian miniatures; relics of the prophet Muhammad (including hair from his beard); and sultans' robes.

The **Fourth Courtyard** was the private realm of the sultan, and the small, elegant pavilions, mosques, fountains, and reflecting pools are scattered amid the gardens that overlook the Bosphorus and Golden Horn. In the **Iftariye** (Golden Cage), also known as the Sofa KÜşkü, the closest relatives of the reigning sultan lived in strict confinement under what amounted to house arrest—superseding an older practice of murdering all possible rivals to the throne. ⊠ *Topkapı Sarayı, Gülhane Park, near Sultanahmet Sq.* ☎ *212/512–0480* ⊕ *www.topkapisarayi. gov.tr* ⊠ *$16 for palace plus another $12 for Harem tour* ☉ *Wed.–Mon. 9–7 in summer and 9–5 in winter for palace itself. The Harem is open Wed.–Mon. 9:30–3:30 all year.*

# SHOPPING

Istanbul has been a shopper's town for, well, centuries—the sprawling Grand Bazaar could easily be called the world's oldest shopping mall—but this is not to say that the city is stuck in the past. Along with its colorful bazaars and outdoor markets, Istanbul also has a wide range of modern options. Whether you're looking for trinkets and souvenirs, kilims and carpets, brass and silverware, leather goods, old books, prints and maps, or furnishings and clothes (Turkish textiles are among the best in the world), you can find them here. **Nuruosmaniye Caddesi,** one of the major streets leading to the Grand Bazaar, is lined with some of Istanbul's most stylish shops, with an emphasis on fine carpets, jewelry, and antiques.

★ **The Arasta Bazaar.** This is one of few markets open on Sunday; you can get a lot of the same items here as at the Grand Bazaar, but the atmosphere is much calmer. ⊠ *Sultanahmet.*

★ **The Egyptian Bazaar.** This bazaar is definitely worth seeing. Also known as the Spice Market, it has stall after enticing stall filled with mounds of exotic spices and dried fruits. ⊠ *Eminönü.*

**Sahaflar Çarşışı.** Just outside the western end of the Grand Bazaar, this is home to a bustling book market, with old and new editions; most are in Turkish, but English is represented, too. The market is open daily, though Sunday has the most vendors. ⊠ *Grand Bazaar.*

## WHERE TO EAT

¢ ✕ **Doy-Doy.** *Doy-doy* is a Turkish expression for "full" and, unlike many
TURKISH other spots in tourist-filled Sultanahmet, this is a place frequented by locals—and you can indeed fill up here for a reasonable sum. The restaurant serves simple kebabs, chicken and lamb stews, and *pide* (Turkish pizza) baked in a wood-burning oven. A variety of mezes are also available, and the meatless pizzas and salads are excellent options for vegetarians. Service is friendly and personable. The two-level rooftop terrace, open in summer, has fine views of the Blue Mosque and the Sea of Marmara. ⊠ *Şifa Hamamı Sok. 13, Sultanahmet* ☎ *212/517–1588* ⊟ *MC, V.*

$ ✕ **Konuk Evi.** A little oasis near Aya Sofya, this inviting restaurant has
TURKISH an outdoor patio with wicker chairs, all shaded by leafy trees. The small menu is comprised of mezes, salads, and grilled meats, as well as an assortment of Turkish desserts. It's a pleasant place to take a break from the hustle and bustle of Sultanahmet. ⊠ *Soğukçeşme Sokak, Sultanahmet* ☎ *212/513–3660* ⊟ *AE, MC, V.*

## WHERE TO STAY

$$$ 🏨 **Ayasofya Pansiyonları & Konuk Evi.** These accommodations are part of the project undertaken by Turkey's Touring and Automobile Club to restore (or authentically re-create) a movie-set-like street of 19th-century wooden houses along the outer wall of Topkapı Palace. The charming, pastel-color houses of Ayasofya Pansiyonları have been turned into *pansiyons* furnished in late Ottoman style. Front rooms have up-close views of Aya Sofya, but the rest do not, so if you want a view, specify when you reserve. The nearby Konuk Evi is an Ottoman mansion that has been restored in similar fashion and has larger rooms. Breakfast is served in the Konuk Evi's shaded garden in summer. **Pros:** unique buildings; location adjacent to Aya Sofya. **Cons:** high room rates because of location. ⊠ *Soğukçeşme Sokak, Sultanahmet* ☎ *212/513–3660* ⊕ *www. ayasofyapensions.com* ⇔ *57 rooms, 7 suites* ⌖ *In-room: no TV, Wi-Fi. In-hotel: 2 restaurants, room service, laundry service, no-smoking rooms* ⊟ *AE, DC, MC, V* ⊠ *BP.*

**$$$$**  ⌂ **Çırağan Palace Kempinski.** This 19th-century Ottoman palace (pro-
★  nounced chi-rahn) is Istanbul's most luxurious hotel. There are two
buildings: the older palace and a newer addition. The ornate public
spaces feel absolutely decadent, and the setting, right on the Bosphorus,
is breathtaking; the outdoor infinity pool seems to hover on the water's
edge. Rooms have Ottoman-inspired wood furnishings and textiles in
warm colors; all have balconies, and the views on the Bosphorus side are
exceptional (rooms on the other side look out on a park and busy road).
Most lodgings are in the new wing, though there are 11 suites in the
palace, including the €25,000 per night Sultan's Suite—start saving now.
**Pros:** incredible location, service, degree of luxury. **Cons:** exorbitant
price of food and drinks. ⊠ *Çırağan Cad. 32, Beşiktaş* ☎ *212/326–4646*
⊕ *www.kempinski-istanbul.com* ⇆ *280 rooms, 33 suites* ⅋ *In-room:
safe, Wi-Fi. In-hotel: 4 restaurants, room service, bar, pools, gym, spa,
children's programs (ages 0–11), laundry service, parking (free), no-
smoking rooms* ▭ *AE, DC, MC, V.*

**$$**  ⌂ **Dersaadet Hotel.** Dersaadet means "place of happiness" in Ottoman
Turkish, and this small hotel lives up to its name. Rooms have an
elegant, even plush, feel, with colorful rugs on the floor, wood fur-
niture, and ceilings hand-painted with Ottoman ornamental motifs.
The top two floors of the hotel have rooms with views, while a cozy
terrace, where breakfast is served and classical music plays in the back-
ground, looks out on the sea. Deniz Duyar, the hotel's young owner
and manager, earned his MBA in New York and runs the place with a
high level of professionalism. **Pros:** extraordinary level of service; lovely
terrace; good value. **Cons:** some rooms modest in size. ⊠ *Küçükayaso-
fya Cad. Kapıağası Sokak 5, Sultanahmet* ☎ *212/458–0760* ⊕ *www.
hoteldersaadet.com* ⇆ *14 rooms, 3 suites* ⅋ *In-room: safe, Wi-Fi.
In-hotel: room service, laundry service, no-smoking rooms* ▭ *MC, V*
⧈ *BP.*

# KATAKOLON, GREECE (FOR OLYMPIA)

Katakolon could not seem less of a cruise port if it tried. A tiny enclave
clinging to the western Peloponnese coast, it's a sleepy place except
when ships dock. But it's a popular cruise destination because of its
proximity to Olympia. Ancient Olympia was one of the most important
cities in classical Greece. The Sanctuary of Zeus was the city's raison
d'être, and attracted pilgrims from around the eastern Mediterranean,
and later the city played host to Olympic Games, the original athletic
games that were the inspiration for today's modern sporting pan-plan-
etary meet. At the foot of the tree-covered Kronion hill, in a valley near
two rivers, Katakolon is today one of the most popular ancient sites
in Greece. If you don't want to make the trip to Olympia, then Kata-
kolon is an ideal place for a leisurely Greek lunch while you watch the
fishermen mend their nets, but there's just not much else to do there.

### ESSENTIALS

CURRENCY  The euro (€1 to US$1.36 at this writing). ATMs are common.

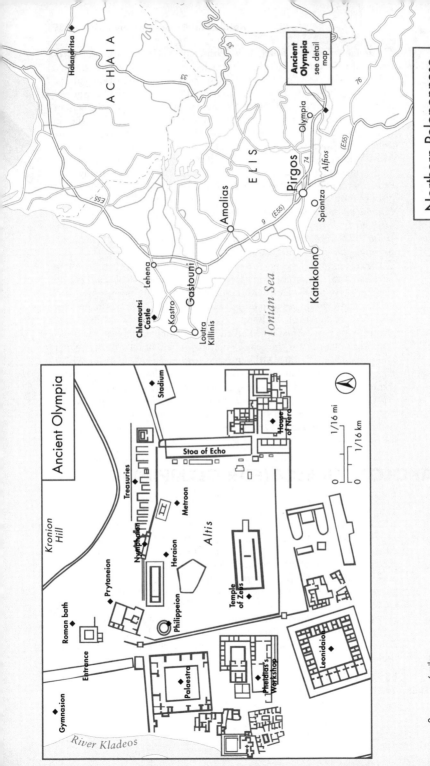

# Northern Peloponnese

ACHAIA

Holandritsa

ELIS

Ancient Olympia
see detail map

Olympia

Pirgos

Amalias

Alfios

Spiantza

Katakolon

Gastouni

Leheng

Chlemoutsi Castle

Kastro

Loutra Killinis

Ionian Sea

# Ancient Olympia

Kronion Hill

Stadium

Treasuries

Stoa of Echo

House of Nero

Metroon

Nymphaion

Altis

Pryhaneion

Heraion

Roman bath

Philippeion

Temple of Zeus

Entrance

Palaestra

Pheidias's Workshop

Leonidaion

Gymnasion

River Kladeos

1/16 mi
1/16 km

6 miles
9 km

HOURS Stores are generally open from 9 to 9 on weekdays and 9 to 6 on Saturday. Museums are generally open from 9 to 5, but many are closed on Monday.

TELEPHONES Tri-band GSM phones work in Greece. You can buy prepaid phone cards at telecom shops, news vendors, and tobacconists in all towns and cities. Phone cards can be used for local or international calls. Vodafone is the leading mobile telecom company. OTE is the national domestic provider. Calls can be made at OTE offices and paid for after completion.

## COMING ASHORE

Katakolon is a very small port. Ships dock at the jetty, from where it is a short walk (five minutes) into Katakolon Town. It's a small Greek town with a lot of character; most residents still make their living from fishing; a few restaurants are along the waterfront, as well as shops selling souvenirs to cruise-ship passengers. There are no passenger facilities at the jetty itself. Though there are refreshment stands, telephones, currency exchange offices, and an ATM in the town.

Taxis are available at the dock to meet ships. However, cabs charge an overinflated fixed fare for the journey to Olympia, so it's often better to go on a ship-sponsored excursion.

**Katakolon Car Rental.** Displas Dionysios runs this agency, but it has a limited number of vehicles, so it's vital to book in advance if you want to drive yourself to Olympia. Prices for a compact manual vehicle are approx €50 per day. ☎ 26210/41727.

### OLYMPIA BEST BETS

**The Twelve Labors of Hercules.** This series now in the archaeological museum is regarded as a high point in classical Greek sculpture.

**Statue of Hermes by Praxiteles.** Also in the museum, this is one of the most complete classical statues to have been unearthed.

**Remains of the Temple of Zeus.** The above-mentioned treasures once adorned this vast temple, which was one of the largest and finest in ancient Greece. Today only the platform remains.

# EXPLORING OLYMPIA

**Ancient Olympia.** Although the first Olympiad is thought to have been held in 776 BC, bronze votive figures of the Geometric period (10th–8th century BC) reveal that the sanctuary was in use before that date. The festival took place every four years over a five-day period in the late summer during a sacred truce, observed by all Greek cities. Initially only native speakers of Greek (excepting slaves) could compete, but Romans were later admitted. The events included the footrace, boxing, chariot and horse racing, the pentathlon (combining running, jumping, wrestling, and both javelin and discus throwing), and the *pankration* (a no-holds-barred style of wrestling in which competitors could break their opponent's fingers and other body parts).

The long decline of Olympia began after the reign of Hadrian. In AD 267, under threat of an invasion, many buildings were dismantled to construct a defensive wall; Christian decrees forbade the functioning of pagan sanctuaries and caused the demolition of the Altis. The Roman emperor Theodosius I, a Christian, banned the games, calling them "pagan rites," in AD 393. Earthquakes settled the fate of Olympia, and the flooding of the Alpheios and the Kladeos, together with landslides off the Kronion hill, buried the abandoned sanctuary.

Olympia's ruins are fairly compact, occupying a flat area at the base of the Kronion hill where the Kladeos and Alpheios rivers join. It's easy to get a quick overview and then investigate specific buildings or head to the museum. The site is pleasant, with plenty of trees providing shade. It is comprised of the sacred precinct, or **Altis**, a large rectangular enclosure south of the Kronion, with **administrative buildings, baths, and workshops** on the west and south and the **Stadium** and **Hippodrome** on the east. In 1829 a French expedition investigated the Temple of Zeus and brought a few metope fragments to the Louvre. The systematic excavation begun by the German Archaeological Institute in 1875 has continued intermittently to this day.

South of the entrance are the remains of a small **Roman bath.**

The **Gymnasion** is essentially a large, open practice field surrounded by stoas.

The large complex opposite the Gymnasion was the **Prytaneion,** where the *prytaneis* (magistrates in charge of the games) feted the winners and where the Olympic flame burned on a sacred hearth.

South is the gateway to the Altis, marked by two sets of four columns. Beyond is the **Philippeion,** a circular shrine started by Philip II and completed after his death by Alexander the Great.

Directly in front of the Philippeion is the large Doric temple of Hera, the **Heraion** (circa 600 BC). It is well preserved, especially considering that it is constructed from the local coarse, porous shell limestone. At first it had wooden columns, which were replaced as needed, so although they are all Doric, the capitals don't exactly match. Three of the columns, which had fallen, have been set back up. A colossal head of a goddess, possibly from the statue of Hera, was found at the temple and is now in the site museum.

There is no doubt about the location of the **Nymphaion,** or Exedra, which brought water to Olympia from a spring to the east. A colonnade around the semicircular reservoir had statues of the family of Herodes Atticus and his imperial patrons.

The 4th-century **Metroon,** at the bottom of the Nymphaion terrace, was originally dedicated to Cybele, Mother of the Gods, and was taken over by the Roman imperial cult. Nearby, at the bottom of the steps leading to the Treasuries and outside the entrance of the Stadium, were **16 bronze statues of Zeus,** called the Zanes, bought with money from fines levied against those caught cheating at the games. Bribery seems to have been the most common offense (steroids not being available).

On the terrace itself are the city-state **Treasuries,** which look like small temples, and were used to store valuables, such as equipment used in rituals.

Just off the northeast corner of the Altis is the **Stadium,** which at first ran along the terrace of the Treasuries and had no embankments for the spectators to sit on; embankments were added later, but were never given seats, and 40,000–50,000 spectators could be accommodated. The starting and finishing lines are still in place, 600 Olympic feet (about 630 feet) apart.

The **House of Nero,** a 1st-century villa off the southeastern corner of the Altis, was hurriedly built for his visit.

In the southwestern corner of the Altis is the **Temple of Zeus.** Only a few column drums are in place, but the huge size of the temple platform is impressive. Designed by Libon, an Elean architect, it was built from about 470 to 456 BC. The magnificent sculptures from the pediments are on view in the site's museum. A gilded bronze statue of Nike (the winged goddess of Victory) stood above the east pediment, matching a marble Nike (in the site museum) that stood on a pedestal in front of the temple. Both were the work of the sculptor Paionios. The cult statue inside the temple, made of gold and ivory, showed Zeus seated on a throne, holding a Nike in his open right hand and a scepter in his left. It was created in 430 BC by Pheidias, sculptor of the statue of Athena in the Parthenon, and was said to be seven times life size; the statue was one of the Seven Wonders of the Ancient World. It is said that Caligula wanted to move the statue to Rome in the 1st century AD and to replace the head with one of his own, but the statue laughed out loud when his men approached it. It was removed to Constantinople, where it was destroyed by fire in AD 475. Pausanias relates that behind the statue there was "a woolen curtain . . . decorated by Assyrian weavers and dyed with Phoenician crimson, dedicated by Antiochos." It is possible this was the veil of the Temple at Jerusalem (Antiochos IV Epiphanes forcibly converted the Temple to the worship of Zeus Olympias in the 2nd century BC).

Outside the gate at the southwestern corner of the Altis stood the **Leonidaion,** at first a guesthouse for important visitors and later a residence of the Roman governor of the province of Achaea.

Immediately north of the Leonidaion was **Pheidias's workshop,** where the cult statue of Zeus was constructed in a large hall of the same size and orientation as the interior of the temple. Tools, clay molds, and Pheidias's own cup (in the site museum) make the identification of this building certain. It was later used as a Byzantine church.

North of Pheidas's workshop is the **Palaestra,** built in the 3rd century BC, for athletic training. The rooms around the square field were used for bathing and cleansing with oil, for teaching, and for socializing. ⊠ *Off Ethnikos Odos 74, ½ km (¼ mi) outside modern Olympia* ☎ *26240/22517* ⊕ *www.culture.gr* ⊠ *€6, combined ticket with Archaeological Museum €9* ☉ *May–Oct., daily 8–7; Nov.–Apr., daily 8:30–5.*

**Archaeological Museum at Olympia.** In a handsome glass and marble pavilion at the edge of the ancient site, this museum has in its magnificent collections the sculptures from the Temple of Zeus and the *Hermes* of Praxiteles, discovered in the Temple of Hera in the place noted by Pausanias. The central gallery of the museum holds one of the greatest sculptural achievements of classical antiquity: the pedimental sculptures and metopes from the Temple of Zeus, depicting Hercules's Twelve Labors. The *Hermes* was buried under the fallen clay of the temple's upper walls, and is one of the best-preserved classical statues. Also on display is the famous *Nike* of Paionios. Other treasures include notable terra-cottas of Zeus and Ganymede; the head of the cult statue of Hera; sculptures of the family and imperial patrons of Herodes Atticus; and bronzes found at the site, including votive figurines, cauldrons, and armor. Of great historic interest are a helmet dedicated by Miltiades, the Athenian general who defeated the Persians at Marathon, and a cup owned by the sculptor Pheidias. ⊠ *Off Ethnikos Odos 74, north of Ancient Olympia site* ☎ *26240/22742* ⛳ *€6, combined ticket with Ancient Olympia €9* ☯ *May–Oct., Mon. 11–7:30, Tues.–Sun. 8–7:30; Nov.–Apr., Mon. 10:30–5:30, Tues.Sun. 8:30–5.*

# SHOPPING

Lovers of handicrafts will really enjoy shopping in Greece. There's an abundance of ceramics, both traditional and modern, wooden bowls, reproductions of ancient statuary, woven rugs, jewelry, lace, and edibles such as delicious honey and olive oil. Cotton clothing is perfect for the summer temperatures, along with strong handcrafted sandals and leather goods that have always been popular purchases here. Around Olympus other popular souvenirs are reproductions of ancient artifacts found at the ancient site. Shop in modern Olympia or in Katakalon before reboarding your ship. There are just a few shops in Kalakon, but they sell a full range of souvenirs.

★ **Archaeological Museum Shop.** The shop at Ancient Olympia carries an appealing line of figurines, bronzes, votives, and other replicas of objects found in the ruins. ⊠ *Off Ethnikos Odos 74, north of Ancient Olympia site* ☎ *26240/22742.*

★ **Atelier Exekias.** At this shop Sakis Doylas sells exquisite handmade and hand-painted ceramic bowls and urns, fashioned after finds in Ancient Olympia; the glazes and colors are beautiful. ⊠ *Kondoli, Olympia* ☎ *6936/314054.*

# WHERE TO EAT

¢ ✕ **Aegean.** Don't let the garish signs depicting menu offerings put you
GREEK off: the far-ranging offerings are excellent. You can eat lightly on a gyro or pizza, but venture into some of the more serious fare, especially such local dishes as fish, oven-baked with onion, garlic, green peppers, and parsley. The house's barrel wine is a nice accompaniment to any meal. ⊠ *Douma, near Hotel New Olympia, Olympia* ☎ *26240/22540* ⊟ *MC, V.*

¢ ✕ **Taverna Melathron.** A nice break from the tourist traps that dominate
GREEK the Olympia dining scene, Melathron offers down-to-earth fare in a simple, traditional taverna. Moussaka and other casseroles, cabbage rolls stuffed with ground beef, and grilled meats dominate the straight-forward menu, and meals can be enjoyed a sidewalk terrace with a view

of animated town life. ✉ *Douma 3* ☏ *26240/22916* ▤ *MC, V* ☉ *Closed mid-Nov.–Mar.*

# KORČULA, CROATIA

Southern Dalmatia's largest, most sophisticated, and most visited island, Korčula was known to the ancient Greeks, who named it *Kerkyra Melaina,* or "Black Corfu." Between the 10th and 18th centuries it spent several periods under Venetian rule. Today most Croatians know it for its traditional sword dances and its excellent white wines. Korčula is also the name of the capital, which is near the island's eastern tip. Eight centuries under Venetian rule bequeathed the town a trove of Gothic and Renaissance churches, palaces, and piazzas, all built from fine local stone. Korčula's main claim to fame, though one still disputed by historians, is that it was the birthplace of Marco Polo (1254–1324). The approach by sea is breathtaking; if the hour isn't too early, make sure you're on deck for this one.

## ESSENTIALS

**CURRENCY** The Croatian kuna (5.3 Kn to US$1 at this writing). ATMs are easy to find, and it is also possible to exchange currency in banks and also in most local travel agencies. Credit cards are accepted at many restaurants and shops.

**HOURS** Offices are open weekdays from 8:30 to 4. Shops often close for lunch around 1, and may close for as long as three hours; banks also sometimes close for lunch. Post offices are open on Saturday during the main summer season, from June through September.

**INTERNET** In summer small temporary Internet cafés spring up. However, many are nothing more than a regular café with a PC in the corner.

**TELEPHONES** Most tri- and quad-band GSM phones will work in Croatia. Public phones use calling cards, which can be purchased at the post office, newsstands, and hotels.

## COMING ASHORE

Smaller ships may be able to dock at two cruise-ship docks in Korčula Town, but larger vessels will have to anchor and tender passengers ashore at the same dock. The dock area is lined with stores, cafés, and tourism offices. If you are staying in town, there's no advantage to having a car for your day in port. If you'd like to explore the island, you can rent a car, scooter, or even abicycle. Expect to pay about €55 per day for a compact manual vehicle. Guided tours can also be arranged, including visits to local vineyards.

# EXPLORING KORČULA TOWN

At first view, Korčula may seem like a much smaller version of Dubrovnik: the same high walls, the circular corner fortresses, and the church tower projecting from within an expanse of red roofs. The main difference lies in the town plan, as narrow side streets run off the main thoroughfare at odd angles to form a herringbone pattern, preventing cold winter winds from whistling unimpeded through town. The center

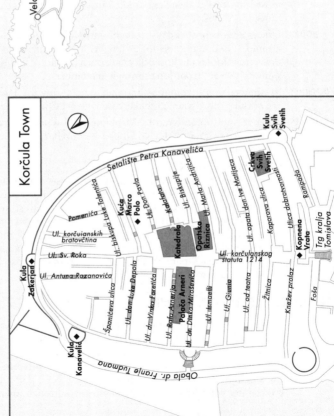

## Korčula Island

## Korčula Town

Šetalište Petra Kanavelića

Pomenića

Ul. biskupa Luke Tolanića

Ul. korčulanskih bratovčtina

Ul. Sv. Roka

Ul. Antuna Razanovića

Španičeva ulica

Ul. dom Luke Depola

Ul. dr Vinka Foretića

Ul. Rafa Arnerija

Ul. dr Dinka Mirošavića

Ul. Ismaeli

Ul. Giunio

Ul. od teatra

Kula Zakerjan ◆

Kula Kanavelić ◆

Kula Svih Svetih ◆

Kuća Marco Polo ◆

Ul. Don Pavla

Katedrala

Ul. Biskupije

Kalafata

Ul. Marka Andrijića

Opatska Riznica

Crkva Svih Svetih

Ul. opata don Ive Matijaca

Palača Arneri

Ul. korčulanskog statuta 1214

Kaporova ulica

Ulica dobronomosti

Rampada

Knežev prolaz

Žitnica

Foša

Kopnena Vrata ◆

Trg kralja Tomislava

Obala dr. Franje Tuđmana

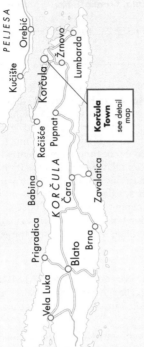

PELJEŠAC

Neretvanski kanal

Korčulanski kanal

Scedro

Kučište

Orebić

Žrnovo

Korčula

Lumbarda

Pupnat

Račišče

KORČULA

Babina

Čara

Zavalatica

Prigradica

Blato

Brna

Vela Luka

Lastovski kanal

Lastovo

Lastovo

Ubli

Korčula Town
see detail map

0   4 miles

0   6 km

is small and compact, and can be explored in an hour.

**Katedrala** *(Cathedral)*. On the main square, the splendid Gothic-Renaissance cathedral is built from a wheat-color stone that turns pale gold in sunlight, amber at sunset. Enter through the beautifully carved Romanesque main portal, which is guarded by Adam and Eve standing upon twin lions. Inside, check out the elegant 15th-century ciborium; within, two paintings are attributed to the Venetian master Tintoretto. ⊠ *Trg Sv Marka* 🖅 *5 Kn* ⊙ *May–Oct., daily 9–2 and 5–8; Nov.–Apr., by appointment.*

**Kopnena Vrata** *(Land Gate)*. The main entrance into the Old Town is topped by the 15th-century Revelin Tower, housing an exhibition connected with the *Moreska* sword dance, and offering panoramic views over the Old Town. ⊠ *Kopnena Vrata* 🖅 *10 Kn* ⊙ *July and Aug., daily 9–9; May, June, Sept., and Oct., daily 9–7; Nov.–Apr., by appointment only.*

**Kuća Marca Pola** *(Marco Polo House)*. A couple of blocks east of the main square is the place where the legendary 13th-century discoverer is said to have been born, when Korčula was part of the Venetian Empire. At present only the tower is open, with a modest exhibition about Polo's life on the first floor, and a belvedere up top offering panoramic views. There were long-standing plans at this writing to restore the entire house and garden to form an educational museum, though no work has yet commenced. ⊠ *Ul Marka Pola* 🖅 *25 Kn* ⊙ *July and Aug., daily 9–9; May, June, Sept., and Oct., daily 9–7; Nov.–Apr., by appointment only.*

**Opatska Riznica** *(Abbot's Treasury)*. Next to the cathedral, the treasury museum occupies the 17th-century Renaissance bishop's palace. This collection of sacral art includes Italian and Croatian Renaissance paintings, the most precious being a 15th-centruy triptych, *Our Lady with Saints,* by the Dalmatian master Blaz Jurjev Trogiranin, plus gold and silver ecclesiastical artifacts and ceremonial vestments. ⊠ *Trg Sv Marka* 🖅 *20 Kn* ⊙ *May–Oct., daily 9–3 and 5–8; Nov.–Apr., by appointment only.*

## SHOPPING

**Cukarin.** This family-run store is renowned for its four different types of delicious handmade biscuits, as well as homemade *rakija* (fruit brandy) flavored with local herbs. ⊠ *Hrvatska Bratske Zajednice* ☎ *020/711–055.*

## SPORTS AND ACTIVITIES

### DIVING

**MM Sub.** This diving center in Lumbarda offers both instruction and trips for those with some experience. Nearby diving destinations include an underwater archaeological site, as well as several sea caves and shipwrecks. ⊠ *Lumbarda* ☏ *020/712–288* ⊕ *www.mm-sub.hr.*

### MOREŠKA DANCES

The Moreška is a colorful sword dance originally performed each year on July 29 (the feast day of the town's protector, St. Theodore). Now it's performed at 9 PM each Monday and Thursday evening from May to October just outside the city walls (tickets 100 Kn), next to the Kopnena Vrata (Land Gate). The word *Moreška* means "Moorish." The dance is said to celebrate the victory of the Christians over the Moors in Spain, but the dance's real roots are conjecture. The dance itself is not native to Croatia, and was performed in many different Mediterranean countries, including Spain, Italy, and Malta. The story of the dance is a clash between the Black (Moorish) king and the White (Christian) king over a young maiden. The dance is done with real swords.

### SAILING

**ACI marina.** The 159-berth marina remains open all year. ⊠ *Korčula* ☏ *020/711–661.*

### WINE TASTING

**Atlas Travel Agency.** This local agency organizes one-day wine tours of either Korčula Island or the Pelješac Peninsula, combining visits to the vineyards, wine tasting, and lunch in a typical Dalmatian *konoba* (pub). Transfers to and from Korčula Town by bus is included. ⊠ *Trg 19 Travanja* ☏ *020/711–060* ⊕ *www.atlas-croatia.com.*

## BEACHES

The closest spot for a quick swim is Banje, a small pebble beach about 10 minutes on foot east of the town walls, close to Hotel Liburnija. For more leisurely bathing, the best beaches lie near the village of **Lumbarda,** which is 6 km (4 mi) southeast of Korčula Town. The most popular of these is the sandy south-facing Przina, 2 km (1 mi) south of Lumbarda, while the smooth-white-stoned Bili Žal lies a short distance east of Lumbarda.

**Rent-a-Djir.** If you don't like the local beach options, you can rent a speedboat and take to the open sea to explore the tiny scattered islets of the nearby Korčula archipelago, which has many secluded bays for swimming. ⊠ *Obala Hrvatskih Mornara* ☏ *020/711–908* ⊕ *www.cro-rent.com.*

## WHERE TO EAT

¢–$

SEAFOOD

**Fodor's**Choice

★

✕**Adio Mare.** A long-standing favorite with locals and visitors alike, Adio Mare occupies a Gothic-Renaissance building in the Old Town, close to Kuca Marca Pola. There's a high-ceiling dining room as well as an open-plan kitchen, so you can watch the cooks while they work.

The menu has not changed since the restaurant opened in 1974: expect Dalmatian classics such as *pasta-fažol* (beans with pasta) and *pašticada* (beef stewed in wine and prunes), as well as fresh fish and seafood. The local wine, *pošip*, is excellent. ⊠ *Ul Marka Pola* ☎ *020/711–253* ▤ *AE, DC, MC, V* ⊙ *Closed Nov.–Mar. No lunch Sun.*

¢  ✕ **Pizzeria Tedeschi.** With tables lining the seafront promenade on the

PIZZA  peninsula just outside Korčula's medieval walls, this family-run eatery serves delicious baked-to-order pizza. ⊠ *Šetalište Petra Kanavelića* ☎ *020/711–586* ▤ *AE, DC, MC, V.*

# KOTOR, MONTENEGRO

Located in Bokor Kotorska (Kotor Bay), Europe's most southerly fjord, Kotor lies 50 mi (80 km) west of Podgorica, the capital of Montenegro, from which it is separated by a belt of dramatic, rugged mountains. Listed as a UNESCO World Heritage Site, Kotor's medieval Stari Grad (Old Town) is enclosed within well-preserved defensive walls built between the 9th and 18th centuries and presided over by a proud hilltop fortress. In the Middle Ages, as Serbia's chief port, Kotor was an important economic and cultural center with its own highly-regarded schools of stone-masonry and iconography. Later, it spent periods under the control of Venice, Austria, and France, though it was undoubtedly the Venetians who left the strongest impression on the city's architecture. Since the breakup of Yugoslavia, some 70% of the stone buildings in the romantic Old Town have been snapped up by foreigners. Fast becoming a celebrity destination, it's been visited recently by such celebrities as Catherine Zeta-Jones and Michael Douglas.

## ESSENTIALS

CURRENCY  The official currency has been the euro since 2002, despite the fact that Montenegro has not yet entered the European Union. At this writing the exchange rate was about €1.46 to U.S.$1.

HOURS  Offices are open weekdays from 8 to 4. Shops are generally open weekdays from 9 to 9, Saturday from 8 to 1, though some some shut for lunch around 2 and may close for as long as three hours. Banks stay open weekdays from 9 to 7, Saturday from 9 to 1.

INTERNET  **Café Forza Club** (⊠ *Trg od Oržja bb, Kotor* ☎ *032/304–352*).

TELEPHONES  The country code for Montenegro is 382. The new area code for Kotor is 032.

## COMING ASHORE

Arriving at Kotor from the water is an impressive experience in itself, so be sure to be up on the deck in advance. Your ship will sail up a 28-km (18-mi) -long bay (often referred to as a fjord), with rugged mountains rising in the background. Cruise ships dock on the quay, immediately in front of Kotor's medieval walled Old Town.

Since the Old Town is compact and pedestrian-friendly, you do not need to rent a car in Kotor. It's easy to reach nearby Perast by bus or taxi.

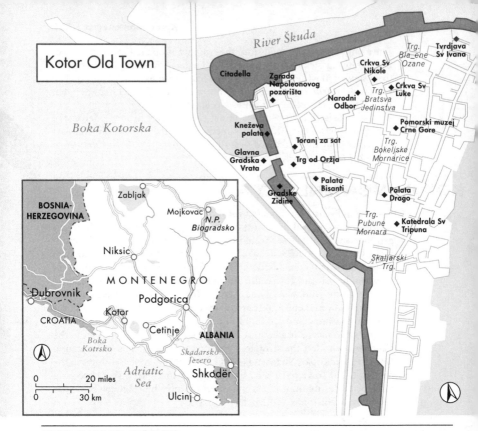

## EXPLORING KOTOR

In the Old Town a labyrinth of winding cobbled streets leads through a series of splendid paved piazzas, rimmed by centuries-old stone buildings, many of which now house trendy cafés and chic boutiques at ground level.

**Crkva Sv Luke** (*St. Luke's Church*). Built in 1195, this delightful Romanesque church is the only building in the Old Town to have withstood all five major earthquakes that afflicted Kotor. Originally a Catholic church, the building later became an Orthodox place of worship. Today there are two altars, one for each faith. ✉ *Trg bratstvo i jedinstva.*

**Crkva Sv Nikole** (*St. Nicholas' Church*). Designed by a Russian architect and built in pseudo-Byzantine style between 1902 and 1909, this is Kotor's most important Orthodox church (the Cathedral, by definition, is Catholic). The gold used to gild the spires was a gift from Russia. ✉ *Trg bratstvo i jedinstva.*

**Glavna Gradska Vrata** (Main Town Gate). The Main Town Gate (also known as the Sea Gate because of its position on the coast), which accesses the Stari Grad (Old Town) via the western facade of the city walls, dates back to the 16th century, and comprises Renaissance and baroque details. Originally, the outer gate bore a relief of the Venetian Lion, but in Tito's time this was replaced by the Socialist star and dates recording the liberation of Kotor on November 21, 1944, at the end of WWII. There are two other entrances to the Stari Grad: the Južna Vrata (South Gate) and the Sjeverna Vrata (North Gate). ⊠ *Jadranski put.*

**Gradske Zidine** (Town Walls). Especially beautiful at night, when they are illuminated, the well-preserved town walls were built between the 9th and 18th century. They measure almost 5 km (3 mi) in length, and reach up to 66 feet in height and 52 feet in width. They form a triangular defense system around the Old Town, then rise up the hill behind it to Tvrdjava Sv Ivana (St.

> ### KOTOR'S BEST BETS
>
> **Kotor Old Town.** Roam the car-free streets of this centuries-old fortified town, now an UNESCO World Heritage Site.
>
> **St John's Fortress.** Follow Kotor's medieval walls uphill to arrive at this small fort, affording magnificent views of the Old Town and the bay below.
>
> **Our Lady of the Rock.** Take a boat ride across the bay from Perast to visit a tiny islet, capped by a church.

John's Fortress), 853 feet above sea level. You can walk up to the fortress along the walls. Allow at least one hour to get up and back down. Wear good hiking shoes and don't forget to bring some water. ⊠ *Old Town, Stari Grad.*

**Katedrala Sv Tripuna** (St. Tryphon's Cathedral). Undoubtedly Kotor's finest building, the Romanesque cathedral dates back to 1166, though excavation work shows that there was already a smaller church here in the 9th century. Due to damage caused by a succession of disastrous earthquakes, the cathedral has been rebuilt several times—the twin baroque bell towers were added in the late 17th century. Inside, the most important feature is the 14th-century Romanesque Gothic ciborium above the main altar. Also look out for fragments of 14th-century frescoes, which would once have covered the entire interior. A collection of gold and silver reliquaries, encasing body parts of various saints and crafted by local masters between the 14th and 18th century, is on display in the treasury. ⊠ *Trg Ustanka Mornara* ☎ *032/322–315* ☉ *May–Oct., daily 7–7; Nov.–Apr., daily 9–2.*

**Kneževa palata** (*Duke's Palace*). Built in the 18th century, the Duke's Palace comprises almost the entire west side of the Old Town. Originally it was the official seat of the Venetian governor. Like the Napoléon Theatre, it is now part of the Cattaro Hotel & Casino. ⊠ *Old Town, Stari Grad.*

**Pomorski Muzej Crne Gore** (Montenegrin Naval Museum). Housed within the 18th-century baroque Grgurina Palace, this museum traces Montenegro's cultural and economic ties to the sea. In the 18th century, tiny Kotor had some 400 ships sailing the world's oceans. The exhibition extends over three floors, and includes model ships; paintings of ships, ship owners, and local naval commanders; navigation equipment; and uniforms worn by Montenegrin admirals and captains. ⊠ *Trg Bokeljeske Mornorice* ☎ *032/304–720* ⊡ *€4* ☉ *May–Sept., Mon.–Sat. 9–8, Sun. 9–1.*

**Toranj za sat** (*Clock Tower*). Built in the 17th century and considered a symbol of Kotor, the Clock Tower stands directly opposite the Main City Gate. You'll still find a watchmaker's shop at ground level (locals claim that the same family of watchmakers have worked here since the 17th century). In front of the Clock Tower, the "Pillar of Shame" was used to subject local criminals to public humiliation. ⊠ *Trg od Oržja, Stari Grad.*

**Trg od Oržja** (Square of Arms). The Main Town Gate leads directly into the Square of Arms, Kotor's main square, today a large paved space animated by popular open-air cafés. Under Venice, arms were repaired and stored here, hence the name. Notable buildings on the square include the 17th-century **Toranj za Sat** (Clock Tower), the 19th-century **Napoleonovog Pozorišta** (Napoleon Theatre), and the 18th-century **Kneževa Palata** (Duke's Palace), the latter two now forming part of the upmarket Hotel Cattaro. ⊠ *Old Town, Stari Grad.*

★ **Tvrdjava Sv Ivana** (St. John's Fortress). On the hill behind Kotor, 853 feet above sea level, this fortress is approached via a series of serpentines and some 1,300 steps. The fantastic view from the top makes the climb worthwhile: the terra-cotta-tile rooftops of the Old Town, the meandering fjord, and the pine-clad mountains beyond. On the way up, you will pass the tiny Crkva Gospe od Zdravlja (Church of Our Lady of Health), built in the 16th century to protect Kotor against the plague. Be sure to wear good walking shoes and take plenty of water. The route up starts from behind the east side of the city walls. ⊠ *Above Old Town.*

**Zgrada Napoleonovog pozorišta** (*Napoléon Theatre Building*). Standing in the north corner of the Square of Arms, this building was turned into a public theater, one of the first of its kind in the Balkans, by the French in 1810. Today, following extensive renovation work, it is part of the upmarket Cattaro Hotel & Casino. ⊠ *Trg od Oržja, Stari Grad.*

## PERAST

Lying 8 mi (13 km) northwest of Kotor, the peaceful little town of Perast is made up of semi-abandoned stone houses built by local sea captains during the 17th and 18th centuries. In the bay in front of Perast lie two charming islets, each with a church.

★ **Gospa od Skrpjela** (Our Lady of the Rock). Unlike its sibling island, St. George, this island is man-made. Folklore has it that in 1452, local sailors found an icon depicting the Virgin and Child cast upon a rock jutting up from the water. Taking this as a sign from God, they began placing stones on and around the rock, slowly building an island over it. By 1630 they had erected a church upon the new island. The original icon (which has been attributed to the 15th-century local artist Lovro Dobričević) is displayed on the altar. Over the centuries, locals have paid their respects to it by donating silver votive offerings, some 2,500 of which are now on display. To get here, hop a boat taxi from the waterfront (a five-minute trip). ⊠ *Kotor Bay* ☎ *032/322–886 Kotor tourist office, for information* 🎫 *€5* ⊙ *June–Sept., daily 9–7; Oct.–May hrs vary.*

**Sveti Djordje** (St. George), a natural islet, is one of Perast's famous pair of islands. It's ringed by a dozen elegant cypress trees and crowned by the Monastery of St. George, dating back to the 12th century and still inhabited by monks. In the 18th century the island became a favorite burial place for local sea captains, whose crypts remain today. The island is closed to the public, but you can snap photos from shore or neighboring Our Lady of the Rock to your heart's content. ⊠ *Kotor Bay.*

## SHOPPING

**Market.** This market that sells fruit and vegetables is just outside the city walls, on the main coastal road, and is filled with colorful, local, seasonal produce: artichokes, asparagus, and cherries in spring; tomatoes, eggplants, and peaches in summer. It takes place every morning but Sunday.

**Travel Agency Forza Kotor.** Although this company's primary duty is as a travel agency, it also stocks souvenirs such as wine and rakija in presentation boxes, as well as ceramics and T-shirts. ⊠ *On left as you enter Old Town through Main City Gate.*

## ACTIVITIES

### BEACHES

The small, pebble **town beach,** which is close to the center, is fine for a quick swim; however, for really decent swimming, locals recommend either **Jaz Beach** or **Plavi Horizonti,** both of which are some 14 mi (23 km) south of Kotor, between Tivat and Budva.

### SAILING

**Avel Yachting.** It is possible to arrange a one-day yacht charter from Kotor marina; Avel is a reliable company. ☎ *032/672–703* ⊕ *www. avelyachting.com.*

## WHERE TO EAT

$  ✕ **Galion.** A five-minute walk along the coast from the Old Town, this
SEAFOOD  sophisticated seafood restaurant occupies an old stone building with a glass-and-steel extension overlooking the bay, offering views of Kotor's medieval walls. Expect funky modern furniture and chill-out music, and a menu featuring favorites such as octopus salad, homemade gnocchi, and barbecued fresh fish. ⊠ *Šuranj bb* ☎ *032/325–054* ▭ *DC, MC, V* ⊗ *Closed Nov.–Mar.*

¢  ✕ **Kantun.** Locals swear by this friendly, down-to-earth eatery in the
EASTERN  Old Town, on a small piazza near the Montenegrin Naval Museum.
EUROPEAN  The menu features a choice of seafood and meat dishes, but ask the waiter to recommend the day's special, which could be anything from *gulaš* (Hungarian goulash) to sarma (cabbage leaves stuffed with rice and minced meat). Get a table outside in summer and soak in the Old Town atmosphere. The restaurant is open year-round. ⊠ *Trg od Muzeja bb* ☎ *032/325–757* ▭ *No credit cards.*

# KUŞADASI, TURKEY (FOR EPHESUS)

The central and southern Aegean is probably the most developed area of Turkey, and the rolling hills, mountains surrounded by clear blue seas, and glorious white-sand beaches are just a few of the reasons why. Wandering through historic ruins, boating, scuba diving, basking in the Anatolian sun, and eating fresh fish are just some of the ways you can fill your day. Kuşadasi itself is the most developed resort along the coast. Surrounding the tiny, atmospheric Old Town, a brash, very touristy development replete with tacky pubs and fish-and-chips restaurants has mushroomed in the last 20 years. On a positive note, Kuşadası is the stepping stone to some of Turkey's most important ancient sites, including Ephesus and the early Christian site of Meryemana. Kuşadası also offers excellent shopping in high-class goods.

## ESSENTIALS

CURRENCY    The New Turkish lira (YTL1.50 to US$1 and YTL 1.92 to €1 at this writing). U.S. dollars are accepted in shops and in some restaurants. ATMs and currency exchange kiosks are common.

HOURS    Most shops are open daily from 9 until 9. Attractions are open daily from 8 to 5 or 6, though some are closed on Monday.

INTERNET    The **Crew Centre** (⊠ *Liman Cad, Kuşadası* ☎ *256/614–2074* ⊕ *www. portofkusadasi.net*) is in the port.

TELEPHONES    Most tri- and quad-band GSM phones will work in Turkey, but the Turkish mobile system is not 3G-compatible, and handsets are single band. Public phones accept tokens or telephone cards, phones accepting cards will also accept credit cards in payment for calls. Tokens and cards can be purchased at newsstands and telepcom shops. Turk Telekom, Turkcell, and Telcim are the major telecom companies.

## COMING ASHORE

Boats dock at the Ephesus town port. The passenger cruise terminal, Scala Nuova, has international shops such as Body Shop, plus a Starbucks and a Burger King. There is also a duty-free shop for reboarding passengers. From the dock it's a short walk of a few minutes to the port gate and into the town directly beyond, with immediate access to taxis, car rental offices, shops, and restaurants.

The public bus service from Kaşadasi to the site at Ephesus and into Selçuk (the town near to Ephesus) is cheap and quick. *Dolmuş* (15-seat minivans) are the bulk of the fleet, and they depart from the bus terminus at Süeyman Demirel Boulevard, a 20-minute walk from the port. There are several services every hour except in mid-afternoon, when services drop to a couple per hour. Journey time is around 15 minutes. Most services stop at the end of the entry road to the archaeological site, leaving passengers with a 10-minute walk to the site entrance.

Taxis are plentiful, and they are metered with prices fixed by the municipality. Check that the meter is set to the day (lower) tariff. There are also numerous tour companies that can provide day tours to surrounding attractions. You can make these arrangements in travel agencies in Kuşadası.

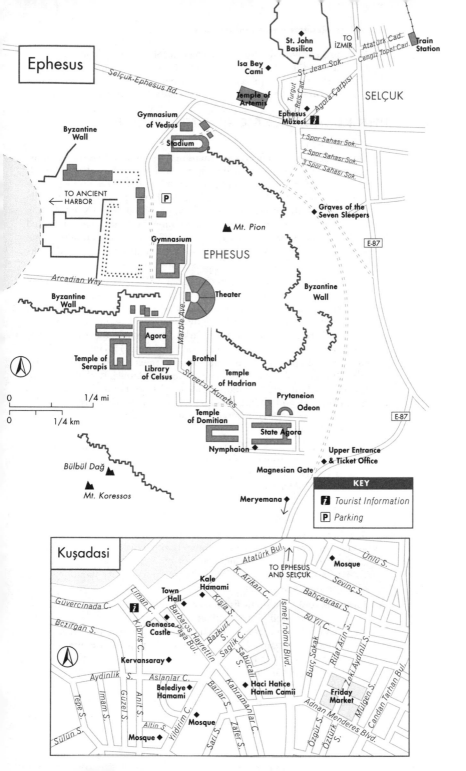

Renting a car would allow you to have a full day of sightseeing and to tailor a schedule to your own desires. Car-rental companies are plentiful. Car rental is approximately $70 per day for a compact manual vehicle. You will be quoted a rate in dollars and can pay in dollars.

## EXPLORING KUŞADASI, SELÇUK, AND EPHESUS

### KUŞADASI

One of the most popular resort towns in the southern Aegean, Kuşadası is an ideal base, geographically, from which to explore the surrounding area. Unfortunately, being popular isn't always easy, and Kuşadası long ago lost its local charm. The huge yacht marina, the largest in the region, has only exacerbated the situation. What was a small fishing village up until the 1970s is now a sprawling, hyperactive town packed with curio shops and a year-round population of around 60,000, which swells several times over in summer with the influx of tourists and Turks with vacation homes.

**Genoese Castle.** There aren't many sights in Kuşadası proper, but the causeway off Kadınlar Denizi, just south of the harbor, connects the town to an old castle on Güvercin Adası (Pigeon Island). Today the site of a popular disco and several teahouses with gardens and sea views, the fortress there was home to three Turkish brothers in the 16th century. These infamous pirates—Barbarossa, Oruc, and Hayrettin—pillaged the coasts of Spain and Italy and sold passengers and crews from captured ships into slavery in Algiers and Constantinople. Rather than fight them, Süleyman the Magnificent (ruled 1520–66) hired Hayrettin as his grand admiral, and set him loose on enemies in the Mediterranean. The strategy worked: Hayrettin won victory after victory and was heaped with honors and riches.

**Kervansaray.** Kuşadası's 300-year-old inn, now the Club Kervansaray, is loaded with Ottoman atmosphere. Its public areas are worth a look even if you're not staying here. And there's a good carpet shop here (⇨ below). ⊠ Atatürk Bul. 1.

### SELÇUK

*20 km (12 mi) northeast of Kuşadası on Rte. 515.*

Selçuk, the closest city to the archaelogical site of Ephesus, lies beneath an ancient fortress, and is, unfortunately, often overlooked. The former farming town has interesting sights of its own to offer—St. John the Evangelist was purportedly buried here, and the city has one of the oldest mosques in Turkey.

★ **Ephesus Müzesi.** The small Ephesus Museum has one of the best collections of Roman and Greek artifacts found anywhere in Turkey. Along with some fine frescoes and mosaics are two white statues of Artemis. In each she is portrayed with several rows of what are alternatively described as breasts or a belt of eggs; in either case, they symbolize fertility. ⊠ Agora Çarsısı, opposite visitor center ☎ 232/892–6010 ☜ YTL5 ☽ Daily 8:30–noon and 1–7.

**Isa Bey Cami.** One of the oldest mosques in Turkey dates from 1375. Its jumble of architectural styles suggests a transition between Seljuk and Ottoman design: like later Ottoman mosques, this one has a courtyard, something not found in Seljuk mosques. The structure is built out of "borrowed" stone: marble blocks with Latin inscriptions, Corinthian columns, black-granite columns from the baths at Ephesus, and pieces from the altar of the Temple of Artemis. ⊠ *St. Jean Sok.* ⊙ *Daily 9–6.*

**Meryemana.** The House of the Virgin Mary is becoming an increasingly popular pilgrimage for Catholics. The site received a papal visit in November 2006. A small church was built above a leafy gully on what had been the site of an ancient house believed by many to have been the place where St. John took the mother of Jesus after the crucifixion and from which she ascended to heaven. ⊠ *Off Rte. E87, 5 km (3 mi) south of Ephesus* ⊙ *Daily 7:30–sunset.*

> ## KUŞADASI BEST BETS
>
> **Kuretes Street, Ephesus.** Follow in the footsteps of millions of Roman citizens and celebrity visitors, including St. Paul of Tarsus.
>
> **The Terrace House, Ephesus.** Venture inside this house to catch a glimpse of high-class interior design, circa the 2nd century AD.
>
> **Ephesus Museum, Selçuk.** Monumental archaeological treasures vie with personal items for prize of best artifact.

**St. John Basilica.** The emperor Justinian built this church over a 2nd-century tomb on Ayasoluk Hill, believed by many to have once held the body of St. John the Evangelist. Eleven domes formerly topped the basilica, which rivaled Istanbul's Aya Sofya in scale. The barrel-vaulted roof collapsed after a long-ago earthquake, but the church is still an incredible sight, with its labyrinth of halls and marble courtyards. ⊠ *Entrance off St. Jean Sok., just east of Isa Bey Cami* ☎ *No phone* 🖃 *YTL 5* ⊙ *Daily 8–5.*

**Temple of Artemis.** The fragments of the temple on display at the Isa Bey Mosque are about all you will see of the holy site that drew hordes of pilgrims and was one of the Seven Wonders of the Ancient World. Begun in the 7th century BC, greatly expanded by the wealthy Lydian king Croesus, and redone in marble in the 6th century BC, the temple was burned down by a disgruntled worshipper in 356 BC. Rebuilt by Alexander the Great, it was sacked by Goths in AD 263 and later stripped for materials to build Istanbul's Aya Sofya and Selçuk's St. John Basilica. Today a lone column towering over a scattering of fallen stones in a green field on the Selçuk–Ephesus road is all that remains of a temple that was once four times larger than the Parthenon in Athens.

### EPHESUS
*20 km (12 mi) north of Kuşadası.*

**Ephesus** (*Efes*, in Turkish), the showpiece of Aegean archaeology, is probably the most evocative ancient city in the eastern Mediterranean, and one of the grandest reconstructed ancient sites in the world. Ancient Ephesus grew from a seaside settlement to a powerful trading port and sacred center for the cult of Artemis. Like most Ionian cities in Asia Minor, Ephesus was conquered by the Romans, and eventually became Christian. St. Paul is believed to have written some of his Epistles here and was later driven out by the city's silversmiths for preaching that their models of Diana were not divine. In 431 Ephesus was the scene of the Third Ecumenical Council, during which Mary was proclaimed the Mother of God. Ephesus was doomed by the silting in its harbor. By the 6th century the port had become useless, and the population had shifted to what is now Selçuk.

The road leading to the parking lot passes a 1st-century AD **stadium,** where chariot and horse races were held on a track 712 feet long and where gladiators and wild beasts met in combat before 70,000 spectators. On your left after you enter the site is the 25,000-seat **theater,** still used for music and dance performances each May during the Selçuk Ephesus Festival of Culture and Art. Leading away from the theater toward the ancient port, now a marsh, is the **Arcadian Way.** This 1,710-foot-long street was once lined with shops and covered archways. Only a long line of slender marble columns remains.

In front of the theater is Marble Avenue. Follow it to the beautiful, two-story **Library of Celsus,** a much-photographed building. The library is near Marble Avenue's intersection with the **Street of Kuretes,** a still-impressive thoroughfare named for the college of priests once located there. At this corner is a large house believed to have been a **brothel.** To the right along the street are the multistoried houses of the nobility, with terraces and courtyards, one of which, **Terrace House,** has been renovated to display its large wall frescoes and mosaic floors in situ (separate fee). A block from the brothel is the facade of the **Temple of Hadrian,** with four Corinthian columns and a serpent-headed hydra above the door to keep out evil spirits. The street then forks and opens into a central square that once held the **Prytaneion,** or town hall; the **Nymphaion,** a small temple decked with fountains; and the **Temple of Domitian,** on the south side of the square, which was once a vast sanctuary with a colossal statue of the emperor for whom it was named. All are now a jumble of collapsed walls and columns.

Returning to the Street of Kuretes, turn right to reach the **Odeon,** an intimate semicircle with just a few rows of seats, where spectators would listen to poetry readings and music. Columns mark the northern edge of the state **agora** (market). Beyond, the **Magnesian Gate** (also known as the Manisa Gate), at the end of the street, was the starting point for a caravan trail and a colonnaded road to the Temple of Artemis. ⊠ *Site entry 4 km (2½ mi) west of Selçuk on Selçuk–Ephesus Rd.* ☎ *232/892–6402 or 232/892–6940* ⊑ *YTL 20, Terrace House YTL 15* ⊙ *Daily 8–5:30.*

**Graves of the Seven Sleepers.** According to legend, seven young Christian men hid in a cave to avoid persecution by the Romans in the 3rd century AD. They fell into a sleep that lasted 200 years, waking only after the Byzantine Empire had made Christianity the official state religion. When they died, they were buried here, and the church that you see was built over them. The tombs in the large cemetery are largely from the Byzantine era. ⊠ *South of Sor Sahasi Sok. 3* ⊑ *Free* ⊙ *Dawn–dusk.*

## SHOPPING

The downtown cores of Kuşadası and Selçuk offer excellent shopping opportunities, though prices and quality vary enormously. Generally, Turkey offers an exceptional range of handicrafts in all price ranges, but is most famed for its hand-woven carpets and kilims in a range of sizes and patterns. The finest are made of silk threads, but more common is cotton or wool. Other traditional wares include items with worked brass and copper articles such as large pots and ornate tables, ceramics, marble items, inlaid wooden articles including jewelry boxes and chess sets, or leatherwear fashioned into bags, shoes, or clothing. For a truly exotic gift, take home a genuine *nargile* (hubble-bubble pipe), or a blue glass *boncuk,* a talisman said to ward off the evil eye.

Kuşadası also has several excellent jewelry shops selling gold, precious stones, and modern jewelry and designer watches at competitive prices. Don't forget to haggle over the price of your souvenirs; never pay the first price asked, whatever you want to buy.

**Caravanserail Carpets.** This shop offers a good range of high-quality carpets in all sizes. ⊠ *Okuz Mehmet Pasa Kervansarayi 2, Kuşadaşı* ☎ *256/614–3110.*

**Orient Bazaar.** This store sells both high-class jewelry and carpets. ⊠ *Dag Mh. Yali Cad. 9, Kuşadası* ☎ *256/612–8298.*

## BEACHES

There are many fine beaches around Kuşadası, and these are also served by dolmuş buses.

**Ladies Beach.** The closest beach to town is Ladies Beach. It has sun beds and umbrellas to rent and a range of bars and restaurants, but it does get very busy. ⊠ *2 mi north of cruise port, Kuşadası.*

**Pamucak.** If you head north from Kuşadası, Pamucak has a long, sandy stretch of beach backed by four- and five-star hotels with good water-sports facilities. ⊠ *7 mi north of Kuşadası.*

## WHERE TO EAT

¢   ✗ **Ejder Restaurant.** Mehmet, the owner, manages this place within sight
TURKISH   of the Selçuk aqueduct, and his wife is the sole cook. It may sometimes take a while to get your food, but the traditional kebabs and Turkish specials are well worth the wait. Mehmet takes much pride in the guest-book filled with customers' comments, so add a few lines. ⊠ *Cengiz Topel Cad. 9/E* ☎ *232/892–3296* ▤ *AE, MC, V.*

¢   ✗ **Özurfa.** The focus at this Turkish fast-food spot is kebabs. The Urfa
TURKISH   kebab—spicy, grilled slices of lamb on pita bread—is the house specialty, and the fish kebabs are tasty, too. The location just off Barbaros Hayrettin Caddesi is convenient to the market and a step away from the crowds. ⊠ *Cephane Sok. No 7, Kuşadası* ☎ *256/612–9881* ⊕ *www. ozurfakebabs.com* ▤ *AE, MC, V.*

# LIMASSOL, CYPRUS

Cyprus, once a center for the cult of the Greek goddess Aphrodite, is a modern island nation that retains an essentially Mediterranean character. Its 3,572 square mi (about the size of Connecticut) encompass citrus and olive groves, pine-forested mountains, and some of Europe's cleanest beaches. Cyprus's strategic position as the easternmost island in the Mediterranean Sea has made it subject to regular invasions by powerful empires. Greeks, Phoenicians, Assyrians, Egyptians, Persians, Romans, Byzantines, the Knights Templar, Venetians, Ottomans and the British—all have either ruled or breezed through here. Vestiges of the diverse cultures that have ruled here dot the island, from remnants of Neolithic settlements and ancient Greek and Roman temple sites, to early Christian basilicas and painted Byzantine churches. But Cyprus isn't limited to its architecture and history; there's also a vibrant lifestyle to be explored.

## ESSENTIALS

CURRENCY  The euro (€1 to US$1.36 at this writing). ATMs are common.

HOURS  Museum hours vary; so it pays to check ahead. Generally, museums are closed for lunch and on Sunday. Most ancient monuments are open from dawn to dusk. During the summer—from about mid-June through August—many shops close for an afternoon break from 2 to 5. In tourist areas, shops may stay open late and on Sunday in the summer.

INTERNET  **Marco Polo Bar** ⌂ *10 Antheon St., Pyla Tourist Area, Larnaca* ☎ *24644633* ⊕ *www.marcopolobar.com.*

TELEPHONES  GSM phones work in Cyprus provided that they can operate at 900 or 1800 mh. Public phones accept Telecards, which can be purchased at post offices, banks, souvenir shops, and kiosks.

## COMING ASHORE

Vessels dock at the main port in Limassol. This is a vast commercial enterprise, but has dedicated cruise berths and offers a shuttle to the passenger terminal. Here you'll find refreshments, tourist information, currency exchange, and a taxi station. Some cruise ships also call at Larnaca, but at this writing Limassol is the major cruise port.

If you want to explore independently, take a taxi from the port into the downtown. Service taxis (four- to eight-seat minibuses) link all major towns for a fixed fee; for instance, Limassol to Larnaca costs €9.90 Monday to Saturday and €11.80 on Sunday. Urban taxis are generally very cheap for local travel, but far more expensive than service taxis between towns. Urban taxis have an initial charge of €3.42 (€4.36 at night) and then €0.73 per km in the daytime, €0.85 at night. The waiting time day-rate is €13.66 per hour. Urban Taxi drivers are bound by law to run their meter, rural taxis are not, but if you engage a taxi in town it will be classed as as urban taxi. Buses are cheaper, with Limassol to Larnaca single fare of €5, but they are slower than service taxis.

You can reach many interesting and ancient attractions in the surrounding Cypriot countryside if you hire a vehicle for the day. Car rentals are about €50 for a subcompact manual vehicle. There will be an extra charge for delivery to the port or pick-up in central Limassol.

Cyprus

Mediterranean Sea

THE REPUBLIC OF CYPRUS

NORTHERN CYPRUS

UN Buffer Zone

KARPASIA PENINSULA

Apostolos Andreas Monastery

Cape Andreas

Kantara Castle

Famagusta Bay

Salamis

Famagusta

Varosha

Cape Greco

Ayia Napa

Kyrenia

Range

Bellapais

Kyrenia

St. Hilarion

Nicosia

Dhali

Phikardou

Stavrovouni Monastery

Larnaca

Kition

Lefkara

Lapithos

Lefkara

Kakopetria

Zygi

Cape Kormakiti

Karavostasi

Lefkara

Olympus

Pano Platres

Pitsilia Foothills

Laneia

A1

Akrotiri Bay

Limassol see detail map

St. Nicholas of the Cats

Cape Gata

Kolossi Castle

Temple of Kourion

Episkopi Bay

Morphou Bay

Kokkina

TROODOS MTS.

Omodos

Apollo Hylates

Ayios Neophytos Monastery

Khima

Petra tou Romiou

Paphos

Polis

Kathikas

Tombs of the Kings

AKAMAS PENINSULA

Latchi

Baths of Aphrodite

Khrysokhou Bay

B7

B9

B3

0    20 miles
0    30 km

Limassol

Folk Art Museum

Zinas Kanther

Ay. Andreas

Znonos

Chr. Sozou

El. Palaiologinas

Vasileiou Makedonos

Kariskaki

Mesolongiou

Kolokotroni

Ay. Kapodistria

Gladstonos

G. Malekidi

Ipeirou

Anexartisias

Natpliou

Leontiou Machaira

Agias Fylaxeos

Victoros Hugo

Gladstonos

Navarinou

Megalou Alexandrou

Vragadinou

Thermo-pylon

Kitious Kyprianou

Kanari

Sariptou

Ellados

Enosis

Spartis

Trenis

Eleftherias

Ay. Trifyllis

Limassol Fort

Akrotiri Bay

Ayias Zonis

Gladstonos

Chr. Chatziprantou

Kitiou Kyprianou

Ioannou

Heroon

Tsiflsa

Spartis

Ay. Aravuxou

0    1/8 mi
0    1/8 km

# EXPLORING CYPRUS FROM LIMASSOL

## LIMASSOL AND VICINITY

A major commercial port, cruise-ship port of call, and wine-making center on the south coast, Limassol, 75 km (47 mi) from Nicosia, is a bustling, cosmopolitan town. Luxury hotels, apartments, and guest houses stretch along 12 km (7 mi) of seafront. In the center, the elegant, modern shops of Makarios Avenue contrast with those of the old part of town, where local handicrafts prevail.

**Apollo Hylates** (*Sanctuary of Apollo of the Woodlands*). This impressive archaeological site stands 3 km (2 mi) west of the Temple of Kourion. ✉ *Main Paphos Rd.* ☎ *25934250* 💰 *€1.70* ⏱ *June–Aug., daily 8–7:30; Apr., May, Sept., and Oct. 8–6; Nov.–May, daily 8–5.*

**Folk Art Museum.** For a glimpse of Cypriot folklore, the collection includes national costumes and fine examples of weaving and other crafts. ✉ *Agiou Andreou 253* ☎ *25362303* 💰 *€0.85* ⏱ *Oct.–May, Mon.–Wed. and Fri. 8:30–1:30 and 3–5:30, Thurs. 8:30–1:30; June–Sept., Mon.–Wed. and Fri. 8:30–1:30 and 4–6:30, Thurs. 8:30–1:30.*

★ **Kolossi Castle.** This Crusader fortress of the Knights of St. John was constructed in the 13th century and rebuilt in the 15th. ✉ *Road to Paphos* ☎ *25934907* 💰 *€1.70* ⏱ *June–Aug., daily 8–7:30; Apr., May, Sept., and Oct. daily 8–6; Nov.–Mar, daily 8–5.*

★ **Limassol Fort.** The 14th-century fort was built on the site of a Byzantine fortification. Richard the Lion-Hearted married Berengaria of Navarre and crowned her Queen of England here in 1191. The **Cyprus Medieval Museum** in the castle displays medieval armor and relics. ✉ *Near Old Port* ☎ *25305419* 💰 *€3.40* ⏱ *Mon.–Sat. 9–5, Sun. 10–1.*

**St. Nicholas of the Cats.** This peaceful convent is seemingly occupied by cats instead of nuns. According to legend, the cats are descendants of the animals St. Helena imported in the 4th century AD to whittle down the area's snake population. Their feline forebears must have done a good job, because today the dozens of cats in residence seem more inclined to laze in the sun than anything else. The little peninsula past the Akrotiri military base is still called Cape Gata (She-Cat). ✉ *Edge of Akrotiri village.*

**Fodor's Choice** **The Temple of Kourion.** The Curium, west of Limassol, has Greek and ★ Roman ruins. Classical and Shakespearean plays are sometimes staged in the **amphitheater.** Next to the theater is the **Villa of Eustolios,** a summer house built by a wealthy Christian. Nearby is the partially rebuilt **Roman stadium.** ✉ *Main Paphos Rd.* ☎ *25934250* 💰 *€1.70* ⏱ *June–Aug., daily 8–7:30; Apr., May, Sept., and Oct. 8–6; Nov.–Mar, daily 8–5.*

## LARNACA

*51 km (32 mi) southeast of Nicosia, 66 km (41 mi) east of Limassol.*

The seaside resort with its own airport has a flamboyant Whitsuntide celebration, called Cataklysmos, as well as fine beaches, a palm-fringed seaside promenade, and a modern harbor.

**Ayios Lazarus** (*Church of Lazarus*). In the town center stands one of the island's more important churches, resplendent with icons. It has a fascinating crypt containing Lazarus's sarcophagus. ⊠ *Plateia Agiou Lazarou* ☎ *24652498* ▣ *Free* ⊙ *Daily 7:30–5:30.*

★ **Hala Sultan Tekke.** On the edge of Salt Lake south of Larnaca, a mosque stands in an oasis of palm trees guarding the burial place of the prophet Muhammad's aunt, Umm Haram; it's an important Muslim shrine. ⊠ *Salt Lake* ▣ *Free* ⊙ *July and Aug., daily 8–7:30; Apr., May, Sept., and Oct., daily 8–6; Nov.– Mar., daily 8–5.*

---

### CYPRUS BEST BETS

**Visit the mosaics of Paphos.** Some of the finest Roman workmanship yet uncovered, they are an awe-inspiring sight.

**Enjoy the galleries at Larnaca Museum.** The museum is stuffed with ancient Greek and Roman artifacts, from monumental statues to precious jewelry to mundane kitchen utensils.

**Browse for souvenirs at Lefkara.** This whitewashed village has a vibrant Greek heartbeat.

---

**Kition.** The old Larnaca of Biblical times was one of the most important ancient city-kingdoms. Architectural remains of temples date from the 13th century BC. ⊠ *Kyman St., north of Larnaca Museum* ☎ *24304115* ▣ *€1.70* ⊙ *Mon., Tues., Thurs., Fri. 8–2:30, Wed. 8–5.*

**Larnaca Museum.** In the marina district, this museum displays treasures, including outstanding sculptures and Bronze Age seals. ⊠ *Kimon and Kilkis Sts.* ☎ *24630169* ▣ *€1.70* ⊙ *Tues., Thurs., and Fri. 8–3, Wed. 8–5, Sat. 9–3.*

**Medieval Museum.** This museum is in a 17th-century Turkish fort, and has finds from Hala Sultan Tekke and Kition. ⊠ *Within sight of marina on seafront* ☎ *24322710* ▣ *€1.70* ⊙ *June–Aug., weekdays 9–7:30; Sept.–May, weekdays 9–5.*

**Panayia Angeloktistos.** The 11th-century church, 11 km (7 mi) south of Larnaca, has extraordinary Byzantine wall mosaics that date from the 6th and 7th centuries. ⊠ *Rte. B4, Kiti* ☎ *24424646* ▣ *Free* ⊙ *Daily 7:30–noon and 2–4.*

**Pierides Collection.** This private assemblage contains more than 3,000 pieces distinguished by its Bronze Age terra-cotta figures. ⊠ *Paul Zenon Kitieos St. 4, near Lord Byron St.* ☎ *24814555* ▣ *€3* ⊙ *Mon.–Thurs. 9–4, Fri. and Sat. 9–1.*

**Stavrovouni** (*Mountain of the Cross*). On a mountain 40 km (25 mi) west of Larnaca stands this monastery. It was founded by St. Helena in AD 326; the present buildings date from the 19th century. The views from here are splendid. Ideally, you should visit the monastery in a spirit of pilgrimage rather than sightseeing, out of respect for the monks. Male visitors are allowed inside the monastery daily sunrise–sunset, except between noon and 3 (or between noon and 2, September–March).

## LEFKARA
*40 km (25 mi) northwest of Larnaca, 64 km (40 mi) north of Limassol.*

Some 40 km west of Larnaca, this picturesque village—one of the prettiest in Cyprus—is best known for its lace: Lefkaritika has been woven by hand here for centuries. Much of it is indeed beautiful, and most shopkeepers are willing to bargain. But considerably more evocative is the village itself, clustered on two hills and split between an upper portion, Kato Lefkara, and lower portion, Pano Lefkara. The tiny streets open up to a small plaza in front of the Church of the Holy Cross in Pano Lefkara, with a stupendous view of the surrounding sun-drenched hills.

## TROODOS MOUNTAINS
*20 km (25 mi) north of Limassol.*

These mountains, which rise to 6,500 feet, have shady cedar and pine forests and cool springs. Small, painted Byzantine churches in the Troodos and Pitsilia foothills are rich examples of a rare indigenous art form. **Asinou Church,** near the village of Nikitari, and **Agios Nikolaos tis Stegis** (St. Nicholas of the Roof), south of Kakopetria, are especially noteworthy. In winter skiers take over the mountains; **Platres,** in the foothills of Mt. Olympus, is the principal resort.

**Kykkos.** At this monastery, founded in 1100, the prized icon of the Virgin is reputed to have been painted by St. Luke. On the southern slopes of the Troodos is the village of Omodos, one of the prettiest in Cyprus, with whitewashed villas, narrow streets, and a broad central square. Laneia is not as beautiful, but its many artisans and craftspeople make it worth a detour.

## PETRA TOU ROMIOU
*20 km (12 mi) west of Limassol.*

The legendary **birthplace of Aphrodite**—Greek goddess of love and beauty—is just off the main road between Limassol and Petra. Signs in Greek and English identify the offshore rock that is viewed from the shoreline. Park in the lot and take the passageway under the highway to the large pebble beach.

## PAPHOS
*68 km (42 mi) west of Limassol.*

In the west of the island Paphos combines a seaside with stellar archaeological sites and a buzzing nightlife. Since the late 1990s it has attracted some of the most lavish resorts on the island. The modern center has a pleasant leisure harbor anchored by a medieval fortress.

**Ayios Neophytos Monastery.** The hermit and scholar Neophytos settled at the site of this monastery in 1159, carving a home for himself out of the rock. Known in his time as the leading critic of Richard the Lion-Hearted and the Byzantine tax collectors, today he is best known for what became a series of grottoes hewn from the hillside rock and the evocative religious frescoes—some actually painted by Neophytos—they contain. The monastery itself, with no more than a half-dozen or so monks, is below the grottoes. ⊠ *10 km (6 mi) north of Paphos.*

★ **Byzantine Museum.** There are notable 6th-century mosaics and icons in the Byzantine Museum. ⊠ *5 Andreas Ioannou St.* ☎ *26931393* ⊠ *€1.71* ⊗ *Weekdays 9–3, Sat. 9–1.*

**Paphos District Archaeological Museum.** The local museum displays pottery, jewelry, and statuettes from Cyprus's Roman villas. ⊠ *43 Grivas Dighenis Ave., Ktima* ☎ *26306215* ⊠ *€1.71* ⊗ *Tues.–Fri. 8–3, Sat. 9–3.*

**Paphos Fort.** The squat 16th-century fortification guards the entrance to the harbor; from the rooftop there's a lovely view. ⊠ *Paphos* ⊠ *€1.71* ⊗ *June–Aug., daily 8–7:30; Apr., May, Sept., and Oct., daily 8–6; Nov.– Mar., daily 8–5.*

Fodor's Choice ★ **Roman Mosaics.** Don't miss the elaborate mosaics in the **Roman Villa of Theseus,** the **House of Dionysos,** and the **House of Aion.** The impressive site is an easy walk from the harbor. ⊠ *Kato Paphos (New Paphos), near harbor* ☎ *26306217* ⊠ *€3.42* ⊗ *June–Aug., daily 8–7:30; Apr., May, and Sept., daily 8–6; Nov.–Mar., daily 8–5.*

★ **Tombs of the Kings.** An early necropolis, this structure date from 300 BC. The coffin niches are empty, but a powerful sense of mystery remains. ⊠ *Kato Paphos (New Paphos)* ☎ *26306295* ⊠ *€1.71* ⊗ *June–Aug., daily 8–7:30; Apr., May, Sept., and Oct., 8–6; Nov.–Mar., daily 8–5.*

## SHOPPING

Cyprus has a great range of handicrafts. Lace and embroidery from Lefkara are still handmade and are widely available. Other items to look for are basketware, ceramics, blown glass, carved wood (the best being olive wood), hand-tied cotton rugs, silverware, and copperware, including beautiful decorative urns. Leather and shoes are excellent value. Museums sell copies of ancient artifacts, and the Orthodox monasteries offer Byzantine icons. Edibles include superb olive oil, honey, and delicious wine.

Shopping in the villages of Lefkara, Omodos, and Laneia is a pleasure, with numerous galleries and shops set along the whitewashed alleyways. In Limassol the main shopping street, Makarios Avenue, has a range of modern boutiques.

**KEO Winery.** The large winery just west of Limassol, welcomes visitors and gives tours weekdays at 10. You can buy KEO wines at many outlets on the island. ⊠ *Roosevelt Ave., toward new port* ☎ *25853100.*

**Lemba Pottery.** This store offers handmade pottery with vibrant glazes. ⊠ *Elefttherias St. 18, Paphos* ☎ *2670822.*

## BEACHES

Cyprus has numerous excellent beaches, but they get busy between June and September with vacationers from across Europe.

**Ladies Mile.** This is the closest beach to the cruise port. ⊠ *Near new port, Limassol.*

## WHERE TO EAT

$ ✕ **Militzis.** This restaurant is popular with locals for its homemade *meze*
MEDITERRANEAN (hot and cold small plates) and other Cypriot specialties. ⊠ *42 Pigiale Pasa Ave., Larnaca* ☎ *24655867* ⊟ *AE, DC, MC, V.*

$ ✕ **Porta.** A varied menu of international and Cypriot dishes, such as
MEDITERRANEAN *foukoudha* barbecue (grilled strips of steak) and trout baked in prawn and mushroom sauce, is served in this (completely) renovated donkey stable. On many nights you'll be entertained by soft live music. ⊠ *17 Yenethliou Mitella, Old Castle, Limassol* ☎ *25360339* ⊟ *MC, V.*

# MYKONOS, GREECE

Put firmly on the map by Jackie O, Mykonos has become one of the most popular of the Aegean islands. Although the dry, rugged island is one of the smallest of the Cyclades—16 km (10 mi) by 11 km (7 mi)—travelers from all over the world are drawn to its sandy beaches, its thatched windmills, and its picturesque, whitewashed port town of Mykonos, whose cubical two-story houses and churches have been long celebrated as some of the best examples of classic Cycladic architecture. Here backpackers rub elbows with millionaires, and the atmosphere is decidedly cosmopolitan. Happily, the islanders seem to have been able to fit cosmopolitan New Yorkers or Londoners gracefully into their way of life. For almost 1,000 years neighboring Delos Island was the religious and political center of the Aegean and host every four years to the Delian games, the region's greatest festival. This is a must-visit site for anyone interested in ancient history.

### ESSENTIALS

CURRENCY The euro (€1 to US$1.36 at this writing). ATMs are common.

HOURS Museums are generally open from 9 to 5, but many are closed on Monday. Shops are open daily in the summer (9 to noon or 1, reopening at 4 or 5 until 9 on weekdays and 9 to 6 on Saturday).

INTERNET **Mykonos Cyber Cafe** (⊠ *26 M Axioti St.* ☎ *22890/27–684*) is open daily from 9 AM to 10 PM, and offers rates by the hour or per 15 minutes.

TELEPHONES Tri-band GSM phones work in Greece. You can buy prepaid phone cards at telecom shops, news vendors, and tobacconists in all towns and cities for local or international calls. Vodafone is the leading mobile telecom company. OTE is the national domestic provider. Calls can be made at OTE offices and paid for after completion.

### COMING ASHORE

The main cruise port is about a mile north of Mykonos Town (on the other side of a very steep hill). Shuttle buses transport passengers to town, where you can catch buses or take a taxi to the beaches. If you anchor offshore and are tendered to the island, you'll alight at the old port in the town itself.

Because the island is so small, journey times anywhere are short. There is a cheap (fares between €1.40 and €1.70) and reliable bus service from the town to all the main beaches, but services can get crowded in July and August. Small boats called *caïques* also act as taxis, taking

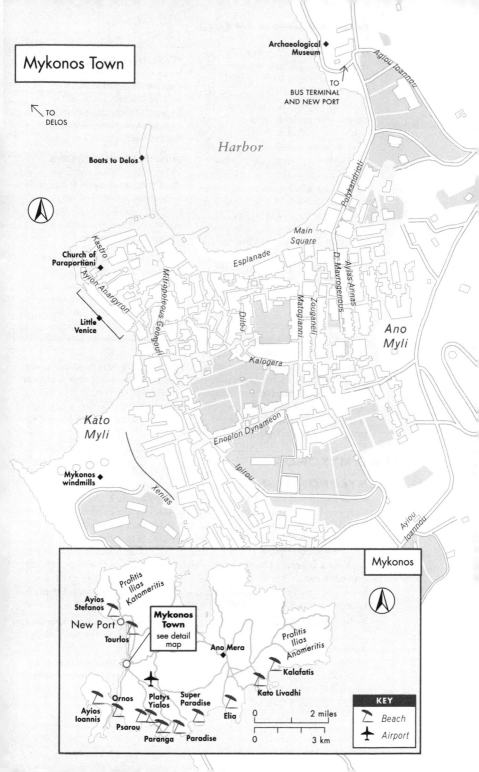

people from the old port to the various beaches. These are reliable and popular services. Commercial taxis operate on fixed fare routes, but the taxi system is easily overburdened when a large ship is in port. These are posted at the taxi rank in Mavro Square, just inland from the old harbor.

Most travel offices in Mykonos Town run guided tours to Delos that cost about €33, including boat transportation and entry fee. Alternatively, take one of the caïques that visit Delos daily from the old port: the round-trip costs about €10, and entry to the site (with no guide) is €6. They leave between 8:30 AM and 1 PM, and return noon to 2 PM.

With reliable transport services, a car rental isn't absolutely necessary, but if you want to do some exploring on your own you can rent an ATV or scooter for two people in town for about €20 to €30, depending on time of the season; motor scooters are not recommended for inexperienced riders (each year people are seriously injured because they don't know how to ride the many hills and narrow roads of Mykonos). A rental car costs about €40 to €50 per day for a subcompact or Smartcar.

> **MYKONOS BEST BETS**
>
> **Explore Ancient Delos.** Delos was the religious center of the Aegean. Large sections of the city have been excavated, revealing treasures magnificent and humble.
>
> **Stroll the streets of Mykonos Town.** Cosmopolitan and bohemian, Mykonos is one of the most fashionable places to be during the European summer, yet the alluring narrow streets retain a vibrant Greek character.
>
> **Spend some time at the beach.** The town sleeps during the heat of the afternoon, so choose one of the island's famous beaches—from fun to hedonism—there's something for every taste.

# EXPLORING MYKONOS

## MYKONOS TOWN

If your ship remains in port late (often the case in Myknos), the best time to visit the central harbor is in the cool of the evening, when the islanders promenade along the esplanade to meet friends and visit the numerous cafés. By the open-air fish market, Petros the Pelican preens and cadges eats. In the 1950s a group of migrating pelicans passed over Mykonos, leaving behind a single exhausted bird; Vassilis the fisherman nursed it back to health, and locals say that the pelican in the harbor is the original Petros, though you'll see several lurking around the fish tavernas right off the esplanade.

**Archaeological Museum.** The museum affords insight into the intriguing history of the Delos shrine. The museum houses Delian funerary sculptures discovered on the neighboring islet of Rhenea, many with scenes of mourning. The most significant work from Mykonos is a 7th-century BC *pithos* (storage jar), showing the Greeks in the Trojan horse and the sack of the city. ⊠ *Ayios Stefanos road, between boat dock and town* ☎ *22890/22325* 🎟 *€3* ۞ *Wed.–Mon. 8:30–2:30.*

★ **Church of Paraportiani.** Mykoniots claim that exactly 365 churches and chapels dot their landscape, one for each day of the year. The most famous of these is Our Lady of the Postern Gate. The sloping, whitewashed conglomeration of four chapels, mixing Byzantine and vernacular idioms, has been described as "a confectioner's dream gone mad," and its position on a promontory facing the sea sets off the unique architecture. ⊠ *Ayion Anargyron, near folk museum.*

★ **Little Venice.** Many of the early ship's captains built distinguished houses directly on the sea here, with wooden balconies overlooking the water. Today this neighborhood, at the southwest end of the port, is full of bars and shops. Many of these fine old houses are now elegant bars or cabarets specializing in sunset drinks, or else they have been turned into shops. Every night crowds head to nearby cafés and clubs, many found a block inland from Little Venice. ⊠ *Mitropoleos Georgouli.*

**Mando Mavrogenous Square** (*Taxi Square*). A bust of Mando Mavroyennis, the island heroine, stands on a pedestal in the town's main square. In the 1821 War of Independence the Mykoniots, known for their seafaring skills, volunteered an armada of 24 ships, and in 1822, when the Ottomans later landed a force on the island, Mando and her soldiers forced them back to their ships. After independence, a scandalous love affair caused her exile to Paros, where she died.

**Mykonos windmills.** Overlooking the town from a high hill are the famous windmills, echoes of a time when wind power was used to grind the island's grain.

## ANO MERA
*8 km (5 mi) east of Mykonos Town.*

Interesting little tavernas line the central square of Ano Mera, which is the "second city" of Mykonos, in the hills near the center of the island.

**Monastery of the Panayia Tourliani.** Monastery buffs should head to Ano Mera, a village in the central part of the island, where the Monastery of the Panayia Tourliani, founded in 1580 and dedicated to the protectress of Mykonos, stands in the central square. Its massive baroque iconostasis (altar screen), made in 1775 by Florentine artists, has small icons carefully placed amid the wooden structure's painted green, red, and gold-leaf flowers. At the top are carved figures of the apostles and large icons depicting New Testament scenes. The hanging incense holders with silver molded dragons holding red eggs in their mouths show an Eastern influence. In the hall of the monastery, an interesting **museum** displays embroideries, liturgical vestments, and wood carvings. ⊠ *Central Square* ☏ *0289/71249* ⊙ *By appointment only; call in advance.*

## DELOS
FodorśChoice  *25-minute boat ride southwest from Mykonos Town.*

★ Why did Delos become the religious and political center of the Aegean? One answer is that Delos provided the safest anchorage for vessels sailing between the mainland and the shores of Asia. But the myth that the Greek deities Artemis and Apollo were born here meant it had a powerful appeal to the ancients. Later the island became the headquarters and bank for the Delian League, but the island was sacked during Roman rule and never recovered.

On the left from the harbor is the **Agora of the Competialists** (circa 150 BC), members of Roman guilds, mostly freedmen and slaves from Sicily who worked for Italian traders. They worshipped the *Lares Competales,* the Roman "crossroads" gods; in Greek they were known as Hermaistai, after the god Hermes, protector of merchants and the crossroads. The **Sacred Way,** east of the agora, was the route, during the holy Delian festival, of the procession to the sanctuary of Apollo.

The **Propylaea,** at the end of the Sacred Way, were once a monumental white marble gateway with three portals framed by four Doric columns. Beyond the Propylaea is the **Sanctuary of Apollo.** Though little of it remains today, when the Propylaea were built in the mid-2nd century BC the sanctuary was crowded with altars, statues, and temples—three of them to Apollo. Inside the sanctuary and to the right is the **House of the Naxians,** a 7th- to 6th-century BC structure with a central colonnade. Dedications to Apollo were stored in this shrine.

One of the most evocative sights on Delos is the 164-foot-long **Avenue of the Lions.** These are replicas; the originals are in the museum. The five Naxian marble beasts crouch on their haunches, their forelegs stiffly upright, vigilant guardians of the Sacred Lake. They are the survivors of a line of at least nine lions, erected in the second half of the 7th century BC by the Naxians. One, removed in the 17th century, now guards the Arsenal of Venice. The **Archaeological Museum** is also on the road south of the gymnasium; it contains most of the antiquities found in excavations on the island: monumental statues of young men and women, stelae, reliefs, masks, and ancient jewelry.

Immediately to the right of the museum is a small **Sanctuary of Dionysos,** erected about 300 BC; outside it is one of the more boggling sights of ancient Greece: several monuments dedicated to Apollo by the winners of the choral competitions of the Delian festivals, each decorated with a huge phallus, emblematic of the orgiastic rites that took place during the Dionysian festivals.

Beyond the path that leads to the southern part of the island is the **ancient theater,** built in the early 3rd century BC in the elegant residential quarter inhabited by Roman bankers and Egyptian and Phoenician merchants. Their one- and two-story houses were typically built around a central courtyard, sometimes with columns on all sides. Floor mosaics of snakes, panthers, birds, dolphins, and Dionysus channeled rainwater into cisterns below; the best-preserved can be seen in the **House of the Dolphins,** the **House of the Masks,** and the **House of the Trident.** A flight of steps goes up 368 feet to the summit of **Mt. Kynthos,** on whose slope the myths say Apollo was born. ☎ *22890/22259* ✉ *€6* ⊙ *Apr.–Oct., Tues.–Sun. 8:30–3.*

## SHOPPING

Mykonos Town has excellent shopping, with many high-class boutiques aimed at the well-heeled sitting side by side with moderately priced shops selling Greek crafts and fashionable clothing. It's a real pleasure for retail junkies, with a seemingly limitless array of choices. Almost every surface of the narrow alleyways is festooned with cotton clothing or cheerful ceramics, leather shoes, or bars of olive-oil soap. Artists are drawn here as much by the clientele as by the beauty and light of the Aegean, so galleries are numerous. The town is especially famed for its jewelry, from simple strings of colourful beads to precious stones in designer settings. Upscale duty-free jewelry shops also abound.

**Anna Gelou.** The eponymous shop, started by her mother 50 years ago, carries Anna's authentic copies of traditional handmade embroideries, all using white Greek cotton, in clothing, tablecloths, curtains, and such. ⊠ *Ayion Anargyron 16, Little Venice* ☎ *22890/26825.*

**Ilias LALAoUNIS.** This store is known internationally for jewelry based on classic ancient designs, especially Greek; the shop is as elegant as a museum. ⊠ *Polykandrioti 14, near taxis* ☎ *22890/22444* ⊕ *www.lalaounismykonos.com.*

**Loco.** This store sells cotton and linen summer wear in lovely colors. The Marla knits are from the family factory in Athens. ⊠ *Kalogera 29 N.* ☎ *22890/23682.*

**Nikoletta.** Mykonos used to be a weaver's island with 500 looms. Only two of these shops remain. In Nikoletta, Nikoletta Xidakis sells her skirts, shawls, and bedspreads made of local wool. ⊠ *Little Venice.*

**Parthenis.** This store was opened by Dimitris Parthenis in 1978, but now features designs by his daughter Orsalia, all showcased in a large Mykonian-style building on the up side of Alefkandra Square in Little Venice. The collection of cotton and silk garments (mostly in black and white) is popular for their soft draping and clinging wrap effect. ⊠ *Alefkandra Sq.* ☎ *22890/23080* ⊕ *www.orsalia-parthenis.gr.*

**Precious Tree.** This tiny shop is aglitter in gems elegantly set at the workshop in Athens. ⊠ *Dilou 2* ☎ *2289024685.*

## ACTIVITIES

There's a full range of water sports on offer in Mykonos, and many concessions operate directly on the beach (from May through September). Windsurfing is particularly popular because of the prevailing *meltemi* winds that blow across the island throughout the summer. The windy northern beaches on Ornos Bay are best for this.

**Aphrodite Beach Hotel.** This hotel has good water sports open even to nonguests. ⊠ *Kalafati Beach* ☎ *28890/71367* ⊕ *www.aphrodite-mykonos.gr.*

**Mykonos Diving Center.** This scuba operation has a variety of courses and excursions at 30 locations. ⊠ *Psarou* ☎ *22890/24808* ⊕ *www.dive.gr.*

## BEACHES

There is a beach for every taste in Mykonos. Beaches near Mykonos Town, within walking distance, are **Tourlos** and **Ayios Ioannis**. **Ayios Stefanos,** about a 45-minute walk from Mykonos Town, has a minigolf course, water sports, restaurants, and umbrellas and lounge chairs for rent. The south coast's **Psarou**, protected from wind by hills and surrounded by restaurants, offers a wide selection of water sports and is often called the finest beach. Nearby **Platys Yialos,** popular with families, is also lined with restaurants and dotted with umbrellas for rent. **Ornos** is also perfect for families.

**Paranga, Paradise, Super Paradise,** and **Elia** are all on the southern coast of the island, and are famously nude, though getting less so. **Super Paradise** is half-gay, half-straight, and swings at night. All have tavernas on the beach. At the easternmost end of the south shores is **Kalafatis,** known for package tours, and between Elia and Kalafatis there's a remote beach at **Kato Livadhi,** which can be reached by road.

## WHERE TO EAT

$$$
GREEK

✕ **Chez Maria's.** If you want a quiet ambience, head to this decades-old restaurant set in the lovely candlelit garden of an aristocratic mansion. Usually the first seating is travelers, the second Mykonians. Sea-urchin salad (with famed urchins from the isle of Delos) is available in season, and not on the menu; the little cheese pies are made with local cheese. The main courses feature local fish and meat. For dessert, try a seasonal delight: the King's Sigh—fresh figs stuffed with almonds, honey, and cream. ⊠ *Kalogera 30* ☎ *22890/27565* ✍ *chezmarias@hotmail.com* ⊟ *AE, MC, V.*

$$
SEAFOOD

✕ **Sea Satin Market–Caprice.** On the far tip of land below the windmills, the restaurant sprawls out onto a seaside terrace and even onto the sand. Prices vary according to weight. Shellfish is a specialty, and everything is beautifully presented. If the wind is up, the waves sing. Live music and dancing add to the liveliness in summer. ⊠ *At seaside under windmills* ☎ *22890/24676* ⊟ *AE, MC, V.*

# PIRAEUS, GREECE (FOR ATHENS)

If you come to Athens in search of gleaming white temples, you may be aghast to find that much of the city has melded into what appears to be a viscous concrete mass. Amid the sprawl and squalor, though, the ancient city gives up its treasures. Lift your eyes 200 feet above the city to the Parthenon, and you behold architectural perfection that has not been surpassed in 2,500 years. Today this shrine of classical form, this symbol of Western civilization and political thought, dominates a 21st-century boomtown. To experience Athens fully is to understand the essence of Greece: tradition juxtaposed with a modernity that the ancients would strain to recognize but would heartily endorse. Ancient Athens is certainly the lure for the millions of visitors to the city, but since the late 1990s, inspired by the 2004 Olympics, the people have gone far toward transforming Athens into a sparkling modern metropolis.

## ESSENTIALS

CURRENCY    The euro (€1 to US$1.36 at this writing). ATMs are common.

HOURS    Most stores are open from 9 to 9 on weekdays, from 9 to 6 on Saturday. Museums are generally open from 9 to 5, but many are closed on Monday.

INTERNET    **C@fe 4U** (✉ *44 Ippokratous St.* ☎ *210/361–1981*) is close to Syntagma Square. It is open 24 hours a day and serves drinks and snacks. You'll find both terminals and Wi-Fi service.

TELEPHONES    Tri-band GSM phones work in Greece. You can buy prepaid phone cards at telecom shops, news vendors, and tobacconists in all towns and cities. Phone cards can be used for local or international calls. Vodafone is the leading mobile telecom company. OTE is the national domestic provider. Calls can be made at OTE offices and paid for after completion.

## COMING ASHORE

Piraeus is the port of Athens, 11 km (7 mi) southwest of the city center, and is itself the third-largest city in Greece, with a population of about 500,000. In anticipation of a flood of visitors during the 2004 Olympics, the harbor district was given a general sprucing up. The cruise port has 12 berths, and the terminal has duty-free shops, information, and refreshments.

The fastest and cheapest way to get to Athens from Piraeus is to take the metro. Line 1 (Green Line) reaches the downtown Athens stops most handy to tourists, including Platia Victorias, near the National Archaeological Museum; Omonia Square; Monastiraki, in the old Turkish bazaar; and Thission, near the ancient Agora. The trip takes 25 to 30 minutes. The Piraeus metro station is off Akti Kallimasioti on the main harbor, a 20-minute walk from the cruise port.

A flat fare covering all forms of public transport within central Athens and valid for 1 hour 30 minutes is €1. A day pass valid on all buses, trams, metro, and suburban railway is €3. Passes should be validated when first used, and are then valid for 24 hours from that time.

KTEL buses run every 30 minutes between the port and the Mavromateon terminal in central Athens, from about 5:30 AM until 9:30 PM, and cost €2.20.

Taxis wait outside the terminal entrance. Taxis into the city are not necessarily quicker than public transport. Taxis rates begin at €1, then €0.48 per km (½ mi), and there are numerous surcharges. A taxi takes longer than the metro because of traffic, and costs around €12–€15. Athens taxi drivers have a reputation for overcharging passengers, so make sure the meter is switched on. It is common practice for drivers to pick up other passengers if there is room in the cab. These extra passengers will also pay the full fare for the trip. Radio taxis also have an additional charge of €3 to €5 for the pick-up.

The best way to get quickly acquainted with Athens is to opt for a ride on the "Athens Sightseeing Public Bus Line," or Bus 400, which stops at all the city's main sights. Those buses run every 30 minutes, from 7:30 AM to 9 PM, and tickets cost €5. The full tour takes 90 minutes,

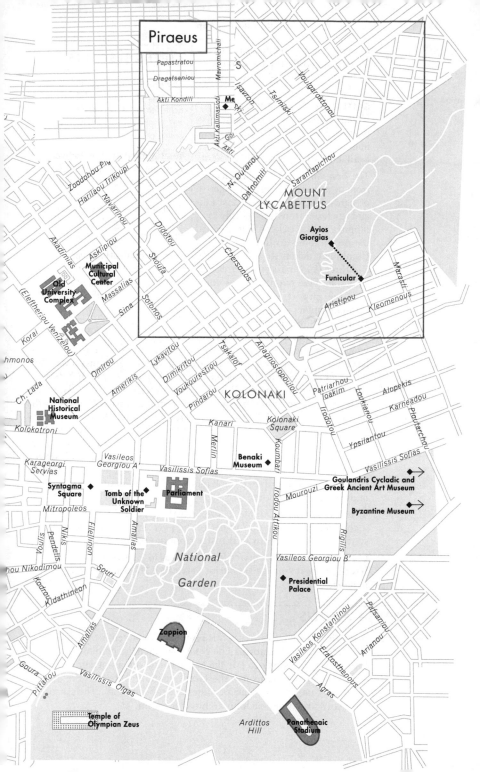

but you can hop on and off as you please. Bus 400 stops are marked by bright-blue waist-high pillars set on the city streets.

### GETTING TO THE AIRPORT

If you choose not to purchase airport transfers from your cruise line, there are inexpensive options available.

The best way to get to the airport from downtown Athens is by metro or light-rail. Single tickets cost €6, and include transfers within 90 minutes of the ticket's initial validation to bus, trolley, or tram. Combined tickets for two (€10) and three (€15) passengers are also available. Five express buses connect the airport with the metro (Ethniki Amyna and Dafni station), Syntagma Square, Kifissia, Kifissos Bus Station, and Piraeus (from which it is a short taxi ride to the port). Express buses leave the arrivals level of the airport every 10 minutes and operate 24 hours a day. Bus X95 will take you to Syntagma Square (Amalias Avenue); X94 goes to the bus terminus at the Ethniki Amyna metro stop (Line 3), which will get you into Syntagma within 10 minutes. Bus X97 goes to the Dafni metro stop; X93 brings voyagers to the dusty Kifissos intercity bus station. Bus X96 goes directly to Piraeus. The Attiki Odos and the expansion of the city's network of bus lanes has made travel times more predictable, and on a good day the X94 can get you to Ethniki Amyna in 40 minutes. Tickets cost €3.20 for any of these buses. Once in the city, pick up Metro line 1 for Pireaus and a 20-minute walk or short taxi transfer to the port.

Taxis are readily available at the arrivals level of the Athens airport; it costs an average of €35 to get to the port. Private limousine service starts at €100 for one-way transfer from the airport to the port.

**Limousines Limousine Service** (📠 210/970–6416 ⊕ www.limousine-service.gr). **Royal Prestige Limousine Service** (📠 210/988–3221 ⊕ www.limousineservices.gr).

> ### ATHENS BEST BETS
>
> **The Parthenon.** Regarded as the pinnacle of ancient architectural achievement, this classical temple has inspired poets, artists, and architects.
>
> **The National Archaeological Museum.** A wide-ranging collection covers Greece's ancient history, from the splendid finds Schliemann excavated at Mycenae to the monumental statues that graced the cities of Attica.
>
> **New Acropolis Museum.** This dazzling new museum at the base of the Acropolis is a welcome development for both Athens and Greece.

## EXPLORING ATHENS

Fodor'sChoice   **Acropolis.** The massive Acropolis remains an emblem of the glories of
★   classical Greek civilization. The great Panathenaic temple that crowns the rise has the power to stir the heart as few other ancient relics can. The term *akropolis* (to use the Greek spelling) refers to the ancient Athenian "upper city" that occupies the tablelike hill. The Akropolis has many structures, each an architectural gem.

The Propylaea is a typical ancient gate, an imposing structure designed to instill proper reverence in worshippers as they crossed from the temporal world into the spiritual world of the Acropolis sanctuary. The Propylaea was used as a garrison during the Turkish period; in 1656 a powder magazine there was struck by lightning, causing much damage; and the Propylaea was again damaged during the Venetian siege of 1687. The view from the inner porch of the Propylaea is stunning: the Parthenon is suddenly revealed in its full glory, framed by the columns.

Designed by Kallikrates, the **Temple of Athena Nike**, or Wingless Victory, was built in 427–424 BC to celebrate peace with Persia. The best sections of the temple's frieze were whisked away to the British Museum two centuries ago and replaced with cement copies.

At the loftiest point of the Acropolis is the **Parthenon,** the architectural masterpiece conceived by Pericles and executed between 447 and 438 BC by the brilliant sculptor Pheidias. Although dedicated to the goddess Athena, the Parthenon was primarily the treasury of the Delian League, an ancient alliance of cities. For the populace, the Parthenon remained Athena's holiest temple.

If the Parthenon is the masterpiece of Doric architecture, the **Erechtheion** is undoubtedly that of the more graceful Ionic order. Here it was that the contest between Poseidon and Athena took place for possession of the city. Athena was declared the winner, and the city was named after her. The Erechtheion was completed in 406 BC. ⊠ *Dionyssiou Areopagitou, Acropolis* ☎ *210/321–4172 or 210/321–0219* ✉ *Joint ticket for all Unification of Archaeological Sites €12* ☽ *Apr.–Oct., daily 8–7:30; Nov.–Mar., daily 8–3* Ⓜ *Acropolis.*

★ **Ancient Agora.** This marketplace was the hub of ancient Athenian life. Besides administrative buildings, it was surrounded by the schools, theaters, workshops, houses, stores, and market stalls of a thriving town. Look for markers indicating the circular Tholos, the seat of Athenian government; the Mitroon, shrine to Rhea, the mother of gods, and the state archives; the Bouleterion, where the Council met; the Monument of Eponymous Heroes, the Agora's information center; and the Sanctuary of the Twelve Gods, a shelter for refugees and the point from which all distances were measured.

Prominent on the grounds is the **Stoa of Attalos II,** a two-story building that holds the Museum of Agora Excavations. It was designed as a retail complex and erected in the 2nd century BC by Attalos, a king of Pergamum. The stoa was reconstructed in 1953–56. The most notable sculptures, of historical and mythological figures from the 3rd and 4th centuries BC, are at ground level outside the museum. In the exhibition hall, chronological displays of pottery and objects from everyday life illustrate the settlement of the area from Neolithic times. ⊠ *Three entrances: from Monastiraki on Adrianou; from Thission on Apostolou Pavlou; and descending from Acropolis on Ayios Apostoloi, Monastiraki* ☎ *210/321–0185* ⊕ *www.culture.gr* ✉ *€4, joint ticket for all Unification of Archaeological Sites €12* ☽ *May–Oct., daily 8–8 (last entrance 7:30); Nov.–Apr., daily 8–sunset; museum closes ½ hr before site* Ⓜ *Thiseio.*

**Fodor'sChoice**  **Benaki Museum.** This immense collection moves chronologically from
★  prehistory to the formation of the modern Greek state. You might see
anything from a 5,000-year-old hammered gold bowl to an austere Byzantine icon of the Virgin Mary. ⊠ *Koumbari 1, Kolonaki* ☎ *210/367–
1000* ⊕ *www.benaki.gr* ⊠ *€6, free Thurs.* ◐ *Mon., Wed., Fri., and Sat.
9–5, Thurs. 9 AM–midnight, Sun. 9–3* Ⓜ *Syntagma or Evangelismos.*

★  **Byzantine and Christian Museum.** One of the few museums in Europe
concentrating exclusively on Byzantine art, this collection displays an
outstanding collection of icons, mosaics, and tapestries. You can also
explore the on-site archaeological dig of Aristotle's Lyceum. ⊠ *Vasilissis Sofias 22, Kolonaki* ☎ *210/721–1027, 210/723–2178, or 210/723–
1570* ⊕ *www.byzantinemuseum.gr* ⊠ *€4* ◐ *Nov.–Mar., Tues.–Sun.
8:30–3; Apr.–Oct., Tues.–Sun. 8:30–7:30* Ⓜ *Evangelismos.*

**Fodor'sChoice**  **Museum of Cycladic Art.** Also known as the Nicholas P. Goulandris Foun-
★  dation, this outstanding collection of 350 Cycladic artifacts dating from
the Bronze Age includes many of the enigmatic marble figurines whose
slender shapes fascinated such artists as Picasso, Modigliani, and Brancusi. ⊠ *Neofitou Douka 4 or Irodotou 1, Kolonaki* ☎ *210/722–8321
through 210/722–8323* ⊕ *www.cycladic.gr* ⊠ *€7* ◐ *Mon., Wed., Fri.,
and Sat. 10–5, Thurs. 10–8, Sun. 11–5* Ⓜ *Evangelismos.*

**Fodor'sChoice**  **National Archaeological Museum.** By far the most important museum in
★  Greece, this collection contains artistic highlights from every period of
ancient Greek civilization, from Neolithic to Roman times.

Holdings are grouped in five major collections: prehistoric artifacts
(7th millennium BC to 1050 BC), sculptures, bronzes, vases and minor
arts, and Egyptian artifacts. The museum's most celebrated display is
the **Mycenaean Antiquities.** Here are the stunning gold treasures from
Heinrich Schliemann's 1876 excavations of Mycenae's royal tombs:
the funeral mask of a bearded king, once thought to be the image of
Agamemnon but now believed to be much older, from about the 15th
century BC; a splendid silver bull's-head libation cup; and the 15th-
century BC Vaphio Goblets, masterworks in embossed gold.

Other stars of the museum include the works of Geometric and Archaic
art (10th–6th centuries BC), and kouroi and funerary stelae (8th–5th
centuries BC), among them the stelae of the warrior Aristion signed by
Aristokles, and the unusual *Running Hoplite* (a hoplite was a Greek
infantry soldier). The collection of classical art (5th–3rd centuries BC)
contains some of the most renowned surviving ancient statues: the bare-
back *Jockey of Artemision*, a 2nd-century BC Hellenistic bronze salvaged
from the sea, and the *Varvakios Athena*, a half-size marble version
of the gigantic gold-and-ivory cult statue that Pheidias erected in the
Parthenon. ⊠ *28 Oktovriou (Patission) 44, Exarchia* ☎ *210/821–7717*
⊕ *www.culture.gr* ⊠ *€6* ◐ *Apr. 15–Oct. 15, Mon. 1–7:30, Tues.–Sun.
8–7:30; Oct. 16–Apr. 14, Mon. 1–7:30, Tues.–Fri. 8:30–7:30, weekends
8:30–3. Closed Jan. 1, Mar. 25, May 1, Easter Sun., Dec. 25–26; open
reduced hrs other holidays* Ⓜ *Victoria, then 10-min walk.*

**New Acropolis Museum.** Designed by the celebrated Swiss architect Bernard Tschumi, the New Acropolis Museum made world headlines when
it opened in June 2009. If some buildings define an entire city in a

particular era, Athens's newest museum boldly sets the tone for the '00s. Occupying a large plot of the city's most prized real estate, the New Acropolis Museum nods to the fabled ancient hill above it but speaks—thanks to a spectacular building—in a contemporary architectural language.

Regal glass walkways, very high ceilings, and panoramic views are all part of the experience. In the five-level museum, every shade of marble is on display and bathed in abundant, UV-safe natural light.

The ground floor exhibit, "The Acropolis Slopes," features objects found in the sanctuaries and settlements around the Acropolis—a highlight is the collection of theatrical masks and vases from the sanctuary of the matrimonial deity Nymphe. The next floor is devoted to the Archaic period (650 BC–480 BC), with rows of precious statues mounted for 360-degree viewing. The floor includes sculptural figures from the Hekatompedon—the temple that may have predated the classical Parthenon—such as the noted group of stone lions gorging a bull from 570 BC. The legendary five Caryatids (or Korai)—the female figures supporting the Acropolis' Erectheion building—symbolically leave a space for their sister, who resides in London's British Museum.

The second floor is devoted to the terrace and small restaurant/bar, which serves mezedes (a more ambitious restaurant is rumored to be in the works). Drifting into the top-floor atrium, the visitor can watch a video on the Parthenon before entering the star gallery devoted to the temple's Pentelic marble decorations, many of which depict a grand procession in the goddess Athena's honor. Frieze pieces (originals and copies), metopes, and pediments are all laid out in their original orientation. This is made remarkably apparent because the gallery consists of a magnificent, rectangle-shaped room tilted to align with the Parthenon itself. Floor-to-ceiling windows provide magnificent vistas of the temple just a few hundred feet away.

Elsewhere on view are other fabled works of art, including the *Rampin Horseman* and the compelling *Hound*, both by the sculptor Phaidimos; the noted pediment sculpted into a calf being devoured by a lioness—a 6th-century BC treasure that brings to mind Picasso's *Guernica*; striking pedimental figures from the Old Temple of Athena (525 BC) depicting the battle between *Athena and the Giants*; and the great *Nike Unfastening Her Sandal*, taken from the parapet of the Acropolis's famous Temple of Athena Nike. With all the ancient and fabled riches now gloriously on view here, a visit of at least three hours to this grand new museum is recommended. ✉ *Dionyssiou Areopagitou 15, Makriyianni, Acropolis* ⊕ *www.theacropolismuseum.gr* 🎫 *€5* ⊙ *Tues.– Sun. 8–8* Ⓜ *Acropolis.*

★ **Roman Agora.** The city's commercial center from the 1st century BC to the 4th century AD, this market's most notable remaining feature is the west entrance's Bazaar Gate, or **Gate of Athena Archegetis**, completed around AD 2. On the north side of the Roman Agora stands one of the few remains of the Turkish occupation, the **Fethiye (Victory) Mosque**, built in the late 15th century on the site of a Christian church to celebrate the Turkish conquest of Athens and to honor Mehmet II (the

Conqueror). The octagonal **Tower of the Winds (Aerides)** is the most appealing and best-preserved of the Roman monuments of Athens, keeping time since the 1st century BC. It was originally a sundial, water clock, and weather vane topped by a bronze Triton with a metal rod in his hand, which followed the direction of the wind. ⊠ *Pelopidas and Aiolou, Plaka* ☎ *210/324–5220* ⊕ *www.culture.gr* ⊠ *€2, joint ticket for all Unification of Archaeological Sites €12* ☉ *May–Oct., daily 8–8; Nov.–Apr., daily 8–3* Ⓜ *Monastiraki.*

★ **Syntagma Square.** At the top of the city's main square (Constitution Square) stands **Parliament,** formerly the royal palace. Here you can watch the **changing of the Evzone guards at the Tomb of the Unknown Soldier**—in front of Parliament on a lower level—which takes place at intervals throughout the day. On Sunday the honor guard of tall young men dons dress costume—a short white *foustanella* (kilt) and red shoes with pompons, arriving in front of Parliament by 11:15 AM. Pop into the gleaming **Syntagma metro station** to examine artfully displayed artifacts uncovered during subway excavations. A floor-to-ceiling cross section of earth behind glass shows finds in chronological layers, ranging from a skeleton in its ancient grave to traces of the 4th-century BC road to Mesogeia to an Ottoman cistern. ⊠ *Vasilissis Amalias and Vasilissis Sofias, Syntagma Sq.* Ⓜ *Syntagma.*

## SHOPPING

Athens has great gifts, particularly handmade crafts. Shops stock copies of traditional Greek jewelry, silver filigree, Skyrian pottery, onyx ashtrays and dishes, woven bags, attractive rugs (including *flokati,* or shaggy goat-wool rugs), wool sweaters, and little blue-and-white pendants designed as amulets to ward off the *mati* (evil eye). Greece is also known for its well-made shoes (most shops are clustered around the Ermou pedestrian zone and in Kolonaki), its furs (Mitropoleos near Syntagma), and its durable leather items (Pandrossou in Monastiraki).

Shops on Pandrossou sell small antiques and icons, but keep in mind that many of these are fakes. You must have government permission to export genuine objects from the ancient Greek, Roman, and Byzantine periods. Many museums sell good-quality reproductions or miniatures of their best pieces.

**Center of Hellenic Tradition.** This is an outlet for quality handicrafts—ceramics, weavings, sheep bells, and old paintings. ⊠ *Mitropoleos 59 and Pandrossou 36, Monastiraki* ☎ *210/321–3023, 210/321–3842 café.*

★ **Goutis.** This store offers an eclectic jumble of jewelry, costumes, embroidery, and old, handcrafted silver objects. ⊠ *Dimokritou 10, Kolonaki* ☎ *210/361–3557.*

Fodor'sChoice **Korres.** Natural beauty products blended in traditional recipes using
★ Greek herbs and flowers have graced the bathroom shelves of celebrities like Nicole Kidman. In Athens they are available at most pharmacies for regular-folk prices. For the largest selection of basil-lemon shower gel, coriander body lotion, olive-stone face scrub, and wild-rose eye cream, go to the original Korres pharmacy behind the Panathenaic

Stadium. ✉ *Eratosthenous 8 and Ivikou, Pangrati* ☎ *210/722-2744* ⊕ *www.korres.com.*

**Thiamis.** Iconographer Aristides Makos creates the beautiful hand-painted, gold-leaf icons on wood and stone that are sold at this boutique. ✉ *Asklipiou 71, Kolonaki* ☎ *210/363-7993.*

## WHERE TO EAT

On Mitropoleos off Monastiraki Square are a handful of counter-front places selling souvlaki—grilled meat rolled in a pita with onions, *tzatziki* (yogurt-garlic dip), and tomatoes—the best bargain in Athens. Make sure you specify whether you want a souvlaki sandwich or a souvlaki plate, which is an entire meal. A contender for the best souvlaki in town is **Thanassis** (✉ *Mitropoleos 69, Monastiraki* ☎ *210/324-4705*), which is always crowded.

$$$
GREEK
**Fodor's**Choice
★

**✗ Daphne's.** Discreet service and refined Mediterranean dishes (such as pork with celery and egg lemon sauce, fricassee of melt-off-the-bone lamb with greens, beef with olives, and rabbit in mavrodaphne wine sauce) help make Daphne's one of the best destinations in Plaka. The Pompeian frescoes on the walls, the fragments of an ancient Greek building in the garden, and the tasteful restoration of the neoclassic building in terra-cotta and ocher hues also contribute to a pleasant evening. ✉ *Lysikratous 4, Plaka* ☎ *210/322-7991* ⊕ *www.daphnesrestaurant. gr* ⊟ *AE, DC, MC, V.*

¢
GREEK
**Fodor's**Choice
★

**✗ O Platanos.** Set on a picturesque pedestrianized square, this is one of the oldest tavernas in Plaka (established 1932)—a welcome sight compared with the many overpriced tourist traps in the area. A district landmark—it is set midway between the Tower of the Winds and the Museum of Greek Popular Musical Instruments—it warms the eye with its pink-hue house, color-coordinated with the bougainvillea-covered courtyard. Although the rooms here are cozily adorned with old paintings and photos, most of the crowd opts to relax under the courtyard's plane trees (which give the place its name). Platanos is packed with locals, who flock here because the food is good Greek home cooking and the waiters fast and polite. Don't miss the oven-baked potatoes, lamb or veal casserole with spinach or eggplant, fresh green beans in savory olive oil, fresh grilled fish, and the exceptionally cheap but delicious barrel retsina. ✉ *Diogenous 4, Plaka* ☎ *210/322-0666* ⊟ *No credit cards* ۩ *Closed Sun. June–Aug. No dinner Sun.*

## WHERE TO STAY

$–$$
**Fodor's**Choice
★

**⊞ Acropolis Select.** For €10 more than many basic budget options, you get to stay in a slick-looking hotel with a lobby full of designer furniture. Bright, comfortable guest rooms have cheery yellow bedspreads with an abstract red poppy design. Similar in color choice, the dramatic restaurant has daffodil-color walls and contemporary, scroll-back chairs in tomato red. About a dozen rooms look toward the Acropolis: ask for Rooms 401–405 for the best views. There are 10 no-smoking rooms in the hotel, all on the fifth floor. The residential neighborhood of Koukaki, south of Filopappou Hill, is a 15-minute walk from the Acropolis.

Pros: lovely rooms, some with breathtaking views; decent gym; friendly staff; in a pretty, low-key neighborhood. **Cons:** few no-smoking rooms. ⊠ *Falirou 37–39, Koukaki* ☎ *210/921–1610* ⊕ *www.acropoliselect.gr* ⤴ *72 rooms* ⚭ *In-room: refrigerator, Internet. In-hotel: restaurant, bar, parking (free)* ⊟ *AE, DC, MC, V.*

**$$$–$$$$**
**Fodor's Choice**
★

⊡ **Electra Palace.** If you want simple elegance, excellent service, and a great location in Plaka, this is the hotel for you. Located on an attractive street close to the area's museums, its guest rooms are comfortable and beautifully decorated, with ample storage space. Rooms from the fifth floor up have a view of the Acropolis—and, in summer, enjoy a once-in-a-lifetime chance to bask in the sunshine at the outdoor swimming pool as you take in a magnificent view of Athens's greatest monument. Before setting out in the morning, fill up with one of the city's best buffet breakfasts—sausage, pancakes, and home fries. In the evening, relax in a steam bath in the hotel spa. **Pros:** gorgeous rooms; great locations; outstanding service. **Cons:** pricey! ⊠ *Nikodimou 18–20, Plaka* ☎ *210/337–0000* ⊕ *www.electrahotels.gr* ⤴ *131 rooms, 19 suites* ⚭ *In-room: refrigerator, Wi-Fi. In-hotel: 2 restaurants, bar, pools, gym, parking (paid)* ⊟ *AE, DC, MC, V* ⦿ *BP.*

**$$$**
⊡ **Sofitel Athens Airport.** This luxury hotel directly across the street from the airport terminal complex makes for a relaxing and stress-free arrival or departure. Rooms are spacious and modern, with large, comfortable beds and amply sized bathrooms. Take time to get over jet lag at the spa or the indoor pool and sauna. There are two good restaurants and bars on-site, or you can head into the terminal for more choices. **Pros:** Ideally placed for flight connections; comfortable rooms for a pre- or post-cruise stopover. **Cons:** It's a long metro ride into Athens for sightseeing; there's some aircraft noise (though the building is sound-proofed); some rooms allow smoking. ⊠ *Airport terminal, Attika Odos Hwy., Spata* ☎ *0210/3544000* ⊕ *www.sofitel.com* ⤴ *345 rooms, 13 suites* ⚭ *In-room: a/c, Internet. In-hotel: 2 restaurants, room service, bars, pool, gym, spa, laundry service, Wi-Fi hotspot, parking (free), some pets allowed* ⊟ *AE, DC, MC, V* ⦿ *EP.*

# PORT SAID, EGYPT (FOR CAIRO)

One of the world's great cosmopolitan cities for well over a thousand years, Cairo is infinite and inexhaustible. Different religions, different cultures—sometimes, it seems, even different eras—coexist amid the jostling crowds and aging monuments gathered here at the start of the Nile delta. But if you come expecting a city frozen in time, you're in for a shock: Cairo's current vitality is as seductive as its rich past. Like so much else in Egypt, Cairo's charm is a product of its history, the physical remains of a thousand years of being conquered and re-conquered by different groups. Cairo gradually reveals its treasures, not with pizzazz and bells and whistles, but with a self-assured understatement. On a one-day visit you'll only be able to take in the tip of a vast iceberg of treasures here.

## ESSENTIALS

CURRENCY The Egyptian pound (£E5.69 to US$1; £E7.31 to €1 at this writing). U.S. currency is accepted for high-value items in shops but not in restaurants and markets. ATMs are not common. You'll need small local bills for tips in Egypt.

HOURS Museums are usually open from 9 to 5. Many museums are closed on Monday. Shops are open from 8 AM until 7 PM. During Ramadan (the Muslim month of fasting), opening times vary; shops close during the day but stay open late into the evening.

INTERNET **Intr@net Cafe** (⊠ *36 Shar'a Sherif, 1st fl., Downtown* ☏ *02/393–9740* ⊕ *www.intranetinfosys.com*).

TELEPHONES Mobile phone coverage is limited to Cairo, the Nile Valley and delta, and the Red Sea coast. The mobile system in Egypt is 3G-supportive. Vodafone, Etisalat Egypt, and Mobinil are the major providers in the country.

## COMING ASHORE

Ships with passengers bound for Cairo generally dock at Port Said, Egypt's premier commercial port. The town was founded at the southern outlet of the Suez Canal as a camp for engineers and workers building the waterway in the mid-19th century. From the port it is a short walk into this unprepossessing town, but there is little to hold the visitor. Most passengers will choose to take a ship-sponsored shore excursion into Cairo.

Taxis wait at the dock entrance, and can offer transfers to Cairo for a day rate, but this is a port where we strongly recommend a ship-sponsored excursion because of the distance and schedule issues. If you decide to travel independently, it's important to agree on a price and to assess the condition of the vehicle first. The journey is long, and a breakdown would be a major inconvenience. We caution strongly against trying to rent a car to visit Cairo. There are too many security issues, and driving in Cairo traffic is not an experience the average cruise passenger is prepared for.

# EXPLORING CAIRO

★ **The Egyptian Antiquities Museum.** This neoclassical building is home to the world's largest collection of ancient Egyptian artifacts. With more than 100,000 items in total, it is said that if you were to spend just one minute on each item, it would take more than nine months to complete the tour. Needless to say, you need to be selective here.

Some of the museum's finest pieces are in the center of the ground floor, below the atrium and rotunda. This area makes a good place to start, acting as a preview for the rest of the museum. Among the prized possessions here are three colossi of the legendary New Kingdom pharaoh Ramesses II (1290–1224 BC); a limestone statue of Djoser (around 2600 BC), the Second Dynasty pharaoh who built the Step Pyramid in Saqqara; several sarcophagi; and a floor from the destroyed palace of Akhenaten (1353–1335 BC), the heretic monotheist king. The Narmer Palette, a piece from about 3000 BC, is thought to document the first unification of northern and southern Egypt.

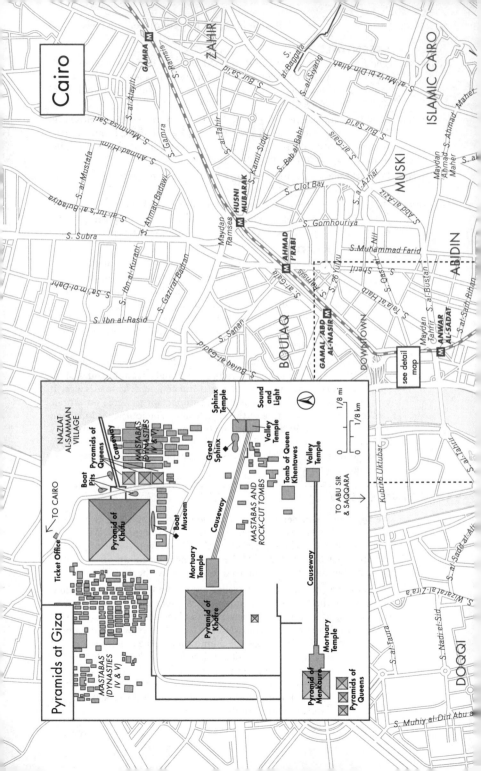

# Cairo

GAMRA Ⓜ

ZAHIR

S. Ramsis
Gamra
S. Ahmad Badawi
S. al-Hayiti
S. al-Muhmisa Sari
S. Ahmad-Hilmi
S. Ahmad-Mustafa
S. al-Tur S. al-Bulaqiya
S. Subra
S. Ahmad Badawi
S. Gazirat Badran
S. Ibn al-Kurani
S. al-m al-Dahr
S. Sa'm al-Dahr
S. Ibn al-Rasid

ISLAMIC CAIRO

S. al-Siyang
al-Baggala
S. al-Mu'iz li-Din Allah
S. Bur Said
Maydan Ahmad S. Ahmad Maher
Maher
S. al-

MUSKI

S. al-Azhar
S. Abd al-Aziz

S. al-Gais
S. Baba al-Babi
S. Kamil-Sidqi
S. Clot Bay
S. Gomhouriya
S. Muhammad Farid
Sherif
S. Qasr
S. Qasr al-Nil
S. 26 Yulyu
S. Talat Harb
S. al-Bustan
S. al-Sadd al-Ali

ABIDIN

Maydan Ahmad
Tahtri
ANWAR
AL-SADAT Ⓜ
S. al-Saih-Rihan

HUSNI
MUBARAK Ⓜ

Maydan
Ramses

AHMAD
FKABI Ⓜ

GAMAL 'ABD
AL-NASIR Ⓜ

S. al-Gala
S. Buraq al-Gadid
S. Sanan
S. Yulyu
S. al-Gala
S. al-Tahir

BOULAQ

DOWNTOWN

see detail
map

DOQQI

S. al-Saad-al-Ali
S. Wizarat al-Zira'a
S. Nadi-el-Sid
S. al-Taura
S. Muhiy al-Din Abu a

## Pyramids at Giza

Ticket Office
←TO CAIRO

NAZLAT
AL-SAMMAN
VILLAGE

Pyramids of
Queens

MASTABAS
(DYNASTIES
IV & V)

Causeway

Boat
Pits

Boat Museum

Pyramid of
Khufu

MASTABAS
(DYNASTIES
IV & V)

Mortuary
Temple

Pyramid of
Khafre

Causeway

Great
Sphinx

Sphinx
Temple

Valley
Temple

Sound
and
Light

MASTABAS
AND
ROCK-CUT TOMBS

Tomb of Queen
Khentawes

Valley
Temple

TO ABU SIR
& SAQQARA

Pyramid of
Menkaure

Mortuary
Temple

Causeway

Pyramids of
Queens

Kubri al-Uktuba

0    1/8 mi
0    1/8 km

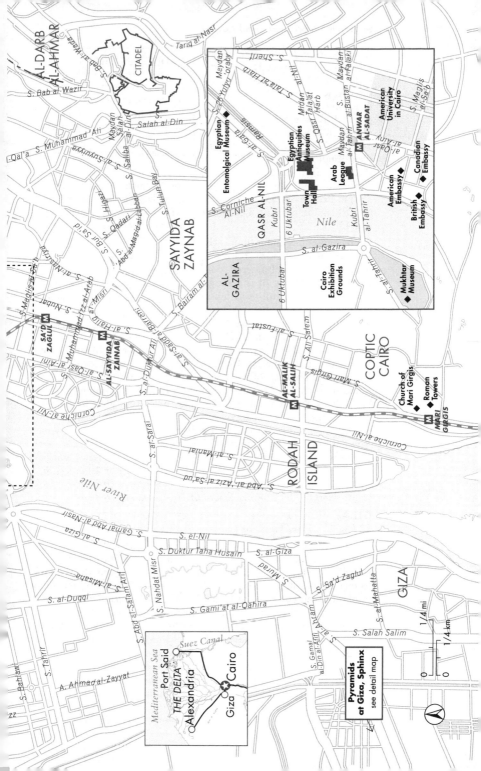

Rooms around the atrium are arranged chronologically, clockwise from the left (west) of the entrance: the Old Kingdom (2575–2134 BC) in Rooms 31, 32, 36, 37, 41, 42, 46, and 47; the Middle Kingdom (2040–1640 BC) in Rooms 11, 12, 16, 17, 21, 22, 26, and 27; the New Kingdom (1550–1070 BC) in Rooms 1–10, 14, 15, 19, and 20; Greco-Roman Egypt (332 BC–c. AD 395) in Rooms 34, 35, 39, and 40; and Nubian Exhibits in Rooms 44 and 45.

On the museum's upper floor is the famous Tutankhamun collection, to date the only unplundered tomb found in the Valley of the Kings. Look for its beautiful gold funerary mask and sarcophagus (Room 3), ancient trumpet (Room 30), thrones (Rooms 20 and 25), the four huge gilded boxes that fit one inside the other (7, 8), and a royal toilet seat to boot (outside Room 30). Also upstairs is the royal Mummy Room, which houses 11 pharaonic dignitaries, including the body of Ramesses II (Room 52). There's an extra fee for the Mummy Room—but well worth it, considering that these preserved rulers initiated the phenomenon of Ancient Egypt as we know it. The Egyptian Antiquities Museum is due to close for renovations once the Grand Egyptian Museum on the Giza Plateau—currently slated in late 2012 or early 2013—when the ancient artifacts will be split between this new museum and the Museum of Egyptian Civilization in Fustat in Islamic Cairo. ⊠ *Al-Mathaf al-Masri, Maydan Tahrir, Downtown* ☎ *02/2578–2452* ⌨ *Museum £E80, Mummy Room £E100* ☉ *Daily 9–6:30.*

## GIZA

*12 km (8 mi) southwest of Cairo.*

The three pyramids of Khufu (Greek name: Cheops), Khafre (Chephren), and Menkaure (Mycerinus) dominate the Giza Plateau. Surrounding the father-son-grandson trio are smaller pyramids belonging to their female dependents, and the *mastabas* (large, trapezoid-shape tombs) of their courtiers and relatives. The word *mastaba* comes from the Arabic word for bench, which these tombs resemble in shape, if not in scale, and the mastabas were often painted and/or decorated with reliefs inside, with the actual burial sites placed in shafts cut into the bedrock. The great Sphinx crouches at the eastern edge of the plateau, guarding the necropolis. A museum south of the Great Pyramid contains one of the most extraordinary artifacts from ancient Egypt, Khufu's own royal boat. The pyramids, Sphinx, and some of the mastabas date from the Fourth Dynasty, while other mastabas date to the Fifth and Sixth Dynasties. South of the Sphinx and its adjacent temples,

---

### CAIRO BEST BETS

**The Cairo Museum.** The most comprehensive collection of ancient Egyptian artifacts in the world, this museum is a must for serious history buffs or curious amateurs keen to catch sight of a mummy.

**The Pyramids.** When you view the Pyramids (and the Sphinx), you are sure to be awed. The mystery of their origin remains, and that's part of the allure.

**Khan al-Khalili souk.** One of the world's oldest and most authentic markets, Khan al-Khalili is a cornucopia of crafts ranging from the mundane to the magnificent.

archaeologists have recently found the living and eating areas of the workmen who built the pyramids, as well as the cemeteries where they were buried.

**Great Sphinx.** Carved from the living rock of the pyramids plateau during the 4th Dynasty, the enigmatic limestone Sphinx is attached to Pharaoh Khafre's funerary complex. The figure of a recumbent lion with a man's face wearing a *nemes* (traditional headdress of the pharaoh) was thought to be Khafre in the guise of Ra-Harakhte, a manifestation of the Sun God. The role of the Sphinx was to guard the vast royal necropolis that incorporated the pyramids and *mastabas* (large trapezoid-shaped tombs) on the Giza plateau, and it's visited as part of the longer visit incorporating these other monuments at the site. It's possible to get close to the Sphinx along a wide viewing platform that has been built around it, but climbing is forbidden, and there's no entry into the small interior chambers (most of the sphinx, however, is solid rock). ✉ *Fayyum Rd., Giza* 🎫 *Sphinx £E60 (includes both Pyramids and Sphinx), Sound & Light Show £E75 ⊘ Daily 8–6:30; Sound & Light Show (in English) Oct.–Apr., Mon.–Wed., Fri., and Sat. 6:30 PM, Thurs. 7:30 PM, Sun. 9:30 PM; May–Sept., Mon.–Wed., Fri., and Sat. 8:30 PM, Thurs. 9:30 PM, Sun. 11:30 PM.*

> ## GRAND EGYPTIAN MUSEUM
>
> The Grand Egyptian Museum will be a fitting home for the mother lode of ancient artifacts excavated in the country in the last 150 years. When opened it will be the world's biggest museum dedicated to ancient Egypt, covering 123 acres (50 hectares) on the Giza Plateau less than 2 mi from the Pyramids. The foundation stone of the museum was laid in 2002, and at this writing only the research labs of the complex are complete. Current estimates are that the museum will open to the public in 2013.

**Fodor's Choice** ★ **Pyramid Plateau.** Three 4th-Dynasty pyramids dominate the skyline of the desert plateau to the southwest of Cairo. The largest is that of **Pharaoh Khufu** (Greek name: Cheops) also known as "The Great Pyramid." The second was built by his son **Khafre** (Greek name: Chephren). The smallest of pyramids was built by **Menkaure** (Greek name: Mycerinus), the grandson of Khufu who reigned from 2490–2472 BC. These are surrounded by smaller pyramids belonging to their respective female dependents, as well as numerous *mastabas* (large trapezoid-shape tombs) of their lesser relatives and courtiers. The site is "guarded" by the monumental carved-limestone Sphinx. A small museum in the shadow of Khufu's Pyramid contains the **Pharaoh's Royal Solar Boat,** by tradition the boat used to transport the Pharaoh on his final journey to the afterlife after his mummy was entombed; the solar boat has its own museum with a separate entrance fee. The pyramid interiors are open on a rotating basis, and ticket numbers are limited to 150 per morning and another 150 per afternoon. A range of *mastabas* will be open to view on any given day. The ticket office will give you current information when you buy your ticket. Buses and cars are no longer allowed on the plateau; electric trams link the ticket office with the plateau, from where you'll be able to explore the site on foot. ✉ *Pyramids Rd., Giza*

No phone ✉ General admission £E60 (includes both Pyramids and Sphinx), Khufu's Pyramid £E100, Khafre's Pyramid £E30, Menkaure's Pyramid £E25, Solar Boat Museum £E50 ⊙ Site daily 8–6:30, pyramid and tomb interiors daily 9–4 (but openings are staggered, so not all pyramid interiors are open every day).

## SHOPPING

Cairo has always been a mercantile and trading town. The hundreds of magnificent mosques and palaces scattered around the city are a testament to Cairo's highly skilled craftspeople. The artisans of Egypt continue this tradition of detailed workmanship, offering a tremendous array of handmade items.

Egyptians specialize in worked brass and copper articles, wood inlay on jewelry boxes and chess sets, and leatherwear. The hookah is also an interesting regional specialty. Egyptian cotton is a byword for quality, and the shops of Cairo are a great place to buy items like bedding and towels. If you want to purchase genuine antiques and antiquities you'll need to have a certificate of approval from the Egyptian authorities to export your purchase, but reproductions are on sale everywhere. These items needn't be expensive: you can buy a lucky alabaster scarab beetle for a few Egyptian pounds—in fact, this small item is almost a compulsory souvenir of your trip to Egypt.

**Fodor's Choice**  **Khan al-Khalili.** Cairo shopping starts at this great medieval souk. ★  Although it has been on every tourist's itinerary for centuries, and some of its more visible wares can seem awfully tacky, the Khan is where everyone—newcomer and age-old Cairene alike—goes to find traditional items: jewelry, lamps, spices, clothes, textiles, handicrafts, water pipes, metalwork, you name it. Whatever it is, you can find it somewhere in this skein of alleys or the streets around them. Every Khan veteran has the shops he or she swears by—usually because of the fact (or illusion) she or he is known there personally and is thus less likely to be overcharged. Go, browse, and bargain hard. Once you buy something, don't ask how much it costs at the next shop; you'll be happier that way. Many shops close Sunday. ⊠ Islamic Cairo North.

## WHERE TO EAT

**$$–$$$**  ✕ **The Fish Market.** On the upper deck of a boat permanently moored on SEAFOOD  the west bank of the Nile, the scene here is decidedly simple: there's no menu, just a display of unbelievably fresh fish, shrimp, crabs, calamari, and shellfish on ice. Pick what appeals, pay by weight, and the kitchen will prepare it however you like, with a slew of Middle Eastern salads on the side. The delicious bread is baked on the premises in a *baladi* (country) oven. ⊠ 26 Shar'a al-Nil, Giza ☎ 02/570–9694 ⚐ Reservations essential ▤ AE, MC, V.

**$$**  ✕ **Naguib Mahfouz Café.** Named after Egypt's most famous novelist and MIDDLE EASTERN  run by the Oberoi Hotel Group, this is a haven of air-conditioned tranquillity in the midst of the sometimes-chaotic Khan al-Khalili. The restaurant serves variations on the usual Egyptian dishes, dressed up in historically resonant names to justify what, by the standards of the area, constitute exorbitant prices. That being said, the food and service are also of higher quality than you'll find in most of the nearby restaurants. The adjoining café serves lighter fare, consisting mostly of sandwiches, at a fraction of the price of the main dishes. ⊠ *5 al-Badestan La., Khan al-Khalili, Islamic Cairo North* ☎ *02/2590–3788* ⊟ *AE, MC, V.*

# RHODES, GREECE

The island of Rhodes (1,400 square km [540 square mi]) is one of the great islands of the Mediterranean. It was long considered a bridge between Europe and the East, and has seen many waves of settlement throughout recorded history. Ancient Rhodes was a powerful city and its political organization became the model for the city of Alexandria in Egypt. When Rome took the city in 42 BC, it was fabled for its beauty and for the sanctuary of Lindos, which drew pilgrims from around the region. Rhodes was a crucial stop on the road to the Holy Land during the Crusades. It came briefly under Venetian influence, then Byzantine, then Genoese, but in 1309, when the Knights of St. John took the city from its Genoese masters, its most glorious modern era began. Today Rhodes is a popular holiday island for Europeans who come for the sun and the beaches.

### ESSENTIALS

CURRENCY The euro (€1 to US$1.36 at this writing). ATMs are common.

HOURS Shops are open from 9 to 9 on weekdays and from 9 to 6 on Saturday. Museums are generally open from 9 to 5, but many are closed on Monday.

INTERNET **Galileo Internet** (⊠ *13 Iroon Politechniou St.* ☎ *22410/20610*) has 25 machines and is open daily from 9 AM to 2 AM.

TELEPHONES Tri-band GSM phones work in Greece. You can buy prepaid phone cards at telecom shops, news vendors, and tobacconists in all towns and cities. Phone cards can be used for local or international calls. Vodafone is the leading mobile telecom company. OTE is the national domestic provider. Calls can be made at OTE offices and paid for after completion.

### COMING ASHORE

Ships dock at the commercial port directly outside the city walls of Rhodes Town. It is a short walk from the port to all the attractions of the walled citadel. For this reason, there are few facilities in the port itself.

The bus station for services down the east coast is found by turning right outside the port and walking for 10 minutes to Rimini Square. There are several services to Lindos each day. Journey time is about one hour, and ticket prices are €3.70

Taxis wait outside the port gates but can also be found at Rimini Square. For a journey to Lindos, prices are fixed at a fare of €35 one way. Journey time is approximately 30 minutes. You could enjoy a full day touring Rhodes island if you rent a car, though both Rhodes's Old Town and Lindos are pedestrian-only or have very limited vehicular

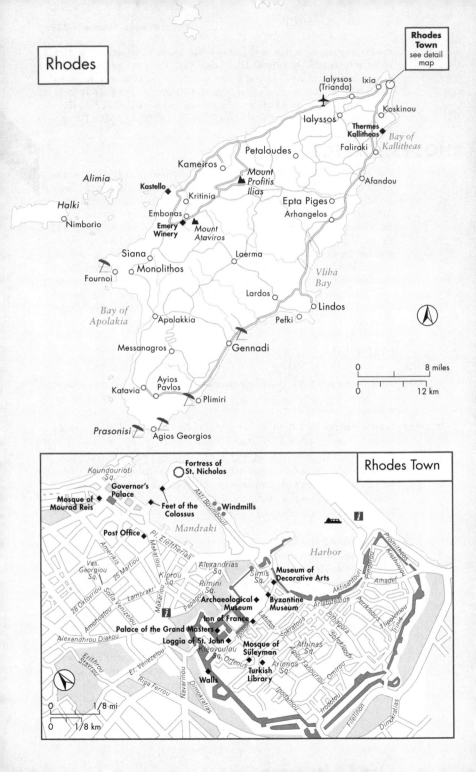

access. Costs are €45 per day for a subcompact vehicle, and the major companies can bring a car to the port for you.

# EXPLORING RHODES

## RHODES TOWN

Rhodes Town is still a city of two parts: the Old Town, a UNESCO World Heritage site, contains exceptional medieval architecture, Orthodox and Catholic churches, and an alluring old Turkish quarter. Spreading away from the walls that encircle the Old Town is the modern metropolis, or new town. You can purchase a multisight ticket (€10), which gets you admission to the Palace of the Grand Masters, Archaeological Museum, Museum of Decorative Arts, and Byzantine Museum.

**Archaeological Museum.** The hospital was the largest of the Knights' public buildings, completed in 1489. The imposing facade opens into a courtyard, where cannonballs remain from the siege of 1522. Today it contains the Archaelogical Museum. On the main floor there's a collection of ancient pottery and sculpture, including two well-known representations of Aphrodite: the *Aphrodite of Rhodes,* who, while bathing, pushes aside her hair as if she's listening; and a standing figure, known as *Aphrodite Thalassia,* or "of the sea," as she was discovered in the water off the northern city beach. Other important works include a 6th-century BC *kouros* (a statue of an idealized male youth, usually nude) that was found in Kameiros, and the beautiful 5th-century BC funerary stele of Timarista bidding farewell to her mother, Crito. ⊠ *Pl. Moussiou* ☎ *22410/25500* ⊕ *www.culture.gr* ⛁ *€6, combined ticket with Byzantine Museum, Decorative Arts Collection, Palace of the Grand Masters €10* ☯ *Apr.–Oct., Tues.–Sun. 8:30–8; Nov.–Mar., Tues.–Sun. 8:30–3.*

**Byzantine Museum.** This collection of icons is displayed within the 11th-century Lady of the Castle church (Panagia tou Kastrou). ⊠ *Off Mouseou Sq.* ☎ *22410/25500* ⛁ *€3* ☯ *Apr.–Oct., Tues.–Sun. 8:30–7; Nov.–Mar., Tues.–Sun. 8:30–3.*

The **Inn of France** was the largest of the Knights' gathering spots and is now the French Consulate. The facade is carved with flowers and heraldic patterns and bears an inscription that dates the building between 1492 and 1509. ⊠ *About halfway down St. of the Knights from Loggia of St. John.*

**Loggia of St. John.** In front of the court of the Palace of the Grand Masters is the Loggia of St. John, on the site where the Knights of St. John were buried in an early church. From the Loggia, the **Street of the Knights** descends toward the **Commercial Port,** bordered on both sides by the **Inns of the Tongues,** where the Knights supped and held their meetings.

**Mosque of Süleyman.** This mosque was built circa 1522 and rebuilt in 1808. At this writing, the restored building was open primarily to groups by appointment only. ⊠ *At top of Sokratous* ☎ *22410/24918* ⛁ *Free* ☯ *By appointment only.*

**Museum of Decorative Arts.** This collection exhibits finely made ceramics, crafts, and artifacts from around the Dodecanese. ⊠ *Argyrokastrou Sq.* ☎ *22410/25500* ⛁ *€2* ☯ *Apr.–Oct., Tues.–Sun. 8:30–7; Nov.–Mar., Tues.–Sun. 8:30–3.*

**Palace of the Grand Masters.** In the castle area, a city within a city, the Knights of St. John built most of their monuments. The Palace of the Grand Masters, at the highest spot of the medieval city, is the best place to begin a tour of Rhodes; here you can get oriented before wandering through the labyrinthine old town. Of great help is the permanent exhibition downstairs, with extensive displays, maps, and plans showing the layout of the city. The palace building withstood the Turkish siege unscathed, but in 1856 an explosion of ammunition stored nearby in the cellars of the Church of St. John devastated it; the present structures are 20th-century Italian reconstructions. Note the Hellenistic and Roman mosaic floors throughout, which came from the Italian excavations in Kos. ⊠ *Ippoton, old town* ☎ *22410/25500* ⊕ *www.culture.gr* ⛭ *€6* ⊗ *May–Oct., Mon. 12:30–7, Tues.–Sun. 8:30–7; Nov.–Apr., Tues.–Sun. 8–3.*

| RHODES BEST BETS |
| --- |
| **Walk down the Street of the Knights.** This medieval street is one of the most complete of its kind in the world. Imagine the crusader knights going about their business here. |
| **Explore the Turkish Quarter.** These narrow alleyways now play host to boutiques and cafés, but it's still a living district with real Aegean character. |
| **Survey Lindos Town from the Acropolis above.** The splendid vista includes a tangle of narrow streets, whitewashed walls, and terra-cotta roofs down to the horseshoe bay with azure waters. |

The **Turkish Library** dates to the late 18th century. Striking reminders of the Ottoman presence, the library and the mosque opposite are still used by those members of Rhodes's Turkish community who stayed behind after the population exchange of 1923. ⊠ *Sokratous opposite Mosque of Süleyman* ☎ *22410/74090* ⛭ *Free* ⊗ *Mon.–Sat. 9:30–4.*

**Walls.** The fortification walls of Rhodes in themselves are one of the great medieval monuments in the Mediterranean. Wonderfully restored, they illustrate the engineering capabilities as well as the financial and human resources available to the Knights. Twentieth-century Italian rulers erased much of the Ottoman influence, preferring to emphasize the Knights' past when restoring architecture. For 200 years the Knights strengthened the walls by thickening them, up to 40 feet in places, and curving them so as to deflect cannonballs. The moat between the inner and outer walls never contained water; it was a device to prevent invaders from constructing siege towers. Part of the road that runs along the top for the entire 4 km (2½ mi) is accessible through municipal guided tours. ⊠ *Old town, tours depart from Palace of the Grand Masters entrance* ☎ *22410/23359* ⛭ *Tour €6* ⊗ *Tours Tues. and Sat. at 2:45 (arrive at least 15 min early).*

## LINDOS

*19 km (12 mi) southwest of Epta Piges, 48 km (30 mi) southwest of Rhodes Town.*

Lindos, cradled between two harbors, had a particular importance in antiquity. It had a revered sanctuary, consecrated to Athena, whose cult probably succeeded that of a pre-Hellenic divinity named Lindia, and the sanctuary was dedicated to Athena Lindia. Lindos prospered during the Middle Ages, and under the Knights of St. John. Only at the beginning of the 19th century did the age-old shipping activity cease. The population decreased radically, reviving only with the 20th-century influx of foreigners.

Lindos is enchanting and remarkably well-preserved. Many 15th-century houses are still in use. Everywhere are examples of Crusader architecture: substantial houses of finely cut Lindos limestone, with windows crowned by elaborate arches. Intermixed with these Crusader buildings are whitewashed, geometric, Cycladic-style houses. Many floors are paved with black-and-white pebble mosaics. The narrow alleyways can get crowded in summer.

**Fodor's**Choice **Acropolis of Lindos.** For about €5 you can hire a donkey for the 15-minute
★ climb from the modern town up to the Acropolis of Lindos. The final approach ascends a steep flight of stairs, past a marvelous 2nd-century BC **relief** of the prow of a Lindian ship carved into the rock, and through the main gate.

The entrance to the Acropolis takes you through the **medieval castle,** with the Byzantine **Chapel of St. John** on the next level above. On the **upper terraces** are the remains of the elaborate **porticoes** and **stoas.** The site and temple command an immense sweep of sea; the lofty white columns on the summit must have presented a magnificent picture. The main portico had 42 Doric columns, at the center of which an opening led to the staircase up to the **propylaea.** The temple at the very top is surprisingly modest, given the drama of the approach. As was common in the 4th century BC, both the front and the rear are flanked by four Doric columns, like the Temple of Athena Nike on the Acropolis of Athens. Numerous inscribed statue bases were found all over the summit, attesting in many cases to the work of Lindian sculptors, who were clearly second to none. ⊠ *Above New Town* ☎ *22440/31258* 🖼 *€6* 🕒 *May–Oct., Tues.–Sun. 8:30–7, Mon. 12:30–7; Nov.–Apr., Tues.–Sun. 8:30–2:40.*

**Church of the Panayia.** This is a graceful building with a beautiful bell tower. The body of the church probably antedates the Knights, although the bell tower bears their arms with the dates 1484–90. The interior has frescoes painted in 1779 by Gregory of Symi. ⊠ *Off main square* 🖼 *No phone* 🕒 *May–Oct., daily 9–2 and 5–9; Nov.–Apr., call number posted on church to have door unlocked.*

## SHOPPING

Lovers of handicrafts will really enjoy shopping in Rhodes. There's an abundance of ceramics, both traditional and modern, wooden bowls, reproductions of ancient statuary, woven rugs, jewelry, lace, and edibles such as delicious honey, olive oil, and of course, olives themselves. Cotton clothing is perfect for the summer temperatures. Strong handcrafted sandals and leather goods are also excellent choices.

Souvenir shopping in Rhodes Town is concentrated on Sokratous Street and the labyrinth of narrow alleyways in the old Turkish Quarter. You'll find the same merchandise in the alleyways of Lindos, where every inch of wall space is used for display—sometimes to the detriment of pedestrian traffic flow. Rhodes Town has a number of high-class jewelers and camera shops, whereas Lindos has more art galleries. The winding path that leads up to the citadel of Lindos is traditionally where Lindian women spread out their lace and embroidery over the rocks like fresh laundry.

**Astero Antiques.** The owner of this shop travels throughout Greece each winter to fill his shop. ⊠ *Ayiou Fanouriou 4, at Sokratous* ☏ *22410/34753.*

**Famous Silver Jewellery.** This store has, as its name suggests, a huge range of silver jewelry for sale. ⊠ *27 Papanikolaou St.* ☏ *22410/70863.*

**Tradition.** Here you can buy delicious olive oil, herbs, olives, wine, and honey, plus some interesting ceramics. ⊠ *8 Ippodamou St.* ☏ *22410/24236.*

# BEACHES

Rhodes is a popular island with European vacationers, and the beaches all around the island have well-developed facilities.

**Faliraki Beach.** With its long stretch of sandy beach and water park, Faliraki has a reputation for its twentysomething, boozing crowds. It's the best place to head for a whole range of water sports. There are some quieter alternatives if you go farther south. ⊠ *16 km (10 mi) south of Rhodes town.*

**Lachania Beach.** Lindos has a lovely sandy crescent flanking the Old Town, but it does get busy in summer. The long Lachania Beach begins a mile before Gennadi and stretches south, uninterrupted for several miles; drive alongside until you come to a secluded spot. ⊠ *48 km (30 mi) southwest of Rhodes town.*

**Prasonisi.** If you head to the southern island tip of the island (around an hour and 15 minutes from Rhodes Town), you'll find beaches known for some of Greece's best windsurfing. Boards and wet suits can be rented at the beach. ⊠ *17 km (10½ mi) south of Plimiri.*

# WHERE TO EAT

**$$$**    ✕ **Dinoris.** The great hall that holds Dinoris was built in AD 310 as a
SEAFOOD    hospital and then converted into a stable for the Knights in 1530. The
★    fish specialties and the spacious, classy setting lure appreciative and demanding clients, from visiting celebs to Middle Eastern sheikhs. For appetizers, try the variety platter, which includes *psarokeftedakia* (fish balls made from a secret recipe), as well as mussels, shrimp, and lobster. Other special dishes are sea-urchin salad and grilled calamari stuffed with cheese. In warm months, cool sea air drifts through the outdoor garden area enclosed by part of the city's walls. ⊠ *Mouseou Sq. 14a* ☏ *22410/25824* ⌂ *Reservations essential* ▭ *AE, MC, V* ☉ *Closed Jan.*

$$$    ✕ **Mavrikos.** The secret of this longtime favorite is an elegant, perfect
GREEK    simplicity. Seemingly straightforward dishes, such as sea-urchin salad, fried *manouri* cheese with basil and pine nuts, swordfish in caper sauce, and lobster risotto, become transcendent with the magic touch of third-generation chef Dimitris Mavrikos. He combines the freshest ingredients with classical training and an abiding love for the best of Greek village cuisine. ⊠ *Main square, Lindos* ☎ *22440/31232* ⊟ *MC, V* ☉ *Closed Nov.–Mar.*

# SANTORINI, GREECE

Undoubtedly the most extraordinary island in the Aegean, crescent-shape Santorini remains a mandatory stop on the Cycladic tourist route—even if it's necessary to enjoy the sensational sunsets from Ia, the fascinating excavations, and the dazzling white towns with a million other travelers. Arriving by boat, you are met by one of the world's truly breathtaking sights, the caldera: a crescent of cliffs, striated in black, pink, brown, white, and pale green, rising 1,100 feet, with the white clusters of the towns of Fira and Ia perched along the top. The encircling cliffs are the ancient rim of a still-active volcano, and you are sailing east across its flooded caldera. Victims of their own success, the main towns of Santorini can at peak times seem overburdened by an unrelenting mass of backpackers and tour groups. Even so, if you look beneath the layers of gimcrack tourism, you'll find that Santorini is still a beautiful place.

## ESSENTIALS

CURRENCY    The euro (€1 to US$1.36 at this writing). ATMs are common.

HOURS    Museums are generally open from 9 to 5, but many are closed on Monday. Shops are open daily in the summer, from 9 to noon or 1, reopening from 4 or 5 until 9 on Monday through Saturday; and from 9 to 6 on Sunday. Many shops and restaurants are closed between October and April.

INTERNET    **Lava Café** (⊠ *Main road, at Fira Sq.* ☎ *22860/25291*) serves snacks and drinks and also has image-editing software.

TELEPHONES    Tri-band GSM phones work in Greece. You can buy prepaid phone cards at telecom shops, news vendors, and tobacconists in all towns and cities. Phone cards can be used for local or international calls. Vodafone is the leading mobile telecom company. OTE is the national domestic provider. Calls can be made at OTE offices and paid for after completion.

## COMING ASHORE

Cruise ships anchor in the spectacular caldera, and in almost all cases passengers are tendered to the small port of Skala Fira, a sheer 1,000 feet below the capital, Fira. You can either take the funicular to the top or take a donkey ride up the steep winding path that claws its way to the top; regardless of your mode of travel, the cost is the same (€4). The donkey drivers are very persistent, but be aware that donkey droppings make the path slippery and smelly (especially relevant if you decide to go up on foot, which is also possible).

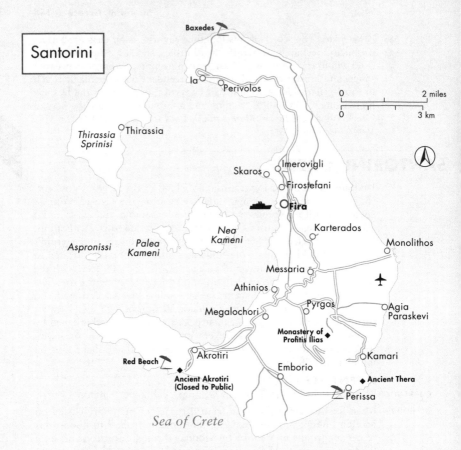

# Santorini

Baxedes

Ia
Perivolos

Thirassia
Sprinisi

Thirassia

Skaros
Imerovigli
Firostefani

Fira

Karterados

Nea
Kameni

Monolithos

Aspronissi

Palea
Kameni

Messaria

Athinios

Pyrgos

Megalochori

Agia
Paraskevi

Monastery of
Profitis Ilias

Red Beach
Akrotiri

Emborio

Kamari

Ancient Akrotiri
(Closed to Public)

Ancient Thera

Perissa

0        2 miles

0      3 km

Sea of Crete

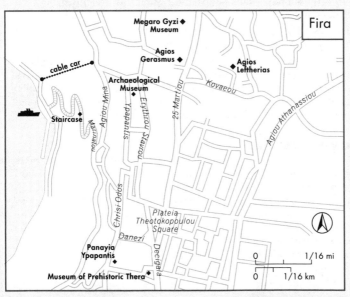

# Fira

Megaro Gyzi ◆
Museum

cable car

Agios
Gerasmus ◆

Agios ◆
Leftherias

Archaeological
Museum

Staircase

Agiou Mina

Mavratzou

Ypapantis

Erythrou Stavrou

25 Martiou

Kovaeou

Agiou Athanassiou

Christi Odos

Plateia
Theotokopoulou
Square

Danezi

Decigala

Panayia
Ypapantis ◆

Museum of Prehistoric Thera ◆

0        1/16 mi

0      1/16 km

Regular bus services (approximately every 30 minutes in summer, dropping to every 1½ hours in winter with shoulder seasons) travel from Thira to Ia and Akrotiri. Schedules are posted in the station. Ticket prices range from €1.10 to €3. The main taxi stand sits next to the bus station in the main town square. Fares are reasonable, with a trip from Fira to Ia costing approximately €15.

If you rented a car for the day, you could probably see most of what Santorini has to offer. The island is compact, and it's difficult to get lost. Prices are €50 per day for a subcompact manual vehicle, but you can get an ATV for around €25 or a motorbike or scooter with prices starting at about €10 a day, including third-party liability coverage. If you rent a quad, bike, or scooter don't wear shorts or sandals, insist on the helmet (which the law requires), and get a phone number, in case of breakdown. Don't rent a scooter if you aren't an experienced rider.

## EXPLORING SANTORINI

### FIRA

Tourism, the island's major industry, adds more than 1 million visitors per year to a population of 7,000. As a result, Fira, the capital, midway along the west coast of the east rim, is no longer only a picturesque village but a major tourist center, overflowing with discos, shops, and restaurants. It soon becomes clear what brings the tourist here: with its white, cubical white houses clinging to the cliff hundreds of feet above the caldera, Fira is a beautiful place. The blocked-off Ypapantis Street (west of Panayia Ypapantis cathedral) leads to Kato Fira (Lower Fira), built into the cliff-side overlooking the caldera, where prices are higher and the vista wonderful. For centuries, the people of the island have been digging themselves rooms with a view right in the cliff face. Along Eikostis Pemptis Martiou (25th March Street), you'll find inexpensive restaurants and accommodations—many bars and hotel rooms now occupy the caves. The farther away from the caldera you get, the cheaper the restaurants.

**Archaeological Museum.** This small museum displays pottery, statues, and grave artifacts found at excavations mostly from ancient Thira and Akrotiri, from the Minoan through the Byzantine periods. ⊠ *Stavrou and Nomikos* ☎ *22860/22217* ☜ *€5, including Museum of Prehistoric Thera* ☉ *Tues.–Sun. 8:30–3.*

★ **The Museum of Prehistoric Thera.** Since the actual archaeological site at ancient Akrotiri is not open, your best bet is to look at the displays of pots and frescoes from there in this museum's collection. Note the fresco fragments with the painted swallows (who flocked here because they loved the cliffs) and the women in Minoan dresses. The fossilized olive leaves from 60,000 BC prove the olive to be indigenous. ⊠ *Mitropoleos, behind big church* ☎ *22860/23217* ⊕ *www.culture.gr* ⊡ *€3* ☉ *Tues.–Sun. 8:30–3.*

**Panayia Ypapantis.** Fira's modern Greek Orthodox cathedral is a major landmark; the local priests, with somber faces, long beards, and black robes, look strangely out of place in summertime Fira. ⊠ *Southern part of town.*

> **ANCIENT AKROTIRI**
>
> The best archaeological site on Santorini is near the tip of the southern horn of the island. Unfortunately, at this writing the site is closed (and has been for some time) for structural repairs. There was some hope that it might reopen, but such hopes have become commonplace for the past few years, so check ahead before you plan a visit.

**Staircase.** To experience life here as it was until only a couple of decades ago, walk down the much-photographed winding staircase that descends from town to the water's edge—walk or take the cable car back up, avoiding the drivers who will try to plant you on the sagging back of one of their bedraggled donkeys. Note, however, that however you choose to return to the top, the price (€4) is the same (cable car or donkey). ⊠ *Marinatou.*

## FIROSTEFANI

Firostefani used to be a separate village, but now it is an elegant suburb north of Fira. The 10-minute walk between it and Fira, along the caldera, is one of Santorini's highlights. From Firostefani's single white cliff-side street, walkways descend to traditional vaulted cave houses, which are fast becoming pensions. Though close to the action, Firostefani feels calm and quiet.

## IMEROVIGLI

Imerovigli, on the highest point of the caldera's rim, is what Firostefani was like a decade and a half ago. It is now being developed, and for good reasons: it is quiet, traditional, and less expensive. The 25-minute walk from Fira, with incredible views, should be on everyone's itinerary. The lodgments, some of them traditional cave houses, are mostly down stairways from the cliff-side walkway. The big rock backing the village was once crowned by Skaros castle, where Venetial the conqueror raised his flag in 1207; it housed the island's administrative offices. It collapsed in an earthquake, leaving only the rock.

## IA

**Fodor's Choice** At the tip of the northern horn of the island sits Ia (or Oia), Santorini's ★ second-largest town and the Aegean's most-photographed village. Ia is more tasteful than Fira (for one thing, no establishment here is allowed to play music that can be heard on the street), and the town's cubical white houses (some vaulted against earthquakes) stand out against the green-, brown-, and rust-color layers of rock, earth, and solid volcanic ash that rise from the sea. Every summer evening, travelers from all over the world congregate at the caldera's rim—sitting on whitewashed fences, staircases, beneath the town's windmill, on the old **Kastro**—each looking out to sea in anticipation of the performance: the Ia sunset. The three-hour rim-edge walk from Ia to Fira at this hour is unforgettable.

In the middle of the quiet caldera, the volcano smolders away eerily, adding an air of suspense to an already awe-inspiring scene. The 1956 earthquake (7.8 on the Richter scale) left 48 people dead (thankfully, most residents were working outdoors at the time), hundreds injured, and 2,000 houses toppled. The island's west side—especially Ia, until then the largest town—was hard hit, and many residents decided to emigrate to Athens, Australia, and America. And although Fira, also damaged, rebuilt rapidly, Ia proceeded slowly, sticking to the traditional architectural style. The perfect example of that style is the restaurant 1800, a renovated ship-captain's villa. In 1900 Ia had nearly 9,000 inhabitants, mostly mariners who owned 164 seafaring vessels and seven shipyards. Now there are about 500 permanent residents, and more than 100 boats. Many of these mariners use the endless flight of stairs from the Kastro to descend down to the water and the small port of **Ammoudi,** where the pebble beach is home to some of the island's nicest fish tavernas. Head east to find the fishing port of **Armeni,** home to all those excursion boats that tour the caldera.

Ia is set up like the other three towns—Fira, Firostefani, and Imerovigli—that adorn the caldera's sinuous rim. There is a car road, which is new, and a cliff-side walkway (Nikolaos Nomikou), which is old. Shops and restaurants are all on the walkway, and hotel entrances mostly descend from it—something to check carefully if you cannot negotiate stairs easily. In Ia there is a lower cliff-side walkway writhing with stone steps, and a long stairway to the tiny blue bay with its dock below. Short streets leading from the car road to the walkway have cheaper eateries and shops. There is a parking lot at either end, and the northern one marks the end of the road and the rim. Nothing is very far from anything else.

The main walkway of Ia can be thought of as a straight river, with a delta at the northern end, where the better shops and restaurants are. The most-luxurious cave-house hotels are at the southern end, and a stroll by them is part of the extended evening promenade. Although it is not as crowded as Fira, where the tour boats deposit their thousands of hasty shoppers, relentless publicity about Ia's beauty and tastefulness, accurate enough, are making it impassable in August. The sunset in Ia may not really be much more spectacular than in Fira, and certainly not better than in higher Imerovigli, but there is something tribally satisfying at the sight of so many people gathering in one spot to celebrate pure beauty. Happily, the night scene isn't as frantic as Fira's—most shop owners are content to sit out front and don't cotton to the few revelers' bars in operation. In winter Ia feels pretty uninhabited.

**Naval Museum of Thera.** This museum is in an old neoclassic mansion, once destroyed in the big earthquake, now risen like a phoenix from the ashes. The collection displays ships' figureheads, seamen's chests, maritime equipment, and models—all revealing the extensive nautical history of the island, Santorini's main trade until tourism took over. ⊠ *Near telephone office* ☎ *22860/71156* ⊠ *€4* ☉ *Tues.–Sun. 8:30–3.*

## NEA KAMENI

To peer into a live, sometimes smoldering volcano, join one of the popular excursions to **Nea Kameni,** the larger of the two Burnt Isles at the center of the caldera. After disembarking, you hike 430 feet to the top and walk around the edge of the crater, wondering if the volcano is ready for its fifth eruption during the last hundred years—after all, the last was in 1956. Some tours continue on to Therasia, where there is a village. ⊠ *In Caldera, 2 km (1 mi) west of Fira.*

# SHOPPING

The dramatic landscapes and light of Santorini are an inspiration to the creative—the archipelago is home to artists working in many genres. There are many galleries selling exquisite one-of-a-kind jewelry and hundreds of others selling artistic accessories for the home.

The locals say that in Santorini there is more wine than water, and it may be true: Santorini produces more wine than any two other Cyclades. Thirty-six varieties of grape thrive here. Farmers twist the vines into a basketlike shape, in which the grapes grow, protected from the wind.

# BEACHES

Santorini's volcanic rocks have produced unusual beaches of black and red sand that make for dramatic vistas. One thing to note is that this sand absorbs the suns rays and gets much hotter than golden sand. The black-sand beaches of **Kamari** (and of Perissa) are popular and consequently overdeveloped. Deck chairs and umbrellas can be rented, and tavernas and refreshment stands abound. **Red Beach,** on the southwest shore below Akrotiri, is quiet and has a taverna.

# WHERE TO EAT

$    ✗ **Lithos.** Dimitris Anastopoulos's restaurant deftly proves you can eat
GREEK    well, inexpensively, and have a caldera view. Start with steamed mussels with ouzo and masticha liquor or pastry flutes with Edam, sun-dried tomatoes, capers, and yogurt. For a main dish, try chicken with artichokes and capers in lemon cream sauce, or Lithos pork tenderloin, with mushrooms and kefalotiri cheese in red-wine sauce. Desserts are a specialty, and cheesecake with wild blackberries tastes as good as it looks. The oil and wine are from Dimitris's farm in the Peloponnese, and the fish is local. From the high caldera street, walk down to the lower until you see the sign. This neighborhood jumps at night. ⊠ *Caldera* ☎ *22860/24421* ⊕ *www.lithossantorini.com* ⊟ *AE, MC, V* ☉ *Closed Nov.–Mar.*

¢–$    ✗ **Skaros Fish Taverna.** This rustic open-air taverna, one of three restau-
GREEK    rants in Imerovigli, has spectacular caldera views. It serves fresh fish and Santorini specialties, such as octopus in onion sauce, and mussels with rice and raisins. ⊠ *On cliff-side walkway* ☎ *22860/23616* ⊟ *AE, MC, V* ☉ *Closed Nov.–Mar.*

# The North Sea

PORTS IN BELGIUM, GREAT BRITAIN, IRELAND, AND THE NETHERLANDS

**WORD OF MOUTH**

"Amsterdam is so walkable and safe, you can easily just 'follow your nose' without needing a walking plan. We loved wandering around that lovely city, at all hours of the day and night."

—MaureenB

"In Edinburgh we walked the Royal Mile (more than once), visited Holyrood Palace, the Britannia, Mary King's Close."

—d1carter

Lindsay
Bennett

Ports in the United Kingdom have long been the starting points for many transatlantic crossings, but these days your ship is more likely to begin its journey in Harwich than Southampton, and may cruise around the North Sea and British Isles or continue to the Baltic or even around the Mediterranean.

Royal Caribbean announced that the line's new ship, *Independence of the Seas,* would make its European home in Southampton and Harwich for the 2008 Mediterranean cruising season. These increasingly busy ports sometimes include more exotic destinations such as the Canary Islands on their itineraries.

### ABOUT THE RESTAURANTS

All the restaurants we recommend serve lunch; they may also serve dinner if your cruise ship stays late in port and you choose to dine off the ship. Europeans tend to eat a leisurely meal at lunch, but in most ports there are quicker and simpler alternatives for those who just want to grab a quick bite before returning to the ship. You'll be able to pay in euros only in Belgium, Ireland, and the Netherlands; prices in England and Scotland are in British pounds. Price categories in those countries are based on the euro-equivalent costs of eating in restaurants.

| WHAT IT COSTS IN EUROS AND POUNDS | | | | | |
|---|---|---|---|---|---|
| | ¢ | $ | $$ | $$$ | $$$$ |
| Restaurants in euros | under €11 | €11–€17 | €17–€23 | €23–€30 | over €30 |
| Restaurants in pounds | under £5 | £5–£8 | £8–£12 | £12–£15 | over £15 |

Restaurant prices are per person for a main course, including tax.

# AMSTERDAM, NETHERLANDS

Amsterdam has as many facets as a 40-carat diamond polished by one of the city's gem cutters: the capital, and spiritual "downtown," of a nation ingrained with the principles of tolerance; a veritable Babylon of Old World charm; a font for homegrown geniuses such as Rembrandt and Van Gogh; a cornucopia bursting with parrot tulips and other greener—more potent—blooms; and a unified social zone that takes in cozy bars, archetypal "brown" cafés, and outdoor markets. Although impressive gabled houses bear witness to the Golden Age of the 17th century, their upside-down images reflected in the waters of the city's canals symbolize and magnify the contradictions within the broader Dutch society. With a mere 730,000 friendly souls and with almost everything a scant 10-minute bike ride away, Amsterdam is actually like a village that happens to pack the cultural wallop of a megalopolis.

### ESSENTIALS

CURRENCY  The euro (€1 to US$1.36). ATMs are common and credit cards are widely accepted.

HOURS  Shops open Tuesday, Wednesday, Friday, and Saturday from 9 or 10 until 6; they are open later on Thursday. Most stores are closed on Sunday and some on Monday. Museums open from 9 until 6, with one late-opening night during the week.

INTERNET  **Underworld Café** ✉ *7–a Voetboogstraat* ☎ *020/6381388.*

TELEPHONES  Most tri- and quad-band GSM mobile phones should work in the Netherlands, which operates a 3G mobile system with dual-band handsets. Public phones take phone cards (available at numerous shops) and credit cards, and will connect international calls. Major telecom companies are Vodafone and Orange.

### COMING ASHORE

Shops dock at the cruise terminal adjacent to the historic Old Town, a five-minute walk from the transport hub of the city. The terminal has tourist information, extensive shopping facilities, and a range of eateries. Passengers can walk directly from the terminal into the town or rent a bike and take to the cycle tracks that crisscross the city. The main train station and city bus station are adjacent for trips to other locations around the Netherlands.

The so-called "Canal Bus" (which is actually a boat) stops at 14 of Amsterdam's major museums, traveling around on the water. A day-ticket for the Canal Bus is €22, including discounts on some museum entrance fees. The bus makes a stop just outside the central train station. Public bus and tram services are also useful for visiting the attractions: single tickets cost €2.60 for a maximum one-hour journey, while a day ticket is €7. In Amsterdam most transit tickets have been replaced with reusable plastic cards, but single tickets and day tickets are disposable paper tickets and can still be bought on board the bus or tram.

### GETTING TO THE AIRPORT

If you chose not to purchase airport transfers from your cruise line, it's simple and inexpensive to make your way from the aiport to the cruise port. There's a train from Schipol Airport direct to the main railway station in the city (Centraal Station) for €3.70. The ticket office is in the main hall of the airport, and there are a number of ticket machines; however, machines do not accept credit cards, so you would need euro coins. It's a 15- to 20-minute journey to the main train station, then a 10-minute walk on foot to the cruise-passenger terminal.

Alternatively, its possible to take a shared airport minibus or a private taxi transfer, which takes about 20 minutes at a cost of around €50.

## EXPLORING AMSTERDAM

Fodor's Choice ★  **Amsterdams Historisch Museum** *(Amsterdam Historical Museum)*. Any city that began in the 13th century as a sinking bog of a fishing village and eventually became the 17th century's most powerful trading city has a fascinating story to tell, and this museum does it superbly. It's housed in a rambling amalgamation of buildings that were used as an orphanage

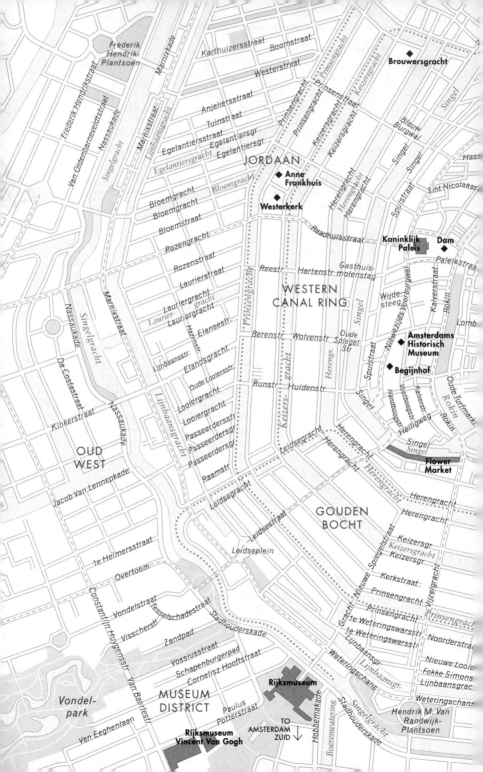

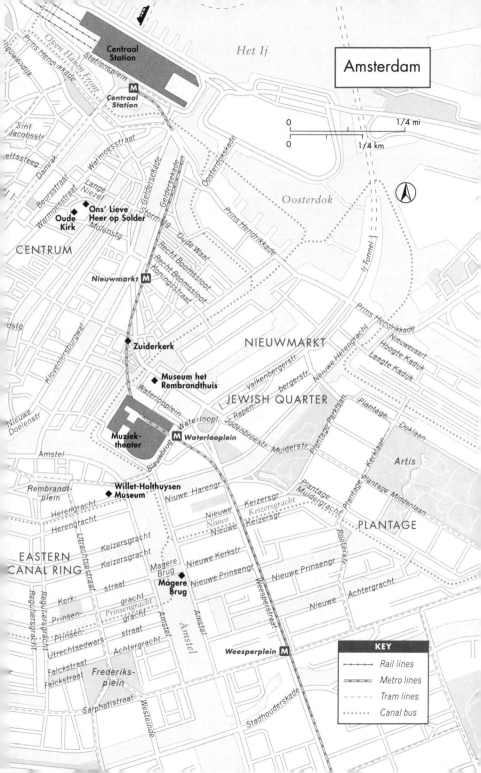

in 1580 and then reopened as a museum in 1975. Although rich with art, models, and plain old treasures, the museum also employs a lot of state-of-the-art technologies: many will delight in the five different **speaking dollhouses** that tell of daily life through the centuries and a "white car" (a small car originally formulated to be a utopian form of urban transportation in the 1960s) in which you can cruise the city's streets. ⊠ *Kalverstraat 92 and Nieuwezijds Voorburgwal 357, Nieuwe Zijde* ☎ *020/523–1822* ⊕ *www.ahm.nl* ⊡ *€10* ☉ *Weekdays 10–5, weekends 11–5.*

> ### AMSTERDAM BEST BETS
>
> **Canal-boat trip.** It may seem kitschy, but this is the best way to get a feel for the canal ring historic area and to take in the wonderful architecture of the Old City.
>
> **Rijksmuseum Vincent van Gogh.** This is the world's richest repository of the tragic artist's work.
>
> **Rijksmuseum.** Though this gallery is currently undergoing a comprehensive renovation program, even the limited display of highlights on show makes it a must-see.

**Fodor's Choice** ★ **Anne Frankhuis** *(Anne Frank House).* In the precious pages of *The Diary of Anne Frank* (published in 1947 as *The Secret Annex* by her father after her death) the young Anne kept her sad record of two increasingly fraught years living in secret confinement from the Nazis. Along with the Van Pels family (called Van Daan in the book), the Frank family felt the noose tighten, so decided to move into a hidden warren of rooms at the back of this 1635-built canal house. Anne's diary has now sold more than 30 million copies and been translated into more than 50 languages. The museum explores the wider issues of genocide and oppression, but visitors flock to feel the reality of Anne's daily existence. Lines can be long in summer, so you may wish to buy tickets in advance online. ⊠ *Prinsengracht 263, Jordaan* ☎ *020/556–7100* ⊕ *www.annefrank.nl* ⊡ *€8.50* ☉ *Sept. 15–Mar. 14, daily 9–7; Mar. 15–June and Sept. 1–Sept. 14, daily 9–9; July and–Aug., daily 9 AM–10 PM.*

**Fodor's Choice** ★ **Brouwersgracht.** The Jordaan (pronounced Yoarh-*dahn*), now a wanderer's paradise lined with quirky boutiques, excellent restaurants, and galleries—has evolved into one of the city's most singular neighborhoods. One of the most-photographed spots in town is Brouwersgracht, a pretty, tree-lined canal at the northern border of the Jordaan district, bordered by residences and historic warehouses of the brewers who traded here in the 17th century, when Amsterdam was the "warehouse of the world." ⊠ *Western Canal Ring, Jordaan.*

**Dam** *(Dam Square).* Home to the Koninklijk Paleis and the Nieuwe Kerk, Amsterdam's official center of town is the Dam, which traces its roots to the 12th century, when wanderers from central Europe came floating in their canoes down the Amstel River and thought to stop to build a dam. The **National Monument,** a towering white obelisk in the center of the square, was erected in 1956 as a memorial to the Dutch victims of World War II. The urns embedded in the monument's rear contain earth from all the Dutch provinces and former colonies (Indonesia, Suriname, and the Antilles). ⊠ *Nieuwe Zijde.*

**Fodor's**Choice **Magere Brug** *(Skinny Bridge).* Of Amsterdam's 60-plus drawbridges, the
★ Magere (which derives from "meager" in Dutch) is the most famous.
It was purportedly built in 1672 by two sisters living on opposite sides
of the Amstel, who wanted an efficient way of sharing that grandest of
Dutch traditions: the *gezellig* (socially cozy) midmorning coffee break.
Nowadays it's spectacularly lighted with electric lights at night, and
often drawn up to let boats pass by. ⊠ *Between Kerkstraat and Nieuwe
Kerkstraat, Eastern Canal Ring.*

**Fodor's**Choice **Museum het Rembrandthuis** *(Rembrandt's House).* One of Amsterdam's
★ more remarkable relics, this house was bought by Rembrandt, flush
with success, for his family and is where he lived and worked between
1639 and 1658. Rembrandt chose this house on what was once the
main street of the Jewish Quarter because he thought he could then
experience daily and firsthand the faces he would use in his Old Testament religious paintings. Rembrandt later lost the house to bankruptcy:
when he showed a quick recovery—and an open taste for servant girls—
after his wife Saskia's death, his uncle-in-law, once his greatest champion, became his biggest detractor. Rembrandt's downfall was sealed.
He came under attack by the Amsterdam burghers, who refused to
accept his liaison with his amour, Hendrickje. Rembrandt's scandal not-
withstanding, the family rooms and the artist's studio have been painstakingly restored. ⊠ *Jodenbreestraat 4–6, Jewish Quarter and Plantage*
☎ *020/520–0400* ⊕ *www.rembrandthuis.nl* ▧ €9 ☉ *Daily 10–5.*

**Fodor's**Choice **Ons' Lieve Heer op Solder** *(Our Lord in the Attic Museum).* With its
★ elegant gray-and-white facade and spout gable, this appears to be
just another canal house, and on the lower floors it is. The attic of
this building, however, contains something unique: the only surviving *schuilkerken* (clandestine church) that dates from the Reformation
in Amsterdam, when open worship by Catholics was outlawed. Since
the Oude Kerk was then relieved of its original patron, St. Nicholas,
when it was de-catholicized, this became the church dedicated to him
until the Sint Nicolaaskerk was built. The chapel itself is a triumph of
Dutch classicist taste, with magnificent marble columns, gilded capitals,
a colored-marble altar, and the *Baptism of Christ* (1716) painting by
Jacob de Wit presiding over all. Sunday services and weddings are still
offered here. The museum is undergoing a renovation through 2012; it
remains open, but not all rooms will be accessible. ⊠ *Oudezijds Voorburgwal 40, Oude Zijde* ☎ *020/624–6604* ⊕ *www.opsolder.nl* ▧ €7
☉ *Mon.–Sat. 10–5, Sun. 1–5.*

★ **Oude Kerk** *(Old Church).* The Oude Kerk is indeed Amsterdam's oldest
church, and has been surrounded by all the trappings of humanity's
oldest trade (i.e., prostitution) for the vast majority of its history—a
history that has seen it chaotically evolve from single-nave chapel to
hall church to a cross basilica. It began as a wooden chapel in 1306,
but was built for the ages between 1366 and 1566 (and fully restored
between 1955 and 1979), when the whole neighborhood was rife with
monasteries and convents. It is now a wholly unique exhibition space
for modern-art exhibitions and the annual World Press Photo competition. Its carillon gets played every Saturday between 4 and 5. ⊠ *Oude-*

*kerksplein 23, Oude Zijde* ☎ *020/625–8284* ⊕ *www.oudekerk.nl* 🖅 *€5* ⊙ *Mon.–Sat. 11–5, Sun. 1–5.*

**Fodor's Choice**  **Rijksmuseum** *(State Museum).* The Netherlands' greatest museum, the
★  Rijksmuseum is home to Rembrandt's *Night Watch,* Vermeer's *The
Kitchen Maid,* and a near infinite selection of world-famous masterpieces by the likes of Steen, Ruisdael, Brouwers, Hals, Hobbema, Cuyp,
Van der Helst, and their Golden Age ilk. This national treasure, however, will be largely closed until 2012 for extensive renovation and
rebuilding, following the plans of Seville's architect duo Antonio Cruz
and Antonio Ortiz. Only the South Wing—which has now through
corporate sponsorship been renamed the Philips Wing—will remain
reliably open to house a "Best of" selection. ⊠ *Stadhouderskade 42;
Entrance during renovations: Jan Luijkenstraat 1, Museum District*
☎ *020/674–7000* ⊕ *www.rijksmuseum.nl* 🖅 *€12.50* ⊙ *Daily 9–6.*

**Fodor's Choice**  **Rijksmuseum Vincent Van Gogh** *(Vincent Van Gogh Museum).* Opened
★  in 1973, this remarkable light-infused building, based on a design by
famed De Stijl architect Gerrit Rietveld, venerates the short, certainly
not sweet, but highly productive career of everyone's favorite tortured
19th-century artist. Although some of the Van Gogh paintings that
are scattered throughout the world's high-art temples are of dubious
provenance, this collection's authenticity is indisputable: its roots trace
directly back to brother Theo van Gogh, Vincent's artistic and financial
supporter. ⊠ *Paulus Potterstraat 7, Museum District* ☎ *020/570–5200*
⊕ *www.vangoghmuseum.nl* 🖅 *€14* ⊙ *Sat.–Thurs. 10–6, Fri. 10–10.*

★  **Westerkerk** *(Western Church).* Built between 1602 and 1631 by the
ubiquitous Hendrick de Keyser and presumed the last resting place of
Rembrandt, the Dutch Renaissance Westerkerk was the largest Protes-
tant church in the world until Christopher Wren came along with his St.
Paul's Cathedral in London. Its tower—endlessly mentioned in Jordaan
songs—is topped by a gaudy copy of the crown of the Habsburg emperor
Maximilian I. The crown's "XXX" marking was quickly exploited by
the city's merchants as a visiting card of quality. ⊠ *Prinsengracht 281
(corner of Westermarkt), Jordaan* ☎ *020/624–7766* ⊕ *www.westerkerk.
nl* 🖅 *€5* ⊙ *Apr.–Oct., weekdays 11–3.*

**Fodor's Choice**  **Willet-Holthuysen Museum.** Few patrician houses are open to the pub-
★  lic along the Herengracht, so make a beeline to this mansion to see
Grachtengordel (Canal Ring) luxury at its best. In 1895 the widow
Sandrina Louisa Willet-Holthuysen donated the house and contents—
which included her husband's extensive art collection—to the city of
Amsterdam. You can now wander through this 17th-century canal
house, now under the management of the Amsterdams Historisch
Museum, and discover all its original 18th-century interiors, complete
with that era's mod-cons from ballroom to *cabinet des merveilles* (rari-
ties cabinet). You can air out the aura of Dutch luxury by lounging in
the French-style garden in the back. ⊠ *Herengracht 605, Eastern Canal
Ring* ☎ *020/523–1822* ⊕ *www.willetholthuysen.nl* 🖅 *€7* ⊙ *Weekdays
10–5, weekends 11–5.*

## SHOPPING

Souvenir shops are filled with wooden clogs and ceramics bearing windmill or tulip motifs, but Amsterdam offers more than just cheap and cheerful items. There's a major market in diamonds and also in antiques. At the lower end of the price scale, there's a market in collectibles and one-of-a-kind items, plus cutting-edge design for the home.

**Kalverstraat,** the city's main pedestrians-only shopping street, is where much of Amsterdam does its day-to-day shopping. Running parallel to Kalverstraat is the **Rokin,** a main tram route lined with shops offering high-priced trendy fashion, jewelry, accessories, antiques, and even an Old Master painting or two. Shoppers will love to explore the **Negen Straatjes** (Nine Streets), nine charming, tiny streets that radiate from behind the Royal Palace. Here, in a sector bordered by Raadhuisstraat and Leidsestraat, specialty and fashion shops are delightfully one-of-a-kind. Heading even farther to the west you enter the chic and funky sector of the **Jordaan,** where generation after generation of experimental designers have set up shop to show their imaginative creations. Though adventurous collectors are increasingly looking to the Jordaan district for unique finds, the more expensive **Spiegelkwartier** is the city's mainstay for high-end antiques. The **De Baarsjes** neighborhood in the western part of the city is progressively attracting small galleries that showcase exciting works of art.

★ Whether hunting for treasures or trash, you could get lucky at one of Amsterdam's flea markets. The best is **Waterlooplein** flea market (Monday–Saturday 9–5), which surrounds the perimeter of the Stopera (Muziektheater/Town Hall complex) building. The **Bloemenmarkt** (along the Singel canal, between Koningsplein and Muntplein), is another of Amsterdam's must-see markets, where flowers and plants are sold from permanently moored barges (Monday–Saturday 9–5).

## WHERE TO EAT

¢ ✗**Bakkerswinkel.** This genteel yet unpretentious bakery/tearoom evokes
DUTCH an English country kitchen, one that lovingly prepares and serves
Fodor'sChoice breakfasts, high tea, hearty-breaded sandwiches, soups, and divine
★ (almost manly) slabs of quiche. This place is a true oasis if you want to indulge in a healthful breakfast or lunch. It opens at 8 AM daily, and there's a second location, complete with garden patio, in the Museum District. ⊠ *Warmoestraat 69, Oude Zijde* ☎ *020/489–8000* ⊕ *www. debakkerswinkel.nl* ⊠ *Roelef Hartstraat 68* ☎ *020/662–3594* ⊠ *Redulateurshuis 1, Polonceaukade 1* ☎ *020/688–0632* ▭ *No credit cards* ⊗ *No dinner. Closed Mon.*

$    ✕ **Café Luxembourg.** One of the city's top grand cafés, Luxembourg has a
DUTCH    stately interior and a view of a bustling square, both of which are maxi-
★    mized for people-watching. Famous for its brunch, its classic café menu
includes a terrific goat-cheese salad, dim sum, and excellent Holtkamp
*krokets* (croquettes, these with a shrimp or meat and potato filling).
The "reading table" is democratically packed with both Dutch and
international newspapers and mags, and there's Wi-Fi available (paid).
⊠ *Spuistraat 24, Nieuwe Zijde and Spui* ☎ *020/620–6264* ⊕ *www.*
*luxembourg.nl* ⊟ *AE, DC, MC, V.*

# WHERE TO STAY

$$$$    🖵 **Dylan Amsterdam.** Known for her chic London properties, Anouska
Fodor's Choice    Hempel opened this Amsterdam outpost as the city's first "designer"
★    hotel. It's located at (and incorporates a stone-arch entranceway from)
the site of the historic Municipal Theater, which burned down in the
17th century. Today the elegant rooms here are decorated with lac-
quered trunks, mahogany screens, modernist hardwood tables, and
luxurious upholstery. One suite commands a view of the canal; many
other rooms overlook a serene central courtyard. The hotel's restaurant
($$$–$$$$) offers an acclaimed French menu in a vogueish setting that
functioned as a bakery between 1787 and 1811. **Pros:** a taste of old
Amsterdam; good for celebrity spotting; updated business facilities.
**Cons:** some parts of the hotel feel overdesigned; not all rooms have
water views. ⊠ *Keizersgracht 384, Western Canal Ring* ☎ *020/530–*
*2010* ⊕ *www.dylanamsterdam.com* ⇥ *33 rooms, 8 suites* ♿ *In-room:*
*safe, refrigerator, DVD (some), Wi-Fi. In-hotel: restaurant, room ser-*
*vice, bar, gym, spa, bicycles, laundry service, Internet terminal, Wi-Fi*
*hotspot, parking (paid), no-smoking rooms* ⊟ *AE, DC, MC, V.*

$$$$    🖵 **Hotel Amsterdam–De Roode Leeuw.** On the corner of Dam Square and
across from the city's leading department store, De Bijenkorf, the Hotel
is a cut above the rest of the competition on the Damrak. The front guest
rooms, showcasing the elegant 18th-century facade, have soundproof
windows that serve as a buffer against the outside world. The rooms
at the back or on the "executive floor" are also safe bets. The hotel's
restaurant, De Roode Leeuw, has built up a sizable following thanks
to its heated terrace, Dutch haute cuisine, and encyclopedic champagne
list. It was the recipient of the coveted *Neerlands Dis* (Netherlands'
Dish) award, and serves a succulent roast Gelderland chicken in tar-
ragon sauce, as well as an array of *stampots* (hotchpotches) made with
smoked sausage, beef steak, and bacon. **Pros:** easy access to transporta-
tion; central location; excellent restaurant. **Cons:** small lobby; lacklus-
ter room decor. ⊠ *Damrak 93–94, Centrum* ☎ *020/555–0666* ⊕ *www.*
*hotelamsterdam.nl* ⇥ *79 rooms, 2 suites* ♿ *In-room: safe, refrigerator,*
*Internet. In-hotel: restaurant, laundry service, Internet terminal, Wi-Fi*
*hotspot, no-smoking rooms, some pets allowed* ⊟ *AE, DC, MC, V.*

$$–$$$    🖵 **Singel.** The three renovated 17th-century canal houses that make up
this property are charmingly lopsided and quirky-looking, with cheer-
ful striped window canopies. The historic exterior belies the modern
furnishings and comforts you'll discover within, which include an eleva-
tor and express ironing and shoeshine service. If you want a view of

the Singel Canal, book a front or side room. From the hotel, it's just a short stroll to the Kalvertoren and Magna Plaza shopping malls, as well as the Dam Square. **Pros:** near Amsterdam's best restaurants and bars; lovely façade; doting service. **Cons:** often noisy on weekends; not all rooms have views. ⊠ *Singel 13–17, Centrum* ☎ *020/626–3108* ⊕ *www. singelhotel.nl* ⇒ *32 rooms* ₺ *In-room: no a/c, safe, Internet, Wi-Fi. In-hotel: room service, bar, laundry service, Wi-Fi hotspot, no-smoking rooms, some pets allowed* ➟ *AE, DC, MC, V* ❘⊘❘ *CP.*

# ANTWERP, BELGIUM

In its heyday, Antwerp (Antwerpen in Flemish, Anvers in French) played second fiddle only to Paris. It became Europe's most important commercial center in the 16th century, and this wealth funded many architectural and artistic projects. Masters such as Rubens and Van Dyck established the city as one of Europe's leading art centers, and its innovative printing presses produced missals for the farthest reaches of the continent. It also became, and has remained, the diamond capital of the world. Antwerp is today Europe's second-largest port, and has much of the zest often associated with a harbor town. The historic Oude Stad, the heart of the city, distils the essence of Antwerp. The narrow, winding streets, many of them restricted to pedestrian traffic, are wonderful for strolling, the squares are full of charm, and the museums and churches are the pride of the city.

## ESSENTIALS

CURRENCY The euro (€1 to US$1.36). ATMs are common.

HOURS Museums and attractions are usually open from 9:30 to 5; many are closed on Monday. Most shops are open Monday–Saturday 9–6.

INTERNET **2zones** ⊠ *Wolstraat 15, Oude Stad* ☎ *03/232–2400.*

TELEPHONES Tri-band GSM phones work in Belgium. You can buy prepaid phone cards at telecom shops, news vendors, and tobacconists in all towns and cities. Phone cards can be used for local or international calls. Proximus and Mobistar are the leading telecom companies.

## COMING ASHORE

The cruise port couldn't be better placed for passengers, as vessels dock directly at the heart of the city. All the major attractions and museums of the historic center are within walking distance of the dock. The commercial port has no facilities for disembarking passengers, but a wealth of shopping options and restaurants lies just outside the gates.

Antwerp's tram and metro public transit system is extensive and reliable. A €1.20 ticket is good for one hour on all forms of public transport, including buses. You'll pay €2 if you buy your ticket on the bus, so prepay at a ticket machine at a bus stop, at the station, at the tourist office, or at news vendors in the city; a day pass buys unlimited travel for one full day. Passes are €5 if you prepay, €6 if you buy on the bus or tram. Car-rental offices are in Antwerp (and are quite expensive at around €100 per day for a compact manual vehicle). Travel by taxi has a per-

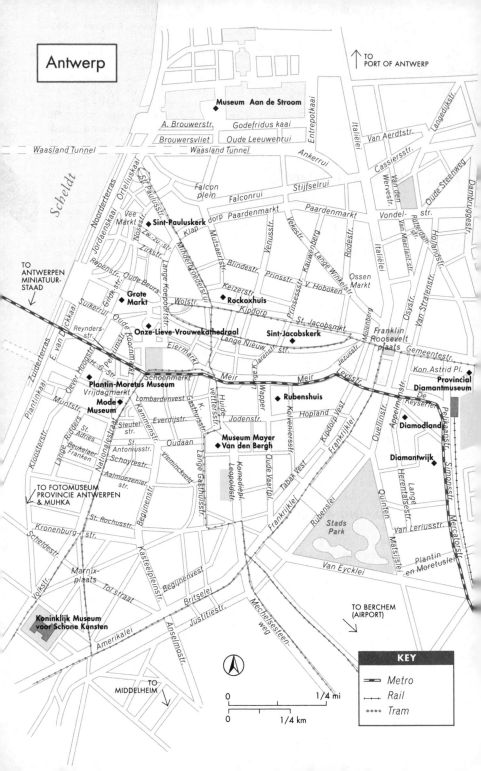

# Antwerp

TO
PORT OF ANTWERP

Museum Aan de Stroom

A. Brouwerstr.
Godefridus kaai
Brouwersvliet
Oude Leeuwenrui

Waasland Tunnel
Waasland Tunnel

Entrepotkaai
Italiëlei
Van Aerdtstr.
Langedijkstr.

Scheldt

Falcon plein
Falconrui
Stijfselrui
Cassiersstr.
Van den Wervestr.
Oude Steenweg
Dambruggestr.

Vee Markt
Sint-Pauluskerk
Zw.zu.str.
Klapdorp
Paardenmarkt
Paardenmarkt
Vondel-str.
Van Maerlant-str.
Rotterdam str.
Hollandstr.

Noordersterras
Ortelluskaai
St.Pauluestr.
Nosestr.
Zirktstr.
Mutsaertstr.
Minderbroedersfui
Venusstr.
Vekestr.
Kauwenberg
Lange Winkelstr.
Rodestr.
Ossen Markt
Italiëlei
Osystr.
Van Stralenstr.

TO
ANTWERPEN
MINIATUUR-
STAAD

Jordaenskaai
Renenstr.
Oude Beurs
Lange Koepoortstr.
Blindestr.
Prinsstr.
Keizerstr.
Prinsessstr.
V. Hoboken
Kon. Astrid Pl.

Grote Markt
Suikerrui
Gridkstr.
Wolstr.
Rockoxhuis
Kipdorp
St. Jacobsmkt.
Molenberg
Franklin Roosevelt plaats
Gemeentestr.

Reynders-str.
Oude Koornmkt
Onze-Lieve-Vrouwekathedraal
Lange Nieuw str.
Sint-Jacobskerk
Jezusstr.
Leysstr.
Provincial Diamantmuseum

Zuiderterras
E. van Dijckkaai
Oever
Hoogstr.
H.G.str.
H.Peperinstr.
Eiermarkt
Klarenstr.
Wijngaard str.
Meir
Kipdorp Vest
De Keyserlei

Plantinkaai
Suikerrui
Schoenmarkt
Meir
Wapper
Appelmstr.
Diamodland

Plantin-Moretus Museum
Vrijdagmarkt
Lombardenvest
Huidevettersstr.
Rubenshuis
Hopland
Quellinstr.
Frankrijkei

Mode Museum
Kammenstr.
K. Gasthuisstr.
Jodenstr.
Kolveniersstr.

Muntstr.
Steutel str.
Everdijstr.
Oudaan
Museum Mayer Van den Bergh
Oude Vaartpl.
Diamantwijk

Lange Ridders
Beukelaer Franken
St. Adries
St. Antoniusstr.
Vliemnckveld
Lange Gasthuisstr.
Komediepl.
Leopoldstr.
Tabak Vest
Lange Herentalsestr.
Mercatorstr.

Kloosterstr.
Nationalestraat
Schoytestr.
Aalmoezenier str.
Beginenstr.
Rubensiei
Quinten Matsijstei
Simonsstr.
Plantin en Moretuslei

TO FOTOMUSEUM
PROVINCIE ANTWERPEN
& MUHKA

St. Rochusstr.
Kasteelpleinstr.
Frankrijklei
Stads Park
Van Leriusstr.

Kronenburg-str.
Beginenvest
Van Eycklei

Marnix-plaats
Tol straat
Britselei
Mechelsesteen weg
TO BERCHEM
(AIRPORT)

Koninklijk Museum voor Schone Kunsten
Scheldestr.
Volkstr.
Amerikalei
Justitiestr.
Anselmostr.

TO
MIDDELHEIM

0 _____ 1/4 mi
0 _____ 1/4 km

## KEY

| | |
|---|---|
| ⊏⊐ | Metro |
| +++ | Rail |
| •••• | Tram |

km charge of around €1.60 on top of an initial pick-up price of €2.75, which makes it expensive for day tours but acceptable for short trips.

## EXPLORING ANTWERP

**Diamondland.** A spectacular showroom, Diamondland was created to enable visitors to get a sense of the activity that goes on behind closed doors in the security-conscious Diamantwijk. All explanations are in English, and you can watch several diamond cutters at work. ⊠ *Appelmansstraat 33A, Diamantwijk* ☎ *03/229–2990* ⊕ *www.diamondland. be* ⊙ *Mon.–Sat. 9:30–5:30.*

**Diamantwijk.** The diamond trade has its own quarter in Antwerp, bounded by De Keyserlei, Pelikaanstraat, Lange Herentalsestraat, and Lange Kievitstraat, where the skills of cutting and polishing the gems have been handed down for generations by a tightly knit community. A large part of the community is Jewish, so you'll see shop signs in Hebrew and Hasidic men with traditional dark clothing and side curls. Some 85% of the world's uncut diamonds pass through Antwerp. Twenty-five million carats are cut and traded here every year, more than anywhere else in the world. A long row of stalls and shops gleams with jewelry and gems.

**Grote Markt.** The heart of the Oude Stad, the Grote Markt is dominated by a huge fountain splashing water onto the paving stones. Atop the fountain stands the figure of the legendary Silvius Brabo, who has been poised to fling the hand of the giant Druon Antigon into the river Scheldt since the 19th century. Another famous monster slayer, St. George, is perched on top of a 16th-century guild house at Grote Markt 5, while the dragon appears to be falling off the pediment.

The triangular square is lined on two sides by guild houses and on the third by the Renaissance **Stadhuis** (⊠ *Grote Markt, Oude Stad* ☎ *03/220–8020*). Antwerp's town hall was built in the 1560s during the city's Golden Age, when Paris and Antwerp were the only European cities with more than 100,000 inhabitants. In its facade, the fanciful fretwork of the late Gothic style has given way to the discipline and order of the Renaissance. It is open to visitors only on Sunday, when it is included in the regular 2 PM walking tour of the city.

★ **Koninklijk Museum voor Schone Kunsten.** The Royal Museum of Fine Arts collection is studded with masterworks of Flemish art. The collection of Flemish "Primitives" includes works by Rubens, Bruegel, Van Dyck, and Memling. There's also a representative survey of Belgian art of the past 150 years—Emile Claus, Rik Wouters, René Magritte, Paul Delvaux, and especially James Ensor. An English-language audioguide is available. ⊠ *Leopold de Waelplaats 2, Het Zuid* ☎ *03/238–7809* ⊕ *www.kmska.be* 🎟 *€6* ⊙ *Tues.–Sat. 10–5, Sun. 10–6.*

**Mode Museum.** To get up to speed on the latest clothing designers, head to MoMu for a fashion crash course. Inside the early-20th-century building you'll find comprehensive exhibits, some highlighting the avant-garde work of contemporary Flemish designers. Also in the museum's complex are the Flanders Fashion Institute, the fashion academy of the

4

## A Major New Museum in Antwerp

**Museum Aan de Stroom.** Housed in a spectacular 196-foot-high (60-meter-high) glass and sandstone tower designed by architects Neutelings Riedijk that overlooks the revitalized docks, this new museum (the "Museum by the River") will bring together several historical collections to present a cohesive portrait of Antwerp and its history when it opens in May 2011. Gallery exhibitions will range from ethnological collections to fine arts to maritime artifacts, and will offer contrasting views of Antwerp through the ages. The upper floors should have magnificent views across the contemporary city skyline. ⊠ *Hanzestedenplaats 1, Eilandje* ☎ *03/338–8600* ⊕ *www.mas.be* ⌨ *Not set at this writing* ☉ *Not set at this writing.*

Royal Academy of Fine Arts (the designer wellspring), a brasserie, and a boutique. You can pick up a brochure with information in English. ⊠ *Nationalestraat 28, Sint-Andrieskwartier* ☎ *03/470–2770* ⊕ *www. momu.be* ⌨ *€6* ☉ *Tues.–Sun. 10–6, every 1st Thurs. of month 10–9.*

**Fodor's Choice**
★ **Museum Mayer Van den Bergh.** Pieter Bruegel the Elder's arguably greatest and most enigmatic painting, *Dulle Griet,* is the showpiece here. Often referred to in English as "Mad Meg," it portrays an irate woman wearing helmet and breastplate—a sword in one hand, and food and cooking utensils in the other—striding across a field strewn with the ravages and insanity of war. In 1894 Mayer Van den Bergh bought *Dulle Griet* for 480 Belgian francs. Today it is priceless. ⊠ *Lange Gasthuisstraat 19, Kruidtuin* ☎ *03/232–4237* ⊕ *museum.antwerpen.be/mayervandenbergh* ⌨ *€4, €6 combination ticket with Rubenshuis* ☉ *Tues.–Sun. 10–5.*

**Fodor's Choice**
★ **Onze-Lieve-Vrouwekathedraal.** A miracle of soaring Gothic lightness, the Cathedral of Our Lady contains some of Rubens's greatest paintings, including four alterpieces, and is topped by a 404-foot-high north spire serving as a beacon that can be seen from far away. Work began in 1352 and continued in fits and starts until 1521. Despite this, it is a homogeneous monument, thanks to a succession of remarkable architects. ⊠ *Handschoenmarkt, Oude Stad* ☎ *03/213–9951* ⊕ *www. dekathedraal.be* ⌨ *€5* ☉ *Weekdays 10–5, Sat. 10–3, Sun. 1–4.*

★ **Plantin-Moretus Museum.** This was the home and printing plant of an extraordinary publishing dynasty. For three centuries, beginning in 1576, the family printed innumerable Bibles, breviaries, and missals. The first three rooms were the family quarters, furnished in 16th-century luxury and containing several portraits by Rubens. Others remain as they were when occupied by accountants, editors, and proofreaders, while many contain Bibles and religious manuscripts dating back to the 9th century. There's a free information brochure available in English. ⊠ *Vrijdagmarkt 22–23, Sint-Andrieskwartier* ☎ *03/221–1450* ⊕ *www. museumplantinmoretus.be* ⌨ *€6, free last Wed. of month* ☉ *Tues.–Sun. 10–5.*

★ **Provinciaal Diamantmuseum.** The high-tech interactive displays in this diamond museum illustrate the entire production process, from mining to gem cutting. A free English-language audioguide explains the wonderful collections of jewelry. ⊠ *Koningin Astridplein 19–23, Centraal Station* ☎ *03/202–4890* ⊕ *www.diamantmuseum.be* ⊠ *€6* ۞ *Thurs.–Tues. 10–5:30.*

**Rockoxhuis.** This was the splendid Renaissance home of Rubens's friend and patron Nicolaas Rockox, seven times mayor of Antwerp. The art on display includes two Rubens pieces and works by Van Dyck, Frans Snyders, Joachim Patinir, Jacob Jordaens, and David Teniers the Younger. The setting makes visiting this collection an exceptional

experience. Rather than being displayed on museum walls, the paintings are shown in the context of an upper-class baroque home, furnished in the style of the period (early 1600s). A documentary slide show in English describes Antwerp at that time. ⊠ *Keizerstraat 10–12, Stadswaag* ☎ *03/201–9250* ⊕ *www.rockoxhuis.be* ⊠ *€2.50* ۞ *Tues.–Sun. 10–5.*

★ **Rubenshuis.** A fabulous picture of Rubens as painter and patrician is presented here at his own house. Only the elaborate portico and temple, designed by Rubens in Italian Baroque style, are original—most of what's here is a reconstruction (completed in 1946) from the master's own design. The most evocative room in Rubens House is the huge studio. In Rubens's day visitors could view completed paintings and watch from the mezzanine while Rubens and his students worked. Rubens completed about 2,500 paintings. A few of his works hang in the house, but unfortunately his widow promptly sold off some 300 pieces after his death in 1640. ⊠ *Wapper 9, Meir* ☎ *03/201–1555* ⊕ *www.rubenshuis. be* ⊠ *€6, free last Wed. of month.* ۞ *Tues.–Sun. 10–5.*

**Sint-Jacobskerk.** Peter Paul Rubens is buried in the white sandstone St. Jacob's Church. A painting depicting him as St. George posed between his two wives, Isabella Brant and Helena Fourment, hangs above his tomb. The three-aisle church blends late-Gothic and baroque styles; the tombs are practically a who's who of prominent 17th-century Antwerp families. ⊠ *Lange Nieuwstraat 73, Meir* ☎ *03/232–1032* ⊕ *www. jacobus-antverpiae.be* ۞ *Daily 2–5.*

**Sint-Pauluskerk.** The late-Gothic St. Paul's Church, built 1530–71, is a repository of more than 50 outstanding paintings. There are three by Rubens, as well as early works by Jordaens and Van Dyck. The church is further enriched by more than 200 17th- and 18th-century sculptures, including the confessionals attributed to Peeter Verbruggen the

Elder. ⊠ *Sint Paulusstraat 20, Oude Stad* ☎ *03/232–3267* ⊕ *www.sint-paulusparochie.be* 🖬 *€2* ☉ *Apr.–mid-Oct., Mon.–Sat. 2–5.*

## SHOPPING

Antwerp has a reputation for edgy chic, due in large part to its clothing designers; followers of fashion consider the city in a league with Milan and Paris. Credit for this development goes to the so-called Antwerp Six (students of Linda Loppa from the class of 1981 at Antwerp's Fashion Academy) and in equal measure to the new wave of talent that has more recently stormed the catwalks. Ready-to-wear by stalwarts Ann Demeulemeester, Dirk Bikkembergs, Dries Van Noten, and relative newcomers Raf Simons, Véronique Branquinho, and Wim Neels command high prices. However, in the shopping area south of Groenplaats, prices are less astronomical. And, of course, the Diamantwijk is prime territory for glittering precious stones.

The elegant **Meir,** together with its extension to the east, **De Keyserlei,** and at the opposite end, **Huidevettersstraat,** is where you will find high-street standbys and long-established names. Shopping galleries branch off all three streets. The area in and around the glamorous **Horta Complex,** on Hopland, is also a popular shopping hub. For avant-garde tastes, the best-known area is **De Wilde Zee,** which straddles the Meir and Oude Stad. The nearby Schuttershofstraat, Kammenstraat, and Nationalestraat are also fizzing with new spots. Another pedestrian area for general shopping is **Hoogstraat.**

**Ann Demeulemeester.** This designer sells her clothes in an elegant corner store in what is her hometown. ⊠ *Leopold de Waelplaats, Het Zuid* ☎ *03/216–0133* ⊕ *www.anndemeulemeester.be.*

**Diamondland.** This is Antwerp's largest diamond showroom. ⊠ *Appelmansstraat 33a, Diamantwijk* ☎ *03/229–2990* ⊕ *www.diamondland. be.*

**Louis.** This was one of the first places to sell the work of Antwerp's top designers in the late 1980s. Today it sells the collections of the city's more recent talent—Martin Margiela, Ann Demeulemeester, A. F. Vandervorst, and Raf Simons. ⊠ *Lombardenstraat 2, Sint-Andrieskwartier* ☎ *03/232–9872.*

**Modepaleis.** The work of Dries Van Noten is in the splendid renovated men's and women's outfitter. ⊠ *Kammenstraat and Nationalestraat 16, Sint-Andrieskwartier* ☎ *03/470–2510* ⊕ *www.driesvannoten.be.*

**Walter.** Owned by Walter Van Beirendonck and Dirk Van Saene, the boutique sells the best of their collections against a futuristic backdrop. ⊠ *Sint-Antoniustraat 12, Sint-Andrieskwartier* ☎ *03/213–2644* ⊕ *www. waltervanbeirendonck.com.*

## WHERE TO EAT

$$ ╳ **'t Brantyser.** This old, two-level café with dark rafters, brick, and
CAFE  stucco, serves more than just drinks and the usual snacks: the tavern fare is supplemented by a range of meal-size salads and affordable

specials. ⊠ *Hendrik Conscienceplein 7, Oude Stad* ☎ *03/233–1833* ⊕ *www.brantyser.be* ⊟ *AE, MC, V.*

**$–$$** ✗ *'t Hofke.* It's worth visiting here for the location alone: the Vlaeykens-
BELGIAN   gang alley, where time seems to have stood still. The cozy dining room has the look and feel of a private home, and the menu includes a large selection of salads and omelets, as well as more substantial fare. Try for a table in the courtyard. ⊠ *Vlaeykensgang, Oude Koornmarkt 16, Oude Stad* ☎ *03/233–8606* ⊕ *www.thofke.com* ⊟ *AE, MC, V.*

# COBH, IRELAND (FOR CORK)

The major metropolis of the South, Cork is Ireland's second-largest city—but it runs a distant second, with a population of 119,400, roughly a tenth the size of Dublin. Cork is a spirited place, with a formidable pub culture, a lively traditional music scene, a respected and progressive university, attractive art galleries, and offbeat cafés. The city received a major boost in 2005 when it was named a Capital of Culture by the EU—the smallest city ever to receive the designation. The result was a burst in development; one of the lasting legacies is a striking but controversial redesign of the city center (Patrick Street and Grand Parade) by Barcelona-based architect Beth Gali. Outside the city, the rolling countryside gives way to rugged coastline hosting tiny villages, each with their own piece of history. Many set sail for the New World from here; some were destined not to arrive.

**ESSENTIALS**

CURRENCY   The euro (€1 to US$1.36 at this writing). ATMs are common.

HOURS   Shops and businesses are generally open Monday through Saturday from 9:30 to 5:30 or 6; some open later and some open on Sunday. Most museums are open Monday–Saturday 9–5 and may have shorter hours on Sunday.

INTERNET   **Internet Exchange** (⊠ *5 Woods St., off Washington St., Cork* ☎ *021/4254666*) is a centrally located Internet café.

TELEPHONES   Most tri- and quad-band GSM phones will work in Ireland, and the country's mobile system is 3G-compatible with excellent coverage. Public phones accept prepaid call cards (available in shops and telecom offices) and credit cards. Eircom, BT Ireland, and Vodafone are the major telecom suppliers.

**COMING ASHORE**

Large ships dock at Cobh's dedicated cruise terminal adjacent to the Cobh Heritage Centre (⇨ *below)*. There are basic facilities for passengers, including restrooms, taxis, and tourist information, but no cafés, restaurants, or shops.

There is a rail link between Cobh and Cork. It runs once or twice an hour throughout the day and costs €6.35, so it would be possible to explore Cork and Cobh in the same day by public transport. Smaller vessels dock at the City Quays in the heart of Cork City; from here you can tour the town on foot.

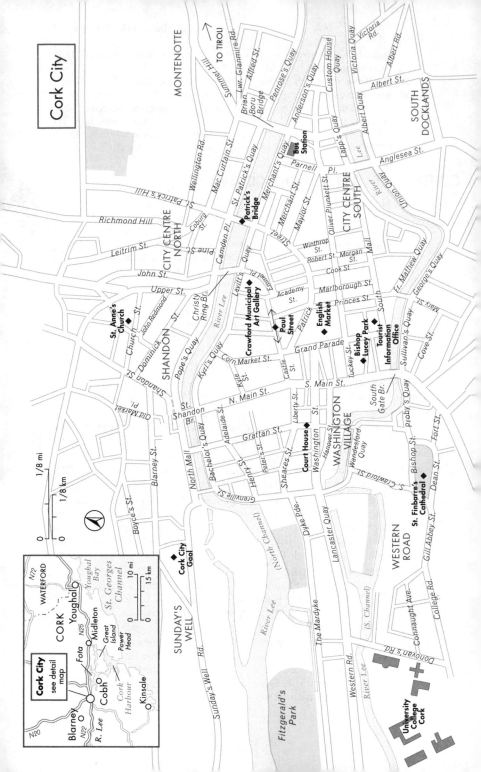

Renting a car would be an advantage for touring the Kerry countryside around the town and the associated attractions. The cost for a compact manual vehicle is approx €50. Taxis can be engaged to run tour itineraries, although charges are complicated. Initial charges are a maximum of €4.10, then €1.03 per km for the first 14 km (9 mi), rising to €1.77 per km (½-mi) once the ride lasts longer than 30 km (19 mi). Drivers can choose to charge by the minute rather than per kilometer.

## EXPLORING COUNTY CORK

### COBH

*24 km (15 mi) southeast of Cork City.*

Many of the people who left Ireland on immigrant ships for the New World departed from Cobh, a pretty fishing port and seaside resort 24 km (15 mi) southeast of Cork City on R624.

**Queenstown Story at Cobh Heritage Center.** The center, in the old Cobh railway station, re-creates the experience of a million emigrants. It also tells the stories of great transatlantic liners, including the *Titanic,* whose last port of call was Cobh, and the *Lusitania,* which was sunk by a German submarine off this coast on May 7, 1915. Many of the *Lusitania's* 1,198 victims are buried in Cobh, which has a memorial to them on the local quay. ☎ *021/481–3591* ⊕ *www.cobhheritage.com* ☞€7.10 ☉ *Oct.–Apr., daily 9:30–5; May–Sept., daily 9:30–6 (sometimes later).*

**St. Colman's Cathedral.** The best view of Cobh is from this exuberant neo-Gothic granite church designed by the eminent British architect E. W. Pugin in 1869 and completed in 1919. Inside, granite niches portray scenes of the Roman Catholic Church's history in Ireland, beginning with the arrival of St. Patrick. ☎ *021/481–3222* ⊕ *www. cobhcathedralparish.ie* ☞ *Free.*

### CORK CITY

**Bishop Lucey Park.** This tiny green park in the heart of the city opened in 1985 in celebration of the 800th anniversary of Cork's Norman charter. During its excavation, workers unearthed portions of the city's original fortified walls, now preserved just inside the arched entrance. Sculptures by contemporary Cork artists are found throughout the park. ⊠ *Grand Parade, Washington Village* ☞ *Free.*

☺ **Cork City Gaol.** This castlelike building contains an austere, 19th-century prison. Life-size figures occupy the cells, and sound effects illustrate the appalling conditions that prevailed here from the early 19th century through the founding of the Free State, after the 1916 Uprising. ⊠ *Sunday's Well Rd., Sunday's Well* ☎ *021/430–5022* ⊕ *www.corkcitygaol. com* ☞€7 ☉ *Nov.–Feb., daily 10–4; Mar.–Oct., daily 9:30–5.*

**Court House.** A landmark in the very center of Cork, this magnificent classical building (1835) has an imposing Corinthian portico and is still used as the district's main courthouse. ⊠ *Washington St., Washington Village* ☎ *021/427–2706* ☉ *Weekdays 9–5.*

★ **Crawford Municipal Art Gallery.** The large redbrick building was built in 1724 as the customs house, and is now home to Ireland's leading provincial art gallery. An imaginative expansion has added an extra 10,000 square feet of gallery space for visiting exhibitions and adventurous shows of modern Irish artists. The permanent collection includes landscape paintings depicting Cork in the 18th and 19th centuries. ⊠ *Emmet Pl., City Center South* ☎ *021/480–5042* ⊕ *www.crawfordartgallery.ie* ▨ *Free* ⊙ *Mon–Wed., Fri., and Sat. 10–5, Thurs. 10–8.*

★ **English Market.** Food lovers: Head for this brick-and-cast-iron Victorian building with the legendary fresh-fish alley, purveying local smoked salmon. O'Reilly's Tripe and Drisheen is the last existing retailer of a Cork specialty, tripe (cow's stomach) and *drisheen* (blood sausage). Upstairs is the Farmgate, an excellent café. ⊠ *Entrances on Grand Parade and Princes St., City Center South* ⊕ *www.corkenglishmarket.ie* ⊙ *Mon.–Sat. 9–5:30.*

⟳ **Fitzgerald's Park.** This small, well-tended park is beside the River Lee's north channel in the west of the city. The park contains the **Cork Public Museum,** a Georgian mansion that houses a well-planned exhibit about Cork's history since ancient times, with a strong emphasis on the city's Republican history. ⊠ *Western Rd., Western Road* ☎ *021/427–0679* ▨ *Free* ⊙ *Museum weekdays 11–1 and 2:15–5, Sat. 11–1 and 2:15–4, Sun. 3–5.*

**Patrick's Bridge.** From here you can look along the curve of Patrick Street and north across the River Lee to St. Patrick's Hill, with its tall Georgian houses. The hill is so steep that steps are cut into the pavement. Tall ships that served the butter trade used to load up beside the bridge at Merchant's Quay before heading downstream to the sea. The design of the large, redbrick shopping center on the site evokes the warehouses of old. ⊠ *Patrick St., City Center South.*

**Paul Street.** A narrow street between the River Lee and Patrick Street and parallel to both, Paul Street is the backbone of the trendy shopping area that now occupies Cork's old French Quarter. The area was first settled by Huguenots fleeing religious persecution in France. Musicians and other street performers often entertain passersby in the Rory Gallagher Piazza, named for the rock guitarist (of the band Taste), whose family was from Cork. The shops here offer the best in modern Irish design—from local fashions to handblown glass—and antiques, particularly in the alley north of the piazza. ⊠ *City Center South.*

**St. Anne's Church.** The church's pepper-pot Shandon steeple is visible throughout the city and is the chief reason why St. Anne's is so frequently visited. The Bells of Shandon were immortalized in a 19th-century

---

**CORK BEST BETS**

**Strolling along Patrick Street.** The historic storefronts along this famous thoroughfare have graced a thousand tourist brochures—it's an atmospheric place to browse for a souvenir or two.

**Kissing the Blarney Stone.** The "magic" stone at Blarney Castle is said to give you the gift of gab to get what you want.

**Visiting the Queenstown Story at Cobh Heritage Center.** This site tells the story of the millions of emigrants who set sail to the United States, and of the tragic last voyage of the *Lusitania*.

ballad of that name. Your reward for climbing the 120-foot-tall tower is the chance to ring the bells out over Cork. ⊠ *Church St., Shandon* ☎ *021/450–5906* ⊕ *www.shandonbells.org* ⊡ *€6* ⊘ *June–Sept., Mon.–Sat. 10–5, Sun. 11:30–4:30; Mar.–May and Oct., Mon.–Sat 10–4, Sun. 11:30–3:30; Nov.–Feb., Mon.–Sat. 10–3.*

**St. Finbarre's Cathedral.** This was once the entrance to medieval Cork. According to tradition, St. Finbarre established a monastery on this site around AD 650, and is credited with being the founder of Cork. The present, compact, three-spire Gothic cathedral, which was completed in 1879, belongs to the Church of Ireland and houses a 3,000-pipe organ. ⊠ *Bishop St., Washington Village* ☎ *021/496–3387* ⊕ *www. cathedral.cork.anglican.org* ⊡ *€4* ⊘ *Nov.–Apr. (Low Sunday), Mon.–Sat. 10–12:45 and 2–5, Sun. 12:30–5; Apr. (Low Sunday)–Oct., Mon.–Sat. 9:30–5:30, Sun. 12:30–5.*

★ **University College Cork.** The porticoed gates of UCC stand about 2 km (1 mi) from the center of the city. The main quadrangle is a fine example of 19th-century university architecture in the Tudor Gothic style, reminiscent of many Oxford and Cambridge colleges. The Honan Collegiate Chapel, east of the quadrangle, was built in 1916 and modeled on the 12th-century Hiberno-Romanesque style. The UCC chapel's stained-glass windows, as well as its collection of art and crafts, altar furnishings, and textiles in the Celtic Revival style, are noteworthy. The **Lewis Glucksman Gallery** opened in late 2004 in a striking new building in a wooded gully beside the college's entrance gates. Besides displaying works from the college's collection, it hosts cutting-edge contemporary art exhibits. ⊠ *Western Road* ☎ *021/490–1876* ⊕ *www.glucksman.org* ⊡ *Free. Guided tours €4* ⊘ *Weekdays 9–5, but call to confirm hrs Easter wk, July and Aug., and mid-Dec.–mid-Jan. Guided tours May–Oct., Mon., Wed., Fri., and Sat. at 3* PM. *Glucksman Gallery Tues.–Sat. 10–5, Sun. 2–5.*

## BLARNEY
*10 km (6 mi) northwest of Cork City.*

**Blarney Castle.** In the center of Blarney is the castle, or what remains of it: the ruined central keep is all that's left of this mid-15th-century stronghold. The castle contains the famed Blarney Stone; kissing the stone, it's said, endows the kisser with the fabled "gift of gab." It's 127 steep steps to the battlements. To kiss the stone, you must lie down on the battlements, hold on to a guardrail, and lean your head way back. It's good fun and not at all dangerous. ☎ *021/438–5252* ⊕ *www.blarneycastle.ie* ⊡ *€10* ⊘ *May and Sept., Mon.–Sat. 9–6:30, Sun. 9–5:30; June–Aug., Mon.–Sat. 9–7, Sun. 9–5:30; Oct.–Apr., daily 9–sundown.*

## KINSALE
*29 km (18 mi) southwest of Cork City on R600.*

Foodies flock to Kinsale, a picturesque port that pioneered the Irish small-town tradition of fine dining in unbelievably small restaurants. In the town center, at the tip of the wide, fjordlike harbor that opens out from the River Bandon, upscale shops and eateries with brightly painted facades line small streets. Kinsale is also a center for sailing.

★ **Charles Fort.** The British built this fort on the east side of the Bandon River estuary in the late 17th century, after their defeat of the Spanish and Irish forces. One of Europe's best-preserved "star forts" encloses some 12 cliff-top acres and is similar to Fort Ticonderoga in New York State. If the sun is shining, take the footpath signposted SCILLY WALK; it winds along the harbor's edge under tall trees and then through the village of Summer Cove. ⊠ *3 km (2 mi) east of town* ☏ *021/477–2263* ⊕ *www.heritageireland.ie* ▧ *€4* ⊘ *Mid-Mar.–Oct., daily 10–6; Nov.– mid-Mar., weekends 10–5.*

**Desmond Castle and the International Museum of Wine.** The "castle" and its wine museum are actually a 15th-century fortified town house— originally a custom house. Now it contains displays that tell the story of the wine trade and its importance to the Irish diaspora to France, America, Australia, and New Zealand. ⊠ *Cork St.* ☏ *021/477–4855* ⊕ *www.winegeese.ie* ▧ *€3* ⊘ *Early-Apr.–late Sept., daily 10–6.*

## SHOPPING

Ireland is *the* place to buy linen and wool products, but the Waterford crystal factory is no longer operating (the name lives on, but no crystal is currently produced in Ireland). The area is still good for ceramics and antiques. Celtic motifs are found on everything from jewelry to coffee cups. In Cork, Paul Street is the backbone of the trendy shopping scene, while Patrick Street has high-end names mixed with antique and souvenir shops. Blarney and Kinsale both have a range of shops selling arts and crafts from around the country.

**Blarney Woolen Mills.** This store has the largest stock of Irish crafts and quality items. It sells everything from Irish-made high fashion to Aran hand-knit items. ⊠ *Blarney* ☏ *021/451–6111* ⊕ *www.blarney.ie.*

**The Philip Gray Gallery of Fine Art.** Philip Gray served as a diver in the Irish navy, and left to paint, which he does extremely well. The sea in all its guises is his subject. His gallery is on a slipway of a dockyard in Cork Harbour. ⊠ *Slipway Two, Cork Dockyard, Rushbrooke, Cobh* ☏ *021/481–4488* ⊕ *www.philipgray.com.*

**Quills.** This boutique has a good selection of Irish-made apparel for women and men. ⊠ *107 Patrick St., City Center South, Cork* ☏ *021/427–1717.*

## WHERE TO EAT

$ ✕ **Farmgate Café.** One of the best—and busiest—informal lunch spots
IRISH in town is on a terraced gallery above the fountain in the English Market. One side of the gallery opens onto the market and is self-service; the other side is glassed-in and has table service (reservations advised). Tripe and drisheen is one dish that is always on the menu; daily specials include similarly traditional dishes, such as corned beef with colcannon (potatoes and cabbage mashed with butter and seasonings) and loin of smoked bacon with *champ* (potatoes mashed with scallions or leeks). ⊠ *English Market, City Center South* ☏ *021/427–8134* ⊕ *www. farmgate.ie* ▤ *DC, MC, V* ⊘ *Closed Sun. No dinner.*

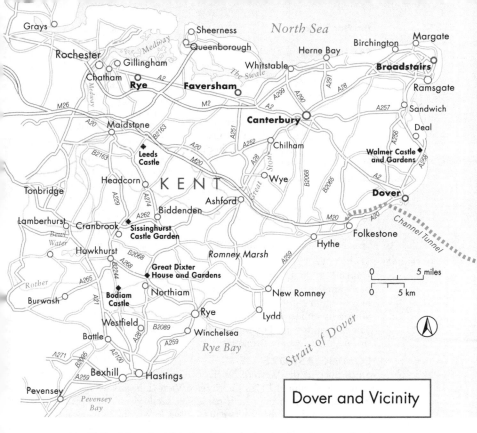

Dover and Vicinity

**$$**

✕ **Jim Edwards.** This is a Kinsale institution, known for its generous

CONTINENTAL portions of local steak, lamb, duck, and fresh seafood, all prepared
under the careful eye of the owner and his wife Paula. Choose from
the daily specials in the busy bar, or have a more relaxed meal in the
attached restaurant. ⊠ *Market Quay, Kinsale* ☎ *021/477–2541* ⊕ *www.
jimedwardskinsale.com* ▭ *AE, DC, MC, V.*

# DOVER, UNITED KINGDOM

In an era when everything small is fashionable, from cell phones to
digital cameras, South East England will inevitably have great appeal.
Here the landscape ravishes the eye in spring with apple blossoms and in
the autumn with lush fields ready for harvest. It is a county of orchards,
market gardens, and round oasthouses with their tilted, pointed roofs,
once used for drying hops (many now converted into pricey homes).
Gentle hills and woodlands are punctuated with farms and storybook
villages rooted in history, while the region's cathedral cities, including
noble Canterbury, wait patiently to be explored. Busy ports, the biggest
of which is Dover, have served for centuries as gateways to continental
Europe. Indeed, because the English Channel is at its narrowest here, a
great deal of British history has been forged in the Southeast.

## ESSENTIALS

CURRENCY The British pound sterling (£1 is $US1.61 at this writing). ATMs are common and credit cards are widely accepted.

HOURS Museums are open daily from 9 until 5, while shops usually open from 9 until 5:30 or 6. Some shops are open on Sunday.

INTERNET **Canterbury Library** ✉ *25 Pound La., Canterbury* ☎ *01227/452747* offers Internet access; however, this is a temporary building. The renovated main library building on High Street should reopen in mid-2011.

TELEPHONES Tri-band GSM phones work in the United Kingdom. You can buy prepaid phone cards at telecom shops, news vendors, and tobacconists in all towns and cities. Phone cards can be used for local or international calls. Vodafone and Orange are the leading telecom companies.

> ### DOVER BEST BETS
>
> **Canterbury Cathedral.** One of Britain's greatest churches, this was an important place of pilgrimage and the scene of one of the country's darkest crimes.
>
> **The White Cliffs of Dover.** Best seen from the water, these iconic cliffs are part of the national psyche and, on a sunny day, an exceptionally breathtaking vista.
>
> **Rye.** Though there are no attractions as such here, the sheer quaintness and "Englishness" of Rye makes it a great place to relax, soak in the atmosphere, and shop for souvenirs.

## COMING ASHORE

Ships dock at the Western Docks in Dover. There are two passenger terminals. Terminal 1 is in a converted Victorian railway station, while Terminal 2 is a purpose-built passenger facility opened in 2001. The terminals have currency exchange facilities, car-rental kiosks, and cafés, plus a taxi stand.

London can be reached in two hours by train. Take a taxi to the station in Dover. Ticket prices start at £16 round-trip but vary depending on the time of the train. The train journey to Canterbury is around 30 minutes, with several trains per hour. Tickets are around €6.50 per single journey.

London (*see* ⇨ *Harwich, below*) can also be reached in 2½ hours by bus. There are bus departures from the Eastern Docks (a taxi ride or a 15-minute walk along the seafront) and, occasionally, directly from the cruise terminal. Prices start at £22.60 round-trip. However, this would not leave you with a great deal of time to explore London, and journey times can be longer depending on traffic. Canterbury is a 30-minute ride away by direct service, with prices starting at £5.30 round-trip. Local buses 15 and 15X link Dover with Canterbury every hour.

A car rental is recommended for exploring the Kent countryside but not for a visit to London, where traffic, congestion charges, and parking difficulties abound. Rental rates are £40 per day for an economy manual vehicle. But given the distance, this is a good opportunity to see the beauty of Kent rather than trek all the way into central London.

### GETTING TO THE AIRPORT

If you choose not to purchase aiport transfers from your cruise line, the easiest way to get to the airport from the cruise port to Heathrow airport is to contract a private taxi or transfer company. Several companies offer the services with prices of a one-way transfer of around €170 for vehicles carrying a maximum of three people. For other transport options, including bus and train, it's necessary to connect through central London, which may be tiring depending how much luggage you are carrying and may not be a money-saving option depending on how many travelers are in your party.

**Contacts Cruise Transfer.com** (☏ 0870/042–2752 ⊕ www.cruisetransfer.com). **Prompt Airport Cars** (☏ 020/7060–6070 ⊕ www.promptexecutivehire.co.uk). **Road Express** (☏ 0844/846–4061 ⊕ www.road-express.co.uk).

## EXPLORING DOVER AND VICINITY

### DOVER

*122 km (76 mi) southeast of London.*

The busy passenger port of Dover has for centuries been Britain's gateway to Europe. Its chalk **White Cliffs** are a famous and inspirational sight, though you may find the town itself a bit disappointing; the savage bombardments of World War II and the shortsightedness of postwar developers left the city center an unattractive place. Roman legacies include a lighthouse adjoining a stout Anglo-Saxon church.

☾ ★ **Dover Castle.** The spectacular castle, towering high above the ramparts of the White Cliffs, was a mighty medieval castle, and it has served as an important strategic center over the centuries, even in World War II. Most of the castle, including the keep, dates to Norman times. It was begun by Henry II in 1181, but incorporates additions from almost every succeeding century. There's a lot to see here besides the castle rooms: exhibits, many of which will appeal to kids, include the "Siege of 1216," the Princess of Wales Regimental Museum, and "Castle Fit for a King." ■TIP→ **Take time to tour the secret wartime tunnels, a medieval and Napoleonic-era system that was used as a World War II command center during the evacuation of Dunkirk in 1940.** ⊠ *Castle Rd.* ☏ *01304/211067* ⊕ *www.english-heritage.org.uk/server/show/nav.14571* 🎟 *£13.90* ☾ *Feb. and Mar., daily 10–4; Apr.–Sept., daily 10–6; Oct., daily 10–5; Nov.–Jan., Thurs.–Mon. 10–4.*

**Roman Painted House.** This house, believed to have been a hotel, includes some wall paintings, along with the remnants of an ingenious heating system. ⊠ *New St.* ☏ *01304/203279* ⊕ *www.theromanpaintedhouse. co.uk* 🎟 *£3.80* ☾ *Apr.–Sept., Tues.–Sat. 10–5, Sun. 1–5.*

### CANTERBURY

*28 km (17 mi) northwest of Dover.*

The cathedral city of Canterbury is an ancient place that has attracted travelers since the 12th century. The city's magnificent cathedral, the Mother Church of England, remains a powerful draw. The mere mention of Canterbury conjures images of Geoffrey Chaucer's *Canterbury Tales*, about medieval pilgrims making their way to Canterbury

Cathedral. Although there is evidence of prosperous society in and around Canterbury as far back as the Bronze Age (around 1000 BC), the height of Canterbury's popularity came in the 12th century, when thousands of pilgrims flocked here to see the shrine of the murdered archbishop St. Thomas à Becket, making this southeastern town one of the most visited in England, if not Europe. Buildings that served as pilgrims' inns (and survived the World War II bombing of the city) still dominate the streets of Canterbury's center.

**Fodor'sChoice**
★
**Canterbury Cathedral.** The nucleus of worldwide Anglicanism—formally the Cathedral Church of Christ Canterbury—is a living textbook of medieval architecture. The building was begun in 1070, demolished, begun anew in 1096, and then systematically expanded over the next three centuries. When the original choir section burned to the ground in 1174, another replaced it, designed in the new Gothic style, with tall, pointed arches. Don't miss the North Choir aisle, which holds two windows that show Jesus in the Temple, the three kings asleep, and Lot's wife turned to a pillar of salt. The windows are among the earliest parts of the cathedral, but only 33 of the original 208 survive.

The cathedral was only a century old, and still relatively small, when Thomas à Becket, the archbishop of Canterbury, was murdered here in 1170. Becket, a defender of ecclesiastical interests, had angered his friend Henry II, who was heard to exclaim, "Who will rid me of this troublesome priest?" Thinking they were carrying out the king's wishes, four knights burst in on Becket in one of the side chapels and killed him. Two years later Becket was canonized, and Henry II's subsequent submission to the authority of the Church helped establish the cathedral as the undisputed center of English Christianity. Becket's tomb, destroyed by Henry VIII in 1538 as part of his campaign to reduce the power of the Church and confiscate its treasures, was one of the most extravagant shrines in Christendom. In **Trinity Chapel,** which held the shrine, you can still see a series of 13th-century stained-glass windows illustrating Becket's miracles. The actual site of Becket's murder is down a flight of steps just to the left of the nave. In the corner, a second flight of steps leads down to the enormous Norman **undercroft,** or vaulted cellarage, built in the early 12th century. A row of squat pillars whose capitals dance with animals and monsters supports the roof.

If time permits, be sure to explore the **cloisters** and other small monastic buildings to the north of the cathedral. The 12th-century octagonal water tower is still part of the cathedral's water supply. The cathedral is popular, so arrive early or late in the day to avoid the worst crowds. ■TIP➜ **You get a map and an overview of the building's history when you enter; audio guides have the most detail, or take a tour for the personal touch.** ⊠ *Cathedral Precincts* ☎ *01227/762862* ⊕ *www.canterbury-cathedral.org* ⛿*£8, free for services and ½ hr before closing; £4 for tour, £3 for audioguide* ☉ *Easter–Sept., Mon.–Sat. 9–5:30, Sun. 12:30–2:30; Oct.–Easter, Mon.–Sat. 9–5, Sun. 12:30–2:30. Restricted access during services.*

**Canterbury Roman Museum.** Below ground, at the level of the remnants of Roman Canterbury, the museum features colorful mosaic Roman pavement and a hypocaust—the Roman version of central heating. Displays of excavated objects (some of which you can hold in the Touch the Past area) and computer-generated reconstructions of Roman buildings and the marketplace help re-create history. ⊠ *Butchery La.* ☎ *01227/785575* ⊕ *www.canterbury-museums.co.uk* ⊠ *£3.10* ⊙ *June–Oct., Mon.–Sat. 10–5, Sun. 1:30–5; Nov.–May, Mon.–Sat. 10–5; last admission at 4. Closed last wk in Dec.*

**The Canterbury Tales.** This is a kitschy audiovisual (and occasionally olfactory) dramatization of 14th-century English life—popular but touristy. You'll "meet" Chaucer's pilgrims at the Tabard Inn near London and view tableaus illustrating five tales. An actor in period costume often performs a charade as part of the scene. ⊠ *St. Margaret's St.* ☎ *01227/479227* ⊕ *www.canterburytales.org.uk* ⊠ *£7.25* ⊙ *Nov.–Feb., daily 10–4:30; Mar.–June, Sept., and Oct., daily 10–5; July and Aug., daily 9:30–5.*

**Medieval city walls.** For an essential Canterbury experience, follow the circuit of the 13th- and 14th-century city walls that were built on the line of the Roman walls. Those to the east survive intact, towering some 20 feet high and offering a sweeping view of the town. You can access these from a number of places, including Castle Street and Broad Street.

## FAVERSHAM
*45 km (28 mi) northwest of Dover.*

In Roman times, Faversham was a thriving seaport. Today the port is hidden from sight, and you could pass through this market town without knowing it was there. Still, Faversham is a worthwhile stop for those in search of Ye Quaint Olde Englande: The town center, with its Tudor houses grouped around the 1574 guildhall and covered market, looks like a perfect stage set. There are no actual sights here, as such, but it's a lovely place to take a break and have a stroll.

## BROADSTAIRS
*36 km (22 mi) north of Dover.*

Like other Victorian seaside towns on this stretch of coast, Broadstairs was once the playground of vacationing Londoners. Charles Dickens spent many summers here between 1837 and 1851 and wrote glowingly of its bracing freshness. Today grand 19th-century houses line the waterfront. In the off-season Broadstairs is a peaceful retreat, but day-trippers pack the town in July and August.

**Dickens House Museum.** This museum was originally the home of Mary Pearson Strong, on whom Dickens based the character of Betsey Trotwood, David Copperfield's aunt. There's a reconstruction of Miss Trotwood's room, a few objects that once belonged to the Dickens family, and prints and photographs commemorating Dickens's association with Broadstairs. ⊠ *2 Victoria Parade* ☎ *01843/863453 or 01843/861232* ⊕ *www.dickensfellowship.org* ⊠ *£3.50* ⊙ *Apr.–Oct., daily 2–5.*

## RYE
★ *64 km (40 mi) south of Dover.*

With cobbled streets and ancient timbered dwellings, Rye is an artist's dream. Once a port (the water retreated, and the harbor is now 2 mi away), the town starts where the sea once lapped at its ankles and then winds its way to the top of a low hill that overlooks the Romney Marshes. Virtually every building in the little town center is intriguingly old; some places were smugglers' retreats. This place can be easily walked without a map, but if you prefer guidance, the local tourist office has an interesting audio tour of the town, as well as maps.

## SHOPPING

The little towns of Kent are great places to browse for collectibles, china, silver and secondhand books. The streets of Canterbury have an excellent selection of souvenirs, some of it decidedly kitsch. Rye has great antiques shops, perfect for an afternoon of rummaging, with the biggest cluster at the foot of the hill near the tourist information center. The English can find bargains; it's harder for Americans, given the exchange rate. The town still has a number of potteries.

**Black Sheep Antiques.** This store has a superior selection of antique crystal and silver. ⊠ *72 The Mint, Rye* ☎ *01797/224508.*

**Cinque Ports Pottery.** Of Rye's working potteries, this is one of the best. ⊠ *The Monastery, Conduit Hill, Rye* ☎ *01797/222033.*

**Collectors Corner.** This shop sells a good mix of furniture, art, and silver. ⊠ *2 Market Rd.Rye* ☎ *01797/225796.*

**David Sharp Pottery.** This company specializes in the ceramic name plaques that are a feature of the town. ⊠ *55 The Mint, Rye* ☎ *01797/222620.*

**Hawkin's Bazaar.** You can choose from an exceptional selection of traditional and modern toys and games at this toy store. ⊠ *34 Burgate, Canterbury* ☎ *01227/785809.*

**National Trust Shop.** This store stocks the National Trust line of household items, ideal for gifts. ⊠ *24 Burgate,Canterbury* ☎ *01227/457120.*

## WHERE TO EAT

¢ ╳ **City Fish Bar.** Long lines and lots of satisfied finger licking attest to the
BRITISH    deserved popularity of this excellent fish-and-chips outlet in the center of town. Everything is freshly fried, the batter crisp and the fish tasty; the fried mushrooms are also surprisingly good. It closes at 7. ⊠ *30 St. Margarets St.,Canterbury* ☎ *01227/760873* ▭ *No credit cards.*

£££ ╳ **Fish Café.** One of Rye's most popular restaurants occupies a brick
SEAFOOD    building that dates to 1907, but the interior has been redone in a sleek, modern style. The ground-floor café has a relaxed atmosphere, and upstairs is a more formal dining room. Most of the seafood here is caught nearby, so it's very fresh. Try modern dishes such as Mediterranean fish stew with tomato and basil, lemon sole with cauliflower purée, or squid-ink risotto. Reservations are recommended for dinner. ⊠ *17 Tower St., Rye* ☎ *08710/756316* ▭ *DC, MC, V* ☯ *Closed Mon. Oct.–Apr. No dinner Sun.*

££–£££ ▥ **Abode Canterbury.** This glossy boutique hotel inside the old city walls brought an up-to-date style to traditional Canterbury. The good-size rooms, modern but not minimal, are classed as Comfortable, Desirable, and Enviable. Enviable rooms have the most space and extras like wood floors, sitting areas, and nibbles. Even Comfortable rooms are nicely designed, with soft bedding in neutral colors, although most have no view. Michael Caines is one of the town's top restaurants because of its elegant atmosphere and French-influenced cuisine. The Old Brewery Tavern, an upscale pub, serves less expensive meals, and there's a champagne bar. **Pros:** central location; luxurious handmade beds; great restaurants and bars. **Cons:** one of the priciest hotels in town; bar gets quite crowded. ⊠ *High St., Canterbury* ☎ *01227/766266* ⊕ *www. abodehotels.co.uk* ⇄ *73 rooms* ⚬ *In-room: DVD (some), Internet. In-hotel: 2 restaurants, bar, laundry service, parking (paid), no-smoking rooms* ☰ *AE, DC, MC, V.*

£  ⊡ **Number One Guest House.** One of the best bargains in the area is this family-run guesthouse. Wallpapers and porcelain collections decorate the cozy corner terrace home built in the early 19th century, and you can even have breakfast in your room. The walled garden has a fine view of the castle. **Pros:** affordable rates; breakfast in bed. **Cons:** rooms are small. ⊠ *1 Castle St., Dover* ☎ *01304/202007* ⊕ *www. number1guesthouse.co.uk* ⇄ *4 rooms* ⚬ *In-room: no a/c, no phone. In-hotel: parking (paid)* ☰ *No credit cards* ⏹ *BP.*

# DUBLIN, IRELAND

In his inimitable, irresistible way, James Joyce immortalized the city of Dublin in works like *Ulysses* and *Dubliners*. He claimed to have chosen Dublin as the setting for his work because it was a "center of paralysis" where nothing much ever changed. What would he make of Temple Bar—the city's erstwhile down-at-the-heels neighborhood, now crammed with restaurants and hotels? Or of the city's newfound status as a bustling hub of the European economy? Yet despite all these advances, traditional Dublin is far from buried. The fundamentals—the Georgian elegance of Merrion Square, the Norman drama of Christ Church Cathedral, the foamy pint at an atmospheric pub—are still on hand to gratify. Most of all, there are the locals themselves: the nod and grin when you catch their eye on the street, the eagerness to share a tale or two, and their paradoxically dark but warm sense of humor.

## ESSENTIALS

CURRENCY   The euro (€1 to US$1.36 at this writing). ATMs are common.

HOURS   Shops and businesses are generally open Monday through Saturday from 9:30 to 5:30 or 6; some open later and some open on Sunday. Most museums open daily Monday through Saturday from 9 until 5; museums may have shorter hours on Sunday.

INTERNET   **Central Café** (⊠ *6 Grafton St.* ☎ *01/6778298*), above Bus Stop News, is a centrally located café.

TELEPHONES   Most tri- and quad-band GSM phones will work in Ireland, and the country's mobile system is 3G compatible with excellent coverage. Public phones accept prepaid call cards (available in shops and telecom offices) and credit crads. Eircom, BT Ireland, and Vodafone are the major telecom suppliers.

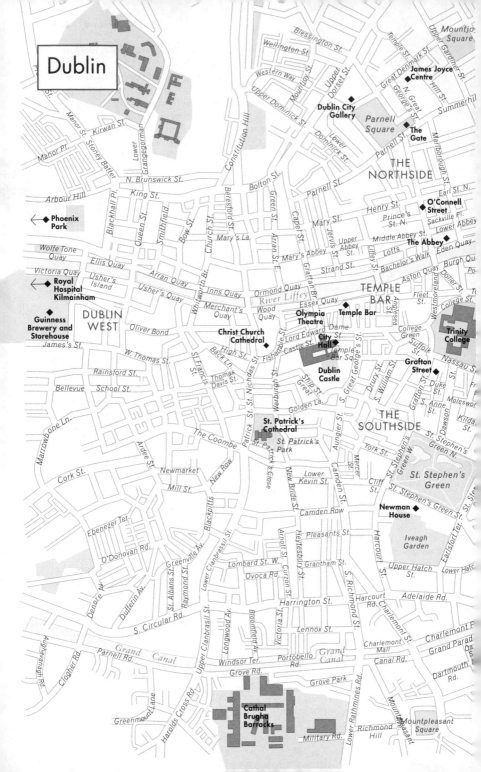

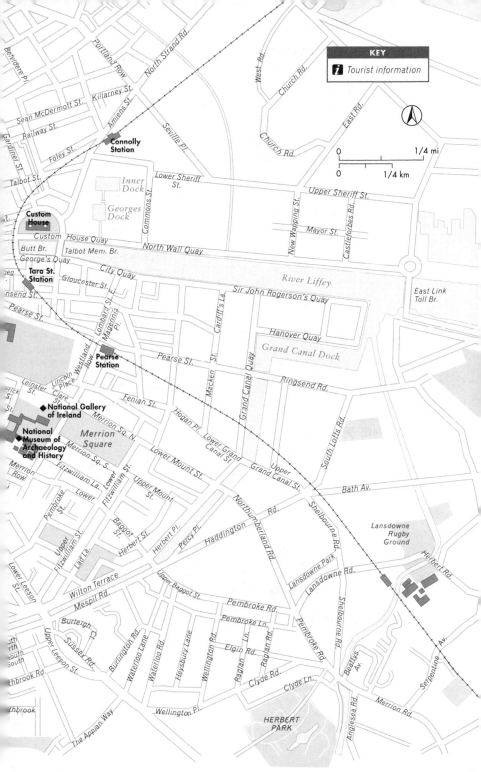

0           1/4 mi

0           1/4 km

Betvidere Pl.

Portland Row

North Strand Rd.

West Rd.

Church Rd.

East Rd.

Sean McDermott St.

Killarney St.

Railway St.

Amiens St.

Church Rd.

Foley St.

Seville Pl.

Gardiner St.

**Connolly Station**

Talbot St.

Lower Sheriff St.

Upper Sheriff St.

**Custom House**

*Inner Dock*

Commons St.

New Wapping St.

Mayor St.

Castleforbes Rd.

*Georges Dock*

Custom House Quay

Butt Br.

Talbot Mem. Br.

North Wall Quay

George's Quay

City Quay

**Tara St. Station**

Gloucester St. L.

*River Liffey*

East Link Toll Br.

Townsend St.

Pearse St.

Sir John Rogerson's Quay

Lombard St.

Magennis Pl.

Cardiff's La.

Hanover Quay

*Grand Canal Dock*

**Pearse Station**

Pearse St.

Macken St.

Grand Canal Quay

Ringsend Rd.

Fenian St.

Lincoln Westland Row

Place

Leinster St.

Clare St.

◆ **National Gallery of Ireland**

Merrion Sq. N.

Hogan Pl.

Lower Grand Canal St.

Upper Grand Canal St.

South Lotts Rd.

Bath Av.

◆ **National Museum of Archaeology and History**

*Merrion Square*

Merrion Sq. S.

Lower Mount St.

Shelbourne Rd.

*Lansdowne Rugby Ground*

Merrion Row

Fitzwilliam La.

Lower Fitzwilliam St.

Upper Mount St.

Northumberland Rd.

Herbert Rd.

Pembroke St.

Lower Baggot St.

Herbert St.

Herbert Pl.

Percy Pl.

Haddington Rd.

Lansdowne Park

Lansdowne Rd.

Upper Fitzwilliam St.

Lad La.

Baggot St.

Shelbourne Rd.

Lower Leeson St.

Wilton Terrace

Upper Baggot St.

Pembroke Rd.

Pembroke Rd.

Beattys Av.

Mespil Rd.

Pembroke Ln.

Serpentine Av.

Burleigh Ct.

Pembroke Rd.

Sussex Rd.

Burlington Rd.

Waterloo Lane

Heysbury Lane

Wellington Rd.

Elgin Rd.

Raglan Ln.

Raglan Rd.

Upper Leeson St.

Waterloo Rd.

Clyde Rd.

Anglesea Rd.

Merrion Rd.

thbrook Rd.

Clyde Ln.

The Appian Way

Wellington Pl.

*HERBERT PARK*

## COMING ASHORE

Small ships dock at the quayside of the River Liffey, close to the downtown area. Larger ships berth at Alexandra Quay, 1.2 mi from downtown. Alexandra Quay is part of the great Dublin Port, with a range of visitor facilities including cafés, shops, information desks, and restrooms. Buses 53 and 53A run from the port into the city. Ticket prices are set according to the number of zones traveled, with a maximum fare of €2.20. Ticket machines on the bus accept only coins.

Taxis can be hired to run tour itineraries, although charges are complicated. Initial charges are a maximum of €4.10, then €1 per km (½-mi) for the first 14 km (9 mi), rising to €1.77 per km once the ride lasts longer than 30 km (19 mi). Drivers can choose to charge by the minute rather than per km, with the initial charge, plus €0.34 per minute for the first 40 minutes, climbing to €0.58 for journeys over 86 minutes. Don't rent a car if you are planning to tour Dublin, but a rental car does offer freedom to explore the countryside and coast around the city. The cost per day for a compact manual vehicle begins at €60.

> ### DUBLIN BEST BETS
>
> **Admire the Georgian architecture.** The magnificent neoclassical buildings form an impressive framework on which the life of the 21st-century city hangs.
>
> **Have a pint of Guinness.** The people of Dublin have a reputation for friendliness and a love of life that's infectious, so find a seat in a pub and enjoy.
>
> **Wander through St. Stephen's Green.** This park offers recreation as well as history—scattered throughout are memorials to the city's literary giants.

## EXPLORING DUBLIN

**City Hall.** This grand Georgian municipal building (1769–79) once housed the Royal Exchange. Today it's the seat of the Dublin Corporation, the elected body that governs the city. The building houses a multimedia exhibition tracing the evolution of Ireland's 1,000-year-old capital. ⊠ *Dame St., Dublin West* ☎ *01/222–2204* ⊕ *www.dublincity.ie* ☞ *€4* ☉ *Mon.–Sat. 10–5:15.*

**Custom House.** The Custom House is the city's most spectacular Georgian building. Note the exquisitely carved lions and unicorns supporting the arms of Ireland at the far ends of the facade. ⊠ *Custom House Quay, Northside* ☎ *01/888–2538* ☞ *Free* ☉ *Mid-Mar.–Oct., weekdays 10–12:30, weekends 2–5; Nov.–mid-Mar., Wed.–Fri. 10–12:30, Sun. 2–5.*

★ **Dublin City Gallery, The Hugh Lane.** Built for the Earl of Charlemont in 1762, this home is now a gallery housing the collection of Sir Hugh Lane. A complicated agreement with the National Gallery in London (reached after heated diplomatic dispute) stipulates that a portion of the 39 French paintings amassed by Lane shuttle between London and here. If you're lucky, you'll be able to see Pissarro's *Printemps,* Manet's *Eva Gonzales,* Morisot's *Jour d'Été,* and, the jewel of the collection, Renoir's *Les Parapluies.*

The late Francis Bacon's partner donated the entire contents of Bacon's studio to the gallery. The studio has been reconstructed here as a permanent display, and includes such masterpieces as *Study After Velázquez* and the tragic splash-and-crash *Triptych.* ✉ *Parnell Sq. N, Northside* ☎ *01/222–5550* ⊕ *www.hughlane.ie* ☜ *Free* ⊙ *Tues.–Thurs. 10–6, Fri. and Sat. 10–5, Sun. 11–5.*

**Grafton Street.** Grafton Street might be the most humming street in the city, if not in all of Ireland. It's one of Dublin's vital spines and the city's premier shopping street. Grafton Street and the smaller alleyways that radiate off it offer dozens of boutiques and some of the Southside's most popular watering holes. In summer, buskers line both sides of the street, pouring out the sounds of drum, whistle, pipe, and string.

**Fodor's** Choice ★ **Guinness Brewery and Storehouse.** Ireland's all-dominating brewer—founded by Arthur Guinness in 1759—spans a 60-acre spread west of Christ Church Cathedral. The brewery itself is closed to the public, but the Guinness Storehouse is a spectacular attraction, designed to woo you with the wonders of the "dark stuff." In a 1904 cast-iron-and-brick warehouse, the exhibit elucidates the brewing process and its history—you even get to enjoy a free pint. ✉ *St. James' Gate, Dublin West* ☎ *01/408–4800* ⊕ *www.guinness-storehouse.com* ☜ *€15* ⊙ *July and Aug., daily 9:30–7; Sept.–June, daily 9:30–5.*

**James Joyce Centre.** Joyce is acknowledged as one of the greatest modern authors, and his *Dubliners, Finnegan's Wake,* and *A Portrait of the Artist as a Young Man* can even be read as quirky "travel guides" to Dublin. This restored 18th-century Georgian town house, once the dancing academy of Professor Denis J. Maginni (which many will recognize from a reading of *Ulysses*), is a center for Joycean studies and events related to the author. ✉ *35 N. Great George's St., Northside* ☎ *01/878–8547* ⊕ *www.jamesjoyce.ie* ☜ *€5, guided tour €10* ⊙ *Tues.–Sat. 10–5, Sun. noon–5.*

**Fodor's** Choice ★ **Merrion Square.** Created between 1762 and 1764, this tranquil square a few blocks east of St. Stephen's Green is lined on three sides by some of Dublin's best-preserved Georgian town houses. Several distinguished Dubliners have lived on the square, including Irish nationalist Daniel O'Connell and author W.B. Yeats. As you walk past the houses, read the plaques on the house facades, which identify former inhabitants. ✉ *Along Upper and Lower Mount Sts., Southside* ⊙ *Daily sunrise–sunset.*

**Fodor's** Choice ★ **National Gallery of Ireland.** Featuring works by Caravaggio, Van Gogh, and Vermeer, the National Gallery of Ireland—the first in a series of major civic buildings on the west side of Merrion Square—is one of Europe's finer small art museums. The collection holds more than 2,500 paintings and some 10,000 other works. ✉ *Merrion Sq. W, Southside* ☎ *01/661–5133* ⊕ *www.nationalgallery.ie* ☜ *Free; special exhibits €10* ⊙ *Mon.–Wed., Fri., and Sat. 9:30–5:30, Thurs. 9:30–8:30, Sun. noon–5:30.*

★ **National Museum of Archaeology and History.** This museum houses a fabled collection of Irish artifacts dating from 7000 BC to the present. Organized around a grand rotunda, the museum is elaborately decorated, with mosaic floors, marble columns, balustrades, and fancy ironwork. It has the largest collection of Celtic antiquities in the world, including gold jewelry, carved stones, bronze tools, and weapons. The newest attraction is "Kinship and Sacrifice," centering on a number of Iron Age "bog bodies" and other objects found in Ireland's peat bogs. The Annex is at 7–9 Merrion Row. ⊠ *Kildare St.,Southside* ☎ *01/677–7444* ⊕ *www.museum.ie* ▧ *Free* ☉ *Tues.–Sat. 10–5, Sun. 2–5.*

**Newman House.** One of the greatest glories of Georgian Dublin, Newman House is actually two imposing town houses joined together. The earlier of the two, No. 85 St. Stephen's Green (1738) was originally known as Clanwilliam House. Designed by Richard Castle, it has two landmarks of Irish Georgian style: the Apollo Room, decorated with stuccowork; and the magnificent Saloon. The Saloon is crowned with an exuberant ceiling aswirl with cupids and gods, created by the Brothers Lafranchini, the finest *stuccadores* (plaster-workers) of 18th-century Dublin. Next door at No. 86 (1765), the staircase, on pastel walls, is one of the city's most beautiful rococo gems. To explore the houses you must join a guided tour. ⊠ *85–86 St. Stephen's Green, Southside* ☎ *01/716-7422* ▧ *House and garden €5* ☉ *Tours June–Aug., Tues.– Fri. at 2, 3, and 4.*

**O'Connell Street.** Dublin's most famous thoroughfare was previously known as Sackville Street, but its name was changed in 1924, two years after the founding of the Irish Free State. A 395-foot-high spire dominates the street. At the south end is a statue dedicated to Daniel O'Connell (1775–1847), "The Liberator," erected as a tribute to the orator's achievement in securing Catholic Emancipation in 1829.

★ **Royal Hospital Kilmainham.** This replica of Les Invalides in Paris is regarded as the most important 17th-century building in Ireland. The entire edifice has been restored to house the **Irish Museum of Modern Art,** which concentrates on the work of contemporary Irish artists. The museum also displays works by some non-Irish 20th-century greats, including Picasso and Miró. ⊠ *Kilmainham La., Dublin West* ☎ *01/612–9900* ⊕ *www.modernart.ie* ▧ *Free* ☉ *Royal Hospital Tues.– Sat. 10–5:30, Sun. noon–5:30. Museum Tues. and Thurs.–Sat. 10–5:30, Wed. 10:30–5:30, Sun. noon–5:30; tours Wed. and Fri. at 2:30, Sat. at 11:30.*

Fodor'sChoice
★ **St. Stephen's Green.** Dubliners call it simply Stephen's Green—a verdant, 27-acre Southside square that was used for the public punishment of criminals before it became a park. On the north side you'll find the legendary Shelbourne Hotel, where you can enjoy afternoon tea. On the south side is the alluring Georgian Newman House. ⊠ *Southside* ▧ *Free* ☉ *Daily sunrise–sunset.*

**Temple Bar.** A visit to modern Dublin wouldn't be complete without spending some time in the city's most vibrant area. This is Dublin's version of New York's SoHo, Paris's Bastille, London's Notting Hill—a thriving mix of high and alternative culture distinct from what you'll find in any other part of the city. Dotting the area's narrow cobblestone streets and pedestrian alleyways are new apartment buildings, vintage clothing stores, postage-stamp-size boutiques, art galleries, hip restaurants, pubs, clubs, European-style cafés, and a smattering of cultural venues. ⊠ *Bound by Liffey, Westmoreland St., Dame St.-College Green, and Fishamble St.*

**Fodor's Choice** ★ **Trinity College.** Founded in 1592, Trinity is Ireland's oldest and most famous college. The memorably atmospheric campus is a must; here you can track the shadows of such noted alumni as Jonathan Swift (1667–1745), Oscar Wilde (1854–1900), and Samuel Beckett (1906–89). Trinity's grounds cover 40 acres. Most of its buildings were constructed in the 18th and early 19th centuries, and together comprise an exceptional collection of neoclassical architecture. The **Old Library** houses Ireland's largest collection of books and manuscripts; its principal treasure is the *Book of Kells,* generally considered to be the most striking manuscript ever produced in the Anglo-Saxon world, and one of the great masterpieces of early Christian art. The book, which dates to the 9th century, is a splendidly illuminated version of the Gospels. The main library room, also known as the **Long Room,** is one of Dublin's most staggering sights. At 213 feet long and 42 feet wide, it contains approximately 200,000 of the 3 million volumes in Trinity's collection. ⊠ *Front Sq., Southside* ☎ *01/896–2320* ⊕ *www.tcd.ie/library* ⊡ *€8* ⊙ *May–Sept., Mon.–Sat. 9:30–5, Sun. 9:30–4:30; Oct.–Apr., Mon.–Sat. 9:30–5, Sun. noon–4:30.*

## SHOPPING

There's a tremendous variety of stores in Dublin, many of which are quite sophisticated. Department stores stock internationally known fashion designer goods and housewares, and small boutiques sell Irish crafts and other merchandise. If you're at all interested in modern and contemporary literature, be sure to leave yourself time to browse through the bookstores. Don't forget a bottle of Irish whiskey or a bottle or two of Guinness.

**Francis Street** is the hub of Dublin's antiques trade. **Grafton Street** has mainly chain stores. The smaller streets off Grafton Street have worthwhile crafts, clothing, and designer houseware shops. **Nassau Street,** Dublin's main tourist-oriented thoroughfare, has some of the best-known stores selling Irish goods. **Temple Bar** is dotted with small boutiques—mainly intimate, quirky shops that traffic in a selection of trendy goods, from vintage clothes to some of the most avant-garde Irish garb anywhere in the city. Note that many museums have excellent gift shops selling crafts, books, and prints, among other items.

**Blarney Woollen Mills.** This store is one of the best places for Belleek china, Waterford and Galway crystal, and Irish linen. ⊠ *21–23 Nassau St., City Center* ☎ *01/671–0068.*

**Cathach Books.** This shop sells first editions of Irish literature and many other books of Irish interest, plus old maps of Dublin and Ireland. ⊠ *10 Duke St., City Center* ☎ *01/671–8676.*

## WHERE TO EAT

¢   ✗ **Busyfeet & Coco Café.** This bustling, quirky bohemian café emphasizes
CAFÉ   good, wholesome food. Organic ingredients play a prominent role on a
**Fodor's Choice**   menu that's laden with delicious salads and sandwiches. Try the grilled
★   goat-cheese salad served with walnut-and-raisin toast and sun-dried-
tomato tapenade on a bed of arugula. The delicious Mediterranean que-
sadilla wrap—with roasted vegetables, napolitana sauce, and mature
cheddar—is a must. It's also one of the city center's best-situated spots
for a bit of people-watching, as Dublin's young and hip stroll by all
day long. ⊠ *41–42 S. William St., Southside* ☎ *01/671–9514* ▤ *No
credit cards.*

$   ✗ **Gruel.** Too many people know about this little joint to call it a secret
ECLECTIC   anymore. The brash, lively staff are masters of knowing when you need
them and when you don't. The atmosphere is chatty and crowded, and
the no-nonsense quality grub focuses on a few reliable classics done to
the highest quality—porridge with plum jam for breakfast, bangers and
mash, Thai fish cakes—along with a couple of new dishes every week
(how about risotto with roast sweet potato, basil, and chili?). They
make their own soup stocks from scratch, and the daily "roast on a
roll" sandwich is a real filler-upper at lunch. ⊠ *67 Dame St., Temple Bar*
☎ *01/670–7119* ⊕ *www.gruel.ie* ⚭ *Reservations not accepted* ▤ *MC, V.*

# GREENOCK, SCOTLAND (FOR GLASGOW)

In the days when Britain still ruled over an empire, Glasgow pronounced
itself the Second City of the Empire. The term "Clyde-built" (from
Glasgow's River Clyde) became synonymous with good workmanship
and lasting quality. Glasgow had fallen into a severely depressed state
by the mid-20th century, but during the century's last two decades
the city cleaned up and started looking forward. Modern Glasgow
has undergone an urban renaissance: A booming cultural life, stylish
restaurants, and an air of confidence make it Scotland's most exciting
city. Glasgow is particularly remarkable for its architecture, from the
unique Victorian cityscapes of Alexander "Greek" Thomson (1817–75)
to the cutting-edge art nouveau vision of Charles Rennie Mackintosh
(1868–1928). The city also has some of the most exciting museum collections outside London.

### ESSENTIALS

CURRENCY   The British pound sterling (£1 is $US1.61 at this writing). ATMs are
common and credit cards are widely accepted.

HOURS   Museums are open from 9 until 5, while shops usually open from 9
until 5:30 or 6. Some shops are open on Sunday.

INTERNET   **Café.com** (⊠ *8 Renfield St., City Center* ☎ *0141/221–5042*).

TELEPHONES   Tri-band GSM phones work in the United Kingdom. You can buy prepaid phone cards at telecom shops, news vendors, and tobacconists in
all towns and cities. Phone cards can be used for local or international
calls. Vodafone and Orange are the leading telecom companies.

**COMING ASHORE**

Vessels dock at Greenock's Ocean Terminal in the main port. Passengers walk the few yards to the terminal building, which has tourist information, refreshments, currency exchange, car-rental kiosks, and a taxi stand. A new waterfront walkway leads into the town of Greenock, where there are shops, restaurants, and some fine Victorian architecture dating from the time when the town was an important transatlantic port. However, there's little to hold visitors here.

A taxi to downtown Glasgow is a fixed-price £40 one way. From the station in Greenock (Greenock West), regular train services run into Glasgow city. From the port to the railway station it's a £4 taxi trip. The journey to Glasgow takes 30 to 40 minutes; trains run three or more times per hour and tickets start at £6 round trip. You can also take bus Numbers 901, 906, and 907 into Glasgow from the Greenock bus station.

Once in Glasgow, metro and bus services (tickets £1.20) can get you around easily. There are also numerous metered taxis. If you want to explore the majestic landscapes of southwestern Scotland independently, it pays to rent a vehicle (approximately £70 per day for a manual economy vehicle) or take a custom guided tour.

## EXPLORING GLASGOW

**Fodor's Choice**
★
**Burrell Collection.** An elegant, ultramodern building of pink sandstone and stainless steel houses thousands of items of all descriptions, from ancient Egyptian, Greek, and Roman artifacts to Chinese ceramics, bronzes, and jade. You'll also find medieval tapestries, stained-glass windows, Rodin sculptures, exquisite French impressionist paintings—Degas's *The Rehearsal*—and Sir Henry Raeburn's *Miss Macartney*. Eccentric millionaire Sir William Burrell (1861–1958) donated the magpie collection to the city in 1944. You can get there via Buses 45, 48, and 57 from Union Street. ⊠ *2060 Pollokshaws Rd., South Side* ☎ *0141/287–2550* ⊕ *www.glasgowlife.org.uk* ✉ *Free* ☉ *Mon.–Thurs. and Sat. 10–5, Fri. and Sun. 11–5.*

**Centre for Contemporary Arts.** This arts, cinema, and performance venue is in a post-industrial-revolution Alexander Thomson building. It has a reputation for unusual visual arts exhibitions, from paintings and sculpture to new media, and has championed a number of emerging artists, including Toby Paterson, winner of the Beck's Futures award in 2001. Simon Starling, the Scottish representative at the Venice Bienale in 2003, has also exhibited work here. The vibrant Tempus Bar Café is designed by Los Angeles-based artist Jorge Pardo. ⊠ *350 Sauchiehall St., City Center* ☎ *0141/352–4900* ⊕ *www.cca-glasgow.com* ✉ *Free* ☉ *Tues.–Sat. 11–6.*

**George Square.** The focal point of Glasgow's business district is lined with an impressive collection of statues of worthies: Queen Victoria; Scotland's national poet, Robert Burns (1759–96); the inventor and developer of the steam engine, James Watt (1736–1819); and towering above them all, Scotland's great historical novelist, Sir Walter Scott (1771–1832). On the square's east side stand the magnificent Italian

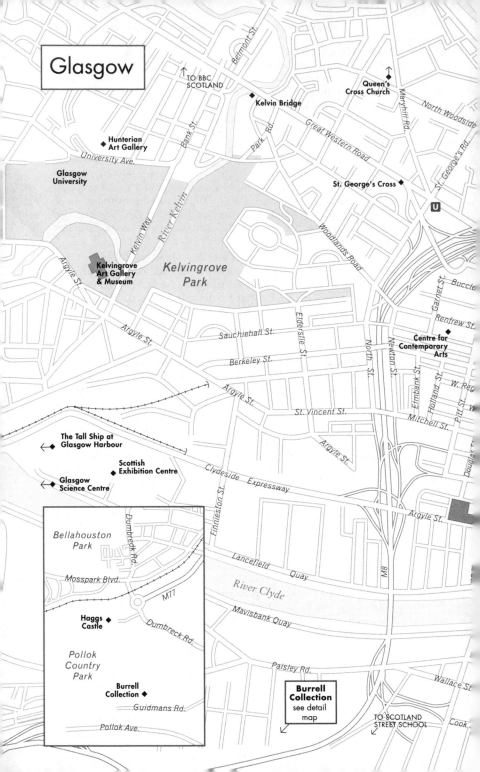

# Glasgow

TO BBC
SCOTLAND

Belmont St.

Queen's
Cross Church

Marryhill Rd.

North Woodside

Kelvin Bridge

Bank St.

Park Rd.

Great Western Road

St. George's Rd.

Hunterian
Art Gallery

University Ave.

Glasgow
University

St. George's Cross

Kelvin Way

River Kelvin

U

Argyle St.

Kelvingrove
Art Gallery
& Museum

Kelvingrove
Park

Woodlands Road

Garnet St.

Buccle

Renfrew St.

Argyle St.

Sauchiehall St.

Eldersile St.

Berkeley St.

North St.

Newton St.

Centre for
Contemporary
Arts

Elmbank St.

Holland St.

Pitt St.

W. Reg

Argyle St.

St. Vincent St.

Mitchell St.

Argyle St.

The Tall Ship at
Glasgow Harbour

Scottish
Exhibition Centre

Glasgow
Science Centre

Clydeside   Expressway

Finnieston St.

Argyle St.

Douglas

Bellahouston
Park

Dumbreck Rd.

Lancefield    Quay

M8

Mosspark Blvd.

M77

River Clyde

Mavisbank Quay

Haggs
Castle

Dumbreck Rd.

Pollok
Country
Park

Paisley Rd.

Wallace St.

Burrell
Collection

Burrell
Collection
see detail
map

Guidmans Rd.

TO SCOTLAND
STREET SCHOOL

Cook

Pollok Ave.

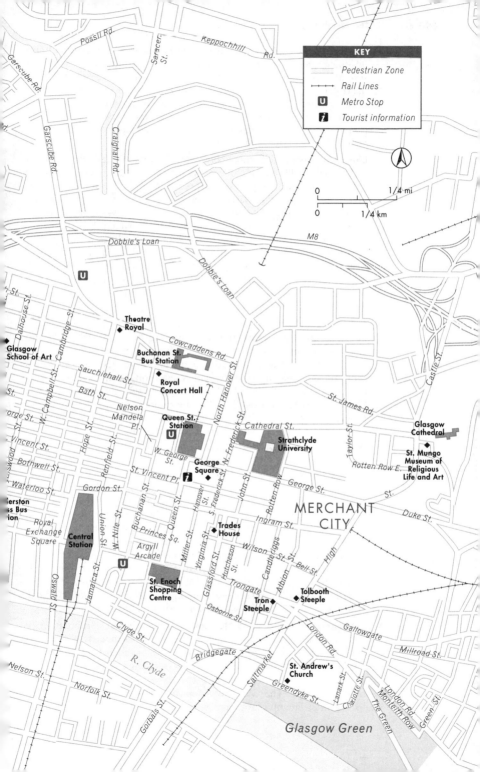

Renaissance–style **City Chambers**; the handsome **Merchants' House** fills the corner of West George Street. Off and around George Square several streets—Virginia Street, Miller Street, Glassford Street—recall the yesterdays of mercantile wealth. The French-style palaces, with their steep mansard roofs and cupolas, were once tobacco warehouses. Inside are shops and offices; here and there you may trace the elaborately carved mahogany galleries where auctions once took place. ⊠ *Between St. Vincent and Argyle Sts., City Center.*

**Glasgow Cathedral.** The most complete of Scotland's cathedrals, this is an unusual double church, one above the other, dedicated to Glasgow's patron saint, St. Mungo. Consecrated in 1136 and completed about 300 years later, it was spared the ravages of the Reformation—which destroyed so many of Scotland's medieval churches—mainly because Glasgow's trade guilds defended it. In the lower church is the splendid crypt of St. Mungo, who features prominently in local legends; Glasgow's coat of arms bears the various symbols of his famous deeds. ⊠ *Cathedral St., City Center* ☎ *0141/552–6891 for Historic Scotland, 0141/552–8198 for Cathedral office* ⊕ *www.glasgow-cathedral.com* ⛭ *Free* ⊙ *Apr.–Sept., Mon.–Sat. 9:30–5:30, Sun. 1–5; Oct.–Mar., Mon.–Sat. 9:30–4:30, Sun. 1–4:30.*

★ **Glasgow School of Art.** The exterior and interior, structure, furnishings, and decoration of this art nouveau building, built between 1897 and 1909, form a unified whole—architect Charles Rennie Mackintosh was only 28 years old when he won a competition for its design. Guided tours are available; it's best to make reservations. You can always visit the four on-site galleries that host frequently changing exhibitions. A block away is Mackintosh's Willow Tearoom. ⊠ *167 Renfrew St., City Center* ☎ *0141/353–4500* ⊕ *www.gsa.ac.uk* ⛭ *£8.75* ⊙ *Tours Oct.–Mar., daily. 11 and 3; Apr.–Sept., daily 10, 11, 12, 2, 3, 4, 5.*

★ **Hunterian Art Gallery.** This Glasgow University gallery houses William Hunter's (1718–83) collection of paintings (his antiquarian collection is housed in the nearby Hunterian Museum), together with prints and drawings by Tintoretto, Rembrandt, Sir Joshua Reynolds, and Auguste Rodin, as well as a major collection of paintings by James McNeill Whistler, who had a great affection for the city that bought one of his earliest paintings. Also in the gallery is a replica of **Charles Rennie Mackintosh's town house,** which once stood nearby. The rooms contain Mackintosh's distinctive art nouveau chairs, tables, beds, and cupboards, and the walls are decorated in the equally distinctive style devised by him and his artist wife Margaret. ⊠ *Hillhead St., West End* ☎ *0141/330–5431* ⊕ *www.hunterian.gla.ac.uk* ⛭ *Free, Mackintosh House £3 (free Wed. afternoon after 2)* ⊙ *Mon.–Sat. 9:30–5.*

★ **Kelvingrove Art Gallery and Museum.** This magnificent combination of cathedral and castle was designed in the Renaissance style and built between 1891 and 1901. The stunning red-sandstone edifice is an appropriate home for an art collection—including works by Botticelli, Rembrandt, and Monet—hailed as one of the greatest civic collections in Europe. The Glasgow Room houses extraordinary works by local artists. The museum has a visitor center, a café, and a restaurant.

⊠ *Argyle St., Kelvingrove Park, West End* ☎ *0141/276–9599* ⊕ *www.glasgowlife.org.uk* ☐ *Free* ⊙ *Mon.–Thurs., Sat. 10–5, Fri.–Sun. 11–5.*

**Queen's Cross Church.** The headquarters of the Charles Rennie Mackintosh Society, this is the only church to have been designed by the Glasgow-born architect and designer. Although one of the leading lights in the turn-of-the-20th-century art nouveau movement, Mackintosh died in 1928 with his name scarcely known. Today he's widely accepted as a brilliant innovator. The church has beautiful stained-glass windows and a light-enhancing, carved-wood interior. The center's library and shop provide further insight into Glasgow's other Mackintosh-designed buildings, which include Scotland Street School, the Martyrs Public School, and the Glasgow School of Art. A cab ride can get you here, or take a bus toward Queen's Cross from stops along Hope Street. ⊠ *870 Garscube Rd., West End* ☎ *0141/946–6600* ⊕ *www.crmsociety.com* ☐ *£4* ⊙ *Mar.–Oct., weekdays 10–5, Sun. 2–5; Nov.–Feb., weekdays 10–5.*

★ **St. Mungo Museum of Religious Life and Art.** An outstanding collection of artifacts, including Celtic crosses and statuettes of Hindu gods, reflects the many religious groups that have settled throughout the centuries in Glasgow and the west of Scotland. This rich history is depicted in the stunning Sharing of Faiths Banner, which celebrates the city's many different creeds. A Zen Garden creates a peaceful setting for rest and contemplation, and elsewhere, stained-glass windows feature a depiction of St. Mungo himself. ⊠ *2 Castle St., City Center* ☎ *0141/553–2557* ⊕ *www.glasgowlife.org.uk* ☐ *Free* ⊙ *Mon.–Thurs. and Sat. 10–5, Fri. and Sun. 11–5.*

---

## GLASGOW BEST BETS

**Kelvingrove Art Gallery and Museum.** A fantastic collection of European art, featuring such luminaries as Rembrandt and Monet, set in a stunning neo-Renaissance edifice.

**Glasgow School of Art.** Designed by Charles Rennie Mackintosh, this building is a tour de force of British art nouveau and one of the finest architectural statements in a city full of fine civic buildings.

**Hunterian Art Gallery.** This gallery features works by Tintoretto, Sir Joshua Reynolds, and Auguste Rodin—all donated by a private collector.

**4**

---

# SHOPPING

Glasgow is a shopper's dream, with its large department stores, designer outlets, quirky boutiques, and unique markets. Choice items include such traditional Scottish crafts as tartans, kilts, knitwear, and of course, whisky. Join the throngs of style-conscious and unseasonably tan locals along Argyle, Buchanan, and Sauchiehall streets. Should the weather turn *dreich,* you can avoid getting *drookit* by sheltering in one of the many covered arcades in the city center. For more unusual items, head to the West End's Byres Road and Great Western Road.

Many of Glasgow's young and upwardly mobile make their home in **Merchant City,** on the edge of the city center. Shopping here is expensive, but the area is worth visiting if you're seeking the youthful Glasgow style. If you're an antiques connoisseur and art lover, a walk along **West Regent Street,** particularly its **Victorian Village,** is highly recommended, as there are various galleries and shops, some specializing in Scottish antiques and paintings.

**Glasgow School of Art.** The school's store sells books, cards, jewelry, and ceramics. Students often display their work in June. ⊠ *167 Renfrew St., City Center* ☎ *0141/353–4526* ⊕ *www.gsa.ac.uk.*

**Hector Russell Kiltmakers.** The company specializes in Highland outfits, wool and cashmere clothing, and women's fashions. ⊠ *110 Buchanan St., City Center* ☎ *0141/221–0217* ⊕ *www.hector-russell.com.*

**National Trust for Scotland.** At the National Trust's shop, many of the items for sale, such as china, giftware, textiles, toiletries, and housewares, are designed exclusively for Trust properties and are often handmade. ⊠ *Hutchesons' Hall, 158 Ingram St., Merchant City* ☎ *0141/552–8391* ⊕ *www.nts.org.uk.*

**Princes Square.** By far the best shopping complex is the art nouveau Princes Square, with high-quality shops alongside pleasant cafés. Look particularly for the Scottish Craft Centre, which carries an outstanding collection of work created by some of the nation's best craftspeople. ⊠ *48 Buchanan St., City Center* ☎ *0141/221–0324* ⊕ *www. princessquare.co.uk.*

**Stockwell Bazaar.** Wander around to view a huge selection of fine china and earthenware, glass, and ornaments. Items can be packed and sent overseas. ⊠ *67–77 Glassford St., Merchant City* ☎ *0141/552–5781.*

## ACTIVITIES

**Royal Troon.** This golf club was founded in 1878, and has two 18-hole courses: the Old, or Championship, Course and the Portland Course. Access for nonmembers is limited between May and mid-October to Monday, Tuesday, and Thursday only; day tickets cost £165, and include two rounds, £55 club hire, and £20 cart hire. The course is 45 km (28 mi) south of Glasgow. ⊠ *Craigend Rd.* ☎ *01292/311555* ⊕ *www.royaltroon.co.uk* ⎱ *Old Course: 18 holes, 7,150 yds, SSS 74. Portland Course: 18 holes, 6,289 yds, SSS 70.*

## WHERE TO EAT

$$    ✕ **Café Gandolfi.** Once the offices of a cheese market, this trendy café
BRITISH  is now popular with the style-conscious crowd. Wooden tables and
★      chairs crafted by Scottish artist Tim Stead are so fluidly shaped it's hard to believe they're inanimate. The menu lists interesting soups, salads, and local specialties, all made with the finest regional produce. Don't miss the smoked venison or the finnan haddie (smoked haddock). ⊠ *64 Albion St., Merchant City* ☎ *0141/552–6813* ⊕ *www.cafegandolfi.com* ▭ *MC, V.*

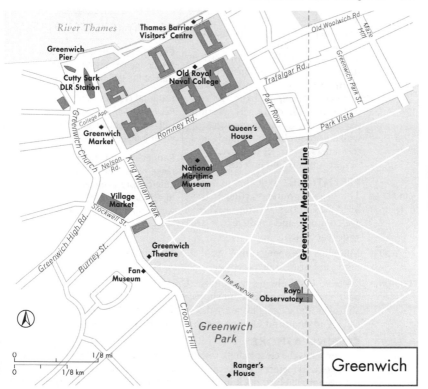

River Thames

Thames Barrier
Visitors' Centre

Greenwich
Pier

Cutty Sark
DLR Station

Old Royal
Naval College

College App.

Greenwich Church

Greenwich
Market

Romney Rd.

Nelson Rd.

Queen's
House

King William Walk

National
Maritime
Museum

Village
Market

Stockwell St.

Greenwich High Rd.

Burney St.

Greenwich
Theatre

Fan
Museum

The Avenue

Croom's Hill

Royal
Observatory

Greenwich
Park

Old Woolwich Rd.

Maze Hill

Greenwich Park St.

Trafalgar Rd.

Park Row

Park Vista

Greenwich Meridian Line

0      1/8 mi
0      1/8 km

Ranger's
House

**Greenwich**

4

**$–$$**    ✕ **Willow Tearoom.** There are two branches of this restaurant, but the
BRITISH    Sauchiehall Street location is the real deal. Conceived by the great
Charles Rennie Mackintosh, the Room De Luxe (the original tearoom)
is kitted out with his trademark furnishings, including high-back chairs
with elegant lines and subtle curves. The St. Andrew's Platter is an
exquisite selection of trout, salmon, and prawns. Scottish and continental breakfasts are available throughout the day, and the scrambled eggs
with salmon is traditional Scots food at its finest. The in-house baker
guarantees fresh scones, cakes, and pastries. ✉ *217 Sauchiehall St.,
City Center* ☎ *0141/332–0521* ⊕ *www.willowtearooms.co.uk* ⊟ *MC,
V* ⊙ *No dinner.*

# GREENWICH, UNITED KINGDOM

Visit Greenwich and you'll discover what makes Londoners tick.
Situated on the Greenwich Meridian Line at 0° longitude, this smart
Thames-side town literally marks the beginning of time. For an island
nation whose reputation was built on seafaring adventure, Britain's
centuries-old maritime tradition lays anchor here. Fans of elegant
architecture will be in heaven-on-sea, while landlubbers can wander
acres of rolling parkland and immaculately kept gardens. And while

the world-famous *Cutty Sark* may have long since unloaded its last tea chest, trading traditions live on in Greenwich's maze of market stalls that sell a Davy Jones locker's worth of bric-a-brac, antiques, and retro gear. Set apart from the rest of London, Greenwich is worth a day to itself, to make the most of walks in the rolling parklands and to immerse yourself in its richness of maritime art and entertainment.

### ESSENTIALS

CURRENCY  The British pound sterling (£1 is $US1.61 at this writing). ATMs are common and credit cards are widely accepted.

HOURS  Museums are open from 9 until 5, while shops usually open from 9 until 5:30 or 6. Some shops are open on Sunday.

TELEPHONES  Tri-band GSM phones work in the United Kingdom. You can buy pre-paid phone cards at telecom shops, news vendors, and tobacconists in all towns and cities. Phone cards can be used for local or international calls. Vodafone and Orange are the leading telecom companies.

### COMING ASHORE

Greenwich is the closest dock to central London for vessels up to a maximum of 240 meters (787 feet), but because most cruise ships are larger, you're more likely to dock in Harwich than Greenwich (⇨ *see Harwich, below, for coverage of central London*). The dock at Greenwich Reach is a mooring point and has no passenger terminal. The attractions of Greenwich itself are all within walking distance of the mooring, but for central London attractions you'll need to take public transport.

A network of buses connects all the attractions of London, but journey times can be slow. A quicker option is to use a combination of the Underground and Docklands Light Railway (DLR) system. The Underground's Jubilee Line runs from north Greenwich's Millennium Dome to Canary Wharf in London. The zippy "driverless" Docklands Light Railway (DLR) runs from Cutty Sark station to Canary Wharf or Bank. Fares from Greenwich DLR to Kings Cross in central London are £4 one way. A one-day travel card costs £7.50. Services run every 10 minutes or so throughout the day. You can also take the DLR to Island Gardens and retrace the steps dockworkers used to take back and forth on the old Victorian Foot Tunnel under the river.

A riverboat service called the *Thames Clipper* is probably the most scenic way to get into central London. The fare from Greenwich to Tower in central London costs £5.30 one way. Services run from 6:16 AM until 0:21 AM (last service from Tower back to Greenwich).

A rental car is both expensive and unadvisable if you are just touring Greenwich or central London. Rental costs approximately £50 per day

---

### GREENWICH BEST BETS

**Greenwich Meridian Line.** Stand astride the line that marks the start of the international date.

**National Maritime Museum.** Relive the *Titanic's* last moments with rescued artifacts and underwater footage of the wreck.

**Ranger's House.** Marvel at the range of treasures in this gem of 18th-century Georgian architecture, including more than 650 works of art.

for an economy manual vehicle, and gasoline is expensive. Taxi fares are regulated and determined by time of day, distance traveled, and taxi speed. Generally fares start at £2.20 and increase by units of 20 pence (per 125 to 191 yards or 24.5 to 37.6 seconds) after a certain initial distance. Surcharges are added around Christmas and New Year's days. Fares also go up between 10 PM and 6 AM. Tips are extra, usually 10% to 15% per ride. The average cost for a journey within central London is £8.

# EXPLORING GREENWICH

Ⓒ **National Maritime Museum.** Following a millennial facelift, one of Green-
★ wich's star attractions has been completely updated to make it one of London's most entertaining museums. Its glass-covered courtyard of grand stone, dominated by a huge revolving propeller from a powerful frigate, is reminiscent of the one in the British Museum. The collection spans everything from seascape paintings to scientific instruments, interspersed with exhibitions on heroes of the waves. A permanent Horatio Nelson gallery contains the uniform he wore, complete with bloodstain, when he met his end at Trafalgar in 1805. Allow at least two hours in this absorbing, adventurous place; if you're in need of refreshment, the museum has a good café with views over Greenwich Park. The **Queen's House** is home to the largest collection of maritime art in the world, including works by William Hogarth, Canaletto, and Joshua Reynolds. Inside, the Tulip Stair, named for the fleur-de-lis–style pattern on the balustrade, is especially fine, spiraling up without a central support to the Great Hall. The Great Hall itself is a perfect cube, exactly 40 feet in all three dimensions, decorated with paintings of the Muses, the Virtues, and the Liberal Arts. ✉ *Romney Rd., Greenwich* ☎ *020/8858–4422, recorded information 020/8312–6565* ⊕ *www.nmm.ac.uk* ✉ *Free* ⊙ *Daily 10–5; last admission 4:30* Ⓜ *DLR: Greenwich.*

★ **Old Royal Naval College.** Begun by Christopher Wren in 1694 as a rest home, or hospital for ancient mariners, this became instead a school for young ones in 1873. Today the University of Greenwich and Trinity College of Music have classes here. You'll notice how the structures part to reveal the Queen's House across the central lawns. Behind the college are two buildings you can visit. The **Painted Hall,** the college's dining hall, derives its name from the baroque murals of William and Mary (reigned 1689–95; William alone 1695–1702) and assorted allegorical figures. James Thornhill's frescoes, depicting scenes of naval grandeur with a suitably pro-British note of propaganda, were painstakingly done over installments in 1708–12 and 1718–26, and good enough to earn him a knighthood. The hall is still used for dinners, parties, schools, and weddings. In the opposite building stands the **College Chapel,** which was rebuilt after a fire in 1779 and is altogether lighter, in a more restrained, neo-Grecian style. ■**TIP**➜ **Trinity College of Music holds free classical music concerts in the chapel every Tuesday lunchtime.** ✉ *Old Royal Naval College, King William Walk, Greenwich* ☎ *020/8269–4747* ⊕ *www.oldroyalnavalcollege.org* ✉ *Free, guided* *tours £5* ⊗ *Painted Hall and Chapel daily 10–5; grounds 8–6* Ⓜ *DLR: Greenwich.*

**Ranger's House.** This handsome, early-18th-century villa, which was the Greenwich Park Ranger's official residence during the 19th century, is hung with Stuart and Jacobean portraits. But the most interesting diversion is the Wernher Collection, more than 650 works of art with a north European flavor, amassed by diamond millionaire Julius Wernher at the turn of the 20th century. After making his money in diamond mining, he chose to buy eclectic objects, sometimes beautiful, often downright quirky, like the silver coconut cup. Sèvres porcelain and Limoges enamels, the largest jewelry collection in the country, and some particularly bizarre reliquaries form part of this fascinating collection. Wernher's American wife, Birdie, was a strong influence and personality during the belle époque, which is easy to imagine from her striking portrait by Sargent. The house also makes a superb setting for concerts, which are regularly scheduled here. ⊠ *Chesterfield Walk, Blackheath, Greenwich* ☎ *020/8853–0035* ⊕ *www.english-heritage.org.uk* ☒ *£6* ⊗ *Apr.–Sept., Mon.–Wed. 11:30–2:30, Sun., 11–5* Ⓜ *DLR: Greenwich; no direct bus access, only to Vanbrugh Hill (from east) and Blackheath Hill (from west).*

☾ **Royal Observatory.** Founded in 1675 by Charles II, this imposing institu-
★ tion was designed the same year by Christopher Wren for John Flamsteed, the first Royal Astronomer. The red ball you see on its roof has been there since 1833, and drops every day at 1 PM, although it started to malfunction in 2006. This Greenwich Timeball and the Gate Clock inside the observatory are the most visible manifestations of Greenwich Mean Time—since 1884, the ultimate standard for time around the world. Greenwich is on the **prime meridian** at 0° longitude. A brass line laid among the cobblestones here marks the meridian, one side the eastern hemisphere, one the western.

In 1948 the Old Royal Observatory lost its official status: London's glow had grown too intense, and the astronomers moved to Sussex, while the Astronomer Royal decamped to Cambridge, leaving various telescopes, chronometers, and clocks for you to view. An excellent exhibition on the solution to the problem of measuring longitude includes John Harrison's famous clocks, H1–H4, now in working order. The museum recently unveiled "Time and Space," a major exhibit that added a planetarium and new galleries to the observatory. ⊠ *Greenwich Park, Greenwich* ☎ *020/8858–4422* ⊕ *www.rog.nmm.ac.uk* ☒ *Observatory free, planetarium £6.50* ⊗ *Daily 10–5; last admission 30 min before closure* Ⓜ *DLR: Greenwich.*

**Thames Barrier Visitors' Centre.** Learn what comes between London and its famous river—a futuristic-looking metal barrier that has been described as the eighth wonder of the world. Multimedia presentations, a film on the Thames's history, working models, and views of the barrier itself put the importance of the relationship between London and its river in perspective. ⊠ *Unity Way, Eastmoor St., Woolwich* ☎ *020/8305–4188* ⊕ *www.environment-agency.gov.uk* ☒ *£3.50* ⊗ *Apr.–Sept., daily*

*10:30–4:30; Oct.–Mar., daily 11–3:30* Ⓜ *National Rail: Charlton (from London Bridge), North Greenwich (Jubilee Line), then Bus 161 or 472.*

## SHOPPING

Greenwich is a collector's paradise, offering everything from English china (manufacturers such as Royal Doulton) and glass to silver and art in the small emporia in the city streets. Don't forget mainstream souvenirs like T-shirts and mugs featuring London buses or the Houses of Parliament (Palace of Westminster). Royal memorabilia is also popular and widespread.

**Antiques Market.** The weekend market, also known as Clocktower Market, on Greenwich High Road, has more vintage shopping, and browsing among the "small collectibles" makes for a good half-hour diversion.

**Greenwich Market.** You'll find the Victorian-era market on College Approach. Established as a fruit-and-vegetable market in 1700, and granted a royal charter in 1849, the glass-roof enclosure now offers arts and crafts Friday through Sunday, and antiques and collectibles on Thursday and Friday. Shopping for crafts is a pleasure, since in most cases you're buying directly from the artist. ✉ *College Approach, Greenwich* ☎ *020/8269–5096* ⊕ *www.greenwichmarket.net* Ⓜ *DLR: Cutty Sark.*

## WHERE TO EAT

¢ ✕ **The Honest Sausage.** Up by the Royal Observatory, beside the Wolfe monument, this spot serves up delicious homemade organic sausages and huge jacket potatoes drenched in onion gravy. The views are great, too. ✉ *Greenwich Park, Greenwich* ☎ *020/858–9695* ⊕ *www.companyofcooks.com* ▭ *No credit cards.*

BRITISH

$$$ ✕ **Trafalgar Tavern.** For the best pub in Greenwich, head to this local favorite, with excellent views of the Thames. It's a grand place to have a pint and some upscale grub. In warm weather the terrace has outdoor seating overlooking the Millenium Dome. ✉ *Park Row* ☎ *020/8858–2909* ⊕ *www.trafalgartavern.co.uk.*

BRITISH

# HARWICH, UNITED KINGDOM (FOR LONDON)

London is an ancient city whose history greets you at every turn. If the city contained only its famous landmarks—the Tower of London or Big Ben—it would still rank as one of the world's top cities. But London is so much more. The foundations of London's character and tradition endure. The British bobby is alive and well. The tall, red, double-decker buses (in an updated model) still lumber from stop to stop. Then there's that greatest living link with the past—the Royal Family with all its attendant pageantry. To ice the cake, swinging-again London is today one of the coolest cities on the planet. The city's art, style, and fashion make headlines around the world, and London's chefs have become superstars. Plus, London's hosting of the 2012 Olympics means the city

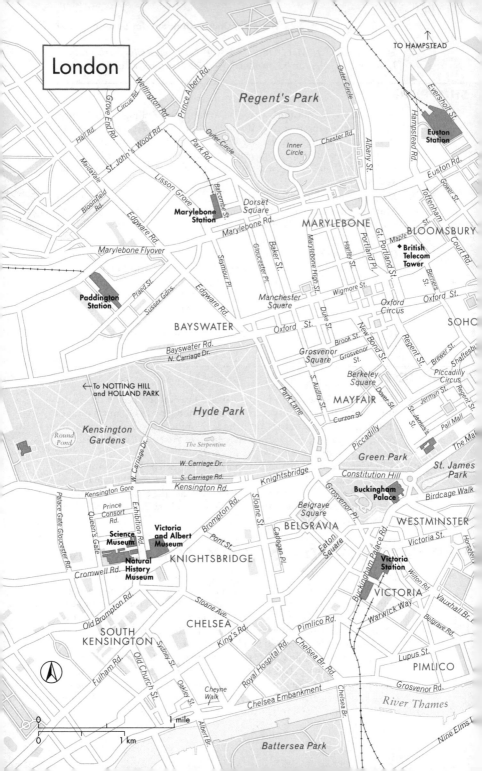

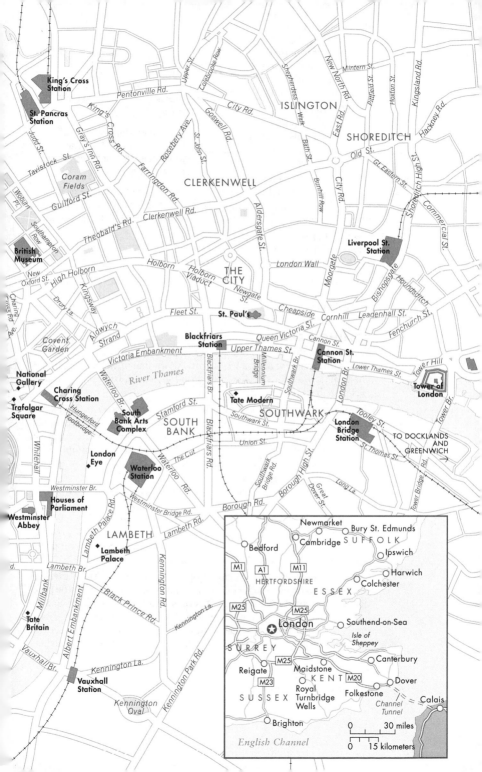

will be a hot spot for years to come. Harwich is now commonly used as the point of embarkation for many ships that use "London" as a base.

### ESSENTIALS

CURRENCY    The British pound sterling (£1 is $US1.61 at this writing). ATMs are common and credit cards are widely accepted.

HOURS    Museums are open from 9 until 5, while shops usually open from 9 until 5:30 or 6. Some shops are open on Sunday.

INTERNET    **Internet Business Lounge** (✉ *116 Gloucester Rd., Kensington* ☎ *020/ 7835-3114* ⊕ *www.bizlounge.co.uk* ⏱ *Daily 9* AM–*11* PM).

TELEPHONES    Tri-band GSM phones work in the UK. You can buy prepaid phone cards at telecom shops, news vendors, and tobacconists in all towns and cities. Phone cards can be used for local or international calls. Vodafone and Orange are the leading telecom companies.

> **LONDON BEST BETS**
>
> **Buckingham Palace.** A prime chance to catch sight of British royalty.
>
> **The British Museum.** One of the world's richest historical and archaeological collections, and it's completely free.
>
> **The Tower of London.** Experience the city's rich history, from dirty deeds to the dazzling Crown Jewels.

### COMING ASHORE

Vessels dock in the commercial port at Harwich, which is small but busy with commercial and ferry traffic. Port amenities include a mainline train station for transfers into London, a café, bar, ATMs, and an exchange bureau.

When larger cruise ships dock, the port schedules extra trains for the transfer into London. The journey time is 80 minutes. Normal rail services involve one change and take one hour 45 minutes. Ticket prices are around £50 round-trip. Taxi transfer to London is prohibitively expensive at around £125 or more.

### GETTING TO THE AIRPORT

If you do not purchase airport transfers from your cruise line there are several ways to reach the Heathrow airport from the cruise port. The most practical way would be to book a private direct tranfer by taxi or private hire company. Costs are around £170, but this covers from one to three people traveling in the same vehicle. Depending on traffic conditions, the transfer should be around one hour.

There are several public transport options, but each of these involves transfer between rail and Underground stations, which may not be practical if you have bulky luggage. There is a rail link between Harwich International Cruise Port and London's Liverpool Street Station. Ticket prices per single journey are around £28. Once at Liverpool Street you need to transfer to your chosen mode of transort to take you from central London to Heathrow airport.

The least expensive option is the London Underground, but carriages can be busy with little luggage space. From Liverpool Street take the Hammersmith and City line to King's Cross. From King's Cross the

Piccadily line takes you directly to Heathrow. The time for the journey is around 1:20 hours and costs £4.

Heathrow Express offers a much quicker journey, 15 minutes from central London to Heathrow because it's a direct service. It also caters more for travelers than for urban commuters. This runs from Paddington Station, and to get here from Liverpool Street you must again take the Hammersmith and City Underground line. Heathrow Express tickets cost £18 single or £32 round-trip.

The Heathrow Connect train links Paddington with Heathrow airport, stopping at selected minor stations along the route. Prices are £7.90 per single journey.

**Contacts Cruise Transfer.com** (☎ 0870/042–2752 ⊕ www.cruisetransfer.com). **Prompt Airport Cars** (☎ 020/7060–6070 ⊕ www.promptexecutivehire.co.uk). **Road Express** (☎ 0844/846–4061 ⊕ www.road-express.co.uk).

## EXPLORING LONDON

Fodor's Choice
★  **British Museum.** This celebrated treasure house is filled with plunder of incalculable value and beauty from around the globe. If you want to navigate the highlights of the almost 100 galleries, join the free **Eyeopener** 50-minute tour by museum guides (details at the information desk).

Here follows a highly edited resume of the British Museum's greatest hits. The **Rosetta Stone,** carved in 196 BC. This inscription provided the French Egyptologist Jean-François Champollion with the key to deciphering hieroglyphics. The **Parthenon Marbles** include the spectacular remains of the Parthenon frieze carved around 440 BC. Close by is one of the Seven Wonders of the Ancient World—in fragment form: the **Mausoleum of Halikarnassos.** There are also galleries of **Egyptian mummies,** the splendid 8th-century Anglo-Saxon **Sutton Hoo Treasure,** and the remains of **Lindow Man**—retrieved from a Cheshire peat marsh—having been ritually slain in the 1st century, probably as a human sacrifice. The museum's **Great Court** is now roofed over and has a lovely, albeit expensive, ourdoor café. ⊠ *Great Russell St., Bloomsbury* ☎ *020/7323–8000* ⊕ *www.thebritishmuseum.ac.uk* ◻ *Free, suggested donation; tickets for special exhibitions vary in price* ◔ *Museum Sat.–Wed. 10–5:30, Thurs. and Fri. 10–8:30. Great Court Sun.–Wed. 9–6, Thurs.–Sat. 9 AM–11 PM* Ⓜ *Holborn, Russell Sq., Tottenham Court Rd.*

Fodor's Choice
★  **Buckingham Palace.** Buckingham Palace tops many must-see lists, although the building itself is no masterpiece. The palace contains some 600 rooms, including the Ballroom and the Throne Room. The state rooms are where much of the business of royalty is played out and these are open to the public while the Royal Family is away during the summer.

The **Changing of the Guard** culminates in front of the palace. ■**TIP→ Get there by 10:30 AM to grab a spot in the best viewing section at the gate facing the palace.** ⊠ *Buckingham Palace Rd., St. James's,* ☎ *020/7766–7300* ⊕ *www.royalcollection.org.uk* ◻ *£17, includes audio tour, credit-card reservations subject to booking charge; prebooking recommended* ◔ *Late*

*July–late Sept., daily 9:45–6, last admission 3:45; confirm dates, which are subject to Queen's mandate. Changing of the Guard Apr.–July, daily 11:30 AM; Aug.–Mar., alternating days only 11:30 AM* ▤*AE, MC, V* Ⓜ *Victoria, St. James's Park.*

FodorśChoice ★ **Houses of Parliament.** Seat of Great Britain's government, the Houses of Parliament are, arguably, the city's most famous and photogenic sights. Designed in glorious, mock-medieval style by two Victorian-era architects, Sir Charles Barry and Augustus Pugin, in the 1830s, the Palace of Westminster, as the complex is still properly called, was first established by Edward the Confessor in the 11th century. It has served as the seat of English administrative power, on and off, ever since. Now virtually the symbol of London, the 1858 **Clock Tower** designed by Pugin contains the bell known as **Big Ben** that chimes the hour (and the quarters). Weighing a mighty 13 tons, the bell takes its name from Sir Benjamin Hall, the far-from-slim Westminster building works commissioner. ⊠ *St. Stephen's Entrance, St. Margaret St., Westminster* ☎ *020/7219–4272 Commons information, 020/7219–3107 Lords information, 020/7222–2219 Jewel Tower, 020/7219–2184 Lord Chancellor's Residence, 0844/847–1672 summer tours* ⊕ *www.parliament. uk* ▤ *Free, £14 summer tours* ☉ *Commons Mon. 2:30–10:30, Tues. and Wed. 11:30–7:30, Thurs. 11:30–6:30, Fri. 9:30–3 (although not every Fri.). Lords Mon.–Thurs. 2:30–10; Lord Chancellor's Residence Tues. and Thurs. 10:30–12:30. Closed Easter wk, late July–early Sept., 3 wks for party conference recess mid-Sept.–early Oct., and 3 wks at Christmas* Ⓜ *Westminster.*

☾ ★ **London Eye.** If you want a pigeon's-eye view of London, this is the place. The highest observation wheel in the world, at 500 feet, towers over the South Bank from the Jubilee Gardens. On a clear day you can take in a range of up to 25 mi, viewing London's most famous landmarks. ■ **TIP→ Buy your ticket online to avoid the long lines.** ⊠ *Jubilee Gardens, South Bank* ☎ *0870/990–8883 customer service, 0871/781– 3000 booking line* ⊕ *www.londoneye.com* ▤ *£17.95, fast track ticket £29.70* ☉ *May and June, Sun.–Thurs. 10–8, Fri. and Sat. 10–9:30; Apr. and Sept., daily 10–9; July and Aug., daily 10–9:30; Oct.–Mar., daily 10–8* Ⓜ *Waterloo.*

FodorśChoice ★ **National Gallery.** Jan Van Eyck's *Arnolfini Marriage,* Leonardo da Vinci's *Virgin and Child,* and Diego Velázquez's *Rokeby Venus* are only a few of the highlights in this priceless collection. There are approximately 2,200 paintings in the museum, many of them among the most treasured works of art anywhere. The National's collection includes paintings of the early Renaissance, the Flemish and Dutch masters, the Spanish school, and the English tradition (notably William Hogarth, Thomas Gainsborough, George Stubbs, and John Constable).

The **Micro Gallery,** a computer information center in the Sainsbury Wing, is a great place to start. You can access information on any work, choose your favorites, and print out a free personal tour map. There's another computer center in the espresso bar in the lower hall. ⊠ *Trafalgar Sq., Westminster* ☎ *020/7747–2885* ⊕ *www.nationalgallery.org. uk* ▤ *Free, charge for special exhibitions* ☉ *Daily 10–6, Wed. until 9;*

*1-hr free guided tour starts at Sainsbury Wing daily at 11:30 and 2:30, and additionally Fri. at 7* Ⓜ *Charing Cross, Leicester Sq.*

**Fodor's** Choice ★ **St. Paul's Cathedral.** The symbolic heart of London, St. Paul's may take your breath away. The structure is Sir Christopher Wren's masterpiece, completed in 1710, and, much later, miraculously spared (mostly) by World War II bombs. Most famous in recent times as the scene of the marriage of Diana to Charles Prince of Wales in 1981, the church has played host to the funerals of English heroes the Duke of Wellington and Admiral Lord Nelson, both of whom lie in the **Crypt.** Behind the high altar is the **American Memorial Chapel,** dedicated in 1958 to the 28,000 GIs stationed in the United Kingdom who lost their lives in World War II. ✉ *St. Paul's Churchyard, The City* ☎ *020/7236–4128* ⊕ *www.stpauls.co.uk* ▤ *£12.50, audio tour £4, guided tour £3* ⊙ *Cathedral Mon.–Sat. 8:30–4 (time of last ticket sold), closed occasionally for special services. Ambulatory, Crypt, and galleries Mon.–Sat. 9–4:15. Shop and Crypt Café also open Sun. 10:30–* Ⓜ *St. Paul's.*

★ **Tate Britain.** This museum is a brilliant celebration of great British artists from the 16th century to the present day. The collection's crowning glory is the Turner Bequest, consisting of Romantic painter J. M. W. Turner's personal collection. ✉ *Millbank, Westminster* ☎ *020/7887–800, 020/7887–8008 recorded information* ⊕ *www.tate.org.uk* ▤ *Free, exhibitions £3–£10* ⊙ *Daily 10–6, last entry 5:15, also Fri. until 10* PM Ⓜ *Pimlico (signposted 5-min walk).*

**Fodor's** Choice ★ **Tate Modern.** This former power station has undergone a dazzling renovation by Herzog de Meuron to provide a grand space for a massive collection of international modern art. On permanent display are classic works from 1900 to the present day by Matisse, Picasso, Dalí, Francis Bacon, Warhol, and the most talked-about upstarts. ✉ *Bankside, South Bank* ☎ *020/7887–8888* ⊕ *www.tate.org.uk* ▤ *Free, special exhibitions £3–£10* ⊙ *Sun.–Thurs. 10–6, Fri. and Sat. 10–10* Ⓜ *Blackfriars, Southwark.*

Ⓒ ★ **Tower of London.** Nowhere else does London's history come to life so vividly as in this minicity of 20 towers filled with heraldry and treasure, the intimate details of lords and dukes and princes and sovereigns etched in the walls (literally, in some places), and quite a few pints of royal blood spilled on the stones. Yeoman Warders, better known as Beefeaters, have been guarding the Tower since Henry VII appointed them in 1485.

The Tower holds the royal gems because it's still one of the royal palaces, although no monarch since Henry VII has called it home. Its best-known and most titillating function has been as a jail and place of torture and execution.

The most famous exhibits are the **Crown Jewels,** in the Jewel House, Waterloo Block. Moving walkways on either side of the jewels hasten progress at the busiest times. Finest of all is the Royal Sceptre, containing the earth's largest cut diamond, the 530-carat Star of Africa.
■ **TIP→** **This is one of Britain's most popular sights, and you can avoid lines by buying a ticket in advance on the Web site, by phone, at any tube station, or at an on-site kiosk. Arriving before 11 can also help at busy times.**
✉ *H.M. Tower of London, Tower Hill, The City* ☎ *0844/482–7799*

*recorded information and advance booking* ⊕ *www.hrp.org.uk* 🎫 *£17*
⊗ *Mar.–Oct., Tues.–Sat. 9–5:30, Sun. and Mon. 10–5:30; Nov.–Feb.,*
*Tues.–Sat. 9–4:30, Sun. and Mon. 10–4:30. Tower closes 1 hr after last*
*admission time and all internal bldgs. close 30 min after last admission.*
*Free guided tours leave daily from Middle Tower (subject to weather*
*and availability) about every 30 min until 3:30 Mar.–Oct., 2:30 Nov.–*
*Feb.* Ⓜ *Tower Hill.*

**Trafalgar Square.** This is the center of London, both geographically and
symbolically. Great events, such as royal weddings, political protests,
and sporting triumphs, always draw crowds to the city's most famous
square. Trafalgar Square takes its name from the Battle of Trafalgar,
Admiral Lord Horatio Nelson's great naval victory over the French, in
1805. Appropriately, the dominant landmark here is **Nelson's Column,**
a 145-foot-high granite perch from which a statue of Nelson keeps
watch. ⊠ *Trafalgar Sq., Westminster* Ⓜ *Charing Cross, Leicester Sq.*

Fodor'sChoice **Westminster Abbey.** A monument to the nation's rich—and often bloody
★ and scandalous—history, this is one of London's most iconic sites.
Nearly all of Britain's monarchs have been crowned here since the coronation of William the Conqueror on Christmas Day 1066—and most
are buried here, too.

The current abbey is a largely 13th- and 14th-century rebuilding of
the 11th-century church founded by Edward the Confessor, with one
notable addition being the 18th-century twin towers over the west
entrance, designed by Sir Christopher Wren and completed by Nicholas Hawksmoor. Highlights of the interior are the **Coronation Chair,**
where monarchs are crowned, plus the tomb of Elizabeth I, buried with
her half-sister, "Bloody" Mary I. The **Chapel of St. Edward** contains
the tombs of more ancient monarchs, while the **Henry VII Chapel** (also
known as the Lady Chapel) offers magnificent sculptures and exquisite
fan vaulting above. In 1400 Geoffrey Chaucer became the first poet to
be buried in **Poets' Corner.** There are memorials to William Shakespeare
and Charles Dickens (who is also buried here). ⊠ *Broad Sanctuary,*
*Westminster* ☎ *020/7222–5152* ⊕ *www.westminster-abbey.org* 🎫 *£15*
⊗ *Abbey Mon., Tues., Thurs., and Fri. 9:30–3:45, Wed. 9:30–6, Sat.*
*9–1:45 (closes 1 hr after last admission). Museum daily 10:30–4. Clois-*
*ters daily 8–6. College Garden Tues.–Thurs. Apr.–Sept. 10–6, Oct.–*
*Mar. 10–4. Separate admission for Chapter House daily 10–4. Abbey*
*closed to visitors during weekday and Sun. services* Ⓜ *Westminster.*

## SHOPPING

Napoléon was being scornful when he called Britain a nation of shopkeepers, but Londoners have had the last laugh. The finest emporiums
are in London still. You can shop like royalty at Her Majesty's glove-
maker, discover an uncommon Toby jug in an antiques shop, or find a
leather-bound edition of *Wuthering Heights* on Charing Cross Road. If
you have limited time, zoom in on one of the city's grand department
stores, such as Harrods or Selfridges, where you can find enough booty
for your entire gift list.

**Chelsea** centers on King's Road, once synonymous with ultra-high fashion; it still harbors some designer boutiques, plus antiques and home furnishings stores. **Covent Garden** has chain clothing stores and top designers, stalls selling crafts, and shops selling gifts of every type. Kensington's main drag, **Kensington High Street,** houses some small, classy shops, with a few larger stores at the eastern end. Try Kensington Church Street for expensive antiques, plus a little fashion.

**Crafts Council Gallery Shop.** This shop showcases a microcosm of British crafts. ✉ *44A Pentonville Rd., Islington* ☎ *020/7806–2559* Ⓜ *Angel.*

Fodor's Choice ★ **Fortnum & Mason.** The Queen's grocer is, paradoxically, the most egalitarian of gift stores, with plenty of luxury foods, stamped with the gold BY APPOINTMENT crest, for less than £5. ✉ *181 Piccadilly, St. James's* ☎ *020/7734–8040* ⊕ *www.fortnumandmason.com* Ⓜ *Piccadilly Circus.*

Fodor's Choice ★ **Harrods.** This is simply one of the world's most famous department stores. The food halls are stunning—so are the crowds and prices. ✉ *87 Brompton Rd., Knightsbridge* ☎ *020/7730–1234* ⊕ *www.harrods.com* Ⓜ *Knightsbridge.*

# WHERE TO EAT

$$$$  MODERN EUROPEAN  ☾  Fodor's Choice ★ ✕ **Boxwood Café.** Attached to the Berkeley and in the Gordon Ramsay stable, the Boxwood is the best uptown but most relaxed place to dine in Knightsbridge, with opulent marble, brown, and greens. The New York–style restaurant is open late (until midnight Thursday–Saturday), and set lunch is useful at £28. Favorite dishes range from Orkney scallops to yellowfin tuna, and from veal burger to treacle tart. Service is top-notch, and you'll find a fashionable buzz. ✉ *The Berkeley, Wilton Pl., Knightsbridge* ☎ *020/7235–1010* ⊕ *www.gordonramsay.com/boxwoodcafe* ⚠ *Reservations essential* ▤ *AE, MC, V* Ⓤ *Knightsbridge.*

$$$  BRITISH ★ ✕ **The Pig's Ear.** This inventive gastro-pub is a Chelsea favorite. Elbow in at the boisterous ground-floor pub area, or choose a restaurant vibe in the wood-panel salon upstairs. You'll find creative dishes on the short menu: shallot and cider soup, roast bone marrow, or skate wing and leeks are all typical, and executed . . . royally. ✉ *35 Old Church St., Chelsea* ☎ *020/7352–2908* ⚠ *Reservations essential* ▤ *AE, DC, MC, V* Ⓜ *Sloane Sq.*

# WHERE TO STAY

$$  ⊞ **B&B Belgravia.** This modern guesthouse a short walk from Victoria Station has cool all-white decor—white chairs and walls, white pillars and desks, white linens and towels. It all looks a bit ethereal, which is what they're aiming for. Rooms are small, but beds are comfortable, and at least nothing you're wearing will clash. There's a modern, open-plan lounge where a fire crackles away in the winter. It's a good place to grab a cup of tea (always available) and check your e-mail on the free computer. **Pros:** free Wi-Fi; nice extras like free use of a laptop in the hotel lounge; coffee and tea always available. **Cons:** bathrooms are small; no hotel restaurant or bar. ✉ *64–66 Ebury St., Victoria* ☎ *020/7259–8780* ⊕ *www.bb-belgravia.com* ⤴ *17 rooms* ♿ *In-room:*

no a/c, Wi-Fi. In-hotel: Wi-Fi, no-smoking rooms ▤ AE, DC, MC, V ⦿⦚ CP Ⓤ Knightsbridge.

$$–$$$ ▣ **Millennium Gloucester.** Recently refurbished in 2007, the hotel has a sleek lobby with polished wood columns, a warming fireplace, and glittering chandeliers. Guest rooms are done in neutral creams and earth tones, and blond-wood desks and leather chairs have a blandly masculine look. The hotel is popular with business travelers, so rooms come equipped with satellite TV and fast broadband connections. Bathrooms are relatively small, but have all you need. There are two bars and several restaurants, which means you don't have to go out if you'd prefer to stay in. **Pros:** good deals available if you book in advance. **Cons:** public areas and restaurant can get crowded. ⊠ 4–18 Harrington Gardens, Kensington ☏ 020/7373–6030 ⊕ www.millenniumhotels. co.uk/millenniumgloucester ⇦ 143 rooms ᴧ In-room: safe, refrigerator, Wi-Fi. In-hotel: restaurant, room service, no-smoking rooms ▤ AE, MC, V ⦿⦚ BP Ⓤ Gloucester Rd.

$$$$ ▣ **One Aldwych.** An understated blend of contemporary and classic
**Fodor's Choice** results in pure, modern luxury here. Flawlessly designed inside an
★ Edwardian building, One Aldwych is coolly eclectic, with an artsy lobby, feather duvets, Italian linen sheets, and ample elegance. It's the ultimate in 21st-century style, from the free, hotel-wide Wi-Fi down to the gorgeous swimming pool in the awesome health club. Suites have amenities such as a private gym, a kitchen, and a terrace. Breakfast is made with organic ingredients. The pool has underwater speakers that play music you can hear only when you dive in. **Pros:** understated (and underwater) luxury. **Cons:** all this luxury doesn't come cheap. ⊠ 1 Aldwych, Covent Garden ☏ 020/7300–1000 ⊕ www.onealdwych. co.uk ⇦ 93 rooms, 12 suites ᴧ In-room: safe, kitchen (some), refrigerator, Wi-Fi. In-hotel: 2 restaurants, room service, bars, pool, gym, spa, laundry service, parking (paid), no-smoking rooms ▤ AE, MC, V Ⓤ Charing Cross, Covent Garden.

# INVERGORDON, SCOTLAND

The port of Invergordon is your gateway to the Great Glen, an area of Scotland that includes Loch Ness and the city of Inverness. Inverness, the capital of the Highlands, has the flavor of a Lowland town, its winds blowing in a sea-salt air from the Moray Firth. The Great Glen is also home to one of the world's most famous monster myths: in 1933, during a quiet news week, the editor of a local paper decided to run a story about a strange sighting of something splashing about in Loch Ness. But there's more to look for here besides Nessie, including inland lochs, craggy and steep-sided mountains, rugged promontories, deep inlets, brilliant purple and emerald moorland, and forests filled with astonishingly varied wildlife, including mountain hares, red deer, golden eagles, and ospreys.

## ESSENTIALS

CURRENCY　The British pound sterling (£1 is $US1.61 at this writing). ATMs are common and credit cards are widely accepted.

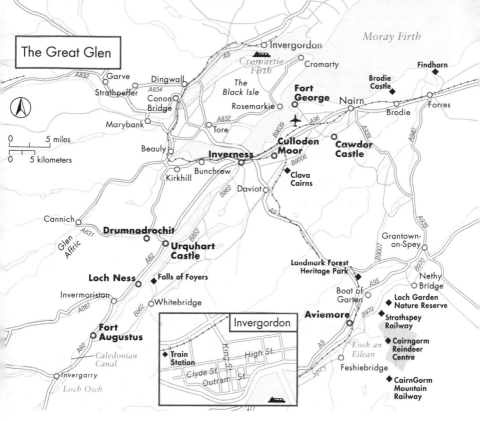

The Great Glen

Invergordon

HOURS      Museums are open from 9 until 5, while shops usually open from 9 until 5:30 or 6. Some shops are open on Sunday.

INTERNET      **Invergordon Naval Museum and Heritage Centre** (✉ *High St., Invergordon* ☎ *01349/8548911* ⊕ *www.invergordonnavalmuseum.co.uk*) is a museum, archive, and library, and it also offers Internet access.

TELEPHONES      Tri-band GSM phones work in the United Kingdom. You can buy prepaid phone cards at telecom shops, news vendors, and tobacconists in all towns and cities. Phone cards can be used for local or international calls. Vodafone and Orange are the leading telecom companies.

## COMING ASHORE

There is no dedicated cruise terminal at Invergordon. Ships dock at one of the town quays—usually Admiralty Quay, the closest to the town. At the pier there is a tourist information kiosk manned only when ships are in dock.

Passengers can walk into the center of Invergordon for public transportation to surrounding sights. The Invergordon railway station is 1 km (½ mi) from the port, and runs five round-trip trains south to Inverness per day, as well as trains north to Dornoch.

A car is a great asset for exploring the Great Glen, especially since the best of the area is away from the main roads. You can use the main A82 from Inverness to Fort William, or use the smaller B862/B852 roads (former military roads) to explore the much quieter east side of Loch Ness. **Ken's Garage** (☎ *014663/717606* ⊕ *www.kensgarage.co.uk*) will meet you at the docks with a car, but you must book in advance. Prices for a small vehicle are £28 per day.

Taxis do not meet the ships as a matter of course. **Duncan Maclean** (☎ *01349/8678645* ⊕ *www.thetaxitourexperience.com*) can provide taxi services at a rate of £35 per hour (one to four people), but he must be prebooked.

# EXPLORING INVERGORDON AND THE GREAT GLEN

## INVERNESS

Inverness seems designed for the tourist, with its banks, souvenirs, high-quality woolens, and well-equipped visitor center. Compared with other Scottish towns, however, Inverness has less to offer visitors who have a keen interest in Scottish history. Throughout its past, Inverness was burned and ravaged by the restive Highland clans competing for dominance in the region. Thus, a decorative wall panel here and a fragment of tower there are all that remain amid the modern shopping facilities and 19th-century downtown developments. The town does make a good base, however, for exploring the northern end of the Great Glen.

**Castle.** One of Inverness's few historic landmarks is its castle (the local Sheriff Court), rising above the river. The current structure is Victorian, built after a former fort was blown up by the Jacobites in the 1745 campaign.

**Inverness Museum & Art Gallery.** The excellent, although small, museum covers archaeology, art, local history, and the natural environment in its lively displays. ⊠ *Castle Wynd* ☎ *01463/237114* ⊕ *www. invernessmuseum.com* 🎫 *Free* ☉ *Mon.–Sat. 10–5.*

## CULLODEN MOOR

Culloden Moor was the scene of the last major battle fought on British soil—to this day considered one of the most infamous and tragic in all of warfare. Here, on a cold April day in 1746, the outnumbered Jacobite forces of Bonnie Prince Charlie were destroyed by the superior firepower of King George II's army. The victorious commander, the Duke of Cumberland (George II's son), earned the name of "Butcher" Cumberland for the bloody reprisals carried out by his men on Highland families—Jacobite or not—caught in the vicinity. In the battle itself, the duke's army—greatly outnumbering the Scots—killed more than 1,000 soldiers. The National Trust for Scotland has re-created a slightly eerie version of the battlefield as it looked in 1746. ⊠ *5 mi east of Inverness via B9006* ☎ *01463/790607* ⊕ *www.nts.org.uk* 🎫 *£10* ☉ *Visitor center Nov.–Mar., daily 10–4; Apr.–Oct., daily 9–6; last entry half hr before closing.*

## FORT GEORGE

Fodor'sChoice
★

As a direct result of the battle at Culloden, the nervous government in London ordered the construction of a large fort on a promontory reaching into the Moray Firth: Fort George was started in 1748 and completed some 20 years later. It survives today as perhaps the best-preserved 18th-century military fortification in Europe. A visitor center and tableaux at the fort portray the 18th-century Scottish soldier's way of life, as does the **Regimental Museum of the Queen's Own Highlanders.** To get here take the B9092 north from A96 west of Nairn. ✉ *Ardersier* ☎ *01667/460232* ⊕ *www.historic-scotland.gov.uk* 🖭 *£6.70* ⊙ *Apr.–Sept., daily 9:30–6:30; Oct.–Mar., daily 9:30–4:30; last admission 45 min before closing.*

### CAWDOR CASTLE

⊙
**Fodor's Choice**
★

Shakespeare's (1564–1616) Macbeth was Thane of Cawdor, but the sense of history within the turreted walls of Cawdor Castle is more than fictional. Cawdor is a lived-in castle, not an abandoned, decaying structure. The earliest part of the castle is the 14th-century central tower; the rooms contain family portraits, tapestries, fine furniture, and paraphernalia reflecting 600 years of history. Outside the castle walls are sheltered gardens and woodland walks. Children will have a ball exploring the lush and mysterious Big Wood, with its wildflowers and varied wildlife. There are lots of creepy stories and fantastic tales amid the dank dungeons and drawbridges. ✉ *Off B9090, 5 mi southwest of Nairn, 24 km (15 mi) northeast of Inverness, Cawdor* ☎ *01667/404401* ⊕ *www.cawdorcastle.com* 🖭 *Grounds £4.50; castle £8.30* ⊙ *May–mid-Oct., daily 10–5.*

### LOCH NESS EXHIBITION CENTRE

⊙ If you're in search of the infamous beast Nessie, head to Drumnadrochit: here you'll find the Loch Ness Monster Exhibition Centre, a visitor center that explores the facts and the fakes, the photographs, the unexplained sonar contacts, and the sincere testimony of eyewitnesses. You'll have to make up your own mind on Nessie. All that's really known is that Loch Ness's huge volume of water has a warming effect on the local weather, making the lake conducive to mirages in still, warm conditions. These are often the circumstances in which the "monster" appears. Whether or not the *bestia aquatilis* lurks in the depths—more than ever in doubt since 1994, when the man who took one of the most convincing photos of Nessie confessed on his deathbed that it was a fake—plenty of camera-toting, sonar-wielding, and submarine-traveling scientists and curiosity seekers haunt the lake. ✉ *Off A82, 23 km (14 mi) southwest of Inverness* ☎ *01456/450573 or 01456/450218* ⊕ *www.loch-ness-scotland.com* 🖭 *£6.50* ⊙ *Easter–May, daily 9:30–5; June and Sept., daily 9–6; July and Aug., daily 9–8; Oct., daily 9:30–5:30; Nov.–Easter, daily 10–3:30; last admission half hr before closing.*

---

## GREAT GLEN BEST BETS

**Monster hunting at Loch Ness.** Even though numerous scientific studies have failed to prove the existence of Scotland's most famous monster, you're sure to be on the lookout, just in case he makes an appearance.

**Urquhart Castle.** A sublime setting on the banks of Loch Ness makes Urquhart one of the world's most romantic and wistful fortresses.

**Aviemore.** The rugged landscapes of the Cairngorm Mountains contrast sharply with the verdant lowland glens; a mountain train takes the strain, so you don't need to work up a sweat.

## URQUHART CASTLE

Urquhart Castle, near Drumnadrochit, is a favorite Loch Ness monster–watching spot. This weary fortress stands on a promontory overlooking the loch, as it has since the Middle Ages. Because of its central and strategic position in the Great Glen line of communication, the castle has a complex history involving military offense and defense, as well as its own destruction and renovation. The castle was begun in the 13th century and was destroyed before the end of the 17th century to prevent its use by the Jacobites. The ruins of what was one of the largest castles in Scotland were then plundered for building material. A visitor center relates these events and gives an idea of what life was like here in medieval times. Today swarms of bus tours pass through after investigating the Loch Ness phenomenon. *⊠ 2 mi southeast of Drumnadrochit on A82 ☎ 01456/450551 ⊕ www.historic-scotland. gov.uk ☁ £7 ⊗ Apr.–Sept., daily 9:30–6; Oct 9:30–5; Nov.–Mar., daily 9:30–4; last admission 45 min before closing.*

## LOCH NESS

**Loch Ness.** From the B862, just east of Fort Augustus, you'll get your first good long view of the formidable and famous Loch Ness, which has a greater volume of water than any other Scottish loch, a maximum depth of more than 800 feet, and its own monster—at least according to popular myth. Early travelers who passed this way included English lexicographer Dr. Samuel Johnson (1709–84) and his guide and biographer James Boswell (1740–95), who were on their way to the Hebrides in 1783, and naturalist Thomas Pennant (1726–98), who noted that the loch kept the locality frost-free in winter. None of these observant early travelers ever made mention of a monster. Clearly, they hadn't read the local guidebooks.

## FORT AUGUSTUS

Fort Augustus, at the southern tip of Loch Ness, is the best place to see the locks of the Caledonian Canal in action. The fort itself was captured by the Jacobite clans during the 1745 Rebellion. It was later rebuilt as a Benedictine abbey, but the monks no longer live here. The **Caledonian Canal Visitor Centre** (⊠ *Ardchattan House, Canalside, Fort Augustus* ☎ *01320/366493* ⊕ *www.scottishcanals.co.uk*), in a converted lock-keeper's cottage, gives the history of the canal and its uses over the years.

## AVIEMORE

Once a quiet junction on the Highland Railway, Aviemore now has all the brashness and concrete boxiness of a year-round holiday resort. The Aviemore area is a versatile walking base, but you must be dressed properly and carry emergency safety gear for high-level excursions onto the near-arctic plateau.

★ **Cairngorm National Park.** For skiing and rugged hiking, follow the B970 to this national park. Past Loch Morlich at the high parking lots on the exposed shoulders of the Cairngorm Mountains are dozens of trails for hiking and cycling. The park is especially popular with birding enthusiasts, as it is the best place to see the Scottish crossbill, the only bird unique to Britain. Cairngorm became Scotland's second national park in March 2003. ⊠ *Aviemore* ☎ *01479/873535* ⊕ *www.cairngorms.co.uk*.

**CairnGorm Mountain Railway.** This funicular railway takes you to the top of Cairn Gorm (the mountain that gives its name to the Cairn-gorms), operates year-round, and affords extensive views of the broad valley of the Spey. At the top is a visitor center and restaurant. Be fore-warned: it can get very cold above 3,000 feet, and weather conditions can change rapidly, even in the middle of summer. Prebooking is recommended. ⊠ *Off B9152* ☎ *01479/861261* ⊕ *www.cairngormmountain. com* 🍴 *£9.75* ⊗ *Daily 10–4:30.*

## SHOPPING

All things "Highland" make the best souvenirs. Tartans and kilts, tweed clothing, and woolen and cashmere knits are made here in the glens. Modern breathable outdoor clothing is also in great abundance. The beauty of the landscape inspires artists and craftspeople, and you'll find their paintings, ceramics, and wooden carved items in markets and specialty shops. Foodies will love the natural smoked salmon.

### BEAULY

★ **Made in Scotland.** It's well worth a 23-km (14-mi) drive west from Inverness (on Route A862) to Beauly to see one of the biggest and best selections of Scottish-made gifts, textiles, and crafts. There's a restaurant here, too. ⊠ *Station Rd., Beauly* ☎ *01463/782821* ⊕ *www. madeinscotland.co.uk.*

### FORT WILLIAM

**Scottish Crafts and Whisky Centre.** This store has lots of crafts and souvenirs, as well as homemade chocolates and a vast range of malt whiskies, including miniatures and limited-edition bottlings. ⊠ *135–139 High St., Fort William* ☎ *01397/704406.*

### INVERNESS

★ **Hector Russell Kiltmakers.** This shop explains the history of the kilt, shows how they are made, and gives you the opportunity to buy from a huge selection or have a kilt made to measure. The firm offers overseas shipping. ⊠ *6–8 Bridge St., Inverness* ☎ *014563/713083* ⊕ *www.hector-russell.com.*

**James Pringle Ltd.** This retailer stocks a vast selection of cashmere, lamb's wool, and Shetland knitwear, tartans, and tweeds. There's a weaving exhibit, as well as an explanation of the history of tartan. ⊠ *Dores Rd., Inverness* ☎ *01463/223311.*

**Riverside Gallery.** The gallery sells paintings, etchings, and prints of Highland landscapes, and contemporary work by Highland artists. ⊠ *11 Bank St.,Inverness* ☎ *01463/224781* ⊕ *www.riverside-gallery.co.uk.*

**Victorian Market.** Don't miss the atmospheric indoor market, built in 1870, which houses more than 40 privately owned specialty shops. ⊠ *Academy St., Inverness.*

## WHERE TO EAT

**$$$**  ✕ **Riva.** With views over the River Ness towards Inverness Castle, Riva
ITALIAN  has a great location; try and get a window seat. The dining room has ele-
gantly lighted deep-red walls lined with black-and-white photographs
of Italian cityscapes. Tasty Italian dishes include pasta carbonara (with
eggs, cream, and bacon), as well as more unusual concoctions like *ravi-
oli alla granchio* (crab and tiger prawn ravioli on a salad of arugula and
garden peas with a chervil olive oil). ⊠ *4–6 Ness Walk* ☎ *01463/237377*
⊟ *MC, V* ☉ *No lunch Sun.*

**$$$$**  ✕ **RocPool Restaurant.** Highly recommended by locals, the RocPool has a
BRASSERIE  calming mix of dark and light woods and cream and pale mint furnish-
ings that creates a welcoming ambience. The frequently changing menus
may include items such as sweet-pea-and-spinach risotto for lunch and
loin of venison with creamed parsnips and wild mushrooms for dinner.
⊠ *1 Ness Walk* ☎ *01463/717274* ⊟ *MC, V* ☉ *Closed Sun.*

# LEITH, SCOTLAND (FOR EDINBURGH)

One of the world's stateliest cities and proudest capitals, Edinburgh is
built—like Rome—on seven hills, making it a striking backdrop for
the ancient pageant of history. In a skyline of sheer drama, Edinburgh
Castle watches over the capital city, frowning down on Princes Street as
if disapproving of its modern razzmatazz. Nearly everywhere in Edin-
burgh (the "-burgh" is always pronounced *burra* in Scotland) there are
spectacular buildings, whose Doric, Ionic, and Corinthian pillars add
touches of neoclassical grandeur to the largely Presbyterian backdrop.
The city is justly proud of its gardens, green lungs that bring a sense
of release to frenetic modern life. Conspicuous from Princes Street is
Arthur's Seat, a child-size mountain with steep slopes and little crags,
like a miniature Highlands set down in the middle of the busy city.
Appropriately, these theatrical elements match Edinburgh's character—
after all, the city has been a stage that has seen its fair share of romance,
violence, tragedy, and triumph.

### ESSENTIALS

CURRENCY  The British pound sterling (£1 is $US1.61 at this writing). ATMs are
common and credit cards are widely accepted.

HOURS  Museums are open from 9 until 5, while shops usually open from 9
until 5:30 or 6. Some shops are open on Sunday.

INTERNET  **E Corner** (⊠ *54 Blackfriars St., Edinburgh* ☎ *0131/5587858* ⊕ *www.e-
corner.co.uk*) is an Internet café in the heart of the old town.

TELEPHONES  Tri-band GSM phones work in the United Kingdom. You can buy pre-
paid phone cards at telecom shops, news vendors, and tobacconists in
all towns and cities. Phone cards can be used for local or international
calls. Vodafone and Orange are the leading telecom companies.

### COMING ASHORE

Currently ships larger than 220 meters (720 feet) must anchor off-
shore at Leith and passengers must be tendered ashore. Smaller ships
can dock at the quayside in Leith Town. The whole waterfront area,

named Ocean Terminal, has received a multimillion-pound redevelopment since the late 1990s, and significantly more is due to be invested in the years up to 2019; a tram system to link the Leith waterfront to central Edinburgh will open during 2012. There are few facilities at the passenger terminal itself, but a huge complex of shopping, eating, and entertainment venues sits right outside the door.

From Leith, Buses 11, 22, 34, 35 and 36 make the 15-minute trip to the Princes Street stop in central Edinburgh; one-way fare is £1.20, and a day ticket £3. Taxis are plentiful and wait at the Ocean Terminal taxi line. Costs include an initial charge of £2.50, then £0.25 for every 225 meters (758 feet) until 2 km (1½ mi), after which charges climb to £0.25 per 210 meters (688 feet). Don't rent a car if you plan to spend your port day in Edinburgh, but a car will open up much of the surrounding countryside to exploration if you want to venture further. Rental rates for a compact manual vehicle are approximately £55 per day.

**4**

## EXPLORING EDINBURGH

**Calton Hill.** Robert Louis Stevenson's favorite view of his beloved city was from the top of this hill. Among the array of Gothic and neoclassical monuments here, the so-called **National Monument,** often referred to as "Edinburgh's (or Scotland's) Disgrace," commands the most attention. Intended to mimic Athens's Parthenon, this monument for the dead of the Napoleonic Wars was started in 1822 to the specifications of a design by William Playfair; in 1830, only 12 columns later, money ran out. The tallest monument on Calton Hill is the 100-foot-high **Nelson Monument,** completed in 1815 in honor of Briatin's naval hero Horatio Nelson; you can climb its 143 steps for sweeping views. ⊠ *Bounded by Leith St. to west and Regent Rd. to south, Calton* ☎ *0131/556–2716* ⊕ *www. edinburgh.gov.uk* ⊠ *Nelson Monument £3* ☉ *Nelson Monument Apr.– Sept., Mon. 1–6, Tues.–Sat. 10–6; Oct.–Mar., Mon.–Sat. 10–3.*

**Charlotte Square.** This is the New Town's centerpiece—an 18th-century square with one of the proudest achievements of Robert Adam, Scotland's noted neoclassical architect. On the north side, Adam designed a palatial facade to unite three separate town houses of such sublime simplicity and perfect proportions that architects come from all over the world to study it. ⊠ *West end of George St., New Town.*

**Fodor'sChoice**

★

**Edinburgh Castle.** The crowning glory of the Scottish capital, Edinburgh Castle is popular not only because it is the symbolic heart of Scotland but also because of the views from its battlements: on a clear day the vistas—stretching to the "kingdom" of Fife—are breathtaking.

Heading over the drawbridge and through the gatehouse, past the guards, you'll find the rough stone walls of the **Half-Moon Battery,** where the one-o'clock gun is fired every day in an impressively anachronistic ceremony; these curving ramparts give Edinburgh Castle its distinctive appearance from miles away. Climb up through a second gateway and you come to the oldest surviving building in the complex, the tiny 11th-century **St. Margaret's Chapel,** named in honor of Saxon queen Margaret (1046–93), who had persuaded her husband, King Malcolm III (circa 1031–93), to move his court from Dunfermline to

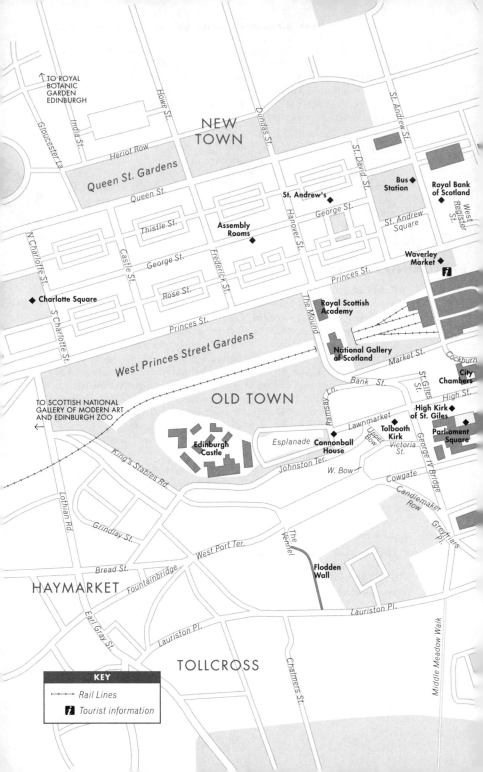

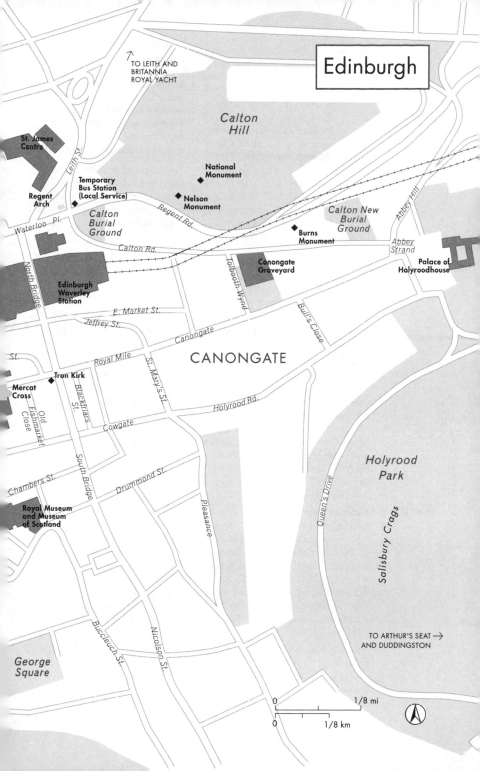

# Edinburgh

TO LEITH AND
BRITANNIA
ROYAL YACHT

*Calton Hill*

St. James Centre

Leith St.

National Monument

Temporary Bus Station (Local Service)

Regent Arch

Nelson Monument

Regent Rd.

*Calton Burial Ground*

Waterloo Pl.

Calton Rd.

Burns Monument

*Calton New Burial Ground*

Abbey Hill

Abbey Strand

North Bridge

Edinburgh Waverley Station

Canongate Graveyard

Tolbooth Wynd

Palace of Holyroodhouse

E. Market St.

Jeffrey St.

Canongate

Bull's Close

Royal Mile

St. Mary's St.

St.

**CANONGATE**

Tron Kirk

Mercat Cross

Blackfriars St.

Holyrood Rd.

Old Fishmarket Close

Cowgate

*Holyrood Park*

South Bridge

Chambers St.

Drummond St.

Queen's Drive

Royal Museum and Museum of Scotland

Pleasance

*Salisbury Crags*

Buccleuch St.

Nicolson St.

*George Square*

TO ARTHUR'S SEAT →
AND DUDDINGSTON

| 0 | | 1/8 mi |
| 0 | | 1/8 km |

Edinburgh. The **Crown Room**, a must-see, contains the "Honours of Scotland"—the crown, scepter, and sword that once graced the Scottish monarch. Upon the **Stone of Scone,** also in the Crown Room, Scottish monarchs once sat to be crowned. In the section now called **Queen Mary's Apartment,** Mary, Queen of Scots, gave birth to James VI of Scotland, who was also to rule England as James I. The **Great Hall** displays arms and armor under an impressive vaulted, beamed ceiling. During the Napoleonic Wars in the early 19th century, the castle held French prisoners of war, whose carvings can still be seen on the vaults under the Great Hall. ✉ *Off Castle Esplanade and Castlehill, Old Town* ☎ *0131/225–9846 Edinburgh Castle, 0131/226–7393 War Memorial* ⊕ *www.edinburghcastle.gov.uk* 🎫 *£14* ☉ *Apr.–Sept., daily 9:30–6; Oct.–Mar., daily 9:30–5.*

**High Kirk of St. Giles** *(St. Giles's Cathedral).* There has been a church here since AD 854, although most of the present structure dates from either 1120 or 1829, when the church was restored. The most elaborate feature is the **Chapel of the Order of the Thistle,** built in 1911 for the exclusive use of Scotland's only chivalric order, the Most Ancient and Noble Order of the Thistle. Inside the church stands a life-size statue of the Scot whose spirit still dominates the place—the great religious reformer and preacher John Knox, before whose zeal all of Scotland once trembled. ✉ *High St., Old Town* ☎ *0131/225–9442* ⊕ *www.stgilescathedral. org.uk* 🎫 *£3 suggested donation* ☉ *May–Sept., weekdays 9–7, Sat. 9–5, Sun. 1–5; Oct.–Apr., Mon.–Sat. 9–5, Sun. 1–5.*

**Fodor's Choice**
★ **National Gallery of Scotland.** The National Gallery presents a wide selection of paintings from the Renaissance to the postimpressionist period within a grand neoclassical building designed by William Playfair. Most famous are the Old Master paintings bequeathed by the Duke of Sutherland, including Titian's *Three Ages of Man.* All the great names are here; works by Velázquez, El Greco, Rembrandt, Goya, Poussin, Clouet, Turner, Degas, Monet, and Van Gogh, among others, complement a fine collection of Scottish art. ✉ *The Mound, Old Town* ☎ *0131/624– 6200 general inquiries, 0131/332–2266 recorded information* ⊕ *www. nationalgalleries.org* 🎫 *Free* ☉ *Fri.–Wed. 10–5, Thurs. 10–7.*

★ **Palace of Holyroodhouse.** Once the haunt of Mary, Queen of Scots, and the setting for high drama—including at least one notorious murder— this is now Queen Elizabeth's official residence in Scotland. When the queen or royal family is not in residence, you can take a guided tour. Many monarchs, including Charles II, Queen Victoria, and George V, have left their mark on its rooms, but it is Mary, Queen of Scots, whose spirit looms largest. For some visitors the most memorable room here is the little chamber in which David Rizzio (1533–66), secretary to Mary, Queen of Scots, met an unhappy end in 1566. Mary's second husband, Lord Darnley (Henry Stewart, 1545–65), burst into the queen's rooms with his henchmen, dragged Rizzio into an antechamber, and stabbed him more than 50 times; a bronze plaque marks the spot. Darnley himself was murdered the next year to make way for the queen's marriage to her lover, Bothwell.

The **King James Tower** is the oldest surviving section, containing the rooms of Mary, Queen of Scots, on the second floor, and Lord Darnley's rooms below. At the south end of the palace front you'll find the **Royal Dining Room,** and along the south side are the **Throne Room** and other drawing rooms now used for social and ceremonial occasions.

At the back of the palace is the **King's Bedchamber.** The 150-foot-long **Great Picture Gallery,** on the north side, displays the portraits of 110 Scottish monarchs by Dutch artist Jacob De Witt. These were commissioned by Charles II—some of the royal figures here are fictional and the likenesses of others imaginary.

**Queen's Gallery,** in a former church and school at the entrance to the palace, holds rotating exhibits from the Royal Collection. ⊠ *Abbey Strand, Holyrood, Old Town* ☎ *0131/556–5100* 🖷 *0131/557–5256* ⊕ *www.royal.gov.uk* 🖾 *£10.25 palace, £14.30 joint ticket with Queen's Gallery* ⊙ *Apr.–Oct., daily 9:30–6; Nov.–Mar., daily 9:30–4:30. Closed during royal visits.*

**Fodor's Choice**
★ **Royal Museum and Museum of Scotland.** In an imposing Victorian building, the Royal Museum houses an internationally renowned collection of art and artifacts. Its treasures include the Lewis Chessmen, 11 intricately carved ivory chessmen found on one of the Western Isles in the 19th century. The museum's main hall, with its soaring roof and "birdcage" design, is architecturally interesting in its own right. Redevelopment, ongoing through 2011, is modernizing many displays. The striking, contemporary building next door houses the Museum of Scotland, with modern displays concentrating on Scotland's own heritage. This state-of-the-art, no-expense-spared museum is full of playful models, complex reconstructions, and paraphernalia ranging from ancient Pictish articles to 21st-century cultural artifacts. ⊠ *Chambers St., Old Town* ☎ *0131/225–7534* ⊕ *www.nms.ac.uk* 🖾 *Free* ⊙ *Daily 10–5.*

**Royal Scottish Academy.** The William Playfair–designed Academy hosts temporary art exhibitions, but is also worth visiting for a look at the imposing, neoclassic architecture. The underground Weston Link connects the museum to the National Gallery of Scotland. ⊠ *The Mound, Old Town* ☎ *0131/225–6671* ⊕ *www.royalscottishacademy.org* 🖾 *Free* ⊙ *Mon.–Sat. 10–5, Sun. noon–5.*

# SHOPPING

Despite its renown as a shopping street, **Princes Street** in the New Town disappoints some visitors with its dull, anonymous modern architecture, average chain stores, and fast-food outlets. It is, however, one of the best spots to shop for tartans, tweeds, and knitwear, especially if your time is limited. One block north of Princes Street, **Rose Street** has many smaller specialty shops; part of the street is a pedestrian zone, so it's a pleasant place to browse.

The streets crossing George Street—Hanover, Frederick, and Castle—are also worth exploring. **Dundas Street,** the northern extension of Hanover Street, beyond Queen Street Gardens, has several antiques shops. **Thistle Street,** originally George Street's "back lane," or service area, has several boutiques and more antiques shops. **Stafford and William streets** form a small, upscale shopping area in a Georgian setting.

As may be expected, many shops along the **Royal Mile** sell what may be politely or euphemistically described as tourist ware—whiskies, tartans, and tweeds. Careful exploration, however, will uncover some worthwhile establishments. Shops here also cater to highly specialized interests and hobbies. Close to the castle end of the Royal Mile, just off George IV Bridge, is **Victoria Street,** with specialty shops grouped in a small area. Follow the tiny West Bow to **Grassmarket** for more specialty stores.

**Edinburgh Crystal.** Ten miles south of the city center, this glassworks is renowned the world over for its fine glass and crystal ware, but Jenners also stocks it if you want to limit your shopping to Edinburgh itself. ⊠ *Eastfield, Penicuik* ☎ *01968/675128* ⊕ *www.edinburgh-crystal. co.uk.*

**Edinburgh Old Town Weaving Company.** Here, you can watch the cloth and tapestry weavers as they work, then buy the products. The company can also provide information on clan histories, and, if your name is a relatively common English or Scottish one, tell you which tartan you are entitled to wear. ⊠ *555 Castlehill, Old Town* ☎ *0131/226–1555.*

**Jenners.** Edinburgh's equivalent of London's Harrods department store, Jenners is noteworthy not only for its high-quality wares and good restaurants but also because of the building's interesting architectural detail. ⊠ *48 Princes St., New Town* ☎ *0844/800–3725* ⊕ *www. houseoffraser.co.uk* ☺ *Mon., Tues., Wed., and Fri., 9:30–6:30, Sat. 9–6:30, Thurs. 9:30–8, Sun. 11–6.*

## WHERE TO EAT

$    ✕ **David Bann.** In the heart of the Old Town, this ultrahip vegetarian and
BRITISH   vegan favorite attracts young locals with its light, airy, modern dining
★    room and creative menu. The food is so flavorful that carnivores may forget they're eating vegetarian. ⊠ *56–58 St. Mary's St., Old Town* ☎ *0131/556–5888* ⊕ *www.davidbann.com* ☐ *AE, DC, MC, V.*

# ROTTERDAM, NETHERLANDS

Rotterdam is the industrial center of Holland and the world's largest port. When Rotterdam's city center and harbor were completely destroyed in World War II, the authorities decided to start afresh rather than try to reconstruct its former maze of canals. The imposing, futuristic skyline along the banks of the Maas River has been developing since then, thanks in large part to the efforts of major figures such as Rem Koolhaas, Eric van Egeraat, and UN Studio. Elsewhere in the region you can step back in time: wander through the ancient cobbled streets in Leiden and buy china in Delft that once colored the world with its unique blue. Many other colors are on view in Holland's fabled tulip fields. Every spring, green thumbs everywhere make a pilgrimage to Lisse to view the noted tulip gardens at Keukenhof and to drive the Bollenstreek Route, which takes them through miles of countryside glowing with gorgeous hues and blooms.

> ## ROTTERDAM BEST BETS
>
> **Modernist architecture.** Rotterdam eschewed rebuilding the city after the destruction of WWII and instead strode resolutely into modernism.
>
> **The Kinderdijk Windmills.** This archetypal Dutch landscape isn't a theme park—the windmills were grouped to pump water out of the polders. Today the vista is picture-perfect.
>
> **Old Delft.** This tangle of canals and medieval streets, with its array of ornate decoration and flower-bedecked windows, offers some of the prettiest views in Holland.

4

## ESSENTIALS

CURRENCY The euro (€1 to US$1.36 at this writing). ATMs are common and credit cards are widely accepted.

HOURS Shops open Tuesday, Wednesday, Friday, and Saturday from 9 or 10 until 6; they are open later on Thursday. Most stores are closed on Sunday and some on Monday. Museums open from 9 until 6 with one late opening night during the week.

INTERNET **Rotterdam Public Library** (✉ *110 Hoogstraat, Rotterdam* ☎ *010/2816100* ⊕ *www.bibliotheek.rotterdam.nl*) offers free Internet service, although the facilities here aren't the newest.

TELEPHONES Most tri- and quad-band GSM mobile phones should work on the Netherlands, which operates a 3G mobile system with dual-band handsets. Public phones take phone cards (available at numerous shops) and credit cards and will connect international calls. Major telecom companies are Vodafone and Orange.

## COMING ASHORE

Ships dock at the historic terminal building in the city dock, once the headquarters of the Holland America Line. The terminal offers handicraft displays, shopping facilities, and an information desk. A shuttle service operates between the terminal and the town. Each bus has an English-speaking host who can answer any questions that you have. A water-taxi service also operates from the port across the River Maas into the heart of the Old Town. A 15-minute round-trip costs approximately €28.

The terminal has a taxi service desk where you can arrange for trips at fixed prices. It is also possible to book journeys and trips ahead of time. All drivers speak English. Public transport is efficient and modern. Tram routes Erasmus, 20, 23, and 25 link the port with Rotterdam Central Station (this station area is currently undergoing a comprehensive

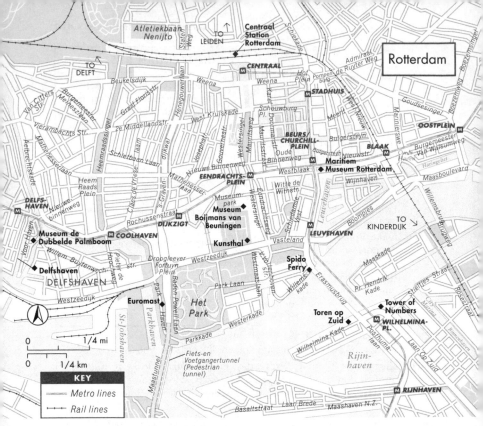

renovation program). All public transport is now paid for with an electronic chip card which deducts the amount of the journey from the amount registered on the card. The easiest option for cruise passengers is to purchase a disposable chip card which can be loaded with a single two-hour travel pass (equivalent to a single ticket), a two-journey metro pass, a one-hour bus/tram pass or a one-day pass. If you intend to use public transport throughout the day, the one-day pass would be simplest. These can be purchased from machines at stations and from personel aboard trams and buses. A day card costs €7. Rotterdam is bicycle-friendly. Bikes can be rented at the central train station at a cost of €6 per day.

The train journey from Rotterdam to Delft takes 15 minutes, and there are several services per hour; ticket prices are €5.10 round-trip. The train journey from Rotterdam to Leiden takes 30 minutes, with several services every hour; ticket prices are €12.70 round-trip. The journey to Amsterdam (⇨ *above*) takes one hour, with several services every hour; round-trip tickets are €25.70.

## EXPLORING ROTTERDAM AND VICINITY

### ROTTERDAM

Cobbled streets, gabled houses, narrow canals overhung with lime trees, and antiques shops give the historic center a tangible feeling of history, and Leiden's university's academic buildings, the historic Waag (Weigh House) and the Burcht fortress, the stately mansions lining the Rapenburg—the most elegant canal in the town—and no fewer than 35 hofjes (groups of houses surrounding little courtyards) make it a rewarding place for a stroll. As you walk about, keep a watch for verses painted on lofty gables, a project started some 10 years ago. The proverbs, sayings, and poems now number more than 70, and are in a multitude of languages.

★ **Delfshaven.** The last remaining nook of old Rotterdam, an open-air museum with rows of gabled houses lining the historic waterfront, Delfshaven is now an area of trendy galleries, cafés, and restaurants. Walk along the Voorhaven and marvel at the many historic buildings; most of the port area has been reconstructed, with many of its 110 buildings now appearing just as they were when originally built.

For historic sights in Delfshaven's environs, check out the working mill of **Korenmolen de Distilleerketel** (open Wednesday and Saturday only), the fascinating **Museum de Dubbelde Palmboom** on Rotterdam city history, and the **Oudekerk/Pilgrimvaders Kerk.** ⊠ *Achterhaven and Voorhaven, Delfshaven.*

**Euromast.** The Euromast provides a spectacular view of the city and harbor, if you can handle the 600-foot-high vista. On a clear day you can just about see the coast from the top. And if you have the stomach for it, you can rappel down the tower. ⊠ *Parkhaven 20, Delfshaven* ☎ *010/436–4811* ⊕ *www.euromast.com* ⬛ *€8.30, rappel €42.50* ⊙ *Apr.–Sept., daily 9:30 AM–11 PM; Oct.–Mar., daily 10 AM–11 PM.*

**Kunsthal.** The corrugated exterior of this "art house" sits at one end of the visitor-friendly museum quarter, and hosts major temporary exhibitions. Designed by architect-prophet Rem Koolhaas, some say the design bridging the gap between the Museumpark and the dike is a clever spatial creation; others consider it ugly. ⊠ *Westzeedijk 341, Museumpark* ☎ *010/440–0301* ⊕ *www.kunsthal.nl* ⬛ *€10* ⊙ *Tues.–Sat. 10–5, Sun. 11–5.*

☾ **Maritiem Museum Rotterdam.** A sea-lover's delight, the Maritime Museum
★ is Rotterdam's noted nautical collection. The museum's prize exhibit is the warship *De Buffel*, moored in the harbor outside, dating back to 1868. The ship has been perfectly restored, and is fitted out sumptuously, as can be seen in the mahogany-deck captain's cabin. ⊠ *Leuvehaven 1, Witte de With* ☎ *010/413–2680* ⊕ *www.maritiemmuseum. nl* ⬛ *€7.50* ⊙ *July and Aug., Mon.–Sat. 10–5, Sun. 11–5; Sept.–June, Tues.–Sat. 10–5, Sun. 11–5.*

Fodor's Choice **Museum Boijmans van Beuningen.** Rotterdam's finest shrine to art, with
★ treasures ranging from Pieter Bruegel the Elder's 16th-century *Tower of Babel* to Mondrian's extraordinary *Composition in Yellow and Blue*, this museum ranks as one of the greatest painting collections in Europe.

Created more than 150 years ago—when Otto Boijmans unloaded a motley collection of objects on the city, then greatly enhanced by the bequest of Daniel van Beuningen in 1955—it is housed in a stunning building ideally designed to hold the collections of painting, sculpture, ceramics, prints, and furnishings.

Fifteenth- and 16th-century art from the northern and southern Netherlands and 17th-century Dutch works are particularly well represented, including painters such as Van Eyck, Rubens, and Rembrandt. Other notable artists include Peter Paul Rubens, Hieronymus Bosch, Claude Monet, René Magritte, Andy Warhol, and Salvador Dalí. ⊠ *Museumpark 18–20, Museumpark* ☎ *010/441–9400* ⊕ *www.boijmans.nl* ☜ *€10* ⊙ *Tues.–Sun. 11–5.*

**Museum de Dubbelde Palmboom.** Devoted to the history of Rotterdam and its role as an international nexus, this museum traces the city's history from prehistoric times to the present. The special and very fascinating focus is on how exotic wares imported by the East India Company affected the city. The building itself is literally redolent of history: not only do its heavy beams and brick floors waft you back to yesteryear, but there even seems to be a faint smell of grains, recalling its many years spent as a warehouse. ⊠ *Voorhaven 12, Delfshaven* ☎ *010/476–1533* ⊕ *www.dedubbeldepalmboom.nl* ☜ *€5* ⊙ *Tues.–Sun. 11–5.*

**Toren op Zuid.** An office complex by celebrated modern architect Renzo Piano, this structure houses the head offices of KPN Telecom. Its eye-catching billboard facade glitters with 1,000-odd green lamps flashing on and off, creating images provided by the city of Rotterdam, in addition to images provided by KPN and an art academy. The facade fronting the Erasmus Bridge leans forward by 6 degrees, which is the same as the angle of the bridge's pylon. It is also said that Piano could have been making a humorous reference to his homeland, as the Tower of Pisa leans at the same angle. ⊠ *Wilhelminakade 123, Kop van Zuid.*

**Tower of Numbers.** Near Piano's Toren op Zuid structure is this creation of Australian architect Peter Wilson. The tower is topped by five LED (light-emitting diodes) boxes, hung from a mast, with digital figures showing—among other things—the time and the world population. This "fluxus" is in contrast to the fixity of the **Garden of Lost Numbers,** found below the yellow bridge-watcher's house designed as a series of numbers set into the pavement. These numbers refer to the city's decommissioned harbors, all of which once were identified by numbers. As Rotterdam has such a heightened awareness of lost identity, these stainless-steel figures serve as a remembrance of things past. ⊠ *Wilhelminakade, Kop van Zuid.*

## DELFT

*15 km (9 mi) northwest of Rotterdam.*

With time-burnished canals and streets, Delft radiates a peaceful calm that recalls the quieter pace of the Golden Age of the 17th century. Back then the town counted among its citizens the artist Johannes Vermeer, who decided one spring day to paint the city gates and landscape across the Kolk harbor from a house's window on the Schieweg (now the Hooikade). The result was the 1660 *View of Delft* (now the star of the

Mauritshuis Museum in The Hague), famously called by Marcel Proust "the most beautiful painting in the world." Spending a few hours in certain parts of Delft, in fact, puts you in the company of Vermeer. Imagine a tiny Amsterdam, canals reduced to dollhouse proportions, narrower bridges, merchants' houses less grand, and you have the essence of Old Delft. But even though the city has one foot firmly planted in the past, another is planted in the present: Delft teems with hip cafés, jazz festivals, and revelers spilling out of bars.

### KINDERDIJK

★ *32 km (20 mi) southeast of Rotterdam.*

The Kinderdijk Windmills are, arguably, the most famous tourist sight in Holland. The 19 mills line Het Nieuwe Waterschap in pairs, each facing another on opposite banks. In 1740, 19 mills were built in the meadows of Kinderdijk to drain the excess water from the Alblasserwaard polders, which lie below sea level. Electrical pumping stations have now taken over water management, but the majority of mills operate at certain times for the delight of tourists. The mills are open in rotation, so there is always one interior to visit during opening hours. Looking around the inside of a mill provides a fascinating insight into how the millers and their families lived. Tours can be taken of the mechanical workings if you want to get a closer look. ✉ *Molenkade, Kinderdijk* ☎ *078/691–5179* ⊕ *www.kinderdijk.com* ✇ *Interior of mill €3.50* ⊙ *Interior Apr.–Oct., daily 9:30–5:30; Nov.–Mar., Sat.–Sun. 11–4 weather permitting.*

### LEIDEN

*37 km (23 mi) north of Rotterdam.*

The town of Leiden owes its first importance to its watery geography—it stands at the junction of two branches of the Rhine—the "Old" and the "New." But as the birthplace of Rembrandt and site of the nation's oldest and most prestigious university, Leiden has long continued to play an important part in Dutch history. A place where windmills still rise over the cityscape, Leiden offers the charm of Amsterdam with little of the sleaze.

★ **Rijksmuseum van Oudheden** *(National Museum of Antiquities),* Leiden's most notable museum, houses the largest archaeological collection in Holland. Collections include pieces from ancient Egypt, the classical world, the Near East, and the Netherlands, from prehistory to the Middle Ages. Among the 6,000 objects on display, exhibits to look out for include the chillingly ghoulish collection of 13 ancient Egyptian human mummies. ✉ *Rapenburg 28* ☎ *071/516–3163* ⊕ *www.rmo.nl* ✇ *€9* ⊙ *Tues.–Sun. 10–5.*

## SHOPPING

Rotterdam is the number-one shopping city in the south of Holland, and it offers some excellent interior design galleries. Its famous **Lijnbaan** and **Beurstraverse** shopping centers, as well as the surrounding areas, offer a dazzling variety of shops. The archways and fountains of the Beurstraverse—at the bottom of the Coolsingel, near the Stadhuis—make this newer, pedestrianized area more pleasing to walk around. **Van Olden-barneveldtstraat** and **Nieuwe Binnenweg** are the places to be if you want something different; there is a huge variety of alternative fashion to be found here. Exclusive shops and boutiques can be found in the Entrepotgebied, Delfshaven, Witte de Withstraat, Nieuwe and Oude Binnenweg, and Van Oldenbarneveldtstraat. **West Kruiskade** and its vicinity offers a wide assortment of multicultural products in the many Chinese, Suriname, Mediterranean, and Arabic shops. You should also walk through the **Entrepot Harbor design district,** alongside the city marina at Kop van Zuid, where there are several interior-design stores.

**De Bijenkorf.** This department store is a favorite, designed by Marcel Breuer (the great Bauhaus architect) with an exterior that looks like its name, a beehive. ⊠ *Coolsingel 105, Centrum* ☎ *0900/0919* ⊕ *www. debijenkorf.nl.*

**De Porceleyne Fles.** If you get out to Delft, this factory is home to the popular blue-and-white Delft pottery. Regular demonstrations of molding and painting pottery are given by the artisans. ⊠ *Royal Delftware Factory, Rotterdamseweg 196Delft* ☎ *015/251–2030* ⊕ *www.royaldelft.com.*

## WHERE TO EAT

$$ ✗ **Annie's Verjaardag.** A low-ceilinged, arched cellar, often full of chatty
DUTCH students, and a water-level canal-side terrace with great views guarantee a special atmosphere no matter where you sit in this popular eatery. During the day there is a modest selection of salads and sandwiches on baguettes, and at least one offering that is more substantial. ⊠ *Hoogstraat 1a, Leiden* ☎ *071/512–5737* ⊕ *www.annies.nu* ⌂ *Reservations not accepted* ⊟ *MC, V.*

¢–$ ✗ **Café Dudok.** Lofty ceilings, a cavernous former warehouse, long read-
CAFE ing tables stacked with international magazines and papers—little won-
★ der this place attracts an artsy crowd. At its most mellow, this spot is perfect for a lazy afternoon treat of delicious homemade pastries, but you can come here for breakfast, lunch, high tea, dinner, or even a snack after midnight. They also offer a small selection for vegetarians. The brasserie, on a mezzanine above the open kitchen at the back, looks out over the Rotte River. Since it's terribly crowded at times, you should get here unfashionably early to avoid disappointment—there's nowhere else like it in Rotterdam. ⊠ *Meent 88, Centrum, Rotterdam* ☎ *010/433–3102* ⊕ *www.dudok.nl* ⊟ *AE, DC, MC, V.*

# SOUTHAMPTON, UNITED KINGDOM

Southampton may not be in every tourist brochure, but this city and its environs hold all kinds of attractions—and not a few quiet pleasures. Two important cathedrals, Winchester and Salisbury (pronounced *sawls*-bree), are found in Hampshire, the county that contains Southampton, as are intriguing market towns and hundreds of haunting prehistoric remains; Stonehenge, the most famous in nearby Wiltshire, should not be missed. However, these are just the tourist brochure superlatives. Like those who migrate here from every corner of the

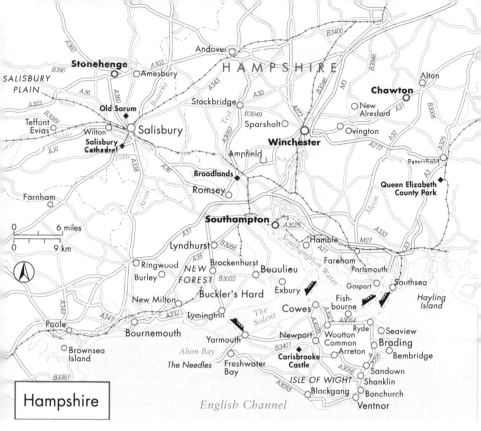

Hampshire

country in search of upward mobility, anyone spending time in the South of England should rent a car and set out to discover the back-road villages not found in brochures. After a drink in the village pub and a look at the cricket game on the village green, stretch out in a field for a nap.

## ESSENTIALS

CURRENCY  The British pound sterling (£1 is $US1.61 at this writing). ATMs are common and credit cards are widely accepted.

HOURS  Museums are open from 9 until 5, while shops usually open from 9 until 5:30 or 6. Some shops are open on Sunday.

INTERNET  Public libraries in all the cities and many of the smaller towns of the region offer free Internet access. **Salisbury Online** (⊠ *14 Endless St., above Endless Life café, Salisbury* ☎ *01722/421328*) is a convenient Internet café.

TELEPHONES  Tri-band GSM phones work in the United Kingdom. You can buy pre-paid phone cards at telecom shops, news vendors, and tobacconists in all towns and cities. Phone cards can be used for local or international calls. Vodafone and Orange are the leading telecom companies.

## COMING ASHORE

Southampton is a busy cruise port, and has four separate cruise terminals, each with its own dock, refreshment facilities, and dedicated taxi rank. City Cruise Terminal and Mayflower Terminal are situated in the Western Docks closest to the city (5 minutes by car), while Ocean Terminal and Queen Elizabeth II Terminal are in the Eastern Docks, a couple of minutes farther away from the downtown. Taxi fares to downtown/railway station are around £6. The Eastern Docks have a public bus link (routes U1 and U6) that runs to downtown.

Southampton is about 90 minutes from central London by train. There are four or five train services every hour, and fares start at £30.50 round-trip. By bus, the journey takes three hours; prices start at £16.50 round-trip. The rail journey from Southampton to Salisbury takes 30 minutes and starts at £10 round-trip; there are trains every half hour. Bus services take around 40 minutes with return ticket prices around £4.80. The rail journey from Southampton to Winchester also takes around 30 minutes; fares start at £7 round-trip. Bus services take around 40 minutes, with return ticket prices around £4.

Renting a car for the day would allow you to explore towns and attractions in the surrounding area more easily. Rental prices are approximately £35 for an economy manual vehicle.

### GETTING TO THE AIRPORT

If you do not purchase airport transfers from your cruise line, the simplest way to reach Heathrow Airport is by private transfer company or taxi. The journey time is around two hours from terminal to terminal, and prices for a vehicle for one to three people are around £130.

Aside from bespoke transfer, the easiest other option is by bus. National Express runs direct services between Southampton Bus Station and Heathrow departing once every 90 minutes or so. Journey time is just over 2 hours. Single journey price is £17.50

Transfer by train is less simple, because you'll need to travel into central London before picking up services to Heathrow. Trains from Southampton terminate at Waterloo Station in London. The journey time is about 90 minutes. There are four or five train services every hour, and fares start at £30.50 round-trip. To reach Heathrow, the least expensive option is the London Underground, but carraiges can be busy with little luggage space. From Waterloo Station take the Bakerloo or Northern lines to pick up the the Piccadily line that takes you directly to Heathrow. The time for the journey is around 1:20 hours and costs £4.

---

### HAMPSHIRE BEST BETS

**Stonehenge.** This world-famous megalithic monument has captured the popular imagination. Although we're sure of its age, its origins and exact purpose remain a mystery.

**Winchester.** Once the capital of England, this diminutive city has many architectural treasures on show, including one of the finest cathedrals in Britain.

**Chawton.** Jane Austen lived here for many years; devotees can be inspired by the atmosphere in the very room where she wrote her greatest works.

Heathrow Express offers a much quicker train journey, only 15 minutes from Heathrow Airport to central London because it's a direct service. It also caters more for travelers than for urban commuters. This runs from Paddington Station, and to get to Waterloo Station from here you must take the Circle or District underground lines and transfer to the Bakerloo line for one station. Heathrow Express tickets cost £18 single or £32 round-trip.

The Heathrow Connect train links Paddington Station with Heathrow airport, stopping at selected minor stations along the route. Prices are £7.90 per single journey.

From the cruise terminal to downtown Southampton (bus or train station) the taxi fare should be around £6. If you are traveling from airport to cruise terminal, be sure to note the name of the terminal your ship is docked at, because the four terminals are a couple of miles apart.

**Contacts Cruise Transfer.com** (☎ *0870/042–2752* ⊕ *www.cruisetransfer.com).* **Prompt Airport Cars** (☎ *020/7060–6070* ⊕ *www.promptexecutivehire.co.uk).* **Road Express** (☎ *0844/846–4061* ⊕ *www.road-express.co.uk).*

## EXPLORING HAMPSHIRE

### SOUTHAMPTON
*Central Southampton is about 2 km (1 mi) from the cruise-ship docks.*

Seafaring Saxons and Romans used Southampton's harbor, Southampton Water, as a commercial trading port for centuries, and the city thrived, becoming one of England's wealthiest. But Plymouth eventually supplanted it, and Southampton has been going downhill ever since. Still, it remains England's leading passenger port, and as the home port of Henry V's fleet bound for Agincourt, the *Mayflower,* the *Queen Mary,* and the ill-fated *Titanic,* along with countless other great ocean liners of the 20th century, Southampton has one of the richest maritime traditions in England. Much of the city center is shoddy, having been hastily rebuilt after World War II bombing, but bits of the city's history peek out from between modern buildings. The Old Town retains its medieval air, and considerable parts of Southampton's castellated town walls remain. Other attractions include an art gallery, extensive parks, and a couple of good museums. The Southampton International Boat Show, a 10-day event in mid-September, draws huge crowds.

**God's House Tower.** Incorporated in the town walls are a number of old buildings, including this one, originally a gunpowder factory and now an archaeology museum. Displays focus on the Roman, Saxon, and medieval periods of Southampton's history, and an interactive computer allows virtual access to the archaeological collections. ⊠ *Winkle St.* ☎ *023/8063–5904* ⊕ *www.southampton.gov.uk* 🎟 *£1.95* ☉ *Tues.–Sat. 10–4, Sun. 1–4.*

**Mayflower Park and the Pilgrim Fathers' Memorial.** This park commemorates the departure of 102 passengers on the North America–bound *Mayflower* from Southampton on August 15, 1620. A plaque also honors the 2 million U.S. troops who left Southampton in World War II. ⊠ *Western Esplanade.*

**Southampton Maritime Museum.** The museum brings together models, mementos, and items of furniture from the age of the great clippers and cruise ships, including a wealth of memorabilia relating to the *Titanic*—footage, photos, crew lists, and so on. Boat buffs will relish plenty of vital statistics dealing with the history of commercial shipping. ⊠ *Bugle St.* ☎ *023/8022–3941* ⊕ *www.southampton.gov.uk* ⌑ *£1.95* ⊙ *Tues.–Sat. 10–4, Sun. 1–4.*

## WINCHESTER

*25 km (16 mi) northeast of Southampton.*

Winchester is among the most historic of English cities. Although it is now merely the county seat of Hampshire, for more than four centuries Winchester served as England's capital. Here, in AD 827, Egbert was crowned first king of England, and his successor, Alfred the Great, held court until his death in 899. After the Norman Conquest in 1066, William I ("the Conqueror") had himself crowned in London, but took the precaution of repeating the ceremony in Winchester.

**Great Hall.** A few blocks west of the cathedral, this hall is all that remains of the city's Norman castle. Here the English Parliament met for the first time in 1246; Sir Walter Raleigh was tried for conspiracy against King James I and condemned to death here in 1603. The hall's greatest relic hangs on its west wall: King Arthur's Round Table has places for 24 knights and features a portrait of Arthur bearing a remarkable resemblance to King Henry VIII. In fact, the table dates back no further than the 13th century and was repainted by order of Henry on the occasion of a visit by the Holy Roman Emperor Charles V. Take time to wander through Queen Eleanor's Medieval Garden—a re-creation of a noblewoman's shady retreat. ⊠ *Castle Hill* ☎ *01962/846476* ⌑ *Free* ⊙ *Daily 10–5.*

★ **Winchester Cathedral.** The city's greatest monument, begun in 1079 and consecrated in 1093, presents a sturdy, chunky appearance in keeping with its Norman construction, so that the Gothic lightness within is even more breathtaking. Its tower, transepts, and crypt, and the inside core of the great Perpendicular nave, reveal some of the world's best surviving examples of Norman architecture. Other features, such as the arcades, the presbytery (behind the choir, holding the high altar), and the windows, are Gothic alterations carried out between the 12th and 14th centuries. Among the many well-known people buried in the cathedral is Jane Austen, whose grave lies in the north aisle of the nave. Special services or ceremonies may mean the cathedral is closed to visits, so telephone first to avoid disappointment. Tours of the bell tower are offered at least two times daily. ⊠ *The Close, Cathedral Precincts* ☎ *01962/857200* ⊕ *www.winchester-cathedral.org.uk* ⌑ *£6; Library and Triforium Gallery free; bell tower tour £6 (combined cathedral and tower tour £9)* ⊙ *Mon.–Sat. 9–5, Sun. 12:30–3, longer for services. Library and Triforium Gallery Apr.–Oct., Mon. 2–4, Tues.–Sat. 11–4; Nov., Dec., and Mar., Wed. and Sat. 11–3:30; Jan. and Feb., Sat. 11–3:30. Free tours on the hr Mon.–Sat. 10–3, bell tower tours late May–Aug., Mon., Wed., and Fri. 2:15, Sat. 11:30 and 2:15; Sept.–late May, Wed. 2:15, Sat. 11:30 and 2:15.*

## CHAWTON
*49 km (30 mi) northeast of Southampton.*

Jane Austen (1775–1817) lived the last eight years of her life in the village of Chawton. The site has always drawn literary pilgrims, but with the ongoing release of successful films based on her novels, the popularity of the town among visitors has grown enormously.

★ **Jane Austen's House.** Now a museum, the rooms of Jane Austen's House retain the atmosphere of restricted gentility suitable to the unmarried daughter of a clergyman. Her mahogany writing desk still resides in the family sitting room. Here, in an unassuming redbrick house, Austen wrote *Emma, Persuasion,* and *Mansfield Park,* and revised *Sense and Sensibility, Northanger Abbey,* and *Pride and Prejudice.* ✉ *Signed off A31/A32 roundabout* ☎ *01420/83262* ⊕ *www.jane-austens-house-museum.org.uk* ✆ *£7* ☉ *Mar.–May and Sept.–Dec., daily 10:30–4:30; June–Aug., daily 10–5; Jan. and Feb., weekends 10:30–4:30; last admission 30 min before closing.*

## SALISBURY CATHEDRAL
Fodor'sChoice *39 km (24 mi) northwest of Southampton.*

★ Salisbury is dominated by the towering cathedral, a soaring hymn in stone. It is unique among cathedrals in that it was conceived and built as a whole, in the amazingly short span of 38 years (1220–58). The spire, added in 1320, is the tallest in England and a miraculous feat of medieval engineering—even though the point, 404 feet above the ground, leans 2½ feet off vertical. ■TIP➔ **You can join a free 45-minute tour of the church leaving two or more times a day, and there are tours to the roof and spire at least once a day.** The **cloisters** are the largest in England, and the octagonal **Chapter House** contains a marvelous 13th-century frieze showing scenes from the Old Testament. In the Chapter House you can also see one of the four original copies of the **Magna Carta,** the charter of rights the English barons forced King John to accept in 1215; it was sent here for safekeeping in the 13th century. ✉ *Cathedral Close* ☎ *01722/555120* ⊕ *www.salisburycathedral.org.uk* ✆ *Cathedral £5 requested donation, roof tour £8.50, Chapter House free* ☉ *Cathedral daily 7:15–6:15. Chapter House Apr.–Oct., Mon.–Sat. 9:30–5:30, Sun. 12:45–5:30; Nov.–Mar., Mon.–Sat. 10–4:30, Sun. 12:45–4:30. Access to cathedral restricted during services.*

## STONEHENGE
Fodor'sChoice *76 km (47 mi) northwest of Southampton.*

★ Mysterious and ancient, Stonehenge has baffled archaeologists for centuries. One of England's most-visited monuments, the circle of giant stones that sits in lonely isolation on the wide sweep of Salisbury Plain still has the capacity to fascinate and move those who view it. Sadly, though, this World Heritage Site is now enclosed by barriers after incidents of vandalism and amid fears that its popularity could threaten its existence. Visitors can no longer walk among the giant stones or see up close the prehistoric carvings, some of which show axes and daggers.

Stonehenge was begun about 3000 BC, enlarged between 2100 and 1900 BC, and altered yet again by 150 BC. It has been excavated and rearranged several times over the centuries. The medieval term "stonehenge" means "hanging stones." Many of the huge stones that ringed the center were brought here from great distances, but it is not certain by what ancient form of transportation they were moved.

Although some of the mysteries concerning the site have been solved, the reason Stonehenge was built remains unknown. It is fairly certain that it was a religious site, and that worship here involved the cycles of the sun; the alignment of the stones to point to sunrise at midsummer and sunset in midwinter makes this clear. The druids certainly had nothing to do with the construction: the monument had already been in existence for nearly 2,000 years by the time they appeared. Excavations at Durrington Walls, another henge a couple of miles northeast (off A345), have unearthed a substantial settlement dating from around 2500 BC, probably built and occupied by the workers who constructed Stonehenge.

A paved path for visitors skirts the stones, ensuring that you don't get very close to the monoliths. Bring a pair of binoculars to help make out the details more clearly. Your ticket entitles you to an informative audio tour, but in general, visitor amenities at Stonehenge are limited, especially for such a major tourist attraction.

The monument stands near the junction with A344. ⊠ *Junction of A303 and A344/A360, near Amesbury* ☎ *0870/333–1181, 01722/343834 for information about private access outside regular hrs* ⊕ *www.english-heritage.org.uk* ⊠ *£6.90* ⊙ *Mid-Mar.–May and Sept.–mid-Oct., daily 9:30–6; June–Aug., daily 9–7; mid-Oct.–mid-Mar., daily 9:30–4.*

## SHOPPING

Almost every town in this part of England has a tempting array of shops selling antiques, collectibles, and one-of-a-kind items. English china makes a fitting souvenir, as do copies of the various Austen novels set in the region. For a post-tour pick-me-up, try English blended teas in presentation sets.

**King's Walk,** off Friarsgate in Winchester, has a number of stalls selling antiques, crafts, gift items, and bric-a-brac.

## WHERE TO EAT

¢    ✕ **Cathedral Refectory.** The bold, modern style of this self-service eatery
BRITISH    next to the cathedral helps make it a refreshing lunch or snack stop. The menu ranges from traditional soups to cottage pie and fish dishes, but do sample the local "trenchers." This thick bread was used in medieval times as a plate from which to eat meat; once soaked in the meat juices, the bread was passed down to the poor. Today the trenchers, soaked in toppings such as pesto or ham and goat's cheese, are grilled. ⊠ *Inner Close, Winchester* ☎ *01962/857200* ▭ *MC, V* ⊙ *No dinner.*

$$$$    ✕ **Chesil Rectory.** The timbered and gabled building may be Old Eng-
MODERN BRITISH    lish—15th or 16th century—but the cuisine is contemporary, mixing classic recipes with local ingredients. Dishes might include lamb shoulder terrine, followed by beetroot risotto or fish pie. Good-value fixed-price lunches and early-evening dinners are available. Service and

the antique charm of the surroundings match the quality of the food.
✉ *1 Chesil St. Winchester* ☎ *01962/851555* ⊕ *www.chesilrectory.co.uk*
⊟ *AE, DC, MC, V* ☽ *Closed Mon. No dinner Sun.*

# ZEEBRUGGE, BELGIUM (FOR BRUGES)

Long thought of as a Sleeping Beauty reawakened, Bruges is an ancient
town where the rhythm of medieval life resonates from every street
corner. The city thrived during the 13th century as a member of the
Hanseatic League, and an era of unprecedented wealth began under
such Burgundian rulers as Philip the Good and Charles the Bold in the
15th century. At this time, Hans Memling and Jan van Eyck took art
in a new direction with the famed Flemish Primitive style of painting,
while fine civil and domestic buildings advertised the wealth generated
by trade. When the city fell into poverty as its rivers silted in the 16th
century, this architecture was preserved as if in aspic. Today Bruges is
a compact and atmospheric maze of tangled streets, narrow canals,
handsome squares, and gabled buildings. The town has not only awak-
ened from its slumbers, but is also bright-eyed with spruced-up shops,
restaurants, and cafés.

## ESSENTIALS

CURRENCY   The euro (€1 to US$1.36 at this writing). ATMs are common and credit
cards are widely accepted.

HOURS   Shops open Tuesday, Wednesday, Friday, and Saturday from 9 or 10
until 6; they are open later on Thursday. Most stores are closed on
Sunday and some on Monday. Museums open from 9 until 6 with one
late opening night during the week.

INTERNET   **Bean Around the World** (✉ *Genthof 5* ☎ *050/70–35–72*) has Wi-Fi and a
computer terminal. It's open every day but Friday.

TELEPHONES   Tri-band GSM phones work in Belgium. You can buy prepaid phone
cards at telecom shops, news vendors, and tobacconists in all towns and
cities. Phone cards can be used for local or international calls. Proximus
and Mobistar are the leading telecom companies.

## COMING ASHORE

Cruise ships dock at Zeebrugge—14 km (9 mi) from the city of Bruges—
at the King Leopold II dam or in Albert II dock, both at the western
outer port. These locations are 2 km (1½ mi) from Zeebrugge train
station. There are no passenger facilities within the port itself. The reliable and modern rail system ensures swift and efficient transfer from
the station to a range of Belgian cities, including Ghent, Antwerp, and
Brussels. The dock is within walking distance of the seafront of Zeebrugge Town, with its seafront promenade, Russian submarine exhibit,
and historic fishing district.

Taxis wait at the dockside to transfer passengers not booked on organized trips into Zeebrugge. By rail from the center of Zeebrugge it is
a 15-minute journey to Bruges at a current cost of €2.70 one way; the
rail journey to Antwerp takes one hour and 45 minutes, at a cost of
€15.40 one-way (⇨ *Antwerp, above*). It is 15 minutes by road from

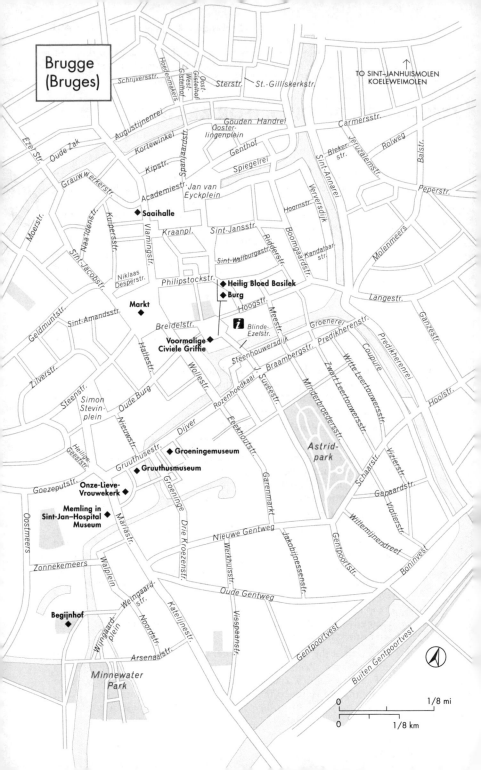

the Zeebrugge docks to Bruges. Travel by taxi has a per-km (per-½-mi) charge of around €2.50, which makes it expensive for day tours but acceptable for short trips.

Vehicle-rental offices are located in Bruges (around €100 per day for a compact manual shift vehicle), but rail transport is most practical for independent travelers unless you really want to see more of the Belgian countryside.

## EXPLORING BRUGES

★ **Begijnhof.** The convent is a pretty and serene cluster of buildings surrounding a pleasant green at the edge of a canal. Founded in 1245 by Margaret, Countess of Constantinople, the beguinage flourished for 600 years. The last of the Beguines died about 50 years ago, and today the site is occupied by Benedictine nuns, who still wear the Beguine habit. Although most of the present-day houses are from the 16th and 17th centuries, they have maintained the architectural style of the houses that preceded them. One house has been set aside as a small museum. The horse-and-carriage rides around the town have a 10-minute stop outside the beguinage—long enough for a quick look around. Visitors are asked to respect the silence. ⊠ *Oude Begijnhof, off Wijngaardstraat* ☎ *050/33–00–11* ⊠ *Free, house visit €2* ☉ *Mon.–Sat. 10–5, Sun. 2:30–5.*

**Fodor'sChoice**
★ **Burg.** A popular daytime meeting place and an enchanting, floodlighted scene after dark, the Burg is flanked by striking civic buildings. Named for the fortress built by Baldwin of the Iron Arm, the Burg was also the former site of the 10th-century Carolingian Cathedral of St. Donaas, which was destroyed by French Republicans in 1799. You can wander through the handsome, 18th-century law court, the Oude Gerechtshof, the Voormalige Civiele Griffie with its 15th-century front gable, the Stadhuis, and the Heilig Bloed Basiliek (⇨ *below*). The Burg is not all historic splendor, though—in sharp contrast to these buildings stands a modern construction by Japanese artist Toyo Ito, added in 2002. Public opinion is sharply divided over Ito's pavilion over a shallow pool; you'll either love it or hate it. ⊠ *Hoogstraat and Breidelstraat.*

**Fodor'sChoice**
★ **Groeningemusem.** The tremendous holdings of this gallery give you the makings for a crash course in the Flemish Primitives and their successors, but for the first half of 2011 the museum will be turned over to a special exhibit "Van Eyck to Dürer"; the exhibit runs to April 2011. Petrus Christus, Hugo van der Goes, Hieronymus Bosch, Rogier van der Weyden, Gerard David, Pieter Bruegel (both Elder and Younger), Pieter Pourbus—all are represented here. Jan van Eyck's wonderfully realistic *Madonna with Canon Van der Paele* vies with Hans Memling's *Moreel Triptych* as best piece. Thoughtfully, there's a play area to keep antsy children busy. An audioguide is available in English. ⊠ *Dijver 12* ☎ *050/44–87–11* ⊠ *€8, includes an audioguide* ☉ *Tues.–Sun. 9:30–5.*

**Gruuthusemuseum.** If you want to understand the daily life of 15th-century Bruges, visit this applied arts museum. The collection is housed in the Gothic former home of Lodewijk Van Gruuthuse, a prominent Dutch nobleman. The home features displays of furniture, tapestries, lace, ceramics, kitchen equipment, weaponry, and musical instruments.

4

The museum is undergoing a major renovation until late 2011, so only a temporary exhibit is open at this writing. ✉ *Dijver 17* ☎ *050/44–87–11* 💷 *€6, includes audioguide* ⊙ *Tues.–Sun. 9:30–5.*

**Heilig Bloed Basiliek.** The Basilica of the Holy Blood plays host to one of Europe's most precious relics. Architecturally bipolar, a 12th-century Lower Chapel retains a sober, Romanesque character while a lavish Gothic Upper Chapel sits above. The basilica's namesake treasure is a vial thought to contain a few drops of the blood of Christ, brought from Jerusalem to Bruges in 1149. It is exposed here every Friday in the Lower Chapel from 8:30 to 10 and in the Upper Chapel from 10 to 11 and from 3 to 4. On Ascension Day it becomes the centerpiece of the magnificent Heilig Bloedprocessie (Procession of the Holy Blood), a major medieval-style pageant in which it is carried through the streets of Bruges. The small **museum** next to the basilica contains the 17th-century reliquary. ✉ *Burg* ☎ *No phone* ⊕ *www.holyblood.org* 💷 *Basilica free, museum €1.25* ⊙ *Apr.–Sept., daily 9:30–noon and 2–6; Oct.–Mar., Thurs.–Tues. 10–noon and 2–4, Wed. 9:30–noon.*

> ### THE NAME GAME
>
> You'll find two spellings of the town name. That's because Belgium has two languages, Flemish and French. In French the spelling is Bruges; in Flemish it's Brugge. Since the city sits in the mainly Flemish-speaking region of Flanders, Brugge is more technically correct—though you won't have a problem if you call the city Bruges, as most tourists do.

**Fodor's Choice** ★ **Markt.** Used as a marketplace since 958, this square is still one of the liveliest places in Bruges. In the center stands a memorial to the city's medieval heroes, Jan Breydel and Pieter De Coninck, who led the commoners of Flanders to a short-lived victory over the aristocrats of France. Old guild houses line the west and north sides of the square, their step-gabled facades overlooking the cafés spilling out onto the sidewalk. These buildings aren't always as old as they seem, though—often they're 19th-century reconstructions. The medieval **Belfort** (Belfry) on the south side of the Markt, however, is the genuine article. The tower dates to the 13th century, its crowning octagonal lantern to the 15th century. Altogether, it rises to a height of 270 feet, commanding the city and the surrounding countryside with more presence than grace. The valuables of Bruges were once kept in the second-floor treasury; now the Belfort's riches are in its remarkable 47-bell carillon. You can climb 366 winding steps to the clock mechanism, and from the carillon enjoy a gorgeous panoramic view. Back down in the square, you may be tempted by the **horse-drawn carriages** that congregate here; a half-hour ride for up to four people, with a short stop at the Begijnhof, costs €30, plus "something for the horse." ✉ *Intersection of Steenstraat, St-Amandstraat, Vlamingstraat, Philipstockstraat, Breidelstraat, and Wollestraat* ☎ *050/44–87–11* 💷 *€8* ⊙ *Tues.–Sun., 9:30–5. Carillon concerts Sun. 2:15–3; June 15–July 1 and Aug. 15–Sept., Mon., Wed., and Sat. 9 PM–10 PM; Oct.–June 14, Wed. and Sat. 2:15–3.*

★ **Memling in Sint-Jan—Hospital Museum.** This collection contains only six works, but they are of breathtaking quality and among the greatest—and certainly the most spiritual—of the Flemish Primitive school. Hans Memling (1440–94) was born in Germany, but spent the greater part of his life in Bruges. In *The Altarpiece of St. John the Baptist and St. John the Evangelist,* two leading personages of the Burgundian court are believed to be portrayed: Mary of Burgundy as St. Catherine, and Margaret of York as St. Barbara. The Memling Museum is housed in **Oud Sint-Janshospitaal,** one of the oldest surviving medieval hospitals in Europe. It was founded in the 12th century and remained in use until the early 20th century. There is a short guide to the museum in English, and also an audioguide in English. ⊠ *Mariastraat 38* ☎ *050/44–87–11* ✉ *€8, includes audioguide* ☉ *Tues.–Sun. 9:30–5.*

> **BRUGES BEST BETS**
>
> **Boat trip on the canals.** The lifeblood of medieval Bruges, the canals now offer some of the finest views of the city's delightful architecture and distinctive streets and alleyways.
>
> **Belfort.** Climb the medieval tower for exceptional views across the tiled rooftops and ornate gables of this tiny enclave.
>
> **Groeningemusem.** The art of the Flemish Primitives and their successors form the core of this gallery, one of the finest of its kind in the world.

**Onze-Lieve-Vrouwekerk.** The towering spire of the plain, Gothic Church of Our Lady, begun about 1220, rivals the Belfry as Bruges's symbol. It is 381 feet high, the tallest brick construction in the world. Look for the small *Madonna and Child* statue, an early work by Michelangelo. The great sculptor sold it to a merchant from Bruges when the original client failed to pay, and now the white-marble figure sits in a black-marble niche behind an altar at the end of the south aisle. The choir contains many 13th- and 14th-century polychrome tombs, as well as two mausoleums: that of Mary of Burgundy, who died in 1482; and that of her father, Charles the Bold, killed in 1477 while laying siege to Nancy in France. Mary was as well loved in Bruges as her husband, Maximilian of Austria, was loathed. Her finely chiseled effigy captures her beauty. ⊠ *Dijver and Mariastraat* ☎ *No phone* ✉ *€2* ☉ *Tues.–Fri. 9:30–5, Sat. 9:30–4:45, Sun. 1:30–5.*

## SHOPPING

Bruges has many trendy boutiques and shops, especially along Nordzandstraat, as well as Steenstraat and Vlamingstraat, both of which branch off from the Markt. Ter Steeghere mall, which links the Burg with Wollestraat, deftly integrates a modern development into the historic center. The largest and most pleasant mall is the Zilverpand off Zilverstraat, where 30-odd shops cluster in Flemish gable houses. Souvenir shops crowd around the Markt, Wollestraat, Breidelstraat, and Minnewater. Bruges has been a center for lace-making since the 15th century. Handmade lace in intricate patterns, however, takes a long time to produce, and this is reflected in the price. For work of this type, you should be prepared to part with €250 or more. Art and antiques abound, with furniture and decorative objects from the surrounding Flanders region.

You also can't go far in the city center without seeing a tempting window display of handmade chocolates, truffles, and pralines. These are delicious to enjoy while you stroll.

**'t Apostelientje.** This is a good shop for the serious lace lover, in the Sint-Anne quarter, behind the church. ⊠ *Balstraat 11* ☎ *050/33–78–60* ⊕ *www.apostelientje.be.*

**The Chocolate Line.** One of the best chocolate shops also sells other delicious handmade candy, as well as handy cases for packing your chocolates to take home. ⊠ *Simon Stevinplein 19* ☎ *050/34–10–90* ⊕ *www. thechocolateline.be.*

**Guyart.** This is both an art gallery and a tavern, so art lovers may browse while the less artistically inclined enjoy the other offerings. ⊠ *Fort Lapin 37* ☎ *050/33–21–59* ⊕ *www.guyart.com.*

**Papyrus.** This shop specializes in antique silverware. ⊠ *Walplein 41* ☎ *050/33–66–87* ⊕ *www.silverantiques.be.*

**'t Leerhuis.** This gallery deals in contemporary art. ⊠ *Groeninge 35* ☎ *050/33–03–02.*

# ACTIVITIES

## CYCLING

The city is easy to explore on two wheels, and many Bruges city dwellers use bicycles daily. Cyclists can go in both directions along more than 50 one-way streets, marked on the tarmac with an image of a bicycle circled in blue. The Bruges tourist office sells a cycling brochure outlining five different routes around the city. The city also offers one-day bike rental and entrance to three municipal museums for €15. You can rent bicycles is several places.

**Koffieboontje.** ⊠ *Hallestraat 4* ☎ *050/33–80–27* ⊕ *www.hotel-koffieboontje.be.*

# WHERE TO EAT

$   ✕ **Eetcafé De Vuyst–Restaurant Bistrot De Serre.** The spires of Bruges are
BELGIAN   dramatically framed within the glass walls of the popular, light-filled Eetcafé. Go through to the back of the building and you'll come to a lovely garden restaurant. The café is ideal for a sandwich or light meal with the kids, while the restaurant homes in on classic Belgian specialties such as waterzooi, mussels, and eel. ⊠ *Simon Stevinplein 15* ☎ *050/34–22–31* ▭ *AE, DC, MC, V* ⊘ *Closed Tues., 1st 2 wks in Feb., and last 2 wks in Nov.*

$   ✕ **Opus Latino.** Though it's on the busy Burg, this café-restaurant man-
CAFÉ   ages to be quiet and secluded. There are two ways of finding it: either through the shopping gallery Ten Steeghere, next to the Heilig Bloed Basiliek, or via De Garre, the little lane off Breidelstraat. Its terrace overlooking a canal makes a good meeting point and rest stop for a restorative snack—a few tapas, perhaps, or a cheese board. ⊠ *Burg 15* ☎ *050/34–72–78* ▭ *MC, V* ⊘ *Closed Wed.* Ⓜ *Bus 1 or 12.*

# The Baltic

PORTS IN DENMARK, ESTONIA, FINLAND, GERMANY, LATVIA, POLAND, RUSSIA & SWEDEN

## WORD OF MOUTH

"We did the Baltic in June,and St. Petersburg was the highlight of the trip. . . . The sights are amazing. . . . For us, we disembarked in every port except St. Petersburg on our own, so we did not have to wait in lines for a tour to assemble and begin."

— jacketwatch

Lindsay
Bennett

Northern European itineraries are increasingly popular. You may depart from Stockholm or Copenhagen and visit several of the Baltic's top ports. A special treat for Baltic cruisers is often a stop in St. Petersburg, Russia, and this is why many people take these cruises.

Some Baltic itineraries begin in a U.K. port or even in Amsterdam (⇨ *Chapter 6 for more information about these ports*). Some may include stops in Norway (⇨ *Chapter 8 for Norwegian ports*). These cruises may be longer than the typical Mediterranean cruise and may cost more, which is one reason why they aren't as popular with first-timers to European cruising. But the number of ships doing Baltic itineraries continues to expand, and there are now some one-week cruises in these northern waters during the summer.

## ABOUT THE RESTAURANTS

All the restaurants we recommend serve lunch; they may also serve dinner if your cruise ship stays late in port and you choose to dine off the ship. Cuisine in Europe is varied, but Europeans tend to eat a leisurely meal at lunch; in most ports there are quicker and simpler alternatives for those who just want to grab a quick bite before returning to the ship. Note that several Baltic countries do not use the euro, including Denmark, Estonia, Finland, Latvia, Poland, Russia, and Sweden. Price categories in those countries are based on the euro-equivalent costs of eating in restaurants.

| WHAT IT COSTS IN EUROS AND KRONER | | | | | |
|---|---|---|---|---|---|
| | ¢ | $ | $$ | $$$ | $$$$ |
| Restaurants in euros | under €11 | €11–€17 | €17–€23 | €23–€30 | over €30 |
| Restaurants in kroner | under Nkr 85 | Nkr 85–Nkr 135 | Nkr 135–Nkr 185 | Nkr 185–Nkr 240 | over Nkr 240 |

Restaurant prices are per person for a main course, including tax.

# ÅRHUS, DENMARK

Århus is Denmark's second-largest city, and, with its funky arts and college community, one of the country's most pleasant ones. The Vikings settled in Århus at the mouth of the river Aros. Traces of Viking life can still be found in Århus. Cutting through the center of town is a canal called the Århus Å (Århus Creek), once an underground aqueduct but now uncovered. An amalgam of bars, cafés, and restaurants has sprouted along its banks, creating one of Denmark's liveliest thoroughfares. At all hours of the day and night this waterfront strip is abuzz with crowds that hang out on the outdoor terraces and steps that lead down to the creek.

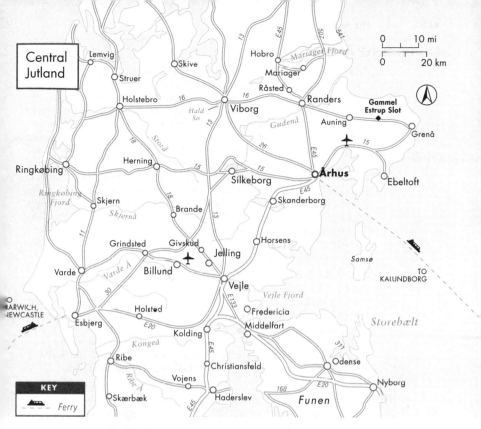

## ESSENTIALS

**CURRENCY** Denmark is an EU country but has opted to keep its currency, the Danish *krone* or *kroner* (DKr 5.86 to US$1; DKr 7.44 to €1); exchange rates were accurate at this writing but are subject to change. ATMs are common, so it's easy to get local currency, but you can't generally use the euro or dollar here.

**HOURS** Most shops are open from 9 or 10 to 5:30 or 6 weekdays, Saturday from 9 to 5, and are closed Sunday.

**INTERNET** **Gate58 APS** (⊠ *Vestergade 58 B* ☎ *87/30–02–80*).

**TELEPHONES** Most tri- and quad-band GSM phones will work in Denmark. If your service provider offers service in Europe, you will likely be able to use your mobile phone in Århus. Pay phones are increasingly rare in Europe, particularly in tech-savvy Scandinavia and Northern Europe.

## COMING ASHORE

Cruise ships dock at Pier 2, a 10-minute walk from the city center. If your ship calls in summer, you may arrive in time for one of Århus' many festivals.

## EXPLORING ÅRHUS

**Århus Domkirke.** Rising gracefully over the center of town, the Århus Cathedral was originally built in 1201 in a Romanesque style, but was later expanded and redesigned into a Gothic cathedral in the 15th century. Its soaring, whitewashed nave is one of the longest in Denmark. The cathedral's highlights include its chalk frescoes, in shades of lavender, yellow, red, and black that grace the high arches and towering walls. Dating from the Middle Ages, the frescoes depict biblical scenes and the valiant St. George slaying a dragon and saving a maiden princess in distress. Also illustrated is the poignant death of St. Clement, who drowned with an anchor tied around his neck; nonetheless, he became the patron saint of sailors. Climb the tower for bird's-eye views of the rooftops and thronged streets of Århus. ⊠ *Bispetorv* ☎ *86/20–54–00* ⊕ *www.aarhus-domkirke.dk* 🎫 *Tower DKr 10* ۞ *Jan.–Apr. and Oct.–Dec., Mon. and Wed.–Sat. 10–3, Tues. 10:30–3; May–Sept., Mon. and Wed.–Sat. 9:30–4, Tues. 10:30–4.*

**ARoS Århus Kunstmuseum.** The city's newest art museum was an immediate hit when it opened in April 2004, and 340,000 people passed through its doors in its first nine months of opening. On the top floor there's a restaurant as well as a rooftop patio—a photographer's dream. The art, of course, is paramount, and comprises the museum's own collection of more than 9,000 works dating from 1770 to the present, as well as internationally known visiting exhibits. ⊠ *Aros Allé 2* ☎ *87/30–66–00* ⊕ *www.aros.dk* 🎫 *DKr 95* ۞ *Tues. and Thurs.–Sun. 10–5, Wed. 10–10.*

★ **Den Gamle By.** Don't miss the town's open-air museum, the only three-star museum outside Copenhagen. Its 75 historic buildings, including 70 half-timber houses, a mill, and millstream, were carefully moved from locations throughout Denmark and meticulously re-created, inside and out. Actors portray people from times past. You can explore the extensive exhibits, and then have a pint in the beer cellar or coffee and cake in the garden. ⊠ *Viborgvej 2* ☎ *86/12–31–88* ⊕ *www.dengamleby.dk* 🎫 *DKr 50–DKr 100 depending on season and activities* ۞ *Late-June–early-Sept., daily 9–6; late Mar.–late June., and early-Sept.–mid-Nov., daily 10–5; late Nov.–late Dec., weekdays 9–7, weekends 10–7; late Dec.–early-Jan., daily 10–5; early-Jan.–early-Feb., daily 11–3, early-Feb.–late Mar., daily 10–4. Grounds always open.*

**Marselisborg Slot.** South of the city is Marselisborg Castle, the palatial summer residence of the royal family. The changing of the guard takes place daily at noon when the queen is staying in the palace. The palace itself is not open for tours, but when the royal family is away (generally in winter and spring) the palace grounds, including a sumptuous rose garden, are open to the public. Take Bus 1, 8, or 19. ⊠ *Kongevejen 100* ☎ *No phone* ⊕ *www.kongehuset.dk* 🎫 *Free* ۞ *Daily dawn–dusk, when Royal Family not in residence.*

**Moesgård Forhistorisk Museum.** In a 250-acre forest south of Århus, the Prehistoric Museum has exhibits on ethnography and archaeology, including the famed Grauballe Man, a 2,000-year-old corpse so well preserved in a bog that scientists could determine his last meal. In fact, when the discoverers of the Graub-alle Man stumbled upon him in 1952 they thought he had recently been murdered and called the police. The Forhistorisk vej (Pre-historic Trail) through the forest leads past Stone- and Bronze Age displays to reconstructed houses from Viking times. ✉ *Moesgård Allé (Bus 6 from center of town)* ☎ *89/42–11–00* ⊕ *www.moesmus. dk* ✆ *DKr 60* ☉ *Apr.–Sept., daily 10–5; Oct.–Mar., Tues.–Sun. 10–4.*

**Rådhus.** Århus's municipal building is probably the most unusual city hall in Denmark. Built in 1941 by noted architects Arne Jacobsen and Erik Møller, the pale Norwegian-marble block building is controversial, but cuts a startling figure when illuminated in the evening. The VisitÅrhus tourist board can arrange for a guide to take you through the building. Tours take about an hour and cost DKr 557. ✉ *Park Allé* ⊕ *www.aarhus.dk* ☉ *Daily by guided tour only.*

☺ **Tivoli Friheden.** If you are in Århus with children, or simply wish to enjoy a young-at-heart activity, visit the provincial amusement park, with more than 40 rides and activities, attractive gardens, and restaurants. Pierrot the Clown entertains, and concerts are given by contemporary artists. ✉ *Skovbrynet* ☎ *86/14–73–00* ⊕ *www.friheden.dk* ✆ *DKr 10 for park entry; multiride ticket DKr 26; individual rides DKr 1.50* ☉ *Call or check Web site, as opening times vary greatly throughout summer.*

> ## ÅRHUS BEST BETS
>
> **Den Gamle By.** Visit this open-air museum to get a sense of what Danish village life was like.
>
> **Tivoli Friheden.** If you have kids, this charming amusement park should be your first destination.
>
> **Meet Grauballe Man.** The Moesgård Museum displays the bog-preserved body of a man who is perhaps 2,000 years old, as well as other relics of the Viking era.

**5**

## SHOPPING

With more than 800 shops and many pedestrian streets (Strøget, Fred-ericksgade, Sct. Clemensgade, Store Torv, and Lille Torv), this city is a great place to play havoc with your credit cards. As befits a student town, Århus also has its "Latin Quarter," a jumble of cobbled streets around the cathedral, with boutiques, antiques shops, and glass and ceramic galleries that may be a little less expensive. In Vestergade street, you can turn on Grønnengade and stroll along Møllestien to see its charming old homes.

The Fredericksbjerg quarter, which includes the streets Bruunsgade, Jægergårdsgade, and Fredericks Allé, is called "the larder of the city" because there are so many specialty food shops here. There's also a shopping center, Bruun's Galleri.

**Bülow Duus Glassworks.** At this glass factory and shop you can browse among delicate and colorful glassworks from fishbowls to candlehold-ers. While there, visit Mette Bülow Duus's workshop and witness the creation of beautiful glassware. ✉ *Studsg. 14* ☎ *86/12–72–86.*

**DesignerTorvet.** This shop has a selection of housewares and gifts, both large and small, primarily by up and coming designers. ⊠ *Badstuegade 11A* ☎ *86/18–28–19* ⊕ *www.designertorvet.dk.*

**Georg Jensen.** For the best selection of Georg Jensen designs, head to the official store. It stocks watches, jewelry, table settings, and art nouveau vases. The textile designs of Georg Jensen Damask, in a separate department, are truly beautiful. ⊠ *Sønderg. 1* ☎ *86/12–01–00* ⊕ *www. georgjensen.com.*

## ACTIVITIES

### FISHING

For the past 24 years the same four friends from England have been fishing in the Silkeborg region on their vacation—surely an excellent endorsement for angling opportunities in the region. The Lake District is a great place for fishing—more than 15 popular species of fish can be found here. License requirements vary, and package tours are also available; contact the local tourist office for details.

## WHERE TO EAT

**$$–$$$**  ✕**Bryggeriet Sct. Clemens.** At this popular pub you can sit among cop-
ECLECTIC  per kettles and quaff the local brew, which is unfiltered and without
★  additives, just as in the old days. Between the spareribs and Australian steaks, you won't go hungry, either. ⊠ *Kannikeg. 10–12* ☎ *86/13–80–00* ⊕ *www.bryggeriet.dk* ▭ *AE, DC, MC, V.*

**$$**  ✕**Restaurant Margueritten.** Tucked into a cobbled courtyard, this cheery
DANISH  restaurant is housed in former stables, which accounts for the low wood-beam ceiling. Well-worn wooden tables and tan walls round out the warm atmosphere. Contemporary Danish fare includes fish, veal, and lobster dishes. In summer and early fall the back garden is open all day. There are fixed-price menus and snacks available. ⊠ *Guldsmedg. 20* ☎ *86/19–60–33* ⊕ *www.margueritten.dk* ▭ *AE, DC, MC, V* ☉ *No lunch Sun. Closed mid-Dec.–mid-Jan.*

# COPENHAGEN, DENMARK

Copenhagen—"København" in Danish—has no glittering skylines, few killer views, and only a handful of meager skyscrapers. Bicycles glide alongside manageable traffic at a pace that's utterly human. The early-morning air in the pedestrian streets of the city's core, Strøget, is redolent of freshly baked bread and soap-scrubbed storefronts. If there's such a thing as a cozy city, this is it. Filled with museums, restaurants, cafés, and lively nightlife, the city has its greatest resource in its spirited inhabitants. The imaginative, unconventional, and affable Copenhageners exude an egalitarian philosophy that embraces nearly all lifestyles and leanings. Despite a tumultuous history, Copenhagen survives as the liveliest Scandinavian capital, with some excellent galleries and museums. With its backdrop of copper towers and crooked rooftops, the venerable city is amused by playful street musicians and performers, soothed by one of the highest standards of living in the world, and spangled by the thousand lights and gardens of Tivoli.

## ESSENTIALS

CURRENCY  The krone (DKr 5.86 to US$1; DKr 7.44 to €1); exchange rates were accurate at this writing but are subject to change. U.S. currency is accepted in some shops and restaurants. ATMs are common.

HOURS  Museum hours vary, though the major collections are open Tuesday through Sunday from 10 to 5. Stores are open weekdays from 9:30 to 5:30 (or sometimes 7).

INTERNET  **Danhostel** (✉ *HC Andersens Blvd. 50, København V* ☎ *33/11–85–85*) has an Internet café.

TELEPHONES  Tri-band GSM phones work in Denmark. You can buy prepaid phone cards at telecom shops, news vendors, and tobacconists in all towns and cities. Phone cards can be used for local or international calls.

## COMING ASHORE

The city's main cruise port at Langelinie Pier is one of the best in Europe. Although it's a 10-minute drive or 30-minute walk from the downtown core, the port is within walking distance of the Little Mermaid and the attractions of the seafront. Taxis wait outside the cruise terminal. The on-site Copenhagen Cruise Information Center is run by the city tourist office, and there is a selection of shops housed in the renovated old wharf warehouses selling typical souvenirs.

Some ships dock at the Freeport Terminal, which is a further 30 minutes on foot from the downtown core (i.e., a full hour's walk from the center). Taxis wait outside the terminal, and the cost is around DKr 125 for the trip into town. A small number of ships (primarily smaller vessels) dock at the quayside at Nordre Toldbod, which sits beside the little Mermaid and is a 10-minute walk from the city center; however, there are no passenger facilities here.

City Bikes is a citywide project offering free bike rental. There's a City Bike rack at Langelinie Pier, so you can pick up a bike here and cycle along the waterfront to the center or take a bike from a rack in the center to cycle back to the ship at the end of your day.

A water-taxi service to the city center leaves from the end of Langelinie Pier hourly. The boat stops at various parts of the city, and you can hop on and hop off as you wish. A one-day ticket costs DKr 40. A taxi direct to downtown (10 to 15 minutes) costs around DKr 70–DKr 90 from Langelinie.

There is a dedicated cruise lounge at the Illum department store on Strøget in the city center, where you can wait for transfers, leave purchases for later collection, have a free coffee, or rest during your day ashore.

Car rentals cost around DKr 1,185 per day for an economy manual vehicle; however, public transport is much more convenient for a short city visit. The metro and bus services are clean and efficient, with tickets costing DKr 23 for a single-ride two-zone ticket, DKr 70 for a one-day City Pass.

**5**

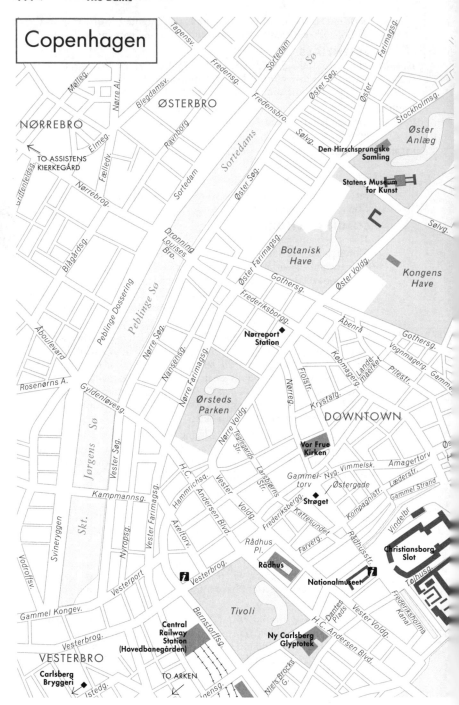

# Copenhagen

NØRREBRO

ØSTERBRO

TO ASSISTENS
KIERKEGÅRD

Den Hirschsprungske
Samling

Statens Museum
for Kunst

Øster
Anlæg

Søvg.

Botanisk
Have

Kongens
Have

Dronning
Louises
Bro.

Frederiksborgg.

Abenrå

Gothersg.

Nørreport
Station

Ørsteds
Parken

DOWNTOWN

Vor Frue
Kirken

Gammel-
torv

Vimmelsk.   Amagertorv

Nyg.

Østergade    Læderstr.

Strøget

Gammel Strand

Rådhus
Pl.

Christiansborg
Slot

Rådhus

Nationalmuseet

Tivoli

Central
Railway
Station
(Hovedbanegården)

Ny Carlsberg
Glyptotek

TO ARKEN

Gammel Kongev.

VESTERBRO

Carlsberg
Bryggeri

Istedg.

**KEY**

🛈 Tourist Information

⊢—⊢ Rail Lines

## GETTING TO THE AIRPORT

If you do not purchase airport transfers from your cruise line, there are easy and inexpensive options for travel between the cruise terminals and the airport.

For Langelinie Pier, take the metro (DKr 30) upstairs in the airport train station at Terminal 3. Trains depart every 4 minutes during the day and every 15 minutes during night hours. There are two possible routes to and from the airport to Langelinie Pier: Either get off at Copenhagen Central Station and then take a taxi to the cruise terminal, or get off at Østerport Station (three more minutes of travel) and take Bus 26 (DKr 25), which stops at the cruise terminal. The 20-minute taxi ride between airport and pier costs around DKr 250.

For Freeport Terminal, take the metro to Copenhagen Central Station (DKr 30); a taxi from the station to the terminal will cost around DKr 75. A taxi direct from the airport to Freeport Terminal will cost around DKr 300.

> ## COPENHAGEN BEST BETS
>
> **Tivoli Gardens.** One of Europe's finest and most famous planned green spaces, Tivoli is part formal garden, part woodland, part theme park.
>
> **Amalienborg Palace.** These rococo palaces, built by the Royal Family at the height of Danish influence, are architectural delights filled with artistic treasures gathered from around Europe.
>
> **The Little Mermaid.** This diminutive statue is the city's most famous landmark, and though she's a little disappointing in real life, you haven't been to Copenhagen if you don't say hello to her.

# EXPLORING COPENHAGEN

**Amalienborg** (*Amalia's Castle*). The four identical rococo buildings occupying this square have housed the royals since 1784. The Christian VIII palace across from the queen's residence houses the **Amalienborg Museum,** which displays part of the Royal Collection and chronicles royal lifestyles between 1863 and 1947.

In the square's center is a magnificent equestrian statue of King Frederik V by the French sculptor Jacques François Joseph Saly. Every day at noon the Royal Guard and band march from Rosenborg Slot through the city for the changing of the guard. On Amalienborg's harbor side are the trees, gardens, and fountains of **Amalienhaven.** ⊠ *Christian VIII's Palace–Amalienborg Pl., Frederiksstaden* ☎ *33/12–21–86* 🖾 *Museum DKr 55* ۞ *Museum Tues.–Sun. 10–4.*

**Carlsberg Bryggeri** (*Carlsberg Brewery*). As you approach the world-famous Carlsberg Brewery, the unmistakable smell of fermenting hops greets you, a pungent reminder that this is beer territory. Nearby, on Gamle Carlsbergvej, is the visitor center, in an old Carlsberg brewery. ⊠ *Gamle Carlsberg Vej 11, Valby* ☎ *33/27–13–14* ⊕ *www.visit-carlsberg.com* 🖾 *DKr 65* ۞ *May–Aug., Tues., Wed., Fri.–Sun. 10–5, Thurs. 10–7:30; Sept.–Apr., Tues.–Sun. 10–5.*

**Fodor's Choice** **Christiansborg Slot** *(Christiansborg Castle).* Surrounded by canals on three
★ sides, the massive granite castle is where the queen officially receives
guests. From 1441 until the fire of 1795, it was used as the royal residence. Even though the first two castles on the site were burned, Christiansborg remains an impressive baroque compound, even by European
standards. The complex contains the Danish Parliament, the Supreme
Court, and Royal Reception Chambers, as well as some ruins. All but
the Supreme Court can be visited. The **Højesteret** *(Supreme Court),* on
the site of the city's first fortress, was built by Bishop Absalon in 1167.

Free tours of the **Folketinget** (Parliament House) are given on Sunday;
the tour at 2 is in English. You can also see a debate when Parliament
is in session (generally Tuesday through Friday from October through
June) if you stop by the receptionist and ask for a free ticket to the public observation gallery. At the **Kongelige Repræsantationlokaler** (Royal
Reception Chambers*)*, you're asked to don slippers to protect the floors.
English-language tours are at 3 PM daily.

While the castle was being rebuilt around 1900, the Nationalmuseet excavated the **ruins of Bishop Absalon's castle,** one of the earlier structures beneath it. The resulting dark, subterranean maze
contains fascinating models and architectural relics. ⊠ *Slotsholmen
(area around Christiansborg; bordered by Boørsgade, Vindebrogade,
and Frederiksholms Kanal), Centrum* ☎ *33/37–55–00 for Parliament
House, 33/92–64–92 for the Royal Reception Chambers and ruins
⊕ www.christiansborgslot.dk* ☜ *Parliament tours free, Royal Reception Chambers DKr 70, ruins DKr 40* ☉ *Danish Parliament tours Sun.
at 2 (in English). Royal Reception Chambers and ruins, May–Sept.,
daily 10–4; Oct.–Apr., Tues.–Sun. 10–4.*

**Christianshavn.** Cobbled avenues, antique street lamps, and Left Bank
charm make up one of the oldest neighborhoods in the city. Today the
area harbors restaurants, cafés, and shops, and its ramparts are edged
with green areas and walking paths, making it the perfect neighborhood
for an afternoon amble.

**Den Hirschsprungske Samling** *(The Hirschsprung Collection).* This
museum showcases paintings from the country's Golden Age—Denmark's mid-19th-century school of naturalism—as well as a collection
of paintings by the late-19th-century artists of the Skagen School. Their
luminous works capture the play of light and water so characteristic
of the Danish countryside. Texts are in English. ⊠ *Stockholmsg. 20,
Østerbro* ☎ *35/42–03–36* ⊕ *www.hirschsprung.dk* ☜ *DKr 50* ☉ *Mon.
and Wed.–Sun. 11–4.*

**Den Lille Havfrue** *(The Little Mermaid).* On the Langelinie promenade,
this 1913 statue commemorates Hans Christian Andersen's lovelorn
creation, and is the subject of hundreds of travel posters. Donated to
the city by Carl Jacobsen, the son of the founder of Carlsberg Brewer-
ies, the innocent waif has also been the subject of some cruel practical
jokes, including decapitation and the loss of an arm, but she is currently
in one piece. Especially on a sunny Sunday, the Langelinie promenade
is thronged with Danes and visitors making their pilgrimage to see the
statue. ⊠ *Langelinie promenade, Østerbro.*

5

C **Nationalmuseet** *(National Museum).* An 18th-century royal resi-
FodorsChoice dence, peaked by massive overhead windows, has contained—since
★ the 1930s—what is regarded as one of the best national museums in
Europe. Extensive permanent exhibits chronicle Danish cultural history
from prehistoric to modern times. The museum has one of the largest
collections of Stone Age tools in the world, as well as Egyptian, Greek,
and Roman antiquities. The exhibit on Danish prehistory features a
great section on Viking times. The children's museum, with replicas
of period clothing and a scalable copy of a real Viking ship, makes
history fun for the under-12 set. Displays have English labels, and the
do-it-yourself walking tour "History of Denmark in 60 Minutes" offers
a good introduction to Denmark; the guide is free at the information
desk. ⊠ *Ny Vesterg. 10, Centrum* ☎ *33/13–44–11* ⊕ *www.natmus.dk*
⊠ *Free* ☉ *Tues.–Sun. 10–5.*

FodorsChoice **Ny Carlsberg Glyptotek** *(New Carlsberg Museum).* Among Copenhagen's
★ most important museums—thanks to its exquisite antiquities and a
world-class collection of impressionist masterpieces—the neoclassical
New Carlsberg Museum was donated in 1888 by Carl Jacobsen, son
of the founder of the Carlsberg Brewery. Surrounding its lush indoor
garden, a series of rooms house works by Pissarro, Degas, Monet, Sisley,
Rodin, and Gauguin. The museum is also renowned for its extensive
assemblage of Egyptian and Greek pieces, not to mention Europe's finest collection of Roman portraits and the best collection of Etruscan art
outside Italy. A modern wing, designed by the acclaimed Danish architect Henning Larsen, provides a luminous entry to the French painting
section. From June to September guided English-language tours start
at 2. ⊠ *Dantes Pl. 7, Vesterbro* ☎ *33/41–81–41* ⊕ *www.glyptoteket.dk*
⊠ *DKr 60* ☉ *Tues.–Sun. 11–5.*

**Statens Museum for Kunst** *(National Art Gallery).* Old Master paintings—
including works by Rubens, Rembrandt, Titian, El Greco, and Frago-
nard—as well as a comprehensive array of antique and 20th-century
Danish art make up the gallery collection. Also notable is the modern
art, which includes pieces by Henri Matisse, Edvard Munch, Henri
Laurens, Emil Nolde, and Georges Braque. ⊠ *Sølvg. 48–50, Østerbro*
☎ *33/74–84–94* ⊕ *www.smk.dk* ⊠ *Free for permanent collection, DKr
80 for special exhibitions* ☉ *Tues. and Thurs.–Sun. 10–5, Wed. 10–8.*

★ **Strøget.** Though it is referred to by one name, the city's pedestrian spine,
pronounced *Stroy-et*, is actually a series of five streets: Frederiksbergs-
gade, Nygade, Vimmelskaftet, Amagertorv, and Østergade. By midmorning, particularly on Saturday, it is congested with people, baby
strollers, and street performers. Past the swank and trendy—and sometimes flashy and trashy—boutiques of **Frederiksberggade** is the double
square of **Gammeltorv** (Old Square) and **Nytorv** (New Square). In addition to shopping, you can enjoy Strøget for strolling, as hundreds do. In
summer the sidewalks have a festive street-fair atmosphere.

C **Tivoli.** Copenhagen's best-known attraction draws an astounding num-
FodorsChoice ber of visitors: 4 million people from mid-April to mid-September and
★ from late-November to Christmas. Tivoli is more sophisticated than a
mere amusement park: Among its attractions are a pantomime theater,

an open-air stage, 38 restaurants (some of them very elegant), and frequent concerts. Fantastic flower exhibits color the lush gardens and float on the swan-filled ponds.

The park was established in the 1840s, when Danish architect George Carstensen persuaded a worried King Christian VIII to let him build an amusement park on the edge of the city's fortifications, rationalizing that "when people amuse themselves, they forget politics." On Wednesday and weekend nights, elaborate fireworks are set off, and the Tivoli Guard, a youth version of the Queen's Royal Guard, performs every day.

The **Nimb** (⊠ *Bernstorffsgade 5, Centrum*), accessed from inside the gardens as well as from outside year-round, is a complex dating from 1909. It has Moorish-inspired architecture and was, indeed, once a bazaar. It was also one of the first buildings here to house a restaurant—a place for the jet-set crowd in the 1920s and '30s. A DKr 100-million investment (roughly $20 million) has transformed the building into a multipurpose high-class playground, with a luxury all-suite hotel, a bar, a gourmet restaurant, a bistro, a dairy, a chocolate factory, and a well-stocked wine cellar. ⊠ *Vesterbrog. 3, Centrum (on border of Vesterbro district)* ☎ *33/15–10–01* ⊕ *www.tivoli.dk* ⊠ *Grounds DKr 95, unlimited ride pass DKr 205* ☉ *Mid-Apr.–mid-Sept., Sun.–Wed. 11–11, Fri. 11 AM–12:30 AM, Sat. 11 AM–midnight.*

**OFF THE BEATEN PATH**

**Museet for Moderne Kunst** (*Arken*). The museum, 20 km (12 mi) southwest of Copenhagen, also known as the Arken, opened in March 1996 to great acclaim, both for its architecture and its collection. The museum's massive sculpture room exhibits both modern Danish and international art, as well as experimental works. Dance, theater, film, and multimedia exhibits are additional attractions. To reach the museum, take the S-train in the direction of either Hundige, Solrød Strand, or Køge to Ishøj Station, then pick up Bus 128 to the museum. ⊠ *Skovvej 100, Ishøj* ☎ *43/54–02–22* ⊕ *www.arken.dk* ⊠ *DKr 85* ☉ *Tues.–Sun. 10–5, Wed. 10–9.*

## SHOPPING

A showcase for world-famous Danish design and craftsmanship, Copenhagen seems to have been designed with shoppers in mind. The best buys are such luxury items as crystal, porcelain, silver, and furs. Although prices are inflated by a hefty 25% Value-Added Tax (Danes call it MOMS), non-European Union citizens can receive about an 18% refund. For more details and a list of all tax-free shops, ask at the tourist office for a copy of the *Tax-Free Shopping Guide.*

The pedestrian-only **Strøget** and adjacent Købmagergade are *the* shopping streets. The most exclusive shops are at the end of Strøget, around Kongens Nytorv, and on Ny Adelgade, Grønnegade, and Pistolstræde. **Kronprinsensgade** has become the in-vogue fashion strip. **Bredgade,** just off Kongens Nytorv, is lined with elegant antiques and silver shops, and furniture stores. A popular mall in the city is the gleaming **Fisketorvet Shopping Center,** built in what was Copenhagen's old fish market.

It includes 100 shops. It's near the canal, south of the city center, and within walking distance of Dybbølsbro Station.

**Birger Christensen.** This company is a purveyor to the royal family and Copenhagen's finest furrier. Denmark, the world's biggest producer of ranched minks, is the place to go for quality furs. ⊠ *Østerg. 38, Downtown* ☎ *33/11–55–55* ⊕ *www.birger-christensen.com.*

**Bodum Hus.** This company's retail showroom displays a wide variety of reasonably priced Danish-designed functional, and especially kitchen-oriented, accoutrements. ⊠ *Østerg. 10, on Strøget, Downtown* ☎ *33/36–40–80* ⊕ *www.bodum.com.*

**Georg Jensen.** One of the most-recognized names in international silver has an elegant, austere shop aglitter with sterling. ⊠ *Amagertorv 4, Downtown* ☎ *33/11–40–80* ⊕ *www.georgjensen.com.*

**Illums Bolighus.** Part gallery, part department store, this store shows off cutting-edge Danish and international design—art glass, porcelain, silverware, carpets, and loads of grown-up toys. ⊠ *Amagertorv 10, Downtown* ☎ *33/14–19–41* ⊕ *www.illumsbolighus.com.*

**Information Center for Danish Crafts and Design.** This center provides helpful information on the city's galleries, shops, and workshops specializing in Danish crafts and design, from jewelry to ceramics to wooden toys to furniture. Its Web site has listings and reviews of the city's best crafts shops. ⊠ *Amagertorv 1, Downtown* ☎ *33/12–61–62* ⊕ *www. danishcrafts.dk.*

**Royal Copenhagen.** This factory outlet sells firsts and seconds of its famous porcelain ware. ⊠ *Amagertorv 6, Downtown* ☎ *33/13–71–81* ⊕ *www.royalcopenhagen.com.*

## WHERE TO EAT

**$$**
**Fodor's Choice**
★
✕ **Ida Davidsen.** Five generations old, this world-renowned lunch spot is synonymous with smørrebrød. Creative sandwiches include the H. C. Andersen, with liver pâté, bacon, and tomatoes. The terrific smoked duck is smoked by the family, and served alongside a horseradish-spiked cabbage salad. ⊠ *Store Kongensg. 70, Sankt Annæ Kvarter* ☎ *33/91–36–55* ⊕ *www.idadavidsen.dk* ⩔ *Reservations essential* ▭ *AE, DC, MC, V* ⊗ *Closed weekends and Dec. 23– Jan 16. No dinner.*

**$**
CAFÉ
**Fodor's Choice**
★
✕ **The Royal Café.** Tucked between the Royal Copenhagen and Georg Jensen shops, this eatery is part Danish design museum, part shop, and part café. High ceilings, Holmegaard glass chandeliers, and a whimsical mural evoke *Alice's Adventures in Wonderland*. Created in collaboration with design legends like Fritz Hansen, Arne Jacobsen, Royal Copenhagen, and Bang & Olufsen, the café is truly a showcase for what is quintessentially Danish. It's perhaps most known for its modern twist on traditional smørrebrød called "smushi." The staff delicately assembles these artful, sushi-ish–size, open-face sandwiches, and a pastry and cake bar tempts sweet tooths. ⊠ *Amagertorv 6, Centrum* ☎ *38/14–95–27* ⊕ *www.theroyalcafe.dk* ⩔ *Reservations not accepted* ▭ *AE, DC, MC, V* ⊗ *No dinner Sun.*

## WHERE TO STAY

**$$$** 🔲 **Copenhagen Marriott Hotel.** This large Marriott on the waterfront is a well-oiled machine. However, the great view of the canal and Christianshavn through floor-to-ceiling windows is the only indication you're in Copenhagen, let alone Denmark. It has superior business and conference facilities and great fitness facilities with separate sauna and steam rooms for men and women. Rooms are comfortable and of a good size. **Pros:** all rooms have both tub and shower combo and either city or canal-side views. **Cons:** no restaurants nearby; small windows in the rooms, slightly institutionalized. ⊠ *Kalvebod Brygge 5, Centrum* 🖾 *88/33–99–00* ⊕ *www.marriott.com/cphdk* 🕾 *383 rooms, 18 suites* ⚿ *In-room: a/c, safe, Internet. In-hotel: restaurant, room service, bar, gym, laundry service, parking (paid), no-smoking rooms, some pets allowed* 🖃 *AE, DC, MC, V* ⅠⓄⅠ *EP.*

**$$** 🔲 **Copenhagen Strand.** You can't stay closer to the harbor than here. A five-minute walk from Nyhavn, this pleasant hotel is housed in a waterfront warehouse dating from 1869. The cozy lobby has brown leather couches and old maritime pictures on the walls. Rooms are small but comfortable, with traditional-style wooden furnishings, blue color schemes, and sparkling baths. **Pros:** close to city attractions; most bathrooms have both a tub and shower. **Cons:** hotel only serves breakfast; tight quarters; morning street noise. ⊠ *Havneg. 37, Centrum* 🖾 *33/48–99–00* ⊕ *www.copenhagenstrand.dk* 🕾 *174 rooms, 2 suites* ⚿ *In-room: Internet. In-hotel: bar, laundry service, Internet terminal, no-smoking rooms, some pets allowed* 🖃 *AE, DC, MC, V* ⅠⓄⅠ *BP.*

**$$$$** 🔲 **Hotel D'Angleterre.** The famed 250-year-old hotel welcomes royalty,

**Fodor's Choice** politicians, and rock stars—from Margaret Thatcher to Madonna. An

★ imposing New Georgian facade leads into an English-style sitting room. Standard guest rooms are individually decorated, many in pastels with overstuffed chairs and a mix of modern and antique furniture. The spit-and-polish staff accommodates every wish. The elegant Restaurant D'Angleterre serves excellent French cuisine. In winter the square in front of the hotel is converted into a skating rink. **Pros:** superb location; rich in history; full-service spa; large fitness center; decent quality restaurant. **Cons:** expensive; formal and straightlaced; some rooms could use a face-lift. ⊠ *Kongens Nytorv 34, Centrum* 🖾 *33/12–00–95* ⊕ *www.dangleterre.com* 🕾 *104 rooms, 19 suites* ⚿ *In-room: a/c, safe, Internet. In-hotel: restaurant, room service, bar, pool, gym, spa, bicycles, laundry service, Internet terminal* 🖃 *AE, DC, MC, V* ⅠⓄⅠ *EP.*

# GDAŃSK, POLAND

Gdańsk is special to Poles—and to Scandinavians and Germans, who visit the region in great numbers. From 1308 to 1945 Gdańsk was an independent city-state called Danzig. In 1997 Gdańsk celebrated its 1,000th year as a Baltic city. It remains well known as the cradle of the anti-Communist workers' movement that came to be known as *Solidarność* (Solidarity)—after the collapse of the Soviet bloc in 1989, Solidarity leader Lech Wałęsa became president of Poland in the nation's first free elections since World War II. Although Gdańsk was almost entirely destroyed during World War II, the streets of its Główne Miasto (Main Town) have been lovingly restored and still retain their historical and cultural richness. The Stare Miasto (Old Town) contains several churches and the beautifully reconstructed Ratusz Główny (Old Town Hall). At the north end of the Old Town sit the shipyards that captivated world attention during the 1970s and '80s but have since undergone a difficult restructuring process. It might be tempting to see its lot as a metaphor to the last few decades of Polish history. Gdańsk is part of the so-called "Tri-city"—the other two of the triplets being Sopot, a fashionable 19th-century resort, and Gdynia, a 1920s, modernist-style port town, where most cruise ships arrive. The three components of the Tri-city are not very far apart, and they are conveniently linked by a suburban rail system (SKM).

## ESSENTIALS

CURRENCY  The Złoty (Zł 3 to US$1; Zł 4 to €1); exchange rates were accurate at this writing but are subject to change. U.S. currency is not accepted, and credit cards are not universally accepted, especially in smaller shops and eateries. ATMs are widespread.

HOURS  Shopping hours are generally weekdays from 7AM until 6 or 7 PM, with shorter hours on the weekend. Museums are typically open Tuesday through Sunday from 10 AM until 4 PM.

INTERNET  **Internet Café** ✉ *ul. Karmelicka 1* ☎ *058/320–9230.*

TELEPHONES  Most international mobile phones (3G included) work in Poland, but do check your roaming charges in advance. Major local telecom companies are Era, Plus, and Orange. It is easy to get a prepaid phone and recharge it as you need it (you can get the cards at mobile operators' shops, newsagents, gas stations, even supermarkets). Due to the fast growth of the mobile network, there are fewer public phones now, but you will still find them. They operate with phone cards, which can be bought at newsstands. Public phones support international calls.

## COMING ASHORE

Most cruise ships arrive at Gdynia, either the Francuskie (French) or Pomorskie (Pomeranian) Quay. The port is within a 20-minute walk (about 1 km) of the SKM (suburban rail) stop, which is right next to the main railway station in Gdynia. This train is the easiest and most economical means of transportation within the Tri-city, and the ride into Gdańsk city center takes about 30 minutes. Taxis are readily available, but a ride between Gdańsk to Gdynia will cost you about 100 złoty.

A few ships arrive in Gdańsk itself. These will dock at two sites in the outer harbor of the city: Oliwskie Quay on the east bank and Westerplatte Quay on the west bank. Both lie 6 km (3.7 mi) from the downtown center. Facilities at Oliwskie Quay, the bigger of the two, include shops and taxi kiosks. It is 1 km (½ mi) to the Oliwa train station for the journey into downtown Gdańsk, or 300 meters to a tram stop (Routes 2, 5, 10, 14, and 15 head into the city). Westerplatte Quay has almost no facilities, with only restrooms and a taxi kiosk. Bus route 106 travels into the city. The downtown core can be easily explored on foot.

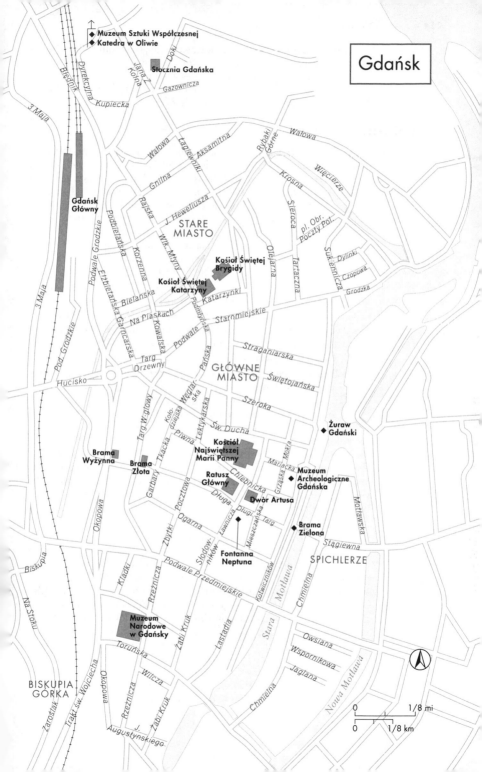

# Gdańsk

- ◆ Muzeum Sztuki Współczesnej
- ◆ Katedra w Oliwie

Stocznia Gdańska

Doki
Jana z Kolna
Gazownicza
Kupiecka
Wałowa
Gnilna
Łagiewniki
Aksamitna
Rybaki Górne
Wałowa
Wieclerze
Krosna
Sieroca
Olejarna
Tartaczna
pl. Obr. Poczty Pol.
Sukiennicza
Dylinki
Czopowa
Grodzka

3 Maja
Biednik
Dyrekcyjna
Podbielańska
Rajska
J. Heweliusza
Wlk. Młyny
STARE MIASTO

Gdańsk Główny

Podwale Grodzkie
Korzenna
Elżbietańska
Bielańska
Garncarska
Na Piaskach
Kowalska
Podwale

**Kościoł Świętej Brygidy**
**Kościoł Świętej Katarzyny**
Katarzynki
Podwójna
Staromicjskie
Straganiarska

3 Maja
Pod. Grodzkie
Hucisko
Targ Drzewny
Pańska
GŁÓWNE MIASTO
Świętojańska
Szeroka
Sw. Ducha

**Brama Wyżynna**
**Brama Złota**
Targ Węglowy
Koło dziejska
Węgiar ska
Lektykarska
Tkacka
Piwna
Garncary
Pocztowa
Chlebnicka
Mariacka
Grząska
Motła
**Żuraw Gdański**

**Kościół Najświętszej Marii Panny**
**Ratusz Główny**
**Dwór Artusa**

**Muzeum Archeologiczne Gdańska**

Okopowa
Zbytki
Ogarna
Długa
Ławnicza
Długi Targ
Mieszczańska
**Brama Zielona**
Motława

Słodowników
Podwale Przedmiejskie
**Fontanna Neptuna**
SPICHLERZE
Kołwiczników
Mottawska
Stągiewna

Biskupia
Na Stoku
Kładki
Rzeźnicza
Żabi Kruk
Lastadia
Stara
Chmielna
Owsiana
Wspornikowa
Jaglana

**Muzeum Narodowe w Gdańsky**
Toruńska

BISKUPIA GÓRKA
Okopowa
Trakt Św. Wojciecha
Wilcza
Rzeźnicza
Żabi Kruk
Chmielna
Nowa Motława

Zaroślak
J. Augustyńskiego

0    1/8 mi
0    1/8 km

Car rentals are not useful for exploring the city, but would allow you to visit the surrounding Pomeranian region. An economy manual vehicle is approximately €63 per day. Companies will pick you up at the port but may add an extra charge. Taxis or limousines can be hired for touring. Taxi rates are Zł 5–Zł 7 at pickup then Zł 3 per km.

## EXPLORING GDAŃSK

★ **Brama Wyżynna** *(High Gate)*. The historic entrance to the old town of Gdańsk is marked by this magnificent Renaissance gate, which marks the beginning of the so-called "Royal Route," along which the king passed through the city on his annual visit. The gate is adorned with the flags of Poland, Gdańsk, and the Prussian kingdom. Its builder, Hans Kramer of Dresden, erected it as a link in the chain of modern fortifications put up to frame the western city borders between 1574 and 1576. The brick gate was renovated and decorated in 1588 by Flemish sculptor Willem van den Blocke, whose decorations you can still see today. ⊠ *Off Wały Jagiellońskie, at ul. Długa, Stare Miasto.*

**Brama Zielona** *(Green Gate)*. The eastern entrance to the medieval city of Gdańsk is at the water's edge. Construction, supervised by Regnier of Amsterdam and Hans Kramer of Dresden, lasted from 1568 to 1571. This 16th-century gate also doubled as a royal residence. Unfortunately, the name no longer fits: the gate is now painted brown. ⊠ *At eastern end of Długi Targ, Stare Miasto.*

**Brama Złota** *(Golden Gate)*. Just behind the Brama Wyżynna, the Golden Gate was the second through which the king passed on the Royal Route. This structure dates from 1614, and combines characteristics of both the Italian and Dutch Renaissance. It was built to the design of Abraham van den Blocke. The stone figures (by Pieter Ringering) along the parapet (on the Wały Jagiellońskie facade) represent allegories of the city's citizen's virtues: Prudence, Justice, Piety, and Concord. On the Długa street facade there are allegories of Peace, freedom, fortune, and fame—the pursuits of Gdańsk city over the centuries. Next to the Golden Gate squats the house of the **St George's Brotherhood**, erected by Glotau between 1487 and 1494 in the late-Gothic style. ⊠ *Off Wały Jagiellońskie, at western end of ul. Długa, Stare Miasto.*

★ **Dwór Artusa** *(Artus Mansion)*. Behind the Fontanna Neptuna on Długi Targ, one of the more significant of the grand houses was constructed over a period from the 15th through the 17th centuries and is now a museum. The mansion was named for mythical English King Arthur, who otherwise has no affiliation with the place. This and the other stately mansions on the Długi Targ are reminders of the traders and aristocrats who once resided in this posh district. The court's elegant interior houses a huge, 40-foot-high Renaissance tiled stove, possibly the world's largest, a mid-16th-century masterpiece by George Stelzener. The mansion's collection also includes Renaissance furnishings, paintings, and holy figures. The building was the meeting place of the Gdańsk city nobles. ⊠ *Długi Targ 43, Stare Miasto* ☎ *058/346–33–58* 🔖 *Zł 10* ⊙ *Mon. 11–3, Tues.–Sat. 10–6, Sun. 11–6.*

🕐 **Fontanna Neptuna** *(Neptune Foun-*
**Fodor's Choice** *tain).* One of the city's most distinc-
★ tive landmarks is the elaborately
gilded, 17th-century fountain at
the western end of Długi Targ.
The fountain itself is perhaps the
best-known symbol of Gdańsk,
emphasizing its bond with the sea.
It was sculpted by Peter Husen and
Johann Rogge. The general conceptual design was developed by
Abraham van den Blocke. The magnificent surrounding fencing was
added in 1634. Between 1757 and
1761 Johann Karl Stender remade
the fountain chalice and plinth in
the rococo style and added a whole
array of sea creatures. ⊠ *ul. Długa,
east of Wały Jagiellońskie, Stare
Miasto.*

5

**Fodor's Choice** **Katedra w Oliwie** *(Oliwa Cathedral).*
★ The district of Oliwa, northwest of the Old Town, is worth visiting if
only for its magnificent cathedral complex. Originally part of a Cistercian monastery, the church was erected during the 13th century. Like
most other structures in Poland, it has been rebuilt many times, resulting in a hodgepodge of styles from Gothic to Renaissance to rococo.
The cathedral houses one of the most impressive rococo organs you're
ever likely to hear—and see. It has more than 6,000 pipes, and when a
special mechanism is activated, wooden angels ring bells and a wooden
star climbs up a wooden sky. Demonstrations of the organ and a brief
narrated church history are given almost hourly on weekdays in summer
(May through September), less frequently on weekends and the rest of
the year. ⊠ *ul. Cysterów 10, Oliwa.*

**Fodor's Choice** **Kościół Najświętszej Marii Panny** *(St. Mary's Church).* The largest brick
★ church in the world—and the largest church of any kind in Poland—St.
Mary's is on the north side of ulica Piwna. The sanctuary can accommodate 25,000 people. This enormous 14th-century church underwent
major restoration after World War II. Although it originally held 22
altars, 15 of them have been relocated to museums in Gdańsk and War-
saw. The highlight of a visit is the climb up the hundreds of steps to
the top of the church tower. The church also contains a 500-year-old,
25-foot-high astronomical clock that has only recently been restored to
working order after years of neglect. It keeps track of solar and lunar
progressions, and it displays the signs of the zodiac, something of an
anomaly in a Catholic church. ⊠ *Podkramarska 5, at ul. Piwna, Stare
Miasto* 🎟 *Tower Zł 3* ⊙ *Daily 9–5.*

**Kościół świętej Brygidy** *(St. Brigitte's Church).* This church, a few blocks
north of the shipyards, is a prime example of the fundamental link in the
Polish consciousness between Catholicism and political dissent. After
the Communist government declared martial law in 1981 in an attempt

to force Solidarity to disband, the union's members began meeting here secretly during celebrations of mass. A statue of Pope John Paul II can be seen in front of the church. At this writing, renovation of the façade and the tower had begun. ⊠ *ul. Profesorska 17, near Ratusz Główny (Old Town Hall), Stare Miasto.*

**Kościół świętej Katarzyny** *(St. Catherine's Church).* The former parish church in Gdańsk's Old Town is supposedly the oldest church in the city: its construction was begun in the 1220s; the tower was constructed in the 1480s; the carillon of 37 bells was added in 1634. The 17th-century astronomer Jan Hevelius is buried in the presbytery of the church, below which lies what's left of the town's oldest Christian cemetery (which dates from the 10th century). ⊠ *Wielki Młyn, Stare Miasto* ☎ *058/301–15–95.*

**Muzeum Archeologiczne Gdańska** *(Gdańsk Archaeological Museum).* Gdańsk's small archaeological museum displays Slavic tribal artifacts, including jewelry, pottery, boats, and bones. ⊠ *ul. Mariacka 25–26, Stare Miasto* ☎ *058/322–21–00* ☜ *Zł 6* ☉ *Tues.–Sun. 10–4.*

★ **Muzeum Narodowe w Gdańsku** *(National Museum in Gdańsk).* The former Franciscan monastery, just south of the old walls of the Main Town, exhibits 14th- to 20th-century art and ethnographic collections. Hans Memling's triptych *Last Judgment* is the jewel of the collection. ⊠ *ul. Toruńska 1, off ul. Okopowa, Stare Miasto* ☎ *058/301–70–61* ☜ *Zł 10, free Sun.* ☉ *Daily 10–3.*

**Muzeum Sztuki Współczesnej** *(Modern Art Museum).* Two museums can be found in a beautiful park surrounding the cathedral in Oliwa in the former Abbots' Palace. The Modern Art Museum has a large collection of works by Polish artists from the inter-war period onward. Connected to the Modern Art Museum, administratively and physically, is the **Muzeum Etnograficzne** *(Ethnographic Museum)* (⊠ *ul. Opacka 12, Oliwa* ☎ *058/552–12–71*), in the former Abbots' Granary. The museum display has fine examples of local crafts from the 19th century and also has an interesting display of amber folk jewelry. It has a separate entrance from the Modern Art Museum and a separate admission fee (Zł 8), but the hours and other contact information are the same for both museums. ⊠ *Pałac Opatów, Cystersów 15A, Oliwa* ☎ *058/552– 12–71* ⊕ *www.muzeum.narodowe.gda.pl* ☜ *Zł 10* ☉ *Tues.–Sun. 9–4.*

★ **Ratusz Główny** *(Old Town Hall).* Although Gdańsk's original town hall was completely destroyed during World War II, a careful reconstruction of the exterior and interior now re-creates the glory of Gdańsk's medieval past. During the summer season the tower is accessible to visitors and well worth climbing for the view. Inside, the **Muzeum Historii Miasta Gdańska** *(Gdańsk Historical Museum)* covers more than five centuries of Gdańsk's history in exhibits that include paintings, sculptures, and weapons. ⊠ *ul. Długa 47, Stare Miasto* ☎ *058/301–48–72* ☜ *Museum Zł 10* ☉ *Tues.–Sun. 11–4.*

Fodor'sChoice **Stocznia Gdańska** *(Gdańsk Shipyard).* Three huge and somber crosses
★ perpetually draped with flowers stand outside the gates of the former Lenin Shipyards, which gave birth to the Solidarity movement. The crosses outside the entrance to the shipyards are the **Pomnik Poległych**

Stoczniowców *(Monument to Fallen Shipyard Workers)*. There are also plaques that commemorate the struggle, and a quotation by Pope John Paul II inspired by his visit to the monument in 1987: "The Grace of God could not have created anything better; in this place, silence is a scream." Formerly inside the shipyard gates (and now a bit further away), the **Roads to Freedom** exhibition once consisted of a number of symbolic gates, which until recently led to a multimedia exhibition in the historic BPH room on Plac Solidarności, where the Gdańsk Agreements were signed. The BPH room, which has been renovated, reopened in 2007 in a new location at Wały Piastowskie Street (a short walk from the shipyard itself, halfway between the shipyards and the Main Railway Station). The exhibition traces the beginning and development of the Solidarity movement, taking you on a virtual tour through 1980s Poland. ⊠ *Wały Piastowskie 24, Stare Miasto* ☎ *058/308–43–19* ⊕ *www.ecs.gda.pl* ⊠ *Zł 6* ⊘ *Oct.–Apr., Tues.–Sun. 10–5; May–Sept., Tues.–Sun. 10–6.*

**Żuraw Gdański** *(Harbor Crane)*. Built in 1444, Gdańsk's crane was medieval Europe's largest—and today it's also Europe's oldest. It used to play the double role of a port crane and city gate. The structure was given its present shape between 1442 and 1444. Today it houses the **Muzeum Morskie** *(Maritime Museum)*, with a collection of models of the ships constructed in the Gdańsk Shipyards since 1945. At the museum ticket office, inquire about tickets for tours of the *Sołdek*, a World War II battleship moored nearby on the canal. ⊠ *Ołowianka 9–13, Stare Miasto* ☎ *058/301–86–11* ⊠ *Zł 8* ⊘ *Oct.–June, Tues.–Sun. 10–3; July–Sept., daily 10–4.*

## SHOPPING

Gdańsk's main souvenir product is amber, sold carved or made into jewelry.

**Wielki Młyn** *(Great Mill)*. On a small island in the canal just north of St. Catherine's Church, the largest mill in medieval Europe operated from the time of its completion in 1350 until 1945. Today it's filled with shops and boutiques. ⊠ *Intersection of Podmłyńska and Na Piaskach, Stare Miasto* ⊘ *Boutiques weekdays 10–7, Sat. 10–4.*

## WHERE TO EAT

¢–$ ✕ **Barracuda.** Although the interior may be rather simple, most people
SEAFOOD agree that this is one of the best restaurants in Gdańsk. The menu offers
★ a tempting array of seafood dishes, which are the specialties of the house. No matter which you choose, you won't go wrong. ⊠ *ul. Piwna 61/63, Stare Miasto* ☎ *058/301–49–62* ☰ *AE, DC, MC, V.*

¢–$ ✕ **Czerwone Drzwi.** Behind the red door (that's what "Czerwone Drzwi"
POLISH means in Polish) is an elegant café-cum-restaurant, a favorite with Gdańsk's fashionable people (with well-stocked wallets). The menu changes with the seasons. ⊠ *ul. Piwna 52/53, Stare Miasto* ☎ *058/301–57–64* ☰ *AE, DC, MC, V.*

# HAMBURG, GERMANY

Water—in the form of the Alster Lakes and the Elbe River—is Hamburg's defining feature and the key to the city's success. A harbor city with an international past, Hamburg is the most tolerant and openminded of German cities. The media have made Hamburg their capital. Add to that the slick world of advertising and you have a populace of worldly and fashionable professionals. Not surprisingly, the city of movers and shakers is also the city with most of Germany's millionaires. Hamburg has been a major port for more than 1,000 years, but it reached the crest of its power during the 19th century. What you see today is the "new" Hamburg. World War II bombing raids destroyed more than half of the city. In spite of the 1940–44 raids, Hamburg now stands as a remarkably faithful replica of that glittering prewar city—a place of enormous style, verve, and elegance, with considerable architectural diversity, including turn-of-the-20th-century art nouveau buildings.

## ESSENTIALS

CURRENCY  The Euro (€1 to US$1.39 at this writing). ATMs are common.

HOURS  Stores are open Monday through Saturday from 8 AM until 8 PM. Museum hours vary, but core hours are 10 AM until 5 PM, with shorter opening on Sundays. Some state museums are closed on Monday.

INTERNET  **Saturn Internet Café** (⌧ *Mönckebergstrasse 1* ☏ *040/3038–2534* ⊕ *www.saturn-internetcafe.de*) is a specialty coffeehouse with Wi-Fi connectivity in addition to computer stations. Closed Sunday.

TELEPHONES  Tri- and quad-band GSM phones should work in Germany, where the mobile system supports 3G technology. Phone cards for public phones are available at newsagents and will allow international calls. Major companies include Vodafone, T2, and T-Mobile.

## COMING ASHORE

Hamburg is constructing a state-of-the-art cruise port and terminal as part of the regeneration of the Überseequartier district and surrounding HafenCity (a totally new city district). This is due to be completed in 2012, and will give the city extensive cruise capacity. The main terminal, to be known as HafnCity 2012, will have a hotel, restaurants, and direct metro access to downtown.

The older Hafn City Terminal is currently the main welcome terminal for cruise passenegers. It has a Welcome Center and a café. Public bus access is a short stroll through the terminal exit gate. Altona Terminal is a modern structure that provides facilities including shops and an information desk, but at present there are no cafés or restaurants. There is a bus stop for public transport into downtown Hamburg. Although city attractions are not far from the terminals, it would be sensible to take transportation to the attractions rather than walking, due to the heavy construction going on in the area.

Passengers exploring the city will find no benefit in renting a car; in fact, many major attractions are within walking distance of each other. But if you want to explore the area by car, a car rental costs €51 for a compact manual vehicle. Taxi meters start at €2.90, and the fare is €1.60 per km (½ mi) for the first 5 km, €1.40 for between 5 and 10 km and

€1.25 for each km thereafter. Waiting time is €22.50 per hour. You can hail taxis on the street or at stands, or order one by phone.

The HVV, Hamburg's public transportation system, includes the U-bahn (subway), the S-bahn (suburban train), and buses. At this writing, a one-way fare starts at €2.40 for a one-zone ticket covers *one* unlimited ride in the Hamburg inner-city area. Tickets are available on all buses and at automatic machines in all stations and at most bus stops. A *Single-Tageskarte* (all-day ticket) for the inner-city districts, valid until 6 AM the next day, costs €5.20. If you're traveling with family or friends, a *Partner Day Ticket* (group or family ticket) is a good value—a group of up to five adults (children count as half an adult) can travel for the entire day for €9.40–€18.80 (depending on the number of fare zones the ticket covers).

## EXPLORING HAMBURG

**Alster** *(Alster Lakes)*. These twin lakes provide downtown Hamburg with one of its most memorable vistas. The two lakes meet at the Lombard and Kennedy bridges. In summer the boat landing at the Jungfernstieg, below the Alsterpavillion, is the starting point for the *Alsterdampfer*, the flat-bottom passenger boats that traverse the lakes. Small sailboats and rowboats, hired from yards on the shores of the Alster, are very much a part of the summer scene.

From April through October, Alster Touristik operates boat trips around the Alster Lakes and through the canals. There are two tour options; both leave from the Jungfernstieg promenade in the city center. The Aussenalster 50-minute lake tour (Alster-Rundfahrt) costs €11 and leaves every half hour, May through October 3, daily from 10 to 6. A two-hour-long *Fleet-Fahrt* costs €16.50, and explores the canals of the historic Speicherstadt (April through October, daily at 10:45, 1:45, and 4:45). From May through September there's also the romantic twilight tour, called Dämmertour, every evening (Wednesday through Saturday in September) at 8 (€16.50). Ⓜ *Jungfernstieg (U-bahn)*.

★ **Deichstrasse.** The oldest residential area in Hamburg's Old Town, which dates from the 14th century, now consists of lavishly restored houses from the 17th through the 19th centuries. Many of the original houses on Deichstrasse were destroyed in the Great Fire of 1842, which broke out in No. 42 and left approximately 20,000 people homeless; only a few of the early dwellings escaped its ravages. Today Deichstrasse and neighboring **Peterstrasse** (just south of Ost-West-Strasse) are of great historical interest. At No. 39 Peterstrasse, for example, is the baroque facade of the Beylingstift complex, built in 1700. Farther along, No. 27, constructed as a warehouse in 1780, is the oldest of its kind in Hamburg. All the buildings in the area have been painstakingly restored, thanks largely to the efforts of individuals. ✉ *Altstadt* Ⓜ *Rödingsmarkt (U-bahn)*.

☼ **Hagenbecks Tierpark** *(Hagenbecks Zoo)*. One of the country's oldest and
★ most popular zoos is family owned. Founded in 1848, it was the world's first city park to let wild animals such as lions, elephants, chimpanzees, and others roam freely in vast, open-air corrals. Weather permitting, you can ride one of the elephants. In the Troparium, an artificial habitat

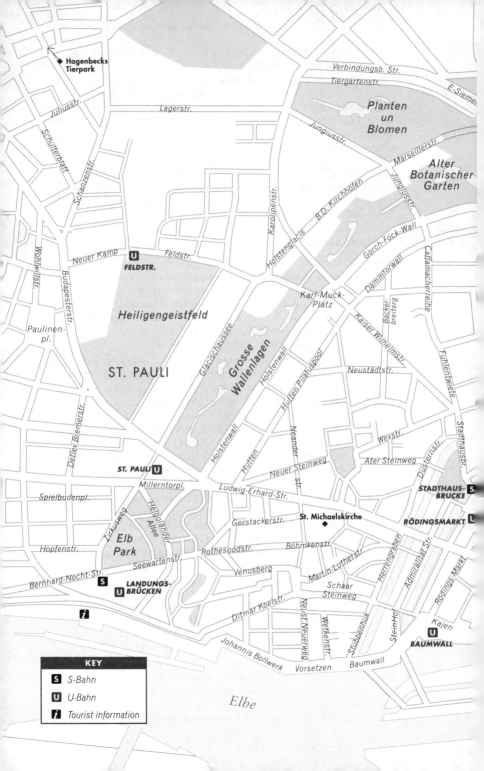

creates a rain forest, an African desert, and a tropical sea. ✉ *Lokstedter Str. at Hamburg-Stellingen, Niendorf* ☎ *040/530–0330* ⊕ *www. hagenbeck.de* 🖾 *€16* ⊙ *Mar.–June, daily 9–6; July and Aug., daily 9–7; Sept. and Oct., daily 9–6; Nov.– Feb., daily 9–4:30* Ⓜ *Hagenbecks Tierpark (U-bahn).*

★ **Jungfernstieg.** This wide promenade looking out over the Alster Lakes is the city's premier shopping boulevard. Laid out in 1665, it used to be part of a muddy millrace that channeled water into the Elbe. Hidden from view behind the sedate facade of Jungfernstieg is a network of nine covered arcades that together account for almost a mile of shops selling everything from souvenirs to haute couture. Many of these air-conditioned passages have sprung up in the past two decades, but some have been here since the 19th century; the first glass-covered arcade, called Sillem's Bazaar, was built in 1845. ✉ *Neustadt* Ⓜ *Jungfernstieg (U-bahn).*

★ **Kunsthalle** *(Art Gallery).* One of the most important art museums in Germany, the Kunsthalle has 3,000 paintings, 400 sculptures, and a coin and medal collection that dates from the 14th century. In the postmodern, cube-shape building designed by Berlin architect O. M. Ungers, the **Galerie der Gegenwart** has housed a collection of international modern art since 1960, including works by Andy Warhol, Joseph Beuys, Georg Baselitz, and David Hockney. Graphic art is well-represented, with a special collection of works by Pablo Picasso and the late Hamburg artist Horst Janssen, famous for his satirical worldview. In the old wing you can view works by local artists dating from the 16th century. The outstanding collection of German Romantic paintings includes works by Runge, Friedrich, and Spitzweg. Paintings by Holbein, Rembrandt, Van Dyck, Tiepolo, and Canaletto are also on view, while late-19th-century impressionism is represented in works by Leibl, Liebermann, Manet, Monet, and Renoir. ✉ *Glockengiesserwall, Altstadt* ☎ *040/4281–31200* ⊕ *www.hamburger-kunsthalle.de* 🖾 *Permanent and special exhibits €10, children under 18 free* ⊙ *Tues., Wed., and Fri.–Sun., 10–6, Thurs. 10–9* Ⓜ *Hauptbahnhof (U-bahn).*

**Fodor'sChoice** **Rathaus** *(Town Hall).* To most Hamburgers this large building is the
★ symbolic heart of the city. As a city-state—an independent city and simultaneously one of the 16 federal states of Germany—Hamburg has a city council and a state government, both of which have their administrative headquarters in the Rathaus. A pompous neo-Renaissance affair, the building dictates political decorum in the city. To this day, the mayor of Hamburg never welcomes VIPs at the foot of its staircase but always awaits them at the very top—whether it's a president or the queen of England.

The immense building, with its 647 rooms (6 more than Buckingham Palace) and imposing central clock tower, is not the most graceful structure in the city, but the sheer opulence of its interior is astonishing. A 45-minute tour begins in the ground-floor Rathausdiele, a vast pillared hall. Although you can only view the state rooms, their tapestries, huge staircases, glittering chandeliers, coffered ceilings, and grand portraits give you a sense of the city's great wealth in the 19th century and its understandable civic pride. ✉ *Rathausmarkt, Altstadt* ☎ *040/428–310* ⊕ *www.hamburgische-buergerschaft.de* ✍ *English-language tour €3* ☉ *Hourly tours on demand in English Mon.–Thurs. 10:15–3:15, Fri.– Sun. 10:15–1:15* Ⓜ *Mönckebergstr. (U-bahn).*

★ **St. Jacobikirche** *(St. James's Church).* This 13th-century church was almost completely destroyed during World War II. Only the furnishings survived, and reconstruction was completed in 1962. The interior is not to be missed—it houses such treasures as the vast baroque organ on which Bach played in 1720 and three Gothic altars from the 15th and 16th centuries. ✉ *Jacobikirchhof 22, at Steinstr., Altstadt* ☎ *040/303–7370* ⊕ *www.jacobus.de* ☉ *Apr.–Sept., Mon.–Sat. 10–5, Sun.10 AM–11 AM; Oct.–Mar., Mon.–Sat. 11–5; tour of organ Thurs. at noon* Ⓜ *Mönckebergstr. (U-bahn).*

**Fodor's**Choice
★ **St. Michaeliskirche** *(St. Michael's Church).* The Michael, as it's called locally, is Hamburg's principal church and northern Germany's finest baroque-style ecclesiastical building. Constructed between 1649 and 1661 (the tower followed in 1669), it was razed after lightning struck almost a century later. It was rebuilt between 1750 and 1786 in the decorative Nordic baroque style but was gutted by a terrible fire in 1906. The replica, completed in 1912, was demolished during World War II. The present church is a reconstruction.

The distinctive 433-foot brick-and-iron tower bears the largest tower clock in Germany, 26 feet in diameter. Just above the clock is a viewing platform (accessible by elevator or stairs) that affords a magnificent panorama of the city, the Elbe River, and the Alster Lakes. ■ TIP→ **Twice a day, at 10 AM and 9 PM (Sunday at noon), a watchman plays a trumpet solo from the tower platform, and during festivals an entire wind ensemble crowds onto the platform to perform.** The **Multivisionsshow** (slide and audio show), one floor beneath the viewing platform, recounts Hamburg's history on a 16-foot screen. ✉ *St. Michaeliskirche, Englische Planke 1, Altstadt* ☎ *040/376–780* ⊕ *www.st-michaelis.de* ✍ *Tower €3.50; crypt and show €3; show, tower, and crypt €5* ☉ *May–Oct., 9–7:30; Nov.–Apr., daily 10–5:30; multimedia screening Thurs. and weekends on the half hr 12:30–3:30* Ⓜ *Landungsbrücken, Rödingsmarkt (U-bahn).*

**Fodor's**Choice
★ **Speicherstadt** *(Warehouse District).* These imposing warehouses in the Freihafen Hamburg reveal yet another aspect of Hamburg's extraordinary architectural diversity. A Gothic influence is apparent here, with a rich overlay of gables, turrets, and decorative outlines. These massive rust-brown buildings are still used to store and process every conceivable commodity, from coffee and spices to raw silks and handwoven oriental carpets. Although you won't be able to enter the buildings,

5

the nonstop comings and goings will give you a good sense of a port at work. If you want to learn about the history and architecture of the old warehouses, detour to the **Speicherstadtmuseum.** ⊠ *St. Annenufer 2, Block R, Speicherstadt* ☎ *040/321–191* ⊕ *www.speicherstadtmuseum. de* 🖃 *€3* ⊘ *Apr.–Oct., Tues.–Fri. 10–5, weekends 10–6; Nov.–Mar., Tues.–Sun. 10–5* Ⓜ *Messberg (U-bahn).*

## SHOPPING

Hamburg's shopping districts are among the most elegant on the continent, and the city has Europe's largest expanse of covered shopping arcades, most of them packed with small, exclusive boutiques. The streets **Grosse Bleichen** and **Neuer Wall**, which lead off Jungfernstieg, are a high-price-tag zone. The Grosse Bleichen leads to six of the city's most important covered (or indoor) malls, many of which are connected. The marble-clad **Galleria** is modeled after London's Burlington Arcade. Daylight streams through the immense glass ceilings of the **Hanse-Viertel,** an otherwise ordinary reddish-brown brick building. The **Kaufmannshaus,** also known as the Commercie, and the upscale (and former first-class hotel) **Hamburger Hof** are two of the oldest and most fashionable indoor malls. There are also the **Alte Post** and the **Bleichenhof,** while over-the-top, stunningly designed **Europa Passage** is the city's latest arrival on the luxury shopping mall scene.

Some of the country's premier designers, such as Karl Lagerfeld, Jil Sander, and Wolfgang Joop, are native Hamburgers, or at least worked here for quite some time, so high-class fashion is well in evidence. For souvenirs, the most famous must-buys are *Buddelschiffe* (ships in bottles) and other maritime memorabilia.

Hamburg's premier shopping street, **Jungfernstieg,** is just about the most expensive in the country. It's lined with jewelers' shops—Wempe, Brahmfeld & Guttruf, and Hintze are the top names—and chic clothing boutiques such as Linette, Ursula Aust, Selbach, Windmöller, and Jäger & Koch. In the fashionable **Pöseldorf** district north of downtown, take a look at Milchstrasse and Mittelweg. Both are filled with small boutiques, restaurants, and cafés. Running from the main train station to Gerhard-Hauptmann-Platz, the boulevard **Spitalerstrasse** is a pedestrian-only street lined with stores. ■ TIP➜ **Prices here are noticeably lower than those on Jungfernstieg.**

**Antik-Center.** This assortment of 39 shops is in the old market hall, close to the main train station, and features a wide variety of antiques from all periods. ⊠ *Klosterwall 9–21, Altstadt* ☎ *172/400–4011* ⊕ *www.antik-center-hamburg.de.*

**Binikowski.** This store specializes in *Buddelschiffe.* There are few better places to shop for one, or for a blue-and-white-stripe sailor's shirt, a sea captain's hat, ship models, or even ships' charts. ⊠ *Lokstedter Weg 68, Eppendorf* ☎ *040/462–852 or 040/4607–1848.*

## WHERE TO EAT

**$$**  ✕ **Rive.** This harborside oyster bar is a Hamburg establishment, known
**GERMAN** for both its German nouvelle cuisine and its classic local fare. Choose
from among dishes such as hearty *Matjes mit drei Saucen* (herring
with three sauces) or *Dorade in der Salzkruste* (dorado fried in salt
crust). Media types come to this shiplike building for the fresh oysters,
clams, and spectacular view. There's a special weekday lunch menu with
items for around €15. ⊠ *Van der Smissen Str. 1, Kreuzfahrt-Center,
Altona* ☎ *040/380–5919* ⊕ *www.rive.de* ⚓ *Reservations essential* ⊟ *AE*
Ⓜ *Königstr. (S-bahn).*

**$$**  ✕ **River-Kasematten.** There is no other restaurant in town that better
**ECLECTIC** embodies Hamburg's international spirit and its lust for style, enter-
★ tainment, and good seafood. Once a legendary jazz club with performances by Ella Fitzgerald and the like, it now hosts a fascinating mix
of hip guests. Sushi, spiced-up regional fish dishes, and exotic soups
are the order of the day. The lunch buffet (weekdays noon–3) for just
€9.90 is a steal; it's even better on the outside terrace. Nighthawks
love the late-night menu (midnight–4 AM). The ambience—black oak
floors, leather seats, and redbrick walls—is elegant yet casual. ⊠ *Fis-
chmarkt 28–32, St. Pauli* ☎ *040/892–760* ⊕ *www.river-kasematten.de*
⚓ *Reservations essential* ⊟ *AE, DC, MC, V* Ⓜ *Reeperbahn or Landungsbrücken (U-bahn).*

# HELSINKI, FINLAND

A city of the sea, Helsinki was built along a series of oddly shaped peninsulas and islands jutting into the Gulf of Finland. Nature dictates life
in this Nordic land, where winter brings perpetual darkness, and summer perpetual light. A disastrous fire in the early 1800s destroyed many
of Helsinki's traditional wooden structures, and as a result, Helsinki
has some of the purest neoclassical architecture in the world. Add to
this foundation the influence of Stockholm and St. Petersburg sprinkled
with the local inspiration of 20th-century Finnish design, and the result
is a European capital city that is as architecturally eye-catching as it is
distinct. Today Helsinki is still a meeting point of eastern and western
Europe, a fact reflected in its cosmopolitan image, its influx of Russians
and Estonians, and its generally multilingual population. Outdoor summer bars (*terrassit*, as the locals call them) and cafés in the city center
are perfect for people-watching on a summer afternoon.

## ESSENTIALS

**CURRENCY**  The euro (€1 is US$1.39). ATMs are common and credit cards are
widely accepted.

**HOURS**  Smaller stores are generally open weekdays from 9 to 6 and Saturday
from 9 to 1; larger department stores are open until 9 weekdays and
until 6 on Saturday. Stores are often open on Sunday from June through
August and during December. The majority of museums are closed on
Monday.

**INTERNET**  You'll find Internet access in the Hernesaari Port cruise terminal building in the West Harbour and at Olympic Quay in the South Harbour.

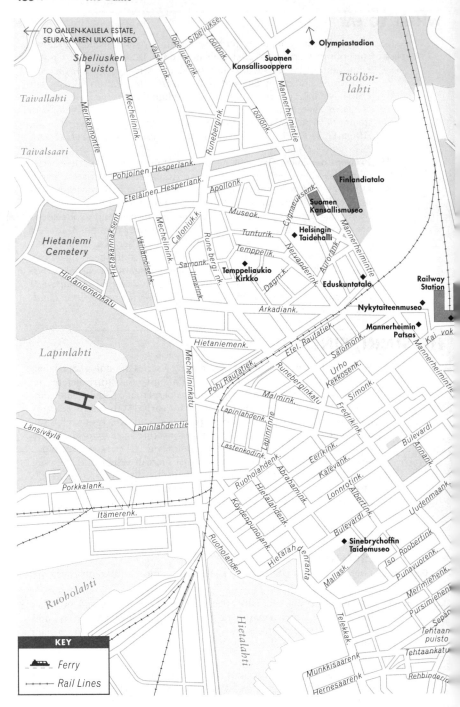

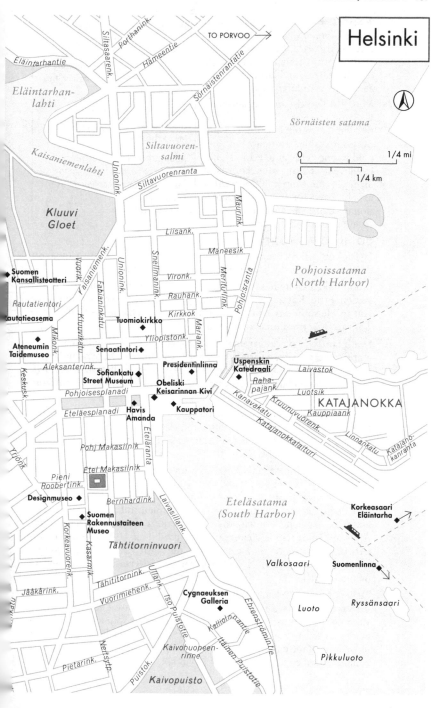

# Helsinki

**Robert's Coffee** (✉ *Aleksanterinkatu 21, Kaytava* ☎ *09/6228–1960* ⊕ *www.robertscoffee.com*) is a stylish spot offering a huge range of coffees, teas, and hot chocolates, as well as computer terminals.

TELEPHONES    Most tri-band and quad-band GSM phones work in Finland, but the Finnish mobile system is not 3G-compatible. You can buy pre-paid phone cards at telecom shops, news vendors and tobacconists in all towns and cities. Phone cards can be used for local or international calls. Major companies include Elisa and Finnish 2G.

---

### HELSINKI BEST BETS

**Temppeliaukio Kirkko.** This church, seemingly rising out of living rock, pushes the boundaries of architecture.

**Senaatintori.** The symmetry of this neoclassical city square is a joy to the eye.

**Kauppatori.** Enjoy a steaming cup of coffee while browsing in the market or immersing yourself in daily life.

---

## COMING ASHORE

Helsinki is a busy cruise destination, and sees many ships throughout the season. Ships dock at one of three distinct areas.

Katajanokka Quay has a terminal with souvenir shop, toilets, and taxi station. From Katajanokka Terminal, local Bus 13 or Tram 4T will take you to Helsinki city center, but this is also reachable on foot. If you want to ride, tram numbers 4 and 4T stop here.

South Harbour has a terminal at Olympia Quay with shopping, information, a taxi rank, currency exchange, and Internet access, and a second quay called Makasiini Quay. It's a 15-minute walk into downtown from the South Harbour port entrance. Trams 1A, 3B, and 3T run from the port into town.

Hernasaari Harbour has two quays with access to the dedicated cruise terminal with shops, information desk, taxi rank, and Internet access. It's a longer walk into Helsinki from here, but the terminal is served by bus routes 14B and 16.

Taxis wait at all terminals to take visitors downtown, and this may be the most convenient way to travel if you don't want to take the cruise shuttle service. Journey times are short from all the terminals, the longest being around 15 minutes. Taxis are plentiful (albeit expensive) and make a convenient way to link attractions. Taxis take credit cards. A 5-km (3-mi) trip is currently €10.30, while a 10-km (6-mi) trip is €16.10. A car rental is not a sensible option if you intend to explore the city, as parking is difficult. Expect to pay €76 per day for a compact manual vehicle.

Tickets for the Helsinki public transport system cost €2.50 from the driver, or €2 from a ticket machine. Day tickets are €6.80—these are valid on trams, buses, the metro, and the ferry to Soumenlinna. Ticket machines sell 1-day tickets. Tram services 3B and 3T link many of the most important city attractions, so in conjunction with a day ticket could be used as hop-on hop-off services.

## EXPLORING HELSINKI

★ **Ateneumin Taidemuseo** *(Atheneum Art Museum of the Finnish National Gallery)*. The best traditional Finnish art is housed in this splendid neo-classical complex, one of three museums organized under the Finnish National Gallery umbrella. The gallery holds major European works, but the outstanding attraction is the Finnish art, particularly the works of Akseli Gallen-Kallela, inspired by the national epic *Kalevala*. The two other museums that make up the National Gallery are **Kiasma** and **Synebrychoff.** ⊠ *Kaivok. 2–4, Keskusta* ☎ *09/1733–6401* ⊕ *www. fng.fi* ✑ *€9, additional charge for special exhibits; combined tickets for 3 museums €12* ⊙ *Tues. and Fri. 10–6, Wed. and Thurs. 10–8, weekends 11–5.*

**Cygnaeuksen Galleria** *(Cygnaeus Gallery)*. This diminutive gallery, in a cottage with a tower overlooking the harbor, is the perfect setting for works by various Finnish painters, sculptors, and folk artists. This was once the summer home of Fredrik Cygnaeus (1807–81), a poet and historian who generously left his cottage and all the art inside to the Finnish public. ⊠ *Kalliolinnantie 8, Kaivopuisto* ☎ *09/4050–9628* ✑ *€5* ⊙ *Daily 11–5.*

**Designmuseo** *(Design Museum)*. The best of Finnish design can be seen here in displays of furnishings, jewelry, ceramics, and more. ⊠ *Korkeavu-orenk. 23, Keskusta* ☎ *09/622–0540* ⊕ *www.designmuseum.fi* ✑ *€8* ⊙ *Sept.–May, Tues. 11–8, Wed.–Sun. 11–6; June–Aug., daily 11–6.*

**Eduskuntatalo** *(Parliament House)*. The imposing, colonnaded Eduskun-tatalo stands on Mannerheimintie. The legislature has one of the world's highest proportions of women. ⊠ *Mannerheimintie 30, Keskusta* ☎ *09/432–2027* ⊕ *www.eduskunta.fi.*

**Finlandiatalo** *(Finlandia Hall)*. This white, winged concert hall was one of Alvar Aalto's last creations. If you can't make it to a concert here, try to take a guided tour. ⊠ *Karamzininkatu 4, Keskusta* ☎ *09/402–41* ⊕ *www.finlandiatalo.fi* ⊙ *Symphony concerts usually held Wed. and Thurs. nights.*

**Havis Amanda.** This fountain's brass centerpiece, a young woman perched on rocks surrounded by dolphins, was commissioned by the city fathers to embody Helsinki. Sculptor Ville Vallgren completed her in 1908. Partying university students annually crown the Havis Amanda with their white caps on the eve of Vappu, the May 1 holiday. ⊠ *Eteläespl. and Eteläranta, Keskusta/Kauppatori.*

**Helsingin Taidehalli** *(Helsinki Art Gallery)*. Here you'll see the best of con-temporary Finnish art, including painting, sculpture, architecture, and industrial art and design. ⊠ *Nervanderink. 3, Keskusta* ☎ *09/454–2060* ✑ *€10, can vary for special exhibitions* ⊙ *Tues., Thurs., and Fri. 11–6, Wed. 11–8, weekends 11–5.*

**Kauppatori** *(Market Square)*. At this Helsinki institution, open year-round, wooden stands with orange and gold awnings bustle in the morning when everyone comes to browse. You can buy a bouquet of bright flowers for a friend, or a fur pelt or hat. ⊠ *Eteläranta and Pohjoisespl., Keskusta/Kauppatori* ⊙ *Sept.–May, weekdays 6:30–2, Sat.*

5

*6:30–3; June–Aug., weekdays 6:30–2 and 3:30–8, Sat. 6:30–3, Sun. 10–4; hrs can vary.*

☾ **Korkeasaari Eläintarha** *(Helsinki Zoo).* Snow leopards and reindeer like the cold climate at one of the world's northernmost zoos, set entirely within the limits of this small island. ⊠ *Korkeasaari (Korkea Island), Korkeasaari* ☏ *09/169–5969* ⊕ *www.korkeasaari.fi* ⊠ *€10, €16 with ferry journey to entrance* ☉ *Apr. and Sept., daily 10–6; May–Aug., daily 10–8; Oct.–Mar., daily 10–4.*

**Mannerheimin Patsas** *(Statue of national hero Marshal Karl Gustaf Mannerheim).* The equestrian gazes down Mannerheimintie, the major thoroughfare named in his honor. ⊠ *Mannerheimintie, in front of main post office and Museum of Contemporary Art, west of main train station, Keskusta/Pääposti.*

★ **Nykytaiteenmuseo (Kiasma)** *(Museum of Contemporary Art).* Praised for the boldness of its curved steel shell, this striking museum displays a wealth of Finnish and foreign art from the 1960s to the present. ⊠ *Mannerheiminaukio 2, Keskusta/Pääposti* ☏ *09/1733–6501* ⊕ *www. kiasma.fi* ⊠ *€8* ☉ *Tues. 10–5, Wed.–Fri. 10–8:30, weekends 10–6.*

**Olympiastadion** *(Olympic Stadium).* At this stadium built for the 1952 Games, take a lift to the top of the tower for sprawling city views. ⊠ *East of Mannerheim, Olympiastadion* ⊕ *www.stadion.fi* ⊠ *€2* ☉ *Weekdays 9–8, weekends 9–6.*

**Presidentinlinna** *(President's Palace).* The long history of this edifice mirrors the history of Finland itself: built between 1813 and 1820 as a private residence for a German businessman, it was redesigned in 1843 as a palace for the czars; then it served as the official residence of Finland's presidents from 1919 to 1993. Today it houses the offices of Finland's first female president, Tarja Halonen. ⊠ *Pohjoisespl. 1, Keskusta/ Kauppatori* ☏ *09/2288–1222.*

**Rautatieasema** *(train station).* The station's huge granite figures are by Emil Wikström; the solid building they adorn was designed by Eliel Saarinen, one of the founders of the early-20th-century National Romantic style. ⊠ *Kaivok., Rautatientori, Keskusta* ☏ *0600/41–902 for information in English (a €1 charge applies), 0307/23703 international fares* ⊕ *www.vr.fi.*

★ **Senaatintori** *(Senate Square).* You've hit the heart of neoclassical Helsinki. The harmony of the three buildings flanking Senaatintori exemplifies one of the purest styles of European architecture, as envisioned and designed by German architect Carl Ludvig Engel. On the square's west side is one of the main buildings of **Helsingin Yliopisto** *(Helsinki University),* and up the hill is the university library. On the east side is the pale yellow **Valtionneuvosto** *(Council of State),* completed in 1822 and once the seat of the Autonomous Grand Duchy of Finland's Imperial Senate. At the lower end of the square, stores and restaurants now occupy former merchants' homes. ⊠ *Bounded by Aleksanterink. to south and Yliopistonk. to north, Senaatintori.*

**Sinebrychoffin Taidemuseo** *(Sinebrychoff Museum of Foreign Art).* The wealthy Russian Sinebrychoffs lived in this splendid yellow-and-white

1840 neo-Renaissance mansion, which is now a public museum filled with their art and furniture. ⊠ *Bulevardi 40, Hietalahti* ☎ *09/1733–6460* ⊕ *www.sinebrychoffintaidemuseo.fi* ⊠ *€8* ☉ *Tues. and Fri. 10–6, Wed. and Thurs. 10–8, weekends 11–5.*

**Suomen Kansallismuseo** *(National Museum of Finland).* Architect Eliel Saarinen and his partners combined the language of Finnish medieval church architecture with elements of art nouveau to create this vintage example of the National Romantic style. The museum's collection of archaeological, cultural, and ethnological artifacts gives insight into Finland's past. ⊠ *Mannerheimintie 34, Keskusta* ☎ *09/4050–9544* ⊕ *www. nba.fi* ⊠ *€7* ☉ *Tues. 11–8, Wed.–Sun. 11–6.*

**Suomen Kansallisooppera** *(Finnish National Opera).* Helsinki's splendid opera house is a striking example of modern Scandinavian architecture. ⊠ *Helsinginkatu 58, Keskusta* ☎ *09/4030–2210 house tours, 09/4030–2211 box office* ⊕ *www.operafin.fi* ☉ *House tours in English by appointment.*

**Suomen Kansallisteatteri** *(National Theater).* The elegant granite facade overlooking the railway station square is decorated with quirky relief typical of the Finnish National Romantic style. In front is a statue of writer Aleksis Kivi. ⊠ *Läntinen Teatterikuja 1, Keskusta/Rautatieasema* ☎ *09/1733–1331* ⊕ *www.nationaltheatre.fi.*

**Fodor'sChoice** **Suomenlinna** *(Finland's Castle).* A former island fortress is now a perennially popular collection of museums, parks, and gardens, which has ★ been designated a UNESCO World Heritage Site. In 1748, the Finnish army helped build the impregnable fortress. Since then, it has expanded into a series of interlinked islands. Although Suomenlinna has never been taken by assault, its occupants surrendered once to the Russians in 1808 and came under fire from British ships in 1855 during the Crimean War. ⊠ *Suomenlinna* ☎ *09/684–1880, 09/684–1850 tours* ⊕ *www. suomenlinna.fi* ☉ *Daily 10–6* ⊠ *Museums €3–€5 each, guided tour €7.*

**Suomen Rakennustaiteen Museo** *(Museum of Finnish Architecture).* Stop in to buy an architectural map of Helsinki that includes the locations of several buildings by Alvar Aalto, the most famous being Finlandiatalo in Töölö. ⊠ *Kasarmik. 24, Keskusta* ☎ *09/8567–5100* ⊕ *www. mfa.fi* ⊠ *€5* ☉ *Tues. and Thurs.–Fri. 10–4, Wed. 10–8, weekends 11–4.*

★ **Temppeliaukio Kirkko** *(Temple Square Church).* Topped with a copper dome, the church looks like a half-buried spaceship from the outside. In truth, it's really a modern Lutheran church carved into the rock outcrops below. ⊠ *Lutherinkatu 3, Töölö* ☎ *09/2340–5920* ⊠ *Free* ☉ *Mon. and Wed. 10–5, Tues. 10–12:45 and 2:15–5, Thurs. and Fri. 10–8, Sat. 10–6, Sun. 11:45–1:45 and 3:30–6; closed during weddings, concerts, and services.*

**Tuomiokirkko** *(Lutheran Cathedral of Finland).* The steep steps and green domes of the church dominate Senaatintori. Completed in 1852, it houses statues of German reformers Martin Luther and Philipp Melancthon, as well as the famous Finnish bishop Mikael Agricola. ⊠ *Unioninkatu 29, Senaatintori* ☎ *09/2340–6120* ☉ *Mon.–Sat. 9–6, Sun.10–6. Closed during some events.*

5

★ **Uspenskin Katedraali** *(Uspenski Cathedral)*. The biggest Orthodox church in Scandinavia is the main cathedral of the Orthodox community in Finland. Its brilliant gold onion domes are its hallmark. ✉ *Kanavak. 1, Katajanokka* ☎ *207/220683* ☉ *May–Sept., weekdays 9:30–4, Sat. 9:30–2, Sun. noon–3; Oct.–Apr., Tues.–Fri. 9:30–4, Sat. 9:30–2, Sun. noon–3; closed for weddings and other special events.*

┌─
│ **OFF THE**
│ **BEATEN**
│ **PATH**

**Seurasaaren Ulkomeseo.** On an island about 3 km (2 mi) northwest of the city center, the Seurasaari Outdoor Museum was founded in 1909 to preserve rural Finnish architecture. The old farmhouses and barns dating from the 17th century were of primary inspiration to the late-19th-century architects of the national revivalist movement in Finland. Guided tours in English are available mid-June through mid-August, at 3, starting at ticket kiosk. ✉ *Seurasaari* ☎ *09/4050–9660* ⊕ *www.nba.fi* 🎫 *€6* ☉ *June–Aug., daily 11–5; early-Sept.–mid-Sept., weekdays 9–3, weekends 11–5. Closed mid-Sept.–end May.*

# SHOPPING

Finnish handicrafts and 21st-century design staples for the home are the must-have souvenirs of your trip. Handicrafts take the form of handwoven woolen rugs, knitted sweaters, glass, ceramics and porcelain, and textiles. There is also a thriving modern jewelry industry, with many young designers. For antiques hunters, Helsinki is an excellent city for tracking down old Russian *objets.*

The southern part of **Senaatintori** has a host of souvenir and crafts stores, with several antiques shops and secondhand bookstores on the adjoining streets. You'll find many smaller boutiques in the streets **west of Mannerheimintie,** Fredrikinkatu and Annankatu, for example. There is one pedestrian shopping street a few blocks south of the Esplanade, on **Iso Roobertinkatu;** stores here are conventional, and are more relaxed than around Mannerheimintie and the Esplanade. **Pohjoisesplanadi,** on the north side of the Esplanade, packs in most of Helsinki's trademark design stores.

**Arabian Tehtaanmyymälä.** The Arabia Factory Shop has Arabia, Hackman, Iittala, and Rörstrand tableware, glassware, cutlery, and cookware for outlet prices. ✉ *Hämeentie 135, Arabia* ☎ *0204/393–507.*

**Hietalahden Tori.** This is Helsinki's famed market and flea market. ✉ *Bulevardi and Hietalahdenk., Hietalahti.*

**Kiseleff Bazaar Hall.** Next to Senaatintori is this attractive shopping gallery. ✉ *Aleksanterinkatu 22–28.*

**Union Design.** This jewelry atelier displays and sells works by the top-notch talent in Finnish design. ✉ *Eteläranta 14, inner courtyard Kauppatori* ☎ *09/6220–0333.*

# ACTIVITIES

Taking a sauna is the big Finnish pastime. It's a place to get cleansed and do some socializing.

**Yrjönkatu Uimahalli.** The oldest and one of the most famous saunas in Helsinki allows swimming and taking saunas in the nude. It's not compulsory to be nude, but the local people will be. The hall periodically closes during the summer months. ⊠ *Yrjönk. 21B, Keskusta* ☏ *09/3108–7400.*

## WHERE TO EAT

$$$

SEAFOOD

**Fodor's**Choice

★

✕ **Havis.** Across the street from the Market Square and the South Harbor close to the cruise terminals, this restaurant specializes in traditional Scandinavian fish dishes with contemporary twists. Begin with the savory blue-mussel soup, and move on to specialties like the slow-fried *lavaret* (whitefish). Vegetarians will appreciate the mushroom crepes with glazed vegetables and the daily vegetarian special. The dessert menu includes old-time Finnish standards like strawberry milk and doughnuts with coffee pudding. ⊠ *Etelärantatie 16, Kauppatori* ☏ *09/6869–5660* ⊕ *www.royalravintolat.com* ⊟ *AE, DC, MC, V* ⊙ *Closed Sun. mid-Sept.–Apr. No lunch weekends.*

¢–$

VEGETARIAN

✕ **Zucchini.** For a vegetarian lunch or just coffee and dessert, Zucchini is a cozy hideaway with quiet music, magazines, and a few sidewalk tables. Pizzas, soups, and salads are all tasty here. ⊠ *Fabianinkatu 4, Keskusta* ☏ *09/622–2907* ⊟ *DC, MC, V* ⊙ *Closed weekends. No dinner.*

# RĪGA, LATVIA

Rīga has an upscale, big-city feel unmatched in the Eastern Baltic region. The capital is almost as large as Tallinn and Vilnius combined, and is the business center of the area. Original, high-quality restaurants and hotels have given Rīga something to brag about. The city has many faces, and is a delight for lovers of both architecture and history, having thrived as a Hanseatic port in the Late Middle Ages. A Baltic trading center in the early 20th century, Rīga eventually re-created itself as the city of art nouveau. This style dominates the city center, and long avenues of complex and sometimes whimsical Jugendstil facades hint at Rīga's grand past. Many were designed by Mikhail Eisenstein, the father of Soviet director Sergei.

### ESSENTIALS

CURRENCY

The Lat (Ls 1 to US$1.79; Ls 1 to €1.41). There are ATMs and exchange kiosks in the passenger terminal of the cruise port. ATMs are widely available in town.

HOURS

Shops are open weekdays from 10 AM until 7 PM and 10 AM until 5 PM on Saturday; most close on Sunday. Museums are generally open from 10 AM until 5 PM; many close on Monday.

INTERNET

There are facilities for checking e-mail and surfing the Internet at the passenger welcome center within the cruise port.

TELEPHONES

The Latvian mobile phone system is 3G-compatible, Tele2 and Latvijas Mobilias Telefons being the main providers. Public phones support international calls. Some kiosks accept credit cards. Phone cards are available at tobacconists/newspaper shops.

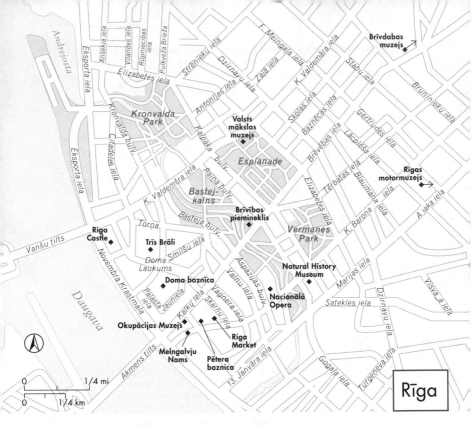

## COMING ASHORE

The cruise port is in the main port, close to the historic downtown core. The walk from port to the downtown core is 15 minutes along the waterfront. The passenger welcome center has good facilities, including restaurants, restrooms, currency exchange facilities, and ATMs.

To reach the Old Town you can take an inexpensive shuttle transfer or taxi. Taxis are more expensive from the port than within the city center. The official rate is 50 Ls per km ½ mi in the daytime with an Ls 1.50 pick-up fee. Drivers must display an operating license and a meter. Stick to the state cabs with orange and black markings. Insist that the meter be turned on; if there is no meter, choose another taxi or decide on a price beforehand. Public transportation costs 45 Ls or 1.90 Ls for a 24-hour pass. Services run from 5:30 AM to midnight. Some routes have 24-hour service. Trams 6 and 11 connect the Old Town with the Esplanāde area and run regularly throughout the day. Buy tickets at numerous outlets and validate them in the machine on board.

# EXPLORING RĪGA

In many ways, the wonder of Rīga resides less in its individual attractions and more in the fabric of the town itself. In the medieval **Old Town,** an ornate gable or architrave catches the eye at every turn. The somber and the flamboyant are both represented in this quarter's 1,000 years of architectural history. Don't hesitate to just follow where your desire leads—the Old Town is compact and bounded by canals, so it's difficult to get totally lost.

When the Old Town eventually became too crowded, the city burst out into the newer inner suburbs. The rich could afford to leave and build themselves fine fashionable mansions in the style of the day; consequently, city planners created a whole new Rīga. Across the narrow canal, you'll find the **Esplanāde,** a vast expanse of parkland with formal gardens and period mansions where the well-heeled stroll and play. Surrounding this is the **art nouveau district.** Encompassing avenues of splendid family homes (now spruced up in the postcommunist era), the collection has been praised by UNESCO as Europe's finest in the art nouveau style. The best examples are at Alberta 2, 2a, 4, 6, 8, and 13; Elizabetes 10b; and Strēlnieku 4a.

## RĪGA BEST BETS

**Stroll around Elizabetes Street.** The heart of art nouveau Rīga has some exceptional period architecture and is a testament to the wealth generated here by shipping and trade in the early 20th century.

**Explore the Old Town.** The fabric of this medieval core remains remarkably intact, with Gothic spires sheltering church naves and winding cobbled streets revealing sturdy gables.

**Relax in the Esplanāde.** The green lung of the city, this huge park has fine formal gardens and planned woodlands. Enjoy a picnic here in warm weather.

5

If the weather permits, eschew public transport and stroll between the two districts, taking in the varied skylines and multifaceted facades, and perhaps stopping at a café or two as you go. The city has churches in five Christian denominations and more than 50 museums, many of which cater to eclectic or specialist tastes.

☺ **Brīvdabas muzejs.** The Open-Air Ethnographic Museum is well worth the 9-km (5-mi) trek from downtown. At this countryside living museum farmsteads and villages have been crafted to look like those in 18th- and 19th-century Latvia, and costumed workers engage in traditional activities (beekeeping, smithing, and so on). ⊠ *Brīvības 440* ☎ *6799–4515* ⌨ *Ls 2* ☉ *Daily 10–5.*

★ **Brīvības piemineklis.** The central Freedom Monument, a 1935 statue whose upheld stars represent Latvia's united peoples (the Kurzeme, Vidzeme, and Latgale), was the rallying point for many nationalist protests during the late 1980s and early 1990s. Watch the changing of the guard every hour on the hour between 9 and 6. ⊠ *Brīvības and Raina.*

**Doma baznīca** *(Dome Cathedral).* In Doma laukums (Dome Square), the nerve center of the Old Town, the stately 1210 cathedral dominates. Reconstructed over the years with Romanesque, Gothic, and baroque elements, this place of worship is astounding as much for its architecture as for its size. The massive 6,768-pipe organ is among the largest in Europe, and it is played nearly every evening at 7 PM. Check at the cathedral for schedules and tickets. ⊠ *Doma laukums* 🕾 *6721–3498* ⊕ *www.omf.lv* ۞ *Tues.–Fri. 1–5, Sat. 10–2.*

**Melngalvju Nams.** The fiercely Gothic Blackheads House was built in 1344 as a hotel for wayfaring merchants (who wore black hats). Partially destroyed during World War II and leveled by the Soviets in 1948, the extravagant, ornate building was renovated and reopened in 2000 for Rīga's 800th anniversary. The facade is a treasured example of Dutch Renaissance work. ⊠ *Ratslaukums 7* 🕾 *6704–4300* ۞ *Tues.– Sun. 10–5.*

**Nacionālā Opera.** Latvia's restored 18th-century National Opera House, where Richard Wagner once conducted, is worthy of a night out. ⊠ *Aspazijas 3* 🕾 *707–3777* ⊕ *www.opera.lv* ۞ *Mon.–Sat. 10–7, Sun. 11–7.*

★ **Okupācijas muzejs.** The Latvian Occupation Museum details the devastation of Latvia at the hands of the Nazis and Soviets during World War II, as well as the Latvians' struggle for independence in September 1991. In front of the museum is a monument to the Latvian sharpshooters who protected Lenin during the 1917 revolution. ⊠ *Strēlnieku laukums 1* 🕾 *6721–2715* 🖳 *Donations accepted* ۞ *May–Sept., daily 11–6; Oct.– Apr., Tues.–Sun. 11–5.*

**Pētera baznīca.** Towering St. Peter's Church, originally built in 1209, had a long history of annihilation and conflagration before being destroyed most recently in 1941. Rebuilt by the Soviets, it lacks authenticity but has a good observation deck on the 200-foot spire. ⊠ *Skārnu 19* 🕾 *6722–9426* ۞ *Tues.–Sun. 10–7.*

**Rīgas motormuzejs.** At the Motor Museum, the Western cars on display can impress, but the Soviet models—including Stalin's iron-plated limo and a Rolls-Royce totaled by Brezhnev himself—are the most fun. ⊠ *Eizensteina 6* 🕾 *6709–7170* ⊕ *www.motormuzejs.lv* 🖳 *Ls 1.5* ۞ *Daily 10–6.*

**Trīs Brāli.** The Three Brothers—a trio of houses on Mazā Pils—show what the city looked like before the 20th century. The three oldest stone houses in the capital (No. 17 is the oldest, dating from the 15th century) span several styles, from the medieval to the baroque. The building at No. 19 is the city's **architecture museum.** ⊠ *Mazā Pils 17, 19, 21* 🕾 *6722–0779* ⊕ *www.archmuseum.lv* ۞ *Mon. 9–6, Tues.–Thurs. 9–5, Fri. 9–4.*

**Valsts mākslas muzejs.** The National Art Museum has a gorgeous interior, with imposing marble staircases linking several large halls of 19th- and 20th-century Latvian paintings. ⊠ *K. Valdemāra 10a* 🕾 *6732–4461* ⊕ *www.lnmm.lv* 🖳 *Ls 1* ۞ *Mon., Wed., Thurs, and weekends 11–5, Fri. 11–8. Closed Tues.*

## SHOPPING

You'll find many souvenir and gift shops in the streets of the Old Town, many of which specifically cater to visitors. Latvia is famed for its linen, which is fashioned into clothes and household items such as tea towels and table runners. Woolen sweaters, mittens, and socks with traditional patterns have been worn by generations of locals during the winter.

Amber items are everywhere, although their quality can vary, so shop around. Also popular are jewelry, carved ornaments, and Rīga Black Balsam, a liqueur made from an ancient recipe incorporating herbs and medicinal roots.

**Galerija Tornis.** This boutique sells a selection of jewelry and gift items featuring amber and other semi-precious stones, along with pretty linen items. ⊠ *Grēcinieku 11–12* ☎ *6722–0270.*

**Souvenirs Klota.** As its name suggests, this is a good general souvenir store. ⊠ *3 Town Hall Sq.* ☎ *6714–4308.*

**Tines.** This company sells an excellent line of linen and woolen clothes and household items. ⊠ *Amatu 5* ☎ *6721–1009* ⊕ *www.tines.lv.*

## WHERE TO EAT

MEXICAN

¢ ✕ **A. Suns.** "Andalusian Dog" has long been an expat hangout in Rīga—and why not? With an art-house cinema upstairs, a breezy restaurant downstairs, and a wall of windows perfect for people-watching, the restaurant is decidedly hip, with a tasty Tex-Mex menu. ⊠ *Elizabetes 83–85* ☎ *6728–8418* ⊕ *www.andaluzijassuns.lv* ▭ *MC, V.*

EASTERN
EUROPEAN

¢ ✕ **Staburags.** In an art nouveau building in downtown Rīga, this may be the capital's best place to sample Latvian national cuisine, with such offerings as roast leg of pork, sauerkraut, an assortment of potato dishes, and smoked chicken. ⊠ *Caka 55* ☎ *6729–9787* ▭ *AE, MC, V.*

# ST. PETERSBURG, RUSSIA

Commissioned by Peter the Great as "a window looking into Europe," St. Petersburg is a planned city built on more than 100 islands in the Neva Delta linked by canals and arched bridges. It was first called the "Venice of the North" by Goethe. Little wonder it's the darling of today's fashion photographers. With its strict geometric lines and perfectly planned architecture, so unlike the Russian cities that came before it, St. Petersburg is almost too European to be Russian. And yet it's too Russian to be European. Memories of revolutionary zeal and one of the worst ordeals of World War II, when the city—then known as Leningrad—withstood a 900-day siege and blockade by Nazi forces, are still fresh in the minds of citizens. Nevertheless, St. Petersburg is filled with pleasures and tantalizing treasures, from golden spires and gilded domes to pastel palaces and candlelit cathedrals.

### ESSENTIALS

CURRENCY

The ruble (RUB 30.82 to US$1). There are ATMs in the city, but exchange bureaus are more plentiful. Credit cards are increasingly accepted, but ask first to be sure.

HOURS

Stores have recently extended their opening hours considerably—many stay open until 8 or 9 PM, or on Sunday.

INTERNET

There's an Internet café in the Hermitage Museum. Check your e-mail at **Quo Vadis** (⊠ *76 Nevsky Prospekt* ☎ *812/3330708* ⊕ *www.quovadis.ru*).

TELEPHONES

Some tri- and quad-band mobile phones may work in St. Petersburg, but mobile service on the whole is patchy. The network does not yet

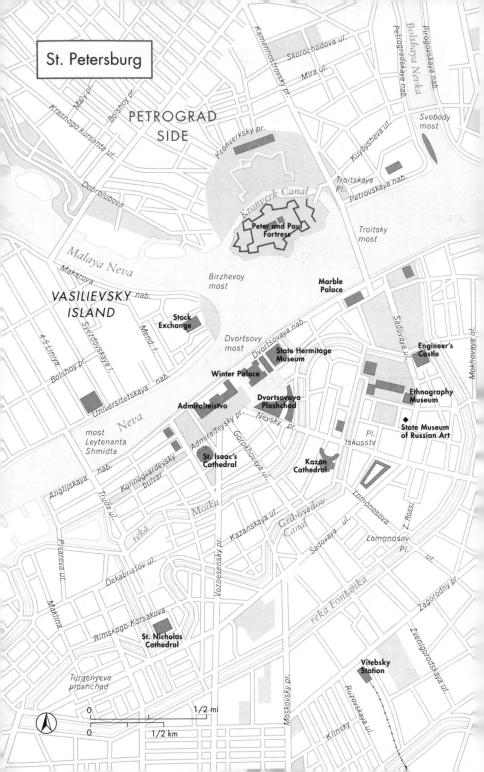

# St. Petersburg

**PETROGRAD SIDE**

**VASILIEVSKY ISLAND**

Maly pr.

Bolshoy pr.

Krasnogo kursanta ul.

Dobrolubova

Makarova

Malaya Neva

4-5 liniya

Bolshoy pr.

Svezdovskaya l.

Mend. l.

Universitetskaya nab.

most
Leytenanta
Shmidta

Neva

Anglijskaya

Truda ul.

Konnogvardeyskiy
bulvar

Pisareva ul.

Maklina

Dekabristov ul.

Rimskogo-Korsakova

St. Nicholas
Cathedral

Turgenyeva
ploshchad

nab.

Kamennostrovsky pr.

Skorochodova ul.

Mira ul.

Kronverksky pr.

Kronverk Canal

Peter and Paul
Fortress

Birzhevoy
most

Stock
Exchange

Dvortsovy
most

Dvortsovaya nab.

Winter Palace

Admiralteistvo

Admiralteysky pr.

St. Isaac's
Cathedral

Gorokhovaya ul.

Voznesensky pr.

Kazanskaya ul.

Moika

teka

Dvortsovaya
Ploshchad

State Hermitage
Museum

Nevsky, pr.

Kazan
Cathedral

Griboyedov
Canal

Sadovaya ul.

Pirogovskaya nab.

Bolshaya Nevka

Petrogradskaya nab.

Svobody
most

Kuybysheva ul.

Troitskaya
Pl.

Petrovskaya nab.

Troitsky
most

Marble
Palace

Sadovaya ul.

Engineer's
Castle

Ethnography
Museum

State Museum
of Russian Art

Pl.
Iskusstv

Mokhovaya ul.

Lomonosova

2. Rossi

Lomonosov
Pl.

ul.

Sadovaya

Zagorodny pr.

reka Fontanka

Vitebsky
Station

Zvenigorodskaya ul.

Ruzovskaya ul.

Moskovsky pr.

Klinsky

0          1/2 mi

0          1/2 km

support 3G services, and handsets are single-band. Public phones take phone cards, which can be bought at newsstands. Note that public phones in Metro stations work on a different system and require a different card.

## COMING ASHORE

Independent travel is not as easy in St. Petersburg as in other destinations, as you need to obtain a tourist visa prior to the cruise departure to explore without a certified guide. Also, independent travelers need to line up for tickets at museums and attractions, while guided groups do not. This can cut down your sightseeing time considerably. Whether you travel independently or with an accredited small tour company, it is approximately 20 minutes on foot to the port entrance, from where you will be able to take a taxi.

---

### ST. PETERSBURG BEST BETS

**Try not to be overwhelmed by the State Hermitage Museum.** This immense and ornate royal palace is one of the finest art repositories in the world.

**Soak in the atmosphere at Dvortsovaya Ploshchad.** The seeds of the revolution were sown in this historic and architecturally stunning square.

**Appreciate the architectural symmetry of the downtown core.** Known by the epithet "Venice of the North," St. Petersburg offers marvelous vistas at every turn.

---

**Explorer-Tour.** If you prebook an independent tour with a certified guide company (so that you aren't with a large group), you don't need a tourist visa if you are visiting St. Petersburg on a cruise ship. Explorer-Tour operates city tours for individuals. This is certainly the safest and most productive way to tour St. Petersburg without being part of a large group. ⊠ *50 ul. Marata, Vladimirskaya* ☎ *812/320–0954* ⊕ *www. explorer-tour.ru* Ⓜ *Mayakovskaya.*

## EXPLORING ST. PETERSBURG

☾ **Dvortsovaya Ploshchad** *(Palace Square).* One of the world's most mag-
★ nificent plazas, the square is a stunning ensemble of buildings and open space, a combination of several seemingly incongruous architectural styles in perfect harmony. It's where the city's imperial past has been preserved in all its glory, but it also resonates with the history of the revolution that followed. Here, on Bloody Sunday in 1905, palace troops opened fire on peaceful demonstrators, killing scores of women and children, kindling the revolutionary movement. It was across Palace Square in October 1917 that Bolshevik revolutionaries stormed the Winter Palace, an event that led to the birth of the Soviet Union. Almost 75 years later huge crowds rallied on Palace Square in support of perestroika and democracy. Today the beautiful square is a bustling hubbub of tourist and marketing activity. Horseback and carriage rides are available for hire here. ⊠ *City Center* Ⓜ *Nevsky prospekt.*

**Kazan Cathedral** *(Kazansky Sobor).* After a visit to Rome, Tsar Paul I (1754–1801) commissioned this magnificent cathedral, wishing to copy—and perhaps present the Orthodox rival to—that city's St. Peter's.

It was erected between 1801 and 1811 from a design by Andrei Voronikhin. Inside and out, the church abounds with sculpture and decoration. On the prospect side the frontage holds statues of St. John the Baptist and the apostle Andrew as well as such sanctified Russian heroes as Grand Prince Vladimir (who advanced the Christianization of Russia) and Alexander Nevsky. Note the enormous bronze front doors—exact copies of Ghiberti's Gates of Heaven at Florence's Baptistery. ⊠ 2 *Kazanskaya Pl., City Center* ☎ *812/314–4663* ☉ *Open daily 8:30–8; services weekdays at 10* AM *and 6* PM, *weekends at 7 and 10* AM *and 6* PM Ⓜ *Nevsky prospekt.*

**Fodor's** Choice
★
**Peter and Paul Fortress** (*Petropavlovskaya Krepost*). The first building in Sankt-Piter-Burkh, as the city was then called, the fortress was erected in just one year, between 1703 and 1704. The date on which construction began on the fortress is celebrated as the birth of St. Petersburg.

The fortifications display several gates, along with arsenal buildings and the **Engineer's House** (*Inzhenerny Dom*), which is now a branch of the Museum of the History of St. Petersburg (as are all exhibits in the fortress) and presents displays about the city's pre-revolutionary history.

The main attraction of the fortress, however, is the **Cathedral of Sts. Peter and Paul** (*Petropavlovsky Sobor*). Constructed between 1712 and 1733 on the site of an earlier wooden church, it's highly unusual for a Russian Orthodox church. Instead of the characteristic bulbous domes, it's adorned by a single, slender, gilded spire whose height (400 feet) made the church the city's tallest building for more than two centuries. Starting with Peter the Great, the cathedral served as the burial place of the tsars.

Several of the fortress's bastions were put to use over the years mainly as political prisons. One of them, **Trubetskoi Bastion,** is open to the public as a museum. Famous prisoners include some of the People's Will terrorists, who killed Alexander II in 1881; plus revolutionaries Leon Trotsky and Maxim Gorky. ⊠ *3 Petropavlovskaya Krepost, Petrograd Side* ☎ *812/238–4511* 🎫 *Cathedral 150R, cathedral and other sights and exhibitions 250R, audioguide in English 250R (purchase guide at Fortress's Information Center located at Ioanovsky Ravelin)* ☉ *Thurs.–Tues. 10–6, kassa open until 5 Thurs.–Mon., until 4 on Tues.; Cathedral of Sts. Peter and Paul closed Wed.; fortress closed last Tues. of month* Ⓜ *Gorkovskaya.*

**Fodor's** Choice
★
**St. Isaac's Cathedral** (*Isaakievsky Sobor*). St. Isaac's is the world's third-largest domed cathedral, and the first monument you see of the city if you arrive by ship. Tsar Alexander I commissioned the construction of the cathedral in 1818 to celebrate his victory over Napoléon.

The interior of the cathedral is lavishly decorated with malachite, lazulite, marble, and other precious stones and minerals. Gilding the dome required 220 pounds of gold. When the city was blockaded during World War II, the gilded dome was painted black to avoid its being targeted by enemy fire. Despite efforts to protect it, the cathedral nevertheless suffered heavy damage, as bullet holes on the columns on the south side attest. ⊠ *1 Isaakievskaya Pl., Admiralteisky* ☎ *812/315–9732* 🎫 *Cathedral 300R, colonade 150R* ☉ *Cathedral May–Sept.,*

*Thurs.–Tues. 10 AM–7 PM and 8 PM–10:30 PM; Oct.–Apr., Thurs.–Tues. 11–6, and 7 PM–9:30 PM* Ⓜ *Sennaya Ploshchad.*

**Fodor's Choice**
★ **State Hermitage Museum** *(Gosudarstvenny Ermitazh Muzey)*. Leonardo's *Benois Madonna* . . . Rembrandt's *Danaë* . . . Matisse's *The Dance* . . . you get the picture. As the former private art collection of the tsars, this is one of the world's most famous museums, virtually wallpapered with celebrated paintings. In addition, the walls are works of art themselves, for this collection is housed in the lavish Winter Palace, one of the most outstanding examples of Russian baroque magnificence. The museum takes its name from Catherine the Great (1729–96), who used it for her private apartments. Between 1764 and 1775 the empress undertook to acquire some of the world's finest works of art.

A wealth of Russian and European art is on show: Florentine, Venetian, and other Italian art through the 18th century, including Leonardos and Michelangelos, two Raphaels, eight Titians, and works by Tintoretto, Lippi, Caravaggio, and Canaletto. The Hermitage also houses a superb collection of Spanish art, of which works by El Greco, Velázquez, Murillo, and Goya are on display. Its spectacular presentation of Flemish and Dutch art contains roomfuls of Van Dycks. Also here are more than 40 canvases by Rubens and an equally impressive number of Rembrandts. There is a smattering of excellent British paintings including works by Joshua Reynolds, Thomas Gainsborough, and George Morland.

Reflecting the Francophilia of the empresses Elizabeth and Catherine, the museum is second only to the Louvre in its assortment of French art. Along with earlier masterpieces by Lorrain, Watteau, and Poussin, the collection runs the whole gamut of 19th-century genius, with Delacroix, Ingres, Corot, and Courbet. There is also a stunning collection of impressionists and postimpressionists, including works by Monet, Degas, Sisley, Pissarro, and Renoir. Sculptures by Auguste Rodin and a host of pictures by Cézanne, Gauguin, and van Gogh are followed by Picasso and a lovely room of Matisse.

Possibly the most-prized section of the Hermitage is the first-floor's **Treasure Gallery,** also referred to as the *Zolotaya Kladovaya* (Golden Room). This spectacular collection of gold, silver, and royal jewels includes ancient Scythian gold and silver treasures, plus precious stones, jewelry, and jewel-encrusted items from the 16th through the 20th centuries. ⊠ *2 Dvortsovaya Pl., City Center* ☎ *812/710–9625, 812/710–9079, 812/571–8446 tours* ⊕ *www.hermitagemuseum.org* ⌦ *State Hermitage Museum 400R (free 1st Thurs. of month); multiaccess ticket 700R; Treasure Gallery 300R, plus 160R for daily English-language tour, which takes place around noon* ☉ *Tues.–Sat. 10:30–6, Sun. 10:30–5 main museum; Tues.–Sat. 11–4, Sun. 11–3 Treasure Gallery* Ⓜ *Nevsky prospekt.*

**Fodor's Choice**
★ **State Museum of Russian Art** *(Gosudarstvenny Russky Muzey)*. In 1898 Nicholas II turned the stupendously majestic neoclassical **Mikhailovsky Palace** *(Mikhailovsky Dvorets)* into a museum that has become one of the country's most important art galleries. The collection at the museum, which is sometimes just referred to as the Russian Museum,

has scores of masterpieces on display, from outstanding icons to mainstream art of all eras. For many years much of this work was unknown in the West, and it's fascinating to see the stylistic parallels and the incorporation of outside influences into a Russian framework. Painters of the World of Art movement—Bakst, Benois, and Somov—are also here. There are several examples of 20th-century art, with works by Kandinsky and Kazimir Malevich. ✉ *4–2 Inzhenernaya ul., City Center* ☎ *812/595–4248* ⊕ *www.rusmuseum.ru* 🎫 *300R* ⊗ *Mon. 10–4, Wed.– Sun. 10–5, kassa open until 1 hr before closing* Ⓜ *Nevsky prospekt.*

**Fodor's Choice** **Winter Palace** *(Zimny Dvorets).* With its 1,001 rooms swathed in mala-
★ chite, jasper, agate, and gilded mirrors, this famous palace—the residence of Russia's rulers from Catherine the Great (1762) to Nicholas II (1917)—is the focal point of Palace Square. The palace, now the site of the State Hermitage Museum, is the grandest monument of that strange hybrid: the Russian rococo, in itself an eye-popping mix of the old-fashioned 17th-century baroque and the newfangled 18th-century neoclassical style. Now "Russianized," the palace's neoclassic ornament lost its early gracefulness and Greek sense of proportion and evolved toward the heavier, more monumental, imperial style. Still, the exterior is particularly successful and pleasing.

The palace, which was created by the Italian architect Bartolomeo Francesco Rastrelli, stretches from Palace Square to the Neva River embankment. It was the fourth royal residence on this site, commissioned in 1754 by Peter the Great's daughter Elizabeth. By the time it was completed, in 1762, Elizabeth had died and the craze for the Russian rococo style had waned. Catherine the Great left the exterior unaltered but had the interiors redesigned in the neoclassical style of her day. In 1837, after the palace was gutted by fire, the interiors were revamped once again. Three of the palace's most celebrated rooms are the **Gallery of the 1812 War,** where portraits of Russian commanders who served against Napoléon are on display; the **Great Throne Room,** richly decorated in marble and bronze; and the **Malachite Room,** designed by the architect Alexander Bryullov. ✉ *Dvortsovaya Pl., City Center* ☎ *812/710–9625, 812/710–9079, 812/571–8446 tours* ⊕ *www.hermitagemuseum.org* 🎫 *60R* ⊗ *Tues.–Sat. 10:30–5, Sun. 10:30–4* Ⓜ *Nevsky prospekt.*

## SHOPPING

Pick up a copy of Russian *Vogue* and you may be surprised to see that it nearly outdoes its Parisian and American counterparts for sheer glitz and trendy garb. And all those nifty threads that the models are wearing are fully stocked in the international boutiques around the city.

A two-tiered system of stores exists in St. Petersburg. "Western-style" shops taking credit-card payment have replaced the old *Beriozkas* (Birch Trees) emporiums, which were stocked only for foreigners. State-run shops are also better stocked now than before. Only rubles (as opposed to credit cards) are accepted here, however, and you'll have a tough time maneuvering through the cashiers if you don't speak some Russian.

The central shopping district is Nevsky prospekt and the streets running off it. Don't expect too many bargains beyond the bootlegged

CDs and videos (which could be confiscated at customs in the United States), however, because prices for items such as clothes and electronic goods are just as high as in the West, and in the chic stores in hotels they are even higher.

For true souvenirs of the city, think quality crafts just like the tsars did. Ceramic painted eggs, á la Fabergé, and almost anything ornate and gilded are typical of the "imperial" style. Look also for good quality linens. Furs may not be to everybody's taste, but wealthy locals still prefer them during the freezing winters. For kitsch, what better than a set of Russian dolls? These vary in quality and in price.

**Guild of Masters.** Jewelry, ceramics, and other types of Russian traditional art, all made by members of the Russian Union of Artists, are sold here. ⊠ *82 Nevsky pr., City Center* ☎ *812/279–0979* Ⓜ *Mayakovskaya.*

**Lena.** A wide selection of furs is sold at this store. Note that some furs from protected species, such as seals, cannot be brought into the United States. ⊠ *50 Nevsky pr., at Malaya Sadovaya, City Center* ☎ *812/312–3234* Ⓜ *Gostinny Dvor.*

## WHERE TO EAT

¢–$ ✕ **James Cook.** Upon entering James Cook you have a choice: turn right for the pub with a decent menu, or left for one of the finest coffee shops in town. Choose from 40 kinds of coffee, elite teas, various coffee cocktails, and desserts. ⊠ *2 Svedsky per., City Center* ☎ *812/312–3200* ▭ *DC, MC, V* Ⓜ *Nevsky prospekt.*

CAFÉ

$$$ ✕ **Tinkoff.** The crowded, loftlike Tinkoff was St. Petersburg's first micro-brewery. Trendy people come to enjoy beer and tasty comfort food in a relaxed, almost clublike dining room. Frequent Western jazz, lounge, and cool pop acts appear at Tinkoff, but when they're here the cover price can be very high, usually around 1,500R. There's a sushi bar, too, with combos starting from 250R, but you're better off sticking with the beer and burgers. ⊠ *7 Kazanskaya ul., City Center* ☎ *812/718–5566* ⊕ *www.tinkoff.ru* ▭ *DC, MC, V* Ⓜ *Nevsky Prospekt.*

AMERICAN

# STOCKHOLM, SWEDEN

Stockholm is a city in the flush of its second youth. In the last 10 years Sweden's capital has emerged from its cold, Nordic shadow to take the stage as a truly international city. The streets are flowing with a young and confident population keen to drink in everything the city has to offer. The glittering feeling of optimism, success, and living in the "here and now" is rampant in Stockholm. Of course, not everyone is looking to live so much in the present; luckily, Stockholm also has plenty of history. Stockholm boasts a glorious medieval Old Town, grand palaces, ancient churches, sturdy edifices, public parks, and 19th-century museums—its history is soaked into the very fabric of its airy boulevards, built as a public display of the city's trading glory.

## ESSENTIALS

**CURRENCY** The krona (SKr 7.30 to US$ 1; SKr 9.43 to €1); exchange rates were accurate at this writing but are subject to change. ATMs are common and credit cards are widely accepted.

**HOURS** General shopping hours are weekdays 10 to 6, Saturday from 10 to 5, Sunday from noon until 3. Museums open at 10 or 11 in the morning, closing at 5 or 6 in the evenings, with most open on Sunday. Places tend to be open longer between mid-May and mid-September and shorter hours other times of the year.

**INTERNET** **Stockholms Stadsbiblioteket** *(Stockholm City Library)* ⊠ *Sveav. 73, Vasastan* ☎ *08/50831100* ⊕ *www.biblioteket.se* ⊙ *Mon.–Thurs. 9–9, Fri. 9–7, weekends noon–4*

**TELEPHONES** Most tri- and quad-band GSM phones will work in Sweden, where the mobile phone system is up to date, with a 3G system and network compatibility. Public phones in Sweden take phone cards or credit cards. Phone cards can be bought at telecom shops, newsstands, and tobacconists. Public phones support international calls. Handsets are single band. Main providers include Telia, Vodafone, and T-Mobile.

## COMING ASHORE

Most vessels dock at various quays in the heart of the Gamla Stan (Old Town). How far you have to walk to the attractions depends on which quay you are moored at. This is one port where you'll want to be out on deck as the ship arrives and the city comes within camera distance. If all berths are full (eight of them), there is a mooring buoy in the harbor, and passengers will be tendered ashore. You can reach everything in the city (museums, shops, restaurants, and cafés) from the quays on foot.

Alternatively, some vessels dock at Nynasham outside the city. It is a 15-minute walk from the port at Nynasham to the railway station for the one-hour journey into central Stockholm. A one-day travel card covers this journey and all other public transport trips within the city. SL (Stockholm Transport) runs a modern and reliable public transit system. Tickets are valid for one hour from validation and cost SKr 30 per journey within Zone 1 (central Stockholm). A one-day card is SKr 100.

Taxis are plentiful but expensive, and most drivers speak some English. Current rates are SKr 45 for pick-up, then around SKr 9 per km depending on the company. So expect to pay SKr100 (over US$14) for about a five-minute taxi ride.

# EXPLORING STOCKHOLM

**Historiska Museet** *(Museum of National Antiquities)*. Viking treasures and the Gold Room are the main draws, but well-presented temporary exhibitions also cover various periods of Swedish history. The gift shop here is excellent. ⊠ *Narvav. 13–17, Östermalm* ☎ *08/51955600* ⊕ *www.historiska.se* ⊠ *SKr 70* ⊙ *May–Sept., daily 10–5; Oct.–Apr., Tues., Wed., and Fri.–Sun. 11–5, Thurs. 11–8.*

○ **Kulturhuset** *(Culture House)*. Stockholm's controversial cultural center is a glass-and-stone monolith on the south side of Sergels Torg. The restaurant Panorama, at the top, has great views and traditional

Swedish cuisine. ⊠ *Sergelstorg 3, Noormalm* ☎ *08/50831508* ⊕ *www. kulturhuset.stockholm.se.*

**Fodor's Choice** **Kungliga Slottet** *(Royal Palace).* Designed by Nicodemus Tessin, the
★ Royal Palace was completed in 1760 and replaced the previous palace that had burned here in 1697. Watch the changing of the guard in the curved terrace entrance, and view the palace's fine furnishings and Gobelin tapestries on a tour of the **Representationsvän** (State Apartments). To survey the crown jewels, which are no longer used in this self-consciously egalitarian country, head to the **Skattkammaren** (Treasury). The **Livrustkammaren** (Royal Armory) has an outstanding collection of weaponry, coaches, and royal regalia. Entrances to the Treasury and Armory are on the Slottsbacken side of the palace. ⊠ *Gamla Stan* ☎ *08/4026130* ⊕ *www.royalcourt.se* ◱ *SKr 100 for each section of palace, SKr 140 for ticket to all three.* ☉ *Mid-May–mid-Sept., daily 10–4; Mid-Sept.–mid-May, Tues.–Sun. noon–3.*

☾ **Kungsträdgården** *(King's Garden).* This is one of Stockholm's smallest and most central parks. Once the royal kitchen garden, it now hosts a large number of festivals and events each season. The park has numerous cafés and restaurants, a playground, and, in winter, an ice-skating rink. ⊠ *Between Hamng. and Operan, Norrmalm.*

★ **Millesgården.** This gallery and sculpture garden north of the city is dedicated to the property's former owner, American-Swedish sculptor Carl Milles (1875–1955), and is one of the most magical places in Stockholm. On display throughout the property are Milles's own unique works, and inside the main building, once his house, is his private collection. Millesgården can be easily reached via subway to Ropsten, where you catch the Lidingö train and get off at Herserud, the second stop. The trip takes about 30 minutes. ⊠ *Herserudsvägen 32, Lidingö* ☎ *08/4467580* ⊕ *www.millesgarden.se* ◱ *SKr 90* ☉ *May 15–Sept., daily 11–5; Oct.–May 15, Tues.–Sun. noon–5.*

★ **Moderna Museet** *(Museum of Modern Art).* This excellent collection includes works by Picasso, Kandinsky, Dalí, Brancusi, and other international artists. You can also view examples of significant Swedish painters and sculptors and an extensive section on photography. The building itself is striking. Designed by the well-regarded Spanish architect Rafael Moneo, it has seemingly endless hallways of blond wood and walls of glass. ⊠ *Skeppsholmen, Lower Norrmalm* ☎ *08/51955200* ⊕ *www.modernamuseet.se* ◱ *SKr 80* ☉ *Tues. 10–8, Wed.–Sun. 10–6.*

**Fodor's Choice** **Nationalmuseum** *(National Museum).* The museum's collection of paint-
★ ings and sculptures is made up of about 12,500 works. The emphasis is on Swedish and Nordic art, but other areas are well represented. Look especially for some fine works by Rembrandt. The print and drawing department is also impressive, with a nearly complete collection of Edouard Manet prints. ⊠ *Södra Blasieholmshamnen, Lower Norrmalm* ☎ *08/51954428* ⊕ *www.nationalmuseum.se* ◱ *SKr 80* ☉ *Jan.–Aug., Tues. 11–8, Wed.–Sun. 11–5; Sept.–Dec., Tues. and Thurs. 11–8, Wed., Fri., and weekends 11–5.*

☾ **Nordiska Museet** *(Nordic Museum).* An imposing late-Victorian structure housing peasant costumes from every region of the country and exhibits on

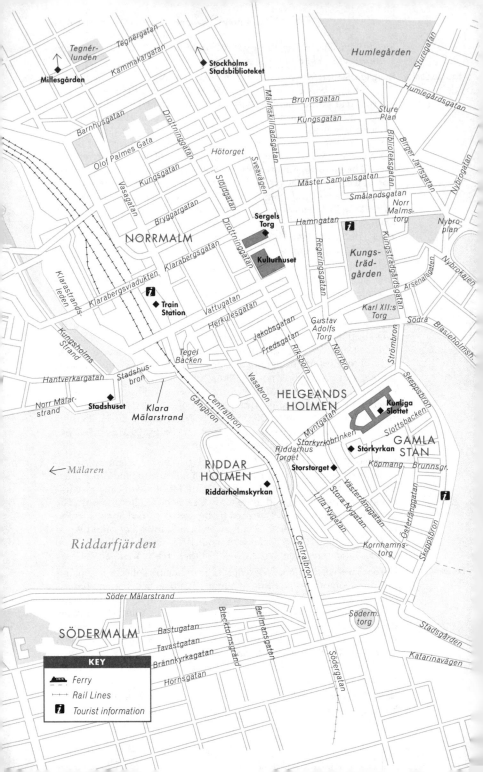

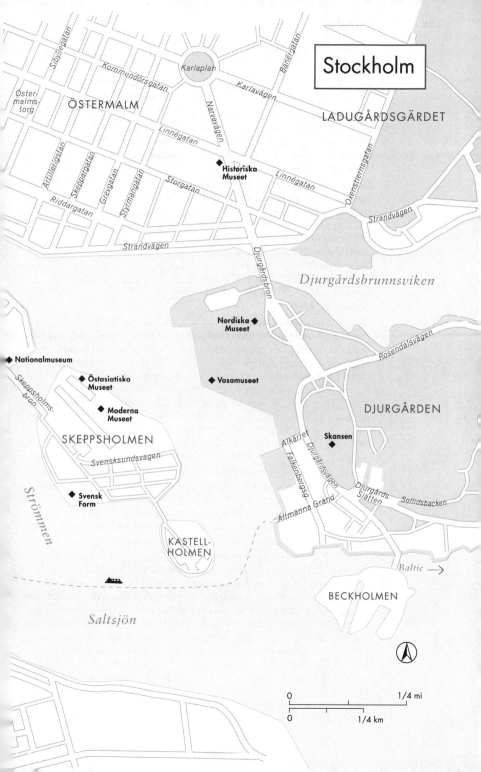

the Sámi (pronounced *sah*-mee), or Lapps—the formerly seminomadic reindeer herders who inhabit the far north—and many other aspects of Swedish life. ✉ *Djurgårdsvagen 6–16, Djurgården* ☎ *08/51954600* ⊕ *www.nordiskamuseet.se* ✒ *SKr 80* ⊘ *June–Aug., daily 10–5; Sept.– May, Mon., Tues., Thurs., and Fri. 10–4, Wed. 10–8, weekends 11–5.*

**Östasiatiska Museet** *(Museum of Far Eastern Antiquities)*. If you have an affinity for Asian art and culture, don't miss this impressive collection of Chinese and Japanese Buddhist sculptures and artifacts. ✉ *Skeppsholmen, Lower Norrmalm* ☎ *08/51955750* ⊕ *www. mfea.se* ✒ *SKr 60* ⊘ *Tues. 11–8, Wed.–Sun. 11–5.*

**Riddarholmskyrkan** *(Riddarholmen Church)*. Dating from 1270, the Grey Friars monastery is the second-oldest structure in Stockholm, and has been the burial place for Swedish kings for more than 400 years. The redbrick structure, distinguished by its delicate iron-fretwork spire, is rarely used for services: it's more like a museum now. The most famous figures interred within are King Gustavus Adolphus, hero of the Thirty Years' War, and the warrior King Karl XII, renowned for his daring invasion of Russia, who died in Norway in 1718. The most recent of the 17 Swedish kings to be put to rest here was Gustav V, in 1950. ✉ *Gamla Stan* ☎ *08/4026167* ✒ *SKr 30* ⊘ *June–Aug., daily 10–5; May 15–May 31, daily 10–4; Sept. 1–15, daily 10–4; Sept 16–May 14 closed.*

**Sergels Torg.** Named after Johan Tobias Sergel (1740–1814), one of Sweden's greatest sculptors, this busy junction in Stockholm's center is dominated by modern, functional buildings and a sunken pedestrian square with subterranean connections to the rest of the neighborhood. Visitors are often put off by its darkened, covered walkways and youths in hooded tops, but it is relatively safe and a great place to witness some real Stockholm street life. ✉ *Norrmalm.*

☾ ★ **Skansen.** The world's first open-air museum, Skansen was founded in 1891 by philologist and ethnographer Artur Hazelius, who is buried here. He preserved examples of traditional Swedish architecture brought from all parts of the country, including farmhouses, windmills, barns, a working glassblower's hut, and churches. Not only is Skansen a delightful trip out of time in the center of a modern city, but it also provides insight into the life and culture of Sweden's various regions. In addition, the park has a zoo, carnival rides, aquarium, theater, and cafés. ✉ *Djurgårdsslätten 49–51, Djurgården* ☎ *08/4428000* ⊕ *www. skansen.se* ✒ *Park and zoo: SKr 100.* ⊘ *Nov.–Feb., daily 10–3; Mar., Apr., and Oct., daily 10–4; May and Sept., daily 10–8; June–Aug., daily 10–10.*

**Fodor's Choice** **Stadshuset** *(City Hall).* The architect Ragnar Östberg, one of the found-
★ ers of the National Romantic movement, completed Stockholm's city
hall in 1923. Headquarters of the city council, the building is functional but ornate: its immense **Blå Hallen** (Blue Hall) is the venue for
the annual Nobel Prize dinner, Stockholm's principal social event.
Take a trip to the top of the 348-foot tower, most of which can be
achieved by elevator, to enjoy a breathtaking panorama of the city and
Riddarfjärden. ✉ *Hantverkargatan 1, Kungsholmen* ☎ *08/50829058*
⊕ *www.stockholm.se/stadshuset* 🎫 *SKr 80 May–Sept., Skr 50 Oct.–
Apr., tower SKr 20* ⊙ *Guided tours only. Tours in English June–Aug.,
daily 10, 11, noon, 1, 2, and 3; Sept., daily 10, noon, and 2; Oct.–May,
daily 10 and noon. Tower May–Sept., daily 10–4:30.*

**Stockholms Stadsbiblioteket** *(Stockholm City Library).* Libraries aren't
always a top sightseeing priority, but the Stockholm City Library is
among the most captivating buildings in town. Designed by the famous
Swedish architect E. G. Asplund and completed in 1928, the building's
cylindrical, galleried main hall gives it the appearance of a large birth-
day cake. ✉ *Sveav. 73, Vasastan* ☎ *08/50831100* ⊕ *www.biblioteket.
se* ⊙ *Mon.–Thurs. 9–9, Fri. 9–7, weekends noon–4.*

**Storkyrkan** *(Great Church).* Swedish kings were crowned in the 15th-cen-
tury Great Church as late as 1907. Today its main attractions are a dramatic wooden statue of St. George slaying the dragon, carved by Bernt
Notke of Lübeck in 1489, and the *Parhelion* (1520), the oldest-known
painting of Stockholm. ✉ *Trångsund 1, Gamla Stan* ☎ *08/7233016*
⊙ *Sept.–Apr., daily 9–4; May–Aug., daily 9–6.*

**Stortorget** *(Great Square).* Here in 1520 the Danish king Christian II
ordered a massacre of Swedish noblemen. The slaughter paved the way
for a national revolt against foreign rule and the founding of Sweden as
a sovereign state. ✉ *Near Kungliga Slottet, Gamla Stan.*

**Svensk Form** *(Swedish Form).* This museum emphasizes the importance
of Swedish form and design, although international works and trends
are also covered. Exhibits include everything from chairs to light fix-
tures to cups, bowls, and silverware. Find out why Sweden is considered
a world leader in industrial design. ✉ *Svensksundsvägen 13, Skeppsholmen, Lower Norrmalm* ☎ *08/4633130* ⊕ *www.svenskform.se* 🎫 *SKr
20* ⊙ *Wed. 5–8, Thurs.–Fri. noon–5, weekends noon–4.*

★ **Vasamuseet** *(Vasa Museum).* The warship *Vasa* sank 10 minutes into its
maiden voyage in 1628, consigned to a watery grave until it was raised
from the seabed in 1961. Its hull was preserved by the Baltic mud, free
of the worms that can eat through ships' timbers. Now largely restored
to her former glory (however short-lived it may have been), the man-of-
war resides in a handsome museum. The political history of the world
may have been different had she made it out of harbor. Daily tours
are available year-round. ✉ *Galärvarsv., Djurgården* ☎ *08/51954800*
⊕ *www.vasamuseet.se* 🎫 *SKr 110* ⊙ *June–Aug., daily 8:30–6; Sept.–
May, Thurs.–Tues. 10–5, Wed. 10–8.*

5

## SHOPPING

Sweden is recognized globally for its unique design sense and has contributed significantly to what is commonly referred to as Scandinavian design. **Kosta Boda and Orrefors** produce the most popular and well-regarded lines of glassware. All of this makes Stockholm one of the best cities in the world for shopping for furniture and home and office accessories. If you like to shop, charge on down to any one of the three main department stores in the central city area, all of which carry top-name Swedish brands for both men and women. For souvenirs and crafts, peruse the boutiques and galleries in Västerlånggatan, the main street of Gamla Stan. For jewelry, crafts, and fine art, hit the shops that line the raised sidewalk at the start of Hornsgatan on Södermalm. Drottninggatan, Birger Jarlsgatan, Biblioteksgatan, Götgatan, and Hamngatan also offer some of the city's best shopping.

**Bruka.** On the corner of Östermalmstorg, in the same building as the marketplace, is this store, which has a wide selection of creative kitchen items, as well as wicker baskets and chairs. ⊠ *Humlegårdsgatan 1, Östermalm* ☎ *08/6601480* ⊕ *www.brukadesign.se/.*

**Crystal Art Center.** This store near the central station, has a great selection of smaller glass items. ⊠ *Tegelbacken 4, Lower Norrmalm* ☎ *08/217169* ⊕ *www.cac.se.*

**Stockhome.** Not just a clever play on words, this store offers a great selection of things with which, well, to stock your home, including china, towels, glass, books, linen, even bicycles and patterned bandages. ⊠ *Kungsg. 25, Norrmalm* ☎ *08/4111300* ⊕ *www.stockhome.se/.*

**Svenskt Tenn.** For elegant home furnishings, affluent Stockholmers tend to favor this boutique, which is best known for its selection of designer Josef Franck's furniture and fabrics. ⊠ *Strandv. 5A, Östermalm* ☎ *08/6701600* ⊕ *www.svenskttenn.se.*

## WHERE TO EAT

Most Stockholm restaurants specialize in the preparation of perennially popular, Swedish-style fish and shellfish. Innovative and traditional herring assortments and locally sourced roe are especially popular as starters. These starters are often large enough for a light, affordable lunch. Note that many restaurants are closed on Sunday.

$ ✕ **Hermans.** Hermans is a haven for vegetarians out to get the most bang for their kronor. The glassed-in back deck and open garden both provide breathtaking vistas across the water of Stockholm harbor, Gamla Stan, and the island of Djurgården. The food is always served buffet style, and includes various vegetable and pasta salads, warm casseroles, and such entrées as Indonesian stew with peanut sauce and vegetarian lasagna. The fruit pies, chocolate cakes, and cookies are delicious. ⊠ *Fjällg. 23A, Södermalm* ☎ *08/6439480* ⊕ *www.gastrogate.com/restaurang/hermans* ⊟ *MC, V.*

VEGETARIAN

Fodor's Choice

★

$$$
SCANDINAVIAN
**Fodor's** Choice
★

✕ **Mathias Dahlgren.** It seemed like all of Stockholm was holding its breath for Mattias Dahlgren to open his new eponymous restaurant at the end of 2007 (his first since he shuttered the legendary Bon Lloc). When the doors finally opened, a collective sigh of relief was audible: success! From the elegant modern dining room to the food—simple, artistically rendered local food which Dahlgren's dubbed "natural cuisine"—this place doesn't disappoint. For his trouble he picked up a Michelin star in his first six months. Don't miss this place. ⊠ *Grand Hotel, S Blasieholmshamen 6* ☎ *08/6793584* ⊕ *www.mathiasdahlgren. com* 🍴 *Reservations essential* ⊟ *AE, DC, MC, V* ۞ *Lunch served weekdays in bar. No lunch weekends. Closed Sun.*

$$
SCANDINAVIAN
**Fodor's** Choice
★

✕ **Pelikan.** Beer, beer, and more beer is the order of the day at Pelikan, a traditional working-class drinking hall, a relic of the days when Södermalm was the dwelling place of the city's blue-collar brigade. Today's more bohemian residents find it just as enticing, with the unvarnished wood-paneled walls, faded murals, and glass globe lights fulfilling all their down-at-the-heel pretensions. The food here is some of the best traditional Swedish fare in the city. The herring, meatballs, and salted bacon with onion sauce are not to be missed. ⊠ *Blekingeg. 40, Södermalm* ☎ *08/55609090* ⊕ *www.pelikan.se* ⊟ *MC, V* ۞ *No lunch Sun.–Thurs.*

$$$
SCANDINAVIAN
★

✕ **Prinsen.** Still in the same location as when it opened in 1897, the Prince serves both traditional and modern Swedish cuisine, but it is for the traditional that most people come. The interior is rich with mellow, warm lighting; dark-wood paneling; and leather chairs and booths. The restaurant is rightly known for its scampi salad and *Wallenbergare*, a classic dish of veal, cream, and peas. Downstairs you'll find a bar and a space for larger parties. ⊠ *Mäster Samuelsg. 4, Normalm* ☎ *08/6111331* ⊕ *www.restaurangprinsen.com/eng* 🍴 *Reservations essential* ⊟ *AE, DC, MC, V* ۞ *No lunch weekends.*

## WHERE TO STAY

Stockholm can be a relatively stagnant town when it comes to hotel development, with few new openings each year. But while the hotel choices here are often not trendily brand-new, they're still plentiful and include everything from grand five-star properties down to basic, affordable hostel accommodation.

$$$
**Fodor's** Choice
★

🏨 **Grand Hotel.** At first glance the Grand seems like any other world-class international hotel, and in many ways it is. Its location is one of the best in the city, on the quayside just across the water from the Royal Palace. It boasts an impressive guest list. The service is slick, professional, and predicts your every need. The large rooms are sumptuous and decadent, with robes so fluffy, beds so soft, and antiques so lovely you may never want to leave. But the Grand offers something else: a touch of the uniquely Scandinavian. You can feel it in the relaxed atmosphere that pervades the hotel, you can smell it in the fresh, salt-tinged air that wafts through the open windows, and you can see it in the purity of the light that penetrates all corners of the hotel. If there is a more exquisite hotel anywhere in town, it is yet to be found. **Pros:** unadulterated luxury; world-class service; great bar. **Cons:** some rooms are small; faded in parts. ⊠ *Södra Blasieholmshamnen 8* ☎ *08/6793500* ⊕ *www. grandhotel.se* ⇝ *386 rooms, 21 suites* ⚭ *In-room: safe, refrigerator, Wi-Fi. In-hotel: 2 restaurants, room service, bar, gym, spa, laundry service, Wi-Fi hotspot, no-smoking rooms* ⊟ *AE, DC, MC, V* |❍| *BP.*

$$$
**Fodor's** Choice
★

**Hotel Stureplan.** Following the demise of the Lydmar Hotel, the undisputed best boutique to have ever graced Stockholm's sidewalks, the city's hotel watchers were left wondering if they would ever recover. Then, along came Hotel Stureplan. Housed in a beautiful 18th-century mansion, Stureplan has pitched itself just right; the perfect mix between modern design, comfortable living, and functional hotel. Rooms come in small, medium, large, or extra large, and are further categorized as classic (Gustavian furniture, stucco features, balconies, fireplaces) and loft (modern, minimal and light-filled). Whichever you choose, Stureplan has perfected the elusive art of making guests feel truly at home. **Pros:** to-die-for design; great service; perfect location. **Cons:** no restaurant; small rooms are very small. ⊠ *Birger Jarlsg. 24* ☎ *08/4406600* ⊕ *www.hotelstureplan.se* ⇝ *102 rooms* ⚭ *In-room: safe, refrigerator, Internet. In-hotel: room service, bar, laundry service, Internet terminal, no-smoking rooms* ⊟ *AE, DC, MC, V* |❍| *BP.*

$$$$ **Sheraton Hotel and Towers.** Popular with business executives, the Sheraton is also an ideal hotel for the tourist on a generous budget looking for comfort and luxury. The Sheraton unveiled a new look in 2008, shaking off its tired 1980s shroud to reveal a much cleaner, more stylish look. The rooms now feature natural tones, cool lighting, refinished bathrooms, and wood detail in all the places you'd expect it. English is the main language at the restaurant and bar, which fill up at night once the piano player arrives. The gift shop sells Swedish crystal and international newspapers. **Pros:** great location; big rooms; extremely comfortable beds. **Cons:** not popular with locals; terrible view from courtyard rooms. ⊠ *Tegelbacken 6* ☎ *08/4123400* ⊕ *www.sheratonstockholm. com* ⇝ *462 rooms, 30 suites* ⚭ *In-room: safe, refrigerator, Internet, Wi-Fi. In-hotel: restaurant, room service, bar, gym, laundry service, Wi-Fi hotspot, parking (paid), no-smoking rooms* ⊟ *AE, DC, MC, V* |❍| *BP.*

$$$–$$$$ **Radisson SAS Strand Hotel.** An art-nouveau monolith, built in 1912 for the Stockholm Olympics, this hotel has been completely and tastefully modernized. It's on the water across from the Royal Dramatic Theater, only a short walk from the Old Town and the museums on Skeppsholmen. No two rooms are alike, but all are furnished with simple and elegant furniture, offset by white woodwork and hues of moss green and cocoa brown. The Strand restaurant has a sharp, urban feel, with a cool color scheme of stone, earth-brown, and natural greens. **Pros:** central location; elegant rooms; lively public areas. **Cons:** has a slight chainhotel feel; beds too soft for some. ⊠ *Nybrokajen 9* ☎ *08/50664000* ⊕ *www.radissonsas.com* ⇝ *152 rooms* ⚭ *In-room: safe, refrigerator, Wi-Fi. In-hotel: restaurant, room service, bar, gym, laundry service, Wi-Fi hotspot, no-smoking rooms* ⊟ *AE, DC, MC, V* |❍| *BP.*

# TALLINN, ESTONIA

Tallinn's tiny gem of an Old Town, the most impressive in the region, is an ideal cruise destination. It has romantic towers, ankle-wrenching cobblestone streets, cozy nooks, city-wall cafés, and a dozen other attractions—all within 1 square km. In many ways still the same town as during the medieval era, it is compact enough to reveal itself on a short visit. In this eminently walkable city it is possible to see the main sights and venture into intimate corners during your trip and feel that you've found your own personal Tallinn. The city has blossomed in the post-Communist era and revels in its resurgent popularity, but it hasn't forgotten its roots. It's still charming and distinctive, despite having strode headlong into the 21st century.

## ESSENTIALS

CURRENCY The Estonian kroon (12.32EEK to US$1; 15.64EEK to €1). Credit cards are widely accepted, and ATMs are common in Tallinn.

HOURS Shops are open from 10 AM until 7 PM, though some close early on Saturday. Museums are open Wednesday through Sunday from 10 AM or 11 AM until 5 PM or 6 PM.

INTERNET Post offices in Tallinn have Internet access. **Toompea Post Office** (✉ *Lossi plats 4*) is the post office for the Old Town; it's open weekdays 9 AM–5 PM. There are more than 100 free Wi-Fi spots in the city, including one at the town hall.

TELEPHONES Most tri- and quad-band mobile phones should work in Estonia. The mobile service is dual-band and supports text and data services. Pay phones take phone cards worth 30EEK, 50EEK, or 100EEK. Buy cards at any kiosk. You can use these to make international calls.

## COMING ASHORE

The Old City Harbor Port sits in the very heart of modern Tallinn and is half a mile from the city center. Terminal facilities are comprehensive, and include a restaurant, bank–exchange facilities, tourist information shops, and restrooms. Taxis wait outside the terminal building for journeys into the Old Town; otherwise, it's only a short walk from the port.

Taxi fares generally start at between 35EEK and 70EEK with an additional charge of 7EEK per km in the daytime, more at night or in bad weather. Drivers are bound by law to display an operating license and a meter. There is no need to rent a car while in Tallinn, as all the major attractions are in the Old Town, which is very close to the dock.

# EXPLORING TALLINN

Tallinn's historic Old Town retains almost 80% of its medieval buildings—impressive enough to gain UNESCO World Heritage status. The city is made up of two parts. Vanalinn (Lower Old Town) was historically the domain of traders, artisans, and ordinary citizens—a workaday commercial hub whose streets were always noisy and busy. The stately, sedate Toompea (Upper Town), a hillock that was the site of the original Estonian settlement, is on the burial mound of Kalev, the epic hero of Estonia. Toompea Castle, crowning the hill, is now the seat of the

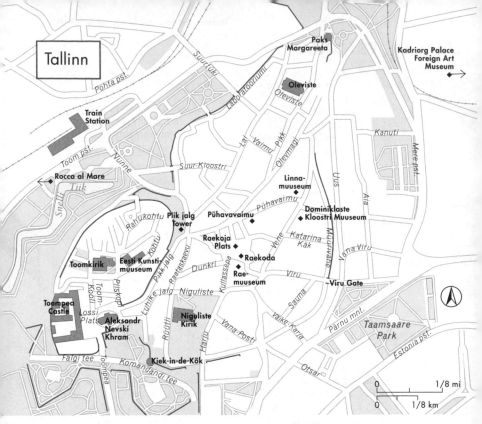

country's parliament and, sadly, not open to visitors. As you wander the cobbled alleyways even with crowds of fellow visitors, it's easy to feel the atmosphere of the Tallinn of old. The commerce of the streets in Vanalinn may disappoint some, but the ancestors of today's gallery and restaurant owners would surely be pleased to see the bustling streets of their city today.

**Aleksandr Nevski Khram.** The 19th-century Russian Orthodox Alexander Nevsky Cathedral, with the country's largest bell, is a symbol of the centuries of Russification endured by Estonia. ⊠ *Lossi pl. 10, Toompea* ☎ *644–3484* ⊙ *Daily 8–7.*

**Dominiiklaste Kloostri Muuseum.** Wander through the ages in the ancient stone galleries and narrow hallways of the Dominican Monastery Museum, founded in 1246 and now displaying 15th- and 16th-century stone carvings. At 5 PM enjoy a half-hour baroque music concert. ⊠ *Vene 16, Vanalinn* ☎ *644–4606* ⊕ *kloostri.ee* ⊙ *Daily 10–6.*

**Kadriorg Palace Foreign Art Museum.** The baroque palace, built for Catherine I by her husband Peter the Great in 1721, merits a visit not just for its impressive and thorough exhibition of 16th- to 20th-century art, but also for the palace's architectural beauty and manicured gardens. Kadriorg Palace offers a glimpse into history, from Russian imperial splendor to Soviet Socialist Realist art, with Estonian and European masterpieces along the way. ✉ *Wei-zenbergi 37* ☎ *606–6400* ⊕ *www.ekm.ee* ✆ *65EEK* ⊙ *May–Sept., Tues.–Sun. 10–5; Oct.–Apr., Wed.–Sun. 10–5.*

★ **Kiek-in-de-Kök.** At the southern end of the Old Town looms this magnificent, six-story tower church (the name is Low German for "peep in the kitchen"), so called because during the 15th century one could peer into the kitchens of lower town houses from here. The tower has a museum of contemporary art and ancient maps and weapons. ✉ *Komandandi 2, Vanalinn* ☎ *644–6686* ⊕ *www.linnamuuseum.ee* ✆ *70EEK* ⊙ *Mar.–Oct., Tues.–Sun. 10:30–6; Nov.–Feb., Tues.–Sun. 10:30–5.*

**TALLINN BEST BETS**

**Shopping in Vanalinn.** These alleyways have been a bustling commercial center for more than 500 years. History practically oozes from every stone and the galleries are a shopper's delight.

**Raekoja Plats.** One of the finest city squares in the Baltic, Raekoja Plats is the social center of the city, hosting markets, concerts, and parades.

**Aleksandr Nevski Khram.** This Orthodox church is a wonderfully ornate example of its type, with onion domes and an interior full of votives and icons.

**Niguliste Kirik.** The 15th-century Church of St. Nicholas, part of the Estonian Art Museum, is famed for its fragment of a treasured frieze, Bernt Notke's (1440–1509) *Danse Macabre*, a haunting depiction of death. ✉ *Niguliste 3, Vanalinn* ☎ *631–4330* ⊕ *www.ekm.ee* ✆ *50EEK* ⊙ *Wed.–Sun. 10–5.*

**Paks Margareeta.** The stocky guardian of the northernmost point of the Old Town, Fat Margaret, is a 16th-century fortification named for a particularly hefty cannon it contained. Now it houses the Maritime Museum and a roof with a view of Old Town. ✉ *Pikk 70, Vanalinn* ☎ *641–1408* ⊕ *www.meremuuseum.ee* ✆ *50EEK* ⊙ *Wed.–Sun. 10–6.*

**Fodor's Choice** ★ **Raekoja Plats.** Tallinn's Town Hall Square has a long history of intrigue, executions, and salt (Tallinn's main export in the Middle Ages). You can tour the only surviving Gothic **town hall** in northern Europe. Old Thomas, its weather vane, has been atop the town hall since 1530. Near the center of the square, an L-shaped stone marks the site of a 17th-century execution, where a priest was beheaded for killing a waitress who had offered him a rock-hard omelet. Across the square stands the town **apothecary,** which dates from 1422. ✉ *Raekoja plats 11* ☎ *645–7900 for town hall, 631–4860 for apothecary* ✆ *Town Hall: July and Aug. 60EEK, 45EEK rest of year* ⊙ *Town Hall: July and Aug., Mon.–Sat. 10–4, tower May–Aug. daily 11–6, rest of year by appointment. Apothecary: weekdays 9–7, Sat. 9–5, Sun. 9–4.*

☞ **Rocca al Mare.** A 15-minute taxi ride from the center, the 207-acre Open-Air Ethnographic Museum provides a breath of fresh air and an informative look into Estonia's past, from farm architecture to World War II–era deportations. ✉ *Vabaõhumuuseumi 12* ☎ *654–9101* ⊕ *www.evm.ee* ✆ *95EEK* ⊙ *Late Apr.–late Sept., daily 10–8; late Sept.–late Apr., daily 10–5.*

**Toomkirik.** The Lutheran Dome Church, the oldest church in the country, was founded by the occupying Danes in the 13th century and rebuilt in 1686. ⊠ *Toom-kooli 6, Toompea* ☎ *644–4140* ⊙ *Tues.–Sun. 9–5.*

## SHOPPING

Travelers from outside the European Union can buy goods from tax-free shops and will receive a tax exemption on purchases over 600.05EEK (which can include more than one item as long as everything is made in a single purchase). The shop will provide you with the paperwork and this must be presented to the customs officials at the port. Purchases must not be unwrapped before you leave the country.

Tallinn has a wide range of crafts on sale. Fragrant juniper wood is carved into bowls and dolomite stone is fashioned into candlesticks and coasters. A whole range of handblown glass, ceramics, delicate wrought iron, and art is sold in tiny galleries. Hand-knitted sweaters, gloves, and socks keep the locals snug in winter and are signature souvenirs here. Warming quilts are also available, as well as a good range of leather goods. Sweet tooths will love the chocolates made by Kalev and the hand-painted marzipan that's sold in presentation boxes. The Old Town is the place to browse, with some excellent shops around Katerina kälk (Catherine Passage).

**Bogapott.** At this store a husband and wife team of artists offer a wide range of Estonian-produced crafts. There's a pretty café on-site. ⊠ *Pikk-jalg 9* ☎ *372 631 3181* ⊕ *www.bogapott.ee.*

**Galerii Kaks.** This boutique stocks locally produced jewelry, glass, textiles, ceramics, and leatherwork. ⊠ *Lühike jalg 1* ☎ *372 641 8308.*

**Saaremaa Sepad.** This store has wrought-iron workshops with a huge selection of objects large and small, ranging from practical to decorative. ⊠ *Nunne tn 7* ☎ *372 64 6 4315* ⊕ *www.sepad.ee.*

## WHERE TO EAT

**$$$**   ✕ **Restoran Gloria.** Voted best restaurant in the Silver Spoon awards by
FRENCH   the Gastronomic Society of Estonia, the Gloria is more expensive than its neighbors but worth the money for the attention to detail and locally sourced ingredients. Chef Dimitri Demjanov happily pays tribute to French cuisine, and the dining room is suitably grand. The adjoining wine celler offers a less formal menu of salads and charcuterie. ⊠ *Muurivahe 2* ☎ *640–6800* ⊕ *www.gloria.ee* ▭ *AE, MC, V* ⊙ *Closed Sun.*

**$**   ✕ **Tristan ja Isolde.** Possibly the most sedate café in Tallinn, Tristan and
CAFÉ   Isolde is inside the medieval stone walls of the town hall. With a dozen varieties of fresh-roasted coffee and soothing jazzy tunes on the sound system, this is a great place to relax morning, noon, or night. ⊠ *Town Hall, Raekoja Plats 1* ☎ *627–9020* ▭ *MC, V.*

# VISBY, SWEDEN

Gotland is Sweden's main holiday island, a place of ancient history with a relaxed summer-party vibe, wide sandy beaches, and wild cliff formations called *raukar*. Measuring 125 km (78 mi) long and 52 km (32 mi) at its widest point, Gotland is where Swedish sheep farming has its home. In its charming glades 35 varieties of wild orchids thrive, attracting botanists from all over the world. The first record of people living on Gotland dates from around 5000 BC. By the Iron Age it had become a leading Baltic trading center. When German marauders arrived in the 13th century, they built most of its churches and established close trading ties with the Hanseatic League in Lübeck. They were followed by the Danes, and Gotland finally became part of Sweden in 1645. Gotland's capital, Visby, reflects this full and fascinating history, and the architecture of its downtown core is classified as a World Heritage Site.

## ESSENTIALS

CURRENCY The Swedish krona (SKr 7.37 to US$1). ATMs are common and credit cards are widely accepted.

HOURS General shopping hours are weekdays from 10 to 6, Saturday from 10 to 5, and Sunday from noon until 3. Museums open at 10 or 11 in the morning, closing at 5 or 6 in the evenings, with most open on Sunday.

TELEPHONES Most tri- and quad-band GSM phones will work in Sweden, where the mobile phone system is up to date and has both 3G and network compatibility. Hand sets are single-band. Public phones in Sweden take phone cards or credit cards, and you can make international calls from them; phone cards can be bought at telecom shops, newsstands and tobacconists. Main providers include Telia, Vodafone, and T-Mobile.

## COMING ASHORE

Vessels dock in the town port; from here it is a 5- to 10-minute walk into the center of town. The port has only the most basic facilities, but shops and restaurants are on hand in town.

You don't need public transport to explore Visby. However, if you want to discover all that Gotland has to offer independently, you'll need transportation. Renting a car would free you up to explore at your own pace. An economy manual vehicle starts at SKr 800 per day.

# EXPLORING GOTLAND

## VISBY

Gotland's capital, Visby, is a delightful hilly town of about 20,000 people. Medieval houses, ruined fortifications, churches, and cottage-lined cobbled lanes make Visby look like a fairy-tale place. Thanks to a very gentle climate, the roses that grow along many of the town's facades bloom even in November. Visby might be better known to some people today as the home of Pippi Longstocking. Movies featuring the popular red-haired girl with pigtails were filmed here.

**Burmeisterska Huset.** The home of the *Burmeister*—or principal German merchant—organizes exhibitions displaying the works of artists from the island and the rest of Sweden. Call the tourist office in Visby to

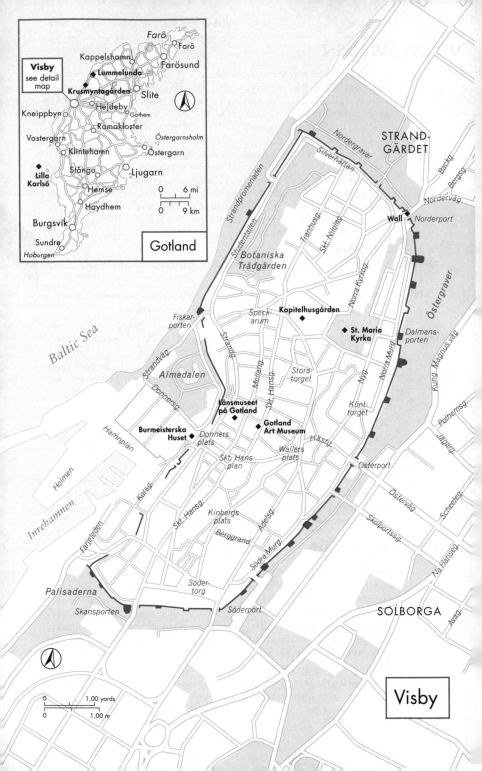

## Gotland (detail map)

Farö
Farö
Kappelshamn
Farösund
**Visby**
see detail
map
**Lummelunda**
**Krusmyntagården**
Slite
Kneippbyn
Hejdeby
Gothem
Romakloster
Östergarnsholm
Vastergarn
Klintehamn
Östergarn
**Lilla Karlsö**
Stånga
Ljugarn
Hemse
Haydhem
Burgsvik
Sundre
Hoburgen

0        6 mi
0        9 km

**Gotland**

## Visby

STRAND-GÄRDET
Nordergravar
Silverhättan
Backg.
Bergsg.
Nordervåg
Strandpromenaden
Tranhusg.
Skt. Nrlolag
Norra Kyrkg.
**Wall** Norderport
Studentallen
Fiskar-porten
Botaniska Trädgården
Speck-arum
**Kapitelhusgården**
**St. Maria Kyrka**
Dalmans-porten
Strandg.
Strandväg
Östergravar
Baltic Sea
Almedalen
Donnersg.
Strandg.
Mellang.
Skt. Hansg.
Stora-torget
Kung Magnus väg
Norra Murg.
Nyg.
Klint-torget
Hamnplan
**Länsmuseet på Gotland**
**Burmeisterska Huset**
Donners plats
**Gotland Art Museum**
Hästg.
Wallers plats
Polhernsg.
Jägarg.
Skt. Hans plan
Österport
Östervåg
Scheeleg.
Holmen
Korsg.
Skt. Hansg.
Kinbergs plats
Adelsg.
Skolportsg.
Inrehamnen
Berggrand
Söder-torg
Södra Murg.
Na Hanseg.
Avag.
Färjeleden
Söderport
SOLBORGA
**Palisaderna**
Skansporten

0        1,00 yards
0        1,00 m

**Visby**

arrange for a viewing. ⊠ *Strandg. 9* ☎ *0498/201700 Visby tourist office* 🖅 *Free.*

**Gotland Art Museum.** The region's primary art museum has some innovative exhibitions of contemporary painting and sculpture. On the first floor is the permanent display, which is mostly uninspiring, save for a beautiful 1917 watercolor by local artist Axel Lindman showing Visby from the beach in all its splendid medieval glory. ⊠ *St. Hansg. 21* ☎ *0498/292700* ⊕ *www. lansmuseetgotland.se* 🖅 *SKr 40* ☉ *June–Sept., Tues.–Sun noon–4.*

☺ **Kapitelhusgården.** Medieval activities are re-created at this museum village. Families can watch and take part in metal- and woodworking, coin making, dressmaking, archery, and hunting. ⊠ *Drottensg. 8* ☎ *0498/247637* 🖅 *Free* ☉ *June–Aug., daily noon–10* PM *(Aug. 8–15 till 1* AM*).*

> **VISBY BEST BETS**
>
> **Follow your whim along the streets of Visby.** The wealth of architectural splendor funded by Hanseatic trade means there's a wonderful vista on almost every corner.
>
> **Explore the dramatic and windswept countryside beyond the city walls.** Wild orchids, rocky coastal precipices, and grassy meadows abound.
>
> **Church-hopping.** Gotland has about 100 old churches that are still in use (Visby itself has 13); exploring them is a major pastime.

**Länsmuseet på Gotland.** Gotland's County Museum contains examples of medieval artwork, prehistoric gravestones and skeletons, and silver hoards from Viking times. Be sure to also check out the ornate "picture stones" from AD 400–600, which depict ships, people, houses, and animals. ⊠ *Strandg. 14* ☎ *0498/292700* ⊕ *www.lansmuseetgotland.se* 🖅 *SKr 80 Old Hall, SKr 40 Art Museum* ☉ *Mid-June–end-Sept., daily 10–6; Oct.–mid-June, Tues.–Sun. noon–4.*

**St. Maria Kyrka.** Visby's cathedral is the only one of the town's 13 medieval churches that is still intact and in use. Built between 1190 and 1225 as a place of worship for the town's German parishioners, the church has few of its original fittings because of the extensive and sometimes clumsy restoration work done over the years. That said, the sandstone font and the unusually ugly angels decorating the pulpit are both original features worth a look. ⊠ *Västra Kyrkogatan 5* ☎ *0498/206800* ☉ *Daily 10–5.*

**Wall.** In its heyday Visby was protected by a wall, of which 3 km (2 mi) survive today, along with 44 towers and numerous gateways. It is considered the best-preserved medieval city wall in Europe after that of Carcassonne, in southern France. Take a stroll to the north gate for an unsurpassed view of the wall.

## GOTLAND

There's a lot to see out on the island, so if you want to spend the day exploring, you can see a fair amount in your day in port. Definitely get out of Visby itself if you want to see some of the island's churches.

## CLOSE UP

# Gotland's Churches

The island has about 100 old churches dating from Gotland's great commercial era that are still in use today. **Barlingbo,** from the 13th century, has vault paintings, stained-glass windows, and a remarkable 12th-century font. The exquisite **Dalhem** was constructed around 1200. **Gothem,** built during the 13th century, has a notable series of paintings of that period. **Grötlingbo** is a 14th-century church with stone sculptures and stained glass (note the 12th-century reliefs on the facade). **Öja,** a medieval church decorated with paintings, houses a famous holy rood from the late-13th century. The massive ruins of a Cistercian monastery founded in 1164 are now called the **Roma Kloster Kyrka** (Roma Cloister Church). **Tingstäde** is a mix of six buildings dating from 1169 to 1300.

**Krusmyntagården.** A pleasant stop along the way to Lummelunda is this garden with more than 200 herbs, 8 km (5 mi) north of Visby. ⊠ *Krusmyntavägen 4, Väskinde* ☎ *0498/296900* ⊕ *www.krusmynta. se* ☞ *Free* ☉ *Mid-May–end-June and mid-Aug.–end-Aug., daily 10–6; July–mid-Aug., daily 10–8.*

**Lilla Karlsö.** Curious rock formations dot the coasts of Gotland, remnants of reefs formed more than 400 million years ago, and two bird sanctuaries, Stora and Lilla Karlsö, stand off the coast south of Visby. The bird population consists mainly of guillemots, which look like penguins. Visits to these sanctuaries are permitted only in the company of a recognized guide. ☎ *0498/240450 for Stora, 0498/241139 for Lilla* ☞ *SKr 350 for Stora, SKr 300 for Lilla* ☉ *May–Aug., daily.*

**Lummelunda.** The 4 km (2½ mi) of stalactite caves, about 18 km (11 mi) north of Visby on the coastal road, are unique in this part of the world and are worth visiting. The largest was discovered in 1950 by three boys out playing. ⊠ *Lummelunds Bruk* ☎ *0498/273050* ⊕ *www. lummelundagrottan.se* ☞ *SKr 120* ☉ *May–early June, daily 10–3; early-June–end June and mid-Aug.–late Aug., daily 10–4; early-July–mid-July, daily 10–5; mid-July–mid-Aug., daily 9–6; late Aug.–end Sept., daily 10–2.*

## SHOPPING

Gotlanders are self-sufficient and resourceful people and have developed many handicrafts, so there is a range of handcrafted souvenirs to choose from, including blown glass, metal objects, sculptures, woven items, and ceramics. Sheepskin and wool items are a particular specialty.

**Antakus.** This store has an excellent range of gifts and housewares made by the Antakus team and other craftspeople based locally around Gotland. ⊠ *St. Hansplein* ☎ *0498/212888.*

**G.A.D.** This boutique (the intials of which stand for "Good Art and Design") sells stunningly simple modern furniture that has been designed and made on Gotland. ⊠ *Södra Kyrkog. 16, Visby* ☎ *0498/249410* ⊕ *www.gad.se.*

## ACTIVITIES

The unspoiled countryside and onshore waters are a perfect playground if you want to get active. Many visitors simply rent a bike and take to the safe open roads, or try kayaking or windsurfing on the water. **Gotlands Cykeluthyrning.** Bicycles can be rented from this cycle shop. ⊠ *Skeppsbron 2* ☎ *0498/214133* ⊕ *www.gotlandscykeluthyrning.com.* **Gotlands Upplevelser.** For an aquatic adventure, this outfitter will rent you a canoe and a life jacket or windsurfing equipment. Call for prices and locations. ☎ *0730/751678* ⊕ *www.gotlandsupplevelser.se.*

## BEACHES

**Fårö and Själsö.** If you do nothing else on Gotland, go for a swim. The island has miles and miles of beautiful golden beaches and unusually warm water for this part of the world. The best and least-crowded beaches are at the north of the island.

## WHERE TO EAT

$$$ ✗**Bakfickan.** Visby's only seafood restaurant offers the excellent daily
SEAFOOD catch plus items like Baltic herring, Gotland bread, pickled herrngs, and potted shrimp. The owners source as many ingredients as possible locally. For example the dessert menu includes a selection of local cheeses. ⊠ *Stora Torget 1* ☎ *0498/271807* ⊕ *www.bakfickan-visby.nu* ☰ *MC, V.*

$-$$$ ✗**Krusmyntagården.** This marvelous little garden café opened in the late
SCANDINAVIAN 1970s and has been passed down through several owners. The garden now has more than 200 organic herbs and plants, many of which are used in the evening BBQ feasts. The menu includes vegan options. ⊠ *Krusmyntavågen 4, Väskinde* ☎ *0498/296901* ⊕ *www.krusmynta.se* ☾ *Closed Sept.–mid-May)* ☰ *AE, DC, MC, V.*

# WARNEMÜNDE, GERMANY (FOR BERLIN)

Since the fall of the Iron Curtain, no city in Europe has seen more development and change. Two Berlins that had been separated for 40 years struggled to meld into one, and in the scar of barren borderland between them sprang government and commercial centers that have become the glossy spreads of travel guides and architecture journals. But even as the capital moves forward, history is always tugging at its sleeve. Between the wealth of neoclassical and 21st-century buildings, there are constant reminders, both subtle and stark, of the events of the 20th century. For every relocated corporate headquarters, a church stands half-ruined, a synagogue is under 24-hour guard, and an empty lot remains where a building either crumbled in World War II or went up in dynamite as East Germany cleared a path for its Wall. There are few other cities where the past and the present collide with such energy.

## ESSENTIALS

CURRENCY   The euro (€1 to US$1.39 at this writing). ATMs are common and credit cards are widely accepted.

HOURS   Stores are open Monday through Saturday from 8 AM to 8 PM. Museum hours vary, but core hours are from 10 AM to 5 PM, with shorter hours on Sunday. Some state museums are closed on Monday.

INTERNET   **Sinn E.V.** (✉ *Hölderlingweg 10, Rostock* ☎ *0381/367–6248* ⊕ *www. sinnev.de*) is closest to the port.

TELEPHONES   Most tri- and quad-band GSM phones will work in Germany, where the mobile system supports 3G technology. Phone cards for public phones are available at newsagents and will allow international calls. Major companies include Vodafone, T2, and T-Mobile.

## COMING ASHORE

A state-of-the-art Warnemünde cruise terminal opened in 2005, but it has limited passenger facilities. The best thing about the terminal is that it is within 300 yards of a railway station for easy onward connections through the town of Rostock. Travel time into Rostock is 20 minutes, with train journeys to Berlin taking 2 hours 45 minutes. Prices to Berlin are €39 round-trip. Trains from Rostock to Berlin run approximately three times per hour depending on time of day.

Once in Berlin, you'll find an integrated network of subway (U-bahn) and suburban (S-bahn) train lines, buses, and trams (in eastern Berlin only). Most visitor destinations are in the broad reach of the fare zones A and B. At this writing, both the €2.10 ticket (fare zones A and B) and the €2.80 ticket (fare zones A, B, and C) allow you to make a one-way trip with an unlimited number of changes between trains, buses, and trams. There are reduced rates for children ages 6–13.

Buy a Kurzstreckentarif ticket (€1.30) for short rides of up to six bus or tram stops or three U-bahn or S-bahn stops. The best deal if you plan to travel around the city extensively is the Tageskarte (day card for zones A and B), for €6.10, good on all transportation. (it's €6.50 for A, B, C zones).

There are no car-rental offices at the port, so you will need to arrange to have a car waiting when the ship docks (extra charges may apply). Alternatively, you can easily travel by train into nearby Rostock and pick up a vehicle there. If you want to visit Berlin, public transport is more practical than a car rental. However, renting a vehicle would allow you to explore the other towns along the Baltic coastline and enjoy the countryside and beaches. The cost for a compact manual vehicle is approximately €80 per day.

## EXPLORING BERLIN

☺ **Berliner Fernsehturm** *(Berlin TV Tower).* Finding Alexanderplatz is no problem: Just head toward the 1,198-foot-high tower piercing the sky. You can get the best view of Berlin from within the tower's disco ball-like observation level; on a clear day you can see for 40 km (25 mi). ⊠ *Panoramastr. 1a, Mitte* ☎ *030/247–5750* ⊕ *www.tv-turm.de* ☜ *€10.50* ☉ *Nov.–Feb., daily 10 AM–midnight; Mar.–Oct., daily 9 AM–midnight; last admission ½ hr before closing* Ⓜ *Alexanderpl. (S-bahn and U-bahn).*

**Fodor's** Choice
★
**Brandenburger Tor** *(Brandenburg Gate).* Once the pride of Prussian Berlin and the city's premier landmark, the Brandenburger Tor was left in a desolate no-man's-land when the Wall was built. Since the Wall's dismantling, the sandstone gateway has become the scene of the city's Unification Day and New Year's Eve parties. This is the sole remaining gate of 14 built by Carl Langhans in 1788–91, designed as a triumphal arch for King Frederick Wilhelm II. Its virile classical style pays tribute to Athens's Acropolis. On the southern side, Berlin's sleek Academy of Arts and the DZ Bank, designed by star architect Frank Gehry, are cheek-by-jowl with the new American embassy built on its prewar location. ⊠ *Pariser Pl., Mitte* Ⓜ *Unter den Linden (S-bahn).*

**Denkmal für die Ermordeten Juden Europas** *(Memorial to the Murdered Jews of Europe).* An expansive and unusual memorial dedicated to the 6 million Jews who were killed in the Holocaust, the monument was designed by American architect Peter Eisenman. The stunning place of remembrance consists of a grid of more than 2,700 concrete stelae, planted into undulating ground. An information center that goes into specifics about the Holocaust lies underground at the southeast corner. ⊠ *Cora-Berliner-Str. 1, Mitte* ☎ *030/2639–4336* ⊕ *www.holocaust-mahnmal.de* ☜ *Free* ☉ *Daily 24 hrs; information center: Oct.–Mar., Tues.–Sun. 10–7; Apr.–Sept., Tues.–Sun. 10–8* Ⓜ *Unter den Linden (S-bahn).*

**Deutsches Historisches Museum** *(German History Museum).* The museum is composed of two buildings. The magnificent pink baroque Prussian arsenal (Zeughaus) was constructed between 1695 and 1730, and is the oldest building on Unter den Linden. The permanent exhibits offer a modern and fascinating view of German history since the early Middle Ages. Behind the arsenal, the granite-and-glass Pei-Bau building by I. M. Pei holds changing exhibits. ⊠ *Unter den Linden 2, Mitte* ☎ *030/203–040* ⊕ *www.dhm.de* ☜ *€5, free Mon.; visitors under 18 free* ☉ *Daily 10–6.*

**Jüdisches Museum** *(Jewish Museum).* The history of Germany's Jews from the Middle Ages through today is chronicled here, from prominent historical figures to the evolution of laws regarding Jews' participation in civil society. An attraction in itself is the highly conceptual building, which was designed by Daniel Libeskind. ⊠ *Lindenstr. 9–14, Kreuzberg* ☎ *030/2599–3300* ⊕ *www.jmberlin.de* ☜ *€5* ☉ *Mon. 10–10, Tues.–Sun. 10–8* Ⓜ *Hallesches Tor (U-bahn).*

**Kaiser-Wilhelm-Gedächtnis-Kirche** *(Kaiser Wilhelm Memorial Church).* A dramatic reminder of World War II's destruction, the ruined bell tower is all that remains of the once massive church, which was dedicated to the emperor Kaiser Wilhelm I. The exhibition revisits World War II's devastation throughout Europe. In stark contrast to the old bell tower (dubbed the Hollow Tooth), are the adjoining Memorial Church and Tower, designed by the noted German architect Egon Eiermann

**5**

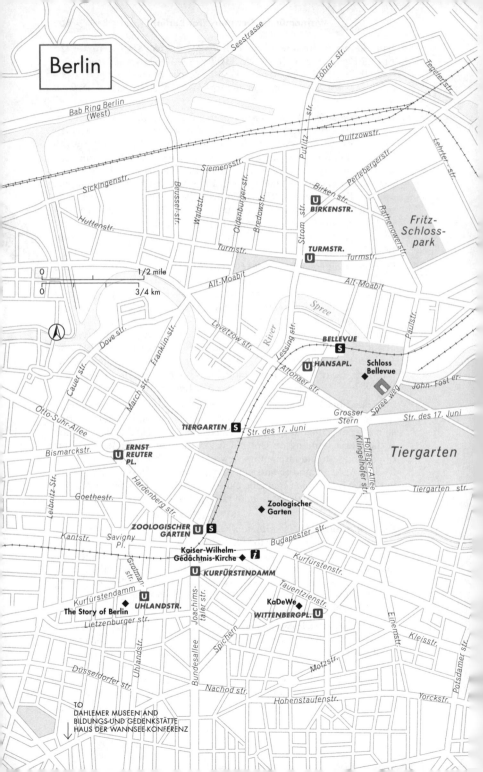

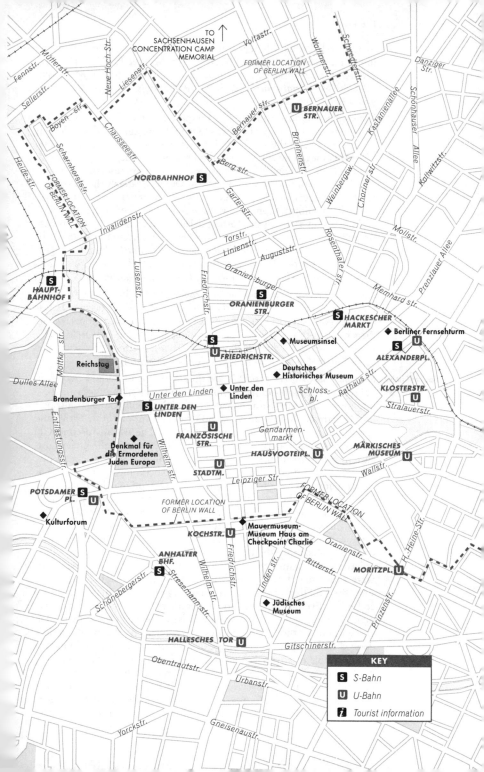

in 1959–61. Brilliant blue stained glass from Chartres dominates the interiors. ✉ *Breitscheidpl., Western Downtown* ☎ *030/218–5023* ⊕ *www.gedaechtniskirche-berlin.de* 🎫 *Free* ☉ *Old Tower, Mon.–Sat. 10–6:30; Memorial Church, daily 9–7* Ⓜ *Zoologischer Garten (U-bahn and S-bahn).*

★ **Kulturforum** *(Cultural Forum).* This unique ensemble of museums, galleries, and the Philharmonic Hall was long in the making. The first designs were submitted in the 1960s, and the last building completed in 1998. The **Gemäldegalerie** *(Picture Gallery)* reunites formerly separated collections from East and West Berlin. Seven rooms are reserved for paintings by German masters, among them Dürer, Cranach the Elder, and Holbein. A special collection has works of the Italian masters—Botticelli, Titian, Giotto, Lippi, and Raphael—as well as paintings by Dutch and Flemish masters of the 15th and 16th centuries: Van Eyck, Bosch, Brueghel the Elder, and van der Weyden. The museum also holds the world's second-largest Rembrandt collection. ✉ *Matthäikirchpl. 4, Tiergarten* ☎ *030/266–2951* ⊕ *www.smb.museum* 🎫 *€8* ☉ *Tues., Wed., and Fri.–Sun. 10–6, Thurs. 10–10* Ⓜ *Potsdamer Pl. (U-bahn and S-bahn).*

★ **Mauermuseum-Museum Haus am Checkpoint Charlie.** Just steps from the famous crossing point between the two Berlins, the Wall Museum–House at Checkpoint Charlie tells the story of the Wall and, even more riveting, the stories of those who escaped through, under, and over it. ✉ *Friedrichstr. 43–45, Kreuzberg* ☎ *030/253–7250* ⊕ *www.mauermuseum.com* 🎫 *€12.50* ☉ *Daily 9* AM*–10* PM Ⓜ *Kochstr. (U-bahn).*

**Fodor's Choice** **Museumsinsel** *(Museum Island).* On the site of one of Berlin's two origi-
★ nal settlements, this unique complex of four state museums is an absolute must. The **Alte Nationalgalerie** (Old National Gallery, entrance on Bodestrasse) houses an outstanding collection of 18th-, 19th-, and early-20th-century paintings and sculptures. The **Altes Museum** (Old Museum), a red marble neoclassical building abutting the green Lustgarten, was Prussia's first building purpose-built to serve as a museum. Designed by Karl Friedrich Schinkel, it was completed in 1830. The newly renovated Neues Museum houses the **Egyptian collection,** whose prize pieces are the exquisite 3,300-year-old bust of Queen Nefertiti, along with a papyrus collection and the finest artifacts from the collection of classical antiquities brought to Germany from around the Mediterranean basin by various archaeological teams. At the northern tip of Museum Island is the **Bode-Museum,** a somber-looking gray edifice graced with elegant columns. Reopened in 2006, it now presents the State Museum's stunning collection of German and Italian sculptures since the Middle Ages, the Museum of Byzantine Art, and a huge coin collection. Even if you think you aren't interested in the ancient world, make an exception for the **Pergamonmuseum** (entrance on Am Kupfergraben), one of the world's greatest museums. The museum's name is derived from its principal display, the Pergamon Altar, a monumental Greek temple discovered in what is now Turkey and dating from 180 BC. Pre-booked tickets give a half-hour time slot for visits to try and minimize crowding; however, your visit is not time-limited once you enter the museums. ✉ *Entrance to Museumsinsel: Am Kupfergraben, Mitte* ☎ *030/2090–5577, 030/226–424242 for ticket purchase* ⊕ *www.*

*smb.museum* 🎫 *All Museum Island museums €10* ⊙ *Pergamonmuseum Fri.–Wed. 10–6, Thurs. 10–10. Alte Nationalgalerie Tues., Wed., and Fri.–Sun. 10–6, Thurs. 10–10. Bode-Museum Fri.–Wed. 10–6, Thurs. 10–10. Neues Museum Sun.–Wed. 10–6, Thurs.–Sat. 10–8* Ⓜ *Hackescher Markt. (S-bahn).*

★ **Reichstag** *(Parliament Building).* After last meeting here in 1933, the Bundestag, Germany's federal parliament, returned to its traditional seat in the spring of 1999. British architect Sir Norman Foster lightened up the gray monolith with a glass dome, which quickly became one of the city's main attractions: you can circle up a gently rising ramp while taking in the rooftops of Berlin and the parliamentary

**BERLIN BEST BETS**

**Brandenburger Tor.** The gate is the symbolic heart of the city, and one of the few survivors of the WWII era.

**Kulturforum.** An assembly of museums, galleries, and the Philharmonic Hall, the Kulturforum features an exceptional gallery of European art with pieces brought together post-reintegration. The Rembrandt collection is the highlight.

**Reichstag.** The historic seat of Germany's federal parliament, the Reichstag is also remarkable for its synthesis of architectural styles.

**5**

chamber below. At the base of the dome is an exhibit on the Reichstag's history, in German and English. ✉ *Pl. der Republik 1, Tiergarten* ☏ *030/2273–2152* 🖷 *030/2273–0027* ⊕ *www.bundestag.de* 🎫 *Free* ⊙ *Daily 8 AM–midnight; last admission 10 PM. Reichstag dome closes for 1 wk 4 times a year* Ⓜ *Unter den Linden (S-bahn).*

🔄 **The Story of Berlin.** Eight hundred years of the city's history, from the first settlers casting their fishing poles to Berliners heaving sledgehammers at the Wall, are conveyed through hands-on exhibits, film footage, and multimedia devices in this unusual venue. Museum placards are also in English. ■ **TIP→** **The eeriest relic is the 1974 nuclear shelter, which you can visit by guided tour on the hour.** ✉ *Ku'damm Karree, Kurfürstendamm 207–208, Western Downtown* ☏ *030/8872–0100* ⊕ *www.story-of-berlin.de* 🎫 *€10* ⊙ *Daily 10–8; last entry at 6* Ⓜ *Uhlandstr. (U-bahn).*

**Tiergarten** *(Animal Garden).* The quiet greenery of the 630-acre Tiergarten is a beloved oasis, with some 23 km (14 mi) of footpaths, meadows, and two beer gardens. The inner park's 6½ acres of lakes and ponds were landscaped by garden architect Joseph Peter Lenné in the mid-1800s. On the shores of the lake in the southwest part you can relax at the **Café am Neuen See** (✉ *Lichtensteinallee*), a café and beer garden. Off the Spree River and bordering the Kanzleramt (Chancellory) is the **Haus der Kulturen der Welt** (✉ *House of World Cultures, John-Foster-Dulles Allee 10* ☏ *030/397–870* ⊕ *www.hkw.de*), referred to as the "pregnant oyster" for its design. Thematic exhibits and festivals take place here, and it's also a boarding point for Spree River cruises.

**Unter den Linden.** The name of this historic Berlin thoroughfare, between the Brandenburg Gate and Schlossplatz, means "under the linden trees"—and as Marlene Dietrich once sang, "As long as the old linden trees still bloom, Berlin is still Berlin." Imagine Berliners' shock when

Hitler decided to fell the trees in order to make Unter den Linden more parade-friendly. The grand boulevard began as a riding path that the royals used to get from their palace to their hunting grounds (now Tiergarten). Lining it now are linden trees planted after World War II.

○ **Zoologischer Garten** *(Zoological Gardens).* Germany's oldest zoo opened
★ in 1844, and today holds more species than any other zoo in Europe, among them stars like the little polar bear Knut, one of the world's few endangered species to be born in captivity. Home to more than 14,000 animals belonging to 1,500 different species, the zoo has been successful at breeding rare and endangered species. The animals' enclosures are designed to resemble their natural habitats, though some structures are ornate, such as the 1910 Arabian-style Zebra House. ⊠ *Hardenbergpl. 8 and Budapester Str. 34, Western Downtown* ☎ *030/254–010* ⊕ *www. zoo-berlin.de* ⌸ *Zoo or aquarium €12, combined ticket €18* ⊙ *Zoo, Nov.–mid-Mar., daily 9–5; mid-Mar.–mid-Oct., daily 9–7. Aquarium, daily 9–6* Ⓜ *Zoologischer Garten (U-bahn and S-bahn).*

# SHOPPING

Although Ku'damm is still touted as the shopping mile of Berlin, many shops are ho-hum retailers. The best stretch for exclusive fashions are the three blocks between Leibnizstrasse and Bleibtreustrasse. For gift items and unusual clothing boutiques, follow this route off Ku'damm: Leibnizstrasse to Mommsenstrasse to Bleibtreustrasse, then on to the ring around Savignyplatz. Fasanenstrasse, Knesebeckstrasse, Schlüterstrasse, and Uhlandstrasse are also fun places to browse.

The finest shops in Mitte (historic Berlin) are along Friedrichstrasse. Nearby, Unter den Linden has just a few souvenir shops and a Meissen ceramic showroom. Smaller clothing and specialty stores populate the Scheunenviertel. The area between Hackescher Markt, Weinmeister Strasse, and Rosa-Luxemburg-Platz alternates pricey independent designers with groovy secondhand shops. Neue Schönhauser Strasse curves into Alte Schönhauser Strasse, and both streets are full of stylish casual wear. Galleries along Gipsstrasse and Sophienstrasse round out the mix.

**Kaufhaus des Westens** *(KaDeWe).* The largest department store in continental Europe surpasses even London's Harrods, and turned 100 in 2007. It has a grand selection of goods on seven floors, as well as food and deli counters, champagne bars, beer bars, and a winter garden on its two upper floors. ⊠ *Tauentzienstr. 21, Western Downtown* ☎ *030/21210* ⊕ *www.kadewe.de.*

**Ködrnigliche Porzellan Manufaktur.** Fine porcelain is still produced bythe former Royal Prussian Porcelain Factory, also called KPM. ⊠ *Unter den Linden 35, Mitte* ☎ *030/206–4150* ⊕ *www.kpm-berlin.de.*

**Puppenstube im Nikolaiviertel** is the ultimate shop for any kind of (mostly handmade) dolls, including designer models as well as old-fashioned German dolls. It's for collectors, not kids. ⊠ *Propststr. 4, Mitte* ☎ *030/242–3967.*

## WHERE TO EAT

**$$**
GERMAN
★

**✗ Café Einstein.** The Einstein is a Berlin landmark and one of the leading coffeehouses in town, serving some of Germany's best coffee (the Einstein has its very own roasting facility) and some great cakes. In summer the fresh strawberry cake is a treat. The Einstein also excels in preparing solid Austrian fare such as schnitzel or goulash for an artsy, highbrow clientele. ⊠ *Kurfürstenstr. 58, Tiergarten* ☎ *030/261–5096* ⊕ *www. cafeeinstein.com* ⊟ *AE, DC, MC, V* Ⓜ *Kurfürstenstrasse (U-bahn).*

**$–$$**
GERMAN
★

**✗ Lubitsch.** One of the few traditional, artsy restaurants left in bohemian Charlottenburg, the Lubitsch—named after the famous Berlin film director Ernst Lubitsch and exuding a similar air of faded elegance—serves hearty Berlin and German food hard to find these days. Reminiscent of good old home cooking, dishes like Königsberger Klopse (cooked dumplings in a creamy caper sauce) or Kasseler Nacken mit Sauerkraut (salted, boiled pork knuckle) are devoured mostly by locals, who don't mind the dingy seating or good-humored, but sometimes cheeky service. In summer the outdoor tables make for some great people-watching in one of Berlin's most beautiful streets. Enjoy a three-course lunch for just €10 or €12. ⊠ *Bleibtreustr. 47, Western Downtown* ☎ *030/882–3756* ⊟ *AE, MC, V* Ⓜ *Savignypl. (S-Bahn).*

5

# Norway

ÅLESUND, BERGEN, FLÅM, GEIRANGER,
HAMMERFEST, HONNINGSVAG, KRISTÌANSAND,
OSLO, TROMSØ, TRONDHEIM

## WORD OF MOUTH

"We sailed from Bergen to Kirkenes in late July.
It never did get dark, just a very long twilight.
By October, say, the days would be quite short.
Some ports—Aalesund, for example—were visited
for several hours. Others, only minutes. It's a won-
derful, scenic voyage, so free of hassles."

—USNR

Paul Rubio

Norway's most renowned cruise itinerary is the *Hurtigruten,* which literally means "Rapid Route." Boats that follow this route, which were historically known as coastal steamers, depart from Bergen and stop at 34 ports along the coast in a week, ending in Kirkenes, near the Russian border, before turning back.

Ships may stop in one port for just a few minutes to load and unload passengers, who use the scenic route for transportation, so these steamers are more than just pleasure cruises for the people who choose to live in the isolated coastal villages in Norway's northern reaches. But many passengers on these routes are Americans here to enjoy the dramatically beautiful Norwegian scenery.

Many of these ships, which are operated primarily by Hurtigruten (the Norwegian cruise line, which was once known in the U.S. as Norwegian Coastal Voyage), are more than just ferries. They do have some cruise-ship-style amenities, though not "big-ship" amenities. So you can expect to find a sauna on board some of the ship but not a full-fledged spa, a restaurant but not a choice of restaurants. And while food is included in your cruise fare (unless you book a transportation-only passage, as some backpackers and short-haul travelers do), you pay extra (and dearly) for alcohol; luckily, the ships allow you to carry your own alcohol on board.

Norway is also a popular destination among major cruise lines—both luxury and mainstream—and many northern European cruises in the summer include some stops in Norway, though they may also include Århus or Copenhagen in Denmark or stops in Sweden, which are covered in the The Baltic chapter.

## ABOUT THE RESTAURANTS

Most of the restaurants we recommend serve lunch; they also serve dinner if your cruise ship stays late in port and you choose to dine off the ship. Cuisine in Europe is varied, though you should expect restaurants in Norway to focus primarily on Norwegian specialties; you'll have more choices in larger cities like Oslo and Bergen. Europeans tend to eat a leisurely meal at lunch, but in most ports there are quicker and simpler alternatives for those who just want to grab a quick bite before returning to the ship. The currency of Norway is the Norwegian krone, and equivalent kroner prices to our regular euro price categories are given below.

| WHAT IT COSTS IN EUROS AND KRONER | | | | |
|---|---|---|---|---|
| ¢ | $ | $$ | $$$ | $$$$ |
| Restaurants in euros | under €11 | €11–€17 | €17–€23 | €23–€30 | over €30 |
| Restaurants in kroner | under Nkr 85 | Nkr 85–Nkr 135 | Nkr 135–Nkr 185 | Nkr 185–Nkr 240 | over Nkr 240 |

Restaurant prices are per person for a main course, including tax

# ÅLESUND, NORWAY

On three islands and between two bright blue fjords is Ålesund, home to 45,000 inhabitants and one of Norway's largest harbors for exporting dried and fresh fish. About two-thirds of its 1,040 wooden houses were destroyed by a fire in 1904. In the rush to shelter the 10,000 homeless victims, Germany's Kaiser Wilhelm II, who often vacationed here, led a swift rebuilding that married German art nouveau (*Jugendstil*) with Viking flourishes. Winding streets are crammed with buildings topped with turrets, spires, gables, dragon heads, and curlicues. Today Ålesund is considered one of the few art nouveau cities in the world. Inquire at the tourism office for one of the insightful guided walking tours.

## ESSENTIALS

CURRENCY   Norway is a non-EU country and has opted to keep its currency, the Norwegian krone (Nkr 6 to US$1). ATMs are readily available.

HOURS   Most shops are open from 10 to 4 or 5 weekdays, Thursday until 7, Saturday from 10 to 3 or 4, and are closed Sunday.

INTERNET   **Ålesund Folkebibliotek** (*Public Library* ⊠ *Rådhuset* ☎ *70–16–22–60* ⊕ *www.alesund.folkebibl.no*). **Ålesund Tourist Office** (⊠ *Skateflukaia* ☎ *70–15–76–00* ⊕ *www.visitalesund.com*).

TELEPHONES   Most tri- and quad-band GSM phones work in Norway, so if your service provider offers service in Europe, you will likely be able to use your mobile phone along the Norwegian coast, even while hugging the shoreline on ship. Public telephones take Nkr 1, 5, 10, and 20 coins, and you need NKr 5 at a minimum. International phone cards are the best value for long-distance calls, and are available at newsstands.

## COMING ASHORE

Ålesund is at the entrance to the world-famous Geirangerfjord. Turrets, spires, and medieval ornaments rise above the skyline of the colorful town and its charming architecture. Cruise ships dock at the cruise terminal at Stornespiren/Prestebrygga, less than a five-minute walk from the city center.

# EXPLORING ÅLESUND

Ⓒ   **Ålesund Akvarium Atlanterhavsparken** (*Atlantic Sea Park*). Teeming with aquatic life, this is one of Scandinavia's largest aquariums. Right on the ocean, 3 km (2 mi) west of town, the park exhibits sea animals of the North Atlantic, including anglerfish, octopus, and lobster. See the daily show when divers feed the huge and sometimes aggressive halibut and wolffish, who become frenzied as they compete for their meals. After your visit, have a picnic, go on a hike, or take a refreshing swim at the adjoining Tueneset Park. Bus 18, which leaves from St. Olavs Plass, makes the 15-minute journey to the park once every hour during the day, Monday through Saturday. ⊠ *Tueneset* ☎ *70–10–70–60* ⊕ *www. atlanterhavsparken.no* ✉ *Nkr 130* ☉ *June–Aug., Sun.–Fri. 10–7, Sat. 10–4; Sept.–May, Mon.–Sat. 11–4, Sun. 11–6.*

**Fodor's** Choice
★
**Ålesunds Museum.** The museum highlights the city's past, including the escape route to the Shetland Islands that the Norwegian Resistance established in World War II. Handicrafts on display are done in the folk-art style of the area. You can also see the art nouveau room and learn more about the town's unique architecture. Next door is the Fisheries Museum. ⊠ *Rasmus Rønnebergsgt. 16* ☎ *70–12–31–70* ⊕ *www. aalesunds.museum.no* ✉ *Nkr 50* ☉ *Mid-June–Sept., weekdays 9–4, Sat. 11–3, Sun. noon–4; Sept.–Dec., weekdays 11–3; May–mid-June, weekdays 9–3, Sun. noon–3.*

**The Art Nouveau Centre.** This museum is beautifully situated by the Brosundet canal in one of Ålesund's most distinctive art nouveau buildings, the former Svaneapoteket pharmacy. The center provides an instructive and fascinating introduction to the history of the great fire of 1904 and the creative art nouveau period. ⊠ *Apotekergt. 16* ☎ *70–10–49–70* ⊕ *www.jugendstilsenteret.no* ✉ *Nkr 60* ☉ *June–Aug. 10–5; Sept.–May, Tues.–Sat. 11–4, Sun. noon–4.*

**Kniven.** You can drive or take a bus up nearby Aksla Mountain to *"the knife,"* a vantage point offering a splendid view of the archipelago, the Sunnmøre Alps, and the beautiful city—which absolutely glitters at night. There is also a restaurant up top. ☎ *70–15–76–00.*

## SHOPPING

The first Saturday of each month is known as "Town Saturday," when shops in the city center are open later than usual.

**Husfliden.** Visit this shop for collections of beautiful Norwegian and Nordic arts and crafts. ⊠ *Parkgt. 1* ☎ *70–12–16–68.*

**Ingrids Glassverksted.** This store has a fine selection of glassware and decorative art glass. ⊠ *Moloveien 15* ☎ *474–16–371.*

**Skinncompagniet.** For leather clothing, handbags, knitwear and souvenirs, drop into this boutique on Ålesund's main pedestrian street. ⊠ *Kongensgt. 14* ☎ *70–12–77–77.*

## ACTIVITIES

### GOLF

**Solnør Gaard Golfbane.** About 30 minutes from Ålesund, this 18-hole golf course has a driving range and pro shop. ⊠ *Skodje 6260, Solnør* ☎ *70–27–42–00* ⊕ *www.aagk.no.*

6

### HIKING

You can trek up the 418 steps to Fjellstua for a panoramic view of the town and the Sunnmøre Alps. A restaurant is at the top.

### WILDLIFE SPOTTING TRIPS

**Safari at Sea.** Experience a wildlife sea safari along the coastline in a high-speed open RIB boat. The trip normally includes visiting a seal colony and Runde's famous bird colonies, where you can see puffins and sea eagles. ⊠ *Skansekaia* ☎ *70–11–44–30* ⊕ *www.fjord-magic.com* 🎫 *Nkr 695* ⊙ *Mid-June–mid-Aug.*

## WHERE TO EAT

**$$** ✕ **Fjellstua.** This mountaintop restaurant has tremendous views over the
NORWEGIAN surrounding peaks, islands, and fjords. There is also a terrace for times when the weather is nice. On the menu, try the Norwegian bacalao (cod), baked salmon, and homemade rissoles (croquettes). ⊠ *Top of Aksla Mountain* ☎ *70–10–74–00* ⊕ *www.fjellstua.no* ▤ *AE, DC, MC, V* ⊙ *Closed Jan. No dinner Feb.–Apr.*

**$$** ✕ **Maki.** The freshest of fresh seafood in town is served in an intimate
NORWEGIAN setting in the heart of Brosundet. ⊠ *Apotekergt. 5* ☎ *70–11–45–00* ⊕ *www.brosundet.no.*

# BERGEN, NORWAY

A place of enchantment, Bergen's many epithets include "Trebyen" (Wooden City; it has many wooden houses), "Regnbyen" (Rainy City, due to its 200 days of rain a year), and "Fjordbyen" (gateway to the fjords). Most visitors quickly learn the necessity of rain jackets and umbrellas, and Bergen has even handily provided the world's first umbrella vending machine. Norway's second-largest city was founded in 1070 by Olav Kyrre as a commercial center. The surviving Hanseatic wooden buildings on Bryggen (the quay) are topped with triangular gingerbread roofs and painted in red, white, and yellow. Monuments in themselves (they are on the UNESCO World Heritage List), the buildings tempt travelers and locals to the shops, restaurants, and museums inside. Evenings, when Bryggen is illuminated, these modest buildings, together with the stocky Rosenkrantz Tower, the Fløyen Funicular, and the yachts lining the pier, are reflected in the water and combine to create one of the loveliest cityscapes in northern Europe.

### ESSENTIALS

CURRENCY Norway is a non-EU country and has opted to keep its currency, the Norwegian *krone* (Nkr 6 to US$1). ATMs are readily available.

HOURS Most shops are open from 10 to 4 and 5 weekdays, Thursday until 7, Saturday from 10 to 3 or 4, and are closed Sunday.

INTERNET **Accezzo Internet Café and Coffee Bar** (⊠ *Galleriet, Torgallm. 8* ☎ *55–31–11–60*).

**Bergen Public Library** (⊠ *Stromgaten* ☎ *55–56–85–00*).

TELEPHONES Most tri- and quad-band GSM phones work in Norway, so if your service provider offers service in Europe, you will likely be able to

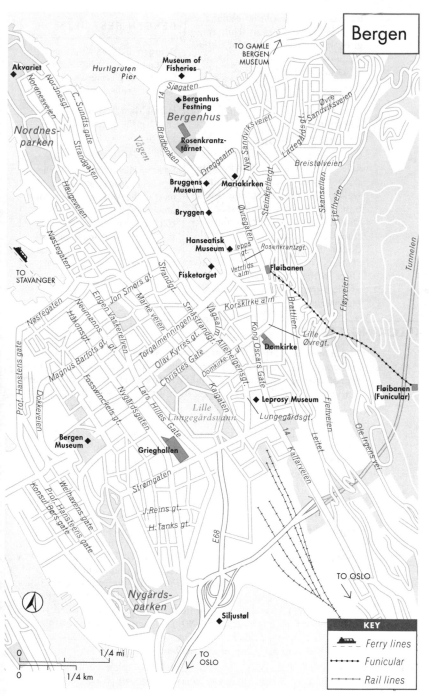

# Bergen

Akvariet

Hurtigruten Pier

Museum of Fisheries

TO GAMLE BERGEN MUSEUM

Nordnesveien

Nordnesgt.

C. Sundts gate

Sjøgaten

14

Bergenhus Festning

*Bergenhus*

Øvre Sandviksveien

Nye Sandviksveien

Ladegårdsgt.

*Nordnes-parken*

Strandgaten

Haugeveien

Bradbenken

*Vågen*

Rosenkrantz-tårnet

Dreggsalm

Breistølveien

Skanselien

Fjellveien

Nøstegaten

Bruggens Museum

Mariakirken

Steinkjellergt.

TO STAVANGER

Bryggen

Øvregaten

Prof. Hanstens gate

Dokkeveien

Nøstegaten

Hansenatisk Museum

Jepps gt.

Rosenkrantzgt.

Vetrlids alm

Fløibanen

Fisketorget

Jon Smørs gt.

Engen Vaskereiven

Neumanns gt.

Magnus Bartols gt.

Håkonsgt.

Fosswinckels gt.

Strandgt.

Marke veien

Torgalmenningen

Olav Kyrres gt.

Christies Gate

Småstrandgt.

Vågsalm Allehelgensgt.

Korskirke alm

Domkirke gt.

Kaigaten

Kong Oscars Gate

Brattlien

*Lille Øvregt.*

Domkirke

Lille Lungegårdsvann

Nygårdsgaten

Lars Hilles Gate

Leprosy Museum

Lungegårdsgt.

14

Fløibanen (Funicular)

Bergen Museum

Grieghallen

Strømgaten

J. Reins gt.

H. Tanks gt.

E68

Kallarveien

Leitet

Fjellveien

Ole Irgens vei

Tunnelen

Fløyveien

*Nygårds-parken*

Welhavens gate

Prof. Hansteens gate

Konsul Børs gate

Siljustøl

TO OSLO

TO OSLO

6

| KEY | |
|---|---|
| ⛴ | *Ferry lines* |
| •••••• | *Funicular* |
| ┼┼┼┼ | *Rail lines* |

0    1/4 mi

0    1/4 km

use your mobile phone along the Norwegian coast, even while hugging the shoreline on ship. Public telephones take Nkr 1, 5, 10, and 20 coins, and you need NKr 5 at a minimum. International phone cards are the best value for long-distance calls, and are available at newsstands.

## COMING ASHORE

Cruise ships dock at Skoltegrunnskaien and Jekteviken/Dokkeskjærskaien. Both are within a 15-minute walk of the city center, and shuttle buses are available from Jekteviken/Dokkeskjærskaien. From Skoltegrunnskaien, buses stop near the docks. The trip to the city center costs NKr 25 on the public bus. Once in the city center, nearly all of the attractions are within walking distance.

# EXPLORING BERGEN

**Bergen Museum.** Part of the University of Bergen, this museum has two collections. The Cultural History Collection has a fascinating collection of archaeological artifacts and furniture and folk art from western Norway, plus exhibits on the Stone Age, Viking Norway, Russian icons, and Church art. Special exhibitions include "Ibsen in Bergen," which focuses on the famous playwright's six years in Bergen working with the local theater. The Natural History Collection is perfect for lovers of the outdoors, since it includes botanical gardens. It also showcases exhibits on minerals, reptiles and bones, Norwegian birds and exotic mammals along with special exhibits such as "The Evolution of Man." ⊠ *Haakon Sheteligs pl. 10 and Musépl. 3, City Center* 🕾 *55–58–81–72 or 55–58–29–05* ⊕ *www.uib.no/bergenmuseum* 🖾 *Nkr 50* ⊙ *June–Aug., Tues.–Fri. 10–4, weekends 11–4; Sept.–May, Tues.–Fri. 10–3, weekends 11–4.*

**Bergenhus Festning** *(Bergenhus Fortress)*. The buildings here date from the mid-13th century. Håkonshallen, a royal ceremonial hall erected during the reign of Håkon Håkonsson, between 1247 and 1261, was badly damaged by the explosion of a German ammunition ship in 1944, but was restored by 1961. Erected in the 1560s by the governor of Bergen Castle (Bergenhus), Erik Rosenkrantz, Rosenkrantztårnet (Rosenkrantz Tower) served as a combined residence and fortified tower. ⊠ *Bergenhus, Bryggen* 🕾 *55–58–80–10* ⊕ *www.bymuseet.no* 🖾 *Nkr 50* ⊙ *Mid-May–Sept., daily 10–4; Oct.–mid-May (Håkonshallen only), Mon.–Wed. and Fri.–Sun. noon–3, Thurs. 3–6.*

**Fodor's Choice** **Bryggen** *(The Quay)*. A trip to Bergen is incomplete without a trip to
★ Bryggen. A row of mostly reconstructed 14th-century wooden buildings

that face the harbor makes this one of the most charming walkways in Europe, especially on a sunny day. The original structures were built by Hansa merchants, while the first reconstruction dates from 1702. Several fires, the latest in 1955, destroyed the original structures. Today the old merchant homes house various boutiques and restaurants. Bryggen has been a UNESCO World Heritage Site since 1979.

**Bryggens Museum.** This museum contains archaeological finds from the Middle Ages. An exhibit on Bergen circa 1300 shows the town at the zenith of its importance, and has reconstructed living quarters as well as artifacts such as old tools and shoes. Back then, Bergen was the largest town in Norway, a cosmopolitan trading center and the national capital. ⊠ *Dreggsalmenning 3* ☎ *55–58–80–10* ⊕ *www.bymuseet.no* 🎫 *Nkr 60* ☉ *May–Aug., daily 10–4; Sept.–mid-May., weekdays 11–3, Sat. noon–3, Sun. noon–4.*

**Domkirke** *(Bergen Cathedral).* The cathedral's long, turbulent history has shaped the eclectic architecture of the current structure. The Gothic-style choir and the lower towers are the oldest sections, dating from the 13th century. Note the cannonball lodged in the tower wall—it dates from a battle between English and Dutch ships in Bergen harbor in 1665. ⊠ *Kong Oscars gt. and Domkirke gt.* ☎ *55–59–32–73* ☉ *June–Aug., Mon.–Sat. 11–4; Sept.–May, Tues.–Fri. 11–12:30.*

**Fisketorget** *(Fish Market).* Turn-of-the-20th-century photographs of this pungent square show fishermen in Wellington boots and raincoats and women in long aprons. Now the fishmongers wear bright-orange rubber overalls as they look over the catches of the day. In summer the selection is mostly limited to shrimp, salmon, and monkfish. There is much greater variety and more locals shop here the rest of the year. There are also fruit, vegetable, and flower stalls, as well as some handicrafts and souvenir vendors at this lively market. You'll also find the world's first umbrella vending machine. Have a classic lunch of smoked shrimp or salmon on a baguette with mayonnaise and cucumber. ⊠ *Zachariasbryggen* ☎ *55–55–20–00* ⊕ *www.torgetibergen.no* ☉ *June–Aug., daily 7–7; Sept.–May, Mon.–Sat. 7–4.*

★ **Hanseatisk Museum.** One of the best-preserved buildings in Bergen, the Hanseatic Museum was the 16th-century office and home of an affluent German merchant. The apprentices lived upstairs, where they slept in boxed-in beds, and windows were cut into the wall. Although claustrophobic, the snug rooms had the benefit of being relatively warm—a blessing in the unheated building. ⊠ *Finnegårdsgaten 1A* ☎ *55–54–46–90* ⊕ *www.museumvest.no* 🎫 *Nkr 50, off-season Nkr 30* ☉ *Mid-May–mid-Sep., daily 9–5; mid-Sept.–mid-May, Tues.–Sat. 11–2, Sun. 11–4.*

**Fodor's Choice**
★ **Mariakirken** *(St. Mary's Church).* Considered one of the most outstanding Romanesque churches in Norway, this is the oldest building in Bergen still used for its original purpose. It was built in the 12th century and eventually gained a Gothic choir, richly decorated portals, and a splendid baroque pulpit—much of which was added by the Hanseatic merchants who owned it from 1408 to 1766. See the gilded triptych at the high altar that dates from the late Middle Ages. Organ recitals are held every Tuesday at 7:30 PM from late June through August.

✉ *Dreggen, Bryggen* ☎ *55–59–32–73* 🖹 *Nkr 20* ⊙ *Late June–Aug., weekdays 9:30–11:30 and 1–4; Sept.–early June, Tues.–Fri. 11–12:30.*

## NIGHTLIFE

Bergen is a university town, and the thousands of students who live and study here year-round contribute to making the city's nightlife livelier than you might expect in a small town. Most nightspots center on Ole Bulls *plass*, the plaza at one end of Torgallmenningen. Within a stone's throw of the plaza you can find dozens of relaxing bars, bustling pubs, dancing, live music, and trendy cafés.

**Altona.** If you prefer a quiet glass of wine in peaceful historic surroundings, try this bar in a 400-year-old wine cellar neighboring the Augustin Hotel. ✉ *Strandgaten 81* ☎ *55–30–40–00.*

**Café Opera** is a classic, both sumptuous and stylish. It's often crowded on Friday and Saturday nights. ✉ *Engen 18* ☎ *55–23–03–15.*

**Havariet Bar.** This is a popular hangout for the hip crowd sipping cocktails and beer at night. ✉ *Torget 2* ☎ *55–55–96–40.*

**Logen Bar.** If you prefer conversation over dancing, try this popular meeting place with live music and/or small cabarets every Sunday and Monday evening. ✉ *Øvre Ole Bulls pl. 6* ☎ *55–23–20–15.*

## SHOPPING

Bergen has several cobblestone pedestrian shopping streets, including Gamle Strandgaten, (Gågaten), Torgallmenningen, Hollendergaten, and Marken. Stores selling Norwegian handicrafts are concentrated along Bryggen boardwalk. Near the cathedral, tiny Skostredet has become popular with young shoppers. The small, independent specialty stores here sell everything from army surplus gear to tailored suits and designer trinkets.

**Bergen Storsenter.** This newer shopping center caters to the day-to-day needs of residents, and is the largest shopping center in the Bergen city center. ✉ *Strømgaten 8.*

**Galleriet.** This is the best of the downtown shopping malls. Here you will find GlasMagasinet and more exclusive small shops along with all the chains, including H&M (Hennes & Mauritz). ✉ *Torgallmenningen 8.*

**Kløverhuset.** Between Strandgaten and the fish market, this shopping center has 40 shops under one roof, including a shop for the ever-so-popular Dale knitwear, as well as shops selling souvenirs, leather, and fur. ✉ *Strandgaten 13/15.*

**Sundt.** This is the closest thing Norway has to a traditional department store, with everything from fashion to interior furnishings. But you can get better value for your kroner if you shop around for souvenirs and sweaters. ✉ *Torgallmenningen 14.*

# ACTIVITIES

Bergen is literally wedged between the mountains and the sea, and there are plenty of opportunities to enjoy the outdoors. Bergensers are quick to do so on sunny days. In summer, don't be surprised to see many Bergensers leaving work early to enjoy sports and other outdoor activities, or to just relax in the parks.

## FISHING

With so much water around, it's no wonder sport fishing is a popular pastime in Bergen. Angling along the coast around Bergen is possible all year, although it is unquestionably more pleasant in summer. In late summer many prefer to fish the area rivers to catch spawning salmon and trout. Whether you prefer fishing in streams, fjords, or the open sea, there are several charter services and fishing tours available. Most can also provide all the fishing gear you need, but be sure to bring warm and waterproof clothes, even in summer.

## GOLF

**Fana Golf Club.** Near Flesland Airport and Siljustøl, this 18-hole course opened in 2004. ✉ *Rådal* ☎ *94–23–10–00* ⊕ *www.fanagolf.no.*

**Meland Golf Club.** North of Bergen at Fløksand, this club has an 18-hole championship course with high-quality golf clubs and carts for rent. ✉ *Frekhaug* ☎ *56–17–46- 10* ⊕ *www.melandgolf.no.*

## HIKING

Like most Norwegians, Bergensers love to go hiking, especially on one or more of the seven mountains that surround the city.

**Mt. Fløyen.** Take the funicular up the mountain, and minutes later you'll be in the midst of a forest. From the nearby gift shop and restaurant, well-marked paths fan out over the mountains. Follow Fløysvingene Road down for an easy stroll with great views of the city and harbor. From mid-June to mid-August, the Floyen Funicular organizes a daily hiking program called "Walk like a Norwegian," where you learn about the history of Bergen, trolls, fairy tales, and the nature surrounding the city, while walking. ✉ *Vetrlidsallmenningen 21* ☎ *55–33–68–00* ⊕ *www.floibanen.com.*

# WHERE TO EAT

$$$$  
NORWEGIAN  ✕ **Bølgen & Moi.** In the same building as the Bergen Art Museum, this local outlet of Norway's Bølgen & Moi restaurant franchise is the perfect place for a break from the galleries. The lunch menu offers excellent value for money, but the brasserie is well worth a visit later in the evening. Try the turbot with asparagus and citrus hollandaise, a modern take on a Norwegian classic. For a hearty lunch, try the fish soup or the crayfish sandwich. The well-stocked bar is a trendy meeting place for local businesspeople. ✉ *Rasmus Meyers Allé 9, Downtown* ☎ *55–59–77–00* ⊕ *www.bolgenogmoi.no* ▤ *AE, DC, MC, V.*

$$$$  
NORWEGIAN  ✕ **Enhjørningen.** This restaurant is named after the unicorn that adorns the doorway of the old wooden building in which it is housed. Enhjørningen has traditions dating back to the Middle Ages, but there's nothing medieval about the menu—it's contemporary Norwegian and it

changes according to the day's catch. Try the famous fish soup to start, followed by herb-fried anglerfish with morel mushroom sauce, or the baked halibut in saffron butter. Enhjørningen is in the running for best seafood restaurant in Bergen. ⊠ *Bryggen 29, Bryggen* ☎ *55–30–69–50* ⊕ *www.enhjorningen.no* 🖃 *AE, DC, MC, V* ⊘ *No lunch.*

# FLÅM

Flåm is on an arm of the world's longest (at 204 km [127 mi]) and deepest (at 1,308 meters [4,291 feet]) fjord. The village of only 500 inhabitants is set against a backdrop of steep mountains, thundering waterfalls, narrow valleys, and deep canyons. Cruise ships—bringing primarily British and German passengers—began transiting the majestic Sognefjord to Flåm in the late 19th century. Today, it's Norway's fourth most popular port of call, a fact that can be attributed not only to the beauty of the fjord but also to the popularity of the Flåm Railway, considered to be one of Europe's most dramatic rail excursions.

## ESSENTIALS

CURRENCY  Norway is a non-EU country and has opted to keep its currency, the Norwegian *krone* (Nkr 6 to US$1). ATMs are readily available.

HOURS  Most shops are open from 10 to 4 or 5 weekdays, Thursday until 7, Saturday from 10 to 3 or 4, and are closed Sunday.

INTERNET  **Saga Souvenirs** (⊠ *Flåm train station* ☎ *57–11–00–11*).

TELEPHONES  Most tri- and quad-band GSM phones work in Norway, so if your service provider offers service in Europe, you will likely be able to use your mobile phone along the Norwegian coast, even while hugging the shoreline on ship. Public telephones take Nkr 1, 5, 10, and 20 coins, and you need Nkr 5 at a minimum. International phone cards are the best value for long-distance calls, and are available at newsstands.

## COMING ASHORE

Ships dock directly in the harbor of Flåm. Sights are easily accessible from the dock. The train station for the famous Flåm Railway is a five-minute walk from the pier.

# EXPLORING FLÅM

**Flåm Church.** This historic church dates back to 1667, its altarpiece to 1681. The wooden church, 3 km outside of Flåm, was restored in the 18th century, and much of the interior decor dates from that period. ⊠ *Hareina station, 3 km from Flåm* ☎ *57–63–29–95* 🎫 *Free* ⊘ *Hrs vary.*

**Flåmsbana** *(Flåm Railway)*. This train trip is only 20 km (12 mi) one way, but it takes 55 minutes to travel the 2,850 feet up the steep mountain gorge. The line includes 20 tunnels. A masterpiece of Norwegian engineering, it took 20 years to complete, and is today one of Norway's prime tourist attractions, with more than 500,000 visiting each year. Built in 1940, the year 2010 marked its 70th anniversary. ⊠ *Flåm train station* ☎ *57–63–14–00* ⊕ *www.visitflam.com.*

**Flåmsbana Museet** *(Flåm Railway Museum).* If you have time to kill before the train departs, make sure you visit the museum. Building the Flåm Railway was a remarkable feat in engineering, and this museum illustrates the challenges the builders faced in detail. You'll find it in the old station building, 300 feet from the present one. ⊠ *Flåm train station* ☎ *57–63–23–10* ⊕ *www.flamsbana-museet.no/default.asp* 🖼 *Free* ⊙ *May–Sept., daily 9–5; Oct.–Apr., daily 1:30–3.*

**Fretheim Hotel.** One of western Norway's most beautiful hotels has a classic, timeless look. If you are looking for a place to stop for an hour and just relax (or even have a quick meal), there's a spectacular view of the Sognefjord from the restaurant and bar. ⊠ *Flåm Harbor, Flåm* ☎ *57–63–63–00* ⊕ *www.fretheim-hotel.no.*

**Aurland.** You can reach the 13th-century fjord village by a scenic drive along the Sognefjord. To reach the village you travel inland along the Aurland River to the innermost part of the Sognefjord. The drive takes you up the beautiful Aurland Valley, past lush flora and fauna en route to Østerbø, a small mountain farm inhabited until the late 1920s.

**Otternes.** Only 4 km (2.5 mi) from Flåm are the farms at this center for traditional handcraft techniques and Norwegian cuisine. The farm consists of 27 houses overlooking the fjord. During the summer months you can walk among the historic buildings and watch while local artisans re-create traditional Norwegian farm crafts.

## SHOPPING

**Saga Souvenirs.** This is one of the largest gift shops in Norway. The selection of traditional items includes knitwear, wood and ceramic trolls, and jewelry. Locally made cloudberry jam and goat cheese from Undredal are favorite purchases, though the goat cheese can't be brought back to the U.S. ⊠ *Flåm train station* ☎ *57–11–00–11* ⊕ *www.sagasouvenir.no.*

## ACTIVITIES

**Njord.** Biking, hiking, kayaking, and fishing are all popular activities in and around Flåm. This local tour company specializes in organizing active adventures within the region. If you are looking for something more exhilarating than a walk or hike, the company also does kayaking and biking tours in the vicinity; the company can even organize glacier walks. ☎ *97–19–45–11* ⊕ *www.njord.as/en.*

# GEIRANGER, NORWAY

★ *85 km (52½ mi) southwest of Åndalsnes.*

The intricate outline of the fjords makes Norway's coastline of 21,347 km (13,264 mi) longer than the distance between the North Pole and the South Pole. The fjords were created by glacier erosion during the ice ages. In spectacular inlets like Geirangerfjord jagged snow-capped peaks blot out the sky and water tumbles down the mountains in an endless variety of colors. Lush, green farmlands edge up the rounded mountainsides, and the chiseled, cragged, steep peaks of the Jotunheimen mountains—Norway's tallest mountain range—seem almost tall enough to touch the blue skies. The first cruise ship sailed in Geiranger in 1869; needless to say, they have kept coming.

The Geirangerfjord made the UNESCO World Heritage List in 2005, and is Norway's most spectacular and perhaps best-known fjord. The 16-km-long (10-mi-long), 960-foot-deep Geirangerfjord's most stunning attractions are its roaring waterfalls—the Seven Sisters, the Bridal Veil, and the Suitor. Perched on mountain ledges along the fjord, deserted farms at Skageflå and Knivsflå are being restored and maintained by local enthusiasts.

## EXPLORING GEIRANGER

The village of Geiranger, at the end of the fjord, is home to only 250 year-round residents, but in spring and summer its population swells to 5,000 due to visitors traveling from Hellesylt to the east. In winter, snow on the mountain roads means that the village is often isolated.

**Mount Dalsnibba.** The drive to this mountain takes you past Lake Djupvatn and then up a hairpin road to the mountain's summit at 4,900 feet above sea level. Nearby is Djupvasshytta Lodge, where you can have refreshments or do a little shopping.

**Norwegian Fjord Center.** The center will give you insights into daily life in Geiranger. You can also board bus trips here to explore the mountain farms in the surrounding area.

★ **Trollstigveien.** The most scenic route to Geiranger is the two-hour drive along Route 63 over the Trollstigveien from Åndalsnes. Once you are here, the Ørneveien (Eagles' Road) road to Geiranger, which has 11 hairpin turns and was completed in 1952, leads directly to the fjord.

## SHOPPING

The handful of shops in Geiranger emphasize traditional Norwegian cottage crafts such as wood carvings and woven and knitted goods, like Norwegian sweaters. All the shops are along the main street.

## ACTIVITIES

### FARM TOURS

**Herdalssetra Mountain Farm.** Tours take you to this traditional farm. Among the specialties produced at the farm are brown and white goat cheese and goat's milk caramels. On a typical tour you will get to sample the foods produced on the farm and admire the animals, including goats, cows, sheep, and Norwegian ponies. ⊠ *Herdalssetra 6214, Nordall* ☏ *70–25–91–08* ⊕ *www.herdalssetra.no.*

### HIKING

Trekking through fjord country can occupy a few hours or several days. Trails and paths are marked by signs or cairns with a red т on them. Area tourist offices and bookshops have maps, and, of course, you can always ask residents for directions or destinations.

### KAYAKING

Geiranger's location near the end of the 16-km-long fjord is the perfect place to kayak alongside steep mountain walls and plunging waterfalls, including the Seven Sisters and Bridal Veil.

**Coastal Odyssey.** This company offers sea-kayak rentals by the hour or the day as well as guided tours. ⊠ *Geiranger Camping, Downtown* ☏ *95–11–80–62* ⊕ *www.coastalodyssey.com* ☉ *May–mid-Sept. 9* AM*–11* PM.

### MOUNTAIN BIKING

Downhill mountain biking exposes riders to the highlights of Geiranger during a 17-km descent from Djupvasshytta to Geiranger called the "sky-to-fjord" trip. The small gift shop by the ferry dock (the one with the green roof) offers this trip, including van transportation to the top of the mountain and a bike rental.

# HAMMERFEST, NORWAY

More than 600 mi north of the Arctic Circle, the world's northernmost town is also one of the most widely visited and oldest places in northern Norway. "Hammerfest" means "mooring place" and refers to the natural harbor (remarkably ice-free year-round thanks to the Gulf Stream) formed by the crags in the mountain. Hammerfest is the gateway to the Barents Sea and the Arctic Ocean, a jumping-off point for Arctic expeditions. Once a hunting town, Hammerfest's town emblem features the polar bear. In 1891 the residents of Hammerfest, tired of the months of darkness that winter always brought, decided to brighten their nights: they purchased a generator from Thomas Edison, and Hammerfest thus became the first city in Europe to have electric street lamps.

### ESSENTIALS

CURRENCY Norway is a non-EU country and has opted to keep its currency, the Norwegian *krone* (Nkr 6 to US$1). ATMs are readily available.

HOURS Most shops are open from 10 to 4 and 5 weekdays, Thursday until 7, Saturday from 10 to 3 or 4, and are closed Sunday.

INTERNET **@-LARM** (⊠ *Nissen Hammerfest Center*) is also a coffee shop.

**Hotel Rica** (⊠ *Sørøygata 15*).

TELEPHONES Most tri- and quad-band GSM phones work in Norway, so if your service provider offers service in Europe, you will likely be able to use your mobile phone along the Norwegian coast, even while hugging the shoreline on ship. Public telephones take Nkr 1, 5, 10, and 20 coins, and you need Nkr 5 at a minimum. International phone cards are the best value for long-distance calls, and are available at newsstands.

### COMING ASHORE

Ships dock either at a pier that is within walking distance of the town center or at Fuglenes, about a mile away. Be prepared to pay about Nkr 84 (US$14) for a taxi if you choose not to walk. Rather than tie up at Fuglenes, ships sometimes anchor and tender passengers ashore to the dock in the town center. There is no terminal in the port area and only

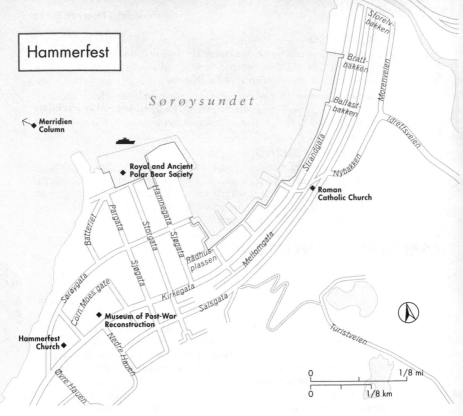

Hammerfest

Sørøysundet

Merridien Column

Royal and Ancient Polar Bear Society

Roman Catholic Church

Museum of Post-War Reconstruction

Hammerfest Church

Storelv-bakken · Bratt-bakken · Ballast-bakken · Mornenveien · Idrettsveien · Strandgata · Nybakken · Hammegata · Pargata · Storgata · Sjøgata · Batteriet · Rådhus plassen · Mellomgata · Sjøgata · Sjøgata · Søroygata · Corn Moes gate · Kirkegata · Salsgata · Nedre Hauen · Øvre Hauen · Turistveien

0    1/8 mi
0    1/8 km

limited facilities, but the town center is only a few steps away and has everything you might need.

## EXPLORING HAMMERFEST

In addition to two museums, there are several shops within Hammerfest's small city center. There is also a market selling souvenirs and other goods outside the town hall. You'll do better if you go back to your ship for lunch.

**Museum of Post-War Reconstruction.** Although it covers the county of Finnmark's history since the Stone Age, this museum primarily focuses on World War II, when the German army forced Finnmark's population to evacuate, and the county was burned to the ground as part of a scorched-earth policy. Through photographs, videos, and sound effects, the museum recounts the residents' struggle to rebuild their lives. The exhibition includes authentic rooms that were built in caves after the evacuation, as well as huts and postwar homes. ⊠ *Kirkegt. 21* ☎ *78–40–29–30* ⊕ *www.gjenreisningsmuseet.no* ⊠ *Nkr 50, free Dec. and Jan.* ☾ *June–mid-Aug., weekdays 9–4, weekends 10–2; mid-Aug.– May, daily 11–2.*

**Royal and Ancient Polar Bear Society.** The society was founded by two businessmen whose goal was to share the town's history as a center for hunting and commerce. Exhibits depict aspects of arctic hunts, including preserved and stuffed polar bears, seals, lynx, puffins, and wolves. ⊠ *Havnegate 3* ☎ *78–41–31–00* ⊕ *www.isbjornklubben.no* 🎫 *Free* ⊙ *June and July, weekdays 6–6, weekends 6–4; Aug.–May weekdays 9–3, weekends 10–2.*

## ACTIVITIES

**Hammerfest Turist Informasjon.** If you stop in the office, you can find out about activities in the region that include golf, walking tours, birdwatching trips, and boating. One of the most popular activities is the Coastal Sightseeing Trip. On this trip a catamaran takes you to the small fishing villages on the island of Sørøya. Another popular tour is the City Tour, whose highlights include the Meridian Column, a UNESCO World Heritage monument, and a ride up Salen mountain for spectacular views of the city. ⊠ *Havnegt. 3* ☎ *78–41–21–85* ⊕ *www.hammerfest-turist.no.*

### FISHING

Fishing trips are organized as private boat rentals with or without guides.

**M/S Amor.** This fishing boat holds up to 12 people, and comes with a guide who will create your bespoke itinerary ☎ *41–80–44–09.*

**Sørøya Gjestestue.** This outfitter offers three boats for rent and guarantees a catch! ☎ *91–88–10–21* ⊕ *www.gjestestua.no.*

### HIKING AND WALKING

Hammerfest is a paradise for those who enjoy long ambles. The tourist office organizes a four-hour scenic walking excursion to reach Kjøttvikvarden, a landmark built in 1850 to help fishermen become oriented on long journeys. They also provide suggested walking routes such as the Gammelveien trail, a 30-minute walk that starts from the town church and heads up an old road. ⊠ *Havnegt. 3* ☎ *78–41–31–00* ⊕ *www.hammerfest-turist.no.*

# HONNINGSVÅG, NORWAY

Searching in 1553 for a northeast passage to India, British navigator Richard Chancellor came upon a crag 307 meters above the Barents Sea. He named the jut of rock North Cape, or *Nordkapp.* Today Europe's northernmost point is a rite-of-passage journey for nearly all Scandinavians. And much of the world has followed. Most cruise passengers visit Nordkapp from Honningsvåg, a fishing village on Magerøya Island. The journey from Honningsvåg to Nordkapp covers about 35 km (22 mi) across a landscape characterized by rocky tundra and grazing reindeer, which are rounded up each spring by Sami herdsmen in boats. The herdsmen force the reindeer to swim across a mile-wide channel from their winter home on the mainland. Honningvåg's northerly location makes for long, dark winter nights and perpetually sun-filled summer

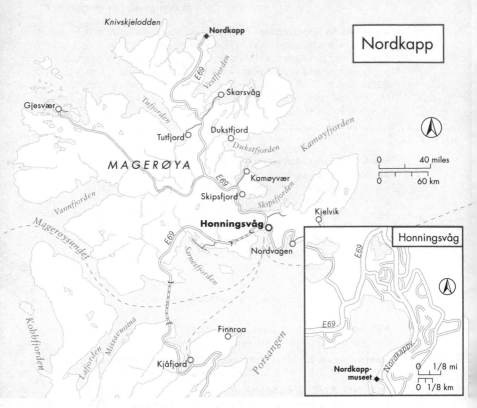

days. The village serves as the gateway to Arctic exploration and the beautiful Nordkapp Plateau, a destination that calls to all visitors of this region.

## ESSENTIALS

CURRENCY    Norway is a non-EU country and has opted to keep its currency, the Norwegian *krone* (Nkr 6 to US$1). ATMs are readily available.

HOURS    Most shops are open from 10 to 4 or 5 weekdays, Thursday until 7, Saturday from 10 to 3 or 4, and are closed Sunday.

INTERNET    **Tourist Information/Nordkapp Reiseliv AS** (✉ *Fiskeriveien 4D, Honningsvåg* ☎ *78–47–70–30*).

TELEPHONES    Most tri- and quad-band GSM phones work in Norway, so if your service provider offers service in Europe, you will likely be able to use your mobile phone along the Norwegian coast, even while hugging the shoreline on ship. Public telephones take Nkr 1, 5, 10, and 20 coins, and you need Nkr 5 at a minimum. International phone cards are the best value for long-distance calls, and are available at newsstands.

## COMING ASHORE

Northern Norway's largest port welcomes about 100 cruise ships annually during the summer season. Ships dock at one of five piers, all within walking distance of the city center. The piers themselves have no services, but within 100 meters are shops, museums, tourist information, post office, banks, restaurants, and an ice bar.

## EXPLORING HONNINGSVÅG AND NORDKAPP

### HONNINGSVÅG

**Nordkappmuseet** *(North Cape Museum)*. On the third floor of Nordkapphuset *(North Cape House)*, this museum documents the history of the fishing industry in the region as well as the history of tourism at Nordkapp. You can learn how the trail of humanity stretches back 10,000 years, and about the development of society and culture in this region. ⊠ *Fiskerivn. 4, Honningsvåg* ☎ *78–47–72–00* ⊕ *www.nordkappmuseet. no* 🖃 *Nkr 50* ⊙ *June–mid-Aug., Mon.–Sat. 10–7, Sun. noon–7; mid-Aug.–May, Mon.–Sat. noon–4.*

### NORDKAPP

*34 km (21 mi) north of Honningsvåg.*

On your journey to Nordkapp you'll see an incredible expanse of treeless tundra, with crumbling mountains and sparse, dwarf plants. The subarctic environment is very vulnerable, so don't disturb the plants. Walk only on marked trails and don't remove stones, leave car marks, or make campfires. The roads are open for buses through most of winter.

**Nordkapphallen** *(North Cape Hall)*. The contrast between this near-barren territory and the tourist center is striking. Blasted into the interior of the plateau, the building is housed in a cave and includes an ecumenical chapel, a souvenir shop, and a post office. Exhibits trace the history of the cape, from Richard Chancellor's discovery in 1533, to Oscar II, king of Norway and Sweden, who climbed to the top of the plateau in 1873. Celebrate your pilgrimage to Nordkapp at Café Kompasset, Restaurant Kompasset, or at the Grotten Bar coffee shop. ⊠ *Nordkapp-platået* ☎ *78–47–68–60* ⊕ *www.rica.no/nordkapphallen* 🖃 *Nkr 235* ⊙ *Mid-May–mid-Aug., daily 11* AM*–1* AM*; mid-Aug.–Sept. daily 11* AM*–10* PM*; Oct.–mid-May daily 11* AM*–3* PM.

## SHOPPING

The small village of Honningsvåg doesn't exactly qualify as a shopper's paradise, but there are shops that sell Norwegian souvenirs and handicrafts.

**Arctic Souvenir.** This shop in the same building as the Nordkappmuseet and the tourist information center, stays open until late at night when cruise ships call. The shop features a range of Norwegian souvenirs, T-shirts, books, knitting products, pewter, and international calling cards—all tax-free. The shop can also mail purchased goods. Accepts all major credit cards and foreign currency. ⊠ *Fiskeriveien 4, Honningsvåg* ☎ *78–47–37–12.*

## ACTIVITIES

### BIRD-WATCHING

**Gjesvær Turistsenter.** This outfitter organizes bird-watching safaris from May to August. ⊠ *Nygårdsveien 38, Gjesvær* 🕾 *78–47–57–73* ⊕ *www. birdsafari.com.*

**Nordkapp Reiseliv.** Headquartered in the North Cape Museum, this company books adventures and activities including bird safaris, deep-sea fishing, boat excursions, and winter expeditions. ⊠ *Fiskeriveien 4, Honningsvåg* 🕾 *78–47–70–30* ⊕ *www.nordkapp.no.*

### DEEP-SEA FISHING

The waters around the North Cape are among the best fishing grounds in the world. Here you can catch large cod, halibut, catfish, and haddock, as well as the *kongekrabbe* or giant crab, a much-prized delicacy. Many operators offer deep-sea fishing tours.

**Destinasjon 71° Nord.** This outfitter offers the unbelievable experience of deep-sea rafting in search of giant king crabs with its King Crab Safari. You also get to eat your catch! 🕾 *78–47–17–00* ⊕ *www.71-nord.no.*

### DEEP-SEA RAFTING

**Nordkapp Safari.** You don't have to fish to experience deep-sea rafting, which is as exhilarating as it is beautiful. After getting a flotation suit to protect against the subarctic wind, board a rubber dinghy at the North Cape Adventure Center and speed toward Nordfågen, an uninhabited fishing hamlet. Continue on to see the Helnes Lighthouse, which was built in 1908 for trading vessels coming from northern Russia and the East. This company organizes three-hour trips to Nordkapp. 🕾 *78–47–52–33* ⊕ *www.nordkappsafari.no/.*

## WHERE TO EAT

**$$**
ECLECTIC

✕**Corner AS.** The daily catch often dictates the menu here, though pizza is always available along with the crispy cod tongue. ⊠ *Fiskeriveien 2A, Honningsvåg* 🕾 *78–47–63–41* ⊕ *www.corner.no* ▤ *AE, MC, V.*

# KRISTIANSAND, NORWAY

Nicknamed "Sommerbyen" ("Summer City"), Norway's fifth-largest city has 80,000 inhabitants. Norwegians come here for its sun-soaked beaches and beautiful harbor. According to legend, in 1641 King Christian IV marked the four corners of Kristiansand with his walking stick, and within that framework the grid of wide streets was laid down. The center of town, called the Kvadraturen, still retains the grid, even after numerous fires. In the northeast corner is Posebyen, one of northern Europe's largest collections of low, connected wooden house settlements, and there's a market here every Saturday in summer. Kristiansand's Fisketorvet (fish market) is near the south corner of the town's grid, right on the sea.

### COMING ASHORE

Cruise ships dock directly at Kristiansand's cruise-ship terminal. The town's main sights are a one-third-mile or 10-minute walk from the terminal.

## EXPLORING KRISTIANSAND

**Agder naturmuseum og botaniske hage** (*Agder Nature Museum and Botanical Gardens*). This museum takes on Sørlandet's natural history from the Ice Age to the present, examining the coast and moving on to the high mountains. There's a rainbow of minerals on display, as well as a rose garden with varieties from 1850. There's even the country's largest collection of cacti. ⊠ *Gimlevn. 23* ☎ *38–05–86–20* ⊕ *www. naturmuseum.no* 🖘 *Nkr 40* ◷ *Mid-June–mid-Aug., daily 11–5; mid-Aug.–mid-June, Tues.–Fri. 10–3, Sun. noon–4.*

**Christiansholm Festning.** This fortress sits on a promontory opposite Festningsgata. Completed in 1674, the circular building with 16-foot-thick walls has played more a decorative role than a defensive one; it was used once, in 1807 during the Napoleonic Wars, to defend the city against British invasion. Now it contains art exhibits. ⊠ *Østre Strandgt.* ☎ *38–07–51–50* ◷ *Mid-May to mid-Sept., daily 9–9.*

**Gimle Gård.** A wealthy merchant-shipowner built Gimle Manor around 1800 in the Empire style. Inside are furnishings from that period, including paintings, silver, and hand-printed wallpaper. To get there from the city center, head north across the Otra River on Bus 22 or drive to Route E18 and cross the bridge over the Otra to Parkveien. Turn left onto Ryttergangen and drive to Gimleveien; take a right. ⊠ *Gimlevn. 23* ☎ *38–10–26–80* ⊕ *www.vestagdermuseet.no* 🖘 *Nkr 40* ◷ *Mid-June–Sept., daily 10–5; weekends noon–5.*

**Kristiansand Domkirke.** The Gothic Revival cathedral dating from 1885 is the third-largest church in Norway. It often hosts summer concerts in addition to the weeklong International Church Music Festival in August. Organ, chamber, and gospel music are on the bill. ⊠ *Kirkegt.* ☎ *38–04–97–00, 38–07–70–40 music festival* 🖘 *Free* ◷ *June–Aug., daily 9–2.*

**Kristiansand Dyreparken.** One of Norway's most popular attractions is actually five separate parks, including a water park (bring bathing suits and towels); a forested park; an entertainment park; a theme park; and a zoo, which contains an enclosure for Scandinavian animals such as wolves, snow foxes, lynxes, and elks. The theme park, **Kardemomme By** (Cardamom Town), is named for a book by Norwegian illustrator and writer Thorbjørn Egner. In the zoo the "My Africa" exhibition allows you to move along a bridge observing native savanna animals such as giraffes, lions, and zebras. The park is 11 km (6 mi) east of town. ⊠ *Kristiansand Dyreparken, Kardemomme By* ☎ *38–04–97–00* ⊕ *www.dyreparken.no* 🖘 *Nkr 280* ◷ *June–Aug., daily 10–7; Sept.–May, weekdays 10–3, weekends 10–5.*

**Kristiansand Kanonmuseum** (*Cannon Museum*). Here you can see the cannon that the occupying Germans rigged up during World War II. With calibers of 15 inches, the cannon was said to be capable of shooting a projectile halfway to Denmark. In the bunkers, related military materials are on display. ⊠ *Møvik* ☎ *38–08–50–90* ⊕ *www. kanonmuseet.no* 🎟 *Nkr 60* ⊙ *Mid-June–mid-Aug., daily 11–6; mid-May–mid-June and mid-Aug.–Sept., Mon.–Wed. 11–3, Thurs.–Sun. 11–5; rest of year Sun. noon–4. Prebooked tours available all year.*

**Oddernes Kirke.** The striking rune stone in the cemetery of this church tells that Øyvind, godson of Saint Olav, built it in 1040 on property he inherited from his father. One of the oldest churches in Norway, it has a baroque pulpit from 1704 and is dedicated to Saint Ola. Organ concerts are held every Sunday in July. ⊠ *Jegersbergvn. 2* ☎ *38–19–68–60* 🎟 *Free* ⊙ *July and Aug., Sun–Fri. 9–2.*

**Ravnedalen.** A favorite with hikers and strolling nannies, the Raven Valley is a lush park that's filled with flowers in springtime. Wear comfortable shoes to hike the narrow, winding paths up the hills and climb the 200 steps up to a 304-foot lookout. There is a café on-site, and open-air concerts in summer. ⊠ *Northwest of Kristiansand.*

**Vest-Agder Fylkesmuseum** (*County Museum*). The region's largest cultural museum has more than 40 old buildings on display. The structures, transported from other locations in the area, include two *tun*—farm buildings traditionally set in clusters around a common area—which suited the extended families. If you have children with you, check out the old-fashioned toys, which can still be played with. The museum is 4 km (2½ mi) east of Kristiansand on Route E18. ⊠ *Vigevn. 22B, Kongsgård* ☎ *38–10–26–80* ⊕ *www.vestagdermuseet.no* 🎟 *Nkr 40* ⊙ *Mid-June–Sept., weekdays 10–5, weekends noon–5; Sept.–Jan., weekdays 9–3, Sun. noon–5.*

## SHOPPING

There are many shops next to Dyreparken in Kristiansand.

**Kvadraturen.** This large mall has 300 stores and eating spots. ⊠ *Rådhus-gaten 6* ☎ *38–02–44–11* ⊕ *www.kvadraturen.no.*

**Sørlandssenteret.** This is one of the region's larger shopping centers, with 100 stores, a pharmacy, and a post office. ⊠ *Barstølveien 31–35* ☎ *38–04–91–00* ⊕ *www.sorlandssenteret.no*).

## ACTIVITIES

### ADVENTURE SPORTS

**Troll Mountain.** About a one-hour drive from Kristiansand, this resort organizes many activities. Be it mountain climbing, sailing, biking, rafting, paintball, or even beaver or deer safaris, this is the place for outdoorsy types. ⊠ *Setesdal Rafting og Aktivitetssenter, Rte. 9, Evje* ☎ *37–93–11–77* ⊕ *www.troll-mountain.no.*

### BIKING

Kristiansand has 70 km (42 mi) of bike trails around the city. The tourist office can recommend routes and rentals.

**Kristiansand Sykkelsenter.** This company rents bicycles and off-road vehicles. ⊠ *Grim Torv 3* ☎ *38–02–68–35* ⊕ *www.sykkelsenter.no.*

### FISHING

Just north of Kristiansand there's excellent trout, perch, and eel fishing at Lillesand's **Vestre Grimevann** lake.

**Lillesand Tourist Office.** You need a license to fish in Norway. You can get a permit at any sports store or at the tourist office in Lillesand. ⊠ *Lillesand* ☎ *37–40–19–10 or 93–01–17–81.*

**Upstream Norway.** This outfitter offers all kinds of fishing experiences, including salmon-, trout-, and fly-fishing. ⊠ *Gimlemoen 19* ☎ *91–10–74–72* ⊕ *www.upstreamnorway.no.*

### HIKING

In addition to the gardens and steep hills of Ravnedalen, the **Baneheia Skog** *(Baneheia Forest)* is full of evergreens, small lakes, and paths that are ideal for a lazy walk or a challenging run. It's a 15-minute walk north from the city center.

# OSLO, NORWAY

What sets Oslo apart from other European cities is not so much its cultural traditions or its internationally renowned museums as its simply stunning natural beauty. How many world capitals have subway service to the forest, or lakes and hiking trails within the city limits? But Norwegians will be quick to remind you that Oslo is a cosmopolitan metropolis with prosperous businesses and a thriving nightlife. During the mid-19th century, Norway and Sweden were ruled as one kingdom, under King Karl Johan. It was then that the grand main street that is his namesake was built, and Karl Johans Gate has been at the center of city life ever since. In 1905 the country separated from Sweden, and in 1925 an act of Parliament finally changed the city's name back to Oslo from Kristiania, its Swedish name. Today Oslo is Norway's political, economic, industrial, and cultural capital. The Norwegian royal family lives in Oslo, and it is also where the Nobel Peace Prize is awarded.

### ESSENTIALS

CURRENCY Norway is a non-EU country and has opted to keep its currency, the Norwegian *krone* (Nkr 6 to US$1). ATMs are readily available.

HOURS Most shops are open from 10 to 4 or 5 weekdays, Thursday until 7, Saturday from 10 to 3 or 4, and are closed Sunday.

INTERNET Most small coffee shops around town offer free Internet access with a purchase.

**Arctic Internet** (⊠ *Oslo S Station, Sentrum* ☎ *22–17–19–40*).

**Hard Rock Cafe** (⊠ *Karl Johans gt. 45Sentrum* ☎ *40–00–62–60*) has Wi-Fi.

TELEPHONES Most tri- and quad-band GSM phones work in Norway, so if your service provider offers service in Europe, you will likely be able to use your mobile phone along the Norwegian coast, even while hugging the shoreline on ship. Public telephones take Nkr 1, 5, 10, and 20 coins, and you need Nkr 5 at a minimum. International phone cards are the best value for long-distance calls, and are available at newsstands.

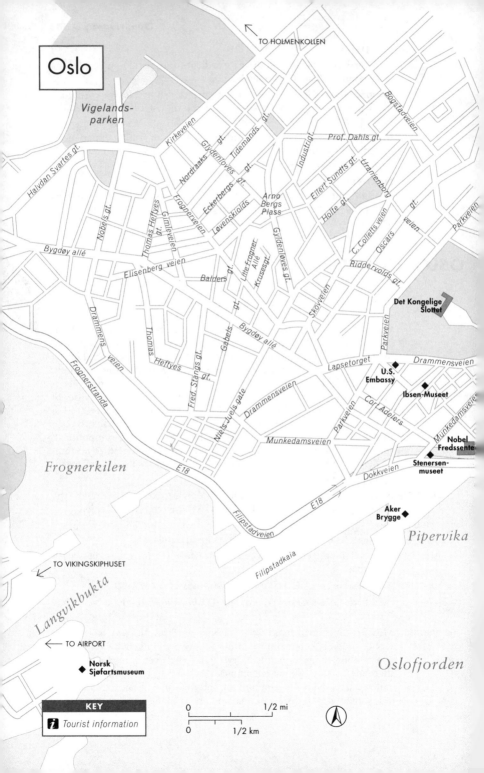

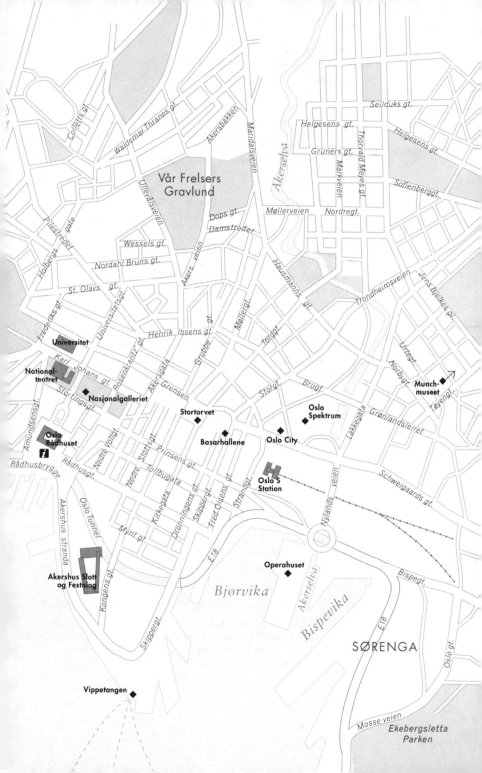

**COMING ASHORE**

Cruise ships navigate beautiful Oslofjord en route to Oslo and dock in the compact city center. Many of Oslo's attractions can be explored on foot from the docks, but Oslo has a good subway system, as well as plentiful buses and taxis.

Taxis are radio dispatched from a central office, and it can take up to 30 minutes to get one during peak hours. Taxi stands are all over town. It is possible to hail a cab on the street, but cabs are not allowed to pick up passengers within 100 yards of a stand. Never take pirate taxis; all registered taxis should have their roof lights on when they're available. Rates start at Nkr 41 for hailed or rank cabs, and Nkr 61 for ordered taxis, depending on the time of day. Minimum fare is Nkr 111.

## EXPLORING OSLO

Fodor's Choice ★ **Aker Brygge.** This area was the site of a disused shipyard until redevelopment saw the addition of residential town houses and a commercial sector. Postmodern steel and glass buildings dominate the skyline now. The area has more than 40 restaurants and 60 shops, including upmarket fashion boutiques, as well as pubs, cinemas, theaters, and an indoor shopping mall. There is outdoor dining capacity for 2,500 as well as an open boulevard for strolling. ⊠ *Aker Brygge* ☎ *22–83–26–80* ⊕ *www. akerbrygge.no* ⊠ *Free* ۞ *Weekdays 10–8, Sat. 10–6.*

**Akershus Slott og Festning** *(Akershus Castle and Fortress).* Dating from 1299, this stone medieval castle and royal residence was developed into a fortress armed with cannons by 1592. After that time, it withstood a number of sieges and then fell into decay. It was finally restored in 1899. Summer tours take guests through its magnificent halls, the castle church, the royal mausoleum, reception rooms, and banquet halls. ⊠ *Akershus Slott, Festningspl., Sentrum* ☎ *22–41–25–21* ⊕ *www.akershusfestning.no* ⊠ *Grounds and concerts free, castle Nkr 65* ۞ *Grounds: daily 6 AM–9 PM. Castle: May–Sept., Mon.–Sat. 10–4, Sun. 12:30–4; Sept.–May, weekends noon–5.*

**Det Kongelige Slottet** *(The Royal Palace).* At one end of Karl Johans Gate, the vanilla- and cream-color neoclassical palace was completed in 1848. Although generally closed to the public, the palace is open for guided tours in summer three times per day. The rest of the time, you can simply admire it from the outside. An equestrian statue of Karl Johan, King of Sweden and Norway from 1818 to 1844, stands in the square in front of the palace. ⊠ *Drammensvn. 1, Sentrum* ☎ *81–53–21–33* ⊕ *www. kongehuset.no* ⊠ *Tour Nkr 95* ۞ *Guided tours mid-June–mid-Aug., Mon.–Thurs. and Sat. noon, 2, 2:20, Fri. and Sun. 2, 2:20, 4.*

**Holmenkollen.** Holmenkollen is the most-visited tourist attraction in Norway, with a ski museum, a ski-jump tower, and ski stimulator, a gorgeous lookout tower, and a souvenir shop in one small enclave. World Cup events are held annually in the Holmenkollen Ski Arena. ⊠ *Kongeveien 5, Holmenkollen* ☎ *22–92–32–00* ⊕ *www.skiforeningen. no* ⊠ *Nkr 60* ۞ *June–Aug., daily 9–8; Sept.–May, daily 10–4.*

**Ibsen-museet** (*Ibsen Museum*). Famed Norwegian dramatist Henrik Ibsen, known for *A Doll's House, Ghosts,* and *Peer Gynt,* among other classic plays, spent his final years here, in the apartment on the second floor, until his death in 1906. Every morning, Ibsen's wife Suzannah would encourage the literary legend to write before allowing him to head off to the Grand Café for his brandy and foreign newspapers. His study provides striking glimpses into his psyche. Huge, intense portraits of Ibsen and his Swedish archrival, August Strindberg, face each other. Take a guided tour (offered hourly) by well-versed and entertaining Ibsen scholars. Afterward, visit the museum's exhibition of Ibsen's drawings and paintings and first magazine writings. ✉ *H. Ibsens gt 26, across Drammensvn. from Royal Palace, Sentrum* ☎ *22–12–35–50* ⊕ *www.ibsenmuseet.no* ✑ *Nkr 85* ☯ *Mid-May–mid-Sept., Tues.–Sun. 11–6; mid-Sept.–mid-May, Tues.–Sun. 11–4, Thurs. 11–6.*

**Fodor's Choice** **Munch-museet** *(Munch Museum)*. Edvard Munch, Norway's most famous
★ artist, bequeathed his enormous collection of works (about 1,100 paintings, 3,000 drawings, and 18,000 graphic works) to the city when he died in 1944. The museum is a monument to his artistic genius, housing the largest collection of his works as well as changing exhibitions. Munch actually painted several different versions of *The Scream,* the image for which he is best known. Although most of the Munch legend focuses on the artist as a troubled, angst-ridden man, he moved away from that pessimistic and dark approach to more optimistic themes later in his career. ✉ *Tøyengt. 53, Tøyen* ☎ *23–49–35–00* ⊕ *www.munch. museum.no* ✑ *Nkr 75* ☯ *June–Sept., daily 10–6; Sept.–June, Tues.–Fri. 10–4, weekends 11–5.*

★ **Nasjonalgalleriet** *(National Gallery)*. The gallery, part of the National Museum of Art, Architecture and Design, houses Norway's largest collection of art created before 1945. The deep-red Edvard Munch room holds such major paintings as *The Dance of Life,* one of two existing oil versions of *The Scream,* and several self-portraits. Classic landscapes by Hans Gude and Adolph Tidemand—including *Bridal Voyage on the Hardangerfjord*—share space in galleries with other works by major Norwegian artists. The museum also has works by Monet, Renoir, Van Gogh, and Gauguin. ✉ *Universitetsgt. 13, Sentrum* ☎ *21–98–20–00* ⊕ *www.nationalmuseum.no* ✑ *Free* ☯ *Tues., Wed., and Fri. 10–6, Thurs. 10–7, weekends 11–5.*

---

### OSLO BEST BETS

**Aker Brygge.** Once a dilapidated shipyard, this is now an upscale residential and commercial district.

**Munch Museet.** Munch is Norway's most famous artist. You can see a version of *The Scream* here; there's another version in the Nasjonalgalleriet if you want a broader introduction to Norwegian art.

**Vigelandsparken.** The 212 bronze, granite, and wrought-iron sculptures by Gustav Vigeland skillfully and artistically detail his life, thoughts, and interpretations of his childhood.

**6**

**Nobel Fredssenter** *(Nobel Peace Center)*. Situated near Oslo's Rådhus (City Hall) in a converted historic train station, the Nobel Peace Center was opened by King Harald on June 11, 2005. With changing exhibits, intriguing digital presentations, and inspiring films and lectures, the Center reflects on the men and women who have been honored over the years. ☒ *Rådhusplassen, Sentrum* ☎ *48–30–10–00* ⊕ *www. nobelpeacecenter.org* ▣ *Tour Nkr 80* ☉ *June–Sept., daily 10–6; Jan.– May, Tues.–Sun. 10–6.*

**Fodor'sChoice**
★
**Operahuset.** Oslo's brand-new opera house opened with great fanfare in April 2008, in the presence of the Norwegian king and a host of celebrities. The white-marble and glass building, designed by renowned Norwegian architect firm Snøhetta, is a stunning addition to the Oslo waterfront and to the pride of Norwegians. It doesn't just look good— acoustics inside the dark oak auditorium are excellent, too. The program includes ballet, orchestra concerts, rock, and opera; the roof is also used for performances ☒ *Kirsten Flagstads pl. 1, City Center* ☎ *21– 42–21–00 or 815–444–88* ⊕ *www.operaen.no* ▣ *Free, tours Nkr 100* ☉ *Tours Juy and Aug., daily at noon and 2; Sept.–mid-Apr., daily at 2.*

**Fodor'sChoice**
★
**Oslo Rådhus** *(City Hall)*. This redbrick building is best known today for the awarding of the Nobel Peace Prize, which takes place here every December. In 1915 the mayor of Oslo made plans for a new city hall and ordered the clearing of slums that stood on the site. The building was finally completed in 1950. Inside, many museum-quality masterpieces hang on the walls. After viewing the frescoes in the main hall, walk upstairs to the banquet hall to see the royal portraits. In the east gallery, Per Krogh's mosaic of a pastoral scene covers all four walls, making you feel like you're part of the painting. On festive occasions the central hall is illuminated from outside by 60 large spotlights that simulate daylight. ☒ *Fr. Nansens plass, Sentrum* ☎ *23–46–12–00* ⊕ *www. rft.oslo.kommune.no* ▣ *Free* ☉ *Daily 9–6.*

**Fodor'sChoice**
★
**Vigelandsparken** *(Vigeland Park)*. Vigelandsparken has 212 bronze, granite, and wrought-iron sculptures by Gustav Vigeland (1869–1943). Most of the stunning park sculptures are placed on a nearly 1-km-long (½ mi-long) axis and depict the stages of life: birth to death, one generation to the next. See the park's 56-foot-high granite *Monolith Plateau*, a column of 121 upward-striving nude figures surrounded by 36 groups on circular stairs. The most beloved sculpture is a bronze of an enraged baby boy stamping his foot and scrunching his face in fury. Known as *Sinnataggen* (*The Angry Boy*), this famous statue has been filmed, parodied, painted red, and even stolen from the park. It is based on a 1901 sketch Vigeland made of a little boy in London. ☒ *Kirkevn., Frogner* ☎ *23–49–37–00* ⊕ *www.vigeland.museum.no* ▣ *Free* ☉ *Daily.*

**Fodor'sChoice**
★
**Vikingskiphuset** *(Viking Ship Museum)*. The Viking legacy in all its glory lives on at this classic Oslo museum. Chances are you'll come away fascinated by the three blackened wooden Viking ships *Gokstad, Oseberg,* and *Tune,* which date to AD 800. Discovered in Viking tombs around the Oslo fjords between 1860 and 1904, the boats are the best-preserved Viking ships ever found, and have been exhibited since the museum's 1957 opening. In Viking times it was customary to bury

the dead with food, drink, useful and decorative objects, and even their horses and dogs. Many of the well-preserved tapestries, household utensils, dragon-style wood carvings, and sledges were found aboard ships. The museum's rounded white walls give the feeling of a burial mound. Avoid summertime crowds by visiting at lunchtime. ⊠ *Huk Aveny 35, Bygdøy* ☎ *22–13–52–80* ⊕ *www.ukm.uio.no/vikingskipshuset* ⛁ *NKr 60* ⊙ *May–Sept., daily 9–6; Oct.–Apr., daily 10–4.*

## SHOPPING

Oslo is the best place in the country for buying anything Norwegian. Popular souvenirs include knitwear, wood and ceramic trolls, wood spoons, rosemaling boxes, gold and silver jewelry, pewter, smoked salmon, caviar, *akvavit* (a caraway seed-flavored liquor), chocolate, and goat cheese. Gold and precious stones are no bargain, but silver and enamel jewelry and Viking period productions can be. Some silver pieces are made with Norwegian stones, particularly pink thulite.

Established Norwegian brands include Porsgrund porcelain, Hadeland and Magnor glass, David Andersen jewelry, and Husfliden handicrafts. You may also want to look for popular, classical, or folk-music CDs; English translations of Norwegian books; or clothing by Norwegian designers.

Prices in Norway, as in all of Scandinavia, are generally much higher than in other European countries. The cost of handmade articles such as knitwear is controlled, making comparison shopping useless. Otherwise, shops have both sales and specials—look for the words *salg* and *tilbud.*

Some popular shopping areas in Oslo are Majorstua and Frogner behind the Royal Palace. The Frogner district has many antiques shops, especially on Skovveien and Thomas Heftyes Gate between Bygdøy Allé and Frogner plass. Deeper in the heart of Majorstuen, Industrigate is famous for its good selection of designer clothing and fashion shops.

**Aker Brygge.** Near the cruise ship docks is Norway's first major shopping center. It's right on the water across from the tourist information center. Shops are open until 8 most days, though few open on Sunday. *Aker Brygge.*

**ByPorten.** This shopping center has more than 70 fashion, food, and gift stores next to Oslo S Station. ⊠ *Jernbanetorget 6, Sentrum* ☎ *23–36– 21–60* ⊕ *www.byporten.no.*

**David-Andersen.** This is Norway's best-known goldsmith. He makes stunning silver and gold designs. ⊠ *Karl Johans gt. 20, Sentrum* ☎ *24– 14–88–00* ⊕ *www.david-andersen.no* ⊠ *Bogstadvn. 23, Majorstuen* ☎ *22–59–50–00* ⊠ *Stranden 3, Aker Brygge* ☎ *22–83–42–00.*

**GlasMagasinet.** If there's no time to visit a glass factory outside of town, department stores are the best option. This one stocks both European and Norwegian designs in glass, pewter, and silver. ⊠ *Stortorvet 8, Sentrum* ☎ *22–90–87–00* ⊕ *www.glasmagasinet.no.*

**Oslo City.** At the other end of downtown, with access to the street from Oslo S Station, this is the city's largest indoor mall, and the country's most-visited one, with almost 100 shops and eateries over five floors. ✉ *Stenersgt. 1, Sentrum* ☎ *815/44–033* ⊕ *www.oslocity.no.*

**Paleet.** This elegant shopping center opens up into a grand, marbled atrium and has many clothing, accessories, and food stores, including a basement food court. ✉ *Karl Johans gt. 37–43, between Universitetsgt. and Rosenkrantz gt., Sentrum* ☎ *22–03–38–88* ⊕ *www.paleet.no.*

## ACTIVITIES

Oslo's natural surroundings and climate make it ideally suited to outdoor pursuits. The Oslofjord and its islands, the forested woodlands called the *marka,* and as many as 18 hours of daylight in summer all make the Norwegian capital an irresistible place for outdoor activities.

### BICYCLING

Oslo is a great biking city. You can rent a city bike from over 100 bike stations in and around the city center by getting a Smartcard at any Tourist Information Office for Nkr 80 for 24 hours. One scenic ride starts at Aker Brygge and takes you along the harbor to the Bygdøy peninsula, where you can visit the museums or cut across the fields next to the royal family's summer house.

**Ski & Guide.** This company at the Voksenkollen station rents mountain bikes for exploration of the Nordmarka forest. ✉ *Tomm Murstadbakken 2, Nordmarka* ☎ *91–51–46–33* ⊕ *www.ski-guide.no.*

**Syklistenes Landsforening.** The National Organization of Cyclists sells books and maps for cycling holidays in Norway and abroad and the staff gives friendly, free advice. ✉ *Storgata 23D, Sentrum* ☎ *22–47–30–30.*

### FISHING

A national fishing license and a local fee are required to fish in the lakes and rivers around Oslo; however, a permit is not required to fish in the Oslo Fjord. No fishing is allowed in lakes that are used as sources for drinking water.

**Dagens Fangst.** This company arranges guided fishing trips in the inner Oslo Fjord. Trips must usually be arranged up to a week in advance. ☎ *95–71–54–04* ⊕ *www.dagensfangst.com.*

**M/S Rina.** This fishing boat offers private fishing trips for up to seven people. ☎ *93–03–04–08.*

**Oslomarkas Fiskeadministrasjon.** For information on fishing areas and on where to buy a license, contact the Oslo Fish Administration, which issues fishing permits. ✉ *Sørkedalen 914, Holmenkollen* ☎ *40–00–67–68* ⊕ *www.ofa.no.*

**Tomm Murstad.** You can fish throughout the Nordmarka woods area in a canoe rented from this company. ✉ *Tryvannsvn. 2, Holmenkollen* ☎ *22–13–95–00.*

### GOLF

**Losby Golfklubb.** This golf club 20 km east of Oslo has two separate courses, both designed by renowned course architect Peter Nordwall, integrating the beauty of the river Losbyelven and Norway's dramatic green landscapes into the courses. ⊠ *Losbyvelen 270, Finstadjordet* ☎ *67–92–33–40* ⊕ *www.losby.no.*

**Oslo Golfklubb Bogstad.** On Bogstad Lake, this course recently reopened after major renovations in 2009. It is a private club; however, it admits members of other golf clubs weekdays before 2 and weekends after 2 if space is available. Visitors must have a handicap certificate of 20 or lower for men, 28 or lower for women. Fees range from Nkr 250 to Nkr 500. ⊠ *Ankerveien 127, Bogstad* ☎ *22–51–05–60* ⊕ *www.oslogk.no.*

### KAYAKING

The Oslo Archipelago is a favorite destination for sunbathing urbanites, who hop ferries to their favorite isles. A ferry to Hovedøya and other islands in the harbor basin leaves from Aker Brygge (take Bus 60 from Jernbanetorget).

**Oslofjord Kayak.** This outfitter offers kayaks for rent directly on the pier at Sjølyst Marina. ⊠ *Sjølyst Marina-Bestumkilen, Oslofjorden* ☎ *95–05–08–21* ⊕ *www.oslofjordkajakk.no.*

## NIGHTLIFE

More than ever, the Oslo nightlife scene is vibrant and varied. Cafés, restaurant-bars, and jazz clubs are laid-back and mellow. But if you're ready to party, there are many pulsating, live-rock and dance clubs to choose from. Day or night, people are usually out on Karl Johans Gate, and many clubs and restaurants in the central area stay open until the early hours. Aker Brygge, the wharf area, has many bars and some nightclubs, attracting both locals and visitors, couples on first dates, and other people willing to spend extra for the waterfront location. Grünerløkka and Grønland have even more bars, pubs, and cafés catering to a younger crowd. A more mature, upmarket crowd ventures out to the less busy west side of Oslo, to Frogner and Bygdøy.

Drinking out is expensive in Oslo, starting at around Nkr 50 for a beer or a mixed drink. Many Norwegians save money by having drinks at friends' houses—called a *vorspiel*—before heading out on the town. Some bars in town remain quiet until 11 PM or midnight when the first groups of vorspiel partiers arrive.

**Bibliotekbaren og Vinterhaven.** If you're more partial to lounging than drinking, the bar at the Hotel Bristol is a stylish hangout with old-fashioned leather armchairs, huge marble columns, and live piano music. ⊠ *Hotel Bristol, Kristian IVs gt. 7, Sentrum* ☎ *22–82–60–00* ⊕ *www. bristol.no.*

**Blå.** On the Akers River, this club is considered the leading destination for jazz and related sounds in the Nordic countries. The riverside patio is popular in summer. ⊠ *Brennerivn. 9C, Grünerløkka* ☎ *40–00–42–77* ⊕ *www.blaaoslo.no.*

**Herr Nilsen.** At this popular venue some of Norway's most celebrated jazz artists perform in a stylish space. There's live music three nights a week and jazz on weekend afternoons. ⊠ *C. J. Hambros pl. 5, Sentrum* ☎ *22–33–54–05* ⊕ *www.herrnilsen.no.*

**Oslo Mikrobryggeri.** Serious beer drinkers may find this microbrewery worth a stop. Eight different beers are brewed on the premises, including the increasingly popular Oslo Pils. ✉ *Bogstadvn. 6, Majorstuen* ☎ *22–56–97–76* ⊕ *www.omb.no.*

## WHERE TO EAT

$$$–$$$$
SEAFOOD
★

✕ **Lofoten Fiskerestaurant.** Named for the Lofoten Islands off the northwest coast, this Aker Brygge restaurant is considered one of Oslo's best for fish, from salmon to cod to monkfish. It has a bright, fresh, minimalist interior with harbor views and a summertime patio. From January through March, try the cod served with its own liver and roe; April through September, the shellfish; and from October through December, the lutefisk. Call ahead, since sometimes only large groups are served. ✉ *Stranden 75, Aker Brygge* ☎ *22–83–08–08* ⊕ *www.lofoten-fiskerestaurant.no* ▤ *AE, DC, MC, V.*

$$–$$$$
NORWEGIAN

✕ **Gamle Raadhus.** Inside Oslo's first city hall, built in 1641, this is the city's oldest restaurant. Its reputation is based mostly on traditional fish and game dishes. The backyard has a charming outdoor area for dining in summer. ✉ *Nedre Slottsgt. 1, Sentrum* ☎ *22–42–01–07* ⊕ *www.gamleraadhus.no* ▤ *AE, DC, MC, V* ◷ *Closed Sun.*

$$
FRENCH

✕ **Markveien Mat og Vinhus.** This restaurant in the heart of the Grünerløkka district serves fresh French-inspired Scandinavian cuisine. It's a relaxed, artsy place with a bohemian vibe. Paintings cover the yellow walls, and the tables are laid with white linen. Veal and baked halibut are both house specialties, but it's the stunning wine list that draws the crowds—it was recently singled out by *Wine Spectator* as among the best in Oslo. ✉ *Torvbakkgt. 12, entrance on Markvn. 57, Grünerløkka* ☎ *22–37–22–97* ⊕ *www.markveien.no* ▤ *AE, DC, MC, V* ◷ *Closed Sun.*

$
PIZZA
★

✕ **Pizza da Mimmo.** Named for owner Domenico Giardina, aka Mimmo, this is Oslo's best pizzeria. In 1993 Mimmo, who's originally from Calabria, was the first to bring thin-crust Italian pizza to the city. Taste his perennially popular panna and prosciutto pizza (with crème fraiche, prosciutto, mushroom, and tomatoes), and the Pizza Calabrizella (with salami, leeks, onions, and eggplant). The casual restaurant is on the basement level in a white-brick building; earthy colors, hanging rugs, and small cellar windows give it a cavelike appearance. ✉ *Behrensgt. 2, entrance on Skovvn., Frogner* ☎ *22–44–40–20* ⊕ *www.pizzadamimmo.no* ⩟ *Reservations essential* ▤ *AE, DC, MC, V.*

## WHERE TO STAY

$$$

▦ **Grand Hotel.** In the center of town on Karl Johans Gate, the Grand opened in 1874, and is the traditional choice of visiting heads of state; there is even a Nobel suite. Ibsen used to drink brandy at the Grand Café in the company of journalists. Munch was also a regular guest; you can see him with his contemporaries in Per Krohg's painting on the café's far wall. Norwegians book several years in advance for National Day, May 17, in order to have a room overlooking the parades below. **Pros:** period features have been preserved throughout the hotel; there's a Ladies Floor, with 13 unique rooms designed for women travelers; beautiful pool in the new Artesia Spa. **Cons:** the hotel is so big you could get lost easily; the gym is tiny for such a large hotel. ✉ *Karl Johans gt. 31, Sentrum* ☎ *23–21–20–00* ⊕ *www.grand.no* ⤳ *290 rooms, 52 suites* ♿ *In-room: Internet. In-hotel: 3 restaurants, bars, pool, gym, spa* ▤ *AE, DC, MC, V* ⦿ *BP.*

**$$$–$$$$** ⛔ **Hotel Continental.** With its elegant early-20th-century facade, the Con-
**★** tinental is an Oslo landmark that continues to attract visitors with its stylish rooms, gracious service, and two wonderful restaurants—Theatercafeen, an Oslo landmark, and (since 2006) Annen Etage. Opposite the Nationaltheatret and close to many cafés, clubs, and movie theaters, the hotel is ideal for leisure travelers. Dagligstuen (the Sitting Room) has original Munch lithographs on the walls and is a popular meeting place for drinks and quiet conversation. **Pros:** exemplary service; beautiful, well-appointed rooms; brand-new gym. **Cons:** steep prices. ✉ *Stortingsgt. 24–26, Sentrum* ☎ *22–82–40–00* ⊕ *www.hotelcontinental.no* ⤳ *155 rooms, 23 suites* ♿ *In-room: Internet. In-hotel: 2 restaurants, bars, gym* ▤ *AE, DC, MC, V* ⦿ *EP.*

**$$$–$$$$** ⛔ **Radisson Blu Plaza Hotel.** Standing out from other buildings on the
**★** city's skyline, northern Europe's largest hotel is the jewel of the Radisson Blu chain. The understated, elegant rooms have gilded fixtures and much marble, and many have spectacular views. Since it's next to Oslo S Station, the hotel is convenient to buses and other local transit. **Pros:** great top-floor bar; fit-for-a-king breakfast buffet; luxuriously grand bathtubs. **Cons:** crowds outside the Oslo Spektrum, opposite the hotel, are a nuisance when there is a concert; the huge reception area looks more like a station concourse than a hotel lobby. ✉ *Sonja Henies pl. 3* ☎ *22–05–80–00* ⊕ *www.radissonblu.com* ⤳ *673 rooms, 20 suites* ♿ *In-room: Internet. In-hotel: 2 restaurants, bars, pool, gym* ▤ *AE, DC, MC, V* ⦿ *BP.*

# TROMSØ, NORWAY

Tromsø surprised visitors in the 1800s: they thought it very sophisticated and cultured for being so close to the North Pole. It looks the way a polar town should, with ice-capped mountain ridges and jagged architecture that is an echo of the peaks. The midnight sun shines from May 20 to July 22, and it is said that the northern lights decorate the night skies over Tromsø more than any other city in Norway. The so-called "Paris of the North" is about the same size as Luxembourg, but home to only 66,000 people. The city's total area—2,558 square km (987 square mi)—is actually the most expansive in Norway. The downtown area is on a small, hilly island connected to the mainland by a slender bridge. The 10,000 students at the world's northernmost university are one reason the nightlife here is uncommonly lively for a northern city.

## ESSENTIALS

CURRENCY  Norway is a non-EU country and has opted to keep its currency, the Norwegian *krone* (Nkr 6 to US$1). ATMs are readily available.

HOURS  Most shops are open from 10 to 4 to 5 weekdays, Thursday until 6 or 7, Saturday from 10 to 3 or 4, and are closed Sunday.

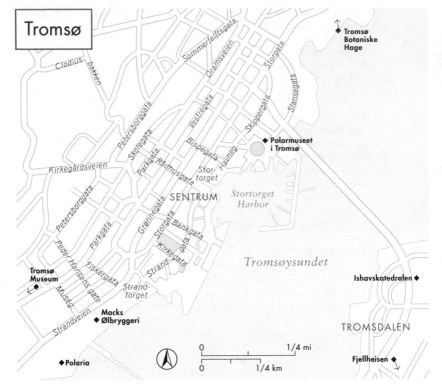

INTERNET **Meieriet Café** (✉ og *Storpub, Grønnegt. 37–39*).

**Tromsø Bibliotek** (✉ *Grønnegt*) is convenient to Breivika.

Passengers disembarking in the city center can check their e-mail at the **Universitetsmuseet** (✉ *Universitetet, Lars Thørings v. 10*), convenient to the City Center.

TELEPHONES   Most tri- and quad-band GSM phones work in Norway, so if your service provider offers service in Europe, you will likely be able to use your mobile phone along the Norwegian coast, even while hugging the shoreline on ship. Public telephones take Nkr 1, 5, 10, and 20 coins, and you need NKr 5 at a minimum. International phone cards are the best value for long-distance calls, and are available at newsstands.

## COMING ASHORE

Cruise ships dock either in the city center at Prostneset or 4 km (2.5 mi) north of the city center at Breivika. Step off the ship in Prostneset, and you're in the city center. A shuttle is offered between Breivika and the city center.

## EXPLORING TROMSØ

☾ **Fjellheisen.** To get a sense of Tromsø's immensity and solitude, take the cable car from behind Tromsø Cathedral up to the mountains, just a few minutes out of the city center. **Storsteinen** *(Big Rock),* 1,386 feet above sea level, has a great city view. In summer a restaurant is open at the top of the lift. ⊠ *Sollivn. 12* 🕿 *77–63–00–00* ⊕ *www.fjellheisen. no* 🖃 *Nkr 99* ☾ *May 20–Aug. 7, daily 10* AM*–1* AM*; Aug. 8–May 19, daily 10* AM*–9:30* PM.

**Ishavskatedralen.** The Arctic Cathedral is the city's signature structure. Designed by Jan Inge Hovig, it's meant to evoke the shape of a Sámi tent as well as the iciness of a glacier. Opened in 1964, it represents northern Norwegian nature, culture, and faith. The immense stained-glass window depicts the Second Coming. Midnight Sun concerts are held every evening from May 15 through August 15, and organ recitals daily throughout July. ⊠ *Hans Nilsens vei 41, Tromsdalen* 🕿 *47–68–06–68* ⊕ *www. ishavskatedralen.no* 🖃 *Nkr 30* ☾ *June–mid-Aug., Mon.–Sat. 9–7, Sun. 1–7; mid-Aug.–mid-Sept., daily 3–6; mid-Sept.–June, daily 4–6.*

**Macks Ølbryggeri.** Ludvik Mack founded Mack's Brewery in 1877, and it is still family-owned. Take a guided tour and afterward receive a beer stein, pin, and a pint of your choice in the Ølhallen pub. Call ahead to reserve a place on the tour. ⊠ *Storgt. 5–13* 🕿 *77–62–45–80* ⊕ *www. olhallen.no* 🖃 *Nkr 150* ☾ *Mon.–Sat. 9–6* ☾ *Guided tours Mon.–Thurs. at 1* PM.

☾ **Polaria.** The adventure center examines life in and around the polar and Barents regions with exhibits on polar travel and arctic research, and a panoramic film from Svalbard. The aquarium has sea mammals, including seals. ⊠ *Hjalmar Johansens gt. 12* 🕿 *77–75–01–00* ⊕ *www. polaria.no* 🖃 *Nkr 100* ☾ *Mid-May–Sept., daily 10–7; Sept.–mid-May, daily noon–5.*

**Polarmuseet i Tromsø.** In an 1830s former customs warehouse, the Polar Museum documents the history of the polar region, focusing on Norway's explorers and hunters. ⊠ *Søndre Tollbugt. 11B* 🕿 *77–60–66–30* ⊕ *www.polarmuseum.no* 🖃 *Nkr 60* ☾ *Mar.–mid-June, daily 11–5; mid-June–mid-Aug., daily 10–7; mid-Aug.–Oct., daily 11–5; Oct.–Mar., daily 11–4.*

★ **Tromsø Botaniske Hage.** Tromsø's Botanic Garden has plants from the Antarctic and Arctic as well as mountain plants from all over the world. Encompassing 4 acres, the garden has been designed as a natural landscape with terraces, slopes, a stream, and a pond. Guides are available by advance arrangement. ⊠ *Tromsø University, Breivika* 🕿 *77–64–40–00* ⊕ *www.uit.no/botanisk* 🖃 *Free* ☾ *Daily 24 hrs.*

☾ **Tromsø Museum, Universitetsmuseet.** Northern Norway's largest museum is dedicated to the nature and culture of the region. Learn about the northern lights, wildlife, fossils and dinosaurs, minerals and rocks, and church art from 1300 to 1800. Outdoors you can visit a Sámi *gamme* (turf hut) and a replica of a Viking longhouse. ⊠ *Universitetet, Lars Thørings v. 10* 🕿 *77–64–50–00* ⊕ *www.uit.no/tmu* 🖃 *Nkr 30* ☾ *June–Aug., daily 9–6; Sept.–May, weekdays 9–4:30, Sat. noon–3, Sun. 11–4.*

6

# ACTIVITIES

## HIKING AND WALKING

With wilderness at its doorstep, Tromsø has more than 100 km (62 mi) of walking and hiking trails in the mountains above the city. They're reachable by funicular.

## HORSEBACK RIDING

**Holmeslet Gård.** This company offers horseback riding, carriage tours, and wildlife-viewing adventures. ⊠ *Innlandsveien 325, Tromsdalen* ☎ *77–61–99–74* ⊕ *www.holmesletgard.com.*

## OUTDOOR ACTIVITY OUTFITTERS

**Arctic Pathfinder.** This outfitter offers kayaking trips, whale-watching excursions, and fly-fishing adventures. ⊠ *Gausdalsveien 32, Tromsdalen* ⊕ *www.arcticpathfinder.no.*

**Tromsø Villmarkssenter.** This company specializes in outdoor adventures, including dogsledding, kayaking, glacier walking, mountain climbing, and mountain hiking excursions. ⊠ *Streetkode 90051-603, Kvaløysletta* ☎ *77–69–60–02* ⊕ *www.villmarkssenter.no.*

# SHOPPING

One of Norway's leading regions for handmade arts and crafts, Tromsø is a treasure trove of shops, particularly along the main pedestrian street Storgata, where a market sells regional and international products. Pick up art from the city's many galleries or craft shops (such as glass-blowing and candle-making studios), or score such Arctic delicacies as reindeer sausages.

**Husfliden.** This store carries traditional handicrafts and souvenirs, as well as traditional folk dress, called *bunads.* ⊠ *Sjørgata 4* ☎ *77–75–88–70.*

**Tromsø Gift and Souvenir Shop.** This boutique sells local handicrafts such as Sámi art and Viking inspired products. ⊠ *Strandgate 39* ☎ *77–67–34–13.*

# WHERE TO EAT

$   ✕**Emma's Under.** Opposite the town cathedral and on the ground floor
NORWEGIAN   of Emma's Drømmekjøkken (Kitchen of Dreams), Emma's Under offers more casual fare from the Norwegian celebrity chef. ⊠ *Kirkegt 8* ☎ *77–63–77–30* ⊕ *www.emmaoglars.no* ⊟ *MC, V.*

$$$   ✕**Vertshuset Skarven.** A Tromsø institution, Vertshuset Skarven features
NORWEGIAN   four restaurants that share the same building. Each restaurant serves different types of Norwegian specialties. Sample the seaweed and shellfish soup, fresh mussels, or seal lasagna. The pleasant terrace is usually packed in summer. ⊠ *Strandtorget 1* ☎ *77–60–07–20* ⊕ *www.skarven. no* ⊟ *AE, DC, MC, V.*

# TRONDHEIM, NORWAY

One of Scandinavia's oldest cities, Trondheim is Norway's third largest, with a population of 162,000. Founded in AD 997 by Viking king Olav Tryggvason, it was first named Nidaros (still the name of the cathedral), a composite word referring to the city's location at the mouth of the Nid River. The city was also the first capital of Norway, from 997 to 1380. Trondheim became a pilgrimage center because of the popularity of King Olaf II Haraldsson (later St. Olaf), who was buried here after being killed in a battle in 1030. Today Trondheim is a university town as well as a center for maritime and medical research, but the wide streets of the historic city center are still lined with brightly painted wood houses and striking warehouses.

## ESSENTIALS

CURRENCY  Norway is a non-EU country and has opted to keep its currency, the Norwegian *krone* (Nkr 6 to US$1). ATMs are readily available.

HOURS  Most shops are open from 10 to 4 or 5 weekdays, Thursday until 7, Saturday from 10 to 3 or 4, and are closed Sunday.

INTERNET  **Trondheim Public Library** (⊠ *Petter Eggens plass 1*).

TELEPHONES  Most tri- and quad-band GSM phones work in Norway, so if your service provider offers service in Europe, you will likely be able to use your mobile phone along the Norwegian coast, even while hugging the shoreline on ship. Public telephones take Nkr 1, 5, 10, and 20 coins, and you need NKr 5 at a minimum. International phone cards are the best value for long-distance calls, and are available at newsstands.

## COMING ASHORE

Cruise ships dock at one of two piers. Both of these are within easy walking distance of the city center. There are no facilities at the piers, but you'll find everything you need—from banks to tourist offices—in the city.

# EXPLORING TRONDHEIM

**Erkebispegården** *(Archbishop's Palace). This* is the oldest secular building in Scandinavia, dating from around 1160. It was the residence of the archbishop until the Reformation in 1537; after that it was a residence for Danish governors, and later a military headquarters. The oldest parts of the palace, which face the cathedral, are used for government functions. A **museum** has original sculptures from Nidaros Cathedral and architectural pieces from throughout the palace's history. The crown jewels are on display here. ⊠ *Bispegata 5* ☎ *73–89–08–00* ⊕ *www. nidarosdomen.no* ⊠ *Nkr 50* ☉ *May, June, Aug., and Sept., weekdays 9–3, Sat. 9–2, Sun. 1–4; June–Aug., weekdays 9–5:30, Sat. 10–3, Sun. noon–4; mid-Sept.–May, weekdays 11–2, Sat. 11–3, Sun. noon–4.*

**Kristiansten Festning** *(Kristiansten Fort).* Built after the great fire of 1681, the fort saved the city from conquest by Sweden in 1718. During Norway's occupation by Germany, from 1940 to 1945, members of the Norwegian Resistance were executed here; there's a plaque in their honor. The fort has a spectacular view of the city, the fjord, and the

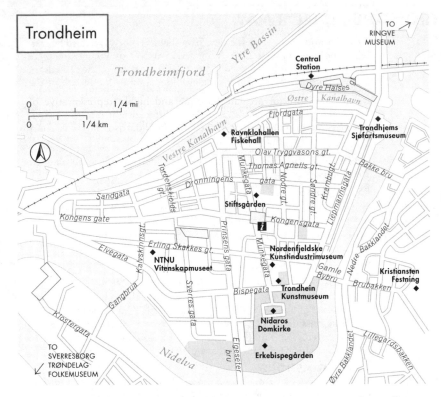

Trondheim

mountains. ⊠ *Kristiansten Festning* ☏ *73–99–52–80* ⌨ *Free* ⊙ *June–Sept., weekdays 11–3.*

**Nidaros Domkirke** *(Nidaros Cathedral).* During his reign, King Olaf formulated a Christian religious code for Norway in 1024. It was on his grave that this cathedral was built. The town became a pilgrimage site for the Christians of northern Europe, and Olaf was canonized in 1164. Although its construction began in 1070, the oldest existing parts of the cathedral date from around 1150. It has been ravaged by fire on several occasions and rebuilt each time, generally in a Gothic style. Since the Middle Ages, Norway's kings have been crowned and blessed in the cathedral. Forty-five minute guided tours are offered in English from mid-June to mid-August, weekdays at 11 and 4. ⊠ *Bispegata 5* ☏ *73–89–08–00* ⊕ *www.nidarosdomen.no* ⌨ *Nkr 50* ⊙ *May, Aug.–mid-Sept., weekdays 9–3, Sat. 9–2, Sun. 1–4; June and July, weekdays 9–5:30, Sat. 9–2, Sun. 1–4; mid-Sept.–May., weekdays 9–3, Sat. 9–2, Sun. 1–3.*

**Ringve Museum.** Norway's national museum of music and musical instruments is on a country estate outside Trondheim. The **Museum in the Manor House,** the oldest section, focuses on instruments in the European musical tradition. Guides demonstrate their use. The Museum in the Barn features modern sound-and-light technology as well as

Norwegian folk instruments. ⊠ *Lade Allé 60* ☎ *73–87–02–80* ⊕ *www. ringve.com* ☏ *Nkr 80* ☉ *July–mid-Aug., daily 11–5; mid-Aug.–mid-Sept., daily 11–4; mid-Sept.–mid-Oct., Sun. 11–4.*

**Fodor'sChoice** **Stiftsgården.** Scandinavia's largest wooden palace was built between
★ 1774 and 1778 as the home of a prominent widow. Sold to the state in 1800, it's now the official royal residence in Trondheim. The architecture and interior are late baroque and highly representative of 18th-century high society's taste. Tours offer insight into the festivities marking the coronations of the kings in Nidaros Domkirke. Tours are conducted on the hour. ⊠ *Munkegt. 23* ☎ *73–84–28–80* ☏ *Nkr 60* ☉ *June–Aug. 20, Mon.–Sat. 10–5, Sun. noon–5.*

**Sverresborg Trøndelag Folkemuseum.** Near the ruins of King Sverre's medieval castle is this outdoor museum, which has re-creations of coastal, inland, and mountain-village buildings that depict life in Trøndelag during the 18th and 19th centuries. The **Haltdalen stave church,** built in 1170, is the northernmost preserved stave church in Norway. In the Old Town you can visit a 1900 dentist's office and an old-fashioned grocery that sells sweets. A special exhibit examines how the stages of life—childhood, youth, adulthood, and old age—have changed over the past 150 years. The audiovisual **Trønderbua** depicts traditional regional wedding ceremonies with artifacts and a 360-degree film. Guided tours are offered from May through September. ⊠ *Sverresborg Allé* ☎ *73–89–01–00* ⊕ *www.sverresborg.no* ☏ *Nkr 85* ☉ *June–Sept., daily 11–6; Sept.–May, weekdays 10–3, weekends noon–4.*

## SHOPPING

**Arne Ronning.** This clothing boutique carries fine sweaters by Dale of Norway. ⊠ *Nordregt. 10* ☎ *73–53–13–30.*

**Husfliden.** Trondheim has a branch of the handicraft store. ⊠ *Olav Tryggvasongt. 18* ☎ *73–83–32–30.*

**Jens Hoff Garn & Ide.** For knitted sweaters by such makers as Oleana and Oda, try this store. ⊠ *Olav Tryggvasongt. 20* ☎ *73–53–15–27.*

**Mercur Centre.** Trondheim's Mercur Centre has about 30 shops. ⊠ *Kongensgt. 8* ☎ *73–87–65–00* ⊕ *www.mercursenteret.no.*

**Møllers Gullsmedforretning.** Founded in 1770, Norway's oldest extant goldsmith sells versions of the Trondheim Rose, the city symbol since the 1700s. ⊠ *Munkegt. 3* ☎ *73–52–04–39* ⊕ *www.gullsmedmoller.no.*

**Trondheim Torg.** This shopping center has a helpful staff and interesting shops. ⊠ *Kongensgt. 11* ☎ *73–80–77–40* ⊕ *www.trondheimtorg.no.*

## ACTIVITIES

### BICYCLING

Some 300 **Trondheim Bysykkel City Bikes** can be borrowed in the city center at a cost of Nkr 70. Parked in easy-to-see stands at central locations, the distinctive green bikes have shopping baskets. You'll need a 20-kroner piece to release the bike (your money's refunded when you return the bike to a parking rack). The Trampe elevator ascends the

6

steep Brubakken Hill near Gamle Bybro and takes cyclists nearly to Kristiansten Festning (Kristiansten Fort). Contact the tourist office to get the card you need in order to use the bicycles and Trampe.

## FISHING
**TOFA** (*Trondheim og Omland Jakt- og Fiskeadministrasjon*). The Nid River is one of Norway's best salmon and trout rivers, famous for its large salmon (the record is 70 pounds). You can fish right in the city, but you need a license. For further information and fishing licenses, contact the fishing administration. ⊠ *Leirfossvn. 76* ☎ *73–96–55–80* ⊕ *www.tofa.org.*

## HIKING AND WALKING
**Bymarka,** a wooded area on Trondheim's outskirts, has a varied and well-developed network of trails—60 km (37 mi) of gravel paths, 80 km (50 mi) of dirtpaths, and 250 km (155 mi) of ski tracks. **Ladestien** *(Lade Trail)* is a 14-km (9-mi) trail that goes along the edge of the Lade Peninsula and offers great views of Trondheimsfjord. **Nidelvstien** *(Nidelv Trail)* runs along the river from Tempe to the Leirfossene waterfalls.

## SWIMMING
**Trondheim Pirbadet.** This is Norway's largest indoor swimming center. There's a wave pool, a sauna, and a Jacuzzi, as well as a gym. ⊠ *Havnegt. 12* ☎ *73–83–18–00* ⊕ *www.pirbadet.no.*

# WHERE TO EAT

Trondheim is known for the traditional dish *surlaks* (marinated salmon served with sour cream). A sweet specialty is *tekake* (tea cake), which looks like a thick-crust pizza topped with a lattice pattern of cinnamon and sugar. The city's restaurant scene is vibrant and evolving, with more and more international restaurants serving continental food, and bars and cafés where the city's considerable student population gathers.

**$$–$$$**
NORWEGIAN
✕ **Egon Tärnet.** An attractive rotating restaurant 74 meters over the city serves a Norwegian rarity—an all-you-can-eat pizza and salad lunch buffet and a breakfast buffet. ⊠ *Otto Nielsens vei 4* ☎ *73–87–35–00* ⊕ *www.egon.no* ⊟ *AE, MC, V.*

**$–$$**
NORWEGIAN
✕ **Vertshuset Grenaderen.** Dine in a 17th-century blacksmith's house on traditional Norwegian food such as reindeer and fish. The restaurant boasts one of the city's most attractive terraces for summer outdoor dining. ⊠ *Kongsgårdsgt. 1* ☎ *73–51–66–80* ⊕ *www.grenaderen.no* ⊟ *AE, MC, V.*

# INDEX